Sales and Service Occupations

© Minister of Supply and Services Canada 1996

Available in Canada through

your local bookseller

or by mail from

Canada Communication Group — Publishing
Ottawa, Canada K1A 0S9

Catalogue No. MP53-25/5-1996E
ISBN 0-660-16300-4

Sales and Service Occupations

**MAJOR GROUP 62
SKILLED SALES AND SERVICE OCCUPATIONS**

621 Sales and Service Supervisors

6211 Retail Trade Supervisors
6212 Food Service Supervisors
6213 Executive Housekeepers
6214 Dry Cleaning and Laundry Supervisors
6215 Cleaning Supervisors
6216 Other Service Supervisors

622 Technical Sales Specialists, Wholesale Trade

6221 Technical Sales Specialists, Wholesale Trade

623 Insurance and Real Estate Sales Occupations and Buyers

6231 Insurance Agents and Brokers
6232 Real Estate Agents and Salespersons
6233 Retail and Wholesale Buyers
6234 Grain Elevator Operators

624 Chefs and Cooks

6241 Chefs
    6241.1 Executive Chefs
    6241.2 Sous-Chefs
    6241.3 Chefs and Specialist Chefs
6242 Cooks

625 Butchers and Bakers

6251 Butchers and Meat Cutters, Retail and Wholesale
6252 Bakers

626 Police Officers and Firefighters

6261 Police Officers (Except Commissioned)
6262 Firefighters

627 Technical Occupations in Personal Service

6271 Hairstylists and Barbers
    6271.1 Hairstylists
    6271.2 Barbers
6272 Funeral Directors and Embalmers
    6272.1 Funeral Directors
    6272.2 Embalmers

MAJOR GROUP 64
INTERMEDIATE SALES AND SERVICE OCCUPATIONS

641 Sales Representatives, Wholesale Trade

6411 Sales Representatives, Wholesale Trade (Non-Technical)

642 Retail Salespersons and Sales Clerks

6421 Retail Salespersons and Sales Clerks

643 Occupations in Travel and Accommodation

6431 Travel Counsellors

6432 Pursers and Flight Attendants
    6432.1 Flight Attendants
    6432.2 Flight Pursers and Passenger Service Directors
    6432.3 Ship Pursers

6433 Airline Sales and Service Agents
    6433.1 Airline Passenger and Ticket Agents
    6433.2 Airline Baggage Agents
    6433.3 Airline Cargo Agents
    6433.4 Airline Reservation Agents
    6433.5 Airline Station Agents
    6433.6 Airline Load Planners

6434 Ticket and Cargo Agents and Related Clerks (Except Airline)
    6434.1 Ticket Agents and Related Clerks (Except Airline)
    6434.2 Cargo Agents (Except Airline)

6435 Hotel Front Desk Clerks

644 Tour and Recreational Guides and Amusement Occupations

6441 Tour and Travel Guides
    6441.1 Tour Guides
    6441.2 Travel Guides

6442 Outdoor Sport and Recreational Guides

6443 Amusement Attraction Operators and Other Amusement Occupations
    6443.1 Amusement Attraction Operators
    6443.2 Gambling Dealers

645 Occupations in Food and Beverage Service

6451 Maîtres d'hôtel and Hosts/Hostesses

6452 Bartenders

6453 Food and Beverage Servers

646 Other Occupations in Protective Service

6461 Sheriffs and Bailiffs

6462 Correctional Service Officers

6463 By-law Enforcement and Other Regulatory Officers, n.e.c.
    6463.1 Animal Control Officers
    6463.2 By-law Enforcement Officers
    6463.3 Commercial Transport Inspectors

            6463.4   Garbage Collection Inspectors
            6463.5   Liquor Licence Inspectors
            6463.6   Parking Control Officers
            6463.7   Taxi Inspectors

6464   Occupations Unique to the Armed Forces

6465   Other Protective Service Occupations
            6465.1   Corporate Security Officers
            6465.2   Private Investigators
            6465.3   Retail Loss Prevention Officers

647   **Childcare and Home Support Workers**

6471   Visiting Homemakers, Housekeepers and Related Occupations
            6471.1   Visiting Homemakers
            6471.2   Housekeepers
            6471.3   Companions
            6471.4   Foster Parents

6472   Elementary and Secondary School Teacher Assistants

6473   Early Childhood Educator Assistants

6474   Babysitters, Nannies and Parents' Helpers
            6474.1   Babysitters
            6474.2   Nannies and Live-in Caregivers
            6474.3   Parents' Helpers

648   **Other Occupations in Personal Service**

6481   Image, Social and Other Personal Consultants
            6481.1   Image Consultants
            6481.2   Make-Up Consultants
            6481.3   Colour Consultants
            6481.4   Wedding Consultants
            6481.5   Weight Loss Consultants

6482   Estheticians, Electrologists and Related Occupations
            6482.1   Estheticians
            6482.2   Cosmeticians
            6482.3   Electrologists
            6482.4   Manicurists and Pedicurists
            6482.5   Scalp Treatment Specialists
            6482.6   Tattoo Artists

6483   Pet Groomers and Animal Care Workers

6484   Other Personal Service Occupations
            6484.1   Astrologers
            6484.2   Psychic Consultants

MAJOR GROUP 66
ELEMENTAL SALES AND SERVICE OCCUPATIONS

661 Cashiers

6611 Cashiers

662 Other Sales and Related Occupations

6621 Service Station Attendants
    6621.1 Automotive Service Station Attendants
    6621.2 Marina Service Station Attendants

6622 Grocery Clerks and Shelf Stockers

6623 Other Elemental Sales Occupations
    6623.1 Direct Distributors and Door-to-Door Salespersons
    6623.2 Street Vendors
    6623.3 Telephone Solicitors and Telemarketers
    6623.4 Demonstrators

663 Elemental Medical and Hospital Assistants

6631 Elemental Medical and Hospital Assistants
    6631.1 Blood Donor Clinic Assistants
    6631.2 Central Supply Aides
    6631.3 Chiropractic Aides
    6631.4 Occupational Therapy Assistants
    6631.5 Physiotherapy Assistants

664 Food Counter Attendants and Kitchen Helpers

6641 Food Service Counter Attendants and Food Preparers

6642 Kitchen and Food Service Helpers
    6642.1 Kitchen Helpers
    6642.2 Food Service Helpers
    6642.3 Dishwashers

665 Security Guards and Related Occupations

6651 Security Guards and Related Occupations

666 Cleaners

6661 Light Duty Cleaners
6662 Specialized Cleaners
    6662.1 Carpet and Upholstery Cleaners
    6662.2 Chimney Cleaners
    6662.3 Furnace and Ventilation System Cleaners
    6662.4 Sandblasters
    6662.5 Vehicle Cleaners
    6662.6 Window Cleaners

6663 Janitors, Caretakers and Building Superintendents

667 **Other Attendants in Travel, Accommodation and Recreation**

6671 Attendants in Recreation and Sport
- 6671.1 Amusement Park Attendants
- 6671.2 Ski Lift Attendants
- 6671.3 Bowling Alley Attendants
- 6671.4 Ice Makers
- 6671.5 Recreational Facility Attendants

6672 Other Attendants in Accommodation and Travel (Except Airline Travel)
- 6672.1 Bellhops
- 6672.2 Baggage Porters
- 6672.3 Ship Attendants
- 6672.4 Train Service Attendants

668 **Other Elemental Service Occupations**

6681 Dry Cleaning and Laundry Occupations
- 6681.1 Dry Cleaning and Laundry Machine Operators
- 6681.2 Dry Cleaning and Laundry Inspectors and Assemblers

6682 Ironing, Pressing and Finishing Occupations

6683 Other Elemental Service Occupations
- 6683.1 Beauty Salon Attendants
- 6683.2 Door Attendants
- 6683.3 Funeral Attendants
- 6683.4 Laundromat Attendants
- 6683.5 Parking Lot Attendants and Car Jockeys
- 6683.6 Ticket Takers and Ushers

6211 Retail Trade Supervisors

Retail Trade Supervisors supervise and co-ordinate the activities of workers in the following groups: *Retail Salespersons and Sales Clerks* (6421), *Cashiers* (6611), *Grocery Clerks and Shelf Stockers* (6622) and *Other Elemental Sales Occupations* (6623).

Profile Summary

APTITUDES

G	V	N	S	P	Q	K	F	M
3	3	3	4	4	3	4	4	4

INTERESTS
SMD

DATA PEOPLE THINGS (DPT)
138

PHYSICAL ACTIVITIES (PA)

V	C	H	B	L	S
3	0	2	3	0	1

ENVIRONMENTAL ACTIVITIES (EC)
L1

EDUCATION/TRAINING
2, 4

Examples of Job Titles

Department Store Supervisor
Head Cashier
Liquor Store Supervisor
Newspaper Delivery Supervisor
Produce Department Supervisor
Rental Service Supervisor
Route Supervisor, Retail Sales
Telemarketing Supervisor

Descriptor Profile

Main Characteristics

Occupations in this group are characterized by the following aptitudes, interests and worker functions as they relate to main duties:

- **General learning ability** to supervise and co-ordinate sales staff and cashiers

- **Verbal** and **numerical ability** to prepare reports on sales volumes, merchandising and personnel matters

- **Clerical perception** to ensure that payments by cheque and inventory control records are accurate

- **Social interest** in selling merchandise to customers and resolving problems such as customer complaints and supply shortages

- **Methodical interest** in **co-ordinating** information to maintain specified inventory, order merchandise and prepare work schedules

- **Directive interest** in **supervising** by assigning duties to workers; and in authorizing payments by cheque and the return of merchandise, and in hiring and training or arranging for the training of new staff

6211

Physical Activities

Vision
  3 Near and far vision

Colour Discrimination
  0 Not relevant

Hearing
  2 Verbal interaction

Body Position
  3 Sitting, standing, walking

Limb Co-ordination
  0 Not relevant

Strength
  1 Limited

Environmental Conditions

Location
  L1 Regulated inside climate

Employment Requirements

Education/Training
2, 4

- Completion of secondary school may be required.

- Previous retail sales experience such as retail salesperson or sales clerk, cashier, telephone solicitor, door-to-door salesperson or rental agent is required.

Workplaces/Employers

Businesses involved in telephone or door-to-door soliciting

Retail establishments

Occupational Options

Progression to management positions such as those in *Retail Trade Managers* (0621) is possible with additional training or experience.

Similar Occupations Classified Elsewhere

Food Service Supervisors (6212)

Retail Trade Managers (0621)

6212 Food Service Supervisors

Food Service Supervisors supervise, direct and co-ordinate the activities of workers who prepare, portion and serve food.

Profile Summary

APTITUDES

G	V	N	S	P	Q	K	F	M
3	3	3	4	4	3	4	4	4

INTERESTS
MDs

DATA PEOPLE THINGS (DPT)
138

PHYSICAL ACTIVITIES (PA)

V	C	H	B	L	S
3	1	2	3	0	1

ENVIRONMENTAL CONDITIONS (EC)
L1, D3

EDUCATION/TRAINING
4, 6

Examples of Job Titles

Cafeteria Supervisor, Food Services
Canteen Supervisor
Catering Supervisor
Food Service Supervisor

Descriptor Profile

Main Characteristics

Occupations in this group are characterized by the following aptitudes, interests and worker functions as they relate to main duties:

- **General learning ability** to supervise, co-ordinate and schedule activities of staff who prepare and portion food

- **Verbal ability** to prepare food order summaries for chefs according to requests from dietitians, patients in hospitals and other customers

- **Numerical ability** to estimate ingredients and supplies required for meal preparation

- **Clerical perception** to order ingredients and supplies and keep accurate records

- **Methodical interest** in **co-ordinating** information to establish methods to meet work schedules and maintain records of stock, repairs, sales and wastage; and in ensuring that food and service meet quality control standards

- **Directive interest** in **supervising** and checking assembly of regular and special diet trays, and delivery of food trolleys to hospital patients

- **Social interest** in training staff in job duties and sanitation and safety procedures

6212

Physical Activities

Vision
3   Near and far vision

Colour Discrimination
1   Relevant

Hearing
2   Verbal interaction

Body Position
3   Sitting, standing, walking

Limb Co-ordination
0   Not relevant

Strength
1   Limited

Environmental Conditions

Location
L1   Regulated inside climate

Discomforts
D3   Odours

Employment Requirements

Education/Training
4, 6

- Completion of secondary school is usually required.

- Completion of a community college program in food service administration, hotel and restaurant management or related discipline
or
several years of experience in food preparation or service are required.

Workplaces/Employers

Cafeterias

Catering companies

Food service establishments

Health care establishments

Hospitals

Similar Occupations Classified Elsewhere

Maîtres d'hôtel and Hosts/Hostesses (6451)

Restaurant and Food Service Managers (0631)

Banquet Captains (in 6453 *Food and Beverage Servers*)

6213 Executive Housekeepers

Executive Housekeepers direct and control the operations of housekeeping departments within establishments.

Profile Summary

APTITUDES

G	V	N	S	P	Q	K	F	M
3	3	3	4	4	3	4	4	4

INTERESTS
MDs

DATA PEOPLE THINGS (DPT)
138

PHYSICAL ACTIVITIES (PA)

V	C	H	B	L	S
2	0	2	1	0	1

ENVIRONMENTAL CONDITIONS (EC)
L1

EDUCATION/TRAINING
1+, 6, 7

Examples of Job Titles

Assistant Executive Housekeeper
Executive Housekeeper
Hospital Executive Housekeeper
Hotel Executive Housekeeper
Housekeeping Director
Housekeeping Manager

Descriptor Profile

Main Characteristics

Occupations in this group are characterized by the following aptitudes, interests and worker functions as they relate to main duties:

- **General learning ability** to plan and co-ordinate the activities of housekeeping supervisors and their crews

- **Verbal** and **numerical ability** to prepare budgets, payroll and employee schedules

- **Clerical perception** to maintain financial records

- **Methodical interest** in co-ordinating information to establish and implement operational procedures; and in co-ordinating the inspection of assigned areas to ensure that safety standards and departmental policies are being met

- **Directive interest** in **supervising** staff; and in selecting and purchasing equipment and supplies

- **Social interest** in hiring staff

6213

Physical Activities

Vision
 2 Near vision

Colour Discrimination
 0 Not relevant

Hearing
 2 Verbal interaction

Body Position
 1 Sitting

Limb Co-ordination
 0 Not relevant

Strength
 1 Limited

Environmental Conditions

Location
 L1 Regulated inside climate

Employment Requirements

Education/Training
 1+, 6, 7

- Completion of secondary school is usually required.

- A university degree or college diploma in hospital management, hotel management or business administration is usually required.

- Extensive experience as a cleaning supervisor may substitute for formal education requirements.

Workplaces/Employers

Hospitals

Hotel

Similar Occupations Classified Elsewhere

Accommodation Service Managers (0632)

Maintenance Managers (0722)

Housekeeping supervisors (in 6215 *Cleaning Supervisors*)

6214 Dry Cleaning and Laundry Supervisors

Dry Cleaning and Laundry Supervisors supervise and co-ordinate the activities of workers in the following groups: *Dry Cleaning and Laundry Occupations* (6681) and *Ironing, Pressing and Finishing Occupations* (6682).

Profile Summary

APTITUDES

G	V	N	S	P	Q	K	F	M
3	3	4	4	4	3	4	4	4

INTERESTS
MDs

DATA PEOPLE THINGS (DPT)
138

PHYSICAL ACTIVITIES (PA)

V	C	H	B	L	S
3	1	2	3	0	1

ENVIRONMENTAL CONDITIONS (EC)
L1, D3

EDUCATION/TRAINING
4

Examples of Job Titles

Dry Cleaning Supervisor

Foreman/woman - Laundry and Dry Cleaning

Laundry Supervisor

Production Supervisor, Dry Cleaning

Descriptor Profile

Main Characteristics

Occupations in this group are characterized by the following aptitudes, interests and worker functions as they relate to main duties:

- **General learning ability** to supervise, co-ordinate and schedule the activities of dry cleaning and laundry staff

- **Verbal** and **numerical ability** to requisition supplies

- **Clerical perception** to complete requisition forms

- **Methodical interest** in co-ordinating information to establish and implement production routines; and in co-ordinating work activities with other departments, and in monitoring quality and production levels

- **Directive interest** in **supervising staff**; and in overseeing the cleaning of suedes, leathers and other difficult-to-clean items

- **Social interest** in hiring and in training or arranging for the training of workers

6214

Physical Activities

Vision
  3   Near and far vision

Colour Discrimination
  1   Relevant

Hearing
  2   Verbal interaction

Body Position
  3   Sitting, standing, walking

Limb Co-ordination
  0   Not relevant

Strength
  1   Limited

Environmental Conditions

Location
  L1 Regulated inside climate

Discomforts
  D3 Odours

Employment Requirements

Education/Training
  4

- Completion of secondary school is usually required.

- Experience as a dry cleaning or laundry machine operator is required.

Workplaces/Employers

Dry cleaning and laundry establishments

Laundries in hotels, hospitals and other institutions

Occupational Options

Progression to managerial positions, such as dry cleaning manager, is possible with additional training or experience.

Similar Occupations Classified Elsewhere

Dry Cleaning and Laundry Occupations (6681)

Dry cleaning services managers (in 0651 *Other Services Managers*)

6215 Cleaning Supervisors

Cleaning Supervisors supervise and co-ordinate the activities of workers in the following groups: *Light Duty Cleaners* (6661), *Specialized Cleaners* (6662) and *Janitors, Caretakers and Building Superintendents* (6663).

Profile Summary

APTITUDES

G	V	N	S	P	Q	K	F	M
3	3	3	4	4	3	4	4	4

INTERESTS
MDs

DATA PEOPLE THINGS (DPT)
137

PHYSICAL ACTIVITIES (PA)

V	C	H	B	L	S
3	0	2	3	0	1

ENVIRONMENTAL CONDITIONS (EC)
L1

EDUCATION/TRAINING
4

Examples of Job Titles

Building Cleaning Supervisor
Carpet Cleaning Supervisor
Cleaning Supervisor
Head Caretaker
Head Custodian
Head Janitor
Window Washing Supervisor

Descriptor Profile

Main Characteristics

Occupations in this group are characterized by the following aptitudes, interests and worker functions as they relate to main duties:

- **General learning ability** to supervise and co-ordinate the work of light duty, industrial and specialized cleaners and janitors

- **Verbal** and **numerical ability** to prepare budgets and estimate costs, and receive payment for specialized cleaning jobs

- **Clerical ability** to keep financial records

- **Methodical interest** in **co-ordinating** information to prepare work schedules and co-ordinate activities with those of other departments; and in inspecting sites and facilities to ensure that they meet established safety and cleanliness standards

- **Directive interest** in **supervising** the activities of workers; and in recommending and arranging for additional services such as painting, repair work, renovations and replacement of furnishings and equipment

- **Social interest** in **handling** to assist cleaners in performing certain duties; and in hiring and training staff

6215

Physical Activities

Vision
   3 Near and far vision

Colour Discrimination
   0 Not relevant

Hearing
   2 Verbal interaction

Body Position
   3 Sitting, standing, walking

Limb Co-ordination
   0 Not relevant

Strength
   1 Limited

Environmental Conditions

Location
   L1 Regulated inside climate

Employment Requirements

Education/Training
   4

- Completion of secondary school is usually required.

- Previous experience as a light duty cleaner, specialized cleaner, janitor or industrial cleaner is required.

Workplaces/Employers

Cleaning companies

Commercial establishments

Hospitals

Hotels

Motels

Office buildings

Schools

Similar Occupations Classified Elsewhere

Executive Housekeepers (6213)

Specialized Cleaners (6662)

Building maintenance supervisors (in 7219 *Contractors and Supervisors, Other Construction Trades, Installers, Repairers and Servicers*)

6216 Other Service Supervisors

Supervisors in this group supervise and co-ordinate the activities of hotel accommodation service clerks, theatre ushers and attendants, reservation clerks, sport and recreation club workers, commissionaires and other service workers not elsewhere classified.

Profile Summary

APTITUDES

G	V	N	S	P	Q	K	F	M
3	3	4	4	4	3	4	4	4

INTERESTS
SMD

DATA PEOPLE THINGS (DPT)
138

PHYSICAL ACTIVITIES (PA)

V	C	H	B	L	S
3	0	2	3	0	1

ENVIRONMENTAL CONDITIONS (EC)
L1

EDUCATION/TRAINING
4

Examples of Job Titles

Camp Ground Supervisor
Hotel Clerk Supervisor
Parking Lot Supervisor
Reservations Supervisor
Supervisor, Club House Attendants
Supervisor, Commissionaires
Supervisor, Security Guards
Supervisor, Theatre Attendants
Supervisor, Ticket Takers
Tour Guide Supervisor
Travel Clerk Supervisor

Descriptor Profile

Main Characteristics

Occupations in this group are characterized by the following aptitudes, interests and worker functions as they relate to main duties:

- **General learning ability** to co-ordinate, assign and review the work of hotel, motel and other accommodation service clerks, theatre ushers and attendants, reservation clerks, sport and recreation club workers, commissionaires and other service workers not elsewhere classified; may perform the same duties as workers

- **Verbal ability** and **clerical perception** to prepare and submit progress and other reports, and to requisition supplies and materials

- **Social interest** in resolving work-related problems and training workers in job duties, safety procedures and company policies

- **Methodical interest** in **co-ordinating** information to establish work schedules and procedures, and in co-ordinating activities with other work units and departments

- **Directive interest** in **supervising** the activities of workers; in ensuring smooth operation of computer systems, equipment and machinery; and in arranging for maintenance and repair work

6216

Physical Activities

Vision
   3   Near and far vision

Colour Discrimination
   0   Not relevant

Hearing
   2   Verbal interaction

Body Position
   3   Sitting, standing, walking

Limb Co-ordination
   0   Not relevant

Strength
   1   Limited

Environmental Conditions

Location
   L1 Regulated inside climate

Employment Requirements

Education/Training
   4

- Completion of secondary school is usually required.

- Completion of college courses related to area supervised may be required.

- Experience in the occupation supervised is usually required.

Workplaces/Employers

Service establishments throughout the public and private sectors

Similar Occupations Classified Elsewhere

Accommodation Service Managers (0632)

Cleaning Supervisors (6215)

Dry Cleaning and Laundry Supervisors (6214)

Executive Housekeepers (6213)

Food Service Supervisors (6212)

Other Services Managers (0651)

Retail Trade Supervisors (6211)

6221 Technical Sales Specialists, Wholesale Trade

Technical Sales Specialists, Wholesale Trade, sell a range of technical goods and services such as scientific and industrial products, electricity, telecommunications services and computer services to governments and commercial and industrial establishments. Technical Sales Specialists who are supervisors are included in this group.

Profile Summary

APTITUDES

G	V	N	S	P	Q	K	F	M
2	2	3	3	3	3	4	4	4

INTERESTS
OSi

DATA PEOPLE THINGS (DPT)
258

PHYSICAL ACTIVITIES (PA)

V	C	H	B	L	S
2	0	2	1	0	1

ENVIRONMENTAL CONDITIONS (EC)
L1

EDUCATION/TRAINING
6, 7

Examples of Job Titles

Aircraft Sales Representative
Communication Equipment Sales Representative
Construction Equipment Sales Representative
Electricity Sales Representative
Heavy Equipment Sales Representative
Industrial Supplies Sales Representative
Medical Instrumentation Sales Engineer
Sales Representative, Technical Sales
Software Sales Representative
Technical Sales Supervisor

Descriptor Profile

Main Characteristics

Occupations in this group are characterized by the following aptitudes, interests and worker functions as they relate to main duties:

- **General learning ability** to assess clients' needs and resources, and to recommend the appropriate goods and services; may supervise the activities of other technical sales specialists

- **Verbal ability** to write reports and proposals as part of sales presentations that illustrate the benefits of goods and services, and to prepare and administer sales contracts

- **Numerical ability** to estimate costs of installing and maintaining equipment and service

- **Spatial** and **form perception** to visualize the layout and functioning of technical equipment, and to interpret plans and operating specifications

- **Clerical perception** to see pertinent detail in reference materials such as diagrams, charts, catalogues, manuals and specifications

- **Objective interest** in providing input for product design where goods and services must be tailored to meet clients' needs

- **Social interest** in **persuading** to promote sales to existing clients

- **Innovative interest** in **analyzing** information to identify and solicit potential clients, and to consult with clients after sale to resolve problems and provide ongoing support

6221

Physical Activities

Vision
  2 Near vision

Colour Discrimination
  0 Not relevant

Hearing
  2 Verbal interaction

Body Position
  1 Sitting

Limb Co-ordination
  0 Not relevant

Strength
  1 Limited

Environmental Conditions

Location
  L1 Regulated inside climate

Employment Requirements

Education/Training
  6, 7

- Completion of secondary school is required.

- A university degree or college diploma in a program related to the product or service is usually required.

- Experience in sales or in a technical occupation related to the product or service may be required.

- Technical sales supervisors require experience as a technical sales specialist.

Workplaces/Employers

Computer services firms

Engineering firms

Hydro-electric companies

Industrial equipment manufacturing companies

Pharmaceutical companies

Occupational Options

Progression to sales management positions is possible with additional training or experience.

Similar Occupations Classified Elsewhere

Retail Salespersons and Sales Clerks (6421)

Sales, Marketing and Advertising Managers (0611)

Sales Representatives, Wholesale Trade (Non-Technical) (6411)

Remarks

Technical sales specialists usually specialize in a particular line of goods or services.

6231　Insurance Agents and Brokers

Insurance Agents and Brokers sell automobile, fire, life, property, marine and other types of insurance to businesses and individuals. Insurance Agents sell individual companies' products to clients. Insurance Brokers seek appropriate insurance products through several insurance companies on behalf of clients.

Profile Summary

APTITUDES

G	V	N	S	P	Q	K	F	M
3	3	3	4	4	3	4	4	4

INTERESTS
MSd

DATA PEOPLE THINGS (DPT)
358

PHYSICAL ACTIVITIES (PA)

V	C	H	B	L	S
2	0	2	1	0	1

ENVIRONMENTAL CONDITIONS (EC)
L1

EDUCATION/TRAINING
4, 5, R

Examples of Job Titles

Insurance Agent
Insurance Broker
Insurance Sales Representative

Descriptor Profile

Main Characteristics

Occupations in this group are characterized by the following aptitudes, interests and worker functions as they relate to main duties:

- **General learning ability** to establish client insurance coverage and method of payment

- **Verbal ability** to provide information concerning group and individual insurance packages, the range of risk coverage, benefits paid and other policy features

- **Numerical ability** and **clerical perception** to calculate premiums using insurance tables and to prepare insurance policies

- **Methodical interest** in **compiling** information to ensure appropriate forms, medical examinations and other policy requirements are completed

- **Social interest** in **persuading** to sell automobile, fire, health, property, marine, aircraft and other types of insurance to clients

- **Directive interest** in responding to clients' questions when claims are made

6231

Physical Activities

Vision
  2   Near vision

Colour Discrimination
  0   Not relevant

Hearing
  2   Verbal interaction

Body Position
  1   Sitting

Limb Co-ordination
  0   Not relevant

Strength
  1   Limited

Environmental Conditions

Location
  L1   Regulated inside climate

Employment Requirements

Education/Training
4, 5, R

- Completion of secondary school is required.

- On-the-job training and completion of insurance industry-sponsored courses and training programs are required.

- Licensing by the Superintendent of Insurance in the province or territory of employment is required.

Workplaces/Employers

Brokerage firms

Insurance companies

Occupational Options

Completion of educational programs through the Insurance Institute of Canada or its provincial counterpart entitles agents to professional recognition as an Associate of the Insurance Institute of Canada (A.I.I.C.) or Fellow of the Insurance Institute of Canada (F.I.I.C.).

Progression to insurance management positions is possible through experience.

Similar Occupations Classified Elsewhere

Insurance Underwriters (1234)

Insurance managers (in 0121 *Insurance, Real Estate and Financial Brokerage Managers*)

6232 Real Estate Agents and Salespersons

Real Estate Agents and Salespersons act as agents for the sale and purchase of houses, apartments, commercial buildings, land and other real estate.

Profile Summary

APTITUDES

G	V	N	S	P	Q	K	F	M
3	3	3	4	4	3	4	4	4

INTERESTS
SMd

DATA PEOPLE THINGS (DPT)
358

PHYSICAL ACTIVITIES (PA)

V	C	H	B	L	S
3	0	2	3	0	1

ENVIRONMENTAL CONDITIONS (EC)
L1

EDUCATION/TRAINING
4, R

Examples of Job Titles

Commercial Real Estate Agent
Estate Agent
Real Estate Agent
Real Estate Broker
Real Estate Sales Representative
Residential Real Estate Agent
Supervisor, Real Estate Agents

Descriptor Profile

Main Characteristics

Occupations in this group are characterized by the following aptitudes, interests and worker functions as they relate to main duties:

- **General learning ability** to assist vendors in selling property by establishing asking price, advertising the property, listing the property with multiple listing services and conducting open houses for prospective buyers

- **Verbal ability** to draw up sales agreements for approval of purchasers and sellers

- **Numerical ability** to calculate data when appraising property and writing up offers to purchase

- **Clerical perception** to prepare sales agreements and related documents

- **Social interest** in **persuading** to solicit property sales listings from prospective vendors; may rent or lease properties on behalf of clients

- **Methodical interest** in **compiling** information to advise clients on market conditions, prices, mortgages, legal requirements and related matters

- **Directive interest** in assisting prospective buyers in selecting, visiting, inspecting and making offers to purchase on real estate properties

6232

Physical Activities

Vision
   3 Near and far vision

Colour Discrimination
   0 Not relevant

Hearing
   2 Verbal interaction

Body Position
   3 Sitting, standing, walking

Limb Co-ordination
   0 Not relevant

Strength
   1 Limited

Environmental Conditions

Location
   L1 Regulated inside climate

Employment Requirements

Education/Training
   4, R

- Completion of secondary school is required.

- Completion of a real estate training course is required.

- Licensing in the province of employment is required.

Workplaces/Employers

Real estate companies

Occupational Options

Real estate agents may operate independently by obtaining a broker's licence in accordance with the regulations of the province of employment. A broker's licence is required to become a manager in real estate.

Similar Occupations Classified Elsewhere

Assessors, Valuators and Appraisers (1235)

Insurance, Real Estate and Financial Brokerage Managers (0121)

Mortgage brokers (in 1114 *Other Financial Officers*)

Rental agents (in 1224 *Property Administrators*)

Right-of-way agents (in 1225 *Purchasing Agents and Officers*)

Remarks

Real estate agents and salespersons normally work on a commission basis.

6233 Retail and Wholesale Buyers

Retail and Wholesale Buyers buy merchandise for resale by retail and wholesale establishments and are usually responsible for the merchandising operations of retail establishments. Buyers who are supervisors and those who are assistants are included in this group.

Profile Summary

APTITUDES

G	V	N	S	P	Q	K	F	M
3	2	3	3	3	3	4	4	4

INTERESTS
MSd

DATA PEOPLE THINGS (DPT)
118

PHYSICAL ACTIVITIES (PA)

V	C	H	B	L	S
2	1	2	3	0	1

ENVIRONMENTAL CONDITIONS (EC)
L1

EDUCATION/TRAINING
6+, 7+

Examples of Job Titles

Appliance Buyer
Assistant Buyer
Buyer - Retail and Wholesale
Chief Buyer
Clothing Buyer
Food Buyer
Merchandiser
Produce Buyer
Senior Buyer
Taster and Buyer, Beverages

Descriptor Profile

Main Characteristics

Occupations in this group are characterized by the following aptitudes, interests and worker functions as they relate to main duties:

- **General learning ability** to review requirements of establishments and determine quantity and type of merchandise to purchase

- **Verbal ability** to establish and maintain contact with suppliers

- **Numerical ability** to purchase merchandise for resale by retail and wholesale establishments

- **Spatial** and **form perception** to select merchandise that best fits the establishments' requirements

- **Clerical perception** to keep records of transactions

- **Methodical interest** in co-ordinating information to study market reports, trade periodicals and sales promotion materials; and in visiting trade shows, showrooms, factories and product design events

- **Social interest** in **negotiating** prices, discounts, credit terms and transportation arrangements when interviewing suppliers

- **Directive interest** in overseeing distribution of merchandise to outlets, in maintaining adequate levels of stock and in supervising the work of other retail buyers

6233

Physical Activities

Vision
  2 Near vision

Colour Discrimination
  1 Relevant

Hearing
  2 Verbal interaction

Body Position
  3 Sitting, standing, walking

Limb Co-ordination
  0 Not relevant

Strength
  1 Limited

Environmental Conditions

Location
  L1 Regulated inside climate

Employment Requirements

Education/Training
6+, 7+

- Completion of secondary school is usually required.

- A university or college diploma in business, marketing or a related program is usually required.

- Experience as a sales supervisor or sales representative is required.

- Supervisors and senior buyers require experience.

Workplaces/Employers

Retail and wholesale establishments

Occupational Options

Retail and wholesale buyers may specialize through experience or product-related training courses.

Progression to *Retail Trade Managers* (0621) or *Sales, Marketing and Advertising Managers* (0611) is possible with additional training or experience.

Similar Occupations Classified Elsewhere

Purchasing Agents and Officers (1225)

Remarks

Retail and wholesale buyers may specialize in a particular merchandise line.

6234 Grain Elevator Operators

Grain Elevator Operators purchase grain from farmers, determine the grade, quality and weight of grain delivered and maintain records for farmers and companies.

Profile Summary

APTITUDES

G	V	N	S	P	Q	K	F	M
3	3	3	4	4	3	4	4	4

INTERESTS
MSd

DATA PEOPLE THINGS (DPT)
232

PHYSICAL ACTIVITIES (PA)

V	C	H	B	L	S
3	0	2	3	1	2

ENVIRONMENTAL CONDITIONS (EC)
L2, H3, D4

EDUCATION/TRAINING
4, R

Examples of Job Titles

Assistant Grain Elevator Manager
District Grain Elevator Manager
Grain Elevator Operator
Primary Grain Elevator Operator

Descriptor Profile

Main Characteristics

Occupations in this group are characterized by the following aptitudes, interests and worker functions as they relate to main duties:

- **General learning ability** to purchase grain and arrange for its transport and storage

- **Verbal ability** to report data to grain companies and the Canadian Wheat Board

- **Numerical ability** to calculate grain quota from information supplied by farmers and the Canadian Wheat Board

- **Clerical perception** to record quota and subsequent deliveries of grain from individual farmers, and to weigh and record type of grain that has been received or is in storage

- **Methodical interest** in **analyzing** information to examine grain samples and conduct tests to determine grade and quality of grain

- **Social interest** in **supervising** the activities of workers; and in acting as a farm sales agent for fertilizers, insecticides and other farm supplies

- **Directive interest** in **controlling** equipment to clean and move grain in elevators, and to load trucks and rail cars

6234

Physical Activities

Vision
   3 Near and far vision

Colour Discrimination
   0 Not relevant

Hearing
   2 Verbal interaction

Body Position
   3 Sitting, standing, walking

Limb Co-ordination
   1 Upper limb co-ordination

Strength
   2 Light

Environmental Conditions

Location
   L2 Unregulated inside climate

Hazards
   H3 Equipment, machinery, tools

Discomforts
   D4 Non-toxic dusts

Employment Requirements

Education/Training
   4, R

- Completion of secondary school is required.

- Several years of experience working in a grain elevator are required.

- On-the-job training is provided.

- A pesticide dispenser's licence is required in Alberta and British Columbia, and may be required in other provinces.

Workplaces/Employers

Licensed grain elevator companies

Occupational Options

Progression from grain elevator manager to district manager is possible with experience.

Similar Occupations Classified Elsewhere

Managers of grain elevator terminals (in 0721 *Facility Operation Managers*)

6241.1 Executive Chefs

Executive Chefs plan and direct food preparation and cooking activities. They may prepare and cook meals and specialty foods.

Profile Summary

APTITUDES

G	V	N	S	P	Q	K	F	M
3	3	3	4	4	3	4	4	4

INTERESTS
DMI

DATA PEOPLE THINGS (DPT)
138

PHYSICAL ACTIVITIES (PA)

V	C	H	B	L	S
2	1	2	1	0	1

ENVIRONMENTAL CONDITIONS (EC)
L1, D3

EDUCATION/TRAINING
4+, 5+, R

Examples of Job Titles

Corporate Chef
Executive Chef
Executive Sous-Chef

Descriptor Profile

Main Characteristics

Occupations in this group are characterized by the following aptitudes, interests and worker functions as they relate to main duties:

- **General learning** and **verbal ability** to plan and direct food preparation and cooking activities of several restaurants in an establishment and for restaurant chains, hospitals and other organizations with food services

- **Numerical ability** to estimate food requirements; may estimate food and labour costs

- **Clerical perception** to read recipes and avoid errors when determining supply requirements and costs

- **Directive interest** in **supervising** the activities of sous-chefs, specialist chefs, chefs and cooks; and in recruiting and hiring staff

- **Methodical interest** in **co-ordinating** information to ensure food meets quality standards; may prepare and cook food on a regular basis or for special guests or functions

- **Innovative interest** in planning menus

6241.1

Physical Activities

Vision
  2 Near vision

Colour Discrimination
  1 Relevant

Hearing
  2 Verbal interaction

Body Position
  1 Sitting

Limb Co-ordination
  0 Not relevant

Strength
  1 Limited

Environmental Conditions

Location
  L1 Regulated inside climate

Discomforts
  D3 Odours

Employment Requirements

Education/Training
  4+, 5+, R

- Completion of secondary school is usually required.

- Completion of a three-year cook's apprenticeship program
  or
  formal training abroad
  or
  equivalent training and experience are required.

- Cook's trade certification is available, but not mandatory, in all provinces and territories.

- Interprovincial trade certification (Red Seal) is also available to qualified cooks.

- Executive chefs usually require several years of experience in commercial food preparation, including two years in a supervisory capacity
  and
  experience as a sous-chef, specialist chef or chef.

Workplaces/Employers

Central food commissaries

Clubs and similar establishments

Hotels

Hospitals and other health care institutions

Restaurants

Ships

Occupational Options

There is some mobility among the various types of chefs in the 6241 group.

Red Seal trade certification allows for interprovincial mobility.

Executive chefs may progress to managerial positions in food preparation establishments.

Similar Occupations Classified Elsewhere

Cooks (6242)

Food Service Counter Attendants and Food Preparers (6641)

6241.2 Sous-Chefs

Sous-Chefs plan and direct food preparation and cooking activities. They may prepare and cook meals and specialty foods.

Profile Summary

APTITUDES

G	V	N	S	P	Q	K	F	M
3	3	3	4	4	4	3	4	3

INTERESTS
MDO

DATA PEOPLE THINGS (DPT)
131

PHYSICAL ACTIVITIES (PA)

V	C	H	B	L	S
2	1	2	2	1	2

ENVIRONMENTAL CONDITIONS (EC)
L1, H3, H7, D3

EDUCATION/TRAINING
4+, 5+, R

Examples of Job Titles

Sous-Chef

Descriptor Profile

Main Characteristics

Occupations in this group are characterized by the following aptitudes, interests and worker functions as they relate to main duties:

- **General learning ability** to acquire and use techniques for planning menus and ordering, storing, preparing and cooking foods

- **Verbal** and **numerical ability** to requisition food and kitchen supplies

- **Motor co-ordination** to cut, decorate and carve food, and to work with kitchen utensils

- **Methodical interest** in **co-ordinating** information on menus, food arrangements and cooking methods; may plan menus and prepare and cook meals or specialty foods

- **Directive interest** in **supervising** activities of specialist chefs, chefs, cooks and other kitchen workers

- **Objective interest** in **precision working** to demonstrate new cooking techniques and equipment to staff

6241.2
Subgroup 2 of 3

Physical Activities

Vision
  2 Near vision

Colour Discrimination
  1 Relevant

Hearing
  2 Verbal interaction

Body Position
  2 Standing and/or walking

Limb Co-ordination
  1 Upper limb co-ordination

Strength
  2 Light

Environmental Conditions

Location
  L1 Regulated inside climate

Hazards
  H3 Equipment, machinery, tools
  H7 Fire, steam, hot surfaces

Discomforts
  D3 Odours

Employment Requirements

Education/Training
  4+, 5+, R

- Completion of secondary school is usually required.

- Completion of a three-year cook's apprenticeship program
  or
  formal training abroad
  or
  equivalent training and experience are required.

- Cook's trade certification is available, but not mandatory, in all provinces and territories.

- Interprovincial trade certification (Red Seal) is also available to qualified cooks.

- Sous-chefs usually require several years of experience in commercial food preparation.

Workplaces/Employers

Central food commissaries

Clubs and similar establishments

Hotels

Hospitals and other health care institutions

Restaurants

Ships

Occupational Options

There is some mobility among the various types of chefs in the 6241 group.

Red Seal trade certification allows for interprovincial mobility.

Similar Occupations Classified Elsewhere

Cooks (6242)

Food Service Counter Attendants and Food Preparers (6641)

6241.3 Chefs and Specialist Chefs

Chefs and Specialist Chefs prepare and cook meals and specialty foods. They also plan and supervise cooking activities.

Profile Summary

APTITUDES

G	V	N	S	P	Q	K	F	M
3	3	3	4	3	4	3	3	3

INTERESTS
MDO

DATA PEOPLE THINGS (DPT)
231

PHYSICAL ACTIVITIES (PA)

V	C	H	B	L	S
2	1	2	2	1	2

ENVIRONMENTAL CONDITIONS (EC)
L1, H3, H7, D3

EDUCATION/TRAINING
4+, 5+, R

Examples of Job Titles

Chef
Chef de cuisine
Chef de partie
Head Chef
Master Chef
Pastry Chef
Saucier
Specialist Chef

Descriptor Profile

Main Characteristics

Occupations in this group are characterized by the following aptitudes, interests and worker functions as they relate to main duties:

- **General learning ability** to acquire and use techniques for planning menus and ordering, storing, preparing and cooking foods

- **Verbal ability** to instruct cooks in the preparation, cooking, garnishing and presentation of food

- **Numerical ability** to estimate food requirements and costs; may requisition food and kitchen supplies

- **Form perception** to examine foods for freshness and proper cooking

- **Motor co-ordination** and **finger dexterity** to cut, decorate and carve food, and to work with kitchen utensils

- **Manual dexterity** to slice and disjoint meat and poultry, mix ingredients, portion foods, knead and stretch dough, and stir soups and sauces

- **Methodical interest** in analyzing information on menus, food arrangements and cooking methods; may plan menus

- **Directive interest** in supervising cooks and other kitchen staff

- **Objective interest** in precision working to prepare and cook complete meals, banquets and specialty foods such as pastries, sauces, soups, salads, vegetables and meat, poultry and fish dishes, and to create decorative food displays

6241.3
Subgroup 3 of 3

Physical Activities

Vision
   2 Near vision

Colour Discrimination
   1 Relevant

Hearing
   2 Verbal interaction

Body Position
   2 Standing and/or walking

Limb Co-ordination
   1 Upper limb co-ordination

Strength
   2 Light

Environmental Conditions

Location
   L1 Regulated inside climate

Hazards
   H3 Equipment, machinery, tools
   H7 Fire, steam, hot surfaces

Discomforts
   D3 Odours

Employment Requirements

Education/Training
   4+, 5+, R

- Completion of secondary school is usually required.

- Completion of a three-year cook's apprenticeship program *or* formal training abroad *or* equivalent training and experience are required.

- Cook's trade certification is available, but not mandatory, in all provinces and territories.

- Interprovincial trade certification (Red Seal) is also available to qualified cooks.

- Specialist chefs and chefs usually require several years of experience in commercial food preparation.

Workplaces/Employers

Central food commissaries

Clubs and similar establishments

Hotels

Hospitals and other health care institutions

Restaurants

Ships

Occupational Options

There is some mobility among the various types of chefs in the 6241 group.

Red Seal trade certification allows for interprovincial mobility.

Similar Occupations Classified Elsewhere

Cooks (6242)

Food Service Counter Attendants and Food Preparers (6641)

6242   Cooks

Cooks prepare and cook a wide variety of foods. Apprentice cooks are included in this group.

Profile Summary

APTITUDES
G	V	N	S	P	Q	K	F	M
3	3	3	4	3	4	3	4	3

INTERESTS
MOd

DATA PEOPLE THINGS (DPT)
331

PHYSICAL ACTIVITIES (PA)
V	C	H	B	L	S
2	1	2	2	1	2

ENVIRONMENTAL CONDITIONS (EC)
L1, H3, H7, D3, D5

EDUCATION/TRAINING
4, 5, 6, R

Examples of Job Titles

Apprentice Cook
Cook
Dietary Cook
First Cook
Grill Cook
Hospital Cook
Institutional Cook
Journeyman/woman Cook
Licensed Cook
Second Cook
Short-Order Cook

Descriptor Profile

Main Characteristics

Occupations in this group are characterized by the following aptitudes, interests and worker functions as they relate to main duties:

- **General learning ability** to acquire and use techniques for preparing and cooking foods, and to determine size of food portions

- **Verbal ability** to order supplies

- **Numerical ability** to estimate food requirements and costs

- **Form perception** to examine foods for freshness and proper cooking

- **Motor co-ordination** to cut, decorate and carve food, and to work with kitchen utensils

- **Manual dexterity** to slice and disjoint meat and poultry, mix ingredients, portion foods, knead and stretch dough, and stir soups and sauces

- **Methodical interest** in **compiling** information to monitor food inventory

- **Objective interest** in **precision working** to prepare and cook complete meals and individual dishes and foods, and to prepare and cook special meals for patients as instructed by dietitians and chefs

- **Directive interest** in **supervising** kitchen helpers; and in overseeing subordinate personnel in the preparation, cooking and handling of food

6242

Physical Activities

Vision
   2 Near vision

Colour Discrimination
   1 Relevant

Hearing
   2 Verbal interaction

Body Position
   2 Standing and/or walking

Limb Co-ordination
   1 Upper limb co-ordination

Strength
   2 Light

Environmental Conditions

Location
   L1 Regulated inside climate

Hazards
   H3 Equipment, machinery, tools
   H7 Fire, steam, hot surfaces

Discomforts
   D3 Odours
   D5 Wetness

Employment Requirements

Education/Training
   4, 5, 6, R

- Completion of secondary school is usually required.

- Completion of a three-year apprenticeship program for cooks
  or
  completion of college or other program in cooking
  or
  several years of commercial cooking experience are required.

- Trade certification is available, but not mandatory, in all provinces and territories.

- Interprovincial trade certification (Red Seal) is also available to qualified cooks.

Workplaces/Employers

Central food commissaries

Construction and logging camp sites

Educational institutions

Hospitals and other health care institutions

Hotels

Restaurants

Ships

Occupational Options

There is mobility among the various types of cooks in this group.

Red Seal trade certification allows for interprovincial mobility.

Progression to supervisory or more senior positions, such as chef, is possible with experience.

Similar Occupations Classified Elsewhere

Chefs (6241)

Food Service Counter Attendants and Food Preparers (6641)

Remarks

Cooks may specialize in preparing and cooking ethnic cuisine or special dishes.

6251 Butchers and Meat Cutters, Retail and Wholesale

Butchers and Meat Cutters, Retail and Wholesale, prepare standard cuts of meat, poultry, fish and shellfish for sale in retail and wholesale food establishments. Butchers who are supervisors and department heads are included in this group.

Profile Summary

APTITUDES

G	V	N	S	P	Q	K	F	M
3	4	4	3	3	5	3	3	3

INTERESTS
MOd

DATA PEOPLE THINGS (DPT)
381

PHYSICAL ACTIVITIES (PA)

V	C	H	B	L	S
2	1	1	2	1	3

ENVIRONMENTAL CONDITIONS (EC)
L1, H3, D3

EDUCATION/TRAINING
2, 5, 6, R

Examples of Job Titles

Butcher Apprentice
Butcher, Retail and Wholesale
Head Butcher, Retail and Wholesale
Meat Cutter, Retail and Wholesale
Supermarket Meat Cutter

Descriptor Profile

Main Characteristics

Occupations in this group are characterized by the following aptitudes, interests and worker functions as they relate to main duties:

- **General learning ability** to cut, trim and otherwise prepare standard cuts of meat, poultry, fish and shellfish for sale at self-serve counters or according to customers' orders

- **Spatial** and **form perception** to prepare special displays of meat, poultry, fish and shellfish

- **Motor co-ordination** and **finger** and **manual dexterity** to shape, lace and tie roasts and other meats, poultry and fish; may wrap prepared meats, poultry, fish and shellfish

- **Methodical interest** in **compiling** information to process customers' orders

- **Objective interest** in **precision working** to grind meats and slice cooked meats using powered grinders and slicing machines

- **Directive interest** in overseeing the work of other butchers and meat cutters

6251

Physical Activities

Vision
  2 Near vision

Colour Discrimination
  1 Relevant

Hearing
  1 Limited

Body Position
  2 Standing and/or walking

Limb Co-ordination
  1 Upper limb co-ordination

Strength
  3 Medium

Environmental Conditions

Location
  L1 Regulated inside climate

Hazards
  H3 Equipment, machinery, tools

Discomforts
  D3 Odours

Employment Requirements

Education/Training
  2, 5, 6, R

- Completion of secondary school may be required.

- Completion of a college or other program in meat cutting may be required.

- On-the-job training in food stores is usually provided for retail butchers and meat cutters.

- Trade certification is available, but voluntary, in British Columbia.

Workplaces/Employers

Butcher shops

Fish stores

Grocery stores

Self-employment

Supermarkets

Similar Occupations Classified Elsewhere

Industrial Butchers and Meat Cutters, Poultry Preparers and Related Workers (9462)

6252 Bakers

Bakers prepare bread, rolls, muffins, pies and cakes for sale in retail food establishments and for serving in restaurants and other establishments. Bakers who are supervisors are included in this group.

Profile Summary

APTITUDES

G	V	N	S	P	Q	K	F	M
3	3	3	3	3	4	3	3	3

INTERESTS
MOd

DATA PEOPLE THINGS (DPT)
382

PHYSICAL ACTIVITIES (PA)

V	C	H	B	L	S
2	1	1	2	1	2

ENVIRONMENTAL CONDITIONS (EC)
L1, H7, D3, D4

EDUCATION/TRAINING
5, 6, R

Examples of Job Titles

Baker
Baker Apprentice
Bakery Supervisor
Head Baker

Descriptor Profile

Main Characteristics

Occupations in this group are characterized by the following aptitudes, interests and worker functions as they relate to main duties:

- **General learning ability** to prepare dough for pies, bread and rolls and sweet goods, and batters for muffins, cookies, cakes, icing and frostings according to recipes and special customer orders

- **Verbal** and **numerical ability** to purchase baking supplies

- **Spatial perception** to visualize and prepare three-dimensional decorating forms for cakes and other baked goods

- **Form perception** to make sure that baked and confectionary goods conform to standards

- **Motor co-ordination** and **finger dexterity** to frost and decorate cakes and other baked goods

- **Manual dexterity** to mix ingredients by hand, measure and weigh ingredients, knead and roll dough, and use various baking utensils

- **Methodical interest** in **compiling** information to record production data and draw up production schedules to determine type and quantity of goods to produce

- **Objective interest** in **controlling** equipment to mix and bake doughs and batters

- **Directive interest** in hiring and training staff; may oversee sales and merchandising of baked goods

6252

Physical Activities

Vision
2 Near vision

Colour Discrimination
1 Relevant

Hearing
1 Limited

Body Position
2 Standing and/or walking

Limb Co-ordination
1 Upper limb co-ordination

Strength
2 Light

Environmental Conditions

Location
L1 Regulated inside climate

Hazards
H7 Fire, steam, hot surfaces

Discomforts
D3 Odours
D4 Non-toxic dusts

Employment Requirements

Education/Training
5, 6, R

- Completion of secondary school is usually required. ✓

- Completion of a three- or four-year apprenticeship program for bakers
  or
  completion of a college or other program for bakers is usually required.

- On-the-job training may be provided.

- Trade certification is available, but voluntary, in Prince Edward Island, Ontario, Alberta, the Northwest Territories, British Columbia and the Yukon.

- Interprovincial trade certification (Red Seal) is also available to qualified bakers.

Workplaces/Employers

Bakeries
Hotels
Restaurants
Self-employment
Supermarkets

Occupational Options

Red Seal trade certification allows for interprovincial mobility.

Similar Occupations Classified Elsewhere

Baking machine operators (in 9461 *Process Control and Machine Operators, Food and Beverage Processing*)

Pastry chefs (in 6241 *Chefs*)

6261 Police Officers (Except Commissioned)

Police Officers protect the public, detect and prevent crime and perform other activities directed at maintaining law and order. This group includes military police, Ports Canada police and railway police.

Profile Summary

APTITUDES

G	V	N	S	P	Q	K	F	M
3	3	3	3	3	4	3	4	3

INTERESTS
MDS

DATA PEOPLE THINGS (DPT)
263

PHYSICAL ACTIVITIES (PA)

V	C	H	B	L	S
4	1	2	3	2	4

ENVIRONMENTAL CONDITIONS (EC)
L1, L3, L4*, H3, H8

EDUCATION/TRAINING
5+, 6+, 7+

Examples of Job Titles

Community Relations Officer
Constable
Crime Prevention Constable
Detective
Harbour Police Officer
Highway Police Officer
Military Police Officer
Police Cadet
Police Diver
Police Officer
Police Sergeant
Railway Police Officer
RCMP Officer

Descriptor Profile

Main Characteristics

Occupations in this group are characterized by the following aptitudes, interests and worker functions as they relate to main duties:

- **General learning ability** to protect the public, detect and prevent crime and perform other activities directed at maintaining law and order

- **Verbal ability** to interview witnesses, compile notes and reports and provide testimony in courts of law

- **Numerical ability** and **spatial** and **form perception** to secure evidence

- **Motor co-ordination** and **finger** and **manual dexterity** to provide emergency assistance to victims of accidents, crimes and natural disasters

- **Methodical interest** in **analyzing** information to investigate crimes and accidents

- **Directive interest** in **driving** when patrolling assigned areas to maintain public safety and order; and in enforcing laws and regulations and arresting criminal suspects; may supervise and co-ordinate the work of other police officers

- **Social interest** in **speaking** to the public when participating in crime prevention, public information and safety programs

6261

Physical Activities

Vision
    4   Total visual field

Colour Discrimination
    1   Relevant

Hearing
    2   Verbal interaction

Body Position
    3   Sitting, standing, walking

Limb Co-ordination
    2   Multiple limb co-ordination

Strength
    4   Heavy

Environmental Conditions

Location
    L1 Regulated inside climate
    L3 Outside
    L4* In a vehicle or cab

Hazards
    H3 Equipment, machinery, tools
    H8 Dangerous locations

Employment Requirements

Education/Training
5+, 6+, 7+

- Completion of secondary school is required.

- Completion of a college program or university degree in law and security or in the social sciences may be required.

- A three-to-six month police training program is provided.

- Physical agility, strength, fitness and vision requirements must be met.

- Experience as a constable is required for detectives and sergeants.

Workplaces/Employers

Canadian Forces

Municipal, provincial and federal governments

Occupational Options

Progression to commissioned police officer positions is possible with additional training and experience.

Similar Occupations Classified Elsewhere

By-law Enforcement and Other Regulatory Officers, n.e.c. (6463)

Commissioned Police Officers (0641)

Sheriffs and Bailiffs (6461)

Private detectives (in 6465 *Other Protective Service Occupations*)

Remarks

*Environmental Conditions

- For some occupations in this group, Location L4 (In a vehicle or cab) may also apply.

6262 Firefighters

Firefighters carry out firefighting and fire prevention activities and assist in other emergencies.

Profile Summary

APTITUDES

G	V	N	S	P	Q	K	F	M
3	3	4	3	3	5	3	4	3

INTERESTS
OMD

DATA PEOPLE THINGS (DPT)
358

PHYSICAL ACTIVITIES (PA)

V	C	H	B	L	S
4	0	2	4	2	4

ENVIRONMENTAL CONDITIONS (EC)
L1, L2, L3, H1, H3, H4, H6, H7, H8, D1, D3, D4, D5

EDUCATION/TRAINING
3+, 5+, 6+

Examples of Job Titles

Airport Firefighter
Fire Captain
Firefighter
Firefighter, Shipboard
Industrial Firefighter
Lieutenant, Firefighter

Descriptor Profile

Main Characteristics

Occupations in this group are characterized by the following aptitudes, interests and worker functions as they relate to main duties:

- **General learning ability** to carry out firefighting and fire prevention activities, and to respond to other calls for assistance such as automobile and industrial accidents

- **Verbal ability** and **spatial** and **form perception** to rescue victims from burning buildings and accident sites

- **Motor co-ordination** and **manual dexterity** to control and extinguish fires using manual and power equipment such as axes, water hoses, aerial ladders and hydraulic equipment

- **Objective interest** in ensuring proper operation and maintenance of firefighting equipment

- **Methodical interest** in **compiling** information to administer first aid and other assistance, and in training to maintain a high level of physical fitness

- **Directive interest** in **persuading** to inform and educate the public on fire prevention; may supervise and co-ordinate the work of other firefighters

6262

Physical Activities

Vision
    4   Total visual field

Colour Discrimination
    0   Not relevant

Hearing
    2   Verbal interaction

Body Position
    4   Other body positions

Limb Co-ordination
    2   Multiple limb co-ordination

Strength
    4   Heavy

Environmental Conditions

Location
    L1 Regulated inside climate
    L2 Unregulated inside climate
    L3 Outside

Hazards
    H1 Dangerous chemical substances
    H3 Equipment, machinery, tools
    H4 Electricity
    H6 Flying particles, falling objects
    H7 Fire, steam, hot surfaces
    H8 Dangerous locations

Discomforts
    D1 Noise
    D3 Odours
    D4 Non-toxic dusts
    D5 Wetness

Employment Requirements

Education/Training
    3+, 5+, 6+

- Completion of secondary school is usually required.

- Completion of a college program in fire protection technology or a related field may be required.

- A municipal firefighter's training course is provided.

- Experience as a volunteer firefighter may be required.

- Physical agility, strength, fitness and vision requirements must be met.

- Several years of experience are required for senior firefighters such as lieutenants and captains.

Workplaces/Employers

Internal firefighting services of large industrial establishments

Municipal, provincial and federal governments

Occupational Options

Progression to senior positions, such as fire chief, is possible with additional training and several years of experience.

Similar Occupations Classified Elsewhere

Fire Chiefs and Senior Firefighting Officers (0642)

Forest firefighters (in 8422 *Silviculture and Forestry Workers*)

6271.1 Hairstylists

Hairstylists cut and style hair and perform related services.

Profile Summary

APTITUDES

G	V	N	S	P	Q	K	F	M
3	3	4	4	3	4	3	2	3

INTERESTS
IOS

DATA PEOPLE THINGS (DPT)
374

PHYSICAL ACTIVITIES (PA)

V	C	H	B	L	S
2	1	2	2	1	1

ENVIRONMENTAL CONDITIONS (EC)
L1, H3, D3, D5

EDUCATION/TRAINING
2, 5, 6, R

Examples of Job Titles

Hair Colour Technician
Hairdresser
Hairdresser Apprentice
Hairstylist
Hairstylist Apprentice
Wig Stylist

Descriptor Profile

Main Characteristics

Occupations in this group are characterized by the following aptitudes, interests and worker functions as they relate to main duties:

- **General learning** and **verbal ability** to suggest hair styles compatible with clients' physical features and to determine styles from clients' instructions and preferences

- **Form perception** to observe detail in facial features and analyze hair and scalp conditions

- **Motor co-ordination** and **finger dexterity** to cut, trim, taper, curl, wave, perm and style hair

- **Manual dexterity** to shampoo and rinse hair and apply bleach, tint, dye and rinses to colour, frost and streak hair

- **Innovative interest** in **compiling** information to provide basic treatment and advice on beauty care treatments for scalp and hair

- **Objective interest** in **manipulating** combs, scissors, clippers, brushes and other devices to cut and style hair

- **Social interest** in **serving** clients by cutting and styling hair and performing related services; may train and supervise other hairstylists, hairdressers and assistants

6271.1

Physical Activities

Vision
   2 Near vision

Colour Discrimination
   1 Relevant

Hearing
   2 Verbal interaction

Body Position
   2 Standing and/or walking

Limb Co-ordination
   1 Upper limb co-ordination

Strength
   1 Limited

Environmental Conditions

Location
   L1 Regulated inside climate

Hazards
   H3 Equipment, machinery, tools

Discomforts
   D3 Odours
   D5 Wetness

Employment Requirements

Education/Training
2, 5, 6, R

- Some secondary school education is required.

- Completion of a two-to-three year hairstyling apprenticeship program or completion of a college or other program in hairstyling combined with on-the-job training is usually required.

- Several years of experience may substitute for formal education or training.

- There are various provincial certification and licensing requirements for hairstylists, ranging from trade certification to licensing by a provincial association.

Workplaces/Employers

Barber shops

Hair replacement clinics and studios

Hairstyling or hairdressing salons

Health care establishments

Theatre, film and television establishments

Vocational schools

Similar Occupations Classified Elsewhere

Estheticians, Electrologists and Related Occupations (6482)

Hairdressing teachers (in 4131 *College and Other Vocational Instructors*)

6271.2 Barbers

Barbers cut and style hair and perform related services.

Profile Summary

APTITUDES

G	V	N	S	P	Q	K	F	M
3	3	4	4	3	4	3	3	3

INTERESTS
OMS

DATA PEOPLE THINGS (DPT)
374

PHYSICAL ACTIVITIES (PA)

V	C	H	B	L	S
2	1	2	2	1	1

ENVIRONMENTAL CONDITIONS (EC)
L1, H3

EDUCATION/TRAINING
2, 5, R

Examples of Job Titles

Barber
Barber Apprentice

Descriptor Profile

Main Characteristics

Occupations in this group are characterized by the following aptitudes, interests and worker functions as they relate to main duties:

- **General learning** and **verbal ability** to cut and trim hair according to clients' instructions and preferences

- **Form perception** to **observe** detail in facial features and analyze hair and scalp conditions

- **Motor co-ordination** and **finger dexterity** to cut and trim hair, and shave and trim beards and moustaches

- **Manual dexterity** to move hands and wrists easily and skillfully; may shampoo hair, provide other hair treatments such as waving, straightening and tinting, and provide scalp conditioning massages

- **Objective interest** in **manipulating** combs, scissors, clippers (hand or electric), brushes, razors and other devices to cut and style hair, and shave and trim beards and moustaches

- **Methodical interest** in **compiling** information to provide advice on services related to the care of hair, face and scalp; may advise on hair problems and suggest grooming aids and appropriate hair styles

- **Social interest** in **serving** clients by providing services related to the care of hair, face and scalp

Physical Activities

Vision
   2 Near vision

Colour Discrimination
   1 Relevant

Hearing
   2 Verbal interaction

Body Position
   2 Standing and/or walking

Limb Co-ordination
   1 Upper limb co-ordination

Strength
   1 Limited

Environmental Conditions

Location
   L1 Regulated inside climate

Hazards
   H3 Equipment, machinery, tools

Employment Requirements

Education/Training
   2, 5, R

- Some secondary school education is required.

- Completion of a two-year apprenticeship or other barber program is usually required.

- On-the-job training may substitute for formal education.

- There are various provincial certification and licensing requirements for barbers, ranging from trade certification to licensing by a provincial association.

Workplaces/Employers

Barber shops

Hair replacement clinics and studios

Hairstyling or hairdressing salons

Health care establishments

Theatre, film and television establishments

Vocational schools

Similar Occupations Classified Elsewhere

Estheticians, Electrologists and Related Occupations (6482)

Hairdressing teachers (in 4131 *College and Other Vocational Instructors*)

6272.1 Funeral Directors

Funeral Directors co-ordinate and arrange all aspects of funeral services.

Profile Summary

APTITUDES

G	V	N	S	P	Q	K	F	M
3	2	3	4	4	3	4	4	4

INTERESTS
DSM

DATA PEOPLE THINGS (DPT)
128

PHYSICAL ACTIVITIES (PA)

V	C	H	B	L	S
2	0	2	1	0	1

ENVIRONMENTAL CONDITIONS (EC)
L1

EDUCATION/TRAINING
5+, R

Examples of Job Titles

Assistant Funeral Director
Funeral Director

Descriptor Profile

Main Characteristics

Occupations in this group are characterized by the following aptitudes, interests and worker functions as they relate to main duties:

- **General learning ability** to oversee the preparation of human remains, plan and schedule funeral services, co-ordinate burials and cremations and complete legal documents

- **Verbal ability** to contact family and friends, issue death notices to newspapers and discuss and negotiate pre-arranged funerals with clients

- **Numerical ability** and **clerical perception** to prepare accounts, keep financial records and order merchandise

- **Directive interest** in **co-ordinating** information to manage funeral home operations; and in hiring and supervising embalmers, funeral attendants and other staff

- **Social interest** in **consulting** with families regarding the nature of the funeral service, disposition of the remains and funeral costs, and to inform survivors of benefits for which they may be eligible

- **Methodical interest** in maintaining financial records; may perform the same duties as embalmers

Physical Activities

Vision
    2 Near vision

Colour Discrimination
    0 Not relevant

Hearing
    2 Verbal interaction

Body Position
    1 Sitting

Limb Co-ordination
    0 Not relevant

Strength
    1 Limited

Environmental Conditions

Location
    L1 Regulated inside climate

Employment Requirements

Education/Training
    5+, R

- Completion of secondary school is usually required for funeral directors.

- Funeral directors usually require a year of training under the supervision of a licensed funeral director
and
completion of a qualifying examination.

- Funeral directors require licensing in all provinces except Prince Edward Island and British Columbia.

- Funeral directors are required to be licensed as embalmers in all provinces except Prince Edward Island, Saskatchewan and British Columbia.

Workplaces/Employers

Funeral homes

Similar Occupations Classified Elsewhere

Bereavement counsellors (in 4153 *Family, Marriage and Other Related Counsellors*)

Funeral attendants (in 6683 *Other Elemental Service Occupations*)

Funeral services general managers (in 0015 *Senior Managers - Trade, Broadcasting and Other Services, n.e.c.*)

6272.2 Embalmers

Embalmers prepare human remains for funerals and burial.

Profile Summary

APTITUDES

G	V	N	S	P	Q	K	F	M
3	4	4	3	3	4	3	3	3

INTERESTS
MOi

DATA PEOPLE THINGS (DPT)
381

PHYSICAL ACTIVITIES (PA)

V	C	H	B	L	S
2	1	2	2	1	2

ENVIRONMENTAL CONDITIONS (EC)
L1, H2, D3

EDUCATION/TRAINING
5+, R

Examples of Job Titles

Apprentice Embalmer

Embalmer

Descriptor Profile

Main Characteristics

Occupations in this group are characterized by the following aptitudes, interests and worker functions as they relate to main duties:

- **General learning ability** to understand, acquire and apply techniques of embalming

- **Spatial** and **form perception** to perform cosmetic and restorative work on human remains

- **Motor co-ordination** and **finger** and **manual dexterity** to prepare bodies for interment

- **Methodical interest** in **compiling** information to maintain records

- **Objective interest** in **precision working** to preserve, sanitize and prepare remains for funeral services

- **Innovative interest** in restoring bodies to their normal appearance

Physical Activities

Vision
  2 Near vision

Colour Discrimination
  1 Relevant

Hearing
  2 Verbal interaction

Body Position
  2 Standing and/or walking

Limb Co-ordination
  1 Upper limb co-ordination

Strength
  2 Light

Environmental Conditions

Location
  L1 Regulated inside climate

Hazards
  H2 Biological agents

Discomforts
  D3 Odours

Employment Requirements

Education/Training
  5+, R

- Completion of secondary school is usually required for embalmers.

- Embalmers usually require completion of a two-to-three year apprenticeship program for embalmers
  and
  completion of a qualifying examination.

- Embalmers require licensing in all provinces except British Columbia.

Workplaces/Employers

Funeral homes

Similar Occupations Classified Elsewhere

Bereavement counsellors (in 4153 *Family, Marriage and Other Related Counsellors*)

Funeral attendants (in 6683 *Other Elemental Service Occupations*)

Funeral services general managers (in 0015 *Senior Managers - Trade, Broadcasting and Other Services, n.e.c.*)

6411 Sales Representatives, Wholesale Trade (Non-Technical)

Sales Representatives, Wholesale Trade (Non-Technical), sell non-technical goods and services to retail, wholesale, commercial, industrial and professional clients. Sales Representatives, Wholesale Trade, who are supervisors are also included in this group.

Profile Summary

APTITUDES

G	V	N	S	P	Q	K	F	M
3	3	3	4	4	3	4	4	4

INTERESTS
SMd

DATA PEOPLE THINGS (DPT)
358

PHYSICAL ACTIVITIES (PA)

V	C	H	B	L	S
2	0	2	3	0	2

ENVIRONMENTAL CONDITIONS (EC)
L1

EDUCATION/TRAINING
4, 5, 6, 7

Examples of Job Titles

Account Executive - Wholesale Trade

Food Products Sales Representative

Freight Sales Agent

Graphic Design Sales Representative

Hotel Accommodations Sales Executive

Liquor Sales Representative - Wholesale

Magazine Sales Representative - Wholesale

Oil Distributor

Periodicals Sales Representative

Security Services Sales Consultant

Supervisor, Wholesale Trade Representatives

Transfer Company Agent

Descriptor Profile

Main Characteristics

Occupations in this group are characterized by the following aptitudes, interests and worker functions as they relate to main duties:

- **General learning ability** to review and adapt to information regarding product innovations, competitors and market conditions

- **Verbal ability** to prepare sales contracts and consult with clients after sales to resolve problems and provide ongoing support

- **Numerical ability** and **clerical perception** to estimate and quote prices, credit terms, warranties and delivery dates

- **Social interest** in **persuading** to promote sales to existing clients; and in providing clients with presentations on the benefits and uses of goods and services

- **Methodical interest** in **compiling** information to identify and solicit potential clients

- **Directive interest** in overseeing the preparation of sales contracts; may supervise the activities of other sales representatives

6411

Physical Activities

Vision
  2 Near vision

Colour Discrimination
  0 Not relevant

Hearing
  2 Verbal interaction

Body Position
  3 Sitting, standing, walking

Limb Co-ordination
  0 Not relevant

Strength
  2 Light

Environmental Conditions

Location
  L1 Regulated inside climate

Employment Requirements

Education/Training
  4, 5, 6, 7

- Completion of secondary school is required.

- A university degree or completion of a college or other program may be required.

- Experience in sales or in an occupation related to the product or service is usually required.

- Supervisors and senior sales representatives require experience.

Workplaces/Employers

Business services firms

Clothing manufacturers

Food, beverage and tobacco producers

Hotels

Motor vehicles and parts manufacturers

Petroleum companies

Transportation companies

Occupational Options

Progression to sales management positions is possible with additional training or experience.

Similar Occupations Classified Elsewhere

Retail Salespersons and Sales Clerks (6421)

Sales, Marketing and Advertising Managers (0611)

Technical Sales Specialists, Wholesale Trade (6221)

6421 Retail Salespersons and Sales Clerks

Retail Salespersons and Sales Clerks sell and rent a range of goods and services to the general public.

Profile Summary

APTITUDES

G	V	N	S	P	Q	K	F	M
3	3	3	4	4	3	4	4	4

INTERESTS
MSd

DATA PEOPLE THINGS (DPT)
457

PHYSICAL ACTIVITIES (PA)

V	C	H	B	L	S
2	1	2	2	1	2

ENVIRONMENTAL CONDITIONS (EC)
L1

EDUCATION/TRAINING
2

Examples of Job Titles

Audio Equipment Salesperson
Automobile Salesperson
Car Rental Agent
Clothing Salesperson
Computer Salesperson - Retail
Counter Clerk - Retail
Department Store Clerk
Furniture Salesperson
Hardware Store Clerk
Jewellery Salesperson
Retail Sales Clerk
Retail Salesperson

Descriptor Profile

Main Characteristics

Occupations in this group are characterized by the following aptitudes, interests and worker functions as they relate to main duties:

- **General learning ability** to greet customers and discuss the type, quality and quantity of merchandise sought for purchase and rental

- **Verbal ability** to advise customers on the use and care of merchandise

- **Numerical ability** to estimate and quote prices, credit terms, trade-in allowances, warranties and delivery dates

- **Clerical perception** to prepare sales contracts and accept cash, cheques, credit cards and automatic debit payments

- **Methodical interest** in **computing** to maintain sales records for inventory control

- **Social interest** in **persuading** to sell and rent merchandise to customers

- **Directive interest** in **handling** to prepare merchandise for purchase and rental, and to assist in the display of merchandise

6421

Physical Activities

Vision
   2 Near vision

Colour Discrimination
   1 Relevant

Hearing
   2 Verbal interaction

Body Position
   2 Standing and/or walking

Limb Co-ordination
   1 Upper limb co-ordination

Strength
   2 Light

Environmental Conditions

Location
   L1 Regulated inside climate

Employment Requirements

Education/Training
2

- Completion of secondary school may be required.

- Demonstrated sales ability and product knowledge are usually required for retail sales persons who sell complex or valuable merchandise, such as automobiles, antiques or computers.

Workplaces/Employers

Stores and other retail businesses

Wholesale businesses that sell on a retail basis

Occupational Options

Progression to retail supervisory positions is possible with additional training or experience.

Similar Occupations Classified Elsewhere

Cashiers (6611)

Retail stock clerks (in 6622 *Grocery Clerks and Shelf Stockers*)

Sales clerk supervisors (in 6211 *Retail Trade Supervisors*)

6431 Travel Counsellors

Travel Counsellors advise clients on travel options and tour packages, make bookings and reservations, prepare tickets and receive payments.

Profile Summary

APTITUDES

G	V	N	S	P	Q	K	F	M
3	3	3	4	4	3	4	4	4

INTERESTS
SMi

DATA PEOPLE THINGS (DPT)
354

PHYSICAL ACTIVITIES (PA)

V	C	H	B	L	S
2	0	2	1	1	1

ENVIRONMENTAL CONDITIONS (EC)
L1

EDUCATION/TRAINING
5, 6, R

Examples of Job Titles

Travel Agent
Travel Consultant
Travel Counsellor

Descriptor Profile

Main Characteristics

Occupations in this group are characterized by the following aptitudes, interests and worker functions as they relate to main duties:

- **General learning ability** to plan and organize vacation travel for individuals and groups

- **Verbal ability** to provide travel tips regarding tourist attractions, foreign currencies, customs, languages and travel safety

- **Numerical ability** to calculate travel costs and receive payments

- **Clerical perception** to perceive detail in verbal and tabular materials when making transportation and accommodation reservations

- **Social interest** in **persuading** clients by promoting particular destinations, tour packages and other travel services, and by selling single-fare tickets and package tours

- **Methodical interest** in **compiling** information to provide travel details to clients regarding destinations, transportation and accommodation options and costs

- **Innovative interest** in **operating** computerized reservation and ticketing system to make bookings and reservations

6431

Physical Activities

Vision
  2   Near vision

Colour Discrimination
  0   Not relevant

Hearing
  2   Verbal interaction

Body Position
  1   Sitting

Limb Co-ordination
  1   Upper limb co-ordination

Strength
  1   Limited

Environmental Conditions

Location
  L1   Regulated inside climate

Employment Requirements

Education/Training
5, 6, R

- Completion of secondary school is required.

- A college diploma or vocational training in travel or tourism is usually required.

- Certification with the Canadian Institute of Travel Counsellors may be required. A Certified Travel Counsellor designation is granted after three years of work experience in the industry and the completion of mandatory courses and examinations.

Workplaces/Employers

Hotel chains

Tourism firms

Transportation firms

Travel agencies

Occupational Options

Progression to managerial positions is possible with experience.

Similar Occupations Classified Elsewhere

Airline ticket agents (in 6433 *Airline Sales and Service Agents*)

Convention co-ordinators (in 1226 *Conference and Event Planners*)

Travel agency managers (in 0621 *Retail Trade Managers*)

6432.1 Flight Attendants

Flight Attendants ensure the safety and comfort of passengers aboard aircraft.

Profile Summary

APTITUDES

G	V	N	S	P	Q	K	F	M
3	3	4	4	4	3	4	4	4

INTERESTS
MSo

DATA PEOPLE THINGS (DPT)
677

PHYSICAL ACTIVITIES (PA)

V	C	H	B	L	S
3	0	2	3	1	2

ENVIRONMENTAL CONDITIONS (EC)
L1, L4, H8, D1, D2

EDUCATION/TRAINING
5

Examples of Job Titles

Flight Attendant

Descriptor Profile

Main Characteristics

Occupations in this group are characterized by the following aptitudes, interests and worker functions as they relate to main duties:

- **General learning ability** to ensure the safety and comfort of passengers

- **Verbal ability** to greet passengers, explain safety features and answer passenger's inquiries

- **Clerical perception** to perceive detail when verifying boarding passes

- **Methodical interest** in **comparing** information to ensure accuracy of inventories of meals, beverages and first-aid supplies

- **Social interest** in **assisting** passengers and attending to their safety during take-offs, landings and emergencies

- **Objective interest** in **handling** equipment to serve food and beverages and make flight announcements

6432.1
Subgroup 1 of 3

Physical Activities

Vision
   3   Near and far vision

Colour Discrimination
   0   Not relevant

Hearing
   2   Verbal interaction

Body Position
   3   Sitting, standing, walking

Limb Co-ordination
   1   Upper limb co-ordination

Strength
   2   Light

Environmental Conditions

Location
   L1   Regulated inside climate
   L4   In a vehicle or cab

Hazards
   H8   Dangerous locations

Discomforts
   D1   Noise
   D2   Vibration

Employment Requirements

Education/Training
5

- Flight attendants require the completion of secondary school and a Transport Canada-approved training program.

- Flight attendants usually require experience working with the public.

Workplaces/Employers

Airline companies

Similar Occupations Classified Elsewhere

Food and beverage servers on trains (in 6453 *Food and Beverage Servers*)

Ship and rail service attendants [in 6672 *Other Attendants in Accommodation and Travel (Except Airline Travel)*]

6432.2 Flight Pursers and Passenger Service Directors

Flight Pursers and Passenger Service Directors ensure the safety and comfort of passengers aboard aircraft.

Profile Summary

APTITUDES

G	V	N	S	P	Q	K	F	M
3	3	4	4	4	3	4	4	4

INTERESTS
MDs

DATA PEOPLE THINGS (DPT)
337

PHYSICAL ACTIVITIES (PA)

V	C	H	B	L	S
3	0	2	3	1	2

ENVIRONMENTAL CONDITIONS (EC)
L1, L4, H8, D1, D2

EDUCATION/TRAINING
5

Examples of Job Titles

Flight Service Director
Passenger Service Director
Purser, Airline

Descriptor Profile

Main Characteristics

Occupations in this group are characterized by the following aptitudes, interests and worker functions as they relate to main duties:

- **General learning ability** to ensure that services are provided for the safety and comfort of passengers

- **Verbal ability** to greet passengers, provide flight information, describe customs and immigration procedures, and answer inquiries regarding connections and schedules

- **Clerical perception** to read schedules and timetables correctly, and to perceive detail when verifying boarding passes

- **Methodical interest** in **compiling** information to prepare records related to en-route services and to complete reports

- **Directive interest** in **supervising** flight attendants and in co-ordinating their activities

- **Social interest** in **handling** equipment to provide services to passengers

6432.2
Subgroup 2 of 3

Physical Activities

Vision
  3   Near and far vision

Colour Discrimination
  0   Not relevant

Hearing
  2   Verbal interaction

Body Position
  3   Sitting, standing, walking

Limb Co-ordination
  1   Upper limb co-ordination

Strength
  2   Light

Environmental Conditions

Location
  L1 Regulated inside climate
  L4 In a vehicle or cab

Hazards
  H8 Dangerous locations

Discomforts
  D1 Noise
  D2 Vibration

Employment Requirements

Education/Training
  5

- Flight pursers require the completion of secondary school and a Transport Canada-approved training program.

- Flight pursers require experience as a flight attendant.

Workplaces/Employers

Airline companies

Occupational Options

There is little mobility between airline pursers and ship pursers.

Similar Occupations Classified Elsewhere

Food and beverage servers on trains (in 6453 *Food and Beverage Servers*)

Ship and rail service attendants [in 6672 *Other Attendants in Accommodation and Travel (Except Airline Travel)*]

6432.3 Ship Pursers

Ship Pursers attend to the safety and comfort of passengers aboard ships.

Profile Summary

APTITUDES

G	V	N	S	P	Q	K	F	M
3	3	4	4	4	3	4	4	4

INTERESTS
MDs

DATA PEOPLE THINGS (DPT)
337

PHYSICAL ACTIVITIES (PA)

V	C	H	B	L	S
3	0	2	3	1	2

ENVIRONMENTAL CONDITIONS (EC)
L1, L4, H8, D1

EDUCATION/TRAINING
2

Examples of Job Titles

Ship Purser

Descriptor Profile

Main Characteristics

Occupations in this group are characterized by the following aptitudes, interests and worker functions as they relate to main duties:

- **General learning ability** to conduct ship's business and attend to the safety and comfort of passengers

- **Verbal ability** and **clerical perception** to assist passengers in preparing customs declarations

- **Methodical interest** in **compiling** information for signing on crew and in maintaining payroll records

- **Directive interest** in **supervising** the activities of a ship's attendants and overseeing the storage of baggage

- **Social interest** in **handling** equipment to provide services to passengers; and in arranging activities for passengers

Physical Activities

Vision
  3   Near and far vision

Colour Discrimination
  0   Not relevant

Hearing
  2   Verbal interaction

Body Position
  3   Sitting, standing, walking

Limb Co-ordination
  1   Upper limb co-ordination

Strength
  2   Light

Environmental Conditions

Location
  L1 Regulated inside climate
  L4 In a vehicle or cab

Hazards
  H8 Dangerous locations

Discomforts
  D1 Noise

Employment Requirements

Education/Training
  2

- Ship pursers may require experience as a ship attendant.

- Ship pursers usually require experience working with the public.

Workplaces/Employers

Tour boat or cruise ship companies

Occupational Options

There is little mobility between airline pursers and ship pursers.

Similar Occupations Classified Elsewhere

Food and beverage servers on trains (in 6453 *Food and Beverage Servers*)

Ship and rail service attendants [in 6672 *Other Attendants in Accommodation and Travel (Except Airline Travel)*]

6433.1 Airline Passenger and Ticket Agents

Airline Passenger and Ticket Agents issue tickets, make reservations, trace missing baggage, arrange for cargo shipments and provide related customer services to assist airline passengers.

Profile Summary

APTITUDES

G	V	N	S	P	Q	K	F	M
3	3	3	4	4	2	4	4	4

INTERESTS
MSO

DATA PEOPLE THINGS (DPT)
564

PHYSICAL ACTIVITIES (PA)

V	C	H	B	L	S
2	0	2	1	1	1

ENVIRONMENTAL CONDITIONS (EC)
L1

EDUCATION/TRAINING
4

Examples of Job Titles

Counter Service Agent, Airline
Customer Service Agent, Airline
Passenger Agent, Airline
Sales and Service Agent, Airline
Ticket Agent, Airline

Descriptor Profile

Main Characteristics

Occupations in this group are characterized by the following aptitudes, interests and worker functions as they relate to main duties:

- **General learning ability** to make reservations and prepare and issue tickets

- **Verbal ability** to provide information on fares, flight schedules and routes; to inform passengers of changes in travelling arrangements; to cancel and confirm reservations; and to direct passengers to designated areas for boarding

- **Numerical ability** to compute cost of tickets

- **Clerical perception** to perceive detail in verbal and tabular materials when using timetables, manuals, reference guides and tariff books; to assign seats; and to avoid errors in the preparation of tickets and boarding passes

- **Methodical interest** in **copying** information to keep inventory of available passenger space

- **Social interest** in **speaking** with passengers while attending boarding gates and in assisting pre-boarding passengers

- **Objective interest** in **operating** equipment to make and confirm reservations; to issue tickets, boarding passes and baggage receipts; and to check baggage

6433.1
Subgroup 1 of 6

Physical Activities

Vision
  2 Near vision

Colour Discrimination
  0 Not relevant

Hearing
  2 Verbal interaction

Body Position
  1 Sitting

Limb Co-ordination
  1 Upper limb co-ordination

Strength
  1 Limited

Environmental Conditions

Location
  L1 Regulated inside climate

Employment Requirements

Education/Training
  4

- Completion of secondary school is usually required.

- Several weeks of on-the-job and classroom training are provided.

Workplaces/Employers

Airline companies

Occupational Options

Depending on the size of the airline or airport, the duties of workers in the 6433 group may overlap.

Progression to supervisory positions is possible with experience.

Similar Occupations Classified Elsewhere

Ticket and Cargo Agents and Related Clerks (Except Airline) (6434)

Travel Counsellors (6431)

Airline cargo and baggage handlers (in 7437 *Air Transport Ramp Attendants*)

Supervisors of airline sales and service agents (in 6216 *Other Service Supervisors*)

6433.2 Airline Baggage Agents

Airline Baggage Agents trace missing baggage and provide related customer services to assist airline passengers.

Profile Summary

APTITUDES

G	V	N	S	P	Q	K	F	M
3	3	3	4	4	2	4	4	4

INTERESTS
MSO

DATA PEOPLE THINGS (DPT)
567

PHYSICAL ACTIVITIES (PA)

V	C	H	B	L	S
2	0	2	1	1	1

ENVIRONMENTAL CONDITIONS (EC)
L1

EDUCATION/TRAINING
4

Examples of Job Titles

Airline Baggage Agent

Baggage Tracer, Airline

Descriptor Profile

Main Characteristics

Occupations in this group are characterized by the following aptitudes, interests and worker functions as they relate to main duties:

- **General learning ability** to trace lost, delayed and misdirected baggage

- **Verbal ability** to receive complaints from passengers regarding lost, mishandled, delayed and damaged baggage

- **Numerical ability** to authorize limited expenditures to provide for emergency assistance to passengers

- **Clerical perception** to prepare lost and found reports, damage reports and forwarding instructions, and to complete tracing forms, customs clearances and other documents

- **Methodical interest** in **copying** information to recover lost baggage, to take corrective measures according to company policies and to arrange for delivery of relocated items to passengers

- **Social interest** in **speaking** with customers to obtain information for tracing lost baggage and to communicate with agents at other locations in the airline system

- **Objective interest** in **handling** equipment to sort and dispatch outbound baggage to departing aircraft, and to dispense inbound baggage being delivered to passengers on arrival at their destinations

6433.2

Physical Activities

Vision
   2 Near vision

Colour Discrimination
   0 Not relevant

Hearing
   2 Verbal interaction

Body Position
   1 Sitting

Limb Co-ordination
   1 Upper limb co-ordination

Strength
   1 Limited

Environmental Conditions

Location
   L1 Regulated inside climate

Employment Requirements

Education/Training
4

- Completion of secondary school is usually required.

- Several weeks of on-the-job and classroom training are provided.

Workplaces/Employers

Airline companies

Occupational Options

Depending on the size of the airline or airport, the duties of workers in the 6433 group may overlap.

Progression to supervisory positions is possible through experience.

Similar Occupations Classified Elsewhere

Ticket and Cargo Agents and Related Clerks (Except Airline) (6434)

Travel Counsellors (6431)

Airline cargo and baggage handlers (in 7437 *Air Transport Ramp Attendants*)

Supervisors of airline sales and service agents (in 6216 *Other Service Supervisors*)

6433.3 Airline Cargo Agents

Airline Cargo Agents arrange for cargo shipments and provide related customer services.

Profile Summary

APTITUDES

G	V	N	S	P	Q	K	F	M
3	3	3	4	4	2	4	4	4

INTERESTS
MOs

DATA PEOPLE THINGS (DPT)
467

PHYSICAL ACTIVITIES (PA)

V	C	H	B	L	S
2	0	1	3	1	3

ENVIRONMENTAL CONDITIONS (EC)
L1

EDUCATION/TRAINING
4

Examples of Job Titles

Airline Cargo Agents

Descriptor Profile

Main Characteristics

Occupations in this group are characterized by the following aptitudes, interests and worker functions as they relate to main duties:

- **General learning ability** to route inbound and outbound air freight shipments to their destinations, to determine and arrange special handling requirements, and to trace lost and misdirected cargo

- **Verbal ability** to take telephone orders from customers and provide information on rate, routing, acceptance requirements, import and export regulations, and documentation requirements

- **Numerical ability** to compute freight costs and calculate charges for services and insurance

- **Clerical perception** to determine shipping costs using rate books and prepare customs documents and cargo manifests

- **Methodical interest** in **computing** information to process bills of lading, and in preparing and maintaining cargo, shipping and other records

- **Objective interest** in **handling** to weigh and assemble outgoing cargo

- **Social interest** in **speaking** with shippers and consignees to notify them of arrival of shipments and to arrange for deliveries

6433.3
Subgroup 3 of 6

Physical Activities

Vision
   2 Near vision

Colour Discrimination
   0 Not relevant

Hearing
   1 Limited

Body Position
   3 Sitting, standing, walking

Limb Co-ordination
   1 Upper limb co-ordination

Strength
   3 Medium

Environmental Conditions

Location
   L1 Regulated inside climate

Employment Requirements

Education/Training
   4

- Completion of secondary school is usually required.

- Several weeks of on-the-job and classroom training are provided.

Workplaces/Employers

Airline companies

Occupational Options

Depending on size of the airline or airport, the duties of workers in the 6433 group may overlap.

Progression to supervisory positions is possible through experience.

Similar Occupations Classified Elsewhere

Ticket and Cargo Agents and Related Clerks (Except Airline) (6434)

Travel Counsellors (6431)

Airline cargo and baggage handlers (in 7437 *Air Transport Ramp Attendants*)

Supervisors of airline sales and service agents (in 6216 *Other Service Supervisors*)

6433.4 Airline Reservation Agents

Airline Reservation Agents issue tickets, make reservations and provide related customer services.

Profile Summary

APTITUDES

G	V	N	S	P	Q	K	F	M
3	3	3	4	4	2	4	4	4

INTERESTS
MSO

DATA PEOPLE THINGS (DPT)
564

PHYSICAL ACTIVITIES (PA)

V	C	H	B	L	S
2	0	2	1	1	1

ENVIRONMENTAL CONDITIONS (EC)
L1

EDUCATION/TRAINING
4

Examples of Job Titles

Reservation Agent, Airline

Sales and Service Agent, Airline

Descriptor Profile

Main Characteristics

Occupations in this group are characterized by the following aptitudes, interests and worker functions as they relate to main duties:

- **General learning ability** to reserve seats for tour companies, travel agencies, wholesalers and the general public

- **Verbal ability** to answer inquiries concerning routes, fares, accommodations and passport requirements

- **Numerical ability** to determine travel and accommodation costs, prepare claim forms for refunds and adjustments, and complete reports of transactions

- **Clerical perception** to review routine invoices of transportation charges and to prepare travel booklets for passengers that contain tickets, copies of itineraries, written lodging confirmations, pertinent credit cards and travel suggestions

- **Methodical interest** in **copying** information to keep a current directory of hotels, motels and timetables

- **Social interest** in **speaking** with customers to provide services and assistance to passengers

- **Objective interest** in **operating** computerized reservation systems to obtain confirmation of travel and lodging space, to issue and validate airline tickets, and to prepare itineraries, claim forms and reports

6433.4

Physical Activities

Vision
  2 Near vision

Colour Discrimination
  0 Not relevant

Hearing
  2 Verbal interaction

Body Position
  1 Sitting

Limb Co-ordination
  1 Upper limb co-ordination

Strength
  1 Limited

Environmental Conditions

Location
  L1 Regulated inside climate

Employment Requirements

Education/Training
  4

- Completion of secondary school is usually required.

- Several weeks of on-the-job and classroom training are provided.

Workplaces/Employers

Airline companies

Occupational Options

Depending on size of the airline or airport, the duties of workers in the 6433 group may overlap.

Progression to supervisory positions is possible through experience.

Similar Occupations Classified Elsewhere

Ticket and Cargo Agents and Related Clerks (Except Airline) (6434)

Travel Counsellors (6431)

Airline cargo and baggage handlers (in 7437 *Air Transport Ramp Attendants*)

Supervisors of airline sales and service agents (in 6216 *Other Service Supervisors*)

6433.5 Airline Station Agents

Airline Station Agents issue tickets, make reservations, trace missing baggage, arrange for cargo shipments and provide related customer services to assist airline passengers.

Profile Summary

APTITUDES

G	V	N	S	P	Q	K	F	M
3	3	3	4	4	2	4	4	4

INTERESTS
MSO

DATA PEOPLE THINGS (DPT)
564

PHYSICAL ACTIVITIES (PA)

V	C	H	B	L	S
2	0	2	1	1	1

ENVIRONMENTAL CONDITIONS (EC)
L1

EDUCATION/TRAINING
4

Examples of Job Titles

Station Agent, Airline

Descriptor Profile

Main Characteristics

Occupations in this group are characterized by the following aptitudes, interests and worker functions as they relate to main duties:

- **General learning ability** to perform duties pertaining to flight servicing, ramp operations, cargo handling and load control, and to perform the duties of ticket, baggage and cargo agents

- **Verbal ability** to receive, transmit and log operational messages to operations control and downline stations

- **Numerical ability** to establish allowable weights and distribution of load in aircraft and ensure that limits are not exceeded

- **Clerical perception** to complete pre-flight documents regarding passenger and load catering counts, special requests and other flight information

- **Methodical interest** in **copying** data to record cargo information on manifest forms and prepare flight cargo plans

- **Social interest** in **speaking** with people to receive, transmit and log messages to and from aircraft and between stations concerning flight movements, arrival and departure times, number of passengers, reservations and other airline operations information

- **Objective interest** in **operating** computer systems and communications equipment to gather load-control information and transmit cargo data to flight destinations

6433.5
Subgroup 5 of 6

Physical Activities

Vision
   2 Near vision

Colour Discrimination
   0 Not relevant

Hearing
   2 Verbal interaction

Body Position
   1 Sitting

Limb Co-ordination
   1 Upper limb co-ordination

Strength
   1 Limited

Environmental Conditions

Location
   L1 Regulated inside climate

Employment Requirements

Education/Training
4

- Completion of secondary school is usually required.

- Several weeks of on-the-job and classroom training are provided.

- Airline station agents usually require experience as a ticket, baggage or cargo agent.

Workplaces/Employers

Airline companies

Occupational Options

Depending on size of the airline or airport, the duties of workers in the 6433 group may overlap.

Progression to supervisory positions is possible through experience.

Similar Occupations Classified Elsewhere

Ticket and Cargo Agents and Related Clerks (Except Airline) (6434)

Travel Counsellors (6431)

Airline cargo and baggage handlers (in 7437 *Air Transport Ramp Attendants*)

Supervisors of airline sales and service agents (in 6216 *Other Service Supervisors*)

6433.6 Airline Load Planners

Airline Load Planners plan the positioning of cargo on aircraft.

Profile Summary

APTITUDES

G	V	N	S	P	Q	K	F	M
3	3	3	4	4	2	4	4	4

INTERESTS
MOD

DATA PEOPLE THINGS (DPT)
484

PHYSICAL ACTIVITIES (PA)

V	C	H	B	L	S
2	0	1	1	1	1

ENVIRONMENTAL CONDITIONS (EC)
L1

EDUCATION/TRAINING
4, R

Examples of Job Titles

Load Planner, Airline

Descriptor Profile

Main Characteristics

Occupations in this group are characterized by the following aptitudes, interests and worker functions as they relate to main duties:

- **General learning** and **verbal ability** to plan cargo loads so cargo is distributed and balanced

- **Numerical ability** to calculate load weights for compartments of aircraft

- **Clerical perception** to read charts and data when determining load-control information

- **Methodical interest** in **computing** load weights so the allowable gross weight of aircraft is not exceeded

- **Objective interest** in **operating** computer equipment to determine load weights

- **Directive interest** in planning load for safe distribution and balance

6433.6
Subgroup 6 of 6

Physical Activities

Vision
    2   Near vision

Colour Discrimination
    0   Not relevant

Hearing
    1   Limited

Body Position
    1   Sitting

Limb Co-ordination
    1   Upper limb co-ordination

Strength
    1   Limited

Environmental Conditions

Location
    L1   Regulated inside climate

Employment Requirements

Education/Training
    4, R

- Completion of secondary school is usually required.

- Several weeks of on-the-job and classroom training are provided.

- Load planners require a restricted radio operator's licence and usually require airline operations experience.

Workplaces/Employers

Airline companies

Occupational Options

Depending on size of the airline or airport, the duties of workers in the 6433 group may overlap.

Progression to supervisory positions is possible through experience.

Similar Occupations Classified Elsewhere

Ticket and Cargo Agents and Related Clerks (Except Airline) (6434)

Travel Counsellors (6431)

Airline cargo and baggage handlers (in 7437 *Air Transport Ramp Attendants*)

Supervisors of airline sales and service agents (in 6216 *Other Service Supervisors*)

6434.1 Ticket Agents and Related Clerks (Except Airline)

Ticket Agents and Related Clerks (Except Airline) quote fares and rates, make reservations, issue tickets, check baggage and provide related customer services to assist travellers.

Profile Summary

APTITUDES

G	V	N	S	P	Q	K	F	M
3	3	3	4	4	3	4	4	4

INTERESTS
MSO

DATA PEOPLE THINGS (DPT)
564

PHYSICAL ACTIVITIES (PA)

V	C	H	B	L	S
2	0	2	1	1	1

ENVIRONMENTAL CONDITIONS (EC)
L1

EDUCATION/TRAINING
4

Examples of Job Titles

Bus Ticket Agent
Counter Services Agent, Railway
Railway Passenger Agent
Reservation Clerk, Railway
Steamship Agent
Ticket Agent

Descriptor Profile

Main Characteristics

Occupations in this group are characterized by the following aptitudes, interests and worker functions as they relate to main duties:

- **General learning ability** to make reservations and sell tickets to passengers travelling by bus, railway and ship

- **Verbal ability** to answer customer inquiries, quote fares and supply information regarding available vacancies when working for wholesale travel companies; and to inform load-control personnel of changes in passenger itinerary

- **Numerical ability** to compute cost of tickets and handle cash transactions

- **Clerical perception** to keep inventories of available passenger space

- **Methodical interest** in **copying** information to receive and record bookings for package tours from retail travel agencies; and in checking baggage

- **Social interest** in **speaking** with customers to assist them in planning travel times and routes

- **Objective interest** in **operating** computer reservation systems to reserve seats for tour companies, travel agencies, wholesalers and the general public, as well as to issue tickets and baggage receipts

6434.1
Subgroup 1 of 2

Physical Activities

Vision
  2   Near vision

Colour Discrimination
  0   Not relevant

Hearing
  2   Verbal interaction

Body Position
  1   Sitting

Limb Co-ordination
  1   Upper limb co-ordination

Strength
  1   Limited

Environmental Conditions

Location
  L1   Regulated inside climate

Employment Requirements

Education/Training
  4

- Completion of secondary school is usually required.

- Up to 10 weeks of training is provided.

Workplaces/Employers

Boat cruise operators

Bus and railway companies

Public transit companies

Steamship lines

Travel wholesalers

Occupational Options

Ticket agents and cargo agents may perform the same duties depending on the size and location of the operation.

Progression to supervisory positions is possible through experience.

Similar Occupations Classified Elsewhere

Airline Sales and Service Agents (6433)

Travel Counsellors (6431)

Baggage handlers in rail, marine and motor transportation [in 6672 *Other Attendants in Accommodation and Travel (Except Airline Travel)*]

Supervisors of ticket and cargo agents and related clerks in this group (in 6216 *Other Service Supervisors*)

6434.2 Cargo Agents (Except Airline)

Cargo Agents quote fares and rates, process cargo shipments, check baggage and provide related customer services to assist travellers.

Profile Summary

APTITUDES

G	V	N	S	P	Q	K	F	M
3	3	3	4	4	3	4	4	4

INTERESTS
MOs

DATA PEOPLE THINGS (DPT)
467

PHYSICAL ACTIVITIES (PA)

V	C	H	B	L	S
2	0	2	4	1	4

ENVIRONMENTAL CONDITIONS (EC)
L1

EDUCATION/TRAINING
4

Examples of Job Titles

Cargo Agents (Except Airline)
Marine Cargo Agent

Descriptor Profile

Main Characteristics

Occupations in this group are characterized by the following aptitudes, interests and worker functions as they relate to main duties:

- **General learning ability** to route inbound and outbound cargo shipments to their destinations, and to trace lost and misdirected passenger baggage and cargo shipments

- **Verbal ability** to quote fares and rates for cargo shipments

- **Numerical ability** to determine costs for shipments using rate tables and schedules

- **Clerical perception** to prepare and maintain shipping and other documents

- **Methodical interest** in **computing** shipment costs including charges for services and insurance

- **Objective interest** in **handling** passenger baggage for checking purposes and to sort for loading by baggage handlers; may load baggage directly onto buses, railway cars and cruise ships

- **Social interest** in **speaking** to provide customer services and assist travellers

Physical Activities

Vision
   2 Near vision

Colour Discrimination
   0 Not relevant

Hearing
   2 Verbal interaction

Body Position
   4 Other body positions

Limb Co-ordination
   1 Upper limb co-ordination

Strength
   4 Heavy

Environmental Conditions

Location
   L1 Regulated inside climate

Employment Requirements

Education/Training
   4

- Completion of secondary school is usually required.

- Up to 10 weeks of training is provided.

Workplaces/Employers

Boat cruise operators

Bus and railway companies

Public transit establishments

Steamship lines

Travel wholesalers

Occupational Options

Ticket agents and cargo agents may perform the same duties depending on the size and location of the operations.

Progression to supervisory positions is possible through experience.

Similar Occupations Classified Elsewhere

Airline Sales and Service Agents (6433)

Travel Counsellors (6431)

Baggage handlers in rail, marine and motor transportation [in 6672 *Other Attendants in Accommodation and Travel (Except Airline Travel)*]

Supervisors of ticket and cargo agents and related clerks in this group (in 6216 *Other Service Supervisors*)

6435 Hotel Front Desk Clerks

Hotel Front Desk Clerks make room reservations, provide information and services to guests and receive payments.

Profile Summary

APTITUDES

G	V	N	S	P	Q	K	F	M
3	3	3	4	4	3	4	4	4

INTERESTS
SMo

DATA PEOPLE THINGS (DPT)
364

PHYSICAL ACTIVITIES (PA)

V	C	H	B	L	S
2	0	2	2	1	1

ENVIRONMENTAL CONDITIONS (EC)
L1

EDUCATION/TRAINING
3, 6

Examples of Job Titles

Front Desk Clerk
Front Office Clerk
Guest Service Agent
Hotel Front Desk Clerk
Night Clerk
Reservations Clerk
Room Clerk

Descriptor Profile

Main Characteristics

Occupations in this group are characterized by the following aptitudes, interests and worker functions as they relate to main duties:

- **General learning ability** to make room reservations, register arriving guests and assign rooms

- **Verbal ability** to answer inquiries regarding hotel services and registration by letter, telephone and in person

- **Numerical ability** and **clerical perception** to prepare statements of charges for departing guests and to receive payments

- **Social interest** in **speaking** with people to provide information and respond to guests' complaints

- **Methodical interest** in **compiling** information for preparing and checking daily record sheets, guests' accounts, receipts and vouchers

- **Objective interest** in **operating** computerized and manual systems to collect and verify guests' accounts

6435

Physical Activities

Vision
   2   Near vision

Colour Discrimination
   0   Not relevant

Hearing
   2   Verbal interaction

Body Position
   2   Standing and/or walking

Limb Co-ordination
   1   Upper limb co-ordination

Strength
   1   Limited

Environmental Conditions

Location
   L1   Regulated inside climate

Employment Requirements

Education/Training
   3, 6

- Completion of secondary school is required.

- Completion of a college program in front desk operations or hotel management may be required.

Workplaces/Employers

Hotels

Motels

Resorts

Occupational Options

Progression to senior positions, such as accommodations manager, is possible with additional training and experience.

Similar Occupations Classified Elsewhere

Travel Counsellors (6431)

Other Attendants in Accommodation and Travel (Except Airline Travel) (6672)

6441.1 Tour Guides

Tour Guides escort individuals and groups on trips, sightseeing tours of cities and tours of historical sites and establishments such as famous buildings, manufacturing plants, cathedrals and theme parks.

Profile Summary

APTITUDES

G	V	N	S	P	Q	K	F	M
3	3	3	4	4	3	4	4	4

INTERESTS
SMd

DATA PEOPLE THINGS (DPT)
568

PHYSICAL ACTIVITIES (PA)

V	C	H	B	L	S
4	1	2	3	2	1

ENVIRONMENTAL CONDITIONS (EC)
L1, L3, L4

EDUCATION/TRAINING
2+

Examples of Job Titles

Calèche Driver
Factory Tour Guide
Sightseeing Guide
Tour Guide
Tourist Guide

Descriptor Profile

Main Characteristics

Occupations in this group are characterized by the following aptitudes, interests and worker functions as they relate to main duties:

- **General learning** and **verbal ability** to transport and escort individuals and groups on tours of cities, waterways and establishments, and to provide descriptive and background information on interesting features

- **Numerical ability** and **clerical perception** to make arithmetical calculations; may collect admission fees

- **Social interest** in **speaking** to sightseers to answer questions; may sell souvenirs

- **Methodical interest** in **copying** information to describe points of interest and supply information

- **Directive interest** in making transportation and other arrangements

Physical Activities

Vision
    4 Total visual field

Colour Discrimination
    1 Relevant

Hearing
    2 Verbal interaction

Body Position
    3 Sitting, standing, walking

Limb Co-ordination
    2 Multiple limb co-ordination

Strength
    1 Limited

Environmental Conditions

Location
    L1 Regulated inside climate
    L3 Outside
    L4 In a vehicle or cab

Employment Requirements

Education/Training
  2+

- On-the-job training is provided.

- Knowledge of both official languages or an additional language may be required for some positions in this group.

Workplaces/Employers

Resorts and similar establishments

Self-employment

Tour operators

Similar Occupations Classified Elsewhere

Outdoor Sport and Recreational Guides (6442)

Museum guides and historical interpreters (in 5212 *Technical Occupations Related to Museums and Galleries*)

Tour operators (in 0621 *Retail Trade Managers*)

6441.2 Travel Guides

Travel Guides escort individuals and groups on trips, sightseeing tours of cities and tours of historical sites and establishments such as famous buildings, manufacturing plants, cathedrals and theme parks.

Profile Summary

APTITUDES

G	V	N	S	P	Q	K	F	M
3	3	3	4	4	3	4	4	4

INTERESTS
SMd

DATA PEOPLE THINGS (DPT)
568

PHYSICAL ACTIVITIES (PA)

V	C	H	B	L	S
3	1	2	3	2	1

ENVIRONMENTAL CONDITIONS (EC)
L1, L3, L4

EDUCATION/TRAINING
2+

Examples of Job Titles

Calèche Driver
Factory Tour Guide
Sightseeing Guide
Travel Guide

Descriptor Profile

Main Characteristics

Occupations in this group are characterized by the following aptitudes, interests and worker functions as they relate to main duties:

- **General learning** and **verbal ability** to escort individuals and groups on vacation and business trips, and to provide descriptions and background information on interesting features

- **Numerical ability** and **clerical perception** to make arithmetical calculations and observe times, dates, locations and other details in correspondence concerning travel arrangements

- **Social interest** in **speaking** to sightseers when visiting and describing points of interest

- **Methodical interest** in **copying** information to confirm reservations for transportation and accommodations, and to meet prepared itineraries

- **Directive interest** in planning and carrying out recreational activities; and in resolving problems with itineraries, service and accommodations

6441.2
Subgroup 2 of 2

Physical Activities

Vision
 3 Near and far vision

Colour Discrimination
 1 Relevant

Hearing
 2 Verbal interaction

Body Position
 3 Sitting, standing, walking

Limb Co-ordination
 2 Multiple limb co-ordination

Strength
 1 Limited

Environmental Conditions

Location
 L1 Regulated inside climate
 L3 Outside
 L4 In a vehicle or cab

Employment Requirements

Education/Training
 2+

- On-the-job training is provided.

- Knowledge of both official languages or an additional language may be required for some positions in this group.

Workplaces/Employers

Resorts and similar establishments

Self-employment

Tour operators

Similar Occupations Classified Elsewhere

Outdoor Sport and Recreational Guides (6442)

Museum guides and historical interpreters (in 5212 *Technical Occupations Related to Museums and Galleries*)

Tour operators (in 0621 *Retail Trade Managers*)

6442 Outdoor Sport and Recreational Guides

Outdoor Sport and Recreational Guides organize and conduct trips and expeditions for sports enthusiasts, adventurers, tourists and resort guests.

Profile Summary

APTITUDES

G	V	N	S	P	Q	K	F	M
3	3	4	3	3	4	3	4	3

INTERESTS
SMO

DATA PEOPLE THINGS (DPT)
167

PHYSICAL ACTIVITIES (PA)

V	C	H	B	L	S
4	0	2	4	2	3

ENVIRONMENTAL CONDITIONS (EC)
L3, H8

EDUCATION/TRAINING
1+, 4, R

Examples of Job Titles

Canoeing Guide
Dude Wrangler
Fishing Guide
Hot Air Balloonist
Hunting Guide
Mountain Climbing Guide
Outfitter
Rafting Guide

Descriptor Profile

Main Characteristics

Occupations in this group are characterized by the following aptitudes, interests and worker functions as they relate to main duties:

- **General learning ability** to organize and conduct trips and expeditions for sports enthusiasts, adventurers, tourists and resort guests

- **Verbal ability** to lead and escort individuals and groups

- **Spatial** and **form perception** to provide first aid in emergency situations

- **Motor co-ordination** and **manual dexterity** to demonstrate and provide instructions on accepted techniques for the use of equipment

- **Social interest** in **speaking** to advise on emergency and safety measures and specific regulations concerning hunting, fishing and boating

- **Methodical interest** in **co-ordinating** information to plan itineraries for trips and expeditions, and to arrange transportation

- **Objective interest** in **handling** to assemble equipment and supplies such as camping gear, rafts, life jackets, fishing tackle and food, and to transport individuals and groups to sites; may prepare meals for groups and set up camps

6442

Physical Activities

Vision
　4　Total visual field

Colour Discrimination
　0　Not relevant

Hearing
　2　Verbal interaction

Body Position
　4　Other body positions

Limb Co-ordination
　2　Multiple limb co-ordination

Strength
　3　Medium

Environmental Conditions

Location
　L3　Outside

Hazards
　H8　Dangerous locations

Employment Requirements

Education/Training
　1+, 4, R

- Knowledge of a particular terrain or body of water and demonstrated ability in the guided activity are required for employment in this group.

- Hot-air-balloon pilots require completion of 10 hours of ground school, 16 hours of pilot-in-command experience and federal licensing.

Workplaces/Employers

Private companies and resorts

Self-employment

Occupational Options

Outdoor sport and recreational guides usually work on a seasonal basis.

Similar Occupations Classified Elsewhere

Tour and Travel Guides (6441)

Program Leaders and Instructors in Recreation and Sport (5254)

6443.1 Amusement Attraction Operators

This group includes amusement occupations such as operators of amusement rides, games and other attractions.

Profile Summary

APTITUDES

G	V	N	S	P	Q	K	F	M
4	4	4	3	4	4	3	4	3

INTERESTS

OMS

DATA PEOPLE THINGS (DPT)

562

PHYSICAL ACTIVITIES (PA)

V	C	H	B	L	S
4	1	2	4	2	3

ENVIRONMENTAL CONDITIONS (EC)

L3, L4, H3, D1

EDUCATION/TRAINING

2

Examples of Job Titles

Amusement Attraction Operator
Amusement Ride Operator
Game Concession Operator

Descriptor Profile

Main Characteristics

Occupations in this group are characterized by the following aptitudes, interests and worker functions as they relate to main duties:

- **General learning ability** and **spatial perception** to set up and operate rides, fun houses, game concessions and other amusement attractions

- Motor co-ordination and manual dexterity to drive trucks, vans and other vehicles in order to transport amusement rides, games and other attractions

- **Objective interest** in **controlling** equipment to operate rides and other attractions

- **Methodical interest** in **copying** information to perform routine maintenance and safety inspections of equipment

- **Social interest** in **speaking** to oversee game activities, ensure safety of participants and supervise amusement attraction attendants; may sell tickets

6443.1
Subgroup 1 of 2

Physical Activities

Vision
   4   Total visual field

Colour Discrimination
   1   Relevant

Hearing
   2   Verbal interaction

Body Position
   4   Other body positions

Limb Co-ordination
   2   Multiple limb co-ordination

Strength
   3   Medium

Environmental Conditions

Location
   L3   Outside
   L4   In a vehicle or cab

Hazards
   H3   Equipment, machinery, tools

Discomforts
   D1   Noise

Employment Requirements

Education/Training
2

- Some secondary school education may be required.

Workplaces/Employers

Amusement parks

Carnivals

Exhibitions

Fairs

Self-employment

Similar Occupations Classified Elsewhere

Amusement ride, sports facility and bingo hall attendants (in 6671 *Attendants in Recreation and Sport*)

Supervisors of attendants in recreation and sport (in 6216 *Other Service Supervisors*)

Remarks

In data provided by Statistics Canada, groups 6443 and 6671 are combined to form 6670 *Attendants in Amusement, Recreation and Sport*.

6443.2 Gambling Dealers

This group includes workers in gambling casinos. Supervisors of gambling casino workers are also included in this group.

Profile Summary

APTITUDES

G	V	N	S	P	Q	K	F	M
3	3	3	4	4	4	4	4	3

INTERESTS
SMD

DATA PEOPLE THINGS (DPT)
367

PHYSICAL ACTIVITIES (PA)

V	C	H	B	L	S
3	1	2	2	1	1

ENVIRONMENTAL CONDITIONS (EC)
L1

EDUCATION/TRAINING
2

Examples of Job Titles

Baccarat Dealer

Blackjack Dealer

Keno Dealer

Supervisor, Gambling Tables

Descriptor Profile

Main Characteristics

Occupations in this group are characterized by the following aptitudes, interests and worker functions as they relate to main duties:

- **General learning ability** and **manual dexterity** to operate gambling tables and games such as roulette, blackjack, keno and baccarat

- **Verbal** and **numerical ability** to determine winners, calculate and pay winning bets and collect losing bets

- **Social interest** in **speaking** with people; may monitor gambling tables

- **Methodical interest** in **compiling** information to make sure that customers follow game rules

- **Directive interest** in **handling** equipment; may supervise staff and train new dealers

6443.2
Subgroup 2 of 2

Physical Activities

Vision
   3   Near and far vision

Colour Discrimination
   1   Relevant

Hearing
   2   Verbal interaction

Body Position
   2   Standing and/or walking

Limb Co-ordination
   1   Upper limb co-ordination

Strength
   1   Limited

Environmental Conditions

Location
   L1   Regulated inside climate

Employment Requirements

Education/Training
2

- Some secondary school education may be required.

- On-the-job training is usually provided for gambling table operators.

Workplaces/Employers

Amusement parks

Carnivals

Exhibitions

Fairs

Gambling casinos

Self-employment

Similar Occupations Classified Elsewhere

Amusement ride, sports facility and bingo hall attendants (in 6671 *Attendants in Recreation and Sport*)

Supervisors of attendants in recreation and sport (in 6216 *Other Service Supervisors*)

Remarks

In data provided by Statistics Canada, groups 6443 and 6671 are combined to form 6670 *Attendants in Amusement, Recreation and Sport*.

6451 Maîtres d'hôtel and Hosts/Hostesses

Maîtres d'hôtel and Hosts/Hostesses greet patrons, escort them to tables, and supervise and co-ordinate the activities of food and beverage servers.

Profile Summary

APTITUDES

G	V	N	S	P	Q	K	F	M
3	3	4	4	4	4	4	4	4

INTERESTS
MSd

DATA PEOPLE THINGS (DPT)
138

PHYSICAL ACTIVITIES (PA)

V	C	H	B	L	S
3	0	2	2	0	1

ENVIRONMENTAL CONDITIONS (EC)
L1

EDUCATION/TRAINING
4

Examples of Job Titles

Host/Hostess, Food Service
Maître d'
Maître d'hôtel
Restaurant Host/Hostess

Descriptor Profile

Main Characteristics

Occupations in this group are characterized by the following aptitudes, interests and worker functions as they relate to main duties:

- **General learning** and **verbal ability** to greet patrons at the entrance of dining rooms, restaurants and lounges, and escort them to tables and other seating areas

- **Form perception** to inspect dining and serving areas for cleanliness

- **Clerical perception** to accept payment for food and beverages

- **Methodical interest** in **co-ordinating** information to receive and record patrons' reservations and assign tables, prepare work schedules and payrolls, and co-ordinate the activities of food and beverage servers and other serving staff

- **Social interest** in speaking with patrons to ensure satisfaction with food and service, and in attending to complaints

- **Directive interest** in **supervising** the activities of food and beverage servers and other serving staff; in interviewing candidates for food and beverage server positions, and in training new employees

6451

Physical Activities

Vision
   3   Near and far vision

Colour Discrimination
   0   Not relevant

Hearing
   2   Verbal interaction

Body Position
   2   Standing and/or walking

Limb Co-ordination
   0   Not relevant

Strength
   1   Limited

Environmental Conditions

Location
   L1   Regulated inside climate

Employment Requirements

Education/Training
4

- Completion of secondary school is usually required.

- Several weeks of on-the-job training are usually provided.

- Maîtres d'hôtel require experience as a formal or captain, server (waiter/waitress) or other food service experience.

Workplaces/Employers

Cocktail lounges

Hotel dining rooms

Private clubs

Restaurants

Similar Occupations Classified Elsewhere

Food and Beverage Servers (6453)

Food Service Supervisors (6212)

6452 Bartenders

Bartenders mix and serve alcoholic and non-alcoholic beverages. Supervisors of Bartenders are included in this group.

Profile Summary

APTITUDES

G	V	N	S	P	Q	K	F	M
4	4	3	4	4	4	3	4	3

INTERESTS
MSd

DATA PEOPLE THINGS (DPT)
477

PHYSICAL ACTIVITIES (PA)

V	C	H	B	L	S
2	0	2	2	1	2

ENVIRONMENTAL CONDITIONS (EC)
L1, D5

EDUCATION/TRAINING
4, 6

Examples of Job Titles

Barkeeper
Bartender
Head Bartender
Service Bartender

Descriptor Profile

Main Characteristics

Occupations in this group are characterized by the following aptitudes, interests and worker functions as they relate to main duties:

- **General learning ability** to acquire a knowledge of wines and liquors, and to understand and apply the techniques of preparing and serving beverages

- **Numerical ability** to collect payment for beverages

- **Motor co-ordination** and **finger dexterity** to mix liquor, soft drinks, water and other ingredients in order to prepare cocktails and other drinks, and to prepare wine, draft and bottled beer and non-alcoholic beverages

- **Manual dexterity** to clean bar areas and wash glassware

- **Methodical interest** in **computing** to maintain inventories of bar stock and order supplies, to record sales and to take beverage orders from serving staff or directly from patrons

- **Social interest** in **serving** alcoholic and non-alcoholic beverages to patrons

- **Directive interest** in **handling** the preparation of alcoholic and non-alcoholic beverages for food and beverage servers; may supervise other bartenders and bar staff

6452

Physical Activities

Vision
 2 Near vision

Colour Discrimination
 0 Not relevant

Hearing
 2 Verbal interaction

Body Position
 2 Standing and/or walking

Limb Co-ordination
 1 Upper limb co-ordination

Strength
 2 Light

Environmental Conditions

Location
 L1 Regulated inside climate

Discomforts
 D5 Wetness

Employment Requirements

Education/Training
4, 6

- Completion of secondary school may be required.

- Completion of college or other program in bartending
 or
 completion of courses in mixing drinks is usually required.

- In some provinces a course or program in the responsible service of alcohol may be required.

Workplaces/Employers

Banquet halls

Bars

Hotels

Licensed establishments

Private clubs

Restaurants

Taverns

Occupational Options

Progression to managerial positions in food and beverage service is possible with experience.

Similar Occupations Classified Elsewhere

Food and Beverage Servers (6453)

6453 Food and Beverage Servers

Food and Beverage Servers take and serve patrons' food and beverage orders.

Profile Summary

APTITUDES
G	V	N	S	P	Q	K	F	M
4	4	4	4	4	4	4	4	4

INTERESTS
MSo

DATA PEOPLE THINGS (DPT)
577

PHYSICAL ACTIVITIES (PA)
V	C	H	B	L	S
3	0	2	2	1	2

ENVIRONMENTAL CONDITIONS (EC)
L1

EDUCATION/TRAINING
2, 4

Examples of Job Titles

Banquet Server
Captain Waiter/Waitress
Chief Wine Steward
Cocktail Waiter/Waitress
Food and Beverage Server
Formal Waiter/Waitress
Waiter/Waitress
Wine Steward

Descriptor Profile

Main Characteristics

Occupations in this group are characterized by the following aptitudes, interests and worker functions as they relate to main duties:

- **General learning** and **verbal ability** to greet patrons, present menus, make recommendations and answer questions regarding food and beverages, as well as to recommend wines that complement patrons' meals

- **Numerical ability** to present bills to patrons and accept payments

- **Methodical interest** in **copying** to take orders and relay them to kitchen and bar staff

- **Social interest** in **serving** food and beverages to patrons

- **Objective interest** in **handling** the preparation of specialty foods at patrons' tables

6453

Physical Activities

Vision
   3   Near and far vision

Colour Discrimination
   0   Not relevant

Hearing
   2   Verbal interaction

Body Position
   2   Standing and/or walking

Limb Co-ordination
   1   Upper limb co-ordination

Strength
   2   Light

Environmental Conditions

Location
   L1   Regulated inside climate

Employment Requirements

Education/Training
   2,4

- Completion of secondary school may be required.

- Formal waiters/waitresses may require completion of college or vocational school courses.

- On-the-job training is usually provided.

- Wine stewards may require courses in wine selection and service
  or
  experience as a captain waiter/waitress or formal waiter/waitress

- In some provinces a course or program in the responsible service of alcohol may be required.

Workplaces/Employers

Banquet halls

Bars

Hotels

Private clubs

Restaurants

Taverns

Similar Occupations Classified Elsewhere

Maîtres d'hôtel and Hosts/Hostesses (6451)

Restaurant and Food Service Managers (0631)

6461 Sheriffs and Bailiffs

Sheriffs and Bailiffs enforce court orders by serving writs and summonses and seizing properties.

Profile Summary

APTITUDES
G	V	N	S	P	Q	K	F	M
3	3	4	4	4	3	4	4	4

INTERESTS
Mds

DATA PEOPLE THINGS (DPT)
567

PHYSICAL ACTIVITIES (PA)
V	C	H	B	L	S
4	1	2	3	2	3

ENVIRONMENTAL CONDITIONS (EC)
L1, L4

EDUCATION/TRAINING
4, 6

Examples of Job Titles

Bailiff
Deputy Sheriff
Sheriff
Sheriff's Bailiff
Sheriff's Officer

Descriptor Profile

Main Characteristics

Occupations in this group are characterized by the following aptitudes, interests and worker functions as they relate to main duties:

- **General learning** and **verbal ability** and **clerical perception** to prepare reports and affidavits

- **Methodical interest** in **copying** to serve statements of claims, summonses, jury summonses, orders to pay alimony and other court orders; and in serving writs of execution by seizing and selling properties and distributing the proceeds according to court decisions

- **Directive interest** in **handling** to locate properties and make seizures and removals under various acts of Parliament; and in providing courthouse security for judges

- **Social interest** in **speaking** while escorting prisoners to and from courts and correctional institutions, and also while attending court, escorting witnesses and assisting in maintaining order

6461

Physical Activities

Vision
   4   Total visual field

Colour Discrimination
   1   Relevant

Hearing
   2   Verbal interaction

Body Position
   3   Sitting, standing, walking

Limb Co-ordination
   2   Multiple limb co-ordination

Strength
   3   Medium

Environmental Conditions

Location
   L1 Regulated inside climate
   L4 In a vehicle or cab

Employment Requirements

Education/Training
4, 6

- Bailiffs usually require completion of secondary school and some work experience related to law enforcement.

- A college diploma in legal studies may be required.

Workplaces/Employers

Provincial courts

Self-employment

Occupational Options

Sheriffs require experience as bailiffs or deputy sheriffs.

Progression to supervisory positions is possible with additional experience and in-house training.

Similar Occupations Classified Elsewhere

Correctional Service Officers (6462)

Court Clerks (1443)

Police Officers (Except Commissioned) (6261)

6462 Correctional Service Officers

Correctional Service Officers guard prisoners and detainees and maintain order in correctional institutions and other places of detention.

Profile Summary

APTITUDES
G	V	N	S	P	Q	K	F	M
3	4	4	4	3	4	4	4	4

INTERESTS
MSd

DATA PEOPLE THINGS (DPT)
538

PHYSICAL ACTIVITIES (PA)
V	C	H	B	L	S
4	0	2	3	2	3

ENVIRONMENTAL CONDITIONS (EC)
L1

EDUCATION/TRAINING
6

Examples of Job Titles

Correctional Facility Guard
Correctional Service Officer
Detention Attendant
Prison Guard
Supervisor, Correctional Officers

Descriptor Profile

Main Characteristics

Occupations in this group are characterized by the following aptitudes, interests and worker functions as they relate to main duties:

- **General learning ability** to observe conduct and behaviour of prisoners to prevent disturbances and escapes

- **Form perception** to recognize signs of tampering when inspecting locks, grills and doors for security

- **Methodical interest** in **copying** to prepare admission and other reports

- **Social interest** in escorting prisoners in transit and during temporary leaves

- **Directive interest** in **supervising** prisoners during work assignments, meals and recreation periods, and in patrolling assigned areas and reporting any problems to supervisors; may supervise and co-ordinate work of other correctional service officers

6462

Physical Activities

Vision
  4 Total visual field

Colour Discrimination
  0 Not relevant

Hearing
  2 Verbal interaction

Body Position
  3 Sitting, standing, walking

Limb Co-ordination
  2 Multiple limb co-ordination

Strength
  3 Medium

Environmental Conditions

Location
  L1 Regulated inside climate

Employment Requirements

Education/Training
  6

- Completion of secondary school is required.

- Completion of a college correctional officer program is usually required.

Workplaces/Employers

Federal government

Municipal governments

Provincial governments

Occupational Options

Correctional service supervisors require experience as a correctional service officer.

Similar Occupations Classified Elsewhere

Managers in Social, Community and Correctional Services (0314)

Social Workers (4152)

Detention home workers (in 4212 *Community and Social Service Workers*)

6463.1 Animal Control Officers

Animal Control Officers enforce animal control by-laws and regulations of provincial and municipal governments.

Profile Summary

APTITUDES

G	V	N	S	P	Q	K	F	M
4	4	4	4	4	4	4	4	3

INTERESTS
MDs

DATA PEOPLE THINGS (DPT)
563

PHYSICAL ACTIVITIES (PA)

V	C	H	B	L	S
3	0	2	4	2	3

ENVIRONMENTAL CONDITIONS (EC)
L1, L3, L4, H2

EDUCATION/TRAINING
4, 6

Examples of Job Titles

Animal Control Officer

Descriptor Profile

Main Characteristics

Occupations in this group are characterized by the following aptitudes, interests and worker functions as they relate to main duties:

- **General learning ability** to acquire knowledge of animal control by-laws and regulations

- **Manual dexterity** to operate vehicles and handle animals

- **Methodical interest** in **copying** to issue warnings and citations to owners

- **Directive interest** in **driving** to impound lost, homeless and dangerous animals

- **Social interest** in **speaking** to citizens in response to complaints concerning stray domestic animals, livestock and wildlife

Physical Activities

Vision
    3   Near and far vision

Colour Discrimination
    0   Not relevant

Hearing
    2   Verbal interaction

Body Position
    4   Other body positions

Limb Co-ordination
    2   Multiple limb co-ordination

Strength
    3   Medium

Environmental Conditions

Location
    L1   Regulated inside climate
    L3   Outside
    L4   In a vehicle or cab

Hazards
    H2   Biological agents

Employment Requirements

Education/Training
    4, 6

- Completion of secondary school is required.

- Completion of a college program or courses in law and security or other related field
 or
 experience in a related administrative or regulatory occupation
 is usually required.

- On-the-job training is provided.

Workplaces/Employers

Municipal and provincial government agencies

Municipal governments

Provincial governments

Similar Occupations Classified Elsewhere

Engineering Inspectors and Regulatory Officers (2262)

Immigration, Unemployment Insurance and Revenue Officers (1228)

Other Protective Service Occupations (6465)

Police Officers (Except Commissioned) (6261)

Sheriffs and Bailiffs (6461)

6463.2 By-law Enforcement Officers

By-law Enforcement Officers enforce by-laws and regulations of provincial and municipal governments.

Profile Summary

APTITUDES

G	V	N	S	P	Q	K	F	M
3	3	4	4	4	4	4	4	4

INTERESTS
MDs

DATA PEOPLE THINGS (DPT)
368

PHYSICAL ACTIVITIES (PA)

V	C	H	B	L	S
3	0	2	3	0	1

ENVIRONMENTAL CONDITIONS (EC)
L1, L3, L4

EDUCATION/TRAINING
4, 6

Examples of Job Titles

By-law Enforcement Officer
Property Standards Inspector
Zoning Inspector

Descriptor Profile

Main Characteristics

Occupations in this group are characterized by the following aptitudes, interests and worker functions as they relate to main duties:

- **General learning ability** to acquire knowledge of by-laws and regulations

- **Verbal ability** to understand the technical language of by-laws and regulations, and to communicate information effectively

- **Methodical interest** in **compiling** information to investigate complaints

- **Directive interest** in enforcing municipal and provincial regulations

- **Social interest** in **speaking** to issue warnings and citations to commercial and residential property owners and occupants

Physical Activities

Vision
    3 Near and far vision

Colour Discrimination
    0 Not relevant

Hearing
    2 Verbal interaction

Body Position
    3 Sitting, standing, walking

Limb Co-ordination
    0 Not relevant

Strength
    1 Limited

Environmental Conditions

Location
    L1 Regulated inside climate
    L3 Outside
    L4 In a vehicle or cab

Employment Requirements

Education/Training
  4, 6

- Completion of secondary school is required.

- Completion of a college program or courses in law and security or other related field
  or
  experience in a related administrative or regulatory occupation is usually required.

- On-the-job training is provided.

Workplaces/Employers

Municipal and provincial government agencies

Municipal governments

Provincial governments

Similar Occupations Classified Elsewhere

Engineering Inspectors and Regulatory Officers (2262)

Immigration, Unemployment Insurance and Revenue Officers (1228)

Other Protective Service Occupations (6465)

Police Officers (Except Commissioned) (6261)

Sheriffs and Bailiffs (6461)

6463.3 Commercial Transport Inspectors

Commercial Transport Inspectors enforce regulations of provincial and municipal governments.

Profile Summary

APTITUDES

G	V	N	S	P	Q	K	F	M
3	3	3	4	4	3	4	4	4

INTERESTS
MDo

DATA PEOPLE THINGS (DPT)
364

PHYSICAL ACTIVITIES (PA)

V	C	H	B	L	S
3	0	2	3	1	1

ENVIRONMENTAL CONDITIONS (EC)
L1, L3, L4, H1

EDUCATION/TRAINING
4, 6

Examples of Job Titles

Commercial Transport Inspector

Descriptor Profile

Main Characteristics

Occupations in this group are characterized by the following aptitudes, interests and worker functions as they relate to main duties:

- **General learning ability** to acquire knowledge of regulations

- **Verbal ability** to understand the technical language of regulations and communicate information effectively

- **Numerical ability** and **clerical perception** to ensure that commercial vehicles meet regulations governing load restrictions

- **Methodical interest** in **compiling** information to inspect commercial vehicles to ensure compliance with regulations governing load restrictions, the transportation of hazardous materials and public safety

- **Directive interest** in **speaking** with transport drivers and companies to advise on standards and adherence to regulations

- **Objective interest** in **operating** equipment to conduct inspections of commercial vehicles

6463.3

Physical Activities

Vision
   3   Near and far vision

Colour Discrimination
   0   Not relevant

Hearing
   2   Verbal interaction

Body Position
   3   Sitting, standing, walking

Limb Co-ordination
   1   Upper limb co-ordination

Strength
   1   Limited

Environmental Conditions

Location
   L1   Regulated inside climate
   L3   Outside
   L4   In a vehicle or cab

Hazards
   H1   Dangerous chemical substances

Employment Requirements

Education/Training
   4, 6

- Completion of secondary school is required.

- Completion of a college program or courses in law and security or other related field
  or
  experience in a related administrative or regulatory occupation is usually required.

- On-the-job training is provided.

Workplaces/Employers

Municipal and provincial government agencies

Municipal governments

Provincial governments

Similar Occupations Classified Elsewhere

Engineering Inspectors and Regulatory Officers (2262)

Immigration, Unemployment Insurance and Revenue Officers (1228)

Other Protective Service Occupations (6465)

Police Officers (Except Commissioned) (6261)

Sheriffs and Bailiffs (6461)

6463.4 Garbage Collection Inspectors

Garbage Collection Inspectors enforce garbage collection by-laws and regulations of provincial and municipal governments.

Profile Summary

APTITUDES

G	V	N	S	P	Q	K	F	M
3	3	4	4	4	4	4	4	4

INTERESTS
MDs

DATA PEOPLE THINGS (DPT)
368

PHYSICAL ACTIVITIES (PA)

V	C	H	B	L	S
3	0	2	3	0	1

ENVIRONMENTAL CONDITIONS (EC)
L1, L3, L4

EDUCATION/TRAINING
4, 6

Examples of Job Titles

Garbage Collection Inspector

Descriptor Profile

Main Characteristics

Occupations in this group are characterized by the following aptitudes, interests and worker functions as they relate to main duties:

- **General learning ability** to acquire knowledge of garbage collection by-laws

- **Verbal ability** to understand the technical language of garbage collection by-laws and communicate information effectively

- **Methodical interest** in **compiling** information to investigate complaints concerning infractions

- **Directive interest** in conducting investigations and enforcing adherence to by-laws

- **Social interest** in **speaking** with the public to advise on garbage collection by-laws

6463.4
Subgroup 4 of 7

Physical Activities

Vision
   3   Near and far vision

Colour Discrimination
   0   Not relevant

Hearing
   2   Verbal interaction

Body Position
   3   Sitting, standing, walking

Limb Co-ordination
   0   Not relevant

Strength
   1   Limited

Environmental Conditions

Location
   L1 Regulated inside climate
   L3 Outside
   L4 In a vehicle or cab

Employment Requirements

Education/Training
   4, 6

- Completion of secondary school is required.

- Completion of a college program or courses in law and security or other related field
  or
  experience in a related administrative or regulatory occupation is usually required.

- On-the-job training is provided.

Workplaces/Employers

Municipal and provincial government agencies

Municipal governments

Provincial governments

Similar Occupations Classified Elsewhere

Engineering Inspectors and Regulatory Officers (2262)

Immigration, Unemployment Insurance and Revenue Officers (1228)

Other Protective Service Occupations (6465)

Police Officers (Except Commissioned) (6261)

Sheriffs and Bailiffs (6461)

6463.5 Liquor Licence Inspectors

Liquor Licence Inspectors enforce liquor laws and regulations of provincial and municipal governments.

Profile Summary

APTITUDES

G	V	N	S	P	Q	K	F	M
3	3	4	4	4	4	4	4	4

INTERESTS
MDs

DATA PEOPLE THINGS (DPT)
368

PHYSICAL ACTIVITIES (PA)

V	C	H	B	L	S
3	0	2	3	0	1

ENVIRONMENTAL CONDITIONS (EC)
L1

EDUCATION/TRAINING
4, 6

Examples of Job Titles

Liquor Licence Inspector

Descriptor Profile

Main Characteristics

Occupations in this group are characterized by the following aptitudes, interests and worker functions as they relate to main duties:

- **General learning ability** to acquire knowledge of liquor laws and regulations

- **Verbal ability** to understand technical language of liquor laws and regulations, and to communicate information effectively

- **Methodical interest** in **compiling** information to conduct inspections of licensed establishments

- **Directive interest** in reporting contravention of laws and regulations to provincial liquor control boards and agencies

- **Social interest** in **speaking** with licensees to advise on laws and regulations

Physical Activities

Vision
  3   Near and far vision

Colour Discrimination
  0   Not relevant

Hearing
  2   Verbal interaction

Body Position
  3   Sitting, standing, walking

Limb Co-ordination
  0   Not relevant

Strength
  1   Limited

Environmental Conditions

Location
  L1   Regulated inside climate

Employment Requirements

Education/Training
  4, 6

- Completion of secondary school is required.

- Completion of a college program or courses in law and security or other related field
  or
  experience in a related administrative or regulatory occupation is usually required.

- On-the-job training is provided.

Workplaces/Employers

Municipal and provincial government agencies

Municipal governments

Provincial governments

Similar Occupations Classified Elsewhere

Engineering Inspectors and Regulatory Officers (2262)

Immigration, Unemployment Insurance and Revenue Officers (1228)

Other Protective Service Occupations (6465)

Police Officers (Except Commissioned) (6261)

Sheriffs and Bailiffs (6461)

6463.6 Parking Control Officers

Parking Control Officers enforce parking control by-laws of provincial and municipal governments.

Profile Summary

APTITUDES

G	V	N	S	P	Q	K	F	M
3	4	4	4	4	4	3	4	4

INTERESTS
MDo

DATA PEOPLE THINGS (DPT)
583

PHYSICAL ACTIVITIES (PA)

V	C	H	B	L	S
3	0	1	3	1	1

ENVIRONMENTAL CONDITIONS (EC)
L1, L3, L4

EDUCATION/TRAINING
4, 6

Examples of Job Titles

Parking Control Officer

Descriptor Profile

Main Characteristics

Occupations in this group are characterized by the following aptitudes, interests and worker functions as they relate to main duties:

- **General learning ability** to acquire knowledge of parking by-laws

- **Motor co-ordination** to operate vehicles and issue tickets

- **Methodical interest** in **copying** to complete tickets indicating information such as dates, meter numbers and space areas, licence numbers and times of infractions

- **Directive interest** in enforcing parking by-laws on city streets, regional roads and municipal properties

- **Objective interest** in **driving** to patrol assigned areas of metered parking lots and sections of the city

6463.6

Physical Activities

Vision
   3 Near and far vision

Colour Discrimination
   0 Not relevant

Hearing
   1 Limited

Body Position
   3 Sitting, standing, walking

Limb Co-ordination
   1 Upper limb co-ordination

Strength
   1 Limited

Environmental Conditions

Location
   L1 Regulated inside climate
   L3 Outside
   L4 In a vehicle or cab

Employment Requirements

Education/Training
   4, 6

- Completion of secondary school is required.

- Completion of a college program or courses in law and security or other related field
  or
  experience in a related administrative or regulatory occupation
  is usually required.

- On-the-job training is provided.

Workplaces/Employers

Municipal and provincial government agencies

Municipal governments

Provincial governments

Similar Occupations Classified Elsewhere

Engineering Inspectors and Regulatory Officers (2262)

Immigration, Unemployment Insurance and Revenue Officers (1228)

Other Protective Service Occupations (6465)

Police Officers (Except Commissioned) (6261)

Sheriffs and Bailiffs (6461)

6463.7 Taxi Inspectors

Taxi Inspectors enforce by-laws and regulations of provincial and municipal governments.

Profile Summary

APTITUDES

G	V	N	S	P	Q	K	F	M
3	3	4	4	4	4	4	4	4

INTERESTS
MDo

DATA PEOPLE THINGS (DPT)
364

PHYSICAL ACTIVITIES (PA)

V	C	H	B	L	S
2	0	2	3	1	1

ENVIRONMENTAL CONDITIONS (EC)
L1, L3, L4

EDUCATION/TRAINING
4, 6

Examples of Job Titles

Taxi Inspector

Descriptor Profile

Main Characteristics

Occupations in this group are characterized by the following aptitudes, interests and worker functions as they relate to main duties:

- **General learning** and **verbal ability** to issue summonses and prepare reports

- **Methodical interest** in **compiling** information to investigate public complaints

- **Directive interest** in **speaking** to give evidence in court and to city councils and taxi commissions

- **Objective interest** in **operating - manipulating** to inspect taxis for mechanical reliability, cleanliness, licensing and meter accuracy

6463.7
Subgroup 7 of 7

Physical Activities

Vision
   2 Near vision

Colour Discrimination
   0 Not relevant

Hearing
   2 Verbal interaction

Body Position
   3 Sitting, standing, walking

Limb Co-ordination
   1 Upper limb co-ordination

Strength
   1 Limited

Environmental Conditions

Location
   L1 Regulated inside climate
   L3 Outside
   L4 In a vehicle or cab

Employment Requirements

Education/Training
   4, 6

- Completion of secondary school is required.

- Completion of a college program or courses in law and security or other related field
or
experience in a related administrative or regulatory occupation is usually required.

- On-the-job training is provided.

Workplaces/Employers

Municipal and provincial government agencies

Municipal governments

Provincial governments

Similar Occupations Classified Elsewhere

Engineering Inspectors and Regulatory Officers (2262)

Immigration, Unemployment Insurance and Revenue Officers (1228)

Other Protective Service Occupations (6465)

Police Officers (Except Commissioned) (6261)

Sheriffs and Bailiffs (6461)

6464 Occupations Unique to the Armed Forces

This group includes personnel in occupations unique to the armed forces such as soldiers in armour, artillery, infantry, airborne and maritime branches, who provide defence measures to protect Canadian waters, land, airspace and other interests.

Profile Summary

APTITUDES

G	V	N	S	P	Q	K	F	M
3	3	4	3	3	4	3	3	3

INTERESTS
MOs

DATA PEOPLE THINGS (DPT)
262

PHYSICAL ACTIVITIES (PA)

V	C	H	B	L	S
1-4*	0-1*	1-3*	1-4*	0-2*	1-4*

ENVIRONMENTAL CONDITIONS (EC)
L1-L4*, H1-H8*, D1-D5*

EDUCATION/TRAINING
5

Examples of Job Titles

Air Defence Technician
Armoured Vehicle Crewmember
Artillery Soldier
Assault Pioneer
Field Engineer
Infantry Soldier
Naval Weapons Technician
Sonar Operator
Tank Driver
Weapons Operator

Descriptor Profile

Main Characteristics

Occupations in this group are characterized by the following aptitudes, interests and worker functions as they relate to main duties:

- **General learning** and **verbal ability** to provide defence measures to protect Canadian waters, land, airspace and other interests, as well as to engage in peacekeeping operations and enforce cease-fire agreements

- **Spatial** and **form perception** to visualize the relative positions of equipment parts and components, and to detect equipment malfunctions

- **Motor co-ordination** and **finger** and **manual dexterity** to use various military combat equipment and defence systems

- **Methodical interest** in **analyzing** information to provide aid in emergency situations such as civil disorder, natural disasters and major accidents, as well as to perform administrative and guard duties

- **Objective interest** in **controlling** armoured vehicles, artillery, hand-held weapons and other military combat and defence equipment

- **Social interest** in **speaking - signalling** to engage in drills and other training in preparation for peacekeeping, combat and natural disaster relief duties

6464

Physical Activities

Vision
  1-4*

Colour Discrimination
  0-1*

Hearing
  1-3*

Body Position
  1-4*

Limb Co-ordination
  0-2*

Strength
  1-4*

Environmental Conditions

Location
  L1-L4*

Hazards
  H1-H8*

Discomforts
  D1-D5*

Employment Requirements

Education/Training
  5

- Completion of secondary school is usually required.

- Three months of basic military training are provided.

- Specialized training in the operation and maintenance of military equipment and systems is provided.

Workplaces/Employers

Canadian Forces

Occupational Options

Progression to commissioned officer occupations is possible with additional training and experience.

Similar Occupations Classified Elsewhere

Commissioned Officers, Armed Forces (0643)

Occupations which exist in the armed forces and for which there are civilian counterparts are classified with those occupations. For example:
Military police officers [in 6261 *Police Officers (Except Commissioned)*]

Musicians - military (in 5133 *Musicians and Singers*)

Vehicle technicians - military (in 7321 *Motor Vehicle Mechanics, Technicians and Mechanical Repairers*)

Remarks

Personnel in this group specialize in specific combat functions.

Data provided by Statistics Canada for *Occupations Unique to the Armed Forces* (6464) include all non-commissioned armed forces personnel.

* Physical Activities and Environmental Conditions

- For occupations in this group, all Physical Activities and Environmental Conditions factors and levels may apply. All soldiers must be prepared in case of war or other military action.

6465.1 Corporate Security Officers

Corporate Security Officers conduct private investigations for clients and employers, implement security measures to protect properties against theft and fire, and provide other protective services.

Profile Summary

APTITUDES

G	V	N	S	P	Q	K	F	M
3	3	4	4	4	4	4	4	4

INTERESTS
MDs

DATA PEOPLE THINGS (DPT)
368

PHYSICAL ACTIVITIES (PA)

V	C	H	B	L	S
3	0	2	3	0	1

ENVIRONMENTAL CONDITIONS (EC)
L1

EDUCATION/TRAINING
3, 4, 6

Examples of Job Titles

Alarm Investigator
Corporate Security Officer
House Detective
Postal Inspection Officer
Security Consultant

Descriptor Profile

Main Characteristics

Occupations in this group are characterized by the following aptitudes, interests and worker functions as they relate to main duties:

- **General learning** and **verbal ability** to understand and apply techniques used to conduct private investigations

- **Methodical interest** in **compiling** information to investigate unlawful acts of employees and patrons of establishments

- **Directive interest** in recommending security systems such as electronic detection devices and access devices

- **Social interest** in **speaking** to question individuals to obtain information and evidence

6465.1
Subgroup 1 of 3

Physical Activities

Vision
   3 Near and far vision

Colour
   0 Not relevant

Hearing
   2 Verbal interaction

Body Position
   3 Sitting, standing, walking

Limb Co-ordination
   0 Not relevant

Strength
   1 Limited

Environmental Conditions

Location
   L1 Regulated inside climate

Employment Requirements

Education/Training
3, 4, 6

- Completion of secondary school is required.

- A college diploma in law and security may be required.

- On-the-job training may be provided.

- Experience as a police officer may be required for corporate security officers.

Workplaces/Employers

Businesses

Hotels

Industrial organizations

Retail establishments

Security and investigation service companies

Self-employment

Similar Occupations Classified Elsewhere

Police Officers (Except Commissioned) (6261)

Security Guards and Related Occupations (6651)

6465.2 Private Investigators

Private Investigators conduct private investigations for clients and employers.

Profile Summary

APTITUDES

G	V	N	S	P	Q	K	F	M
3	3	4	4	3	4	4	4	4

INTERESTS
MIS

DATA PEOPLE THINGS (DPT)
368

PHYSICAL ACTIVITIES (PA)

V	C	H	B	L	S
3	0	2	3	0	1

ENVIRONMENTAL CONDITIONS (EC)
L1, L3, H8

EDUCATION/TRAINING
3, 4, 6, R

Examples of Job Titles

Private Investigator

Security Officer, Private

Descriptor Profile

Main Characteristics

Occupations in this group are characterized by the following aptitudes, interests and worker functions as they relate to main duties:

- **General learning** and **verbal ability** to understand and apply the principles and techniques of private investigations

- **Form perception** to note pertinent details in materials and objects

- **Methodical interest** in **compiling** information for use in civil and criminal litigation matters

- **Innovative interest** in conducting investigations to locate missing persons

- **Social interest** in **speaking** to question individuals to obtain information and evidence

6465.2
Subgroup 2 of 3

Physical Activities

Vision
   3   Near and far vision

Colour Discrimination
   0   Not relevant

Hearing
   2   Verbal interaction

Body Position
   3   Sitting, standing, walking

Limb Co-ordination
   0   Not relevant

Strength
   1   Limited

Environmental Conditions

Location
   L1 Regulated inside climate
   L3 Outside

Hazards
   H8 Dangerous locations

Employment Requirements

Education/Training
   3, 4, 6, R

- Completion of secondary school is required.

- A college diploma in law and security may be required.

- On-the-job training may be provided.

- Provincial licensing is required for private investigators.

Workplaces/Employers

Businesses

Hotels

Industrial organizations

Retail establishments

Security and investigation service companies

Self-employment

Similar Occupations Classified Elsewhere

Police Officers (Except Commissioned) (6261)

Security Guards and Related Occupations (6651)

6465.3 Retail Loss Prevention Officers

Retail Loss Prevention Officers conduct private investigations for clients and employers, implement security measures to protect properties against theft and fire, and provide other protective services.

Profile Summary

APTITUDES

G	V	N	S	P	Q	K	F	M
3	3	4	4	4	4	4	4	4

INTERESTS
Mds

DATA PEOPLE THINGS (DPT)
367

PHYSICAL ACTIVITIES (PA)

V	C	H	B	L	S
3	0	2	3	1	1

ENVIRONMENTAL CONDITIONS (EC)
L1

EDUCATION/TRAINING
3, 4, 6

Examples of Job Titles

Retail Loss Prevention Officer

Store Detective

Descriptor Profile

Main Characteristics

Occupations in this group are characterized by the following aptitudes, interests and worker functions as they relate to main duties:

- **General learning ability** to prevent and detect shoplifting and theft in retail establishments

- **Verbal ability** to prepare reports of investigations for authorities

- **Methodical interest** in **compiling** information to conduct investigations on own initiative or on employers' requests

- **Directive interest** in **handling** to perform duties of regular employees such as selling and stock checking

- **Social interest** in **speaking** to question individuals and suspects in attempts to secure evidence and personal admissions relating to cases being investigated

Physical Activities

Vision
　3　Near and far vision

Colour Discrimination
　0　Not relevant

Hearing
　2　Verbal interaction

Body Position
　3　Sitting, standing, walking

Limb Co-ordination
　1　Upper limb co-ordination

Strength
　1　Limited

Environmental Conditions

Location
　L1　Regulated inside climate

Employment Requirements

Education/Training
　3, 4, 6

- Completion of secondary school is required.

- A college diploma in law and security may be required.

- On-the-job training may be provided.

Workplaces/Employers

Businesses

Hotels

Industrial organizations

Retail establishments

Security and investigation service companies

Self-employment

Similar Occupations Classified Elsewhere

Police Officers (Except Commissioned) (6261)

Security Guards and Related Occupations (6651)

6471.1 Visiting Homemakers

Visiting Homemakers provide ongoing and short-term home support services for individuals and families during periods of incapacitation, convalescence and family disruption.

Profile Summary

APTITUDES

G	V	N	S	P	Q	K	F	M
3	3	4	4	4	4	4	4	4

INTERESTS
SMo

DATA PEOPLE THINGS (DPT)
377

PHYSICAL ACTIVITIES (PA)

V	C	H	B	L	S
2	0	2	4	1	3

ENVIRONMENTAL CONDITIONS (EC)
L1

EDUCATION/TRAINING
2, 4, 6, R

Examples of Job Titles

Home Support Worker
Home-Health Aide
Visiting Homemaker

Descriptor Profile

Main Characteristics

Occupations in this group are characterized by the following aptitudes, interests and worker functions as they relate to main duties:

- **General learning** and **verbal ability** to care for individuals and families during periods of incapacitation, convalescence and family disruption

- **Social interest** in **serving - assisting** clients by administering bedside and personal care such as aid in walking, bathing and personal hygiene under the direction of home-care agency supervisors and nurses; and in demonstrating infant care to new parents

- **Methodical interest** in **compiling** information to maintain client files and plan meals and special diets

- **Objective interest** in **handling** the preparation of meals and special diets; may perform routine housekeeping duties such as laundry, washing dishes and making beds

6471.1

Physical Activities

Vision
   2 Near vision

Colour Discrimination
   0 Not relevant

Hearing
   2 Verbal interaction

Body Position
   4 Other body positions

Limb Co-ordination
   1 Upper limb co-ordination

Strength
   3 Medium

Environmental Conditions

Location
   L1 Regulated inside climate

Employment Requirements

Education/Training
2, 4, 6, R

- Some secondary school education may be required.

- Child-care or home-management experience may be required.

- Visiting homemakers may require college or other courses in home support.

- First-aid certification may be required.

Workplaces/Employers

Government organizations

Home-care agencies

Non-profit agencies

Self-employment

Occupational Options

There is mobility among the occupations in the 6471 group.

Visiting homemakers may move into occupations such as health care aide or long-term care aide in nursing homes and long-term care institutions.

Similar Occupations Classified Elsewhere

Babysitters, Nannies and Parents' Helpers (6474)

Housekeepers who are house cleaners (in 6661 *Light Duty Cleaners*)

6471.2 Housekeepers

Housekeepers perform housekeeping and other home management duties.

Profile Summary

APTITUDES

G	V	N	S	P	Q	K	F	M
3	4	4	4	4	4	3	4	3

INTERESTS
MOs

DATA PEOPLE THINGS (DPT)
577

PHYSICAL ACTIVITIES (PA)

V	C	H	B	L	S
2	0	1	4	1	3

ENVIRONMENTAL CONDITIONS (EC)
L1

EDUCATION/TRAINING
2, R

Examples of Job Titles

Housekeeper

Descriptor Profile

Main Characteristics

Occupations in this group are characterized by the following aptitudes, interests and worker functions as they relate to main duties:

- **General learning ability, motor co-ordination** and **manual dexterity** to carry out home management duties

- **Methodical interest** in **copying** information to work under general direction of employers, and to plan and prepare meals independently or with employers

- **Objective interest** in **handling** cleaning materials and equipment to perform housekeeping tasks

- **Social interest** in **serving - assisting** to perform housekeeping duties; may serve meals and care for children

6471.2

Physical Activities

Vision
  2 Near vision

Colour Discrimination
  0 Not relevant

Hearing
  1 Limited

Body Position
  4 Other body positions

Limb Co-ordination
  1 Upper limb co-ordination

Strength
  3 Medium

Environmental Conditions

Location
  L1 Regulated inside climate

Employment Requirements

Education/Training
  2, R

- Some secondary school education may be required.

- Child-care or home-management experience may be required.

- First-aid certification may be required.

Workplaces/Employers

Embassies

Private households

Residential establishments

Occupational Options

There is mobility among the occupations in the 6471 group.

Similar Occupations Classified Elsewhere

Babysitters, Nannies and Parents' Helpers (6474)

Housekeepers who are house cleaners (in 6661 *Light Duty Cleaners*)

6471.3 Companions

Companions provide elderly and convalescent clients with companionship and personal care in residential and institutional settings.

Profile Summary

APTITUDES

G	V	N	S	P	Q	K	F	M
4	4	4	4	4	4	4	4	4

INTERESTS
SMo

DATA PEOPLE THINGS (DPT)
577

PHYSICAL ACTIVITIES (PA)

V	C	H	B	L	S
2	0	2	4	1	3

ENVIRONMENTAL CONDITIONS (EC)
L1, L3

EDUCATION/TRAINING
2, R

Examples of Job Titles

Companion

Personal Aide

Descriptor Profile

Main Characteristics

Occupations in this group are characterized by the following aptitudes, interests and worker functions as they relate to main duties:

- **General learning** and **verbal ability** to provide elderly and convalescent clients with companionship and personal care in clients' homes

- **Social interest** in **serving - assisting** clients by providing aid with walking, bathing and other aspects of personal hygiene

- **Methodical interest** in **copying** to carry out activities under general direction of home-care agency supervisor or family members

- **Objective interest** in **handling** to perform various activities related to the provision of personal care

6471.3
Subgroup 3 of 4

Physical Activities

Vision
   2 Near vision

Colour Discrimination
   0 Not relevant

Hearing
   2 Verbal interaction

Body Position
   4 Other body positions

Limb Co-ordination
   1 Upper limb co-ordination

Strength
   3 Medium

Environmental Conditions

Location
   L1 Regulated inside climate
   L3 Outside

Employment Requirements

Education/Training
   2, R

- Some secondary school education may be required.

- Child-care or home-management experience may be required.

- First-aid certification may be required.

Workplaces/Employers

Home-care agencies
Self-employment

Occupational Options

There is mobility among the occupations in the 6471 group.

Similar Occupations Classified Elsewhere

Babysitters, Nannies and Parents' Helpers (6474)

Housekeepers who are house cleaners (in 6661 *Light Duty Cleaners*)

6471.4 Foster Parents

Foster parents care for children as family members under the direction of foster-parent agencies.

Profile Summary

APTITUDES

G	V	N	S	P	Q	K	F	M
3	3	4	4	4	4	3	4	3

INTERESTS
SID

DATA PEOPLE THINGS (DPT)
378

PHYSICAL ACTIVITIES (PA)

V	C	H	B	L	S
3	0	2	4	1	3

ENVIRONMENTAL CONDITIONS (EC)
L1, L3

EDUCATION/TRAINING
2, R

Examples of Job Titles

Foster Parent

Descriptor Profile

Main Characteristics

Occupations in this group are characterized by the following aptitudes, interests and worker functions as they relate to main duties:

- **General learning** and **verbal ability** to care for foster children, usually on an emergency or temporary basis, as family members under the general direction of foster-parent agencies

- **Motor co-ordination** and **manual dexterity** to carry out various child-care activities

- **Social interest** in consulting foster-parent agency supervisors for advice and when problems arise

- **Innovative interest** in **compiling** information to apply knowledge and techniques of child care

- **Directive interest** in **serving - assisting** to administer therapeutic programs for foster children as directed by foster-agency social workers

6471.4
Subgroup 4 of 4

Physical Activities

Vision
   3   Near and far vision

Colour Discrimination
   0   Not relevant

Hearing
   2   Verbal interaction

Body Position
   4   Other body positions

Limb Co-ordination
   1   Upper limb co-ordination

Strength
   3   Medium

Environmental Conditions

Location
   L1   Regulated inside climate
   L3   Outside

Employment Requirements

Education/Training
   2, R

- Some secondary school education may be required.

- Child-care or home-management experience may be required.

- First-aid certification may be required.

Workplaces/Employers

Within own homes for foster-parent agencies

Occupational Options

There is mobility among the occupations in the 6471 group.

Similar Occupations Classified Elsewhere

Babysitters, Nannies and Parents' Helpers (6474)

Housekeepers who are house cleaners (in 6661 *Light Duty Cleaners*)

6472 Elementary and Secondary School Teacher Assistants

This group includes workers who assist elementary and secondary school teachers and counsellors.

Profile Summary

APTITUDES
G	V	N	S	P	Q	K	F	M
3	3	3	3	3	3	4	3	3

INTERESTS
SMi

DATA PEOPLE THINGS (DPT)
577

PHYSICAL ACTIVITIES (PA)
V	C	H	B	L	S
3	0	2	3	1	2

ENVIRONMENTAL CONDITIONS (EC)
L1, L3

EDUCATION/TRAINING
4, 5

Examples of Job Titles

Educational Resources Assistant
Lunch Room Supervisor
Program Assistant, Education
Secondary School Teacher's Assistant
Special Education Assistant
Staff Assistant, Education
Teacher's Aide
Teacher's Assistant

Descriptor Profile

Main Characteristics

Occupations in this group are characterized by the following aptitudes, interests and worker functions as they relate to main duties:

- **General learning, verbal,** and **numerical ability** to help students with lessons, assist in school libraries and offices, and perform other duties assigned by school principals

- **Finger** and **manual dexterity** to operate, or assist teachers in the operation of, projectors, tape recorders and other audio-visual and electronic equipment

- **Social interest** in **assisting** special-needs students such as those with mental and physical disabilities with mobility, communication and personal hygiene

- **Methodical interest** in **copying** information to work under direct supervision of classroom teachers and under the supervision of professionals such as special education instructors, psychologists and speech-language pathologists; and in monitoring students during recess and noon hour

- **Innovative interest** in **handling** techniques of behaviour modification, personal development and other therapeutic programs; and in accompanying and supervising students during activities in school gymnasiums, laboratories, libraries and resource centres, and on field trips

6472

Physical Activities

Vision
 3 Near and far vision

Colour Discrimination
 0 Not relevant

Hearing
 2 Verbal interaction

Body Position
 3 Sitting, standing, walking

Limb Co-ordination
 1 Upper limb co-ordination

Strength
 2 Light

Environmental Conditions

Location
 L1 Regulated inside climate
 L3 Outside

Employment Requirements

Education/Training
 4, 5

- Completion of secondary school is usually required.

- College courses in child care or related fields may be required for some positions.

- Teacher assistants who aid students with special needs may require specialized training and experience.

Workplaces/Employers

Public and private elementary schools

Public and private secondary schools

Occupational Options

Mobility to other occupations related to child and adolescent care is possible with experience.

Similar Occupations Classified Elsewhere

Early Childhood Educator Assistants (6473)

Early Childhood Educators (4214)

Elementary School and Kindergarten Teachers (4142)

Post-Secondary Teaching and Research Assistants (4122)

6473 Early Childhood Educator Assistants

Early Childhood Educator Assistants supervise pre-school children and, under the supervision of early childhood educators, lead children in activities to stimulate and develop their intellectual, physical and emotional growth.

Profile Summary

APTITUDES

G	V	N	S	P	Q	K	F	M
3	3	4	4	4	4	4	4	4

INTERESTS

SMd

DATA PEOPLE THINGS (DPT)

577

PHYSICAL ACTIVITIES (PA)

V	C	H	B	L	S
4	1	2	4	1	2

ENVIRONMENTAL CONDITIONS (EC)

L1, L3

EDUCATION/TRAINING

4

Examples of Job Titles

Child-Care Worker Assistant

Day-Care Helper

Day-Care Worker's Assistant

Early Childhood Educator Assistant

Early Childhood Program Staff Assistant

Pre-School Helper

Descriptor Profile

Main Characteristics

Occupations in this group are characterized by the following aptitudes, interests and worker functions as they relate to main duties:

- **General learning** and **verbal ability** to submit written observations on children to supervisors, and to attend staff meetings to discuss children's progress and problems

- **Social interest** in **assisting** children in the development of proper eating and dressing habits and personal hygiene

- **Methodical interest** in **copying** information to assist supervisors in keeping records; and in preparing and serving snacks, maintaining day-care equipment and assisting with housekeeping duties

- **Directive interest** in **handling** to lead children's activities by telling stories, teaching songs and preparing craft materials; and in supervising children in indoor and outdoor play and during rest periods

6473

Physical Activities

Vision
　4　Total visual field

Colour Discrimination
　1　Relevant

Hearing
　2　Verbal interaction

Body Position
　4　Other body positions

Limb Co-ordination
　1　Upper limb co-ordination

Strength
　2　Light

Environmental Conditions

Location
　L1　Regulated inside climate
　L3　Outside

Employment Requirements

Education/Training
4

- Completion of secondary school is usually required.

- Experience in child care, such as babysitting, is required.

Workplaces/Employers

Day-care centres

Nursery schools

Similar Occupations Classified Elsewhere

Early Childhood Educators (4214)

Elementary School and Kindergarten Teachers (4142)

Teacher aides (in 6472 *Elementary and Secondary School Teacher Assistants*)

Remarks

In data provided by Statistics Canada, groups 4214 and 6473 are combined to form 6470 *Early Childhood Educators and Assistants*.

6474.1 Babysitters

Babysitters care for children on an ongoing and short-term basis.

Profile Summary

APTITUDES

G	V	N	S	P	Q	K	F	M
4	4	4	4	4	5	4	4	3

INTERESTS
SMd

DATA PEOPLE THINGS (DPT)
577

PHYSICAL ACTIVITIES (PA)

V	C	H	B	L	S
3	0	2	4	1	3

ENVIRONMENTAL CONDITIONS (EC)
L1

EDUCATION/TRAINING
2+, R

Examples of Job Titles

Babysitter

Descriptor Profile

Main Characteristics

Occupations in this group are characterized by the following aptitudes, interests and worker functions as they relate to main duties:

- **General learning ability** to supervise and care for children in the absence of regular caregivers

- **Manual dexterity** to bathe, diaper and feed infants and children

- **Social interest** in **assisting** children with their needs while providing care

- **Methodical interest** in **copying** to perform housekeeping duties and prepare meals according to employers' instructions

- **Directive interest** in **handling** the organization of activities and outings to provide amusement and exercise

6474.1

Physical Activities

Vision
  3 Near and far vision

Colour Discrimination
  0 Not relevant

Hearing
  2 Verbal interaction

Body Position
  4 Other body positions

Limb Co-ordination
  1 Upper limb co-ordination

Strength
  3 Medium

Environmental Conditions

Location
  L1 Regulated inside climate

Employment Requirements

Education/Training
  2+, R

- Completion of secondary school may be required.

- Child-care or home-management experience may be required.

- Demonstrated ability to perform work is usually required.

- First-aid certification may be required.

Workplaces/Employers

Babysitting agencies

Self-employment

Occupational Options

There is mobility among occupations in the 6474 group.

Similar Occupations Classified Elsewhere

Early Childhood Educator Assistants (6473)

Visiting Homemakers, Housekeepers and Related Occupations (6471)

Companions and foster parents (in 6471 *Visiting Homemakers, Housekeepers and Related Occupations*)

Day-care workers (in 4214 *Early Childhood Educators*)

6474.2 Nannies and Live-in Caregivers

Nannies care for children and provide for their health and physical and social development.

Profile Summary

APTITUDES

G	V	N	S	P	Q	K	F	M
4	3	4	4	4	5	4	4	3

INTERESTS
SMd

DATA PEOPLE THINGS (DPT)
577

PHYSICAL ACTIVITIES (PA)

V	C	H	B	L	S
3	0	2	4	1	3

ENVIRONMENTAL CONDITIONS (EC)
L1, L3

EDUCATION/TRAINING
2+, 5+, R

Examples of Job Titles

Live-in Caregiver
Nanny

Descriptor Profile

Main Characteristics

Occupations in this group are characterized by the following aptitudes, interests and worker functions as they relate to main duties:

- **General learning ability** to acquire and apply knowledge of child-care principles and techniques

- **Verbal ability** to instruct children in personal hygiene and social development

- **Manual dexterity** to bathe, diaper and feed infants and children

- **Social interest** in **assisting** to care for children in employers' residences; may reside in employers' homes

- **Methodical interest** in **handling** the preparation of meals, laundering of clothes and other housekeeping duties

- **Directive interest** in **copying** employers' instructions to oversee children's activities such as meals and rest periods; and in organizing games, activities and outings to provide amusement and exercise

6474.2
Subgroup 2 of 3

Physical Activities

Vision
  3 Near and far vision

Colour Discrimination
  0 Not relevant

Hearing
  2 Verbal interaction

Body Position
  4 Other body positions

Limb Co-ordination
  1 Upper limb co-ordination

Strength
  3 Medium

Environmental Conditions

Location
  L1 Regulated inside climate
  L3 Outside

Employment Requirements

Education/Training
2+, 5+, R

- Completion of secondary school may be required.

- Nannies and live-in caregivers may require completion of a training program in child care or a related field.

- Child-care or home-management experience may be required.

- Demonstrated ability to perform work is usually required.

- First-aid certification may be required.

Workplaces/Employers

Private households where they may also reside

Occupational Options

There is mobility among occupations in the 6474 group.

Similar Occupations Classified Elsewhere

Early Childhood Educator Assistants (6473)

Visiting Homemakers, Housekeepers and Related Occupations (6471)

Companions and foster parents (in 6471 *Visiting Homemakers, Housekeepers and Related Occupations*)

Day-care workers (in 4214 *Early Childhood Educators*)

6474.3 Parents' Helpers

Parents' Helpers assist parents with child care and household duties.

Profile Summary

APTITUDES

G	V	N	S	P	Q	K	F	M
4	4	4	4	4	5	4	4	3

INTERESTS
SMo

DATA PEOPLE THINGS (DPT)
577

PHYSICAL ACTIVITIES (PA)

V	C	H	B	L	S
3	0	2	4	1	3

ENVIRONMENTAL CONDITIONS (EC)
L1

EDUCATION/TRAINING
2+, R

Examples of Job Titles

Parent's Helper

Descriptor Profile

Main Characteristics

Occupations in this group are characterized by the following aptitudes, interests and worker functions as they relate to main duties:

- **General learning ability** to acquire and apply knowledge of child care and household management procedures

- **Manual dexterity** to bathe, diaper and feed infants and children

- **Social interest** in **assisting** to help parents in child supervision and household management

- **Methodical interest** in **copying** instructions to assist with meal preparation, laundry, washing dishes, running errands and other routine housekeeping duties

- **Objective interest** in **handling** cooking, laundry and other household equipment

6474.3

Physical Activities

Vision
   3   Near and far vision

Colour Discrimination
   0   Not relevant

Hearing
   2   Verbal interaction

Body Position
   4   Other body positions

Limb Co-ordination
   1   Upper limb co-ordination

Strength
   3   Medium

Environmental Conditions

Location
   L1   Regulated inside climate

Employment Requirements

Education/Training
   2+, R

- Completion of secondary school may be required.

- Child-care or home-management experience may be required.

- Demonstrated ability to perform work is usually required.

- First-aid certification may be required.

Workplaces/Employers

Babysitting agencies

Private households where they may also reside

Self-employment

Occupational Options

There is mobility among occupations in the 6474 group.

Similar Occupations Classified Elsewhere

Early Childhood Educator Assistants (6473)

Visiting Homemakers, Housekeepers and Related Occupations (6471)

Companions and foster parents (in 6471 *Visiting Homemakers, Housekeepers and Related Occupations*)

Day-care workers (in 4214 *Early Childhood Educators*)

6481.1 Image Consultants

Image Consultants advise clients on their personal appearance, speaking style, manners or other behaviour in order to improve personal or business images.

Profile Summary

APTITUDES

G	V	N	S	P	Q	K	F	M
3	3	4	4	3	4	4	4	4

INTERESTS
ISD

DATA PEOPLE THINGS (DPT)
358

PHYSICAL ACTIVITIES (PA)

V	C	H	B	L	S
2	1	2	1	0	1

ENVIRONMENTAL CONDITIONS (EC)
L1

EDUCATION/TRAINING
3, 4

Examples of Job Titles

Etiquette Consultant
Image Consultant
Professional Image Consultant
Public Speaking Consultant

Descriptor Profile

Main Characteristics

Occupations in this group are characterized by the following aptitudes, interests and worker functions as they relate to main duties:

- **General learning ability** to acquire and apply techniques to help clients improve their personal or business images

- **Verbal ability** to arrange appointments, meet clients and explain services and fees

- **Form perception** to study overall appearance of clients

- **Innovative interest** in **compiling** information to assist clients in identifying personal-image goals through discussion

- **Social interest** in **persuading** clients by advising them on hair colour, hairstyle, make-up and clothing accessories; may advise on posture, general appearance and manner

- **Directive interest** in recommending colours for clothing and make-up using seasonal colour techniques

6481.1
Subgroup 1 of 5

Physical Activities

Vision
   2 Near vision

Colour Discrimination
   1 Relevant

Hearing
   2 Verbal interaction

Body Position
   1 Sitting

Limb Co-ordination
   0 Not relevant

Strength
   1 Limited

Environmental Conditions

Location
   L1 Regulated inside climate

Employment Requirements

Education/Training
   3, 4

- Completion of secondary school is usually required.

- Specialized training courses are available for occupations in this group.

- Experience and expertise in fashion, art, modelling or related fields are usually required.

Workplaces/Employers

Beauty salons

Fashion boutiques

Image consulting companies

Modelling schools

Self-employment

Similar Occupations Classified Elsewhere

Hairstylists and Barbers (6271)

Cosmeticians and manicurists (in 6482 *Estheticians, Electrologists and Related Occupations*)

Modelling school instructors (in 4216 *Other Instructors*)

6481.2 Make-Up Consultants

Make-Up Consultants advise clients on their personal appearance to improve their personal and business images.

Profile Summary

APTITUDES

G	V	N	S	P	Q	K	F	M
3	3	4	4	3	3	4	3	4

INTERESTS
SMd

DATA PEOPLE THINGS (DPT)
374

PHYSICAL ACTIVITIES (PA)

V	C	H	B	L	S
2	1	2	1	1	1

ENVIRONMENTAL CONDITIONS (EC)
L1

EDUCATION/TRAINING
3, 4

Examples of Job Titles

Fashion and Wardrobe Consultant

Descriptor Profile

Main Characteristics

Occupations in this group are characterized by the following aptitudes, interests and worker functions as they relate to main duties:

- **General learning ability** to understand and use make-up application techniques

- **Verbal ability** to arrange appointments, meet clients and explain services and fees

- **Form perception** to observe detail in skin and facial features

- **Finger dexterity** to apply make-up

- **Social interest** in **assisting** clients by advising on type, colour and application of make-up

- **Methodical interest** in **manipulating** to apply make-up for special occasions such as weddings, parties and photography sessions

- **Directive interest** in **compiling** information to recommend and arrange for manicures, pedicures, silkwraps, facials, massages and other esthetic services

6481.2
Subgroup 2 of 5

Physical Activities

Vision
   2 Near vision

Colour Discrimination
   1 Relevant

Hearing
   2 Verbal interaction

Body Position
   1 Sitting

Limb Co-ordination
   1 Upper limb co-ordination

Strength
   1 Limited

Environmental Conditions

Location
   L1 Regulated inside climate

Employment Requirements

Education/Training
   3, 4

- Completion of secondary school is usually required.

- Specialized training courses are available for make-up and skin-care consultants.

- Experience and expertise in fashion, art, modelling or related fields are usually required.

Workplaces/Employers

Beauty salons

Fashion boutiques

Image consulting companies

Modelling schools

Self-employment

Similar Occupations Classified Elsewhere

Hairstylists and Barbers (6271)

Cosmeticians and manicurists (in 6482 *Estheticians, Electrologists and Related Occupations*)

Modelling school instructors (in 4216 *Other Instructors*)

6481.3 Colour Consultants

Colour Consultants advise clients on their personal appearance to improve their personal and business images.

Profile Summary

APTITUDES

G	V	N	S	P	Q	K	F	M
4	3	4	4	4	4	4	4	4

INTERESTS
SMd

DATA PEOPLE THINGS (DPT)
378

PHYSICAL ACTIVITIES (PA)

V	C	H	B	L	S
2	1	2	1	0	1

ENVIRONMENTAL CONDITIONS (EC)
L1

EDUCATION/TRAINING
3, 4

Examples of Job Titles

Colour Consultant, Fashion
Fashion and Wardrobe Consultant
Wardrobe Consultant

Descriptor Profile

Main Characteristics

Occupations in this group are characterized by the following aptitudes, interests and worker functions as they relate to main duties:

- **General learning ability** to understand and use techniques related to the selection of colours most becoming to clients' natural body tones

- **Verbal ability** to arrange appointments, meet clients and explain services and fees

- **Social interest** in **assisting** clients to choose colours for clothing that will complement their appearance; may advise clients on the selection and purchase of clothing, accessories, make-up and other fashion-related items

- **Methodical interest** in **compiling** information to pick colours that are best suited to the clients' skin tone, hair colour and lip and eye colours

- **Directive interest** in recommending personal colour charts for clients' use in purchasing clothing, accessories and make-up

6481.3
Subgroup 3 of 5

Physical Activities

Vision
  2 Near vision

Colour Discrimination
  1 Relevant

Hearing
  2 Verbal interaction

Body Position
  1 Sitting

Limb Co-ordination
  0 Not relevant

Strength
  1 Limited

Environmental Conditions

Location
  L1 Regulated inside climate

Employment Requirements

Education/Training
  3, 4

- Completion of secondary school is usually required.

- Specialized training courses are available for colour consultants.

- Experience and expertise in fashion, art, modelling or related fields are usually required.

Workplaces/Employers

Beauty salons

Fashion boutiques

Image consulting companies

Modelling schools

Self-employment

Similar Occupations Classified Elsewhere

Hairstylists and Barbers (6271)

Cosmeticians and manicurists (in 6482 *Estheticians, Electrologists and Related Occupations*)

Modelling school instructors (in 4216 *Other Instructors*)

6481.4 Wedding Consultants

Wedding Consultants advise clients on their wedding plans.

Profile Summary

APTITUDES

G	V	N	S	P	Q	K	F	M
3	3	3	4	3	3	4	4	4

INTERESTS
SDI

DATA PEOPLE THINGS (DPT)
358

PHYSICAL ACTIVITIES (PA)

V	C	H	B	L	S
2	1	2	1	0	1

ENVIRONMENTAL CONDITIONS (EC)
L1

EDUCATION/TRAINING
3, 4

Examples of Job Titles

Wedding Consultant

Descriptor Profile

Main Characteristics

Occupations in this group are characterized by the following aptitudes, interests and worker functions as they relate to main duties:

- **General learning ability** to understand and apply knowledge as it relates to wedding consulting

- Verbal and **numerical ability** and **clerical perception** to arrange appointments, meet clients and explain services and fees

- **Form perception** to study overall appearance of clients and to maintain client records

- **Social interest** in **persuading** clients by advising them on all aspects of the planning and organization of weddings

- **Directive interest** in recommending choice of wedding gowns, floral arrangements, banquet facilities, wedding invitations and other items related to weddings

- **Innovative interest** in **compiling** information to assist clients to identify wedding-related goals through discussion

6481.4

Physical Activities

Vision
   2   Near vision

Colour Discrimination
   1   Relevant

Hearing
   2   Verbal interaction

Body Position
   1   Sitting

Limb Co-ordination
   0   Not relevant

Strength
   1   Limited

Environmental Conditions

Location
   L1   Regulated inside climate

Employment Requirements

Education/Training
   3, 4

- Completion of secondary school is usually required.

- Specialized training courses are available for this occupation.

- Experience and expertise in fashion, art, modelling or related fields are usually required.

Workplaces/Employers

Beauty salons

Fashion boutiques

Image consulting companies

Modelling schools

Self-employment

Similar Occupations Classified Elsewhere

Hairstylists and Barbers (6271)

Cosmeticians and manicurists (in 6482 *Estheticians, Electrologists and Related Occupations*)

Modelling school instructors (in 4216 *Other Instructors*)

6481.5 Weight Loss Consultants

Weight Loss Consultants advise clients on their personal appearance and weight-loss goals to improve their personal or business images.

Profile Summary

APTITUDES

G	V	N	S	P	Q	K	F	M
4	3	4	4	4	3	4	4	4

INTERESTS
SMD

DATA PEOPLE THINGS (DPT)
358

PHYSICAL ACTIVITIES (PA)

V	C	H	B	L	S
2	0	2	1	0	1

ENVIRONMENTAL CONDITIONS (EC)
L1

EDUCATION/TRAINING
3, 4

Examples of Job Titles

Weight Loss Consultant

Descriptor Profile

Main Characteristics

Occupations in this group are characterized by the following aptitudes, interests and worker functions as they relate to main duties:

- **General learning ability** to understand and apply knowledge as it relates to weight-loss consulting

- **Verbal ability** to arrange appointments, meet clients and explain services and fees

- **Clerical perception** to take accurate weight and body measurements

- **Social interest** in **persuading** clients by advising them on diet, eating behaviour and exercise

- **Methodical interest** in **compiling** information to assist clients to determine weight-loss goals

- **Directive interest** in administering commercial weight-loss programs and providing appropriate support services

6481.5
Subgroup 5 of 5

Physical Activities

Vision
   2 Near vision

Colour Discrimination
   0 Not relevant

Hearing
   2 Verbal interaction

Body Position
   1 Sitting

Limb Co-ordination
   0 Not relevant

Strength
   1 Limited

Environmental Conditions

Location
   L1 Regulated inside climate

Employment Requirements

Education/Training
   3, 4

- Completion of secondary school is usually required.

- Specialized training courses are available for weight-loss consultants.

- Experience and expertise in fashion, art, modelling or related fields are usually required.

Workplaces/Employers

Beauty salons

Fashion boutiques

Image consulting companies

Modelling schools

Self-employment

Similar Occupations Classified Elsewhere

Hairstylists and Barbers (6271)

Cosmeticians and manicurists
(in 6482 *Estheticians, Electrologists and Related Occupations*)

Modelling school instructors
(in 4216 *Other Instructors*)

6482.1 Estheticians

Estheticians provide facial and body treatments designed to enhance their clients' physical appearance.

Profile Summary

APTITUDES

G	V	N	S	P	Q	K	F	M
3	3	4	4	3	4	3	3	3

INTERESTS
MSO

DATA PEOPLE THINGS (DPT)
374

PHYSICAL ACTIVITIES (PA)

V	C	H	B	L	S
2	0	2	4	1	1

ENVIRONMENTAL CONDITIONS (EC)
L1, D3

EDUCATION/TRAINING
2, 3, 4, 5, 6, R

Examples of Job Titles

Esthetician

Descriptor Profile

Main Characteristics

Occupations in this group are characterized by the following aptitudes, interests and worker functions as they relate to main duties:

- **General learning ability** to understand and use specialized techniques to enhance physical appearance

- **Verbal ability** to communicate with clients

- **Form perception** to assess facial and skin condition of clients

- **Motor co-ordination** and **finger** and **manual dexterity** to apply specialized products to clients' face and skin

- **Methodical interest** in **compiling** information on clients' facial and skin conditions

- **Social interest** in **serving - assisting** clients by offering facial and other skin treatment services

- **Objective interest** in **manipulating** various products and using specialized techniques

6482.1
Subgroup 1 of 6

Physical Activities

Vision
  2 Near vision

Colour Discrimination
  0 Not relevant

Hearing
  2 Verbal interaction

Body Position
  4 Other body positions

Limb Co-ordination
  1 Upper limb co-ordination

Strength
  1 Limited

Environmental Conditions

Location
  L1 Regulated inside climate

Discomforts
  D3 Odours

Employment Requirements

Education/Training
2, 3, 4, 5, 6, R

- Completion of high school, college or beauty school programs for estheticians, is required
  or
  on-the-job training is provided.

- Skin care specialists in Nova Scotia require provincial licensing.

Workplaces/Employers

Beauty salons

Self-employment

Occupational Options

There is little or no mobility among the different occupations in the 6482 group without additional specialized training.

Similar Occupations Classified Elsewhere

Hairstylists and Barbers (6271)

Image, Social and Other Personal Consultants (6481)

6482.2 Cosmeticians

Cosmeticians provide facial and body treatments designed to enhance their clients' physical appearance.

Profile Summary

APTITUDES

G	V	N	S	P	Q	K	F	M
3	3	4	4	3	4	3	2	3

INTERESTS
MSO

DATA PEOPLE THINGS (DPT)
374

PHYSICAL ACTIVITIES (PA)

V	C	H	B	L	S
2	1	2	3	1	1

ENVIRONMENTAL CONDITIONS (EC)
L1, D3

EDUCATION/TRAINING
2, 3, 4, 5, 6, R

Examples of Job Titles

Beauty Treatment Operator
Cosmetician

Descriptor Profile

Main Characteristics

Occupations in this group are characterized by the following aptitudes, interests and worker functions as they relate to main duties:

- **General learning ability** to understand and use the techniques of make-up application

- **Verbal ability** to communicate with clients

- **Form perception** to observe detail in skin and facial features

- **Motor co-ordination** and **finger and manual dexterity** to apply make-up to clients' face and skin

- **Methodical interest** in **compiling** information on clients' facial features and skin conditions

- **Social interest** in **serving - assisting** by advising clients on the use of make-up

- **Objective interest** in **manipulating** various products and using make-up application techniques

6482.2
Subgroup 2 of 6

Physical Activities

Vision
  2 Near vision

Colour Discrimination
  1 Relevant

Hearing
  2 Verbal interaction

Body Position
  3 Sitting, standing, walking

Limb Co-ordination
  1 Upper limb co-ordination

Strength
  1 Limited

Environmental Conditions

Location
  L1 Regulated inside climate

Discomforts
  D3 Odours

Employment Requirements

Education/Training
  2, 3, 4, 5, 6, R

- Completion of high school, college or beauty school programs for cosmeticians is required
  or
  on-the-job training is provided.

- Beauty treatment operators in Manitoba require provincial licensing.

Workplaces/Employers

Beauty salons

Self-employment

Occupational Options

There is little or no mobility among the different occupations in the 6482 group without additional specialized training.

Similar Occupations Classified Elsewhere

Hairstylists and Barbers (6271)

Image, Social and Other Personal Consultants (6481)

6482.3 Electrologists

Electrologists provide electrolysis treatments to enhance their clients' physical appearance.

Profile Summary

APTITUDES

G	V	N	S	P	Q	K	F	M
3	3	4	4	2	4	3	2	3

INTERESTS
MSO

DATA PEOPLE THINGS (DPT)
371

PHYSICAL ACTIVITIES (PA)

V	C	H	B	L	S
1	0	2	4	1	1

ENVIRONMENTAL CONDITIONS (EC)
L1, H3

EDUCATION/TRAINING
2, 3, 4, 5, 6

Examples of Job Titles

Electrologist
Electrologist Technician

Descriptor Profile

Main Characteristics

Occupations in this group are characterized by the following aptitudes, interests and worker functions as they relate to main duties:

- **General learning ability** to understand and use the techniques of electrolysis

- **Verbal ability** to communicate with clients

- **Form perception** to remove hairs from follicles using electrolysis

- **Finger** and **manual dexterity** to use needles and tweezers, to swab skin areas with antiseptic solutions or alcohol, and to press switches and adjust timing and rheostat controls of electrical equipment

- **Methodical interest** in **compiling** information for clients' treatment files

- **Social interest** in **serving - assisting** clients by permanently removing unwanted hair from faces and bodies

- **Objective interest** in **precision working** when using specialized electrical equipment

6482.3
Subgroup 3 of 6

Physical Activities

Vision
  1 Close visual acuity

Colour Discrimination
  0 Not relevant

Hearing
  2 Verbal interaction

Body Position
  4 Other body positions

Limb Co-ordination
  1 Upper limb co-ordination

Strength
  1 Limited

Environmental Conditions

Location
  L1 Regulated inside climate

Hazards
  H3 Equipment, machinery, tools

Employment Requirements

Education/Training
  2, 3, 4, 5, 6

- Completion of high school, college or beauty school programs for electrologists is required
  or
  on-the-job training is provided.

Workplaces/Employers

Beauty salons

Electrolysis studios

Self-employment

Occupational Options

There is little or no mobility among the different occupations in the 6482 group without additional specialized training.

Similar Occupations Classified Elsewhere

Hairstylists and Barbers (6271)

Image, Social and Other Personal Consultants (6481)

6482.4 Manicurists and Pedicurists

Manicurists and Pedicurists provide treatment to hands and feet to enhance their clients' physical appearance.

Profile Summary

APTITUDES

G	V	N	S	P	Q	K	F	M
4	4	5	4	3	5	3	3	3

INTERESTS
MSO

DATA PEOPLE THINGS (DPT)
674

PHYSICAL ACTIVITIES (PA)

V	C	H	B	L	S
2	1	2	1	1	1

ENVIRONMENTAL CONDITIONS (EC)
L1, D3

EDUCATION/TRAINING
2, 3, 4, 5, 6, R

Examples of Job Titles

Manicurist
Pedicurist

Descriptor Profile

Main Characteristics

Occupations in this group are characterized by the following aptitudes, interests and worker functions as they relate to main duties:

- **General learning ability** to acquire and apply manicuring and pedicuring techniques

- **Form perception** to determine nail and cuticle condition

- **Motor co-ordination** to shape and smooth ends of fingernails and toenails

- **Finger dexterity** to use cuticle knives, scissors, files, emery boards and nail polish brushes

- **Manual dexterity** to clean and polish fingernails and toenails

- **Methodical interest** in **comparing** to clean, shape and polish fingernails and toenails and provide related treatments

- **Social interest** in **serving - assisting** clients by providing body treatments designed to enhance physical appearance

- **Objective interest** in **manipulating** and applying various specialized products

6482.4

Physical Activities

Vision
 2 Near vision

Colour Discrimination
 1 Relevant

Hearing
 2 Verbal interaction

Body Position
 1 Sitting

Limb Co-ordination
 1 Upper limb co-ordination

Strength
 1 Limited

Environmental Conditions

Location
 L1 Regulated inside climate

Discomforts
 D3 Odours

Employment Requirements

Education/Training
 2, 3, 4, 5, 6, R

- Completion of high school, college or beauty school programs for manicurists and pedicurists is required
 or
 on-the-job training is provided.

- Manicurists in Manitoba and Nova Scotia require provincial licensing.

Workplaces/Employers

Beauty salons

Self-employment

Occupational Options

There is little or no mobility among the different occupations in the 6482 group without additional specialized training.

Similar Occupations Classified Elsewhere

Hairstylists and Barbers (6271)

Image, Social and Other Personal Consultants (6481)

6482.5 Scalp Treatment Specialists

Scalp Treatment Specialists provide scalp treatments to enhance their clients' physical appearance.

Profile Summary

APTITUDES

G	V	N	S	P	Q	K	F	M
3	3	4	4	3	4	3	3	3

INTERESTS
MOS

DATA PEOPLE THINGS (DPT)
574

PHYSICAL ACTIVITIES (PA)

V	C	H	B	L	S
2	0	2	2	1	1

ENVIRONMENTAL CONDITIONS (EC)
L1, D3

EDUCATION/TRAINING
2, 3, 4, 5, 6, R

Examples of Job Titles

Scalp Treatment Specialist

Descriptor Profile

Main Characteristics

Occupations in this group are characterized by the following aptitudes, interests and worker functions as they relate to main duties:

- **General learning ability** to understand and use specialized techniques for scalp treatment

- **Verbal ability** to communicate with clients

- **Form perception** to assess scalp conditions

- **Finger** and **manual dexterity** to massage, shampoo and steam hair and scalp of clients

- **Methodical interest** in **copying** information to maintain clients' treatment records

- **Objective interest** in **operating - manipulating** specialized equipment; and in using hands to apply medications and massage scalps

- **Social interest** in **serving - assisting** clients by applying medicated lotions to treat scalp conditions and hair loss

6482.5

Physical Activities

Vision
2   Near vision

Colour Discrimination
0   Not relevant

Hearing
2   Verbal interaction

Body Position
2   Standing and/or walking

Limb Co-ordination
1   Upper limb co-ordination

Strength
1   Limited

Environmental Conditions

Location
L1   Regulated inside climate

Discomforts
D3   Odours

Employment Requirements

Education/Training
2, 3, 4, 5, 6, R

- Completion of high school, college or a beauty school program is required
  or
  on-the-job training is provided.

- Skin care specialists in Nova Scotia require provincial licensing.

Workplaces/Employers

Beauty salons

Scalp treatment clinics

Self-employment

Occupational Options

There is little or no mobility among the different occupations in the 6482 group without additional specialized training.

Similar Occupations Classified Elsewhere

Hairstylists and Barbers (6271)

Image, Social and Other Personal Consultants (6481)

6482.6 Tattoo Artists

Tattoo Artists provide tattoos to enhance their clients' physical appearance.

Profile Summary

APTITUDES

G	V	N	S	P	Q	K	F	M
4	4	4	3	3	4	3	2	3

INTERESTS
MOd

DATA PEOPLE THINGS (DPT)
571

PHYSICAL ACTIVITIES (PA)

V	C	H	B	L	S
1	1	2	4	1	1

ENVIRONMENTAL CONDITIONS (EC)
L1, H3, D3

EDUCATION/TRAINING
2, 3, 4, 5, 6

Examples of Job Titles

Tattoo Artist

Descriptor Profile

Main Characteristics

Occupations in this group are characterized by the following aptitudes, interests and worker functions as they relate to main duties:

- **General learning ability** to understand and use the techniques of tattooing

- **Form perception** to perceive pertinent detail when applying tattoo designs

- **Motor co-ordination** and **finger dexterity** to draw and cut out original designs to form patterns and stencils

- **Manual dexterity** to prepare skin to be tattooed by shaving and washing with germicidal solutions and applying protective creams to sterile areas

- **Methodical interest** in **copying** information to mark outlines of designs on customers' skin

- **Objective interest** in **precision working** to apply permanent designs to customers' skin using electric needles and chemical dyes

- **Directive interest** in **serving - assisting** customers by providing tattooing services

6482.6

Physical Activities

Vision
  1 Close visual acuity

Colour Discrimination
  1 Relevant

Hearing
  2 Verbal interaction

Body Position
  4 Other body positions

Limb Co-ordination
  1 Upper limb co-ordination

Strength
  1 Limited

Environmental Conditions

Location
  L1 Regulated inside climate

Hazards
  H3 Equipment, machinery, tools

Discomforts
  D3 Odours

Employment Requirements

Education/Training
  2, 3, 4, 5, 6

- Completion of high school, college or a beauty school program is required
  or
  on-the-job training is provided.

Workplaces/Employers

Beauty salons

Self-employment

Occupational Options

There is little or no mobility among the different occupations in the 6482 group without additional specialized training.

Similar Occupations Classified Elsewhere

Hairstylists and Barbers (6271)

Image, Social and Other Personal Consultants (6481)

6483 Pet Groomers and Animal Care Workers

Pet Groomers and Animal Care Workers feed, handle, train and groom animals and assist veterinarians, animal health technologists and animal breeders.

Profile Summary

APTITUDES
G	V	N	S	P	Q	K	F	M
4	4	4	4	4	4	4	4	3

INTERESTS
MOD

DATA PEOPLE THINGS (DPT)
677

PHYSICAL ACTIVITIES (PA)
V	C	H	B	L	S
2	0	1	4	1	2

ENVIRONMENTAL CONDITIONS (EC)
L1, L3, H2, D3, D4

EDUCATION/TRAINING
3, 4

Examples of Job Titles

Animal Care Worker
Dog Groomer
Dog Trainer
Kennel Attendant
Laboratory Animal Attendant
Pet Groomer
Pound Attendant
Veterinary Attendant
Zoo Attendant

Descriptor Profile

Main Characteristics

Occupations in this group are characterized by the following aptitudes, interests and worker functions as they relate to main duties:

- **General learning ability** to understand and apply techniques required to feed, handle, train and groom animals

- **Motor co-ordination** and **finger dexterity** to assist veterinarians and animal health technologists to inoculate and treat animals

- **Manual dexterity** to clean and disinfect cages, pens and surrounding areas, and to shampoo, clip and groom animals

- **Methodical interest** in **comparing** information to monitor and document animal behaviour, and to prepare food and feed animals, fish and birds at scheduled intervals

- **Objective interest** in **assisting** scientists and researchers in conducting laboratory tests with animals

- **Directive interest** in **handling** and nurturing animals when assisting breeders; and in training dogs to obey commands and perform specific duties in response to signals

6483

Physical Activities

Vision
   2 Near vision

Colour Discrimination
   0 Not relevant

Hearing
   1 Limited

Body Position
   4 Other body positions

Limb Co-ordination
   1 Upper limb co-ordination

Strength
   2 Light

Environmental Conditions

Location
   L1 Regulated inside climate
   L3 Outside

Hazards
   H2 Biological agents

Discomforts
   D3 Odours
   D4 Non-toxic dusts

Employment Requirements

Education/Training
   3, 4

- Completion of secondary school is usually required.

- Depending on the type of work performed, training courses in animal handling, grooming or dog training may be required.

Workplaces/Employers

Animal clinics

Animal hospitals

Animal shelters

Breeding and boarding kennels

Laboratories

Pet grooming service companies

Zoos

Occupational Options

Progression to animal health technology occupations is possible with additional training.

Similar Occupations Classified Elsewhere

Animal Health Technologists (3213)

Animal nutritionists (in 2121 *Biologists and Related Scientists*)

Horse trainers (in 8253 *Farm Supervisors and Specialized Livestock Workers*)

Horseshoers (in 7383 *Other Trades and Related Occupations*)

Marine mammal trainers (in 2221 *Biological Technologists and Technicians*)

Sheep shearers (in 8431 *General Farm Workers*)

6484.1 Astrologers

Astrologers provide astrological services.

Profile Summary

APTITUDES

G	V	N	S	P	Q	K	F	M
3	3	3	3	4	3	4	4	4

INTERESTS
ISD

DATA PEOPLE THINGS (DPT)
358

PHYSICAL ACTIVITIES (PA)

V	C	H	B	L	S
2	0	2	1	0	1

ENVIRONMENTAL CONDITIONS (EC)
L1

EDUCATION/TRAINING
2

Examples of Job Titles

Astrologer

Descriptor Profile

Main Characteristics

Occupations in this group are characterized by the following aptitudes, interests and worker functions as they relate to main duties:

- **General learning ability** to understand principles and apply techniques of astrology

- **Verbal ability** to communicate with clients and the general public; may prepare general forecasts for regular publications

- **Numerical ability** and **spatial** and **clerical perception** to chart horoscopes showing the relative positions of planets and stars to each other and to signs of the zodiac at specified times and places

- **Innovative interest** in **compiling** information to interpret stellar and planetary positions on horoscopes

- **Social interest** in predicting future events and trends for clients and the general public

- **Directive interest** in **persuading** clients by recommending favourable dates for pursuit of particular objectives

Physical Activities

Vision
　2　Near vision

Colour Discrimination
　0　Not relevant

Hearing
　2　Verbal interaction

Body Position
　1　Sitting

Limb Co-ordination
　0　Not relevant

Strength
　1　Limited

Environmental Conditions

Location
　L1　Regulated inside climate

Employment Requirements

Education/Training
2

- A period of training under the guidance of a practitioner is usually required.

Workplaces/Employers

Self-employment

6484.2 Psychic Consultants

Psychic Consultants provide psychic consulting services.

Profile Summary

APTITUDES

G	V	N	S	P	Q	K	F	M
3	3	4	4	3	4	4	4	4

INTERESTS
ISD

DATA PEOPLE THINGS (DPT)
358

PHYSICAL ACTIVITIES (PA)

V	C	H	B	L	S
2	0	2	1	0	1

ENVIRONMENTAL CONDITIONS (EC)
L1

EDUCATION/TRAINING
2

Examples of Job Titles

Fortune Teller
Psychic Consultant
Psychic Reader

Descriptor Profile

Main Characteristics

Occupations in this group are characterized by the following aptitudes, interests and worker functions as they relate to main duties:

- **General learning ability** to understand principles and apply techniques of psychic consulting

- **Verbal ability** to communicate psychic information to clients

- **Innovative interest** in compiling information to interpret psychic phenomena as it relates to clients' personal readings

- **Social interest** in providing personal advice to clients

- **Directive interest** in persuading clients by recommending certain courses of action to follow based on various schools of thought

6484.2

Physical Activities

Vision
  2 Near vision

Colour Discrimination
  0 Not relevant

Hearing
  2 Verbal interaction

Body Position
  1 Sitting

Limb Co-ordination
  0 Not relevant

Strength
  1 Limited

Environmental Conditions

Location
  L1 Regulated inside climate

Employment Requirements

Education/Training
  2

- A period of training under the guidance of a practitioner is usually required.

Workplaces/Employers

Self-employment

6611 Cashiers

Cashiers record and receive payment from customers for the purchase of goods, services and admission fees.

Profile Summary

APTITUDES

G	V	N	S	P	Q	K	F	M
4	4	3	4	4	3	3	3	4

INTERESTS
MOs

DATA PEOPLE THINGS (DPT)
664

PHYSICAL ACTIVITIES (PA)

V	C	H	B	L	S
2	0	2	3	1	2

ENVIRONMENTAL CONDITIONS (EC)
L1

EDUCATION/TRAINING
2

Examples of Job Titles

Box Office Cashier
Cafeteria Cashier
Grocery Store Cashier
Office Cashier
Race Track Cashier
Self-Serve Gas Bar Cashier
Theatre Cashier

Descriptor Profile

Main Characteristics

Occupations in this group are characterized by the following aptitudes, interests and worker functions as they relate to main duties:

- **General learning** and **numerical ability** to establish or identify price of goods, services and admissions, and to receive payment by cash, cheques, credit cards and automatic debits

- **Clerical perception** to observe and correct errors and omissions in statements and accounts

- **Motor co-ordination** and **finger dexterity** to use calculators, cash registers and optical price scanners

- **Methodical interest** in **comparing** to calculate total payments received at the end of the work shift and reconcile with total sales

- **Objective interest** in **manipulating - operating** to wrap and place merchandise in bags, and to tabulate bills using calculators, cash registers and optical price scanners

- **Social interest** in **speaking** with customers to provide information

6611

Physical Activities

Vision
  2 Near vision

Colour Discrimination
  0 Not relevant

Hearing
  2 Verbal interaction

Body Position
  3 Sitting, standing, walking

Limb Co-ordination
  1 Upper limb co-ordination

Strength
  2 Light

Environmental Conditions

Location
  L1 Regulated inside climate

Employment Requirements

Education/Training
  2

- Some secondary school education is usually required.

- Eligibility for bonding may be required.

Workplaces/Employers

Business offices

Establishments that charge admissions

Restaurants

Stores

Theatres

Wholesale establishments

Occupational Options

Cashiers may progress to supervisory positions, such as head cashier, with additional training or experience.

Similar Occupations Classified Elsewhere

Retail Salespersons and Sales Clerks (6421)

Service Station Attendants (6621)

Tellers, Financial Services (1433)

Head cashiers (in 6211 *Retail Trade Supervisors*)

6621.1 Automotive Service Station Attendants

Automotive Service Station Attendants sell fuel and other automotive products, and perform such services as fuelling, cleaning, lubricating and performing minor repairs to motor vehicles.

Profile Summary

APTITUDES

G	V	N	S	P	Q	K	F	M
4	4	4	4	4	4	4	4	3

INTERESTS
MOs

DATA PEOPLE THINGS (DPT)
674

PHYSICAL ACTIVITIES (PA)

V	C	H	B	L	S
3	0	2	2	1	2

ENVIRONMENTAL CONDITIONS (EC)
L1, L3, H1, D3

EDUCATION/TRAINING
2, R

Examples of Job Titles

Gas Station Attendant (Except Self-Serve)

Service Station Attendant

Descriptor Profile

Main Characteristics

Occupations in this group are characterized by the following aptitudes, interests and worker functions as they relate to main duties:

- **General learning ability** to understand and apply simple motor-vehicle servicing instructions

- **Numerical ability** to receive payment from customers

- **Manual dexterity** to lubricate and make minor adjustments to motor vehicles

- **Methodical interest** in **comparing** information to check oil levels, tire pressures and fluid levels

- **Objective interest** in **operating - manipulating** to refuel vehicles and replace parts such as light bulbs, oil filters, windshield wiper blades and fan belts

- **Social interest** in **serving** customers by performing minor repairs and maintenance work on motor vehicles, and by selling fuel and other automotive products

6621.1

Physical Activities

Vision
  3 Near and far vision

Colour Discrimination
  0 Not relevant

Hearing
  2 Verbal interaction

Body Position
  2 Standing and/or walking

Limb Co-ordination
  1 Upper limb co-ordination

Strength
  2 Light

Environmental Conditions

Location
  L1 Regulated inside climate
  L3 Outside

Hazards
  H1 Dangerous chemical substances

Discomforts
  D3 Odours

Employment Requirements

Education/Training
  2, R

- Some secondary school education is usually required.

- Propane and natural gas pump attendants may require an operator's licence.

Workplaces/Employers

Automotive service stations

Similar Occupations Classified Elsewhere

Auto technicians (in 7321 *Motor Vehicle Mechanics, Technicians and Mechanical Repairers*)

Self-serve gas bar cashiers (in 6611 *Cashiers*)

Service station managers (in 0621 *Retail Trade Managers*)

Service station supervisors (in 6211 *Retail Trade Supervisors*)

6621.2 Marina Service Station Attendants

Marina Service Station Attendants sell fuel, rent boats and related equipment, and maintain marina facilities.

Profile Summary

APTITUDES

G	V	N	S	P	Q	K	F	M
4	4	4	4	4	4	4	4	3

INTERESTS
MOs

DATA PEOPLE THINGS (DPT)
674

PHYSICAL ACTIVITIES (PA)

V	C	H	B	L	S
3	0	2	4	1	2

ENVIRONMENTAL CONDITIONS (EC)
L1, L3, H1, D3

EDUCATION/TRAINING
2, R

Examples of Job Titles

Marina Attendant
Service Station Attendant

Descriptor Profile

Main Characteristics

Occupations in this group are characterized by the following aptitudes, interests and worker functions as they relate to main duties:

- **General learning ability** to understand and apply simple boat-servicing instructions

- **Numerical ability** to receive payments from customers

- **Manual dexterity** to maintain dock areas and marina facilities, and to assist in seasonal moving of ramps and docks

- **Methodical interest** in **comparing** information to check such things as oil levels and to record rental data

- **Objective interest** in **operating - manipulating** to refuel boats and pump marine septic systems

- **Social interest** in **serving** customers by performing routine maintenance work on boats and by renting boats, life jackets and other equipment

Physical Activities

Vision
    3   Near and far vision
Colour Discrimination
    0   Not relevant
Hearing
    2   Verbal interaction
Body Position
    4   Other body positions
Limb Co-ordination
    1   Upper limb co-ordination
Strength
    2   Light

Environmental Conditions

Location
    L1 Regulated inside climate
    L3 Outside
Hazards
    H1 Dangerous chemical substances
Discomforts
    D3 Odours

Employment Requirements

Education/Training
    2, R

- Some secondary school education is usually required.

- Propane and natural gas pump attendants may require an operator's licence

Workplaces/Employers

Marinas

Similar Occupations Classified Elsewhere

Auto technicians (in 7321 *Motor Vehicle Mechanics, Technicians and Mechanical Repairers*)

Self-serve gas bar cashiers (in 6611 *Cashiers*)

Service station managers (in 0621 *Retail Trade Managers*)

Service station supervisors (in 6211 *Retail Trade Supervisors*)

6622 Grocery Clerks and Shelf Stockers

Grocery Clerks and Shelf Stockers pack customers' purchases, price items, stock shelves with merchandise and fill mail orders.

Profile Summary

APTITUDES

G	V	N	S	P	Q	K	F	M
4	4	4	4	4	4	3	4	3

INTERESTS
Mso

DATA PEOPLE THINGS (DPT)
677

PHYSICAL ACTIVITIES (PA)

V	C	H	B	L	S
3	0	1	4	1	3

ENVIRONMENTAL CONDITIONS (EC)
L1, L3*

EDUCATION/TRAINING
2

Examples of Job Titles

Bag Clerk
Grocery Clerk
Grocery Packer
Order Filler
Price Clerk - Retail
Produce Clerk
Shelf Stocker - Retail
Supermarket Clerk
Warehouse Stock Picker

Descriptor Profile

Main Characteristics

Occupations in this group are characterized by the following aptitudes, interests and worker functions as they relate to main duties:

- **General learning ability** to understand and apply on-the-job training instructions

- **Motor co-ordination** to price items using stamps and stickers

- **Manual dexterity** to bag, box and parcel purchases for customers and for delivery to customers, and to carry customers' purchases to parking lots and pack in vehicles

- **Methodical interest** in **comparing** to price merchandise according to price lists, fill mail orders from warehouse stock and obtain articles for customers from shelves and stockrooms

- **Social interest** in **serving - assisting** by directing customers to the location of articles

- **Objective interest** in **handling** merchandise to stock shelves and display areas, and to keep stock clean and in order; and in sweeping aisles and performing other general cleaning duties

6622

Physical Activities

Vision
  3   Near and far vision

Colour Discrimination
  0   Not relevant

Hearing
  1   Limited

Body Position
  4   Other body positions

Limb Co-ordination
  1   Upper limb co-ordination

Strength
  3   Medium

Environmental Conditions

Location
  L1 Regulated inside climate
  L3* Outside

Employment Requirements

Education/Training
2

- Some secondary school education is usually required.

Workplaces/Employers

Department stores

Grocery stores

Hardware stores

Mail-order warehouses

Similar Occupations Classified Elsewhere

Cashiers (6611)

Comparison shopper (in 6623 *Other Elemental Sales Occupations*)

Meat counter clerk (in 6421 *Retail Salespersons and Sales Clerks*)

Stock handler (in 7452 *Material Handlers*)

Supervisor, stock clerks (in 6211 *Retail Trade Supervisors*)

Remarks

* Environmental Conditions

- For some occupations in this group, Location L3 (Outside) may also apply.

6623.1 Direct Distributors and Door-to-Door Salespersons

Direct Distributors and Door-to-Door Salespersons include workers who sell goods and services during home demonstrations or by going door-to-door.

Profile Summary

APTITUDES

G	V	N	S	P	Q	K	F	M
4	3	4	4	4	4	4	4	4

INTERESTS
MSd

DATA PEOPLE THINGS (DPT)
557

PHYSICAL ACTIVITIES (PA)

V	C	H	B	L	S
2	0	2	3	1	2

ENVIRONMENTAL CONDITIONS (EC)
L1, L3

EDUCATION/TRAINING
2, R

Examples of Job Titles

Canvasser - Retail
Direct Distributor - Retail
Door-to-Door Salesperson

Descriptor Profile

Main Characteristics

Occupations in this group are characterized by the following aptitudes, interests and worker functions as they relate to main duties:

- **General learning ability** to acquire and apply knowledge of selling techniques, and to become familiar with products

- **Verbal ability** to communicate with customers when describing products

- **Methodical interest** in **copying** information to present sample products and catalogues, and to explain desirable qualities of products

- **Social interest** in **persuading** customers by soliciting sales of goods and services in private homes

- **Directive interest** in **handling** merchandise to canvass prospective customers; may develop lists of prospective customers or follow leads supplied by management, and may distribute advertising literature and provide samples

6623.1
Subgroup 1 of 4

Physical Activities

Vision
   2 Near vision

Colour Discrimination
   0 Not relevant

Hearing
   2 Verbal interaction

Body Position
   3 Sitting, standing, walking

Limb Co-ordination
   1 Upper limb co-ordination

Strength
   2 Light

Environmental Conditions

Location
   L1 Regulated inside climate
   L3 Outside

Employment Requirements

Education/Training
   2, R

- Some secondary school education is usually required.

- Self-employed door-to-door salespersons may require a municipal merchant's permit.

Workplaces/Employers

Retail establishments

Self-employment

Wholesale establishments

Occupational Options

Progression to related supervisory positions is possible with additional training or experience.

Similar Occupations Classified Elsewhere

Cashiers (6611)

Retail Trade Managers (0621)

Retail Trade Supervisors (6211)

Kiosk sales clerks (in 6421 *Retail Salespersons and Sales Clerks*)

6623.2 Street Vendors

Street Vendors sell goods and services by street vending from street-corner carts or kiosks, at arenas, rinks and ballparks.

Profile Summary

APTITUDES

G	V	N	S	P	Q	K	F	M
4	4	4	4	4	4	4	4	4

INTERESTS
MSd

DATA PEOPLE THINGS (DPT)
657

PHYSICAL ACTIVITIES (PA)

V	C	H	B	L	S
2	0	2	2	1	2

ENVIRONMENTAL CONDITIONS (EC)
L1, L3

EDUCATION/TRAINING
2, R

Examples of Job Titles

Street Vendor

Descriptor Profile

Main Characteristics

Occupations in this group are characterized by the following aptitudes, interests and worker functions as they relate to main duties:

- **General learning ability** to acquire and apply knowledge of selling techniques, and to become familiar with products

- **Verbal ability** to communicate with customers when describing products

- **Numerical ability** to receive payments and make change

- **Methodical interest** in **comparing** information to explain products' desirable qualities, and set up and display merchandise on sidewalks and at public events

- **Social interest** in **persuading** customers by selling products

- **Directive interest** in **handling** products by loading goods into baskets, pushcarts and trucks, and by handing goods to customers

6623.2
Subgroup 2 of 4

Physical Activities

Vision
  2 Near vision

Colour Discrimination
  0 Not relevant

Hearing
  2 Verbal interaction

Body Position
  2 Standing and/or walking

Limb Co-ordination
  1 Upper limb co-ordination

Strength
  2 Light

Environmental Conditions

Location
  L1 Regulated inside climate
  L3 Outside

Employment Requirements

Education/Training
  2, R

- Some secondary school education is usually required.

- Self-employed street vendors may require a municipal merchant's permit.

Workplaces/Employers

Retail establishments

Self-employment

Wholesale establishments

Occupational Options

Progression to related supervisory positions is possible with additional training or experience.

Similar Occupations Classified Elsewhere

Cashiers (6611)

Retail Trade Managers (0621)

Retail Trade Supervisors (6211)

Kiosk sales clerks (in 6421 Retail Salespersons and Sales Clerks)

6623.3 Telephone Solicitors and Telemarketers

Telephone Solicitors and Telemarketers sell goods and services by telephone.

Profile Summary

APTITUDES

G	V	N	S	P	Q	K	F	M
4	3	4	5	4	4	4	4	4

INTERESTS
Msd

DATA PEOPLE THINGS (DPT)
658

PHYSICAL ACTIVITIES (PA)

V	C	H	B	L	S
2	0	2	1	0	1

ENVIRONMENTAL CONDITIONS (EC)
L1

EDUCATION/TRAINING
2

Examples of Job Titles

Telemarketer
Telephone Solicitor

Descriptor Profile

Main Characteristics

Occupations in this group are characterized by the following aptitudes, interests and worker functions as they relate to main duties:

- **General learning ability** to acquire and apply knowledge of selling techniques, and to become familiar with goods and services being offered

- **Verbal ability** to contact businesses and private individuals by telephone

- **Methodical interest** in **comparing** information to quote prices and follow a prepared sales talk

- **Social interest** in **persuading** customers by soliciting sales for goods and services

- **Directive interest** in distributing sales orders to other workers for further processing; may develop lists of prospective customers from city and telephone directories

6623.3
Subgroup 3 of 4

Physical Activities

Vision
   2 Near vision

Colour Discrimination
   0 Not relevant

Hearing
   2 Verbal interaction

Body Position
   1 Sitting

Limb Co-ordination
   0 Not relevant

Strength
   1 Limited

Environmental Conditions

Location
   L1 Regulated inside climate

Employment Requirements

Education/Training
2

- Some secondary school education is usually required.

Workplaces/Employers

Retail establishments

Wholesale establishments

Occupational Options

Progression to related supervisory positions is possible with additional training or experience.

Similar Occupations Classified Elsewhere

Cashiers (6611)

Retail Trade Managers (0621)

Retail Trade Supervisors (6211)

Kiosk sales clerks (in 6421 *Retail Salespersons and Sales Clerks*)

6623.4 Demonstrators

Demonstrators sell goods and services during home demonstrations and retail exhibitions.

Profile Summary

APTITUDES

G	V	N	S	P	Q	K	F	M
4	3	4	4	4	4	4	4	4

INTERESTS
MSo

DATA PEOPLE THINGS (DPT)
557

PHYSICAL ACTIVITIES (PA)

V	C	H	B	L	S
2	0	2	3	1	2

ENVIRONMENTAL CONDITIONS (EC)
L1

EDUCATION/TRAINING
2

Examples of Job Titles

Demonstrator - Retail
Home Demonstrator - Retail

Descriptor Profile

Main Characteristics

Occupations in this group are characterized by the following aptitudes, interests and worker functions as they relate to main duties:

- **General learning ability** to acquire and apply knowledge of selling techniques, and to become familiar with goods and services being offered

- **Verbal ability** to communicate with prospective customers when describing goods and services

- **Methodical interest** in **copying** information to demonstrate and explain products' features

- **Social interest** in **persuading** customers by organizing demonstration parties in private homes and describing qualities and merits of products

- **Objective interest** in **handling** products to arrange displays in wholesale, retail and industrial establishments, at exhibitions and trade shows, and in homes

6623.4
Subgroup 4 of 4

Physical Activities

Vision
  2 Near vision

Colour Discrimination
  0 Not relevant

Hearing
  2 Verbal interaction

Body Position
  3 Sitting, standing, walking

Limb Co-ordination
  1 Upper limb co-ordination

Strength
  2 Light

Environmental Conditions

Location
  L1 Regulated inside climate

Employment Requirements

Education/Training
2

- Some secondary school education is usually required.

Workplaces/Employers

Retail establishments

Wholesale establishments

Occupational Options

Progression to related supervisory positions is possible with additional training or experience.

Similar Occupations Classified Elsewhere

Cashiers (6611)

Retail Trade Managers (0621)

Retail Trade Supervisors (6211)

Kiosk sales clerks (in 6421 *Retail Salespersons and Sales Clerks*)

6631.1 Blood Donor Clinic Assistants

Blood Donor Clinic Assistants perform a variety of support functions to assist health care professionals and other health care staff.

Profile Summary

APTITUDES

G	V	N	S	P	Q	K	F	M
4	4	4	4	4	3	4	4	3

INTERESTS
OMs

DATA PEOPLE THINGS (DPT)
577

PHYSICAL ACTIVITIES (PA)

V	C	H	B	L	S
2	0	1	3	1	2

ENVIRONMENTAL CONDITIONS (EC)
L1, H2

EDUCATION/TRAINING
2, 4, 6

Examples of Job Titles

Blood Donor Clinic Assistant
Clinic Assistant

Descriptor Profile

Main Characteristics

Occupations in this group are characterized by the following aptitudes, interests and worker functions as they relate to main duties:

- **General learning ability** to understand instructions to assist with blood donor clinic functions

- **Clerical perception** to record information on donors and label donated blood

- **Manual dexterity** to operate equipment

- **Objective interest** in **handling** to set up equipment and process donated blood

- **Methodical interest** in **copying** information to monitor donors throughout procedure under the supervision of registered nurses; and in maintaining supplies

- **Social interest** in **assisting** other health care staff to perform a variety of support functions as members of blood donor clinic teams

6631.1
Subgroup 1 of 5

Physical Activities

Vision
  2   Near vision

Colour Discrimination
  0   Not relevant

Hearing
  1   Limited

Body Position
  3   Sitting, standing, walking

Limb Co-ordination
  1   Upper limb co-ordination

Strength
  2   Light

Environmental Conditions

Location
  L1   Regulated inside climate

Hazards
  H2 Biological agents

Employment Requirements

Education/Training
2, 4, 6

- Some secondary school education and on-the-job training are required for occupations in this group.

- Health care courses or short-term college programs related to the work of medical aides may be required by employers.

Workplaces/Employers

Blood donor clinics

Hospitals

Medical clinics

Similar Occupations Classified Elsewhere

Other Aides and Assistants in Support of Health Services (3414)

6631.2 Central Supply Aides

Central Supply Aides perform a variety of support functions to assist health care professionals and other health care staff.

Profile Summary

APTITUDES

G	V	N	S	P	Q	K	F	M
4	4	4	4	4	4	4	4	4

INTERESTS
OMd

DATA PEOPLE THINGS (DPT)
574

PHYSICAL ACTIVITIES (PA)

V	C	H	B	L	S
2	0	1	2	1	2

ENVIRONMENTAL CONDITIONS (EC)
L1, H2

EDUCATION/TRAINING
2, 4, 6

Examples of Job Titles

Central Supply Aide
Clinical Laboratory Helper
Supply, Processing and Distribution Aide

Descriptor Profile

Main Characteristics

Occupations in this group are characterized by the following aptitudes, interests and worker functions as they relate to main duties:

- **General learning ability** to understand instructions to assist with central supply support functions

- **Objective interest** in **operating** machines such as instrument washers, sonic sinks, cart washers and steam autoclaves to clean, reprocess and sterilize supplies for reuse

- **Methodical interest** in **copying** information to assemble packs of sterile supplies and instruments for delivery to hospital departments

- **Directive interest** in **assisting** health care staff by collecting and sorting soiled supplies and instruments from hospital departments

Physical Activities

Vision
  2 Near vision

Colour Discrimination
  0 Not relevant

Hearing
  1 Limited

Body Position
  2 Standing and/or walking

Limb Co-ordination
  1 Upper limb co-ordination

Strength
  2 Light

Environmental Conditions

Location
  L1 Regulated inside climate

Hazards
  H2 Biological agents

Employment Requirements

Education/Training
  2, 4, 6

- Some secondary school education and on-the-job training are required for occupations in this group.

- Health care courses or short-term college programs related to the work of medical aides, such as the central supply service techniques program, are available and may be required by employers.

Workplaces/Employers

Hospitals

Medical clinics

Similar Occupations Classified Elsewhere

Other Aides and Assistants in Support of Health Services (3414)

6631.3 Chiropractic Aides

Chiropractic Aides perform a variety of support functions to assist chiropractors.

Profile Summary

APTITUDES

G	V	N	S	P	Q	K	F	M
4	4	4	4	4	3	4	4	4

INTERESTS
MSo

DATA PEOPLE THINGS (DPT)
577

PHYSICAL ACTIVITIES (PA)

V	C	H	B	L	S
2	0	2	4	1	2

ENVIRONMENTAL CONDITIONS (EC)
L1

EDUCATION/TRAINING
2, 4, 6

Examples of Job Titles

Chiropractic Aide

Descriptor Profile

Main Characteristics

Occupations in this group are characterized by the following aptitudes, interests and worker functions as they relate to main duties:

- **General learning ability** to understand instructions to assist chiropractors

- **Clerical perception** to perceive pertinent details in patient records; may perform clerical duties

- **Methodical interest** in **copying** information to connect treatment machines to patients as directed by chiropractors

- **Social interest** in **assisting** elderly and incapacitated patients to dress and undress

- **Objective interest** in **handling** patients when positioning them on tables and chairs for treatments by chiropractors or for machine treatments

6631.3
Subgroup 3 of 5

Physical Activities

Vision
2 Near vision

Colour Discrimination
0 Not relevant

Hearing
2 Verbal interaction

Body Position
4 Other body positions

Limb Co-ordination
1 Upper limb co-ordination

Strength
2 Light

Environmental Conditions

Location
L1 Regulated inside climate

Employment Requirements

Education/Training
2, 4, 6

- Some secondary school education and on-the-job training are required for occupations in this group.

- Health care courses or short-term college programs related to the work of medical aides, such as the chiropractic college assistants course, are available and may be required by employers.

Workplaces/Employers

Hospitals

Medical clinics

Offices of chiropractors

Similar Occupations Classified Elsewhere

Other Aides and Assistants in Support of Health Services (3414)

6631.4 Occupational Therapy Assistants

Occupational Therapy Assistants perform a variety of support functions to assist health care professionals and other health care staff.

Profile Summary

APTITUDES

G	V	N	S	P	Q	K	F	M
4	3	4	4	4	4	4	4	3

INTERESTS
MSo

DATA PEOPLE THINGS (DPT)
577

PHYSICAL ACTIVITIES (PA)

V	C	H	B	L	S
2	0	2	3	1	1

ENVIRONMENTAL CONDITIONS (EC)
L1

EDUCATION/TRAINING
2, 4, 6

Examples of Job Titles

Occupational Therapy Aide

Descriptor Profile

Main Characteristics

Occupations in this group are characterized by the following aptitudes, interests and worker functions as they relate to main duties:

- **General learning ability** to understand instructions to assist occupational therapists

- **Verbal ability** to communicate with patients

- **Manual dexterity** to prepare and lay out work materials and supplies

- **Methodical interest** in copying information to assist patients as directed by occupational therapists

- **Social interest** in assisting in the administration of occupational therapy programs; may assist patients in crafts and other activities

- **Objective interest** in handling the preparation and maintenance of work materials and supplies

6631.4
Subgroup 4 of 5

Physical Activities

Vision
    2 Near vision

Colour Discrimination
    0 Not relevant

Hearing
    2 Verbal interaction

Body Position
    3 Sitting, standing, walking

Limb Co-ordination
    1 Upper limb co-ordination

Strength
    1 Limited

Environmental Conditions

Location
    L1 Regulated inside climate

Employment Requirements

Education/Training
    2, 4, 6

- Some secondary school education and on-the-job training are required for occupations in this group.

- Health care courses or short-term college programs related to the work of medical aides are available and may be required by employers.

Workplaces/Employers

Hospitals

Medical clinics

Offices of occupational therapists

Similar Occupations Classified Elsewhere

Other Aides and Assistants in Support of Health Services (3414)

6631.5 Physiotherapy Assistants

Physiotherapy Assistants perform a variety of support functions to assist health care professionals and other health care staff.

Profile Summary

APTITUDES

G	V	N	S	P	Q	K	F	M
4	3	4	4	4	4	4	4	3

INTERESTS
MSo

DATA PEOPLE THINGS (DPT)
577

PHYSICAL ACTIVITIES (PA)

V	C	H	B	L	S
2	0	2	4	1	1

ENVIRONMENTAL CONDITIONS (EC)
L1

EDUCATION/TRAINING
2, 4, 6

Examples of Job Titles

Physical Therapy Aide
Physiotherapy Helper

Descriptor Profile

Main Characteristics

Occupations in this group are characterized by the following aptitudes, interests and worker functions as they relate to main duties:

- **General learning ability** to understand instructions in order to assist physiotherapists

- **Verbal ability** to communicate with patients

- **Manual dexterity** to clean physiotherapy equipment and change linen

- **Methodical interest** in **copying** information to assist patients with maintenance programs as directed and supervised by physiotherapists; and in maintaining appointment schedules

- **Social interest** in **assisting** patients by accompanying them to treatment rooms

- **Objective interest** in **handling** to assist patients in the use of therapeutic equipment

Physical Activities

Vision
  2 Near vision

Colour Discrimination
  0 Not relevant

Hearing
  2 Verbal interaction

Body Position
  4 Other body positions

Limb Co-ordination
  1 Upper limb co-ordination

Strength
  1 Limited

Environmental Conditions

Location
  L1 Regulated inside climate

Employment Requirements

Education/Training
  2, 4, 6

- Some secondary school education and on-the-job training are required for occupations in this group.

- Health care courses or short-term college programs related to the work of medical aides are available and may be required by employers.

Workplaces/Employers

Hospitals

Medical clinics

Offices of physiotherapists

Similar Occupations Classified Elsewhere

Other Aides and Assistants in Support of Health Services (3414)

6641 Food Service Counter Attendants and Food Preparers

Food Service Counter Attendants and Food Preparers prepare, heat and cook simple food items and serve customers at food counters.

Profile Summary

APTITUDES

G	V	N	S	P	Q	K	F	M
4	4	4	4	4	4	4	4	4

INTERESTS
Mso

DATA PEOPLE THINGS (DPT)
677

PHYSICAL ACTIVITIES (PA)

V	C	H	B	L	S
2	0	2	2	1	2

ENVIRONMENTAL CONDITIONS (EC)
L1

EDUCATION/TRAINING
2

Examples of Job Titles

Counter Attendant, Cafeteria
Fast-Food Preparer
Food Counter Attendant
Food Preparer
Ice Cream Counter Attendant
Salad Bar Attendant
Sandwich Maker

Descriptor Profile

Main Characteristics

Occupations in this group are characterized by the following aptitudes, interests and worker functions as they relate to main duties:

- **General learning ability** to acquire knowledge of menu items and food preparation techniques, and to take customers' orders

- **Numerical ability** to do simple arithmetic; may receive payment for food items

- **Motor co-ordination** and **finger dexterity** to prepare and cook food items

- **Methodical interest** in **comparing** information to prepare food according to set standards; and in taking customers' orders

- **Social interest** in **serving** food to customers at counters and buffet tables

- **Objective interest** in **handling** the preparation of food such as sandwiches, hamburgers, salads, milkshakes and ice cream dishes

6641

Physical Activities

Vision
  2 Near vision

Colour Discrimination
  0 Not relevant

Hearing
  2 Verbal interaction

Body Position
  2 Standing and/or walking

Limb Co-ordination
  1 Upper limb co-ordination

Strength
  2 Light

Environmental Conditions

Location
  L1 Regulated inside climate

Employment Requirements

Education/Training
2

- Some secondary school education is usually required.
- On-the-job training is provided.

Workplaces/Employers

Cafeterias

Fast-food outlets

Hospitals

Hotels

Restaurants

Occupational Options

There is considerable mobility among jobs in this group.

Movement into other occupations within food preparation and service, such as cook or waiter, is possible with further training and experience.

Similar Occupations Classified Elsewhere

Chefs (6241)

Cooks (6242)

Kitchen and Food Service Helpers (6642)

Street food-vendors (in 6623 *Other Elemental Sales Occupations*)

6642.1 Kitchen Helpers

Kitchen Helpers clean kitchen areas and assist workers who prepare or serve food and beverages.

Profile Summary

APTITUDES

G	V	N	S	P	Q	K	F	M
4	4	5	4	4	5	4	4	3

INTERESTS
OMs

DATA PEOPLE THINGS (DPT)
677

PHYSICAL ACTIVITIES (PA)

V	C	H	B	L	S
2	0	1	4	1	3

ENVIRONMENTAL CONDITIONS (EC)
L1, H3, D3, D5

EDUCATION/TRAINING
2

Examples of Job Titles

Cook's Helper
Kitchen Helper

Descriptor Profile

Main Characteristics

Occupations in this group are characterized by the following aptitudes, interests and worker functions as they relate to main duties:

- **General learning ability** to understand instructions to keep kitchen areas clean and neat

- **Manual dexterity** to work with cooking and cleaning utensils

- **Objective interest** in **handling** to remove trash and clear kitchen garbage containers, and to unpack and store supplies in refrigerators, cupboards and other storage areas

- **Methodical interest** in **comparing** to wash and peel vegetables and fruit, clean work tables, cupboards and appliances, and sweep and mop floors

- **Social interest** in **assisting** cook and kitchen staff

6642.1
Subgroup 1 of 3

Physical Activities

Vision
  2   Near vision

Colour Discrimination
  0   Not relevant

Hearing
  1   Limited

Body Position
  4   Other body positions

Limb Co-ordination
  1   Upper limb co-ordination

Strength
  3   Medium

Environmental Conditions

Location
  L1 Regulated inside climate

Hazards
  H3 Equipment, machinery, tools

Discomforts
  D3 Odours
  D5 Wetness

Employment Requirements

Education/Training
2

- Some secondary school education may be required.

Workplaces/Employers

Cafeterias

Fast-food outlets

Hospitals

Hotels

Restaurants

Occupational Options

There is considerable mobility among jobs in this group.

Movement into other occupations within food preparation and service, such as cook or food server, is possible with further training and experience.

Similar Occupations Classified Elsewhere

Food and Beverage Servers (6453)

Food Service Counter Attendants and Food Preparers (6641)

6642.2 Food Service Helpers

Food Service Helpers clear tables and assist workers who prepare and serve food and beverages.

Profile Summary

APTITUDES

G	V	N	S	P	Q	K	F	M
4	4	5	4	4	5	4	4	4

INTERESTS
OMs

DATA PEOPLE THINGS (DPT)
677

PHYSICAL ACTIVITIES (PA)

V	C	H	B	L	S
2	0	1	2	1	3

ENVIRONMENTAL CONDITIONS (EC)
L1

EDUCATION/TRAINING
2

Examples of Job Titles

Bartender Helper
Bus Boy/Girl
Food Service Helper

Descriptor Profile

Main Characteristics

Occupations in this group are characterized by the following aptitudes, interests and worker functions as they relate to main duties:

- **General learning ability** to understand instructions to assist workers who prepare and serve food and beverages

- **Objective interest** in **handling** to clear tables and trays in eating establishments, to bring clean dishes, flatware and other items to serving areas, to remove dishes before and after courses, and to perform duties such as scraping and stacking dishes and carrying linen to and from laundry areas

- **Methodical interest** in **comparing** to clean tables and trays, and to replenish condiments and other supplies at tables and serving areas

- **Social interest** in **assisting** other staff by running errands

6642.2
Subgroup 2 of 3

Physical Activities

Vision
   2   Near vision

Colour Discrimination
   0   Not relevant

Hearing
   1   Limited

Body Position
   2   Standing and/or walking

Limb Co-ordination
   1   Upper limb co-ordination

Strength
   3   Medium

Environmental Conditions

Location
   L1   Regulated inside climate

Employment Requirements

Education/Training
2

- Some secondary school education may be required.

Workplaces/Employers

Cafeterias

Fast-food outlets

Hospitals

Hotels

Restaurants

Occupational Options

There is considerable mobility among jobs in this group.

Movement into other occupations within food preparation and service, such as cook or food server, is possible with further training and experience.

Similar Occupations Classified Elsewhere

Food and Beverage Servers (6453)

Food Service Counter Attendants and Food Preparers (6641)

6642.3 Dishwashers

Dishwashers wash dishes and assist workers who prepare and serve food and beverages.

Profile Summary

APTITUDES

G	V	N	S	P	Q	K	F	M
4	5	5	4	4	5	4	4	4

INTERESTS
OMs

DATA PEOPLE THINGS (DPT)
674

PHYSICAL ACTIVITIES (PA)

V	C	H	B	L	S
2	0	1	2	1	3

ENVIRONMENTAL CONDITIONS (EC)
L1, D5

EDUCATION/TRAINING
2

Examples of Job Titles

Dishwasher

Descriptor Profile

Main Characteristics

Occupations in this group are characterized by the following aptitudes, interests and worker functions as they relate to main duties:

- **General learning ability** to understand instructions to assist workers who prepare and serve food and beverages

- **Objective interest** in **operating** dishwashers to clean dishes, glassware, flatware, pots and pans

- **Methodical interest** in **comparing** to clean and scour pots and pans; may clean and polish silverware

- **Social interest** in **assisting** workers who prepare and serve food and beverages

6642.3
Subgroup 3 of 3

Physical Activities

Vision
  2 Near vision

Colour Discrimination
  0 Not relevant

Hearing
  1 Limited

Body Position
  2 Standing and/or walking

Limb Co-ordination
  1 Upper limb co-ordination

Strength
  3 Medium

Environmental Conditions

Location
  L1 Regulated inside climate

Discomforts
  D5 Wetness

Employment Requirements

Education/Training
  2

- Some secondary school education may be required.

Workplaces/Employers

Cafeterias

Fast-food outlets

Hospitals

Hotels

Restaurants

Occupational Options

There is considerable mobility among jobs in this group.

Movement into other occupations within food preparation and service, such as cook or food server, is possible with further training and experience.

Similar Occupations Classified Elsewhere

Food and Beverage Servers (6453)

Food Service Counter Attendants and Food Preparers (6641)

6651 Security Guards and Related Occupations

This group includes Security Guards and other related workers who guard property against theft and vandalism, control access to establishments, maintain order and enforce regulations at public events and within organizations or areas.

Profile Summary

APTITUDES

G	V	N	S	P	Q	K	F	M
4	3	4	4	4	4	4	4	4

INTERESTS
Msd

DATA PEOPLE THINGS (DPT)
563

PHYSICAL ACTIVITIES (PA)

V	C	H	B	L	S
4	0	3	3	1	2

ENVIRONMENTAL CONDITIONS (EC)
L1, L2, L3, L4, H3*, H8*

EDUCATION/TRAINING
2

Examples of Job Titles

Airport Security Guard
Armoured Car Guard
Bodyguard
Bouncer
Commissionaire
Crossing Guard
Gate Attendant
Night Watchman/woman
Pre-boarding Security Guard
Security Guard
Security Officer

Descriptor Profile

Main Characteristics

Occupations in this group are characterized by the following aptitudes, interests and worker functions as they relate to main duties:

- **General learning ability** to understand and apply security regulations

- **Verbal ability** to communicate with police, fire and civil defence authorities and the general public

- **Form perception** to patrol assigned areas against theft, shoplifting, vandalism and fire

- **Methodical interest** in **copying** to perform security checks of passengers and luggage at airports, and to enforce regulations of establishments to maintain order

- **Social interest** in **speaking** with visitors to control access to organizations, issue passes and direct them to appropriate areas

- **Directive interest** in **driving** and guarding armoured trucks when delivering cash and valuables to banks, automated teller machines and retail establishments; may supervise and co-ordinate the activities of other security guards

6651

Physical Activities

Vision
   4 Total visual field

Colour Discrimination
   0 Not relevant

Hearing
   3 Other sound discrimination

Body Position
   3 Other body positions

Limb Co-ordination
   1 Upper limb co-ordination

Strength
   2 Light

Environmental Conditions

Location
   L1 Regulated inside climate
   L2 Unregulated inside climate
   L3 Outside
   L4 In a vehicle or cab

Hazards
   H3* Equipment, machinery, tools
   H8* Dangerous locations

Employment Requirements

Education/Training
2

- Some secondary school education is usually required.

- Training is provided for airport security guards and may be provided for other occupations in this group.

- Armoured car drivers require a driver's licence.

- Security guards carrying firearms require a licence.

Workplaces/Employers

Businesses

Industrial establishments

Museums

Private security agencies

Retail stores

Occupational Options

Senior security guards and supervisors require experience.

Similar Occupations Classified Elsewhere

Correctional Service Officers (6462)

Managers of security agencies (in 0123 *Other Business Services Managers*)

Private investigators (in 6465 *Other Protective Service Occupations*)

Remarks

* Environmental Conditions

- For some occupations in this group, Hazards H3 (Equipment, machinery and tools) and H8 (Dangerous locations) may apply.

6661 Light Duty Cleaners

Light Duty Cleaners clean the lobbies, hallways, offices and rooms of hotels, hospitals, schools, office buildings and private residences.

Profile Summary

APTITUDES

G	V	N	S	P	Q	K	F	M
4	4	5	4	4	5	4	4	3

INTERESTS
MOi

DATA PEOPLE THINGS (DPT)
587

PHYSICAL ACTIVITIES (PA)

V	C	H	B	L	S
2	0	1	4	1	3

ENVIRONMENTAL CONDITIONS (EC)
L1, D3, D5

EDUCATION/TRAINING
1

Examples of Job Titles

Cleaner
Hospital Cleaner
Hotel Cleaner
House Cleaner
Light Duty Cleaner
Office Cleaner
Room Attendant
Sweeper

Descriptor Profile

Main Characteristics

Occupations in this group are characterized by the following aptitudes, interests and worker functions as they relate to main duties:

- **General learning ability** to understand and follow instructions

- **Manual dexterity** to dust furniture, clean, disinfect and polish kitchen and bathroom fixtures and appliances, wash windows, walls and ceilings, make beds, change sheets, distribute clean towels and toiletries, pick up debris and empty trash containers

- **Methodical interest** in **copying** instructions to clean lobbies, hallways, offices and rooms of hotels, hospitals, schools, office buildings and private residences, and to disinfect operating rooms and other hospital areas

- **Objective interest** in **handling** equipment to sweep, mop, wash, wax and polish floors, and to vacuum carpeting and area rugs, draperies and upholstered furniture

- **Innovative interest** in inspecting surfaces and objects for dust, dirt and grease to determine appropriate cleaning products to use

6661

Physical Activities

Vision
    2 Near vision

Colour Discrimination
    0 Not relevant

Hearing
    1 Limited

Body Position
    4 Other body positions

Limb Co-ordination
    1 Upper limb co-ordination

Strength
    3 Medium

Environmental Conditions

Location
    L1 Regulated inside climate

Discomforts
    D3 Odours
    D5 Wetness

Employment Requirements

Education/Training
1

- There are no specific educational requirements for occupations in this group.

Workplaces/Employers

Cleaning service companies

Hospitals

Hotels

Motels

Office-building management companies

School boards

Occupational Options

Progression to supervisory cleaning positions is possible with additional training or experience.

Similar Occupations Classified Elsewhere

Cleaning Supervisors (6215)

Janitors, Caretakers and Building Superintendents (6663)

Specialized Cleaners (6662)

6662.1 Carpet and Upholstery Cleaners

Carpet and Upholstery Cleaners clean carpets and upholstery using specialized equipment and techniques.

Profile Summary

APTITUDES

G	V	N	S	P	Q	K	F	M
4	4	4	4	4	4	4	4	3

INTERESTS
OMd

DATA PEOPLE THINGS (DPT)
684

PHYSICAL ACTIVITIES (PA)

V	C	H	B	L	S
2	0	1	4	1	2

ENVIRONMENTAL CONDITIONS (EC)
L1, D1, D4

EDUCATION/TRAINING
2

Examples of Job Titles

Carpet Cleaner
Upholstery Cleaner

Descriptor Profile

Main Characteristics

Occupations in this group are characterized by the following aptitudes, interests and worker functions as they relate to main duties:

- **General learning ability** to understand and apply carpet- and upholstery-cleaning techniques

- **Manual dexterity** to apply various cleaning techniques to clean carpets, rugs and upholstered furniture

- **Objective interest** in **operating** specialized cleaning machines

- **Methodical interest** in **comparing** to clean carpets, rugs and upholstered furniture on customers' premises or in carpet- and upholstery-cleaning establishments

- **Directive interest** in selecting appropriate cleaning agents to remove stains from materials

6662.1
Subgroup 1 of 6

Physical Activities

Vision
   2 Near vision

Colour Discrimination
   0 Not relevant

Hearing
   1 Limited

Body Position
   4 Other body positions

Limb Co-ordination
   1 Upper limb co-ordination

Strength
   2 Light

Environmental Conditions

Location
   L1 Regulated inside climate

Discomforts
   D1 Noise
   D4 Non-toxic dusts

Employment Requirements

Education/Training
2

- There are no specific educational requirements for occupations in this group.

- On-the-job training is usually provided.

- Previous experience in a related position may be required.

Workplaces/Employers

Self-employment

Specialized cleaning services companies

Occupational Options

Progression to supervisory positions is possible with additional training or experience.

Similar Occupations Classified Elsewhere

Cleaning Supervisors (6215)

Janitors, Caretakers and Building Superintendents (6663)

Light Duty Cleaners (6661)

6662.2 Chimney Cleaners

Chimney Cleaners clean chimneys using specialized equipment and techniques.

Profile Summary

APTITUDES

G	V	N	S	P	Q	K	F	M
4	4	4	4	4	5	4	4	3

INTERESTS
OMd

DATA PEOPLE THINGS (DPT)
684

PHYSICAL ACTIVITIES (PA)

V	C	H	B	L	S
2	0	1	4	1	2

ENVIRONMENTAL CONDITIONS (EC)
L1, L3, H3, H6, H8, D1, D4

EDUCATION/TRAINING
2

Examples of Job Titles

Chimney Cleaner

Descriptor Profile

Main Characteristics

Occupations in this group are characterized by the following aptitudes, interests and worker functions as they relate to main duties:

- **General learning ability** to understand and apply chimney cleaning techniques

- **Manual dexterity** to clean soot and creosote from chimneys and fireplaces

- **Objective interest** in **operating** hand tools and industrial vacuum cleaners

- **Methodical interest** in **comparing** to inspect surfaces for soot and creosote deposits; and in cleaning chimneys and fireplaces

- **Directive interest** in selecting appropriate chimney cleaning techniques

6662.2

Physical Activities

Vision
  2 Near vision

Colour Discrimination
  0 Not relevant

Hearing
  1 Limited

Body Position
  4 Other body positions

Limb Co-ordination
  1 Upper limb co-ordination

Strength
  2 Light

Environmental Conditions

Location
  L1 Regulated inside climate
  L3 Outside

Hazards
  H3 Equipment, machinery, tools
  H6 Flying particles, falling objects
  H8 Dangerous locations

Discomforts
  D1 Noise
  D4 Non-toxic dusts

Employment Requirements

Education/Training
  2

- There are no specific educational requirements for occupations in this group.

- On-the-job training is usually provided.

- Previous experience in a related position may be required.

Workplaces/Employers

Self-employment

Specialized cleaning services companies

Occupational Options

Progression to supervisory positions is possible with additional training or experience.

Similar Occupations Classified Elsewhere

Cleaning Supervisors (6215)

Janitors, Caretakers and Building Superintendents (6663)

Light Duty Cleaners (6661)

6662.3 Furnace and Ventilation System Cleaners

Furnace and Ventilation System Cleaners clean furnaces and ventilation systems using specialized equipment and techniques.

Profile Summary

APTITUDES

G	V	N	S	P	Q	K	F	M
4	4	5	4	4	5	3	4	3

INTERESTS
OMd

DATA PEOPLE THINGS (DPT)
684

PHYSICAL ACTIVITIES (PA)

V	C	H	B	L	S
2	0	1	4	1	2

ENVIRONMENTAL CONDITIONS (EC)
L1, H3, D1, D4

EDUCATION/TRAINING
2

Examples of Job Titles

Furnace Cleaner
Ventilation System Cleaner

Descriptor Profile

Main Characteristics

Occupations in this group are characterized by the following aptitudes, interests and worker functions as they relate to main duties:

- **General learning ability** to understand and apply furnace and ventilation-system cleaning techniques

- **Motor co-ordination** and **manual dexterity** to clean ducts, vents and filters of furnaces in residences and commercial buildings

- **Objective interest** in **operating** hand tools and industrial vacuum cleaners

- **Methodical interest** in **comparing** to inspect surfaces for dust, dirt, grease and other deposits; and in cleaning furnaces and ventilation systems

- **Directive interest** in selecting appropriate furnace and ventilation-system cleaning techniques

6662.3

Physical Activities

Vision
　2　Near vision

Colour Discrimination
　0　Not relevant

Hearing
　1　Limited

Body Position
　4　Other body positions

Limb Co-ordination
　1　Upper limb co-ordination

Strength
　2　Light

Environmental Conditions

Location
　L1　Regulated inside climate

Hazards
　H3　Equipment, machinery, tools

Discomforts
　D1　Noise
　D4　Non-toxic dusts

Employment Requirements

Education/Training
2

- There are no specific educational requirements for occupations in this group.

- On-the-job training is usually provided.

- Previous experience in a related position may be required.

Workplaces/Employers

Self-employment

Specialized cleaning services companies

Occupational Options

Progression to supervisory positions is possible with additional training or experience.

Similar Occupations Classified Elsewhere

Cleaning Supervisors (6215)

Janitors, Caretakers and Building Superintendents (6663)

Light Duty Cleaners (6661)

6662.4 Sandblasters

Sandblasters clean and refurbish building exteriors, chimneys, industrial equipment and other surfaces using specialized equipment and techniques.

Profile Summary

APTITUDES

G	V	N	S	P	Q	K	F	M
4	4	5	4	4	5	4	4	3

INTERESTS
OMd

DATA PEOPLE THINGS (DPT)
684

PHYSICAL ACTIVITIES (PA)

V	C	H	B	L	S
3	0	1	4	1	2

ENVIRONMENTAL CONDITIONS (EC)
L3, H3, H6, H7, H8, D1, D2, D4

EDUCATION/TRAINING
2

Examples of Job Titles

Building Exterior Cleaner
Laboratory Equipment Cleaner
Sandblaster
Septic Tank Cleaner

Descriptor Profile

Main Characteristics

Occupations in this group are characterized by the following aptitudes, interests and worker functions as they relate to main duties:

- **General learning ability** to understand and apply various sandblasting techniques

- **Manual dexterity** to clean building exteriors, tanks, chimneys and industrial equipment

- **Objective interest** in **operating** sandblasting, pressurized steam and hydroblasting equipment

- **Methodical interest** in **comparing** to inspect surfaces for dust, dirt, grease and other deposits; and in cleaning building exteriors and other surfaces

- **Directive interest** in selecting appropriate sandblasting equipment and techniques

6662.4

Physical Activities

Vision
   3 Near and far vision

Colour Discrimination
   0 Not relevant

Hearing
   1 Limited

Body Position
   4 Other body positions

Limb Co-ordination
   1 Upper limb co-ordination

Strength
   2 Light

Environmental Conditions

Location
   L3 Outside

Hazards
   H3 Equipment, machinery, tools
   H6 Flying particles, falling objects
   H7 Fire, steam, hot surfaces
   H8 Dangerous locations

Discomforts
   D1 Noise
   D2 Vibration
   D4 Non-toxic dusts

Employment Requirements

Education/Training
2

- There are no specific educational requirements for occupations in this group.

- On-the-job training is usually provided.

- Previous experience in a related position may be required.

Workplaces/Employers

Self-employment

Specialized cleaning services companies

Occupational Options

Progression to supervisory positions is possible with additional training or experience.

Similar Occupations Classified Elsewhere

Cleaning Supervisors (6215)

Janitors, Caretakers and Building Superintendents (6663)

Light Duty Cleaners (6661)

6662.5 Vehicle Cleaners

Vehicle Cleaners clean interiors and exteriors of vehicles using specialized equipment and techniques.

Profile Summary

APTITUDES

G	V	N	S	P	Q	K	F	M
4	4	5	4	4	5	4	4	3

INTERESTS
OMd

DATA PEOPLE THINGS (DPT)
684

PHYSICAL ACTIVITIES (PA)

V	C	H	B	L	S
2	0	1	4	1	2

ENVIRONMENTAL CONDITIONS (EC)
L3, L4, D1, D4, D5

EDUCATION/TRAINING
2

Examples of Job Titles

Freight Car Cleaner
Vehicle Cleaner

Descriptor Profile

Main Characteristics

Occupations in this group are characterized by the following aptitudes, interests and worker functions as they relate to main duties:

- **General learning ability** to understand and apply various vehicle cleaning techniques

- **Manual dexterity** to clean the interior and exterior of automobiles, trucks and other vehicles

- **Objective interest** in **operating** specialized cleaning equipment

- **Methodical interest** in **comparing** to inspect surfaces for dust, dirt, grease and other deposits; and in cleaning the interior and exterior of vehicles

- **Directive interest** in selecting appropriate vehicle cleaning equipment

6662.5
Subgroup 5 of 6

Physical Activities

Vision
    2 Near vision

Colour Discrimination
    0 Not relevant

Hearing
    1 Limited

Body Position
    4 Other body positions

Limb Co-ordination
    1 Upper limb co-ordination

Strength
    2 Light

Environmental Conditions

Location
    L3 Outside
    L4 In a vehicle or cab

Discomforts
    D1 Noise
    D4 Non-toxic dusts
    D5 Wetness

Employment Requirements

Education/Training
    2

- There are no specific educational requirements for occupations in this group.

- On-the-job training is usually provided.

- Previous experience in a related position may be required.

Workplaces/Employers

Self-employment

Specialized cleaning services companies

Occupational Options

Progression to supervisory positions is possible with additional training or experience.

Similar Occupations Classified Elsewhere

Cleaning Supervisors (6215)

Janitors, Caretakers and Building Superintendents (6663)

Light Duty Cleaners (6661)

6662.6 Window Cleaners

Window Cleaners clean windows and other glass surfaces using specialized equipment and techniques.

Profile Summary

APTITUDES

G	V	N	S	P	Q	K	F	M
4	4	5	4	4	5	3	4	3

INTERESTS
OMd

DATA PEOPLE THINGS (DPT)
684

PHYSICAL ACTIVITIES (PA)

V	C	H	B	L	S
3	0	1	4	1	2

ENVIRONMENTAL CONDITIONS (EC)
L1, L3, H8, D5

EDUCATION/TRAINING
2

Examples of Job Titles

Window Cleaner

Descriptor Profile

Main Characteristics

Occupations in this group are characterized by the following aptitudes, interests and worker functions as they relate to main duties:

- **General learning ability** to understand and apply various window cleaning techniques

- **Motor co-ordination** and **manual dexterity** to wash and clean interior and exterior windows and other glass surfaces of buildings

- **Objective interest** in **operating** specialized equipment

- **Methodical interest** in **comparing** to inspect glass surfaces for dust, dirt, grease and other deposits; and in cleaning glass surfaces

- **Directive interest** in applying appropriate window cleaning techniques

6662.6
Subgroup 6 of 6

Physical Activities

Vision
    3   Near and far vision

Colour Discrimination
    0   Not relevant

Hearing
    1   Limited

Body Position
    4   Other body positions

Limb Co-ordination
    1   Upper limb co-ordination

Strength
    2   Light

Environmental Conditions

Location
    L1 Regulated inside climate
    L3 Outside

Hazards
    H8 Dangerous locations

Discomforts
    D5 Wetness

Employment Requirements

Education/Training
    2

- There are no specific educational requirements for occupations in this group.

- On-the-job training is usually provided.

- Previous experience in a related position may be required.

Workplaces/Employers

Self-employment

Specialized cleaning services companies

Occupational Options

Progression to supervisory positions is possible with additional training or experience.

Similar Occupations Classified Elsewhere

Cleaning Supervisors (6215)

Janitors, Caretakers and Building Superintendents (6663)

Light Duty Cleaners (6661)

6663 Janitors, Caretakers and Building Superintendents

Janitors, Caretakers and Building Superintendents clean and maintain the interior and exterior of commercial, institutional and residential buildings and their grounds.

Profile Summary

APTITUDES

G	V	N	S	P	Q	K	F	M
4	4	4	4	4	4	4	4	3

INTERESTS
MOI

DATA PEOPLE THINGS (DPT)
584

PHYSICAL ACTIVITIES (PA)

V	C	H	B	L	S
3	0	1	4	1	3

ENVIRONMENTAL CONDITIONS (EC)
L1, L3, H3, D1, D3, D5

EDUCATION/TRAINING
2

Examples of Job Titles

Building Caretaker
Building Superintendent
Custodian
Handyman/woman
Heavy Duty Cleaner
Industrial Cleaner
Janitor
Plant Cleaner

Descriptor Profile

Main Characteristics

Occupations in this group are characterized by the following aptitudes, interests and worker functions as they relate to main duties:

- **General learning ability** to understand and follow instructions related to building maintenance; may advertise vacancies, show apartments and offices to prospective tenants and collect rent

- **Manual dexterity** to empty trash cans and other waste containers, wash windows, interior walls and ceilings, and clean and disinfect washrooms and fixtures

- **Methodical interest** in **copying** instructions to clean and maintain the interior and exterior of commercial, institutional and residential buildings and their grounds

- **Objective interest** in **operating - manipulating** industrial vacuum cleaners to remove scraps, dirt, heavy debris and other refuse; to sweep, mop, scrub and wax hallways, floors and stairs; to clear snow and ice from walkways and parking area; and to cut grass and tend grounds

- **Innovative interest** in making adjustments and minor repairs to heating, cooling, ventilating, plumbing and electrical systems, and in performing routine maintenance jobs and repairs such as painting

6663

Physical Activities

Vision
   3   Near and far vision

Colour Discrimination
   0   Not relevant

Hearing
   1   Limited

Body Position
   4   Other body positions

Limb Co-ordination
   1   Upper limb co-ordination

Strength
   3   Medium

Environmental Conditions

Location
    L1 Regulated inside climate
    L3 Outside

Hazards
    H3 Equipment, machinery, tools

Discomforts
    D1 Noise
    D3 Odours
    D5 Wetness

Employment Requirements

Education/Training
2

- Completion of secondary school may be required.

- Some occupations in this group, such as building superintendents, require previous cleaning and maintenance experience.

Workplaces/Employers

Apartment building management companies

Hospitals

Office-building management companies

Recreational facilities

School boards

Shopping malls

Occupational Options

Progression to supervisory positions is possible with additional training or experience.

Similar Occupations Classified Elsewhere

Cleaning Supervisors (6215)

Light Duty Cleaners (6661)

Specialized Cleaners (6662)

6671.1 Amusement Park Attendants

Amusement Park Attendants supervise entry into amusement parks and the use of park equipment.

Profile Summary

APTITUDES

G	V	N	S	P	Q	K	F	M
4	4	5	4	4	5	4	4	4

INTERESTS
MSd

DATA PEOPLE THINGS (DPT)
667

PHYSICAL ACTIVITIES (PA)

V	C	H	B	L	S
3	0	2	3	1	2

ENVIRONMENTAL CONDITIONS (EC)
L1, L2, L3

EDUCATION/TRAINING
2

Examples of Job Titles

Amusement Park Attendant

Descriptor Profile

Main Characteristics

Occupations in this group are characterized by the following aptitudes, interests and worker functions as they relate to main duties:

- **General learning ability** to collect tickets and assist patrons

- **Methodical interest** in **comparing** to admit patrons to amusement parks and rides

- **Social interest** in **speaking - signalling** to assist patrons to get on and off rides

- **Directive interest** in **handling** to secure and release safety belts and bars

6671.1
Subgroup 1 of 5

Physical Activities

Vision
   3 Near and far vision

Colour Discrimination
   0 Not relevant

Hearing
   2 Verbal interaction

Body Position
   3 Sitting, standing, walking

Limb Co-ordination
   1 Upper limb co-ordination

Strength
   2 Light

Environmental Conditions

Location
   L1 Regulated inside climate
   L2 Unregulated inside climate
   L3 Outside

Employment Requirements

Education/Training
2

- Some secondary school education may be required.

Workplaces/Employers

Amusement parks

Similar Occupations Classified Elsewhere

Other Elemental Service Occupations (6683)

Other Personal Service Occupations (6484)

Program Leaders and Instructors in Recreation and Sport (5254)

Amusement ride operators (in 6443 *Amusement Attraction Operators and Other Amusement Occupations*)

Supervisors of attendants in recreation and sport (in 6216 *Other Service Supervisors*)

Remarks

In data provided by Statistics Canada, groups 6443 and 6671 are combined to form 6670 *Attendants in Amusement, Recreation and Sport*.

6671.2 Ski Lift Attendants

Ski Lift Attendants supervise the use of ski lift equipment.

Profile Summary

APTITUDES

G	V	N	S	P	Q	K	F	M
4	4	4	3	4	4	3	4	4

INTERESTS
MOs

DATA PEOPLE THINGS (DPT)
667

PHYSICAL ACTIVITIES (PA)

V	C	H	B	L	S
3	0	2	3	1	2

ENVIRONMENTAL CONDITIONS (EC)
L2, L3

EDUCATION/TRAINING
2

Examples of Job Titles

Ski Lift Attendant

Descriptor Profile

Main Characteristics

Occupations in this group are characterized by the following aptitudes, interests and worker functions as they relate to main duties:

- **General learning ability, spatial perception** and **motor co-ordination** to operate ski lifts

- **Methodical** interest in **comparing** to monitor equipment to detect wear and damage

- **Objective** interest in **handling** ski lift equipment to transport skiers up hills

- **Social** interest in **speaking - signalling** to assist passengers on and off ski lifts

6671.2
Subgroup 2 of 5

Physical Activities

Vision
  3 Near and far vision

Colour Discrimination
  0 Not relevant

Hearing
  2 Verbal interaction

Body Position
  3 Sitting, standing, walking

Limb Co-ordination
  1 Upper limb co-ordination

Strength
  2 Light

Environmental Conditions

Location
  L2 Unregulated inside climate
  L3 Outside

Employment Requirements

Education/Training
  2

- Some secondary school education may be required.

Workplaces/Employers

Ski centres

Similar Occupations Classified Elsewhere

Other Elemental Service Occupations (6683)

Other Personal Service Occupations (6484)

Program Leaders and Instructors in Recreation and Sport (5254)

Amusement ride operators (in 6443 *Amusement Attraction Operators and Other Amusement Occupations*)

Supervisors of attendants in recreation and sport (in 6216 *Other Service Supervisors*)

Remarks

In data provided by Statistics Canada, groups 6443 and 6671 are combined to form 6670 *Attendants in Amusement, Recreation and Sport.*

6671.3 Bowling Alley Attendants

Bowling Alley Attendants supervise the use of bowling alley facilities.

Profile Summary

APTITUDES

G	V	N	S	P	Q	K	F	M
4	4	3	4	4	4	4	4	4

INTERESTS

MSd

DATA PEOPLE THINGS (DPT)

667

PHYSICAL ACTIVITIES (PA)

V	C	H	B	L	S
3	0	2	3	1	2

ENVIRONMENTAL CONDITIONS (EC)

L1

EDUCATION/TRAINING

2

Examples of Job Titles

Bowling Alley Attendant

Descriptor Profile

Main Characteristics

Occupations in this group are characterized by the following aptitudes, interests and worker functions as they relate to main duties:

- **General learning ability** to understand the operations of bowling alleys and explain rules of the game to patrons

- **Numerical ability** to collect fees

- **Methodical interest** in **comparing** to assign bowling alleys to patrons and rent bowling shoes

- **Social interest** in **speaking** to attend to the requests of patrons

- **Directive interest** in **handling** bowling equipment and issuing score sheets

6671.3
Subgroup 3 of 5

Physical Activities

Vision
   3 Near and far vision

Colour Discrimination
   0 Not relevant

Hearing
   2 Verbal interaction

Body Position
   3 Sitting, standing, walking

Limb Co-ordination
   1 Upper limb co-ordination

Strength
   2 Light

Environmental Conditions

Location
   L1 Regulated inside climate

Employment Requirements

Education/Training
   2

- Some secondary school education may be required.

Workplaces/Employers

Amusement parks

Bowling alleys

Recreational and sports facilities

Similar Occupations Classified Elsewhere

Other Elemental Service Occupations (6683)

Other Personal Service Occupations (6484)

Program Leaders and Instructors in Recreation and Sport (5254)

Amusement ride operators (in 6443 *Amusement Attraction Operators and Other Amusement Occupations*)

Supervisors of attendants in recreation and sport (in 6216 *Other Service Supervisors*)

Remarks

In data provided by Statistics Canada, groups 6443 and 6671 are combined to form 6670 *Attendants in Amusement, Recreation and Sport.*

6671.4 Ice Makers

Ice Makers operate ice making equipment for skating and curling rinks.

Profile Summary

APTITUDES

G	V	N	S	P	Q	K	F	M
4	4	5	4	4	5	3	4	3

INTERESTS
MOd

DATA PEOPLE THINGS (DPT)
684

PHYSICAL ACTIVITIES (PA)

V	C	H	B	L	S
3	0	1	3	2	3

ENVIRONMENTAL CONDITIONS (EC)
L1, L3, H3

EDUCATION/TRAINING
2

Examples of Job Titles

Ice Maker, Rink

Descriptor Profile

Main Characteristics

Occupations in this group are characterized by the following aptitudes, interests and worker functions as they relate to main duties:

- **General learning ability** to understand and apply the techniques of preparing ice surfaces of rinks for activities such as skating, hockey and curling

- **Motor co-ordination** and **manual dexterity** to operate equipment for spraying surfaces of rinks

- **Methodical interest** in **comparing** to clean, smooth and prepare ice surfaces

- **Objective interest** in **operating** machines equipped with scraper blades and water spraying devices to clean and smooth ice surfaces

- **Directive interest** in maintaining quality of ice surfaces and the proper functioning of ice making equipment

6671.4
Subgroup 4 of 5

Physical Activities

Vision
  3 Near and far vision

Colour Discrimination
  0 Not relevant

Hearing
  1 Limited

Body Position
  3 Sitting, standing, walking

Limb Co-ordination
  2 Multiple limb co-ordination

Strength
  3 Medium

Environmental Conditions

Location
  L1 Regulated inside climate
  L3 Outside

Hazards
  H3 Equipment, machinery, tools

Employment Requirements

Education/Training
2

- Some secondary school education may be required.

Workplaces/Employers

Amusement parks

Arenas

Recreational and sports facilities

Similar Occupations Classified Elsewhere

Other Elemental Service Occupations (6683)

Other Personal Service Occupations (6484)

Program Leaders and Instructors in Recreation and Sport (5254)

Amusement ride operators (in 6443 *Amusement Attraction Operators and Other Amusement Occupations*)

Supervisors of attendants in recreation and sport (in 6216 *Other Service Supervisors*)

Remarks

In data provided by Statistics Canada, groups 6443 and 6671 are combined to form 6670 *Attendants in Amusement, Recreation and Sport*.

6671.5 Recreational Facility Attendants

Recreational Facility Attendants supervise the use of recreational facilities.

Profile Summary

APTITUDES

G	V	N	S	P	Q	K	F	M
4	4	3	4	4	3	4	4	4

INTERESTS
MSo

DATA PEOPLE THINGS (DPT)
667

PHYSICAL ACTIVITIES (PA)

V	C	H	B	L	S
2	0	2	3	1	1

ENVIRONMENTAL CONDITIONS (EC)
L1, L3

EDUCATION/TRAINING
2

Examples of Job Titles

Athletic Equipment Custodian
Billiard Parlour Attendant
Bingo Hall Attendant
Campground Attendant
Recreation Attendant
Recreational Facility Attendant
Sport Attendant
Tennis Court Attendant

Descriptor Profile

Main Characteristics

Occupations in this group are characterized by the following aptitudes, interests and worker functions as they relate to main duties:

- **General learning ability** to understand the operation of recreational facilities and attend to patrons' requests

- **Numerical ability** to collect fees

- **Clerical perception** to record schedules, and equipment rental and sales

- **Methodical interest** in **comparing** to schedule the use of golf courses, tennis courts, fitness clubs and other recreational facilities

- **Social interest** in **speaking** to attend to patrons' requests

- **Objective interest** in **handling** sports equipment

6671.5
Subgroup 5 of 5

Physical Activities

Vision
  2 Near vision

Colour Discrimination
  0 Not relevant

Hearing
  2 Verbal interaction

Body Position
  3 Sitting, standing, walking

Limb Co-ordination
  1 Upper limb co-ordination

Strength
  1 Limited

Environmental Conditions

Location
  L1 Regulated inside climate
  L3 Outside

Employment Requirements

Education/Training
  2

- Some secondary school education may be required.

Workplaces/Employers

Amusement parks

Arenas

Billiard parlours

Bowling alleys

Golf courses

Recreational and sports facilities

Ski centers

Tennis clubs

Similar Occupations Classified Elsewhere

Other Elemental Service Occupations (6683)

Other Personal Service Occupations (6484)

Program Leaders and Instructors in Recreation and Sport (5254)

Amusement ride operators (in 6443 *Amusement Attraction Operators and Other Amusement Occupations*)

Supervisors of attendants in recreation and sport (in 6216 *Other Service Supervisors*)

Remarks

In data provided by Statistics Canada, groups 6443 and 6671 are combined to form 6670 *Attendants in Amusement, Recreation and Sport.*

6672.1 Bellhops

Bellhops carry hotel guests' luggage and escort guests to their rooms.

Profile Summary

APTITUDES

G	V	N	S	P	Q	K	F	M
4	4	5	4	4	5	4	4	4

INTERESTS
OSM

DATA PEOPLE THINGS (DPT)
677

PHYSICAL ACTIVITIES (PA)

V	C	H	B	L	S
2	0	2	4	1	3

ENVIRONMENTAL CONDITIONS (EC)
L1

EDUCATION/TRAINING
2

Examples of Job Titles

Bellhop
Doorkeeper, Hotel

Descriptor Profile

Main Characteristics

Occupations in this group are characterized by the following aptitudes, interests and worker functions as they relate to main duties:

- **General learning ability** to understand and apply standard procedures to perform the duties of a bellhop

- **Objective interest** in **handling** luggage for hotel guests

- **Social interest** in **assisting** guests by escorting them to their rooms, and offering information regarding features of rooms, services of hotel and points of interest

- **Methodical interest in comparing** to check rooms to make sure they are in order

6672.1

Physical Activities

Vision
    2   Near vision

Colour Discrimination
    0   Not relevant

Hearing
    2   Verbal interaction

Body Position
    4   Other body positions

Limb Co-ordination
    1   Upper limb co-ordination

Strength
    3   Medium

Environmental Conditions

Location
    L1   Regulated inside climate

Employment Requirements

Education/Training
2

- Some secondary school education may be required.

Workplaces/Employers

Hotels

Occupational Options

Progression to supervisory positions is possible with experience.

Similar Occupations Classified Elsewhere

Pursers and Flight Attendants (6432)

Ticket and Cargo Agents and Related Clerks (Except Airline) (6434)

Tour and Travel Guides (6441)

Supervisors of attendants in this group (in 6216 *Other Service Supervisors*)

6672.2 Baggage Porters

Baggage Porters carry travellers' luggage at railway stations.

Profile Summary

APTITUDES

G	V	N	S	P	Q	K	F	M
4	4	5	4	4	5	4	4	4

INTERESTS
OSM

DATA PEOPLE THINGS (DPT)
677

PHYSICAL ACTIVITIES (PA)

V	C	H	B	L	S
2	0	2	4	1	3

ENVIRONMENTAL CONDITIONS (EC)
L1, L3

EDUCATION/TRAINING
2

Examples of Job Titles

Baggage Porter
Luggage Attendant (Except Airline)
Porter
Redcap

Descriptor Profile

Main Characteristics

Occupations in this group are characterized by the following aptitudes, interests and worker functions as they relate to main duties:

- **General learning ability** to understand and apply standard procedures to perform the duties of a baggage porter

- **Objective interest** in handling travellers' luggage at railway stations by hand or handcart

- **Social interest** in assisting travellers by arranging for ground transportation

- **Methodical interest** in comparing to make sure luggage is transported according to standard procedures

6672.2
Subgroup 2 of 4

Physical Activities

Vision
    2   Near vision

Colour Discrimination
    0   Not relevant

Hearing
    1   Limited

Body Position
    4   Other body positions

Limb Co-ordination
    1   Upper limb co-ordination

Strength
    3   Medium

Environmental Conditions

Location
    L1   Regulated inside climate
    L3   Outside

Employment Requirements

Education/Training
  2

- Some secondary school education may be required.

Workplaces/Employers

Railway companies

Occupational Options

Progression to supervisory positions is possible with experience.

Similar Occupations Classified Elsewhere

Pursers and Flight Attendants (6432)

Ticket and Cargo Agents and Related Clerks (Except Airline) (6434)

Tour and Travel Guides (6441)

Supervisors of attendants in this group (in 6216 *Other Service Supervisors*)

6672.3 Ship Attendants

Ship Attendants carry travellers' luggage aboard ships and clean and maintain public areas and passengers' rooms aboard ships.

Profile Summary

APTITUDES

G	V	N	S	P	Q	K	F	M
4	4	4	4	4	5	4	4	3

INTERESTS
OSM

DATA PEOPLE THINGS (DPT)
677

PHYSICAL ACTIVITIES (PA)

V	C	H	B	L	S
2	0	2	4	1	3

ENVIRONMENTAL CONDITIONS (EC)
L1, L3

EDUCATION/TRAINING
2

Examples of Job Titles

Passenger Attendant, Cruise Line
Passenger Attendant, Ship

Descriptor Profile

Main Characteristics

Occupations in this group are characterized by the following aptitudes, interests and worker functions as they relate to main duties:

- **General learning ability** to understand and apply standard procedures to perform the duties of a ship attendant

- **Manual dexterity** to use cleaning equipment

- **Objective interest** in **handling** luggage for passengers aboard ships

- **Social interest** in **serving** food and beverages

- **Methodical interest** in **comparing** to clean cabins, make beds and wash dishes

6672.3

Physical Activities

Vision
   2 Near vision

Colour Discrimination
   0 Not relevant

Hearing
   2 Verbal interaction

Body Position
   4 Other body positions

Limb Co-ordination
   1 Upper limb co-ordination

Strength
   3 Medium

Environmental Conditions

Location
    L1 Regulated inside climate
    L3 Outside

Employment Requirements

Education/Training
  2

- Some secondary school education may be required.

Workplaces/Employers

Water transport companies

Occupational Options

Progression to supervisory positions is possible with experience.

Similar Occupations Classified Elsewhere

Pursers and Flight Attendants (6432)

Ticket and Cargo Agents and Related Clerks (Except Airline) (6434)

Tour and Travel Guides (6441)

Supervisors of attendants in this group (in 6216 *Other Service Supervisors*)

6672.4 Train Service Attendants

Train Service Attendants clean and maintain public areas and sleeping cars aboard trains.

Profile Summary

APTITUDES

G	V	N	S	P	Q	K	F	M
4	4	4	4	4	5	4	4	4

INTERESTS
OSM

DATA PEOPLE THINGS (DPT)
677

PHYSICAL ACTIVITIES (PA)

V	C	H	B	L	S
2	0	2	4	1	2

ENVIRONMENTAL CONDITIONS (EC)
L1

EDUCATION/TRAINING
2

Examples of Job Titles

Train Service Attendant

Descriptor Profile

Main Characteristics

Occupations in this group are characterized by the following aptitudes, interests and worker functions as they relate to main duties:

- **General learning ability** to understand and apply standard procedures to perform the duties of a train service attendant

- **Objective interest** in **handling** supplies to set and clear tables

- **Social interest** in **assisting** passengers as required

- **Methodical interest** in **comparing** to clean sleeping cars and maintain washroom supplies

6672.4

Physical Activities

Vision
  2 Near vision

Colour Discrimination
  0 Not relevant

Hearing
  2 Verbal interaction

Body Position
  4 Other body positions

Limb Co-ordination
  1 Upper limb co-ordination

Strength
  2 Light

Environmental Conditions

Location
  L1 Regulated inside climate

Employment Requirements

Education/Training
  2

- Some secondary school education may be required.

Workplaces/Employers

Railway companies

Occupational Options

Progression to supervisory positions is possible with experience.

Similar Occupations Classified Elsewhere

Pursers and Flight Attendants (6432)

Ticket and Cargo Agents and Related Clerks (Except Airline) (6434)

Tour and Travel Guides (6441)

Supervisors of attendants in this group (in 6216 *Other Service Supervisors*)

6681.1 Dry Cleaning and Laundry Machine Operators

Dry Cleaning and Laundry Machine Operators operate machines to dry-clean and launder garments and household articles.

Profile Summary

APTITUDES

G	V	N	S	P	Q	K	F	M
4	4	5	4	4	5	4	4	3

INTERESTS
OMd

DATA PEOPLE THINGS (DPT)
684

PHYSICAL ACTIVITIES (PA)

V	C	H	B	L	S
2	1	1	2	1	2

ENVIRONMENTAL CONDITIONS (EC)
L1, H1, D3

EDUCATION/TRAINING
2, 5

Examples of Job Titles

Cleaning Machine Operator
Drapery Cleaner
Dry Cleaner
Dyer, Laundry and Dry Cleaning
Fur Cleaner
Laundry Machine Operator
Laundry Worker
Leather Cleaner
Machine Operator, Laundry and Dry Cleaning
Spotter
Sprayer, Leather or Suede
Suede Cleaner

Descriptor Profile

Main Characteristics

Occupations in this group are characterized by the following aptitudes, interests and worker functions as they relate to main duties:

- **General learning ability** to acquire and apply knowledge of fabrics and techniques of dry cleaning and stain removal

- **Manual dexterity** to load and unload machines, rub articles with brushes and sponges, and use steam guns and air hoses to remove stains

- **Objective interest** in operating machines to dry-clean dresses, suits, coats, sweaters, draperies, cushion covers and other garments and household articles, and to use washing machines and dryers to clean and dry shirts, sheets, blankets and towels

- **Methodical interest** in comparing to dry-clean and launder garments and household articles

- **Directive interest** in using specialized machines to clean, blow-dry and glaze fur garments, and to dry-clean, dye, spray, re-oil, press and re-buff suede and leather garments

6681.1
Subgroup 1 of 2

Physical Activities

Vision
  2 Near vision

Colour Discrimination
  1 Relevant

Hearing
  1 Limited

Body Position
  2 Standing and/or walking

Limb Co-ordination
  1 Upper limb co-ordination

Strength
  2 Light

Environmental Conditions

Location
  L1 Regulated inside climate

Hazards
  H1 Dangerous chemical substances

Discomforts
  D3 Odours

Employment Requirements

Education/Training
  2, 5

- Some secondary school education is required.

- Three-to-six months of on-the-job training are usually provided.

- Dry cleaners in British Columbia may require completion of a one-year apprenticeship program.

- Dry cleaning and laundry machine operators may require experience as inspectors or assemblers.

- Suede, leather and fur cleaners may require experience as dry cleaning or laundry machine operators.

Workplaces/Employers

Dry cleaning and laundry establishments

Laundries of hotels, hospitals and similar institutions.

Occupational Options

- Progression to supervisory dry cleaning and laundry occupations is possible with additional training and experience.

Similar Occupations Classified Elsewhere

Dry Cleaning and Laundry Supervisors (6214)

Ironing, Pressing and Finishing Occupations (6682)

Alterers (in 7342 *Tailors, Dressmakers, Furriers and Milliners*)

Dry cleaning service managers (in 0651 *Other Services Managers*)

6681.2 Dry Cleaning and Laundry Inspectors and Assemblers

Dry Cleaning and Laundry Inspectors and Assemblers check finished garments to make sure that they meet required standards for cleaning and pressing, and assemble and bag finished garments.

Profile Summary

APTITUDES

G	V	N	S	P	Q	K	F	M
4	4	5	4	4	4	4	4	4

INTERESTS
Mod

DATA PEOPLE THINGS (DPT)
687

PHYSICAL ACTIVITIES (PA)

V	C	H	B	L	S
2	1	1	2	1	2

ENVIRONMENTAL CONDITIONS (EC)
L1, H3, H7

EDUCATION/TRAINING
2

Examples of Job Titles

Assembler, Laundry and Dry Cleaning
Bagger, Laundry and Dry Cleaning
Inspector, Laundry and Dry Cleaning
Laundry Worker

Descriptor Profile

Main Characteristics

Occupations in this group are characterized by the following aptitudes, interests and worker functions as they relate to main duties:

- **General learning ability** to understand and apply procedures to inspect and assemble dry-cleaned and laundered articles

- **Methodical interest** in **comparing** to check finished garments to make sure that they are properly cleaned, dried and pressed, to match invoices with garment tags, and to record damaged and improperly cleaned and laundered garments

- **Objective interest** in **handling** to assemble and bag finished garments and household articles; and in using hand-held steam irons to touch up rough finishes

- **Directive interest** in sending improperly cleaned and damaged articles for further processing and repair

6681.2
Subgroup 2 of 2

Physical Activities

Vision
  2 Near vision

Colour Discrimination
  1 Relevant

Hearing
  1 Limited

Body Position
  2 Standing and/or walking

Limb Co-ordination
  1 Upper limb co-ordination

Strength
  2 Light

Environmental Conditions

Location
  L1 Regulated inside climate

Hazards
  H3 Equipment, machinery, tools
  H7 Fire, steam, hot surfaces

Employment Requirements

Education/Training
  2

- Some secondary school education is required.

- Three-to-six months of on-the-job training are usually provided.

- Dry cleaners in British Columbia may require completion of a one-year apprenticeship program.

- Dry cleaning and laundry machine operators may require experience as inspectors or assemblers.

- Suede, leather and fur cleaners may require experience as dry cleaning or laundry machine operators.

Workplaces/Employers

Dry cleaning and laundry establishments

Laundries of hotels, hospitals and similar institutions

Occupational Options

Progression to supervisory dry cleaning and laundry occupations is possible with additional training and experience.

Similar Occupations Classified Elsewhere

Dry Cleaning and Laundry Supervisors (6214)

Ironing, Pressing and Finishing Occupations (6682)

Alterers (in 7342 *Tailors, Dressmakers, Furriers and Milliners*)

Dry cleaning service managers (in 0651 *Other Services Managers*)

6682 Ironing, Pressing and Finishing Occupations

This group includes workers who press garments and household articles using hand irons and pressing machines.

Profile Summary

APTITUDES

G	V	N	S	P	Q	K	F	M
4	4	5	4	4	5	3	4	3

INTERESTS
MOi

DATA PEOPLE THINGS (DPT)
584

PHYSICAL ACTIVITIES (PA)

V	C	H	B	L	S
2	0	1	2	1	2

ENVIRONMENTAL CONDITIONS (EC)
L1, H3, H7

EDUCATION/TRAINING
2

Examples of Job Titles

Finisher
Laundry Finisher
Pleats Finisher
Presser
Silk Finisher
Steam Finisher

Descriptor Profile

Main Characteristics

Occupations in this group are characterized by the following aptitudes, interests and worker functions as they relate to main duties:

- **General learning ability** to understand and follow instructions for machine and hand-pressing work

- **Motor co-ordination** and **manual dexterity** to use hand irons and handle garments, flatwork and other articles

- **Methodical interest** in **copying** procedures to fold and bag shirts and sheets

- **Objective interest** in **operating** pressing machines to press garments such as pants, shirts and skirts, and household articles such as sheets and cushion covers

- **Innovative interest** in understanding the qualities of fabrics, and in hand-ironing fine lace and silk garments

6682

Physical Activities

Vision
  2 Near vision

Colour Discrimination
  0 Not relevant

Hearing
  1 Limited

Body Position
  2 Standing and/or walking

Limb Co-ordination
  1 Upper limb co-ordination

Strength
  2 Light

Environmental Conditions

Location
  L1 Regulated inside climate

Hazards
  H3 Equipment, machinery, tools
  H7 Fire, steam, hot surfaces

Employment Requirements

Education/Training
2

- Some secondary school education is required.
- On-the-job training is provided.

Workplaces/Employers

Dry cleaning establishments

Hospitals

Hotels

Laundry establishments

Occupational Options

Progression to supervisory dry cleaning and laundry positions is possible with additional training or experience.

Similar Occupations Classified Elsewhere

Dry Cleaning and Laundry Occupations (6681)

Dry Cleaning and Laundry Supervisors (6214)

6683.1 Beauty Salon Attendants

Beauty Salon Attendants provide services in beauty salons.

Profile Summary

APTITUDES

G	V	N	S	P	Q	K	F	M
4	4	5	4	4	5	4	4	4

INTERESTS
MSO

DATA PEOPLE THINGS (DPT)
677

PHYSICAL ACTIVITIES (PA)

V	C	H	B	L	S
2	0	1	2	1	1

ENVIRONMENTAL CONDITIONS (EC)
L1, D3, D4, D5

EDUCATION/TRAINING
1

Examples of Job Titles

Beauty Salon Attendant
Tanning Salon Attendant

Descriptor Profile

Main Characteristics

Occupations in this group are characterized by the following aptitudes, interests and worker functions as they relate to main duties:

- **General learning ability** to understand and apply standard procedures to perform the duties of a beauty salon attendant

- Methodical interest in **comparing** to keep work areas clean

- Social interest in **assisting** hairdressers

- Objective interest in **handling** to wash, condition and dry customers' hair

6683.1
Subgroup 1 of 6

Physical Activities

Vision
    2   Near vision

Colour Discrimination
    0   Not relevant

Hearing
    1   Limited

Body Position
    2   Standing and/or walking

Limb Co-ordination
    1   Upper limb co-ordination

Strength
    1   Limited

Environmental Conditions

Location
    L1   Regulated inside climate

Discomforts
    D3 Odours
    D4 Non-Toxic Dusts
    D5 Wetness

Employment Requirements

Education/Training
    1

- There are no specific educational requirements for occupations in this group.

Workplaces/Employers

Beauty salons

Retail service establishments

Similar Occupations Classified Elsewhere

Attendants in Recreation and Sport (6671)

6683.2 Door Attendants

Door attendants provide services in retail service establishments.

Profile Summary

APTITUDES

G	V	N	S	P	Q	K	F	M
4	4	5	4	4	5	4	4	4

INTERESTS
MSo

DATA PEOPLE THINGS (DPT)
677

PHYSICAL ACTIVITIES (PA)

V	C	H	B	L	S
2	0	1	2	1	1

ENVIRONMENTAL CONDITIONS (EC)
L1, L3

EDUCATION/TRAINING
1

Examples of Job Titles

Door Attendant

Elevator Operator

Descriptor Profile

Main Characteristics

Occupations in this group are characterized by the following aptitudes, interests and worker functions as they relate to main duties:

- **General learning ability** to understand and follow instructions

- **Methodical interest** in **comparing** to prevent entry of unauthorized and undesirable guests

- **Social interest** in **assisting** people entering and leaving hotels, theatres and similar establishments

- **Objective interest** in **handling** to open doors for people entering and leaving establishments

6683.2

Physical Activities

Vision
   2 Near vision

Colour Discrimination
   0 Not relevant

Hearing
   1 Limited

Body Position
   2 Standing and/or walking

Limb Co-ordination
   1 Upper limb co-ordination

Strength
   1 Limited

Environmental Conditions

Location
   L1 Regulated inside climate
   L3 Outside

Employment Requirements

Education/Training
   1

- There are no specific educational requirements for occupations in this group.

Workplaces/Employers

Retail service establishments

Similar Occupations Classified Elsewhere

Attendants in Recreation and Sport (6671)

6683.3 Funeral Attendants

Funeral Attendants provide services for funeral homes.

Profile Summary

APTITUDES

G	V	N	S	P	Q	K	F	M
4	4	5	4	4	4	4	4	4

INTERESTS
OMs

DATA PEOPLE THINGS (DPT)
673

PHYSICAL ACTIVITIES (PA)

V	C	H	B	L	S
4	0	1	3	2	2

ENVIRONMENTAL CONDITIONS (EC)
L1, L3, L4

EDUCATION/TRAINING
1, R

Examples of Job Titles

Funeral Attendant

Descriptor Profile

Main Characteristics

Occupations in this group are characterized by the following aptitudes, interests and worker functions as they relate to main duties:

- **General learning ability** to understand and follow instructions and standard procedures

- **Objective interest** in **driving** hearses and other vehicles

- **Methodical interest** in **comparing** to clean funeral parlours and chapels, and to arrange lights and floral displays

- **Social interest** in **assisting** to escort mourners; and in acting as pallbearers

Physical Activities

Vision
    4   Total visual field

Colour Discrimination
    0   Not relevant

Hearing
    1   Limited

Body Position
    3   Sitting, standing, walking

Limb Co-ordination
    2   Multiple limb co-ordination

Strength
    2   Light

Environmental Conditions

Location
    L1 Regulated inside climate
    L3 Outside
    L4 In a vehicle or cab

Employment Requirements

Education/Training
    1, R

- There are no specific educational requirements for occupations in this group.

- A valid driver's licence is required for funeral attendants.

Workplaces/Employers

Funeral homes or parlours

Similar Occupations Classified Elsewhere

Attendants in Recreation and Sport (6671)

6683.4 Laundromat Attendants

Laundromat Attendants provide services in laundromats.

Profile Summary

APTITUDES

G	V	N	S	P	Q	K	F	M
4	4	4	4	4	4	4	4	4

INTERESTS
MOs

DATA PEOPLE THINGS (DPT)
667

PHYSICAL ACTIVITIES (PA)

V	C	H	B	L	S
2	0	2	4	1	2

ENVIRONMENTAL CONDITIONS (EC)
L1

EDUCATION/TRAINING
1

Examples of Job Titles

Laundromat Attendant

Descriptor Profile

Main Characteristics

Occupations in this group are characterized by the following aptitudes, interests and worker functions as they relate to main duties:

- **General learning ability** to understand and follow standard procedures

- **Methodical interest** in **comparing** to clean laundromats; and in arranging for the repair of broken machines

- **Objective interest** in **handling** to replenish vending machines

- **Social interest** in **speaking** to customers when providing change and explaining operation of machines

6683.4

Physical Activities

Vision
   2 Near vision

Colour Discrimination
   0 Not relevant

Hearing
   2 Verbal interaction

Body Position
   4 Other body positions

Limb Co-ordination
   1 Upper limb co-ordination

Strength
   2 Light

Environmental Conditions

Location
   L1 Regulated inside climate

Employment Requirements

Education/Training
1

- There are no specific educational requirements for occupations in this group.

Workplaces/Employers

Laundromats

Retail service establishments

Similar Occupations Classified Elsewhere

Attendants in Recreation and Sport (6671)

6683.5 Parking Lot Attendants and Car Jockeys

Parking Lot Attendants and Car Jockeys provide services in parking lots.

Profile Summary

APTITUDES

G	V	N	S	P	Q	K	F	M
4	4	4	4	4	4	4	4	4

INTERESTS
MOs

DATA PEOPLE THINGS (DPT)
663

PHYSICAL ACTIVITIES (PA)

V	C	H	B	L	S
4	0	1	3	2	1

ENVIRONMENTAL CONDITIONS (EC)
L1, L2, L3

EDUCATION/TRAINING
1, R

Examples of Job Titles

Car Jockey
Hotel Valet
Parking Lot Attendant
Toll Booth Attendant

Descriptor Profile

Main Characteristics

Occupations in this group are characterized by the following aptitudes, interests and worker functions as they relate to main duties:

- **General learning ability** to understand and follow standard procedures

- **Methodical interest** in **comparing** to issue ticket stubs and collect parking fees

- **Objective interest** in **driving** to park cars

- **Social interest** in **speaking** to customers when directing them to parking spaces

6683.5
Subgroup 5 of 6

Physical Activities

Vision
    4   Total visual field

Colour Discrimination
    0   Not relevant

Hearing
    1   Limited

Body Position
    3   Sitting, standing, walking

Limb Co-ordination
    2   Multiple limb co-ordination

Strength
    1   Limited

Environmental Conditions

Location
    L1   Regulated inside climate
    L2   Unregulated inside climate
    L3   Outside

Employment Requirements

Education/Training
    1, R

- There are no specific educational requirements for occupations in this group.

- A valid driver's licence is required for some occupations in this group.

Workplaces/Employers

Hotels

Parking Lots

Retail service establishments

Similar Occupations Classified Elsewhere

Attendants in Recreation and Sport (6671)

6683.6 Ticket Takers and Ushers

Ticket Takers and Ushers provide services in retail service establishments.

Profile Summary

APTITUDES

G	V	N	S	P	Q	K	F	M
4	4	5	4	4	4	4	4	4

INTERESTS
Msd

DATA PEOPLE THINGS (DPT)
668

PHYSICAL ACTIVITIES (PA)

V	C	H	B	L	S
2	0	2	2	1	1

ENVIRONMENTAL CONDITIONS (EC)
L1

EDUCATION/TRAINING
1

Examples of Job Titles

Cloakroom Attendant
Fur Storage Attendant
Ticket Taker
Usher

Descriptor Profile

Main Characteristics

Occupations in this group are characterized by the following aptitudes, interests and worker functions as they relate to main duties:

- **General learning ability** to understand and follow standard procedures

- **Methodical interest** in **comparing** to collect admission tickets and passes from patrons at entertainment events

- **Social interest** in **speaking** to patrons when answering questions

- **Directive interest** in maintaining order in lobbies and waiting areas, and in directing patrons to their seats

6683.6

Physical Activities

Vision
  2 Near vision

Colour Discrimination
  0 Not relevant

Hearing
  2 Verbal interaction

Body Position
  2 Standing and/or walking

Limb Co-ordination
  1 Upper limb co-ordination

Strength
  1 Limited

Environmental Conditions

Location
  L1 Regulated inside climate

Employment Requirements

Education/Training
  1

- There are no specific educational requirements for occupations in this group.

Workplaces/Employers

Retail service establishments

Similar Occupations Classified Elsewhere

Attendants in Recreation and Sport (6671)

Trades, Transport and Equipment Operators and Related Occupations

Trades, Transport and Equipment Operators and Related Occupations

MAJOR GROUP 72-73
TRADES AND SKILLED TRANSPORT AND EQUIPMENT OPERATORS

721 **Contractors and Supervisors, Trades and Related Workers**

7211 Supervisors, Machinists and Related Occupations
7212 Contractors and Supervisors, Electrical Trades and Telecommunications Occupations
7213 Contractors and Supervisors, Pipefitting Trades
7214 Contractors and Supervisors, Metal Forming, Shaping and Erecting Occupations
7215 Contractors and Supervisors, Carpentry Trades
7216 Contractors and Supervisors, Mechanic Trades
7217 Contractors and Supervisors, Heavy Construction Equipment Crews
7218 Supervisors, Printing and Related Occupations
7219 Contractors and Supervisors, Other Construction Trades, Installers, Repairers and Servicers

722 **Supervisors, Railway and Motor Transportation Occupations**

7221 Supervisors, Railway Transport Operations
7222 Supervisors, Motor Transport and Other Ground Transit Operators

723 **Machinists and Related Occupations**

7231 Machinists and Machining and Tooling Inspectors
    7231.1 Machinists
    7231.2 Machining and Tooling Inspectors
7232 Tool and Die Makers

724 **Electrical Trades and Telecommunication Occupations**

7241 Electricians (Except Industrial and Power System)
7242 Industrial Electricians
7243 Power System Electricians
7244 Electrical Power Line and Cable Workers
7245 Telecommunications Line and Cable Workers
7246 Telecommunications Installation and Repair Workers
    7246.1 Telephone Installers and Repairers
    7246.2 Switch Network Installers and Repairers
    7246.3 Telecommunications Service Testers
    7246.4 Telecommunications Equipment Technicians
7247 Cable Television Service and Maintenance Technicians
    7247.1 Cable Television Service Technicians
    7247.2 Cable Television Maintenance Technicians

725 **Plumbers, Pipefitters and Gas Fitters**

7251 Plumbers
7252 Steamfitters, Pipefitters and Sprinkler System Installers
    7252.1 Steamfitters and Pipefitters
    7252.2 Sprinkler System Installers
7253 Gas Fitters

726 Metal Forming, Shaping and Erecting Occupations

- 7261 Sheet Metal Workers
- 7262 Boilermakers
- 7263 Structural Metal and Platework Fabricators and Fitters
- 7264 Ironworkers
- 7265 Welders
- 7266 Blacksmiths and Die Setters
  - 7266.1 Blacksmiths
  - 7266.2 Die Setters

727 Carpenters and Cabinetmakers

- 7271 Carpenters
- 7272 Cabinetmakers

728 Masonry and Plastering Trades

- 7281 Bricklayers
- 7282 Cement Finishers
- 7283 Tilesetters
- 7284 Plasterers, Drywall Installers and Finishers and Lathers
  - 7284.1 Plasterers
  - 7284.2 Drywall Installers and Finishers
  - 7284.3 Lathers

729 Other Construction Trades

- 7291 Roofers and Shinglers
  - 7291.1 Roofers
  - 7291.2 Shinglers
- 7292 Glaziers
- 7293 Insulators
- 7294 Painters and Decorators
- 7295 Floor Covering Installers

731 Machinery and Transportation Equipment Mechanics (Except Motor Vehicle)

- 7311 Construction Millwrights and Industrial Mechanics (Except Textile)
- 7312 Heavy-Duty Equipment Mechanics
- 7313 Refrigeration and Air Conditioning Mechanics
- 7314 Railway Carmen/women
- 7315 Aircraft Mechanics and Aircraft Inspectors
  - 7315.1 Aircraft Mechanics
  - 7315.2 Aircraft Inspectors
- 7316 Machine Fitters
- 7317 Textile Machinery Mechanics and Repairers
- 7318 Elevator Constructors and Mechanics

732 Motor Vehicle Mechanics

- 7321 Motor Vehicle Mechanics, Technicians and Mechanical Repairers
  - 7321.1 Motor Vehicle Mechanics and Technicians
  - 7321.2 Mechanical Repairers, Motor Vehicle Manufacturing

7322 Motor Vehicle Body Repairers

733 Other Mechanics

7331 Oil and Solid Fuel Heating Mechanics

7332 Electric Appliance Servicers and Repairers
    7332.1 Small Appliance Servicers and Repairers
    7332.2 Major Appliance Repairers/Technicians

7333 Electrical Mechanics

7334 Motorcycle and Other Related Mechanics

7335 Other Small Engine and Equipment Mechanics

734 Upholsterers, Tailors, Shoe Repairers, Jewellers and Related Occupations

7341 Upholsterers

7342 Tailors, Dressmakers, Furriers and Milliners
    7342.1 Tailors and Dressmakers
    7342.2 Furriers
    7342.3 Milliners
    7342.4 Seamstresses

7343 Shoe Repairers and Shoemakers
    7343.1 Shoemakers
    7343.2 Shoe Repairers

7344 Jewellers, Watch Repairers and Related Occupations
    7344.1 Jewellers and Related Workers
    7344.2 Watch Repairers

735 Stationary Engineers and Power Station and System Operators

7351 Stationary Engineers and Auxiliary Equipment Operators

7352 Power Systems and Power Station Operators
    7352.1 Power Systems Operators
    7352.2 Power Station Operators

736 Train Crew Operating Occupations

7361 Railway and Yard Locomotive Engineers
    7361.1 Railway Locomotive Engineers
    7361.2 Yard Locomotive Engineers

7362 Railway Conductors and Brakemen/women
    7362.1 Railway Conductors
    7362.2 Brakemen/women

737 Crane Operators, Drillers and Blasters

7371 Crane Operators

7372 Drillers and Blasters – Surface Mining, Quarrying and Construction
    7372.1 Drillers – Surface Mining, Quarrying and Construction
    7372.2 Blasters – Surface Mining, Quarrying and Construction

7373 Water Well Drillers

738 Printing Press Operators, Commercial Divers and Other Trades and Related Occupations, n.e.c.

7381 Printing Press Operators

7382 Commercial Divers

7383 Other Trades and Related Occupations
- 7383.1 Gunsmiths
- 7383.2 Locksmiths
- 7383.3 Recreational Vehicle Repairers
- 7383.4 Safe and Vault Servicers
- 7383.5 Saw Fitters

MAJOR GROUP 74
INTERMEDIATE OCCUPATIONS IN TRANSPORT, EQUIPMENT OPERATION, INSTALLATION AND MAINTENANCE

741 Motor Vehicle and Transit Drivers

7411 Truck Drivers

7412 Bus Drivers and Subway and Other Transit Operators
- 7412.1 Bus and Streetcar Drivers
- 7412.2 School Bus Drivers
- 7412.3 Subway Train and Light Rail Transit Operators

7413 Taxi and Limousine Drivers and Chauffeurs
- 7413.1 Taxi and Limousine Drivers
- 7413.2 Chauffeurs

7414 Delivery Drivers

742 Heavy Equipment Operators

7421 Heavy Equipment Operators (Except Crane)

7422 Public Works Maintenance Equipment Operators

743 Other Transport Equipment Operators and Related Workers

7431 Railway Yard Workers

7432 Railway Track Maintenance Workers

7433 Deck Crew, Water Transport

7434 Engine Room Crew, Water Transport

7435 Lock and Cable Ferry Operators and Related Occupations
- 7435.1 Lock Equipment Operators
- 7435.2 Cable Ferry Operators
- 7435.3 Ferry Terminal Workers

7436 Boat Operators

7437 Air Transport Ramp Attendants

744 Other Installers, Repairers and Servicers

7441 Residential and Commercial Installers and Servicers

7442 Waterworks and Gas Maintenance Workers
- 7442.1 Waterworks Maintenance Workers
- 7442.2 Gas Maintenance Workers

7443	Automotive Mechanical Installers and Servicers
7444	Pest Controllers and Fumigators
7445	Other Repairers and Servicers

745　Longshore Workers and Material Handlers

7451	Longshore Workers
7452	Material Handlers
	7452.1　Material Handlers (Manual)
	7452.2　Material Handlers (Equipment Operators)

MAJOR GROUP 76
TRADES HELPERS, CONSTRUCTION LABOURERS AND RELATED OCCUPATIONS

761　Trades Helpers and Labourers

7611	Construction Trades Helpers and Labourers
7612	Other Trades Helpers and Labourers

762　Public Works and Other Labourers, n.e.c.

7621	Public Works and Maintenance Labourers
7622	Railway and Motor Transport Labourers
	7622.1　Railway Labourers
	7622.2　Motor Transport Labourers

7211 Supervisors, Machinists and Related Occupations

Supervisors in this group direct and co-ordinate the activities of workers classified in the following groups: *Machinists and Machining and Tooling Inspectors* (7231) and *Tool and Die Makers* (7232).

Profile Summary

APTITUDES

G	V	N	S	P	Q	K	F	M
3	3	4	3	3	3	3	3	3

INTERESTS
Dio

DATA PEOPLE THINGS (DPT)
130

PHYSICAL ACTIVITIES (PA)

V	C	H	B	L	S
3	0	2	3	1	2

ENVIRONMENTAL CONDITIONS (EC)
L1, D1

EDUCATION/TRAINING
5+, R

Examples of Job Titles

Foreman/woman, Automotive Machine Shop

Foreman/woman, Machinists

Foreman/woman, Maintenance Machine Shop

Foreman/woman, Tool and Die Makers

Supervisor, Machine Shop

Supervisor, Machinists

Supervisor, Metal Mould and Patternmakers

Supervisor, Tool and Die Makers

Descriptor Profile

Main Characteristics

Occupations in this group are characterized by the following aptitudes, interests and worker functions as they relate to main duties:

- **General learning ability** to establish methods to meet work schedules and co-ordinate activities with other departments, and to recommend measures for improved productivity

- **Verbal ability** to recommend personnel actions, such as hirings and promotions, and to train and arrange for training of workers

- **Clerical perception** to prepare production and other reports and to requisition materials and supplies

- **Directive interest** in **supervising** activities of workers who machine metal into parts, products, tools and dies and moulds with precise dimensions; and in ensuring that standards for safe working conditions are observed; may also supervise activities of related apprentices, helpers and labourers

- **Innovative interest** in **co-ordinating** and scheduling the activities of workers; and in resolving work problems

- **Objective interest** in **setting up** machines and equipment

7211

Physical Activities

Vision
   3 Near and far vision

Colour Discrimination
   0 Not relevant

Hearing
   2 Verbal interaction

Body Position
   3 Sitting, standing, walking

Limb Co-ordination
   1 Upper limb co-ordination

Strength
   2 Light

Environmental Conditions

Location
   L1 Regulated inside climate

Discomforts
   D1 Noise

Employment Requirements

Education/Training
   5+, R

- Completion of secondary school is usually required.

- Several years of experience as a qualified machinist or tool and die maker are required.

- Trade certification in machining or tool and die making is required.

Workplaces/Employers

Machine shops

Metal products manufacturing companies

7212 Contractors and Supervisors, Electrical Trades and Telecommunications Occupations

Contractors in this group include telecommunication and electrical trade contractors who own and operate their own businesses. Supervisors in this group direct and co-ordinate the activities of workers classified in the following groups: *Electricians* (7241), *Industrial Electricians* (7242), *Power System Electricians* (7243), *Electrical Power Line and Cable Workers* (7244), *Telecommunications Line and Cable Workers* (7245), *Telecommunications Installation and Repair Workers* (7246) and *Cable Television Service and Maintenance Technicians* (7247).

Profile Summary

APTITUDES

G	V	N	S	P	Q	K	F	M
3	3	3	3	3	3	3	4	3

INTERESTS
Dio

DATA PEOPLE THINGS (DPT)
138

PHYSICAL ACTIVITIES (PA)

V	C	H	B	L	S
3	1	2	3	0	1

ENVIRONMENTAL CONDITIONS (EC)
L1, L3

EDUCATION/TRAINING
5+, R

Examples of Job Titles

Electrical Contractor

Foreman/woman, Cablevision Technicians

Foreman/woman, Construction Electricians

Foreman/woman, Industrial Electricians

Foreman/woman, Power Line and Cable Workers

Foreman/woman, Power System Electricians

Foreman/woman, Telecommunications Installation and Repair Workers

Supervisor, Cable Maintenance and Repair

Supervisor, Plant Electricians

Supervisor, Residential Electricians

Descriptor Profile

Main Characteristics

Occupations in this group are characterized by the following aptitudes, interests and worker functions as they relate to main duties:

- **General learning ability** to establish methods to meet work schedules and co-ordinate activities with other subcontractors and departments, and to recommend measures for improved productivity; may manage the operations of own company

- **Verbal ability** to recommend personnel actions, such as hirings and promotions, and to train and arrange for training of workers

- **Clerical perception** to prepare progress reports and requisition materials and supplies

- **Directive interest** in **supervising** the activities of workers who install, repair and maintain electrical wiring, fixtures and control devices, power systems, telecommunication systems and cablevision systems; and in ensuring that standards for safe working conditions are observed; may supervise activities of related workers

- **Innovative interest** in **co-ordinating** and scheduling the activities of workers; and in resolving problems; may co-ordinate and schedule activities of apprentices, helpers and labourers

- **Objective interest** in understanding the functioning of equipment and machinery and the production procedures used in electrical trades and telecommunications

7212

Physical Activities

Vision
   3 Near and far vision

Colour Discrimination
   1 Relevant

Hearing
   2 Verbal interaction

Body Positionl
   3 Sitting, standing, walking

Limb Co-ordination
   0 Not relevant

Strength
   1 Limited

Environmental Conditions

Location
   L1 Regulated inside climate
   L3 Outside

Employment Requirements

Education/Training
   5+, R

- Completion of secondary school is usually required.

- Several years of experience as a qualified tradesperson in a relevant trade are required.

- Journeyman/woman trade certification in a relevant trade is required.

Workplaces/Employers

For workplaces/employers, refer to individual groups supervised

Self-employment

Occupational Options

There is some mobility among jobs within a specific trade; however, there is little or no inter-trade mobility.

7213 Contractors and Supervisors, Pipefitting Trades

Contractors in this group include plumbing and other pipefitting trade contractors who own and operate their own businesses. Supervisors in this group direct and co-ordinate the activities of workers classified in the following groups: *Plumbers (7251), Steamfitters, Pipefitters and Sprinkler System Installers (7252)* and *Gas Fitters (7253)*.

Profile Summary

APTITUDES

G	V	N	S	P	Q	K	F	M
3	3	3	3	3	3	3	4	3

INTERESTS
Dio

DATA PEOPLE THINGS (DPT)
138

PHYSICAL ACTIVITIES (PA)

V	C	H	B	L	S
3	0	2	3	0	1

ENVIRONMENTAL CONDITIONS (EC)
L1, H3

EDUCATION/TRAINING
5+, R

Examples of Job Titles

Contractor, Pipefitting
Contractor, Plumbing
Foreman/woman, Gas Fitters
Foreman/woman, Pipefitters
Foreman/woman, Plumbers
Foreman/woman, Sprinkler System Installers
Foreman/woman, Steamfitters
Supervisor, Gas Fitters
Supervisor, Plumbers
Supervisor, Steamfitters

Descriptor Profile

Main Characteristics

Occupations in this group are characterized by the following aptitudes, interests and worker functions as they relate to main duties:

- **General learning ability** to establish methods to meet work schedules and co-ordinate activities with other departments, and to recommend measures for improved productivity; may manage the operations of own company

- **Verbal ability** to recommend personnel actions, such as hirings and promotions, and to train and arrange for training of workers

- **Clerical perception** to requisition materials and supplies, and to prepare schedules and other reports

- **Directive interest** in supervising the activities of workers who install, repair and maintain piping systems used for the transmission of steam, heat, water, oil and other liquids and gases in residential, commercial, industrial and other installations; and in ensuring that standards for safe working conditions are observed; may supervise activities of related workers

- **Innovative interest** in co-ordinating and scheduling the activities of workers; and in resolving problems; may co-ordinate and schedule the activities of apprentices, helpers and labourers

- **Objective interest** in understanding the functioning of equipment and machinery used in the plumbing and pipefitting trades

7213

Physical Activities

Vision
   3 Near and far vision

Colour Discrimination
   0 Not relevant

Hearing
   2 Verbal interaction

Body Position
   3 Sitting, standing, walking

Limb Co-ordination
   0 Not relevant

Strength
   1 Limited

Environmental Conditions

Location
   L1 Regulated inside climate

Hazards
   H3 Equipment, machinery, tools

Employment Requirements

Education/Training
   5+, R

- Completion of secondary school is usually required.

- Several years of experience as a qualified tradesperson in a relevant trade are required.

- Journeyman/woman trade certification in a relevant trade is required.

Workplaces/Employers

Construction companies

Maintenance departments of industrial, commercial and manufacturing establishments

Plumbing and pipefitting trade contractors

Self-employment

Occupational Options

There is little or no inter-trade mobility among supervisors in this group.

7214 Contractors and Supervisors, Metal Forming, Shaping and Erecting Occupations

Contractors in this group include sheet-metal, ironwork, welding and boilermaking trade contractors who own and operate their own businesses. Supervisors in this group direct and co-ordinate the activities of workers classified in the following groups: *Sheet Metal Workers* (7261), *Boilermakers* (7262), *Structural Metal and Platework Fabricators and Fitters* (7263), *Ironworkers* (7264), *Welders* (7265) and *Blacksmiths and Die Setters* (7266).

Profile Summary

APTITUDES

G	V	N	S	P	Q	K	F	M
3	3	3	3	3	3	3	4	3

INTERESTS
Dio

DATA PEOPLE THINGS (DPT)
130

PHYSICAL ACTIVITIES (PA)

V	C	H	B	L	S
3	0	2	3	1	2

ENVIRONMENTAL CONDITIONS (EC)
L1, D1

EDUCATION/TRAINING
5+, R

Examples of Job Titles

Contractor, Ironwork
Foreman/woman, Blacksmiths
Foreman/woman, Boilermakers
Foreman/woman, Ironworkers
Supervisor, Boilermakers
Supervisor, Sheet-Metal Workers
Supervisor, Structural Metal Fitters
Supervisor, Welders

Descriptor Profile

Main Characteristics

Occupations in this group are characterized by the following aptitudes, interests and worker functions as they relate to main duties:

- **General learning ability** to establish methods to meet work schedules and co-ordinate activities with other departments, and to recommend measures for improved productivity; may manage operations of own company

- **Verbal ability** to recommend personnel actions, such as hirings and promotions, and to train and arrange for training of workers

- **Clerical perception** to requisition materials and supplies, and to prepare production and other reports

- **Directive interest** in **supervising** the activities of workers who shape, form and join metal parts and products to specified dimensions and erect light and heavy metal products and structures; and in ensuring that standards for safe working conditions are observed; may also supervise activities of related workers

- **Innovative interest** in **co-ordinating** and scheduling activities of workers; and in resolving problems; may co-ordinate and schedule activities of apprentices, machine operators, helpers and labourers

- **Objective interest** in **setting up** machines and equipment

7214

Physical Activities

Vision
   3 Near and far vision

Colour Discrimination
   0 Not relevant

Hearing
   2 Verbal interaction

Body Position
   3 Sitting, standing, walking

Limb Co-ordination
   1 Upper limb co-ordination

Strength
   2 Light

Environmental Conditions

Location
   L1 Regulated inside climate

Discomforts
   D1 Noise

Employment Requirements

Education/Training
   5+, R

- Completion of secondary school is usually required.

- Several years of experience as a qualified tradesperson in a relevant trade are required.

- Journeyman/woman trade certification in a relevant trade is required.

Workplaces/Employers

Structural, platework and related metal-products fabrication, manufacturing and erecting companies

Self-employment

Occupational Options

There is little or no inter-trade mobility among the supervisors in this group.

7215 Contractors and Supervisors, Carpentry Trades

Contractors in this group include carpentry trade contractors who own and operate their own businesses. Supervisors in this group direct and co-ordinate the activities of carpenters.

Profile Summary

APTITUDES

G	V	N	S	P	Q	K	F	M
3	3	3	3	3	3	3	4	3

INTERESTS
Dio

DATA PEOPLE THINGS (DPT)
138

PHYSICAL ACTIVITIES (PA)

V	C	H	B	L	S
3	0	2	3	0	1

ENVIRONMENTAL CONDITIONS (EC)
L1, L2, L3, D1

EDUCATION/TRAINING
5+, R

Examples of Job Titles

Carpenter Supervisor
Carpentry Contractor
Foreman/woman, Finish Carpenters
Foreman/woman, Framers
Foreman/woman, Form Builders
Foreman/woman, Maintenance Carpenters
Supervisor, Carpenters

Descriptor Profile

Main Characteristics

Occupations in this group are characterized by the following aptitudes, interests and worker functions as they relate to main duties:

- **General learning ability** to establish methods to meet work schedules and co-ordinate activities with other departments, and to recommend measures for improved productivity; may manage the operations of own company

- **Verbal ability** to recommend personnel actions such as hirings and promotions, and to train and arrange for training of workers

- **Clerical perception** to requisition materials and supplies, and to prepare schedules and other reports

- **Directive interest** in **supervising** the activities of carpenters who construct, renovate and maintain structures of wood and other building materials and who build and install interior finishing in residential, commercial and industrial buildings; and in ensuring that standards for safe working conditions are observed; may supervise related workers

- **Innovative interest** in **co-ordinating** and scheduling the activities of carpenters; and in resolving problems; may co-ordinate and schedule the activities of apprentices, helpers and labourers

- **Objective interest** in understanding the functioning of equipment and machinery and production procedures used in carpentry

7215

Physical Activities

Vision
   3 Near and far vision

Colour Discrimination
   0 Not relevant

Hearing
   2 Verbal interaction

Body Position
   3 Sitting, standing, walking

Limb Co-ordination
   0 Not relevant

Strength
   1 Limited

Environmental Conditions

Location
   L1 Regulated inside climate
   L2 Unregulated inside climate
   L3 Outside

Discomforts
   D1 Noise

Employment Requirements

Education/Training
   5+, R

- Completion of secondary school is usually required.

- Several years of experience as a qualified carpenter are usually required.

- Journeyman/woman trade certification as a carpenter is usually required.

Workplaces/Employers

Carpentry contractors

Construction companies

Self-employment

Similar Occupations Classified Elsewhere

Construction Managers (0711)

Residential Home Builders and Renovators (0712)

Supervisors of cabinetmakers (in 9224 *Supervisors, Furniture and Fixtures Manufacturing*)

7216 Contractors and Supervisors, Mechanic Trades

Contractors in this group include heating, refrigeration, air-conditioning, millwrighting and elevator-installation trade contractors who own and operate their own businesses. Supervisors in this group direct and co-ordinate the activities of workers classified in groups within the following minor groups: *Machinery and Transportation Equipment Mechanics (Except Motor Vehicle)* (731), *Motor Vehicle Mechanics* (732) and *Other Mechanics* (733).

Profile Summary

APTITUDES

G	V	N	S	P	Q	K	F	M
3	3	3	3	3	3	3	4	3

INTERESTS
Dio

DATA PEOPLE THINGS (DPT)
138

PHYSICAL ACTIVITIES (PA)

V	C	H	B	L	S
3	0	2	3	0	1

ENVIRONMENTAL CONDITIONS (EC)
L1

EDUCATION/TRAINING
5+, R

Examples of Job Titles

Contractor, Heating Systems

Foreman/woman, Air-Conditioning and Refrigeration Mechanics

Foreman/woman, Aircraft Mechanics and Inspectors

Foreman/woman, Electrical Mechanics

Foreman/woman, Heating Systems Mechanics

Foreman/woman, Heavy-Duty Equipment Mechanics

Foreman/woman, Printing Machine Repairers

Foreman/woman, Railway Car Repairers

Foreman/woman, Railway Equipment Maintenance Inspectors

Foreman/woman, Textile Mechanics

Supervisor, Aircraft Maintenance Mechanics

Supervisor, Appliance Repair Shop

Supervisor, Industrial Mechanics

Supervisor, Motor Vehicle Repair Shop

Supervisor, Small-Engine Repair Shop

Descriptor Profile

Main Characteristics

Occupations in this group are characterized by the following aptitudes, interests and worker functions as they relate to main duties:

- **General learning ability** to establish methods to meet work schedules and co-ordinate activities with other departments, and to recommend measures for improved productivity; may manage the operations of own company

- **Verbal ability** to recommend personnel actions, such as hiring and promotions, and to train and arrange for training of workers

- **Clerical perception** to prepare production and other reports, and to requisition materials and supplies

- **Directive interest** in **supervising** the activities of workers who repair and maintain aircraft, railway locomotives and cars, industrial machinery and equipment, construction and other heavy equipment, textile equipment, printing machines, transformers and other electrical equipment, motor vehicles, air-conditioning and refrigeration equipment, electric appliances and other equipment such as motorcycles, outboard motors and snowmobiles; and in ensuring that standards for safe working conditions are observed; may supervise the activities of related workers

- **Innovative interest** in **co-ordinating** and scheduling the activities of workers in the mechanical trades; and in resolving problems; may co-ordinate and schedule the activities of apprentices, helpers and labourers

7216

- Objective interest in understanding the functioning of equipment and machinery and production procedures used in mechanical trades

Physical Activities

Vision
   3 Near and far vision

Colour Discrimination
   0 Not relevant

Hearing
   2 Verbal interaction

Body Position
   3 Sitting, standing, walking

Limb Co-ordination
   0 Not relevant

Strength
   1 Limited

Environmental Conditions

Location
   L1 Regulated inside climate

Employment Requirements

Education/Training
   5+, R

- Completion of secondary school is usually required.

- Several years of experience as a qualified tradesperson in a relevant trade are usually required.

- Provincial trade certification in a relevant trade is required.

Workplaces/Employers

For workplaces/employers, refer to individual groups supervised

Self-employment

Occupational Options

There is little or no inter-trade job mobility among the supervisors classified in this group.

7217 Contractors and Supervisors, Heavy Construction Equipment Crews

Contractors in this group include excavating, grading, paving, drilling and blasting contractors who own and operate their own businesses. Supervisors in this group direct and co-ordinate the activities of workers classified in the following groups: *Crane Operators* (7371), *Drillers and Blasters - Surface Mining, Quarrying and Construction* (7372), *Heavy Equipment Operators (Except Crane)* (7421), *Longshore Workers* (7451), *Public Works Maintenance Equipment Operators* (7422), *Railway Track Maintenance Workers* (7432) and *Water Well Drillers* (7373).

Profile Summary

APTITUDES

G	V	N	S	P	Q	K	F	M
3	3	3	3	3	3	3	4	3

INTERESTS
Dio

DATA PEOPLE THINGS (DPT)
138

PHYSICAL ACTIVITIES (PA)

V	C	H	B	L	S
3	0	2	3	0	1

ENVIRONMENTAL CONDITIONS (EC)
L1, L3, H8, D1, D4

EDUCATION/TRAINING
2+, 5+, R

Examples of Job Titles

Excavating Contractor
Foreman/woman, Demolition
Foreman/woman, Drilling and Blasting Construction
Foreman/woman, Logging Road Construction
Foreman/woman, Railway Gang
Foreman/woman, Railway Track Maintenance
Paving Contractor
Pipeline Construction Supervisor
Road Maintenance Foreman/woman
Section Foreman/woman, Railway
Supervisor, Heavy Equipment Operators
Supervisor, Oilfield Construction
Supervisor, Water Well Drilling
Track Foreman/woman, Railway

Descriptor Profile

Main Characteristics

Occupations in this group are characterized by the following aptitudes, interests and worker functions as they relate to main duties:

- **General learning ability** to establish methods to meet work schedules and co-ordinate activities with other project supervisors and managers, and to recommend measures for improved productivity; may manage the operations of own company

- **Verbal ability** to recommend personnel actions, such as hirings and promotions, and to train and arrange for training of workers

- **Clerical perception** to prepare production and other reports, and to requisition materials and supplies

- **Directive interest** in **supervising** the activities of workers who operate cranes and construction, paving, drilling, railway maintenance and other similar heavy equipment; may supervise activities of related workers

- **Innovative interest** in **co-ordinating** and scheduling the activities of workers on heavy construction equipment crews; and in resolving problems; may co-ordinate and schedule the activities of apprentices, helpers and labourers

- **Objective interest** in understanding the functioning of equipment and machinery and procedures used by heavy construction equipment crews

7217

Physical Activities

Vision
   3 Near and far vision

Colour Discrimination
   0 Not relevant

Hearing
   2 Verbal interaction

Body Position
   3 Sitting, standing, walking

Limb Co-ordination
   0 Not relevant

Strength
   1 Limited

Environmental Conditions

Location
   L1 Regulated inside climate
   L3 Outside

Hazards
   H8 Dangerous locations

Discomforts
   D1 Noise
   D4 Non-toxic dusts

Employment Requirements

Education/Training
2+, 5+, R

- Completion of secondary school may be required.

- Several years of experience in the occupation supervised is required.

- Provincial trade certification in a relevant trade may be required.

Workplaces/Employers

For workplaces/employers, refer to individual groups supervised

Self-employment

Occupational Options

There is some mobility between occupations classified in this group.

Similar Occupations Classified Elsewhere

Supervisors of heavy equipment mechanics (in 7216 *Contractors and Supervisors, Mechanic Trades*)

Supervisors of logging machinery operators (in 8211 *Supervisors, Logging and Forestry*)

7218 Supervisors, Printing and Related Occupations

Supervisors in this group direct and co-ordinate the activities of workers who produce camera work, printing plates and cylinders, process film, print text and illustrations on paper, metal and other material, and bind and finish printed products.

Profile Summary

APTITUDES
G	V	N	S	P	Q	K	F	M
3	3	4	3	3	3	3	3	3

INTERESTS
Dio

DATA PEOPLE THINGS (DPT)
138

PHYSICAL ACTIVITIES (PA)
V	C	H	B	L	S
3	1	2	3	0	1

ENVIRONMENTAL CONDITIONS (EC)
L1

EDUCATION/TRAINING
4+, 5+, 6+, R

Examples of Job Titles

- Bindery Foreman/woman - Printing
- Bindery Supervisor - Printing
- Composing Room Supervisor - Printing
- Film Processing Supervisor
- Finishing Supervisor - Printing
- Foreman/woman, Photographic and Film Processing
- Platemaking Supervisor - Printing
- Preparatory Supervisor - Printing
- Pre-Press Supervisor - Printing
- Pressroom Supervisor - Printing
- Printing Supervisor

Descriptor Profile

Main Characteristics

Occupations in this group are characterized by the following aptitudes, interests and worker functions as they relate to main duties:

- **General learning ability** to establish methods to meet work schedules and co-ordinate activities with other departments, and to recommend measures for improved productivity and product quality

- **Verbal ability** to recommend personnel actions, such as hirings and promotions, and to train staff in job duties, safety procedures and company policies

- **Clerical perception** to prepare production and other reports, and to requisition materials and supplies

- **Directive interest** in **supervising** the activities of workers who produce camera work, printing plates and cylinders, process film and print, bind and finish books, newspapers, business forms and other printed products; and in reviewing job proofs and samples to ensure quality of work meets client specifications

- **Innovative interest** in **co-ordinating** and scheduling the activities of workers involved in printing and related occupations; and in resolving problems

- **Objective interest** in providing technical advice and hands-on training to staff; may set up machines and equipment

7218

Physical Activities

Vision
   3 Near and far vision

Colour Discrimination
   1 Relevant

Hearing
   2 Verbal interaction

Body Position
   3 Sitting, standing, walking

Limb Co-ordination
   0 Not relevant

Strength
   1 Limited

Environmental Conditions

Location
   L1 Regulated inside climate

Employment Requirements

Education/Training
4+, 5+, 6+, R

- Completion of secondary school is required.

- Completion of a college program in graphic arts technology may be required.

- Several years of experience in the work area supervised is usually required.

- Provincial trade certification may be required for some occupations in this group.

Workplaces/Employers

Commercial printing companies

In-house printing departments of public- and private-sector establishments

Magazines

Newspapers

Publishing companies

Occupational Options

Progression to management positions, such as department, production or plant manager, is possible with experience.

Similar Occupations Classified Elsewhere

Supervisors of typesetters (in 1211 *Supervisors, General Office and Administrative Support Clerks*)

Printing plant, department and production managers (in 0911 *Manufacturing Managers*)

7219 Contractors and Supervisors, Other Construction Trades, Installers, Repairers and Servicers

Contractors in this group include roofing, masonry, painting and other construction trade contractors, not elsewhere classified, who own and operate their own businesses. Supervisors in this group direct and co-ordinate the activities of tradespersons, installers, repairers and servicers classified in the following minor groups: *Masonry and Plastering Trades* (728), *Other Construction Trades* (729) and *Other Installers, Repairers and Servicers* (744). This group also includes prefabricated product installation and service contractors and proprietors of some repair and service establishments.

Profile Summary

APTITUDES

G	V	N	S	P	Q	K	F	M
3	3	3	3	3	3	3	4	3

INTERESTS
Dio

DATA PEOPLE THINGS (DPT)
138

PHYSICAL ACTIVITIES (PA)

V	C	H	B	L	S
3	1	2	3	1	1

ENVIRONMENTAL CONDITIONS (EC)
L1, L3

EDUCATION/TRAINING
4+, 5+, R

Examples of Job Titles

Bricklaying Contractor
Cement Finishing Contractor
Foreman/woman, Glaziers
Foreman/woman, Insulators
Foreman/woman, Plasterers
Painting Contractor
Pest Control Supervisor
Roofing Contractor
Supervisor, Bicycle Repair Shop
Supervisor, Painters and Decorators
Supervisor, Tilesetters

Descriptor Profile

Main Characteristics

Occupations in this group are characterized by the following aptitudes, interests and worker functions as they relate to main duties:

- **General learning ability** to establish methods to meet work schedules and co-ordinate activities with other subcontractors, and to recommend measures for improved productivity and product quality; may manage the operations of own company

- **Verbal ability** to recommend personnel actions such as hirings and promotions, and to conduct staff training

- **Clerical perception** to prepare work progress reports and requisition materials and supplies

- **Directive interest** in **supervising** the activities of construction workers engaged in bricklaying, roofing, cement finishing, tilesetting, plastering, drywall installation, glazing, insulating and painting, workers who install and service prefabricated products in residential and commercial properties, and workers who repair a wide variety of products such as musical instruments, sports equipment, vending machines, bicycles and cameras; may supervise the activities of related workers

- **Innovative interest** in **co-ordinating** and scheduling the activities of workers in construction trades, installers, repairers and servicers; and in resolving problems; may co-ordinate and schedule the activities of apprentices, helpers and labourers

- **Objective interest** in training workers in duties, safety procedures and company policies

7219

Physical Activities

Vision
  3 Near and far vision

Colour Discrimination
  1 Relevant

Hearing
  2 Verbal interaction

Body Position
  3 Sitting, standing, walking

Limb Co-ordination
  1 Upper limb co-ordination

Strength
  1 Limited

Environmental Conditions

Location
  L1 Regulated inside climate
  L3 Outside

Employment Requirements

Education/Training
  4+, 5+, R

- Completion of secondary school is usually required.

- Several years of experience in the trade or in the work area supervised are usually required.

- Provincial trade certification may be required for some occupations in this group.

Workplaces/Employers

For workplaces/employers, refer to individual groups supervised

Occupational Options

There is little or no mobility among supervisors in this group.

Similar Occupations Classified Elsewhere

Contractors and Supervisors, Carpentry Trades (7215)

Contractors and Supervisors, Pipefitting Trades (7213)

Electrical contractors and supervisors of electricians (in 7212 *Contractors and Supervisors, Electrical Trades and Telecommunications Occupations*)

Ironwork contractors and supervisors of ironworkers (in 7214 *Contractors and Supervisors, Metal Forming, Shaping and Erecting Trades*)

7221 Supervisors, Railway Transport Operations

Supervisors in this group direct and co-ordinate the activities of railway and yard locomotive engineers, railway yard workers and railway labourers.

Profile Summary

APTITUDES

G	V	N	S	P	Q	K	F	M
3	3	4	3	3	3	4	4	3

INTERESTS
DMi

DATA PEOPLE THINGS (DPT)
138

PHYSICAL ACTIVITIES (PA)

V	C	H	B	L	S
3	0	2	3	1	1

ENVIRONMENTAL CONDITIONS (EC)
L1

EDUCATION/TRAINING
4+, R

Examples of Job Titles

Railway Transport Operations Supervisor
Road Foreman/woman, Freight Train
Stationmaster
Trainmaster
Yard Foreman/woman, Railway
Yardmaster, Railway

Descriptor Profile

Main Characteristics

Occupations in this group are characterized by the following aptitudes, interests and worker functions as they relate to main duties:

- **General learning ability** to establish methods to meet work schedules and co-ordinate activities with other units, and to recommend measures for improved performance

- **Verbal ability** to recommend personnel actions such as hirings and promotions, and to conduct staff training

- **Clerical perception** to prepare reports and requisition materials and supplies

- **Directive interest** in supervising the activities of workers who operate trains, drive locomotives in railway yards and perform other duties related to railway operations

- **Methodical interest** in training staff in duties, safety procedures and company policies

- **Innovative interest** in co-ordinating and scheduling the activities of workers in railway transport operations; and in resolving problems

7221

Physical Activities

Vision
  3 Near and far vision

Colour Discrimination
  0 Not relevant

Hearing
  2 Verbal interaction

Body Position
  3 Sitting, standing, walking

Limb Co-ordination
  1 Upper limb co-ordination

Strength
  1 Limited

Environmental Conditions

Location
  L1 Regulated inside climate

Employment Requirements

Education/Training
  4+, R

- Completion of secondary school is usually required.

- Several years of railway operations experience are required.

- Level A Certificate of the Canadian Rail Operating Rules is required.

- Certification in Qualification Standards for Operating Crews is required.

Workplaces/Employers

Railway transport companies

Similar Occupations Classified Elsewhere

Supervisors of locomotive mechanics (in 7216 *Contractors and Supervisors, Mechanic Trades*)

Supervisors of railway track maintenance crews (in 7217 *Contractors and Supervisors, Heavy Construction Equipment Crews*)

7222 Supervisors, Motor Transport and Other Ground Transit Operators

Supervisors in this group direct and co-ordinate activities of truck drivers, bus drivers, delivery drivers, subway and other transit operators, chauffeurs and taxi and limousine drivers. This group also includes bus dispatchers who co-ordinate the activities of transit system bus drivers and subway traffic controllers who operate and monitor signal and track switch-control panels.

Profile Summary

APTITUDES

G	V	N	S	P	Q	K	F	M
3	3	4	3	4	3	3	4	3

INTERESTS
DMi

DATA PEOPLE THINGS (DPT)
138

PHYSICAL ACTIVITIES (PA)

V	C	H	B	L	S
2	0	2	1	1	1

ENVIRONMENTAL CONDITIONS (EC)
L1, L3

EDUCATION/TRAINING
4+

Examples of Job Titles

Bus Inspector
Dispatcher, Bus
Foreman/woman, Truck Drivers
Foreman/woman, Urban Transit System
Mobile Inspector, Transit
Subway Traffic Controller
Supervisor, Light Rail Transit Operators
Supervisor, School Bus Drivers
Supervisor, Subway Operators

Descriptor Profile

Main Characteristics

Occupations in this group are characterized by the following aptitudes, interests and worker functions as they relate to main duties:

- **General learning ability** to establish methods to meet work schedules and co-ordinate activities with other units, and to recommend measures for improved performance

- **Verbal ability** to recommend personnel actions such as hirings and promotions, and to train staff in duties, safety procedures and company policies

- **Spatial perception** and **finger and manual dexterity** to operate signal and track switch-control panels of subway systems

- **Clerical perception** to prepare reports and requisition materials and supplies

- **Directive interest** in **supervising** the activities of workers who operate trucks, buses, subway trains, light rail transit, taxicabs and other transport vehicles; and in dispatching bus drivers, monitoring routes to ensure schedules are met and resolving operating problems

- **Methodical interest** in monitoring routes, signal and track switch control panels

- **Innovative interest** in **co-ordinating** and scheduling the activities of workers in motor transport and other ground transit operations; and in resolving work problems

7222

Physical Activities

Vision
   2 Near vision

Colour Discrimination
   0 Not relevant

Hearing
   2 Verbal interaction

Body Position
   1 Sitting

Limb Co-ordination
   1 Upper limb co-ordination

Strength
   1 Limited

Environmental Conditions

Location
   L1 Regulated inside climate
   L3 Outside

Employment Requirements

Education/Training
   4+

- Completion of secondary school is usually required.

- Several years of experience as a driver or operator of motor transport or ground transit equipment are usually required.

Workplaces/Employers

Government departments

Ground transit companies

Motor transportation companies

Occupational Options

There is little mobility among occupations in the different transportation sectors of this group.

Similar Occupations Classified Elsewhere

Supervisors, Railway Transport Operations (7221)

Train dispatchers (in 2275 *Railway and Marine Traffic Controllers*)

Truck transport and taxi dispatchers (in 1475 *Dispatchers and Radio Operators*)

7231.1 Machinists

Machinists set up and operate a variety of machine tools to cut and grind metal and similar materials into parts and products with precise dimensions. Apprentices are included in this group.

Profile Summary

APTITUDES

G	V	N	S	P	Q	K	F	M
3	3	3	2	2	4	3	2	2

INTERESTS
OIM

DATA PEOPLE THINGS (DPT)
380

PHYSICAL ACTIVITIES (PA)

V	C	H	B	L	S
1	0	1	4	1	3

ENVIRONMENTAL CONDITIONS (EC)
L1, H3, H6, D1

EDUCATION/TRAINING
5, R

Examples of Job Titles

Automotive Machinist
General Machinist
Machine Tool Set-Up Operator
Machinist
Machinist Apprentice
Maintenance Machinist

Descriptor Profile

Main Characteristics

Occupations in this group are characterized by the following aptitudes, interests and worker functions as they relate to main duties:

- **General learning ability** to set up and operate a variety of machine tools including computer numerically controlled tools for precision machining operations

- **Numerical ability** to compute dimensions and tolerances, and to measure and lay out work pieces

- **Spatial** and **form perception** to read and interpret blueprints, charts and tables and to study sample parts in order to determine necessary machining operations

- **Finger** and **manual dexterity** to fit and assemble machined metal parts and subassemblies using hand and power tools

- **Objective interest** in **setting up** and adjusting machine tools for use by machining tool operators

- **Innovative interest** in performing precision machining operations such as turning, milling, boring, planing, drilling, precision grinding and other operations

- **Methodical interest** in **compiling** information to verify dimensions of products for accuracy and conformance to specifications using precision measuring instruments

7231.1
Subgroup 1 of 2

Physical Activities

Vision
1 Close visual acuity

Colour Discrimination
0 Not relevant

Hearing
1 Limited

Body Position
4 Other body positions

Limb Co-ordination
1 Upper limb co-ordination

Strength
3 Medium

Environmental Conditions

Location
L1 Regulated inside climate

Hazards
H3 Equipment, machinery, tools
H6 Flying particles, falling objects

Discomforts
D1 Noise

Employment Requirements

Education/Training
5, R

- Some secondary school education is required.

- Completion of a four-year apprenticeship program
or
a combination of over four years of work experience in the trade and some college or industry courses in machining is usually required to be eligible for trade certification.

- Trade certification is available, but not compulsory, in all provinces and territories except Quebec.

- Interprovincial trade certification (Red Seal) is also available to qualified machinists.

Workplaces/Employers

Machine shops

Machinery, equipment, motor vehicle, automotive parts, aircraft and other metal-products manufacturing companies

Occupational Options

Red Seal certification allows for interprovincial mobility.

Progression to supervisory positions is possible with experience.

Similar Occupations Classified Elsewhere

Machining Tool Operators (9511)

Tool and Die Makers (7232)

Woodworking Machine Operators (9513)

Supervisors of machinists and machining and tooling inspectors (in 7214 *Contractors and Supervisors, Metal Forming, Shaping and Erecting Trades*)

7231.2 Machining and Tooling Inspectors

Machining and Tooling Inspectors examine machined parts and tooling to maintain quality control standards.

Profile Summary

APTITUDES

G	V	N	S	P	Q	K	F	M
3	3	3	3	2	3	3	3	3

INTERESTS
OMi

DATA PEOPLE THINGS (DPT)
381

PHYSICAL ACTIVITIES (PA)

V	C	H	B	L	S
2	0	1	3	1	2

ENVIRONMENTAL CONDITIONS (EC)
L1, D1

EDUCATION/TRAINING
5+, R

Examples of Job Titles

Machine Shop Inspector
Machined Parts Inspector
Machining Inspector
Tooling Inspector

Descriptor Profile

Main Characteristics

Occupations in this group are characterized by the following aptitudes, interests and worker functions as they relate to main duties:

- **General learning** and **verbal ability** to inspect machined parts and tooling, and to report deviations from specifications and tolerances to supervisor

- **Form perception** to notice physical defects such as wear, surface defects and warping, and to recognize finish and completeness when inspecting products, tools, parts, materials and assemblies

- **Clerical perception** to maintain inspection records and complete reports

- **Objective interest** in **precision working** to maintain and calibrate precision instruments such as dial indicators, fixed gauges, height gauges and other measuring devices

- **Methodical interest** in **compiling** information to verify dimensions of machined parts and tooling using micrometers, verners, callipers, height gauges, optical comparators and other specialized measuring instruments

- **Innovative interest** in repairing precision measuring instruments

7231.2
Subgroup 2 of 2

Physical Activities

Vision
2   Near vision

Colour Discrimination
0   Not relevant

Hearing
1   Limited

Body Position
3   Sitting, standing, walking

Limb Co-ordination
1   Upper limb co-ordination

Strength
2   Light

Environmental Conditions

Location
L1   Regulated inside climate

Discomforts
D1   Noise

Employment Requirements

Education/Training
5+, R

- Some secondary school education is required.

- Completion of a four-year apprenticeship program
  or
  a combination of over four years of work experience in the trade and some college or industry courses in machining is usually required to be eligible for trade certification.

- Trade certification is available, but not compulsory, in all provinces and territories except Quebec.

- Interprovincial trade certification (Red Seal) is also available to qualified machinists.

- Several years of experience as a machinist, tool and die maker or machining tool operator may be required for machining and tooling inspectors.

Workplaces/Employers

Machine shops

Machinery, equipment, motor vehicle, automotive parts, aircraft and other metal-products manufacturing companies

Occupational Options

Red Seal certification allows for interprovincial mobility.

Progression to supervisory positions is possible with experience.

Similar Occupations Classified Elsewhere

Machining Tool Operators (9511)

Tool and Die Makers (7232)

Woodworking Machine Operators (9513)

Supervisors of machinists and machining and tooling inspectors (in 7214 *Contractors and Supervisors, Metal Forming, Shaping and Erecting Trades*)

7232 Tool and Die Makers

Tool and Die Makers repair, modify and make custom-made, prototype and special tools, dies, jigs, fixtures and gauges that require precise dimensions. Patternmakers, metal mould makers and tool and die maker apprentices are included in this group.

Profile Summary

APTITUDES

G	V	N	S	P	Q	K	F	M
3	3	3	2	2	4	3	2	2

INTERESTS
OIM

DATA PEOPLE THINGS (DPT)
280

PHYSICAL ACTIVITIES (PA)

V	C	H	B	L	S
2	0	1	2	1	3

ENVIRONMENTAL CONDITIONS (EC)
L1, H3, H6, D1

EDUCATION/TRAINING
5, 6, R

Examples of Job Titles

Die Finisher
Die Maker
Jig Maker
Metal Mould Maker
Metal Patternmaker
Mould Maker - Plastics Processing
Tool and Die Maker
Tool and Die Maker Apprentice
Tool Maker

Descriptor Profile

Main Characteristics

Occupations in this group are characterized by the following aptitudes, interests and worker functions as they relate to main duties:

- **General learning ability** to operate machine tools to cut, turn, mill, plane, bore, grind and otherwise shape pieces to prescribed dimensions and finishes

- **Numerical ability** to compute dimensions and tolerances

- **Spatial** and **form perception** to read and interpret drawings and specifications of tools, dies, prototypes and models

- **Finger** and **manual dexterity** to position, secure, measure and work metal stock and castings to lay out for machining, as well as to fit and assemble parts using hand tools

- **Objective interest** in **setting up** machine tools to machine, fit and assemble casting and other parts to make metal patterns, core boxes, match plates, metal moulds for plastic injection moulding and other production processes

- **Innovative interest** in inspecting and testing completed tools, dies, jigs and fixtures for proper operation

- **Methodical interest** in **analyzing** information to verify machined parts for conformance to specifications using precision measuring instruments

7232

Physical Activities

Vision
  2 Near vision

Colour Discrimination
  0 Not relevant

Hearing
  1 Limited

Body Position
  2 Standing and/or walking

Limb Co-ordination
  1 Upper limb co-ordination

Strength
  3 Medium

Environmental Conditions

Location
  L1 Regulated inside climate

Hazards
  H3 Equipment, machinery, tools
  H6 Flying particles, falling objects

Discomforts
  D1 Noise

Employment Requirements

Education/Training
  5, 6, R

- Some secondary school education is required.

- Completion of a four-year tool-and-die-making apprenticeship program
  or
  a combination of over five years of work experience in the trade and some high school, college or industry courses in tool and die making is usually required to be eligible for trade certification.

- Mould makers may require completion of an apprenticeship or a college program in mouldmaking.

- Patternmakers may require completion of an apprenticeship or a college program in patternmaking.

- Tool and die making trade certification is available, but not compulsory, in Nova Scotia, Ontario, Manitoba and Alberta.

- Interprovincial trade certification (Red Seal) is also available to qualified tool and die makers.

- Mouldmaking and patternmaking trade certification is available, but not compulsory, in Ontario.

Workplaces/Employers

Manufacturing industries

Tool and die, mouldmaking and machine shops

Occupational Options

Red Seal trade certification allows for interprovincial mobility.

Progression to supervisory positions is possible with experience.

Similar Occupations Classified Elsewhere

Machinists and Machining and Tooling Inspectors (7231)

Supervisors of tool and die makers (in 7214 *Contractors and Supervisors, Metal Forming, Shaping and Erecting Trades*)

7241 Electricians (Except Industrial and Power System)

Electricians in this group lay out, assemble, install, test, troubleshoot and repair electrical wiring, fixtures, control devices and related equipment in buildings and other structures. Apprentices are included in this group.

Profile Summary

APTITUDES
G	V	N	S	P	Q	K	F	M
3	3	3	3	3	4	3	3	3

INTERESTS
Oim

DATA PEOPLE THINGS (DPT)
261

PHYSICAL ACTIVITIES (PA)
V	C	H	B	L	S
2	1	1	4	1	2

ENVIRONMENTAL CONDITIONS (EC)
L1, L2, H4

EDUCATION/TRAINING
5, R

Examples of Job Titles

Apprentice Electrician
Construction Electrician
Electrician

Descriptor Profile

Main Characteristics

Occupations in this group are characterized by the following aptitudes, interests and worker functions as they relate to main duties:

- **General learning ability** to determine wiring layouts for new and existing installations and to install, replace and repair lighting fixtures and electrical control and distribution equipment such as switches, relays and circuit breaker panels

- **Spatial** and **form perception** to read and interpret drawings and electrical code specifications

- **Motor co-ordination** to connect electrical power to sound and visual communication equipment, signalling devices and heating and cooling systems

- **Finger** and **manual dexterity** to pull wire through conduits and holes in walls and floors, and to splice, join and connect wire to fixtures and components to form circuits

- **Objective interest** in **precision working** to test continuity of circuits using test equipment to ensure compatibility and safety of a system, following installation, replacement and repair

- **Innovative interest** in **analyzing** to troubleshoot and isolate faults in electrical and electronic systems, and to remove and replace faulty components

- **Methodical interest** in **speaking - signalling** to conduct preventive maintenance programs and keep maintenance records

7241

Physical Activities

Vision
   2 Near vision

Colour Discrimination
   1 Relevant

Hearing
   1 Limited

Body Position
   4 Other body positions

Limb Co-ordination
   1 Upper limb co-ordination

Strength
   2 Light

Environmental Conditions

Location
   L1 Regulated inside climate
   L2 Unregulated inside climate

Hazards
   H4 Electricity

Employment Requirements

Education/Training
   5, R

- Some secondary school education is required.

- Completion of a four-to-five year apprenticeship program is usually required.

- Trade certification is compulsory in Nova Scotia, Prince Edward Island, New Brunswick, Quebec, Ontario, Manitoba, Saskatchewan and Alberta and available, but voluntary, in Newfoundland, British Columbia, the Northwest Territories and the Yukon.

- Interprovincial trade certification (Red Seal) is also available to qualified electricians.

Workplaces/Employers

Electrical contractors

Maintenance departments of buildings

Self-employment

Occupational Options

Red Seal trade certification allows for interprovincial mobility.

Progression to supervisory positions is possible with experience.

Similar Occupations Classified Elsewhere

Electrical Mechanics (7333)

Industrial Electricians (7242)

Power System Electricians (7243)

Supervisors of electricians (in 7212 *Contractors and Supervisors, Electrical Trades and Telecommunications Occupations*)

7242 Industrial Electricians

Industrial Electricians install, maintain, test, troubleshoot and repair industrial electrical equipment and associated electrical and electronic controls. Apprentices are included in this group.

Profile Summary

APTITUDES

G	V	N	S	P	Q	K	F	M
3	3	3	3	3	4	3	3	3

INTERESTS
Oim

DATA PEOPLE THINGS (DPT)
261

PHYSICAL ACTIVITIES (PA)

V	C	H	B	L	S
2	1	1	4	1	3

ENVIRONMENTAL CONDITIONS (EC)
L1, L2, H3, H4

EDUCATION/TRAINING
5, R

Examples of Job Titles

Electrician, Shipyard
Industrial Electrician
Marine Electrician
Mill Electrician
Mine Electrician
Plant Electrician
Plant Maintenance Electrician

Descriptor Profile

Main Characteristics

Occupations in this group are characterized by the following aptitudes, interests and worker functions as they relate to main duties:

- **General learning ability** to install, test, troubleshoot, maintain and repair electrical equipment and electronic controls

- **Spatial** and **form perception** to read and interpret drawings and electrical code specifications to determine layout of industrial electrical equipment installations

- **Motor co-ordination** to test electrical and electronic equipment and components for continuity, current, voltage and resistance

- **Finger** and **manual dexterity** to maintain, repair, test and install switchgears, transformers, switchboard meters, regulators, reactors, electrical motors, generators, industrial storage batteries, and hydraulic and pneumatic electrical control systems

- **Objective interest** in **precision working** to install, examine, replace and repair electrical wiring, receptacles, switch boxes, conduits, feeders, cable assemblies, lighting fixtures and other electrical components

- **Innovative interest** in **analyzing** to troubleshoot, maintain and repair industrial electrical and electronic control systems and devices

- **Methodical interest** in **speaking - signalling** to conduct preventive maintenance programs and keep maintenance records

7242

Physical Activities

Vision
  2   Near vision

Colour Discrimination
  1   Relevant

Hearing
  1   Limited

Body Position
  4   Other body positions

Limb Co-ordination
  1   Upper limb co-ordination

Strength
  3   Medium

Environmental Conditions

Location
  L1 Regulated inside climate
  L2 Unregulated inside climate

Hazards
  H3 Equipment, machinery, tools
  H4 Electricity

Employment Requirements

Education/Training
  5, R

- Some secondary school education is required.

- Completion of a four-year industrial electrician apprenticeship program
  or
  a combination of over five years of work experience in the trade and some high school, college or industry courses in industrial electrical equipment is usually required to be eligible for trade certification.

- Marine electricians in New Brunswick may require completion of a marine-electrician apprenticeship program.

- Mine electricians in Nova Scotia may require completion of a mine-electrician apprenticeship program.

- Trade certification is compulsory in Prince Edward Island and available, but voluntary, in Newfoundland, Nova Scotia, New Brunswick, Quebec, Ontario, Manitoba and the Yukon.

- Interprovincial trade certification (Red Seal) is also available to qualified industrial electricians.

Workplaces/Employers

Electrical contractors

Maintenance departments of factories, plants, mines, shipyards and other industrial companies

Occupational Options

Red Seal trade certification allows for interprovincial mobility.

Progression to supervisory positions is possible with experience.

Similar Occupations Classified Elsewhere

Power System Electricians (7243)

Construction electricians [in 7241 *Electricians (Except Industrial and Power System)*]

Supervisors of industrial electricians (in 7212 *Contractors and Supervisors, Electrical Trades and Telecommunications Occupations*)

7243 Power System Electricians

Power System Electricians install, maintain, test and repair equipment and apparatus for electric power distribution systems. Apprentices are included in this group.

Profile Summary

APTITUDES

G	V	N	S	P	Q	K	F	M
3	3	3	3	3	4	3	3	3

INTERESTS
Oim

DATA PEOPLE THINGS (DPT)
261

PHYSICAL ACTIVITIES (PA)

V	C	H	B	L	S
2	1	1	4	1	2

ENVIRONMENTAL CONDITIONS (EC)
L1, L3, H1, H4

EDUCATION/TRAINING
5, R

Examples of Job Titles

Apprentice Power System Electrician
Power Electrician
Power Station Electrician
Power System Electrician

Descriptor Profile

Main Characteristics

Occupations in this group are characterized by the following aptitudes, interests and worker functions as they relate to main duties:

- **General learning ability** to install and maintain electrical equipment and apparatus in generating stations and powerhouses

- **Clerical perception** to complete test and maintenance reports

- **Motor co-ordination** and **finger** and **manual dexterity** to use voltmeters, ammeters and other electrical test instruments and equipment

- **Objective interest** in **precision working** to inspect and test installed electrical equipment and apparatus to locate electrical faults

- **Innovative interest** in **analyzing** power systems to repair and replace faulty electrical equipment and apparatus

- **Methodical interest** in **speaking** with co-workers when installing and maintaining transformers, generators, voltage regulators and other electric power distribution equipment

7243

Physical Activities

Vision
 2 Near vision

Colour Discrimination
 1 Relevant

Hearing
 1 Limited

Body Position
 4 Other body positions

Limb Co-ordination
 1 Upper limb co-ordination

Strength
 2 Light

Environmental Conditions

Location
 L1 Regulated inside climate
 L3 Outside

Hazards
 H1 Dangerous chemical substances
 H4 Electricity

Employment Requirements

Education/Training
 5, R

- Completion of secondary school is usually required.

- Completion of a four-year apprenticeship program for power system electricians
 or
 a combination of up to four years of work experience in the trade and some college or industry courses in electrical technology is usually required.

- Trade certification is available, but not mandatory, in Manitoba and Alberta.

Workplaces/Employers

Electric power generation, transmission and distribution companies

Similar Occupations Classified Elsewhere

Electrical Mechanics (7333)

Electricians (Except Industrial and Power System) (7241)

Industrial Electricians (7242)

Supervisors of power system electricians (in 7212 Contractors and Supervisors, Electrical Trades and Telecommunications Occupations)

7244 Electrical Power Line and Cable Workers

Electrical Power Line and Cable Workers construct, maintain and repair overhead and underground electric power transmission and distribution systems. Apprentices are included in this group.

Profile Summary

APTITUDES

G	V	N	S	P	Q	K	F	M
3	3	4	3	3	4	2	3	3

INTERESTS
Oim

DATA PEOPLE THINGS (DPT)
361

PHYSICAL ACTIVITIES (PA)

V	C	H	B	L	S
3	1	1	4	2	3

ENVIRONMENTAL CONDITIONS (EC)
L3, H3, H4, H8

EDUCATION/TRAINING
5, R

Examples of Job Titles

Apprentice Lineman/woman, Electrical Power Line

Cable Installer, Electrical Power

Cable Splicer, Electrical Power

Construction Lineman/woman, Electrical Power Line

Power Line Patroller

Power Lineman/woman

Descriptor Profile

Main Characteristics

Occupations in this group are characterized by the following aptitudes, interests and worker functions as they relate to main duties:

- **General learning ability** to construct, install, maintain and repair electric distribution and transmission systems including overhead and underground power lines and cables, insulators, conductors, lightning arrestors, switches, transformers and other associated equipment

- **Verbal ability** to communicate with other workers to co-ordinate the preparation and completion of assignments

- **Spatial** and **form perception** to erect and maintain steel, wood and concrete poles, towers and guy wires

- **Motor co-ordination** to climb ladders and operate hydraulic buckets when working aloft on poles and towers, and to work in confined spaces such as trenches and tunnels when installing power lines, cables and associated equipment

- **Objective interest** in **precision working** to splice, solder and insulate conductors and related wiring in order to connect power distribution and transmission networks using splicing tools, related electrical equipment and tools

- **Innovative interest** in **speaking** with other workers to inspect and test overhead and underground power lines and cables and auxiliary equipment using electrical testing equipment

- **Methodical interest** in **compiling** information to install and maintain street lighting systems; and in adhering to safety practices and procedures.

7244

Physical Activities

Vision
   3   Near and far vision

Colour Discrimination
   1   Relevant

Hearing
   1   Limited

Body Position
   4   Other body positions

Limb Co-ordination
   2   Multiple limb co-ordination

Strength
   3   Medium

Environmental Conditions

Location
   L3 Outside

Hazards
   H3 Equipment, machinery, tools
   H4 Electricity
   H8 Dangerous locations

Employment Requirements

Education/Training
5, R

- Completion of secondary school is usually required.

- Completion of a provincial four-year lineman/woman apprenticeship program *or* a combination of up to four years of work experience in the trade and some high school, college or industry courses in electrical technology is usually required for electric power line and cable workers.

- Trade certification is available but not mandatory, in Newfoundland, Nova Scotia, Prince Edward Island, New Brunswick, Ontario, Saskatchewan, Alberta, British Columbia, the Northwest Territories and the Yukon.

- Interprovincial trade certification (Red Seal) is available for qualified linemen/women.

Workplaces/Employers

Electric power generation, transmission and distribution companies

Electrical contractors

Public utility commissions

Occupational Options

Red Seal certification allows for interprovincial mobility.

Similar Occupations Classified Elsewhere

Power System Electricians (7243)

Other linemen/women and cable installers (in 7245 *Telecommunications Line and Cable Workers*)

Supervisors of electric power line and cable workers (in 7212 *Contractors and Supervisors, Electrical Trades and Telecommunications Occupations*)

7245 Telecommunications Line and Cable Workers

Telecommunications Line and Cable Workers install, repair and maintain telecommunication lines and cables. Apprentices are included in this group.

Profile Summary

APTITUDES

G	V	N	S	P	Q	K	F	M
3	3	4	3	4	4	3	3	3

INTERESTS
Oim

DATA PEOPLE THINGS (DPT)
361

PHYSICAL ACTIVITIES (PA)

V	C	H	B	L	S
3	1	1	4	2	3

ENVIRONMENTAL CONDITIONS (EC)
L2, L3, H3, H4, H8

EDUCATION/TRAINING
5, R

Examples of Job Titles

- Apprentice Lineman/woman, Telecommunications
- Cable Repairer, Telecommunications
- Communication Technician, Construction
- Construction Technician, CATV
- Lineman/woman, Telecommunications
- Splicer Technician, Telephone
- Telecommunications Line Installer
- Telephone Line Technician

Descriptor Profile

Main Characteristics

Occupations in this group are characterized by the following aptitudes, interests and worker functions as they relate to main duties:

- **General learning ability** to install, remove, maintain and repair aerial and underground telephone and other telecommunication transmission and distribution lines, cables and associated hardware, and to install cable television lines and cables

- **Verbal ability** to communicate with other workers in order to co-ordinate the preparation and completion of assignments

- **Spatial perception** to assist in the erection and removal of telecommunication poles, towers and associated support structures

- **Motor co-ordination** and **finger** and **manual dexterity** to climb and work aloft on poles, ladders and other support structures, and to work in confined spaces such as trenches, tunnels and crawl spaces

- **Objective interest** in **precision working** to splice and repair various types and sizes of telephone and other telecommunication cables including single line, coaxial and fibre optic

- **Innovative interest** in **compiling** information to repair telecommunication lines, cables and various types of telephone and other telecommunication cables

- **Methodical interest** in **speaking** with other workers to analyze and record test results and communicate findings

7245

Physical Activities

Vision
   3 Near and far vision

Colour Discrimination
   1 Relevant

Hearing
   1 Limited

Body Position
   4 Other body positions

Limb Co-ordination
   2 Multiple limb co-ordination

Strength
   3 Medium

Environmental Conditions

Location
   L2 Unregulated inside climate
   L3 Outside

Hazards
   H3 Equipment, machinery, tools
   H4 Electricity
   H8 Dangerous locations

Employment Requirements

Education/Training
   5, R

- Completion of secondary school is usually required.

- Completion of a four-year telecommunication line and cable apprenticeship program *or* a combination of over three years of work experience in the trade and some industry-related or other specialized courses is usually required.

- Trade certification is available, but not mandatory, in Alberta and the Yukon.

Workplaces/Employers

Cable television companies

Telephone and other telecommunication services companies

Occupational Options

Progression to supervisory positions is possible with experience.

Similar Occupations Classified Elsewhere

Cable Television Service and Maintenance Technicians (7247)

Telecommunication Installation and Repair Workers (7246)

Supervisors of telecommunication line and cable workers (in 7212 *Contractors and Supervisors, Electrical Trades and Telecommunications Occupations*)

7246.1 Telephone Installers and Repairers

Telephone Installers and Repairers install, test, maintain and repair telephones. Apprentices are included in this group.

Profile Summary

APTITUDES

G	V	N	S	P	Q	K	F	M
3	3	4	3	3	4	3	3	3

INTERESTS
Oim

DATA PEOPLE THINGS (DPT)
361

PHYSICAL ACTIVITIES (PA)

V	C	H	B	L	S
2	1	1	4	1	2

ENVIRONMENTAL CONDITIONS (EC)
L1, H3

EDUCATION/TRAINING
5, R

Examples of Job Titles

Line and Station Installer, Telephone
Telephone Installer

Descriptor Profile

Main Characteristics

Occupations in this group are characterized by the following aptitudes, interests and worker functions as they relate to main duties:

- **General learning ability** to understand and apply the principles of electrical theory to the installation, repair and adjustment of telephone equipment and wiring

- **Spatial perception** to visualize circuits, equipment functions and layouts and to locate transmission faults

- **Form perception** to notice defective electrical connections and worn and damaged parts

- **Motor co-ordination** and **finger** and **manual dexterity** to install, arrange, remove and maintain telephone equipment, wiring and associated hardware

- **Objective interest** in **precision working** to use hand and power tools, and to test meters when repairing equipment and wires

- **Innovative interest** in **compiling** information to repair and replace defective and damaged telephones, wires and associated equipment

- **Methodical interest** in **speaking** to test installed telephone systems

7246.1

Physical Activities

Vision
2 Near vision

Colour Discrimination
1 Relevant

Hearing
1 Limited

Body Position
4 Other body positions

Limb Co-ordination
1 Upper limb co-ordination

Strength
2 Light

Environmental Conditions

Location
L1 Regulated inside climate

Hazards
H3 Equipment, machinery, tools

Employment Requirements

Education/Training
5, R

- Completion of secondary school is usually required.

- Telephone installers and repairers require completion of an apprenticeship program ranging from three to four years
or
a combination of over three years of work experience in the trade and some high school, college or industry-related courses.

- Trade certification is available, but not mandatory in Alberta, the Northwest Territories and the Yukon.

Workplaces/Employers

Telephone, telegraph and other telecommunication transmission services

Similar Occupations Classified Elsewhere

Telecommunications Line and Cable Workers (7245)

Supervisors of telecommunication installation and repair workers (in 7212 *Contractors and Supervisors, Electrical Trades and Telecommunications Occupations*)

7246.2 Switch Network Installers and Repairers

Switch Network Installers and Repairers install, test, maintain and repair telephone switching equipment. Apprentices are included in this group.

Profile Summary

APTITUDES

G	V	N	S	P	Q	K	F	M
3	3	4	3	3	4	3	3	3

INTERESTS
Oim

DATA PEOPLE THINGS (DPT)
261

PHYSICAL ACTIVITIES (PA)

V	C	H	B	L	S
2	1	1	4	1	2

ENVIRONMENTAL CONDITIONS (EC)
L1, H3, H4

EDUCATION/TRAINING
5, R

Examples of Job Titles

Apprentice Communication Electrician, Switching

Central Office Technician

Private Branch Exchange (PBX) Installer

Switch Network Installer and Repairer

Descriptor Profile

Main Characteristics

Occupations in this group are characterized by the following aptitudes, interests and worker functions as they relate to main duties:

- **General learning ability** to apply the principles of electrical theory to the installation, repair and adjustment of trunking systems, circuits and equipment

- **Spatial perception** to visualize circuits, equipment functions and layouts from drawings and specifications

- **Form perception** to notice defective connections and worn and damaged parts

- **Motor co-ordination** and **finger** and **manual dexterity** to install and repair electromechanical, analog and digital trunking systems, circuits and equipment in telecommunication central offices and switching centres

- **Objective interest** in **precision working** to adjust, change and repair switching systems and associated equipment

- **Innovative interest** in **analyzing** test results

- **Methodical interest** in **signalling** to inspect and test trunking systems, circuits and equipment

7246.2
Subgroup 2 of 4

Physical Activities

Vision
  2 Near vision

Colour Discrimination
  1 Relevant

Hearing
  1 Limited

Body Position
  4 Other body positions

Limb Co-ordination
  1 Upper limb co-ordination

Strength
  2 Light

Environmental Conditions

Location
  L1 Regulated inside climate

Hazards
  H3 Equipment, machinery, tools
  H4 Electricity

Employment Requirements

Education/Training
  5, R

- Completion of secondary school is required.

- Switch network installers and repairers require completion of an apprenticeship program ranging from three to four years
  or
  a combination of over three years of work experience in the trade and some high school, college or industry-related courses.

- Trade certification is available, but not mandatory in Alberta, the Northwest Territories and the Yukon.

Workplaces/Employers

Telephone, telegraph and other telecommunication transmission services

Similar Occupations Classified Elsewhere

Telecommunications Line and Cable Workers (7245)

Supervisors of telecommunication installation and repair workers (in 7212 *Contractors and Supervisors, Electrical Trades and Telecommunications Occupations*)

7246.3 Telecommunications Service Testers

Telecommunications Service Testers check telephones and telephone switching equipment. Apprentices are included in this group.

Profile Summary

APTITUDES

G	V	N	S	P	Q	K	F	M
3	3	4	3	3	4	3	3	3

INTERESTS
Oim

DATA PEOPLE THINGS (DPT)
364

PHYSICAL ACTIVITIES (PA)

V	C	H	B	L	S
2	1	1	4	1	1

ENVIRONMENTAL CONDITIONS (EC)
L1

EDUCATION/TRAINING
5+, R

Examples of Job Titles

Communication Technician, Telephone

Exchange Tester

Descriptor Profile

Main Characteristics

Occupations in this group are characterized by the following aptitudes, interests and worker functions as they relate to main duties:

- **General learning ability** to apply the knowledge of electrical inspection and testing principles to detect and determine the causes of defects and service problems

- **Spatial perception** to interpret test instruments and how they relate to the function and operation of electrical components

- **Form perception** to detect defects and irregularities on customer lines and equipment

- **Motor co-ordination** and **finger** and **manual dexterity** to use test instruments; may assist repair personnel to test lines, circuits and systems and to isolate and clear cable faults

- **Objective interest** in **operating** computerized testing systems to conduct service tests on customer lines and equipment

- **Innovative interest** in **compiling** information to determine the nature, cause and location of service problems

- **Methodical interest** in **speaking** to initiate the dispatch of repair personnel; and in completing test reports and maintaining test and service records

7246.3
Subgroup 3 of 4

Physical Activities

Vision
　2　Near vision

Colour Discrimination
　1　Relevant

Hearing
　1　Limited

Body Position
　4　Other body positions

Limb Co-ordination
　1　Upper limb co-ordination

Strength
　1　Limited

Environmental Conditions

Location
　L1　Regulated inside climate

Employment Requirements

Education/Training
　5+, R

- Completion of secondary school is usually required.

- Experience as an installer and repairer (telephone and switch network) is usually required for service testers.

- Telephone and switch network installers and repairers require completion of an apprenticeship program ranging from three to four years
  or
  a combination of over three years of work experience in the trade and some high school, college or industry related courses.

- Trade certification is available, but not mandatory in Alberta, the Northwest Territories and the Yukon.

Workplaces/Employers

Telephone, telegraph and other telecommunication transmission services companies

Similar Occupations Classified Elsewhere

Telecommunications Line and Cable Workers (7245)

Supervisors of telecommunication installation and repair workers (in 7212 Contractors and Supervisors, Electrical Trades and Telecommunications Occupations)

7246.4 Telecommunications Equipment Technicians

Telecommunications Equipment Technicians install, test, maintain and repair telephones and other telecommunication equipment.

Profile Summary

APTITUDES

G	V	N	S	P	Q	K	F	M
3	3	4	3	3	4	3	3	3

INTERESTS
Oim

DATA PEOPLE THINGS (DPT)
261

PHYSICAL ACTIVITIES (PA)

V	C	H	B	L	S
2	1	1	4	1	2

ENVIRONMENTAL CONDITIONS (EC)
L1, H3

EDUCATION/TRAINING
6, R

Examples of Job Titles

Cellular Telephone Technician
Mobile Radio Installer
Telecommunications Equipment Technician

Descriptor Profile

Main Characteristics

Occupations in this group are characterized by the following aptitudes, interests and worker functions as they relate to main duties:

- **General learning ability** to understand and apply principles of telecommunications to the installation, repair and adjustment of telecommunications equipment and related systems

- **Spatial perception** to visualize circuits, functions and layouts of equipment and systems

- **Form perception** to detect defects, irregularities and damaged parts

- **Motor co-ordination** and **finger** and **manual dexterity** to install, remove and maintain various telecommunications equipment and related systems such as telex and facsimile machines, teletypewriters, mobile radios, cellular telephones and other equipment

- **Objective interest** in **precision working** to adjust, replace and repair telecommunications equipment

- **Innovative interest** in **analyzing** information to inspect equipment and diagnose and locate equipment faults

- **Methodical interest** in **speaking** to test operations of telecommunications equipment

7246.4

Physical Activities

Vision
  2 Near vision

Colour Discrimination
  1 Relevant

Hearing
  1 Limited

Body Position
  4 Other body positions

Limb Co-ordination
  1 Upper limb co-ordination

Strength
  2 Light

Environmental Conditions

Location
  L1 Regulated inside climate

Hazards
  H3 Equipment, machinery, tools

Employment Requirements

Education/Training
  6, R

- Completion of secondary school is usually required.

- Telecommunications equipment technicians usually require completion of a college electrical and electronics program and several months of on-the-job training.

Workplaces/Employers

Telephone, telegraph and other telecommunication transmission services

Similar Occupations Classified Elsewhere

Telecommunications Line and Cable Workers (7245)

Supervisors of telecommunication installation and repair workers (in 7212 *Contractors and Supervisors, Electrical Trades and Telecommunications Occupations*)

7247.1 Cable Television Service Technicians

Cable Television Service Technicians install, maintain and repair cable television signals and associated equipment in homes and commercial buildings. Apprentices are included in this group.

Profile Summary

APTITUDES

G	V	N	S	P	Q	K	F	M
3	3	4	3	4	4	3	3	3

INTERESTS
Oms

DATA PEOPLE THINGS (DPT)
364

PHYSICAL ACTIVITIES (PA)

V	C	H	B	L	S
2	0	1	4	1	2

ENVIRONMENTAL CONDITIONS (EC)
L1

EDUCATION/TRAINING
4, 5, 6, R

Examples of Job Titles

Apprentice Community Antenna Television (CATV) Technician

Cable Television Installer

Cablevision Servicer

CATV Technician

Installation Technician, Cable Television

Descriptor Profile

Main Characteristics

Occupations in this group are characterized by the following aptitudes, interests and worker functions as they relate to main duties:

- **General learning ability** to install, maintain and repair cable television signals and associated equipment

- **Spatial perception** to visualize circuits, equipment functions and layouts at subscribers' premises

- **Motor co-ordination** and **finger** and **manual dexterity** to bend, position and splice cables and wires to install splitters, converters, pay-TV equipment and other hardware

- **Objective interest** in **operating** hand tools, power tools and test equipment to install cable hardware and systems

- **Methodical interest** in **compiling** information to inspect, test and repair cable television signals and associated equipment at subscribers' premises

- **Social interest** in **speaking** with cable television subscribers and company personnel to determine assignments

7247.1
Subgroup 1 of 2

Physical Activities

Vision
  2   Near vision

Colour Discrimination
  0   Not relevant

Hearing
  1   Limited

Body Position
  4   Other body positions

Limb Co-ordination
  1   Upper limb co-ordination

Strength
  2   Light

Environmental Conditions

Location
  L1   Regulated inside climate

Employment Requirements

Education/Training
4, 5, 6, R

- Completion of secondary school is usually required.

- Completion of a college program in electronics
  or
  a combination of college, correspondence or industry courses related to electronics and electrical systems and on-the-job training
  or
  completion of a four-year CATV-technician apprenticeship program is required.

- Trade certification is available, but not mandatory, in British Columbia.

Workplaces/Employers

Cable television companies

Occupational Options

Progression to supervisory positions is possible with experience.

Similar Occupations Classified Elsewhere

Supervisors of cable television service and maintenance technicians (in 7212 *Contractors and Supervisors, Electrical Trades and Telecommunications Occupations*)

Workers who install aerial or underground cable television lines (in 7245 *Telecommunications Line and Cable Workers*)

7247.2 Cable Television Maintenance Technicians

Cable Television Maintenance Technicians maintain and repair cable television transmission and distribution systems and associated hardware. Apprentices are included in this group.

Profile Summary

APTITUDES

G	V	N	S	P	Q	K	F	M
3	4	4	3	4	4	3	3	3

INTERESTS
Oim

DATA PEOPLE THINGS (DPT)
361

PHYSICAL ACTIVITIES (PA)

V	C	H	B	L	S
3	1	1	4	2	3

ENVIRONMENTAL CONDITIONS (EC)
L2, L3, H3, H4, H8

EDUCATION/TRAINING
4, 5, 6, R

Examples of Job Titles

Maintenance Technician, Cable Television

Descriptor Profile

Main Characteristics

Occupations in this group are characterized by the following aptitudes, interests and worker functions as they relate to main duties:

- **General learning abilities** to maintain and repair main aerial and underground cable television transmission lines, trunking and related distribution and interconnecting systems including power supplies and amplifiers

- **Spatial perception** to visualize circuits, equipment functions and layouts

- **Motor co-ordination** and **finger** and **manual dexterity** to climb and work aloft on poles, ladders and other support structures

- **Objective interest** in **precision working** to inspect, monitor, test and adjust cable transmission and distribution systems

- **Innovative interest** in **speaking** with other workers to co-ordinate the preparation and completion of assignments

- **Methodical interest** in **compiling** information to repair and replace faulty cables, power supplies, amplifiers and other associated transmission and distribution equipment

7247.2
Subgroup 2 of 2

Physical Activities

Vision
   3   Near and far vision

Colour Discrimination
   1   Relevant

Hearing
   1   Limited

Body Position
   4   Other body positions

Limb Co-ordination
   2   Multiple limb co-ordination

Strength
   3   Medium

Environmental Conditions

Location
   L2 Unregulated inside climate
   L3 Outside

Hazards
   H3 Equipment, machinery, tools
   H4 Electricity
   H8 Dangerous locations

Employment Requirements

Education/Training
4, 5, 6, R

- Completion of secondary school is usually required.

- Completion of a college program in electronics
or
a combination of college, correspondence or industry courses related to electronics and electrical systems and on-the-job training
or
completion of a four-year CATV-technician apprenticeship program is required.

- Trade certification is available, but not mandatory, in British Columbia.

Workplaces/Employers

Cable television companies

Occupational Options

Progression to supervisory positions is possible with experience.

Similar Occupations Classified Elsewhere

Supervisors of cable television service and maintenance technicians (in 7212 *Contractors and Supervisors, Electrical Trades and Telecommunications Occupations*)

Workers who install aerial or underground cable television lines (in 7245 *Telecommunications Line and Cable Workers*)

7251 Plumbers

Plumbers install, repair and maintain pipes, fixtures and other plumbing equipment used for water distribution and waste-water disposal in residential, commercial and industrial buildings. Apprentices are included in this group.

Profile Summary

APTITUDES

G	V	N	S	P	Q	K	F	M
3	4	3	3	3	4	3	3	3

INTERESTS
Oim

DATA PEOPLE THINGS (DPT)
361

PHYSICAL ACTIVITIES (PA)

V	C	H	B	L	S
2	0	1	4	1	4

ENVIRONMENTAL CONDITIONS (EC)
L1, H3

EDUCATION/TRAINING
5, R

Examples of Job Titles

Maintenance Plumber
Plumber
Plumber Apprentice
Plumbing Mechanic

Descriptor Profile

Main Characteristics

Occupations in this group are characterized by the following aptitudes, interests and worker functions as they relate to main duties:

- **General learning ability** to install, repair and maintain domestic, commercial and industrial plumbing fixtures and systems

- **Spatial** and **form perception** to read blueprints, drawings and specifications to determine layout of plumbing systems, water supply networks and waste and drainage systems

- **Motor co-ordination** and **finger and manual dexterity** to join pipes using couplings, clamps, screws, bolts, cement, and soldering, brazing and welding equipment

- **Objective interest** in **precision working** to measure, cut, bend and thread pipes using machines and hand and power tools

- **Innovative interest** in **compiling** information to repair plumbing fixtures and systems, and to test pipes for leaks using air and water pressure gauges

- **Methodical interest** in **speaking - signalling** to locate and mark positions for pipe connections, passage holes and fixtures in walls and floors

7251

Physical Activities

Vision
    2 Near vision

Colour Discrimination
    0 Not relevant

Hearing
    1 Limited

Body Position
    4 Other body positions

Limb Co-ordination
    1 Upper limb co-ordination

Strength
    4 Heavy

Environmental Conditions

Location
    L1 Regulated inside climate

Hazards
    H3 Equipment, machinery, tools

Employment Requirements

Education/Training
5, R

- Some secondary school education is required.

- Completion of a four-to-five year apprenticeship program
  or
  a combination of over five years of work experience in the trade and some high school, college or industry courses in plumbing is usually required to be eligible for trade certification.

- Trade certification is compulsory in Nova Scotia, Prince Edward Island, New Brunswick, Quebec, Ontario, Saskatchewan, Alberta and British Columbia and available, but voluntary, in Newfoundland, Manitoba, the Northwest Territories and the Yukon.

- Interprovincial trade certification (Red Seal) is available to qualified plumbers.

Workplaces/Employers

Maintenance departments of factories or plants

Plumbing contractors

Self-employment

Occupational Options

Red Seal trade certification allows for interprovincial mobility.

Progression to supervisory positions is possible with experience.

Similar Occupations Classified Elsewhere

Steamfitters, Pipefitters and Sprinkler System Installers (7252)

Supervisors of plumbers (in 7213 *Contractors and Supervisors, Pipefitting Trades*)

7252.1 Steamfitters and Pipefitters

Steamfitters and Pipefitters lay out, assemble, fabricate, maintain and repair piping systems carrying water, steam, chemicals and fuel in heating, cooling, lubricating and other process piping systems. Apprentices are included in this group.

Profile Summary

APTITUDES

G	V	N	S	P	Q	K	F	M
3	3	3	3	3	4	3	3	3

INTERESTS
Oim

DATA PEOPLE THINGS (DPT)
381

PHYSICAL ACTIVITIES (PA)

V	C	H	B	L	S
3	0	1	4	2	4

ENVIRONMENTAL CONDITIONS (EC)
L1, H3, H6, H7

EDUCATION/TRAINING
4+, 5, R

Examples of Job Titles

Marine Pipefitter
Pipefitter
Steamfitter

Descriptor Profile

Main Characteristics

Occupations in this group are characterized by the following aptitudes, interests and worker functions as they relate to main duties:

- **General learning ability** to lay out, assemble, fabricate, maintain and repair piping systems

- **Verbal** and **numerical ability** to prepare cost estimates for customers

- **Spatial** and **form perception** to read and interpret drawings and specifications to determine layout requirements

- **Motor co-ordination** to cut openings for pipe in walls, floors and ceilings using hand and power tools and machines

- **Finger** and **manual dexterity** to weld, braze, cement, solder and thread joints to join pipes and fabricate sections of piping systems

- **Objective interest** in **precision working** to measure, cut, thread and bend pipe to required shape using hand and power tools

- **Innovative interest** in **compiling** information to select types and sizes of pipe required and to test systems for leaks using testing equipment

- **Methodical interest** in removing and replacing worn components and in cleaning and maintaining pipe units and fittings

7252.1

Physical Activities

Vision
  3 Near and far vision

Colour Discrimination
  0 Not relevant

Hearing
  1 Limited

Body Position
  4 Other body positions

Limb Co-ordination
  2 Multiple limb co-ordination

Strength
  4 Heavy

Environmental Conditions

Location
  L1 Regulated inside climate

Hazards
  H3 Equipment, machinery, tools
  H6 Flying particles, falling objects
  H7 Fire, steam, hot surfaces

Employment Requirements

Education/Training
4+, 5, R

- Some secondary school education is required.

- Completion of a four-to-five year apprenticeship program
  or
  a combination of over five years of work experience in the trade and some high school, college or industry courses in steamfitting or pipefitting is usually required to be eligible for trade certification.

- Steamfitter-pipefitter trade certification is compulsory in Quebec, Ontario, Alberta and British Columbia and available, but voluntary, in all other provinces and the territories.

- Interprovincial trade certification (Red Seal) is also available to qualified steamfitters-pipefitters.

Workplaces/Employers

Maintenance departments of factories and plants

Pipefitting contractors

Self-employment

Occupational Options

Red Seal trade certification allows for interprovincial mobility.

Progression to supervisory positions is possible with experience.

Similar Occupations Classified Elsewhere

Plumbers (7251)

Gas Fitters (7253)

Supervisors of steamfitters, pipefitters and sprinkler system installers (in 7213 *Contractors and Supervisors, Pipefitting Trades*)

7252.2 Sprinkler System Installers

Sprinkler System Installers fabricate, install, test, maintain and repair water, foam, carbon-dioxide and dry-chemical sprinkler systems in buildings for fire protection purposes. Apprentices are included in this group.

Profile Summary

APTITUDES

G	V	N	S	P	Q	K	F	M
3	3	3	3	3	4	3	3	3

INTERESTS
Oim

DATA PEOPLE THINGS (DPT)
381

PHYSICAL ACTIVITIES (PA)

V	C	H	B	L	S
3	0	1	4	2	4

ENVIRONMENTAL CONDITIONS (EC)
L1, H3, H6, H7

EDUCATION/TRAINING
4+, 5, R

Examples of Job Titles

Fire Sprinkler Fitter
Sprinkler System Fitter
Sprinkler System Installer

Descriptor Profile

Main Characteristics

Occupations in this group are characterized by the following aptitudes, interests and worker functions as they relate to main duties:

- **General learning ability** to understand and apply techniques used in the installation, maintenance and repair of sprinkler systems

- **Verbal** and **numerical ability** to prepare cost estimates for customers

- **Spatial** and **form perception** to read and interpret drawings and specifications to determine layout requirements

- **Motor co-ordination** to connect piping systems to water mains, supply tanks, pumps, compressors and control equipment and to mount prepared pipe in supports

- **Finger** and **manual dexterity** to install sprinklers and fire protection equipment and clamps, brackets and hangers to support piping systems using hand and power tools

- **Objective interest** in **precision working** to join pipes and piping sections using soldering and welding equipment

- **Innovative interest** in **compiling** information to select, measure, cut, ream and thread pipe

- **Methodical interest** in testing systems for leaks using air and liquid pressure equipment

7252.2
Subgroup 2 of 2

Physical Activities

Vision
  3 Near and far vision

Colour Discrimination
  0 Not relevant

Hearing
  1 Limited

Body Position
  4 Other body positions

Limb Co-ordination
  2 Multiple limb co-ordination

Strength
  4 Heavy

Environmental Conditions

Location
  L1 Regulated inside climate

Hazards
  H3 Equipment, machinery, tools
  H6 Flying particles, falling objects
  H7 Fire, steam, hot surfaces

Employment Requirements

Education/Training
4+, 5, R

- Some secondary school education is required.

- Completion of a four-to-five year apprenticeship program
or
a combination of over five years of work experience in the trade and some high school, college or industry courses in sprinkler system installation is usually required to be eligible for trade certification.

- Sprinkler-system-installer trade certification is compulsory in Quebec and British Columbia and available, but voluntary, in all other provinces and the Yukon.

- Interprovincial trade certification (Red Seal) is also available to qualified sprinkler system installers.

Workplaces/Employers

Maintenance departments of factories and plants

Self-employment

Sprinkler system contractors

Occupational Options

Red Seal trade certification allows for interprovincial mobility.

Progression to supervisory positions is possible with experience.

Similar Occupations Classified Elsewhere

Plumbers (7251)

Gas Fitters (7253)

Supervisors of steamfitters, pipefitters and sprinkler system installers (in 7213 *Contractors and Supervisors, Pipefitting Trades*)

7253   Gas Fitters

Gas Fitters install, inspect, repair and maintain gas lines and gas equipment such as meters, regulators, heating units and appliances in residential, commercial and industrial establishments. Apprentices are included in this group.

Profile Summary

APTITUDES

G	V	N	S	P	Q	K	F	M
3	3	3	3	3	3	3	3	3

INTERESTS
Oim

DATA PEOPLE THINGS (DPT)
361

PHYSICAL ACTIVITIES (PA)

V	C	H	B	L	S
3	0	1	4	1	3

ENVIRONMENTAL CONDITIONS (EC)
L1, L3, H1, H3

EDUCATION/TRAINING
4+, 5, R

Examples of Job Titles

Gas Customer Servicer
Gas Fitter
Gas Fitter Apprentice
Gas Servicer

Descriptor Profile

Main Characteristics

Occupations in this group are characterized by the following aptitudes, interests and worker functions as they relate to main duties:

- **General learning ability** to install and maintain gas meters and regulators and the gas lines between units and meters, as well as to install, maintain and service gas heating units and their components such as burners, valves and automatic controls

- **Verbal ability** to advise customers on standards, safety features and maintenance of gas units and systems

- **Clerical perception** to prepare reports on work done and condition of facilities

- **Spatial** and **form perception** to study drawings and specifications to determine the installation layouts and required materials

- **Motor co-ordination** and **finger** and **manual dexterity** to measure and mark reference points for installation of gas lines and equipment

- **Objective interest** in **precision working** to test and adjust control mechanisms and to check pipes and piping connections for gas leaks using gas-detecting devices

- **Innovative interest** in **compiling** information to repair and service gas appliances and related equipment

- **Methodical interest** in **speaking** to respond to calls about leaking gas and assist in the investigation of gas fires and explosions

7253

Physical Activities

Vision
　3　Near and far vision

Colour Discrimination
　0　Not relevant

Hearing
　1　Limited

Body Position
　4　Other body positions

Limb Co-ordination
　1　Upper limb co-ordination

Strength
　3　Medium

Environmental Conditions

Location
　L1　Regulated inside climate
　L3　Outside

Hazards
　H1　Dangerous chemical substances
　H3　Equipment, machinery, tools

Employment Requirements

Education/Training
4+, 5, R

- Completion of secondary school may be required.

- Completion of a three-year gas-fitter apprenticeship program *or* several years of work experience in a pipefitting trade plus completion of a high school, college or industry gas fitter program are required.

- Gas-fitter trade certification is compulsory in Alberta and available, but voluntary, in British Columbia, the Northwest Territories and the Yukon.

- A provincial gas fitter licence is required in all other provinces.

Workplaces/Employers

Gas servicing companies

Gas utility companies

Occupational Options

Mobility between provinces may be restricted due to the differing licensing requirements.

Progression to supervisory positions is possible with experience.

Similar Occupations Classified Elsewhere

Plumbers (7251)

Steamfitters, Pipefitters and Sprinkler System Installers (7252)

Supervisors of gas fitters (in 7213 *Contractors and Supervisors, Pipefitting Trades*)

7261 Sheet Metal Workers

Sheet Metal Workers fabricate, assemble, install and repair sheet-metal products. Apprentices are included in this group.

Profile Summary

APTITUDES

G	V	N	S	P	Q	K	F	M
3	4	3	2	3	4	3	3	2

INTERESTS
OMI

DATA PEOPLE THINGS (DPT)
381

PHYSICAL ACTIVITIES (PA)

V	C	H	B	L	S
3	0	1	4	1	3

ENVIRONMENTAL CONDITIONS (EC)
L1, L2, L3, H3, H6, H7, D1

EDUCATION/TRAINING
4+, 5, R

Examples of Job Titles

Apprentice Sheet Metal Worker
Coppersmith
Sheet Metal Fabricator
Sheet Metal Mechanic
Sheet Metal Worker

Descriptor Profile

Main Characteristics

Occupations in this group are characterized by the following aptitudes, interests and worker functions as they relate to main duties:

- **General learning ability** to fabricate, assemble, install and repair sheet metal products

- **Spatial perception** to read drawings and sketches and lay out sheet metal according to drawings and templates

- **Manual dexterity** to operate light metalworking machines, such as shears, brakes, punches and drill presses, to cut, bend, punch, drill, shape and straighten sheet metal; and to fit and join sheet-metal parts using riveting, welding, soldering and similar equipment to fabricate products such as ventilation shafts, eavestroughs, partition frames, air and heat ducts, roof decking and sheet-metal buildings

- **Objective interest** in **precision working** to measure and mark sheet metal, and to operate laser and plasma cutting equipment to cut sheet metal

- **Methodical interest** in grinding and buffing seams, joints and rough surfaces

- **Innovative interest** in **compiling** information to inspect product quality and installation to ensure products conform to specifications

7261

Physical Activities

Vision
   3 Near and far vision

Colour Discrimination
   0 Not relevant

Hearing
   1 Limited

Body Position
   4 Other body positions

Limb Co-ordination
   1 Upper limb co-ordination

Strength
   3 Medium

Environmental Conditions

Location
   L1 Regulated inside climate
   L2 Unregulated inside climate
   L3 Outside

Hazards
   H3 Equipment, machinery, tools
   H6 Flying particles, falling objects
   H7 Fire, steam, hot surfaces

Discomforts
   D1 Noise

Employment Requirements

Education/Training
4+, 5, R

- Some secondary school education is required.

- Completion of a three-to-four year apprenticeship program
 or
 a combination of over four years of work experience in the trade and some high school, college or industry courses in sheet-metal working is usually required to be eligible for trade certification.

- Trade certification is compulsory in Quebec, Ontario, Saskatchewan, Alberta and British Columbia and available, but voluntary, in all other provinces and territories.

- Interprovincial trade certification (Red Seal) is also available to qualified sheet-metal workers.

Workplaces/Employers

Sheet-metal fabrication shops

Sheet-metal products manufacturing companies

Sheet-metal work contractors

Occupational Options

Red Seal certification allows for interprovincial mobility.

Progression to supervisory positions is possible with experience.

Similar Occupations Classified Elsewhere

Metalworking Machine Operators (9514)

Structural Metal and Platework Fabricators and Fitters (7263)

Aircraft sheet-metal technicians (in 7315 *Aircraft Mechanics and Aircraft Inspectors*)

Metal roofers (in 7291 *Roofers and Shinglers*)

Supervisors of sheet-metal workers (in 7214 *Contractors and Supervisors, Metal Forming, Shaping and Erecting Trades*)

7262 Boilermakers

Boilermakers fabricate, assemble, erect and repair boilers, vessels, tanks, heat exchangers and other heavy-metal structures. Apprentices are included in this group.

Profile Summary

APTITUDES

G	V	N	S	P	Q	K	F	M
3	3	3	2	3	4	3	3	2

INTERESTS
OMI

DATA PEOPLE THINGS (DPT)
360

PHYSICAL ACTIVITIES (PA)

V	C	H	B	L	S
3	0	1	4	1	4

ENVIRONMENTAL CONDITIONS (EC)
L1, L2, H3, H7, D1

EDUCATION/TRAINING
4+, 5, R

Examples of Job Titles

Boiler Fitter
Boiler Installer
Boilermaker
Boilermaker Apprentice
Construction Boilermaker
Industrial Boilermaker
Marine Boilermaker

Descriptor Profile

Main Characteristics

Occupations in this group are characterized by the following aptitudes, interests and worker functions as they relate to main duties:

- **General learning ability** to understand the physical properties of structural metal and methods of assembly

- **Spatial perception** to read blueprints and specifications to plan a sequence of operations

- **Form perception** to erect and install boilers and other heavy-metal products according to specifications

- **Motor co-ordination** and **finger dexterity** to fit and weld metal parts and sections together in order to fabricate boilers, vessels, tanks, heat exchanges, piping and other heavy-metal products

- **Manual dexterity** to use hand and power tools to lay out plate, sheet steel and other heavy metals, and to mark bending and cutting lines on metal using protractors, compasses, drawing instruments and templates

- **Objective interest** in setting up and operating heavy-duty metalworking machines such as brakes, rolls, shears, flame cutters and drill presses to cut, shape and form metal into parts and sections

- **Methodical interest** in **speaking** to direct the activities of hoist operators, crane operators and other workers during fabrication, assembly, installation and repair of structures

- **Innovative interest** in **compiling** information to repair and perform maintenance work on boilers and other heavy-metal products

7262

Physical Activities

Vision
   3   Near and far vision

Colour Discrimination
   0   Not relevant

Hearing
   1   Limited

Body Position
   4   Other body positions

Limb Co-ordination
   1   Upper limb co-ordination

Strength
   4   Heavy

Environmental Conditions

Location
   L1   Regulated inside climate
   L2   Unregulated inside climate

Hazards
   H3   Equipment, machinery, tools
   H7   Fire, steam, hot surfaces

Discomforts
   D1   Noise

Employment Requirements

Education/Training
4+, 5, R

- Some secondary school education is required.

- Completion of a three-to-four year apprenticeship program *or* a combination of over four years of work experience in the trade and some high school, college or industry courses in boilermaking is usually required to be eligible for trade certification.

- Marine boilermakers in New Brunswick may require completion of a separate apprenticeship program and trade certification.

- Trade certification is compulsory in Quebec and Alberta and available, but voluntary, in all other provinces.

- Interprovincial trade certification (Red Seal) is also available to qualified boilermakers.

Workplaces/Employers

Boiler fabrication companies

Industrial establishments

Manufacturing companies

Ship building companies

Occupational Options

Red Seal trade certification allows for interprovincial mobility.

Progression to supervisory positions is possible with experience.

Similar Occupations Classified Elsewhere

Structural Metal and Platework Fabricators and Fitters (7263)

Supervisors of boilermakers (in 7214 *Contractors and Supervisors, Metal Forming, Shaping and Erecting Trades*)

7263 Structural Metal and Platework Fabricators and Fitters

Structural Metal and Platework Fabricators and Fitters make, assemble and fit steel and other metal components for buildings, bridges, tanks, boilers, pressure vessels and other similar structures and products. Apprentices are included in this group.

Profile Summary

APTITUDES

G	V	N	S	P	Q	K	F	M
3	4	3	3	3	4	3	3	3

INTERESTS
OMI

DATA PEOPLE THINGS (DPT)
380

PHYSICAL ACTIVITIES (PA)

V	C	H	B	L	S
3	0	1	4	1	3

ENVIRONMENTAL CONDITIONS (EC)
L1, H3, H6, H7, D1

EDUCATION/TRAINING
5, R

Examples of Job Titles

Metal Fabricator
Plater
Platework Fitter
Shipfitter
Shipfitter Apprentice
Steel Fabricator
Structural Steel Fitter

Descriptor Profile

Main Characteristics

Occupations in this group are characterized by the following aptitudes, interests and worker functions as they relate to main duties:

- **General learning ability** to understand the physical properties of structural metal and methods of assembly and to carry out procedures for fabrication

- **Spatial** and **form perception** to lay out reference points and patterns on heavy metal according to component specifications

- **Motor co-ordination** and **finger** and **manual dexterity** to assemble and fit metal sections and plates to form complete units and subunits using tack welding, bolting and other methods

- **Objective interest** in setting up and operating heavy-duty, metalworking machines such as brake presses, shears, cutting torches, grinders, drills and computer numerical control (CNC) equipment to bend, cut, form, punch, drill and otherwise form heavy-metal components

- **Methodical interest** in forming heavy-metal components using heavy-duty metalworking machines, and in assembling components to form subunits and complete units

- **Innovative interest** in compiling information to construct patterns and templates as guides for layouts

7263

Physical Activities

Vision
   3 Near and far vision

Colour Discrimination
   0 Not relevant

Hearing
   1 Limited

Body Position
   4 Other body positions

Limb Co-ordination
   1 Upper limb co-ordination

Strength
   3 Medium

Environmental Conditions

Location
   L1 Regulated inside climate

Hazards
   H3 Equipment, machinery, tools
   H6 Flying particles, falling objects
   H7 Fire, steam, hot surfaces

Discomforts
   D1 Noise

Employment Requirements

Education/Training
   5, R

- Some secondary school education is required.

- Completion of a three-to-four year apprenticeship program *or* a combination of over four years of work experience in the trade and some college or industry courses in structural steel and platework fabrication is usually required to be eligible for trade certification.

- Trade certification is available, but not compulsory, in Newfoundland, Nova Scotia, New Brunswick, Ontario, Alberta and British Columbia.

- Interprovincial trade certification (Red Seal) is also available to qualified fabricators and fitters.

Workplaces/Employers

Boiler fabrication plants

Heavy-machinery manufacturing companies

Platework fabrication plants

Shipbuilding companies

Structural-steel fabrication plants

Occupational Options

Red Seal certification allows for interprovincial mobility.

Progression to supervisory positions is possible with experience.

Similar Occupations Classified Elsewhere

Boilermakers (7262)

Skilled Welders (7265)

Structural steel erectors
(in 7264 *Ironworkers*)

Supervisors of structural metal and platework fabricators and fitters
(in 7214 *Contractors and Supervisors, Metal Forming, Shaping and Erecting Trades*)

7264 Ironworkers

Ironworkers fabricate, erect, hoist, install, repair and service structural ironwork, precast concrete, concrete reinforcing materials, curtain walls, ornamental iron and other metals used in the construction of buildings, bridges and other structures and equipment. Apprentices are included in this group.

Profile Summary

APTITUDES

G	V	N	S	P	Q	K	F	M
3	4	4	3	4	5	3	4	3

INTERESTS
OMI

DATA PEOPLE THINGS (DPT)
361

PHYSICAL ACTIVITIES (PA)

V	C	H	B	L	S
3	0	1	4	1	4

ENVIRONMENTAL CONDITIONS (EC)
L2, L3, H3, H6, H7, H8, D1

EDUCATION/TRAINING
4+, 5, R

Examples of Job Titles

Ironworker
Ironworker Apprentice
Ornamental Ironworker
Reinforcing Ironworker
Structural Steel Erector

Descriptor Profile

Main Characteristics

Occupations in this group are characterized by the following aptitudes, interests and worker functions as they relate to main duties:

- **General learning ability** to understand and apply methods and techniques associated with the use of structural ironwork, concrete and other metals in construction

- **Spatial** and **form perception** to understand specifications according to blueprints; to erect and install scaffolding, hoisting equipment and rigging; and to erect structural and architectural precast-concrete components for buildings, bridges, towers and other structures

- **Motor co-ordination** to assemble and erect prefabricated metal structures

- **Finger** and **manual dexterity** to position and secure steel bars and metal mesh in concrete forms to reinforce concrete structures

- **Objective interest** in **precision working** to align, weld and bolt steel units into place

- **Methodical interest** in **signalling** crane operators to position steel units according to blueprints

- **Innovative interest** in **compiling** information to install ornamental and other structural metalwork such as curtain walls, metal stairways, railings and power doors

7264

Physical Activities

Vision
   3 Near and far vision

Colour Discrimination
   0 Not relevant

Hearing
   1 Limited

Body Position
   4 Other body positions

Limb Co-ordination
   1 Upper limb co-ordination

Strength
   4 Heavy

Environmental Conditions

Location
   L2 Unregulated inside climate
   L3 Outside

Hazards
   H3 Equipment, machinery, tools
   H6 Flying particles, falling objects
   H7 Fire, steam, hot surfaces
   H8 Dangerous locations

Discomforts
   D1 Noise

Employment Requirements

Education/Training
4+, 5, R

- Some secondary school education is required.

- Completion of a two-to-three year apprenticeship program *or* over three years of work experience in the trade and some high school, college or industry courses in ironworking are usually required to be eligible for trade certification.

- Trade certification is compulsory in Quebec and Alberta and available, but voluntary, in Newfoundland, Nova Scotia, New Brunswick, Ontario, Saskatchewan and British Columbia.

- Interprovincial trade certification (Red Seal) is also available to qualified ironworkers.

Workplaces/Employers

Construction ironwork contractors

Occupational Options

Red Seal trade certification allows for interprovincial mobility.

Progression to supervisory positions is possible with experience.

Similar Occupations Classified Elsewhere

Supervisors of ironworkers (in 7214 *Contractors and Supervisors, Metal Forming, Shaping and Erecting Trades*)

7265 Welders

Welders operate equipment to weld ferrous and non-ferrous metals. Apprentices are included in this group.

Profile Summary

APTITUDES

G	V	N	S	P	Q	K	F	M
3	4	3	2	3	4	3	4	3

INTERESTS
OMI

DATA PEOPLE THINGS (DPT)
381

PHYSICAL ACTIVITIES (PA)

V	C	H	B	L	S
1	0	1	4	1	3

ENVIRONMENTAL CONDITIONS (EC)
L1, L2, L3, H3, H7, D3, D4

EDUCATION/TRAINING
5, R

Examples of Job Titles

Aircraft Welder
Electric Arc Welder
Gas-Shielded Arc Welder
Precision Welder
Pressure Vessel Welder
Welder
Welder-Fitter

Descriptor Profile

Main Characteristics

Occupations in this group are characterized by the following aptitudes, interests and worker functions as they relate to main duties:

- **General learning ability** to understand the properties of metals and the effects of expansion and shrinkage due to heat, and to understand and apply methods and techniques of welding, brazing, soldering and flame cutting

- **Spatial** and **form perception** to read and interpret blueprints and welding process specifications

- **Motor co-ordination** and **manual dexterity** to operate manual and semi-automatic welding, flame-cutting, brazing and soldering equipment

- **Objective interest** in **precision working** to fuse metal segments using processes such as gas tungsten arc (GTAW), gas metal arc (GMAW), flux-cored arc (FAW), plasma arc (PAW), shielded metal arc (SMAW), resistance welding and submerged arc welding (SAW)

- **Methodical interest** in cleaning and preparing pieces for welding

- **Innovative interest** in **compiling** information from specifications to shape metal by operating metal-shaping machines such as brakes, shears and other metal straightening and bending machines

7265

Physical Activities

Vision
1 Close visual acuity

Colour Discrimination
0 Not relevant

Hearing
1 Limited

Body Position
4 Other body positions

Limb Co-ordination
1 Upper limb co-ordination

Strength
3 Medium

Environmental Conditions

Location
L1 Regulated inside climate
L2 Unregulated inside climate
L3 Outside

Hazards
H3 Equipment, machinery, tools
H7 Fire, steam, hot surfaces

Discomforts
D3 Odours
D4 Non-toxic dusts

Employment Requirements

Education/Training
5, R

- Some secondary school education is usually required.

- Completion of a three-year apprenticeship program
or
a combination of over three years of work experience in the trade and some college or industry courses in welding is usually required to be eligible for trade certification.

- Trade certification is compulsory in Nova Scotia and Alberta and available, but voluntary, in Newfoundland, Prince Edward Island, New Brunswick, Manitoba, Saskatchewan, the Northwest Territories and the Yukon.

- Interprovincial trade certification (Red Seal) is also available to qualified welders.

Workplaces/Employers

Manufacturers of structural steel and platework, boilers, heavy machinery, aircraft and ships

Welding contractors

Welding shops and other industrial sectors

Self-employment

Occupational Options

Red Seal trade certification allows for interprovincial mobility.

Progression to supervisory positions is possible with experience.

Similar Occupations Classified Elsewhere

Welding, Brazing and Soldering Machine Operators (9515)

Supervisors of welders in this group (in 7214 *Contractors and Supervisors, Metal Forming, Shaping and Erecting Trades*)

Underwater welders (in 7382 *Commercial Divers*)

Remarks

Welders may specialize in certain types of welding such as custom fabrication, ship building and repair, aerospace precision welding, pressure vessel welding, pipeline construction welding, structural construction welding, or machinery and equipment repair welding.

In data provided by Statistics Canada, groups 7265 and 9515 are combined to form 9510 *Welders and Soldering Machine Operators*.

7266.1 Blacksmiths

Blacksmiths forge a variety of metal items such as tools, chains, wrought iron fixtures, agricultural implements and structural components.

Profile Summary

APTITUDES

G	V	N	S	P	Q	K	F	M
3	4	3	2	3	4	2	4	2

INTERESTS
OMI

DATA PEOPLE THINGS (DPT)
381

PHYSICAL ACTIVITIES (PA)

V	C	H	B	L	S
2	1	1	4	1	4

ENVIRONMENTAL CONDITIONS (EC)
L2, H3, H7, D1, D2, D3, D4

EDUCATION/TRAINING
2, 4

Examples of Job Titles

Anvilsmith
Blacksmith
Hammersmith
Toolsmith

Descriptor Profile

Main Characteristics

Occupations in this group are characterized by the following aptitudes, interests and worker functions as they relate to main duties:

- **General learning ability** to understand forging processes and apply forging techniques

- **Spatial perception** to form work pieces into desired shapes and sizes

- **Motor co-ordination** to temper, harden and anneal forged items

- **Manual dexterity** to hammer, punch, cut and otherwise form metal workpieces into desired shapes and sizes

- **Objective interest** in **precision working** to shape metal using power-forging machinery

- **Methodical interest** in heating metal items in forges and in forge-welding structural components

- **Innovative interest** in **compiling** information to forge special tools from metal and devise special jigs and fixtures

7266.1

Physical Activities

Vision
   2 Near vision

Colour Discrimination
   1 Relevant

Hearing
   1 Limited

Body Position
   4 Other body positions

Limb Co-ordination
   1 Upper limb co-ordination

Strength
   4 Heavy

Environmental Conditions

Location
   L2 Unregulated inside climate

Hazards
   H3 Equipment, machinery, tools
   H7 Fire, steam, hot surfaces

Discomforts
   D1 Noise
   D2 Vibration
   D3 Odours
   D4 Non-toxic dusts

Employment Requirements

Education/Training
2, 4

- Completion of secondary school may be required.

- Several years of experience as a forging machine operator may be required.

Workplaces/Employers

Fabricated metal-products manufacturing companies

Machinery manufacturing companies

Transportation equipment manufacturing companies

Occupational Options

Progression to supervisory positions is possible with experience.

Similar Occupations Classified Elsewhere

Forging Machine Operators (9512)

Agriculture blacksmiths, farriers and horseshoers (in 7383 *Other Trades and Related Occupations*)

Supervisors of blacksmiths and die setters (in 7214 *Contractors and Supervisors, Metal Forming, Shaping and Erecting Trades*)

7266.2 Die Setters

Die Setters set up forging machines such as forging presses, drop hammers, forging rolls and upsetters.

Profile Summary

APTITUDES

G	V	N	S	P	Q	K	F	M
3	4	4	2	3	4	3	3	3

INTERESTS
OMi

DATA PEOPLE THINGS (DPT)
380

PHYSICAL ACTIVITIES (PA)

V	C	H	B	L	S
2	0	1	4	1	4

ENVIRONMENTAL CONDITIONS (EC)
L1, H3, D1

EDUCATION/TRAINING
2, 4

Examples of Job Titles

Die Setter

Descriptor Profile

Main Characteristics

Occupations in this group are characterized by the following aptitudes, interests and worker functions as they relate to main duties:

- **General learning ability** to understand and apply forging processes and techniques

- **Spatial perception** to verify dimensions of sample work pieces according to die set-up specifications

- **Motor co-ordination** and **finger** and **manual dexterity** to position, align and bolt dies to the ram and anvil of power presses and hammers

- **Objective interest** in **setting up** and repairing forging machines

- **Methodical interest** in checking initial operations of forging machines to ensure machines are set up properly for use by forging machine operators

- **Innovative interest** in **compiling** information to select dies for forging according to work orders and specifications

7266.2
Subgroup 2 of 2

Physical Activities

Vision
   2 Near vision

Colour Discrimination
   0 Not relevant

Hearing
   1 Limited

Body Position
   4 Other body positions

Limb Co-ordination
   1 Upper limb co-ordination

Strength
   4 Heavy

Environmental Conditions

Location
   L1 Regulated inside climate

Hazards
   H3 Equipment, machinery, tools

Discomforts
   D1 Noise

Employment Requirements

Education/Training
2, 4

- Completion of secondary school may be required.

- Several years of experience as a forging machine operator may be required.

Workplaces/Employers

Fabricated metal-products manufacturing companies

Machinery manufacturing companies

Transportation equipment manufacturing companies

Occupational Options

Progression to supervisory positions is possible with experience.

Similar Occupations Classified Elsewhere

Forging Machine Operators (9512)

Agriculture blacksmiths, farriers and horseshoers (in 7383 *Other Trades and Related Occupations*)

Supervisors of blacksmiths and die setters (in 7214 *Contractors and Supervisors, Metal Forming, Shaping and Erecting Trades*)

7271 Carpenters

Carpenters construct, erect, install, maintain and repair structures and components of structures made of wood, wood substitutes and other materials. Apprentices are included in this group.

Profile Summary

APTITUDES

G	V	N	S	P	Q	K	F	M
3	3	3	3	3	4	3	3	3

INTERESTS
OMI

DATA PEOPLE THINGS (DPT)
361

PHYSICAL ACTIVITIES (PA)

V	C	H	B	L	S
3	0	1	4	1	3

ENVIRONMENTAL CONDITIONS (EC)
L1, L2, L3, H3, H8*, D1, D4

EDUCATION/TRAINING
5, R

Examples of Job Titles

Apprentice Carpenter
Carpenter
Finish Carpenter
Journeyman/woman Carpenter
Maintenance Carpenter
Renovation Carpenter
Rough Carpenter

Descriptor Profile

Main Characteristics

Occupations in this group are characterized by the following aptitudes, interests and worker functions as they relate to main duties:

- **General learning ability** to measure, cut, shape, assemble and join materials made of wood, wood substitutes and other materials

- **Verbal** and **numerical ability** to calculate requirements from specifications and prepare cost estimates for clients

- **Spatial** and **form perception** to read and interpret blueprints, drawings and sketches to determine specifications

- **Motor co-ordination** to fit and install trim items such as doors, stairs, mouldings and hardware

- **Finger** and **manual dexterity** to maintain, repair and renovate residences and wood structures in mills, mines, hospitals, industrial plants and other establishments

- **Objective interest** in **precision working** to prepare layouts that conform to building codes using measuring tools

- **Methodical interest** in **speaking** to apprentices and other construction workers to supervise their activities

- **Innovative interest** in **compiling** information to build foundations, install floor beams, lay subflooring and erect walls and roof systems

7271

Physical Activities

Vision
   3 Near and far vision

Colour Discrimination
   0 Not relevant

Hearing
   1 Limited

Body Position
   4 Other body positions

Limb Co-ordination
   1 Upper limb co-ordination

Strength
   3 Medium

Environmental Conditions

Location
   L1 Regulated inside climate
   L2 Unregulated inside climate
   L3 Outside

Hazards
   H3 Equipment, machinery, tools
   H8*Dangerous locations

Discomforts
   D1 Noise
   D4 Non-toxic dusts

Employment Requirements

Education/Training
5, R

- Some secondary school education is usually required.

- Completion of a three-to-four year apprenticeship program
  or
  a combination of over four years of work experience in the trade and some high school, college or industry courses in carpentry is usually required to be eligible for trade certification.

- Trade certification is compulsory in Quebec and available but voluntary, in all other provinces and the territories.

- Interprovincial trade certification (Red Seal) is also available to qualified carpenters.

Workplaces/Employers

Construction companies

Carpentry contractors

Maintenance departments of factories, plants and other establishments

Self-employment

Occupational Options

Red Seal trade certification allows for interprovincial mobility.

Progression to supervisory positions is possible with experience.

Similar Occupations Classified Elsewhere

Cabinetmakers (7272)

Supervisors of carpenters (in 7215 *Contractors and Supervisors, Carpentry Trades*)

Remarks

*Environmental Conditions

- For some occupations in this group, Hazards H8 (Dangerous locations) may also apply.

7272 Cabinetmakers

Cabinetmakers construct and repair wooden cabinets, furniture, fixtures and related products. Apprentices are included in this group.

Profile Summary

APTITUDES

G	V	N	S	P	Q	K	F	M
3	4	3	3	3	4	3	3	2

INTERESTS
OMI

DATA PEOPLE THINGS (DPT)
381

PHYSICAL ACTIVITIES (PA)

V	C	H	B	L	S
2	0	1	4	1	3

ENVIRONMENTAL CONDITIONS (EC)
L1, H3, D1, D3, D4

EDUCATION/TRAINING
4+, 5, R

Examples of Job Titles

Cabinetmaker
Cabinetmaker Apprentice
Custom Wood Furniture Maker
Furniture Cabinetmaker

Descriptor Profile

Main Characteristics

Occupations in this group are characterized by the following aptitudes, interests and worker functions as they relate to main duties:

- **General learning ability** to identify different types of wood, understand their characteristics, and apply the techniques and procedures involved in the construction, assembly and repair of wood furniture, fixtures and equipment

- **Spatial** and **form perception** to prepare and study plans, specifications and drawings of articles to be made

- **Motor co-ordination** to sand wood surfaces and apply veneer, stain and polish to finished products

- **Manual dexterity** to operate woodworking machines such as power saws, jointers, mortisers and shapers, and to use hand tools to cut, shape and form parts and components

- **Objective interest** in **precision working** to trim joints and fit parts and subassemblies together to form complete units using glue and clamps, and to reinforce joints using nails, screws and other fasteners

- **Methodical interest** in marking outlines for dimensions of parts on wood

- **Innovative interest** in **compiling** information to repair and restyle wood furniture, fixtures and related products

7272

Physical Activities

Vision
   2 Near vision

Colour Discrimination
   0 Not relevant

Hearing
   1 Limited

Body Position
   4 Other body positions

Limb Co-ordination
   1 Upper limb co-ordination

Strength
   3 Medium

Environmental Conditions

Location
   L1 Regulated inside climate

Hazards
   H3 Equipment, machinery, tools

Discomforts
   D1 Noise
   D3 Odours
   D4 Non-toxic dusts

Employment Requirements

Education/Training
   4+, 5, R

- Some secondary school education is usually required.

- Completion of a three-to-four year apprenticeship program
  or
  a combination of over four years of work experience in the trade and some high school or college courses in cabinetmaking is usually required to be eligible for trade certification.

- Trade certification is available, but voluntary, in Prince Edward Island, New Brunswick, Ontario, Alberta, British Columbia, the Northwest Territories and the Yukon.

- Interprovincial trade certification (Red Seal) is also available to qualified cabinetmakers.

Workplaces/Employers

Cabinetmaking contractors

Construction companies

Furniture manufacturing or repair companies

Self-employment

Occupational Options

Red Seal trade certification allows for interprovincial mobility.

Progression to supervisory positions is possible with experience.

Similar Occupations Classified Elsewhere

Carpenters (7271)

Woodworking Machine Operators (9513)

Supervisors of cabinetmakers (in 7215 *Contractors and Supervisors, Carpentry Trades*)

7281 Bricklayers

Bricklayers lay bricks, concrete blocks, stone and other similar materials to construct and repair walls and other structures according to blueprints and specifications. Apprentices are included in this group.

Profile Summary

APTITUDES

G	V	N	S	P	Q	K	F	M
3	4	3	3	4	4	3	4	3

INTERESTS
OMI

DATA PEOPLE THINGS (DPT)
381

PHYSICAL ACTIVITIES (PA)

V	C	H	B	L	S
3	1	1	4	2	4

ENVIRONMENTAL CONDITIONS (EC)
L1, L2, L3, H3, H8*, D4

EDUCATION/TRAINING
5, R

Examples of Job Titles

Apprentice Bricklayer
Bricklayer
Brickmason
Marble Mason
Refractory Bricklayer
Stonecutter
Stonemason

Descriptor Profile

Main Characteristics

Occupations in this group are characterized by the following aptitudes, interests and worker functions as they relate to main duties:

- **General learning ability** to prepare and lay bricks, concrete blocks, stone, structural tiles and similar materials to construct and repair walls, foundations and other structures in residential, industrial and commercial construction

- **Spatial** and **form perception** to visualize a structure from drawings and specifications and the positioning of materials and sequences of operation required to form the structure

- **Objective interest** in **precision working** to lay bricks and other masonry units to build residential and commercial chimneys and fireplaces; to lay radial bricks to build masonry shells of industrial chimneys; to lay and install firebricks to line industrial chimneys and smokestacks; to lay bricks, stone and similar materials to provide veneers to walls and other surfaces; and to lay bricks and other masonry units to build patios, garden walls and other decorative installations

- **Methodical interest** in lining and relining furnaces, kilns, boilers and similar installations using refractory and acid-resistant bricks, refractory concretes, plastic refractories and other materials

- **Innovative interest** in **compiling** information to construct and install prefabricated masonry units

7281

Physical Activities

Vision
   3   Near and far vision

Colour Discrimination
   1   Relevant

Hearing
   1   Limited

Body Position
   4   Other body positions

Limb Co-ordination
   2   Multiple limb co-ordination

Strength
   4   Heavy

Environmental Conditions

Location
   L1   Regulated inside climate
   L2   Unregulated inside climate
   L3   Outside

Hazards
   H3   Equipment, machinery, tools
   H8*Dangerous locations

Discomforts
   D4   Non-toxic dusts

Employment Requirements

Education/Training
   5, R

- Some secondary school education is required.

- Completion of a three-to-four year apprenticeship program
  or
  a combination of over four years of work experience in the trade and some high school, college or industry courses in bricklaying is usually required to be eligible for trade certification.

- Trade certification is compulsory in Nova Scotia, New Brunswick and Quebec and available, but voluntary, in all other provinces and the Yukon.

- Interprovincial trade certification (Red Seal) is also available to qualified bricklayers.

Workplaces/Employers

Construction companies

Bricklaying contractors

Self-employment

Occupational Options

Red Seal trade certification allows for interprovincial mobility.

Progression to supervisory positions is possible with experience.

Similar Occupations Classified Elsewhere

Tilesetters (7283)

Supervisors of bricklayers (in 7219 *Contractors and Supervisors, Other Construction Trades, Installers, Repairers and Servicers*)

Remarks

*Environmental Conditions

- For some occupations in this group, **Hazard** H8 (Dangerous locations) may also apply.

7282 Cement Finishers

Cement Finishers smooth and finish freshly poured concrete, apply curing and surface treatments, and restore, repair and replace hardened concrete structures. Apprentices are included in this group.

Profile Summary

APTITUDES

G	V	N	S	P	Q	K	F	M
3	4	4	4	4	5	3	4	3

INTERESTS
OMi

DATA PEOPLE THINGS (DPT)
584

PHYSICAL ACTIVITIES (PA)

V	C	H	B	L	S
3	0	1	4	1	3

ENVIRONMENTAL CONDITIONS (EC)
L2, L3, H3, H8*, D1, D2, D4

EDUCATION/TRAINING
5, R

Examples of Job Titles

Cement Finisher Apprentice
Cement Mason
Concrete Finisher
Concrete Mason
Precast Concrete Finisher

Descriptor Profile

Main Characteristics

Occupations in this group are characterized by the following aptitudes, interests and worker functions as they relate to main duties:

- **General learning ability** to pour, smooth, cast, cure and finish concrete and concrete structures, and to waterproof, damp-proof and restore concrete surfaces

- **Motor co-ordination** to check formwork, granular base and steel reinforcement materials, and to direct placement of concrete into forms and onto surfaces according to grade

- **Manual dexterity** to install anchor bolts, steel plates, door sills and other fixtures in freshly poured concrete, and to apply finish to concrete surfaces using hand and power tools

- **Objective interest** in **operating** hand tools, power tools and power vibrators to compact concrete

- **Methodical interest** in **copying** information to fill hollows and remove high spots to smooth freshly poured concrete; and in applying hardening and sealing compounds to cure concrete surfaces

- **Innovative interest** to repair, resurface and replace worn and damaged sections of floors, walls, roads and other concrete structures

7282

Physical Activities

Vision
   3 Near and far vision

Colour Discrimination
   0 Not relevant

Hearing
   1 Limited

Body Position
   4 Other body positions

Limb Co-ordination
   1 Upper limb co-ordination

Strength
   3 Medium

Environmental Conditions

Location
   L2 Unregulated inside climate
   L3 Outside

Hazards
   H3 Equipment, machinery, tools
   H8*Dangerous locations

Discomforts
   D1 Noise
   D2 Vibration
   D4 Non-toxic dusts

Employment Requirements

Education/Training
   5, R

- Some secondary school education is required.

- Completion of a two-to-three year apprenticeship program
or
over three years of work experience in the trade and some high school, college or industry courses in cement finishing are usually required to be eligible for trade certification.

- Trade certification is compulsory in Quebec and available, but voluntary, in Ontario, Saskatchewan and Alberta.

Workplaces/Employers

Cement and concrete contractors

Construction companies

Manufacturers of precast concrete products

Self-employment

Occupational Options

Progression to supervisory positions is possible with experience.

Similar Occupations Classified Elsewhere

Supervisors of cement finishers (in 7219 *Contractors and Supervisors, Other Construction Trades, Installers, Repairers and Servicers*)

Remarks

*Environmental Conditions

- For some occupations in this group, **Hazards** H8 (Dangerous locations) may also apply.

7283 Tilesetters

Tilesetters cover interior and exterior walls, floors and ceilings with ceramic, marble and quarry tile, mosaics and terrazzo. Apprentices are included in this group.

Profile Summary

APTITUDES

G	V	N	S	P	Q	K	F	M
3	4	4	3	4	4	3	4	3

INTERESTS
OMi

DATA PEOPLE THINGS (DPT)
381

PHYSICAL ACTIVITIES (PA)

V	C	H	B	L	S
3	1	1	4	2	3

ENVIRONMENTAL CONDITIONS (EC)
L1, L2, L3, H1, H3, D4

EDUCATION/TRAINING
4+, 5, R

Examples of Job Titles

Apprentice Tilesetter
Ceramic Tile Installer
Marble Setter
Terrazzo Polisher
Terrazzo Worker
Tile Installer
Tilesetter

Descriptor Profile

Main Characteristics

Occupations in this group are characterized by the following aptitudes, interests and worker functions as they relate to main duties:

- **General learning ability** to prepare, measure and mark surfaces to be covered, and to build underbeds and install anchor bolts, wires, brackets and tile strips

- **Spatial perception** to lay and set mosaic tiles to create decorative wall, mural and floor designs

- **Motor co-ordination** to set tiles in position, to apply pressure to affix tiles to base, and to mix, lay and polish terrazzo surfaces

- **Manual dexterity** to mix, apply and spread mortar, cement, mastic, glue and other adhesives using hand trowels, as well as to align and straighten tile using levels, squares and straightedges

- **Objective interest** in **precision working** to cut and fit tiles around obstacles and openings

- **Methodical interest** in **compiling** information to pack grout into joints between tiles and remove the excess

- **Innovative interest** in removing and replacing damaged tiles

7283

Physical Activities

Vision
   3 Near and far vision

Colour Discrimination
   1 Relevant

Hearing
   1 Limited

Body Position
   4 Other body positions

Limb Co-ordination
   2 Multiple limb co-ordination

Strength
   3 Medium

Environmental Conditions

Location
   L1 Regulated inside climate
   L2 Unregulated inside climate
   L3 Outside

Hazards
   H1 Dangerous chemical substances
   H3 Equipment, machinery, tools

Discomforts
   D4 Non-toxic dusts

Employment Requirements

Education/Training
4+, 5, R

- Some secondary school education is required.

- Completion of a three-year apprenticeship program
 or
 a combination of over three years of work experience in the trade and some high school, college or industry courses in tilesetting is usually required to be eligible for trade certification.

- Trade certification is compulsory in Quebec and available, but voluntary, in Saskatchewan and Alberta.

Workplaces/Employers

Construction companies

Masonry contractors

Self-employment

Occupational Options

In provinces where there is no apprenticeship, this trade is usually learned through several years of on-the-job training.

Progression to supervisory positions is possible with experience.

Similar Occupations Classified Elsewhere

Bricklayers (7281)

Supervisors of tilesetters (in 7219 *Contractors and Supervisors, Other Construction Trades, Installers, Repairers and Servicers*)

7284.1 Plasterers

Plasterers apply coats of plaster to interior and exterior walls, ceilings and building partitions to produce plain and decorative surfaces. Apprentices are included in this group.

Profile Summary

APTITUDES

G	V	N	S	P	Q	K	F	M
3	4	4	3	4	5	3	4	3

INTERESTS
MOI

DATA PEOPLE THINGS (DPT)
581

PHYSICAL ACTIVITIES (PA)

V	C	H	B	L	S
3	0	1	4	2	3

ENVIRONMENTAL CONDITIONS (EC)
L1, D4

EDUCATION/TRAINING
5, R

Examples of Job Titles

Plasterer

Descriptor Profile

Main Characteristics

Occupations in this group are characterized by the following aptitudes, interests and worker functions as they relate to main duties:

- **General learning ability** to clean and prepare surfaces, to apply, level and smooth coats of plaster, and to cure freshly plastered surfaces

- **Spatial perception** to mould and install ornamental plaster panels, cornices and trims

- **Motor co-ordination** to spray acoustic materials and texture finish over walls and ceilings

- **Manual dexterity** to trowel and spray coats of stucco over exteriors of buildings to form weatherproof surfaces

- **Methodical interest** in **copying** information to mix plaster ingredients in troughs to desired consistency

- **Objective interest** in **precision working** to finish corners and angles

- **Innovative interest** in creating decorative textures and designs

7284.1
Subgroup 1 of 3

Physical Activities

Vision
   3 Near and far vision

Colour Discrimination
   0 Not relevant

Hearing
   1 Limited

Body Position
   4 Other body positions

Limb Co-ordination
   2 Multiple limb co-ordination

Strength
   3 Medium

Environmental Conditions

Location
   L1 Regulated inside climate

Hazards
   D4 Non-toxic dusts

Employment Requirements

Education/Training
   5, R

- Some secondary school education is required.

- Completion of a three-year apprenticeship program in plastering
  or
  a combination of over three years of work experience and some high school, college or industry courses in plastering is usually required.

- Plasterer trade certification is compulsory in Quebec and available, but not compulsory, in Ontario, Manitoba, Saskatchewan and Alberta.

Workplaces/Employers

Construction companies

Plastering contractors

Self-employment

Occupational Options

Progression to supervisory positions is possible with experience.

Similar Occupations Classified Elsewhere

Supervisors of trade workers in this group (in 7219 *Contractors and Supervisors, Other Construction Trades, Installers, Repairers and Servicers*)

7284.2 Drywall Installers and Finishers

Drywall Installers and Finishers install and finish drywall sheets and ceiling systems. Apprentices are included in this group.

Profile Summary

APTITUDES

G	V	N	S	P	Q	K	F	M
3	4	4	3	4	5	3	4	3

INTERESTS
MOi

DATA PEOPLE THINGS (DPT)
581

PHYSICAL ACTIVITIES (PA)

V	C	H	B	L	S
3	0	1	4	2	4

ENVIRONMENTAL CONDITIONS (EC)
L1, L2, H3, D4

EDUCATION/TRAINING
5, R

Examples of Job Titles

Acoustical Ceiling Installer
Ceiling Installer
Drywall Applicator
Drywall Finisher
Drywall Taper
Sheetrock Applicator

Descriptor Profile

Main Characteristics

Occupations in this group are characterized by the following aptitudes, interests and worker functions as they relate to main duties:

- **General learning ability** to measure, cut and fit drywall sheets for installation on walls and ceilings

- **Spatial perception** to install suspended metal ceiling grids and to fit and place panels to form acoustical and coffered ceilings

- **Motor co-ordination** to position and secure sheets to metal and wood studs and joists

- **Manual dexterity** to tape over joints using taping machines, embed tape in compound and smooth out excess compound

- **Methodical interest** in copying information to apply successive coats of compound and to sand seams and joints

- **Objective interest** in **precision working** to fill joints, nail indentations, holes and cracks with joint compound using trowels and broad knives

- **Innovative interest** in fabricating suspended metal ceiling grids, and in cutting and installing metal corner beads to protect exterior corners

7284.2
Subgroup 2 of 3

Physical Activities

Vision
  3 Near and far vision

Colour Discrimination
  0 Not relevant

Hearing
  1 Limited

Body Position
  4 Other body positions

Limb Co-ordination
  2 Multiple limb co-ordination

Strength
  4 Heavy

Environmental Conditions

Location
  L1 Regulated inside climate
  L2 Unregulated, inside climate

Hazards
  H3 Equipment, machinery, tools

Discomforts
  D4 Non-toxic dusts

Employment Requirements

Education/Training
  5, R

- Some secondary school education is required.

- Completion of a three-year apprenticeship program in drywalling
  or
  a combination of over three years of work experience and some high school, college or industry courses in drywalling is usually required.

- Drywall installer and finisher trade certification is available, but not compulsory, in Manitoba and Saskatchewan.

Workplaces/Employers

Construction companies

Drywalling contractors

Self-employment

Occupational Options

Progression to supervisory positions is possible with experience.

Similar Occupations Classified Elsewhere

Supervisors of trade workers in this group (in 7219 *Contractors and Supervisors, Other Construction Trades, Installers, Repairers and Servicers*)

7284.3 Lathers

Lathers install support framework for ceiling systems, interior and exterior walls and building partitions. Apprentices are included in this group.

Profile Summary

APTITUDES

G	V	N	S	P	Q	K	F	M
3	4	4	3	4	4	3	4	3

INTERESTS
OMi

DATA PEOPLE THINGS (DPT)
581

PHYSICAL ACTIVITIES (PA)

V	C	H	B	L	S
3	0	1	4	2	3

ENVIRONMENTAL CONDITIONS (EC)
L1, L2, H3

EDUCATION/TRAINING
5, R

Examples of Job Titles

Interior Systems Mechanic
Lather
Wood Lather

Descriptor Profile

Main Characteristics

Occupations in this group are characterized by the following aptitudes, interests and worker functions as they relate to main duties:

- **General learning ability** to install metal stud framing and furring for interior drywall and plaster walls and ceilings

- **Spatial perception** to prepare wall and ceiling layouts

- **Motor co-ordination** and **manual dexterity** to use hand and power tools to install framing and furring

- **Objective interest** in **precision working** to cut openings in lath for heating and ventilation piping, ducts and electrical outlets

- **Methodical interest** in **copying** information to attach metal and gypsum lath to studs and furring using nails, screws, clips and wire ties

- **Innovative interest** in installing corner beads and wire mesh around beams for plastering

7284.3
Subgroup 3 of 3

Physical Activities

Vision
3   Near and far vision

Colour Discrimination
0   Not relevant

Hearing
1   Limited

Body Position
4   Other body positions

Limb Co-ordination
2   Multiple limb co-ordination

Strength
3   Medium

Environmental Conditions

Location
L1   Regulated inside climate
L2   Unregulated, inside climate

Hazards
H3   Equipment, machinery, tools

Employment Requirements

Education/Training
5, R

- Some secondary school education is required.

- Completion of a three-year apprenticeship program in lathing
  or
  a combination of over three years of work experience and some high school, college or industry courses in lathing is usually required.

- Lather trade certification is compulsory in Quebec and available, but not compulsory, in Ontario, Manitoba, Alberta and the Yukon.

- Interprovincial trade certification (Red Seal) is also available to qualified lathers.

Workplaces/Employers

Construction companies

Lathing contractors

Self-employment

Occupational Options

Red Seal trade certification for lathers allows interprovincial mobility.

Progression to supervisory positions is possible with experience.

Similar Occupations Classified Elsewhere

Supervisors of trade workers in this group (in 7219 *Contractors and Supervisors, Other Construction Trades, Installers, Repairers and Servicers*)

7291.1 Roofers

Roofers install, repair and replace flat roofs and shingles, shakes and other roofing tiles on sloped roofs. Apprentices are included in this group.

Profile Summary

APTITUDES

G	V	N	S	P	Q	K	F	M
3	4	3	3	3	4	3	3	3

INTERESTS
Moi

DATA PEOPLE THINGS (DPT)
584

PHYSICAL ACTIVITIES (PA)

V	C	H	B	L	S
3	0	1	4	2	4

ENVIRONMENTAL CONDITIONS (EC)
L3, H3, H7, H8, D1, D3

EDUCATION/TRAINING
5, R

Examples of Job Titles

Apprentice Roofer
Asphalt Roofer
Built-Up Roofer
Flat Roofer
Metal Roofer
Roofer
Single-Ply Roofer

Descriptor Profile

Main Characteristics

Occupations in this group are characterized by the following aptitudes, interests and worker functions as they relate to main duties:

- **General learning ability** to install, repair and replace built-up roofing systems using materials such as asphalt-saturated felts and hot asphalt and gravel, and single-ply roofing systems using waterproof sheet materials such as modified plastics, elastometric and other asphaltic compositions

- **Spatial** and **form perception** to set up scaffolding to provide safe access to roofs

- **Motor co-ordination** and **finger** and **manual dexterity** to install, repair and replace roofing systems and tiles and sheet metal flashings

- **Methodical interest** in **copying** information to apply waterproof coatings to concrete and other masonry surfaces above, and below, ground level

- **Objective interest** in **operating** hand and power tools to install and repair metal roofs

- **Innovative interest** in repairing roofing systems, and in installing, repairing and replacing shingles, shakes and other roofing tiles on sloped roofs

7291.1
Subgroup 1 of 2

Physical Activities

Vision
  3 Near and far vision

Colour Discrimination
  0 Not relevant

Hearing
  1 Limited

Body Position
  4 Other body positions

Limb Co-ordination
  2 Multiple limb co-ordination

Strength
  4 Heavy

Environmental Conditions

Location
  L3 Outside

Hazards
  H3 Equipment, machinery, tools
  H7 Fire, steam, hot surfaces
  H8 Dangerous locations

Discomforts
  D1 Noise
  D3 Odours

Employment Requirements

Education/Training
  5, R

- Some secondary school education is required.

- Completion of a two-to-three year apprenticeship program *or* over three years of work experience in the trade are usually required to be eligible for trade certification.

- Roofing trade certification is compulsory in Quebec and British Columbia and available, but voluntary, in Nova Scotia, Prince Edward Island, New Brunswick, Manitoba, Saskatchewan, Alberta and the Northwest Territories.

- Interprovincial trade certification (Red Seal) is also available to qualified roofers.

Workplaces/Employers

Roofing contractors

Self-employment

Occupational Options

Red Seal trade certification for roofers allows for interprovincial mobility.

Progression to supervisory positions is possible with experience.

Similar Occupations Classified Elsewhere

Supervisors of roofers and shinglers (in 7219 *Contractors and Supervisors, Other Construction Trades, Installers, Repairers and Servicers*)

7291.2 Shinglers

Shinglers install and replace shingles, tiles and similar coverings on sloped roofs.

Profile Summary

APTITUDES

G	V	N	S	P	Q	K	F	M
3	4	3	3	4	4	3	3	3

INTERESTS
Moi

DATA PEOPLE THINGS (DPT)
684

PHYSICAL ACTIVITIES (PA)

V	C	H	B	L	S
3	0	1	4	2	4

ENVIRONMENTAL CONDITIONS (EC)
L3, H3, H8, D1

EDUCATION/TRAINING
2

Examples of Job Titles

Shingler

Descriptor Profile

Main Characteristics

Occupations in this group are characterized by the following aptitudes, interests and worker functions as they relate to main duties:

- **General learning ability** to cover structures with shingles to form waterproof surfaces

- **Spatial** and **form perception** to set up scaffolding to provide safe access to roofs

- **Motor co-ordination** and **finger** and **manual dexterity** to lay and secure shingles and apply waterproofing and sealing compounds

- **Methodical interest** in **operating** hand and power tools to install and replace asphalt shingles, wood shingles and shakes, and masonry and baked-clay roofing tiles on sloped roofs

- **Objective interest** in **comparing** information to determine designs and patterns when laying shingles

- **Innovative interest** in cutting shingles to fit around vent stacks, chimneys and corners

7291.2
Subgroup 2 of 2

Physical Activities

Vision
   3 Near and far vision

Colour Discrimination
   0 Not relevant

Hearing
   1 Limited

Body Position
   4 Other body positions

Limb Co-ordination
   2 Multiple limb co-ordination

Strength
   4 Heavy

Environmental Conditions

Location
   L3 Outside

Hazards
   H3 Equipment, machinery, tools
   H8 Dangerous locations

Discomforts
   D1 Noise

Employment Requirements

Education/Training
  2

- Some secondary school education is required.

- Shinglers require one-to-two years of on-the-job training.

Workplaces/Employers

Roofing contractors

Self-employment

Occupational Options

Progression to supervisory positions is possible with experience.

Similar Occupations Classified Elsewhere

Supervisors of roofers and shinglers (in 7219 *Contractors and Supervisors, Other Construction Trades, Installers, Repairers and Servicers*)

7292 Glaziers

Glaziers prepare, install and replace glass in residential, commercial and industrial buildings, on exterior walls of buildings and other structures, and in vehicles, furniture and other products. Apprentices are included in this group.

Profile Summary

APTITUDES

G	V	N	S	P	Q	K	F	M
3	4	3	3	3	4	3	4	3

INTERESTS
MOi

DATA PEOPLE THINGS (DPT)
361

PHYSICAL ACTIVITIES (PA)

V	C	H	B	L	S
3	0*	1	4	2	3

ENVIRONMENTAL CONDITIONS (EC)
L1, L2, L3, H3, H8*

EDUCATION/TRAINING
4+, 5, R

Examples of Job Titles

Auto Glass Glazier
Glazier
Glazier and Metal Mechanic
Glazier Apprentice
Plate Glass Installer
Stained Glass Glazier
Structural Glass Glazier

Descriptor Profile

Main Characteristics

Occupations in this group are characterized by the following aptitudes, interests and worker functions as they relate to main duties:

- **General learning ability** to assemble and install prefabricated glass, mirrors and glass products on walls, ceilings and exteriors of buildings, and to fabricate metal frames for glass installation

- **Numerical ability** to prepare cost estimates for customers

- **Spatial** and **form perception** to read and interpret specifications to determine type and thickness of glass, frames and materials

- **Motor co-ordination** and **manual dexterity** to position glass panes into frames and secure glass using clips, points and mouldings

- **Methodical interest** in **compiling** information to install pre-cut mirrors and opaque and transparent glass in furniture and other products

- **Objective interest** in **precision working** to measure, mark and cut glass using glass cutters, and to replace windows and windshields in vehicles, furniture and other products

- **Innovative interest** in **speaking** with customers when preparing estimates; and in preparing and installing skylights and stained and other special glass in churches, museums and other establishments

7292

Physical Activities

Vision
   3 Near and far vision

Colour Discrimination
   0* Not relevant

Hearing
   1 Limited

Body Position
   4 Other body positions

Limb Co-ordination
   2 Multiple limb co-ordination

Strength
   3 Medium

Environmental Conditions

Location
   L1 Regulated inside climate
   L2 Unregulated inside climate
   L3 Outside

Hazards
   H3 Equipment, machinery, tools
   H8*Dangerous locations

Employment Requirements

Education/Training
   4+, 5, R

- Some secondary school education is required.

- Completion of a four-year apprenticeship program
or
a combination of over four years of work experience in the trade and some high school, college or industry courses in glazing is usually required to be eligible for trade certification.

- Trade certification is available, but not compulsory, in Prince Edward Island, Ontario, Manitoba, Saskatchewan, Alberta, British Columbia, the Northwest Territories and the Yukon.

- Interprovincial trade certification (Red Seal) is also available to qualified glaziers.

Workplaces/Employers

Construction glass installation contractors

Glass fabrication shops

Retail service and repair shops

Occupational Options

Red Seal trade certification allows for interprovincial mobility.

Progression to supervisory positions is possible with experience.

Similar Occupations Classified Elsewhere

Glass Forming and Finishing Machine Operators and Glass Cutters (9413)

Supervisors of glaziers (in 7219 *Contractors and Supervisors, Other Construction Trades, Installers, Repairers and Servicers*)

Remarks

*Physical Activities

- For some occupations in this group, Colour Discrimination 1 (Relevant) may apply.

*Environmental Conditions

- For some occupations in this group, Hazards H8 (Dangerous locations) may also apply.

7293 Insulators

Insulators apply insulation materials to plumbing, heating, cooling and refrigeration systems, piping equipment and pressure vessels, and walls, floors and ceilings of buildings and other structures in order to prevent or reduce the passage of heat, cold, sound and fire. Apprentices are included in this group.

Profile Summary

APTITUDES

G	V	N	S	P	Q	K	F	M
3	4	4	4	4	5	3	4	3

INTERESTS
MOi

DATA PEOPLE THINGS (DPT)
584

PHYSICAL ACTIVITIES (PA)

V	C	H	B	L	S
3	0	1	4	2	3

ENVIRONMENTAL CONDITIONS (EC)
L1, L2, H1*, H3, D4

EDUCATION/TRAINING
4+, 5, R

Examples of Job Titles

Boiler and Pipe Insulator
Building Insulator
Fire Insulator
Heat and Frost Insulator
Insulation Applicator
Insulation Mechanic
Insulator
Insulator Apprentice
Sound Insulator

Descriptor Profile

Main Characteristics

Occupations in this group are characterized by the following aptitudes, interests and worker functions as they relate to main duties:

- **General learning ability** to read and interpret drawings and specifications to determine insulation requirements and select type of insulation

- **Motor co-ordination** and **manual dexterity** to apply and secure insulation using spraying, blowing, pasting, strapping, taping and other application and installation methods, as well as to remove asbestos and other types of insulation from buildings

- **Methodical interest** in **copying** information to brush waterproofing cement over insulating materials to finish surfaces, and to install vapour barriers

- **Objective interest** in **operating** hand and power tools to measure and cut insulating material to required dimensions

- **Innovative interest** in fitting insulation around obstructions and between studs and joints

7293

Physical Activities

Vision
   3 Near and far vision

Colour Discrimination
   0 Not relevant

Hearing
   1 Limited

Body Position
   4 Other body positions

Limb Co-ordination
   2 Multiple limb co-ordination

Strength
   3 Medium

Environmental Conditions

Location
   L1 Regulated inside climate
   L2 Unregulated inside climate

Hazards
   H1*Dangerous chemical substances
   H3 Equipment, machinery, tools

Discomforts
   D4 Non-toxic dusts

Employment Requirements

Education/Training
4+, 5, R

- Some secondary school education is required.

- Completion of a three-to-four year apprenticeship program
  or
  a combination of over four years of work experience in the trade and some high school, college or industry courses in insulating is usually required to be eligible for trade certification.

- Trade certification is compulsory in Quebec and Saskatchewan and available, but voluntary, in New Brunswick, Alberta and British Columbia.

- Interprovincial trade certification (Red Seal) is also available to qualified insulators.

Workplaces/Employers

Construction companies

Insulation contractors

Self-employed

Occupational Options

Red Seal trade certification allows for interprovincial mobility.

Progression to supervisory positions is possible with experience.

Similar Occupations Classified Elsewhere

Supervisors of insulators (in 7219 *Contractors and Supervisors, Other Construction Trades, Installers, Repairers and Servicers*)

Remarks

*Environmental Conditions

- For some occupations in this group, Hazards H1 (Dangerous chemical substances) may also apply.

7294 Painters and Decorators

Painters and Decorators apply paint, wallpaper and other finishes to interior and exterior surfaces of buildings and other structures. Apprentices are included in this group.

Profile Summary

APTITUDES

G	V	N	S	P	Q	K	F	M
3	3	3	3	3	5	3	3	3

INTERESTS
MOi

DATA PEOPLE THINGS (DPT)
564

PHYSICAL ACTIVITIES (PA)

V	C	H	B	L	S
3	1	1	4	2	3

ENVIRONMENTAL CONDITIONS (EC)
L1, L3, H1, H3, H8*, D3, D4

EDUCATION/TRAINING
4+, 5, R

Examples of Job Titles

Construction Painter
Maintenance Painter
Painter
Painter and Decorator
Painter and Decorator Apprentice
Paperhanger

Descriptor Profile

Main Characteristics

Occupations in this group are characterized by the following aptitudes, interests and worker functions as they relate to main duties:

- **General learning ability** to apply paint and other materials such as fibreglass, metal coating and fire retardant to interior and exterior surfaces of buildings and other structures

- **Verbal ability** to advise customers on colour schemes and wall coverings

- **Numerical ability** to provide cost estimates and determine quantities of required materials

- **Motor co-ordination** to assemble and erect scaffolding and swing gates

- **Finger** and **manual dexterity** to measure, cut and apply wallpaper and fabric to walls

- **Methodical interest** in **copying** information to mix paint to obtain desired colour and texture

- **Objective interest** in **operating** spray equipment and other associated equipment and in using brushes and rollers to apply paint and other materials

- **Innovative interest** in **speaking** to customers to provide cost estimates and give advice on colour schemes and wall coverings

7294

Physical Activities

Vision
   3   Near and far vision

Colour Discrimination
   1   Relevant

Hearing
   1   Limited

Body Position
   4   Other body positions

Limb Co-ordination
   2   Multiple limb co-ordination

Strength
   3   Medium

Environmental Conditions

Location
   L1   Regulated inside climate
   L3   Outside

Hazards
   H1   Dangerous chemical substances
   H3   Equipment, machinery, tools
   H8*Dangerous locations

Discomforts
   D3   Odours
   D4   Non-toxic dusts

Employment Requirements

Education/Training
   4+, 5, R

- Some secondary school education is usually required.

- Completion of a two-to-three year apprenticeship program
  or
  over three years of work experience in the trade are usually required to be eligible for trade certification.

- Trade certification is compulsory in Quebec and voluntary in all other provinces and territories.

- Interprovincial trade certification (Red Seal) is also available to qualified painters and decorators.

Workplaces/Employers

Building maintenance contractors

Construction companies

Decorating contractors

Decorators

Painting contractors

Self-employment

Occupational Options

Red Seal trade certification allows for interprovincial mobility.

Progression to a supervisory position is possible with experience.

Similar Occupations Classified Elsewhere

Painters and Coaters, Manufacturing (9496)

Interior decorators (in 6421 *Retail Salespersons and Sales Clerks*)

Supervisors of painters and decorators (in 7219 *Contractors and Supervisors, Other Construction Trades, Installers, Repairers and Servicers*)

Remarks

*Environmental Conditions

- For some occupations in this group, Hazards H8 (Dangerous Locations) may also apply.

7295 Floor Covering Installers

Floor Covering Installers install carpet, wood, linoleum, vinyl and other resilient floor coverings in residential, commercial, industrial and institutional buildings. Apprentices are included in this group.

Profile Summary

APTITUDES

G	V	N	S	P	Q	K	F	M
3	4	3	3	3	4	3	4	3

INTERESTS
MOi

DATA PEOPLE THINGS (DPT)
464

PHYSICAL ACTIVITIES (PA)

V	C	H	B	L	S
3	0	1	4	2	4

ENVIRONMENTAL CONDITIONS (EC)
L1, L2, H3

EDUCATION/TRAINING
4+, 5, R

Examples of Job Titles

Carpet Installer
Carpet Layer
Floor Covering Installer
Floor Covering Mechanic
Resilient Floor Installer
Rug Installer
Vinyl Floor Installer

Descriptor Profile

Main Characteristics

Occupations in this group are characterized by the following aptitudes, interests and worker functions as they relate to main duties:

- **General learning ability** to measure, cut and install carpeting, resilient floor covering and hardwood floors

- **Numerical ability** to estimate material and labour costs

- **Motor co-ordination** to stretch carpeting using knee-kickers and power stretchers to secure carpeting to floors and other surfaces and to install hardwood floors, such as strip floors, block floors and plank floors, using glue, staples, nails and other means

- **Manual dexterity** to measure, cut and fasten underlay and underpadding and to install floor coverings using adhesive, rollers and other hand tools

- **Methodical interest** in **computing** to estimate costs for material and labour

- **Objective interest** in **operating** hand and machine stitchers, staple guns and seaming irons and in using bonding tape and bonding materials to install carpeting; and in operating power stretchers and other devices to stretch carpeting

- **Innovative interest** in **speaking** with customers and other workers to inspect and repair damaged floor coverings and to inspect, measure and mark surfaces to be covered

7295

Physical Activities

Vision
   3 Near and far vision

Colour Discrimination
   0 Not relevant

Hearing
   1 Limited

Body Position
   4 Other body positions

Limb Co-ordination
   2 Multiple limb co-ordination

Strength
   4 Heavy

Environmental Conditions

Location
   L1 Regulated inside climate
   L2 Unregulated inside climate

Hazards
   H3 Equipment, machinery, tools

Employment Requirements

Education/Training
4+, 5, R

- Some secondary school education is usually required.

- Completion of a two-to-three year apprenticeship program
or
over three years of work experience in the trade are usually required to be eligible for trade certification.

- Trade certification is compulsory in Quebec and voluntary in Alberta, British Columbia and the Northwest Territories.

- Interprovincial trade certification (Red Seal) is also available to qualified floor covering installers.

Workplaces/Employers

Carpet outlets

Construction companies

Floor-covering contractors

Self-employment

Occupational Options

Red Seal trade certification allows for interprovincial mobility.

Progression to supervisory positions is possible with experience.

Similar Occupations Classified Elsewhere

Supervisors of floor covering installers (in 7219 *Contractors and Supervisors, Other Construction Trades, Installers, Repairers and Servicers*)

7311 Construction Millwrights and Industrial Mechanics (Except Textile)

Construction Millwrights and Industrial Mechanics install, maintain and repair stationary industrial machinery and mechanical equipment. Apprentices are included in this group.

Profile Summary

APTITUDES

G	V	N	S	P	Q	K	F	M
3	4	3	2	3	4	3	3	3

INTERESTS
OIM

DATA PEOPLE THINGS (DPT)
260

PHYSICAL ACTIVITIES (PA)

V	C	H	B	L	S
3	0	1	4	1	4

ENVIRONMENTAL CONDITIONS (EC)
L1, L2, H3, H6, D1, D4*

EDUCATION/TRAINING
4+, 5, R

Examples of Job Titles

Construction Millwright
Industrial Mechanic
Maintenance Millwright
Millwright
Millwright Apprentice
Plant Equipment Mechanic
Treatment Plant Mechanic

Descriptor Profile

Main Characteristics

Occupations in this group are characterized by the following aptitudes, interests and worker functions as they relate to main duties:

- **General learning** and **numerical ability** to install stationary industrial machinery and mechanical equipment according to layout plans using hand and power tools

- **Spatial perception** to read diagrams and schematic drawings to determine work procedures

- **Form perception** to fabricate parts required during overhaul, maintenance and set-up of machinery

- **Motor co-ordination** and **finger** and **manual dexterity** to operate hoisting and lifting devices to position machinery and parts during the installation, set-up and repair of machinery; to operate machine tools and to construct foundations

- **Objective interest** in **setting up** and assembling machinery and equipment before installation using hand tools, power tools and welding equipment

- **Innovative interest** in analyzing information to inspect and examine machinery and equipment to detect and investigate irregularities and malfunctions, to adjust machinery and to repair and replace defective parts

- **Methodical interest** in **speaking** with other workers to direct them in constructing foundations for machinery; and in cleaning, lubricating and performing other routine maintenance work on machinery

7311

Physical Activities

Vision
3   Near and far vision

Colour Discrimination
0   Not relevant

Hearing
1   Limited

Body Position
4   Other body positions

Limb Co-ordination
1   Upper limb co-ordination

Strength
4   Heavy

Environmental Conditions

Location
L1   Regulated inside climate
L2   Unregulated inside climate

Hazards
H3   Equipment, machinery, tools
H6   Flying particles, falling objects

Discomforts
D1   Noise
D4*Non-toxic dusts

Employment Requirements

Education/Training
4+, 5, R

- Some secondary school education is required.

- Completion of a three-to-four year apprenticeship program
  or
  a combination of over five years of work experience in the trade and some high school, college or industry courses in industrial machinery repair or millwrighting is usually required to be eligible for trade certification.

- Industrial-mechanic trade certification is compulsory in Quebec and available, but voluntary, in all other provinces and territories.

- Construction millwright trade certification is available, but not compulsory, in New Brunswick and Ontario.

- Interprovincial trade certification (Red Seal) is also available to qualified industrial mechanics or millwrights.

Workplaces/Employers

Industrial establishments

Manufacturing plants

Millwrighting contractors

Utilities

Occupational Options

Red Seal certification allows for interprovincial mobility.

Progression to supervisory positions is possible with experience.

Similar Occupations Classified Elsewhere

Heavy-Duty Equipment Mechanics (7312)

Industrial Instrument Technicians and Mechanics (2243)

Textile Machinery Mechanics and Repairers (7317)

Supervisors of industrial mechanics and millwrights (in 7216 *Contractors and Supervisors, Mechanic Trades*)

Remarks

Construction millwrights are mostly engaged in the initial installation of industrial plant machinery and equipment; industrial mechanics are more concerned with post-installation maintenance and repair of machinery and equipment.

*Environmental Conditions

- For some occupations in this group, **D**iscomforts D4 (Non-toxic dusts) may also apply.

7312 Heavy-Duty Equipment Mechanics

Heavy-Duty Equipment Mechanics repair, overhaul and maintain mobile heavy-duty equipment used in construction, forestry, mining, material handling, landscaping, land clearing, farming and similar activities. Apprentices are included in this group.

Profile Summary

APTITUDES

G	V	N	S	P	Q	K	F	M
3	4	3	3	2	4	3	3	3

INTERESTS
OMI

DATA PEOPLE THINGS (DPT)
281

PHYSICAL ACTIVITIES (PA)

V	C	H	B	L	S
2	0	3	4	1	4

ENVIRONMENTAL CONDITIONS (EC)
L1, L3, H3, D1

EDUCATION/TRAINING
4+, 5, R

Examples of Job Titles

Construction Equipment Mechanic
Diesel Mechanic, Heavy Equipment
Farm Equipment Mechanic
Heavy-Duty Equipment Mechanic Apprentice
Heavy Equipment Mechanic
Heavy Mobile Logging Equipment Mechanic
Heavy Mobile Mining Equipment Mechanic
Tractor Mechanic

Descriptor Profile

Main Characteristics

Occupations in this group are characterized by the following aptitudes, interests and worker functions as they relate to main duties:

- **General learning ability** to check bulldozers, cranes, graders and other heavy construction, logging and mining equipment for proper performance

- **Form perception** to inspect equipment to detect faults and malfunctions

- **Motor co-ordination** to perform repair work on heavy trucks

- **Finger** and **manual dexterity** to test repaired equipment for proper performance and to ensure that work meets manufacturers' specifications

- **Objective interest** in **precision working** with hand and power tools to adjust equipment and repair and replace defective parts, components and systems

- **Methodical interest** in cleaning, lubricating and performing other routine maintenance work

- **Innovative interest** in **analyzing** to diagnose faults and malfunctions to determine how much repair is required

7312

Physical Activities

Vision
2 Near vision

Colour Discrimination
0 Not relevant

Hearing
3 Other sound discrimination

Body Position
4 Other body positions

Limb Co-ordination
1 Upper limb co-ordination

Strength
4 Heavy

Environmental Conditions

Location
L1 Regulated inside climate
L3 Outside

Hazards
H3 Equipment, machinery, tools

Discomforts
D1 Noise

Employment Requirements

Education/Training
4+, 5, R

- Some secondary school education is required.

- Completion of a four-year apprenticeship program
  or
  a combination of over four years of work experience in the trade and some high school, college or industry courses in heavy equipment repair is usually required to be eligible for trade certification.

- Heavy-duty equipment mechanic trade certification is compulsory in Quebec and Alberta and available, but voluntary, in all other provinces and territories.

- Farm equipment mechanic trade certification is available, but voluntary in Prince Edward Island, Ontario, Saskatchewan and Alberta.

- Interprovincial trade certification (Red Seal) is also available to qualified heavy equipment and form equipment mechanics.

- Mine equipment mechanics in Nova Scotia may require completion of a mine-equipment-repair apprenticeship program and trade certification.

Workplaces/Employers

Establishments that own and operate heavy equipment

Heavy equipment dealers

Heavy equipment rental and service establishments

Occupational Options

Red Seal certification allows for interprovincial mobility.

Progression to supervisory positions is possible with experience.

Similar Occupations Classified Elsewhere

Construction Millwrights and Industrial Mechanics (Except Textile) (7311)

Diesel mechanics, motor vehicles (in 7321 *Motor Vehicle Mechanics, Technicians and Mechanical Repairers*)

Supervisors of heavy-duty equipment mechanics (in 7216 *Contractors and Supervisors, Mechanic Trades*)

7313 Refrigeration and Air Conditioning Mechanics

Refrigeration and Air Conditioning Mechanics install, maintain, repair and overhaul residential central air-conditioning systems, commercial and industrial refrigeration and air-conditioning systems, and combined heating and cooling systems. Apprentices are included in this group.

Profile Summary

APTITUDES

G	V	N	S	P	Q	K	F	M
3	3	3	3	3	4	3	3	3

INTERESTS
OMI

DATA PEOPLE THINGS (DPT)
261

PHYSICAL ACTIVITIES (PA)

V	C	H	B	L	S
2	1	1	4	2	3

ENVRIONMENTAL CONDITIONS (EC)
L1, L2, H3, H7

EDUCATION/TRAINING
4+, 5, R

Examples of Job Titles

Central Air Conditioning Mechanic
Commercial Air Conditioning Mechanic
Heating and Cooling Mechanic
Refrigeration and Air Conditioning Mechanic
Refrigeration and Air Conditioning Mechanic Apprentice
Refrigeration Mechanic

Descriptor Profile

Main Characteristics

Occupations in this group are characterized by the following aptitudes, interests and worker functions as they relate to main duties:

- **General learning ability** to assemble and install refrigeration and air-conditioning components such as motors, controls, gauges, valves, pumps, condensers and compressors using hand and power tools

- **Spatial perception** to read and interpret blueprints, drawings and other specifications

- **Motor co-ordination** to install and maintain combined heating and cooling units, and to start up systems and test for leaks using testing devices

- **Finger** and **manual dexterity** to connect piping using welding and brazing equipment

- **Objective interest** in **precision working** to measure and cut piping and to measure and lay out reference points for installation

- **Methodical interest** in **speaking** to provide cost estimates to customers; and in recharging systems with refrigerant and in performing routine maintenance and servicing

- **Innovative interest** in **analyzing** information to repair and replace parts and components or overhaul entire refrigeration, air-conditioning and heat-pump systems, and to repair heating and cooling units

7313

Physical Activities

Vision
   2 Near vision

Colour Discrimination
   1 Relevant

Hearing
   1 Limited

Body Position
   4 Other body positions

Limb Co-ordination
   2 Multiple limb co-ordination

Strength
   3 Medium

Environmental Conditions

Location
   L1 Regulated inside climate
   L2 Unregulated inside climate

Hazards
   H3 Equipment, machinery, tools
   H7 Fire, steam, hot surfaces

Employment Requirements

Education/Training
4+, 5, R

- Some secondary school education is usually required.

- Completion of a four-year apprenticeship program
or
a combination of over five years of work experience in the trade and some high school, college or industry courses in refrigeration and air-conditioning repair is usually required to be eligible for trade certification.

- Trade certification is compulsory in Nova Scotia, Quebec, Ontario, Saskatchewan, Alberta and British Columbia and available, but voluntary, in all other provinces and territories.

- Interprovincial trade certification (Red Seal) is also available to qualified refrigeration and air-conditioning mechanics.

Workplaces/Employers

Refrigeration and air-conditioning installation contractors

Refrigeration and air-conditioning retail and servicing businesses

Occupational Options

Red Seal trade certification allows for interprovincial mobility.

Progression to supervisory positions is possible with experience.

Similar Occupations Classified Elsewhere

Domestic refrigeration and window air-conditioner servicers and repairers (in 7332 *Electric Appliance Servicers and Repairers*)

Supervisors of refrigeration and air-conditioning mechanics (in 7216 *Contractors and Supervisors, Mechanic Trades*)

7314 Railway Carmen/women

Railway Carmen/women inspect, maintain and repair railway passenger and freight cars. Apprentices are included in this group.

Profile Summary

APTITUDES

G	V	N	S	P	Q	K	F	M
3	4	4	3	3	4	3	3	3

INTERESTS
OMi

DATA PEOPLE THINGS (DPT)
381

PHYSICAL ACTIVITIES (PA)

V	C	H	B	L	S
3	0	1	4	1	3

ENVIRONMENTAL CONDITIONS (EC)
L1, L2, L3, H3

EDUCATION/TRAINING
2, 4, 5

Examples of Job Titles

Carman/woman
Railway Carman/woman
Railway Carman/woman Apprentice

Descriptor Profile

Main Characteristics

Occupations in this group are characterized by the following aptitudes, interests and worker functions as they relate to main duties:

- **General learning ability** to understand the construction and function of railway rolling stock and related equipment and to apply the appropriate techniques to repair, rebuild and adjust equipment and components

- **Spatial perception** to visualize the sequence of actions necessary to repair and replace mechanical and structural components

- **Form perception** to inspect the interiors and exteriors of passenger and freight cars to determine defects, wear and damage

- **Motor co-ordination** and **finger** and **manual dexterity** to use hand and power tools when repairing metal, wood and mechanical components

- **Objective interest** in **precision working** to test and adjust parts using test gauges and other test equipment

- **Methodical interest** in replacing damaged windows, repairing upholstery and repainting wood fixtures

- **Innovative interest** in **compiling** information to repair defective and damaged metal and wood components and to repair and install railway car parts such as compressors, air valves, bearings, air cylinders and piping

7314

Physical Activities

Vision
   3 Near and far vision

Colour Discrimination
   0 Not relevant

Hearing
   1 Limited

Body Position
   4 Other body positions

Limb Co-ordination
   1 Upper limb co-ordination

Strength
   3 Medium

Environmental Conditions

Location
   L1 Regulated inside climate
   L2 Unregulated inside climate
   L3 Outside

Hazards
   H3 Equipment, machinery, tools

Employment Requirements

Education/Training
2, 4, 5

- Some secondary school education is usually required.

- Completion of an internal company apprenticeship program or three-to-four years of on-the-job training are usually required.

Workplaces/Employers

Railway transport companies

Occupational Options

Progression to supervisory positions is possible with experience.

Similar Occupations Classified Elsewhere

Supervisors of railway carmen/women (in 7216 *Contractors and Supervisors, Mechanic Trades*)

7315.1 Aircraft Mechanics

Aircraft Mechanics maintain, repair and overhaul aircraft structures and mechanical and hydraulic systems.

Profile Summary

APTITUDES

G	V	N	S	P	Q	K	F	M
3	4	3	2	2	4	3	3	2

INTERESTS
OIM

DATA PEOPLE THINGS (DPT)
281

PHYSICAL ACTIVITIES (PA)

V	C	H	B	L	S
3	0	3	4	1	3

ENVIRONMENTAL CONDITIONS (EC)
L1, H3, D1

EDUCATION/TRAINING
6+, R

Examples of Job Titles

Aircraft Maintenance Engineer
Aircraft Mechanic, Engine Overhaul
Certified Aircraft Technician
Hydraulics Mechanic
Mechanic, Aircraft Maintenance

Descriptor Profile

Main Characteristics

Occupations in this group are characterized by the following aptitudes, interests and worker functions as they relate to main duties:

- **General learning ability** to understand the principles of aircraft construction and operation, and to apply the appropriate techniques for servicing, repairing and overhauling engines and accessories

- **Spatial perception** to visualize the arrangement and relationship of parts and assemblies when repairing and overhauling aircraft structural, mechanical and hydraulic systems

- **Form perception** to disassemble and inspect parts for wear, warping and other defects

- **Manual dexterity** to use hand and power tools to repair, replace and assemble parts, and to dismantle airframes, aircraft engines and other aircraft systems in order to repair, overhaul and then reassemble them

- **Objective interest** in **precision working** to reassemble, adjust and test engine operations to conform with specifications

- **Innovative interest** in **analyzing** information to troubleshoot aircraft structural, mechanical and hydraulic systems to identify problems, and to adjust and repair systems according to specifications and established procedures

- **Methodical interest** in installing and modifying aircraft engines and other aircraft systems

7315.1

Physical Activities

Vision
   3 Near and far vision

Colour Discrimination
   0 Not relevant

Hearing
   3 Other sound discrimination

Body Position
   4 Other body positions

Limb Co-ordination
   1 Upper limb co-ordination

Strength
   3 Medium

Environmental Conditions

Location
   L1 Regulated inside climate

Hazards
   H3 Equipment, machinery, tools

Discomforts
   D1 Noise

Employment Requirements

Education/Training
6+, R

- Completion of secondary school is required.

- A college diploma in aircraft maintenance is usually required.

- Several years of on-the-job training are required for aircraft mechanics.

- Aircraft mechanics who sign maintenance releases require an Aircraft Maintenance Engineer's (AME) licence issued by Transport Canada.

Workplaces/Employers

Aircraft manufacturing, maintenance and overhaul establishments

Aircraft operators

Airlines

Occupational Options

Aircraft mechanics may progress to foreman/woman or shop supervisor or, with an AME licence, to aircraft inspector.

Similar Occupations Classified Elsewhere

Aircraft Assemblers and Aircraft Assembly Inspectors (9481)

Aircraft engine assemblers (in 7316 *Machine Fitters*)

Aircraft mechanics and aircraft maintenance engineers specializing in maintaining electrical or avionics systems (in 2244 *Aircraft Instrument, Electrical and Avionics Mechanics, Technicians and Inspectors*)

Government airworthiness inspectors (in 2262 *Engineering Inspectors and Regulatory Officers*)

Supervisors of aircraft mechanics and aircraft inspectors (in 7216 *Contractors and Supervisors, Mechanic Trades*)

Remarks

Aircraft mechanics usually specialize in working on specific aircraft systems such as engines, engine accessories, airframes or hydraulic systems.

AME licences are issued in the following categories:

   General Maintenance
   M - Aircraft

   Specialized Maintenance
   E - Avionics Systems
   S - Structures
   P - Propulsion Systems

7315.2 Aircraft Inspectors

Aircraft Inspectors examine aircraft and aircraft systems following manufacture, modification, maintenance, repair and overhaul.

Profile Summary

APTITUDES

G	V	N	S	P	Q	K	F	M
3	3	3	2	2	4	3	3	3

INTERESTS
OMD

DATA PEOPLE THINGS (DPT)
281

PHYSICAL ACTIVITIES (PA)

V	C	H	B	L	S
3	0	3	3	1	1

ENVIRONMENTAL CONDITIONS (EC)
L1

EDUCATION/TRAINING
6+, R

Examples of Job Titles

Aircraft Inspector
Inspector, Flight Test
Inspector, Repair and Overhaul
Shop Inspector, Aircraft Repair

Descriptor Profile

Main Characteristics

Occupations in this group are characterized by the following aptitudes, interests and worker functions as they relate to main duties:

- **General learning ability** to understand the function and use of mechanical equipment and related test equipment to determine operating conditions and necessary repairs

- **Spatial perception** to visualize the arrangement and relationship of parts and assemblies when inspecting aircraft and aircraft systems

- **Form perception** to inspect, examine and test mechanical equipment and to check disassembled units for wear, cracks, splits and other damage

- **Objective interest** in **precision working** to inspect structural and mechanical systems and certify that these systems meet Transport Canada and company standards of performance and safety

- **Methodical interest** in maintaining detailed repair, inspection and certification records and reports

- **Directive interest** in **analyzing** information to inspect work of aircraft mechanics performing maintenance, repairs, overhauls and modifications of aircraft and aircraft mechanical systems to make sure they have followed standards and procedures

7315.2

Physical Activities

Vision
   3 Near and far vision

Colour Discrimination
   0 Not relevant

Hearing
   3 Other sound discrimination

Body Position
   3 Sitting, standing, walking

Limb Co-ordination
   1 Upper limb co-ordination

Strength
   1 Limited

Environmental Conditions

Location
   L1 Regulated inside climate

Employment Requirements

Education/Training
   6+, R

- Aircraft inspectors require several years of experience as an aircraft mechanic.

- Aircraft inspectors require an Aircraft Maintenance Engineer's (AME) licence with endorsements for specific aircraft types and systems.

Workplaces/Employers

Aircraft manufacturing, maintenance and overhaul establishments

Aircraft operators

Airlines

Occupational Options

With experience, aircraft inspectors may progress to shop inspector.

Similar Occupations Classified Elsewhere

Aircraft Assemblers and Aircraft Assembly Inspectors (9481)

Aircraft engine assemblers (in 7316 *Machine Fitters*)

Aircraft mechanics and aircraft maintenance engineers specializing in maintaining electrical or avionics systems (in 2244 *Aircraft Instrument, Electrical and Avionics Mechanics, Technicians and Inspectors*)

Government airworthiness inspectors (in 2262 *Engineering Inspectors and Regulatory Officers*)

Supervisors of aircraft mechanics and aircraft inspectors (in 7216 *Contractors and Supervisors, Mechanic Trades*)

Remarks

Aircraft inspectors may acquire further endorsements to their AME licence, allowing them to inspect and certify a broader range of aircraft and aircraft systems.

AME licences are issued in the following categories:

   General Maintenance
   M - Aircraft

   Specialized Maintenance
   E - Avionics Systems
   S - Structures
   P - Propulsion

7316 Machine Fitters

Machine Fitters fit, assemble and otherwise build heavy industrial machinery and transportation equipment including aircraft engines.

Profile Summary

APTITUDES

G	V	N	S	P	Q	K	F	M
3	3	3	3	3	4	3	3	3

INTERESTS
OMI

DATA PEOPLE THINGS (DPT)
381

PHYSICAL ACTIVITIES (PA)

V	C	H	B	L	S
3	0	1	4	1	4

ENVIRONMENTAL CONDITIONS (EC)
L1, H3, D1

EDUCATION/TRAINING
4, 5, 6, R

Examples of Job Titles

Aircraft Engine Fitter
Assembly Fitter
Heavy Equipment Fitter
Machine Builder
Machine Fitter
Mechanical Fitter

Descriptor Profile

Main Characteristics

Occupations in this group are characterized by the following aptitudes, interests and worker functions as they relate to main duties:

- **General learning ability** to fit and assemble prefabricated metal parts to build heavy industrial machinery and equipment such as construction, farming and processing machinery, and railway vehicles and aircraft engines

- **Spatial** and **form perception** to read and interpret blueprints, sketches and diagrams to determine assembly operations

- **Objective interest** in **precision working** to move and align subassemblies and components using lifting and transporting devices such as overhead cranes

- **Methodical interest** in inspecting parts, subassemblies and finished products to ensure quality

- **Innovative interest** in **compiling** information to install major components such as gears, pumps, motors and hydraulic assemblies

7316

Physical Activities

Vision
3   Near and far vision

Colour Discrimination
0   Not relevant

Hearing
1   Limited

Body Position
4   Other body positions

Limb Co-ordination
1   Upper limb co-ordination

Strength
4   Heavy

Environmental Conditions

Location
L1   Regulated inside climate

Hazards
H3   Equipment, machinery, tools

Discomforts
D1   Noise

Employment Requirements

Education/Training
4, 5, 6, R

- Completion of secondary school is usually required.

- Completion of a mechanical apprenticeship program, such as millwrighting, machining, pipefitting, auto mechanics or heavy equipment repair
  or
  five years of on-the-job training are usually required.

- Completion of a two-to-three year college program in aircraft manufacturing or general fabrication is required for aircraft engine fitters.

- Certification in a related trade may be required.

Workplaces/Employers

Industrial machinery manufacturing companies

Transportation equipment manufacturing companies

Occupational Options

Progression to supervisory positions is possible with experience.

Similar Occupations Classified Elsewhere

Mechanical Assemblers and Inspectors (9486)

Welders (7265)

Aircraft assemblers (in 9486 *Mechanical Assemblers and Inspectors*)

Assemblers of electrical industrial equipment (in 9485 *Assemblers, Fabricators and Inspectors, Industrial Electrical Motors and Transformers*)

Supervisors of machine fitters (in 7216 *Contractors and Supervisors, Mechanic Trades*)

7317 Textile Machinery Mechanics and Repairers

Textile Machinery Mechanics and Repairers install, maintain, repair, overhaul and set up textile machinery such as looms, knitting machines, spinning frames and carding machines.

Profile Summary

APTITUDES

G	V	N	S	P	Q	K	F	M
3	4	3	3	2	4	3	3	3

INTERESTS
OMI

DATA PEOPLE THINGS (DPT)
260

PHYSICAL ACTIVITIES (PA)

V	C	H	B	L	S
2	0	1	4	1	3

ENVIRONMENTAL CONDITIONS (EC)
L1, H3, D1

EDUCATION/TRAINING
4+, 5

Examples of Job Titles

Card Fixer
Card Grinder
Fixer, Textile Machinery
Knitting Machine Mechanic
Loom Fixer
Loom Technician
Mechanic, Textile Machines
Open-End Technician
Spinning Fixer
Textile Fixer

Descriptor Profile

Main Characteristics

Occupations in this group are characterized by the following aptitudes, interests and worker functions as they relate to main duties:

- **General learning ability** to understand and apply mechanical repair principles and procedures to make sure that machinery runs properly

- **Form perception** to detect defects and excessive wear in machinery and to see slight differences in dimensions and shapes of component parts

- **Manual dexterity** to repair and overhaul machinery

- **Objective interest** in **setting up** and adjusting complex machinery for new patterns and products

- **Methodical interest** in **analyzing** information to perform routine adjustments and maintenance

- **Innovative interest** in **speaking** with management to recommend equipment changes and modifications; and in evaluating new equipment

7317

Physical Activities

Vision
  2 Near vision

Colour Discrimination
  0 Not relevant

Hearing
  1 Limited

Body Position
  4 Other body positions

Limb Co-ordination
  1 Upper limb co-ordination

Strength
  3 Medium

Environmental Conditions

Location
  L1 Regulated inside climate

Hazards
  H3 Equipment, machinery, tools

Discomforts
  D1 Noise

Employment Requirements

Education/Training
  4+, 5

- Completion of secondary school is usually required.

- Up to three years of on-the-job training
  or
  several years of experience as a mechanic in other industries are usually required.

- Mechanics hired from other industries may require additional training in textile processes.

- Experience as a textile operator, such as weaver or tufting operator, may be required.

Workplaces/Employers

Textile manufacturing companies

Occupational Options

Progression to supervisory positions is possible with experience.

Similar Occupations Classified Elsewhere

Industrial mechanics or millwrights [in 7311 *Construction Millwrights and Industrial Mechanics (Except Textile)*]

Supervisors of textile machinery mechanics and repairers (in 7216 *Contractors and Supervisors, Mechanic Trades*)

7318 Elevator Constructors and Mechanics

Elevator Constructors and Mechanics assemble, install, maintain and repair freight and passenger elevators, escalators, moving walk-ways and other related equipment. Apprentices are included in this group.

Profile Summary

APTITUDES
G	V	N	S	P	Q	K	F	M
3	4	3	3	3	4	3	3	3

INTERESTS
OMI

DATA PEOPLE THINGS (DPT)
281

PHYSICAL ACTIVITIES (PA)
V	C	H	B	L	S
3	1	1	4	1	3

ENVIRONMENTAL CONDITIONS (EC)
L1, H3, H8

EDUCATION/TRAINING
4+, 5, R

Examples of Job Titles

Elevator Constructor
Elevator Mechanic
Elevator Mechanic Apprentice
Escalator Repairer

Descriptor Profile

Main Characteristics

Occupations in this group are characterized by the following aptitudes, interests and worker functions as they relate to main duties:

- **General learning ability** to install elevators, escalators, moving walk-ways, dumbwaiters and related equipment according to specifications

- **Spatial perception** to read and interpret blueprints to determine layout of system components

- **Motor co-ordination** to install, test and adjust safety control devices

- **Finger dexterity** to install and wire electrical control system devices

- **Manual dexterity** to disassemble defective units and to repair and replace worn and suspect parts

- **Objective interest** in **precision working** to adjust valves, ratchets, seals, brake linings and other components

- **Methodical interest** in carrying out preventive maintenance to ensure public safety

- **Innovative interest** in **analyzing** information to troubleshoot electrical and mechanical system failures and test the operation of newly installed equipment

7318

Physical Activities

Vision
  3 Near and far vision

Colour Discrimination
  1 Relevant

Hearing
  1 Limited

Body Position
  4 Other body positions

Limb Co-ordination
  1 Upper limb co-ordination

Strength
  3 Medium

Environmental Conditions

Location
  L1 Regulated inside climate

Hazards
  H3 Equipment, machinery, tools
  H8 Dangerous locations

Employment Requirements

Education/Training
4+, 5, R

- Some secondary school education is required.

- Completion of a four-to-five year apprenticeship program
  or
  a combination of over four years of work experience in the trade and some high school, college or industry courses in elevator construction or repair is usually required to be eligible for trade certification.

- Elevator-constructor-and-mechanic trade certification is compulsory in Quebec and Alberta.

- There is no provincial apprenticeship program for elevator construction and repair in the other provinces and territories.

Workplaces/Employers

Elevator construction and maintenance companies

Occupational Options

Progression to supervisory positions is possible with experience.

Similar Occupations Classified Elsewhere

Supervisors of elevator constructors and mechanics (in 7216 *Contractors and Supervisors, Mechanic Trades*)

7321.1 Motor Vehicle Mechanics and Technicians

Motor Vehicle Mechanics diagnose, repair and service mechanical, electrical and electronic systems and components of cars, buses and trucks. Apprentices are included in this group.

Profile Summary

APTITUDES
G	V	N	S	P	Q	K	F	M
3	3	4	3	3	4	3	3	3

INTERESTS
OIM

DATA PEOPLE THINGS (DPT)
261

PHYSICAL ACTIVITIES (PA)
V	C	H	B	L	S
2	1	3	4	1	3

ENVIRONMENTAL CONDITIONS (EC)
L1, H3, D1, D3

EDUCATION/TRAINING
4+, 5, R

Examples of Job Titles

Automobile Mechanic
Automotive Service Technician
Bus Mechanic
Car Mechanic
Motor Vehicle Mechanic
Transmission Mechanic
Truck Mechanic
Tune-Up Specialist, Motor Vehicle

Descriptor Profile

Main Characteristics

Occupations in this group are characterized by the following aptitudes, interests and worker functions as they relate to main duties:

- **General learning ability** to understand and apply mechanical repair principles and procedures to ensure that motor vehicles run properly

- **Verbal ability** to advise customers on work done, general vehicle conditions and future repair requirements

- **Spatial perception** to visualize the sequence of parts assembly and relative positions of machinery components

- **Form perception** to inspect motors in operation and to test systems and components using testing devices to diagnose and isolate faults

- **Motor co-ordination** and **finger** and **manual dexterity** to road-test motor vehicles, and to use hand tools and specialized automotive repair equipment when adjusting parts and components of automotive systems including fuel, brake, steering and suspension systems, transmissions, differentials, drive axles and shafts, emission-control and exhaust systems, engines and electrical, cooling and climate-control systems

- **Objective interest** in **precision working** to test and adjust repaired systems to manufacturers' performance specifications

- **Innovative interest** in **speaking** with supervisors to discuss work and review work orders; and in repairing and replacing parts and components of automotive systems

- **Methodical interest** in **analyzing** information to perform scheduled maintenance services such as oil changes, lubrication and tune-ups

7321.1
Subgroup 1 of 2

Physical Activities

Vision
  2 Near vision

Colour Discrimination
  1 Relevant

Hearing
  3 Other sound discrimination

Body Position
  4 Other body positions

Limb Co-ordination
  1 Upper limb co-ordination

Strength
  3 Medium

Environmental Conditions

Location
  L1 Regulated inside climate

Hazards
  H3 Equipment, machinery, tools

Discomforts
  D1 Noise
  D3 Odours

Employment Requirements

Education/Training
  4+, 5, R

- Completion of secondary school is usually required.

- Completion of a four-year motor-vehicle-mechanic apprenticeship program
  or
  a combination of over four years of work experience in the trade and high school, college or industry courses in automotive technology is required to be eligible for trade certification.

- Motor-vehicle-mechanic trade certification is compulsory in Newfoundland, Nova Scotia, Prince Edward Island, New Brunswick, Ontario and Alberta and available, but voluntary, in Manitoba, Saskatchewan, British Columbia, the Northwest Territories and the Yukon.

- Truck-and transport-mechanic trade certification is compulsory in Nova Scotia and available, but voluntary, in Prince Edward Island, New Brunswick, Saskatchewan and British Columbia.

- Interprovincial trade certification (Red Seal) is also available to qualified automobile mechanics and truck and transport mechanics.

Workplaces/Employers

Automotive service shops of retail establishments

Automotive specialty shops

Garages

Motor vehicle dealers

Service stations

Occupational Options

Motor-vehicle-mechanic Red Seal trade certification allows for interprovincial mobility of motor vehicle mechanics.

Truck- and transport-mechanic Red Seal trade certification allows for interprovincial mobility of truck and bus mechanics.

With additional training, mobility is possible among automobile, truck and transport mechanics.

With experience, motor vehicle mechanics may progress to supervisory positions.

Similar Occupations Classified Elsewhere

Motor Vehicle Assemblers, Inspectors and Testers (9482)

Motor Vehicle Body Repairers (7322)

Supervisors of automobile assembly metal repairers (in 9221 *Supervisors, Motor Vehicle Assembling*)

Supervisors of motor vehicle mechanics (in 7216 *Contractors and Supervisors, Mechanic Trades*)

Remarks

Motor vehicle mechanics may specialize in one of the following areas: engine and fuel systems, transmission systems, air-conditioning, cooling and heating systems, brakes, drive lines, suspension, electrical and electronic systems or diagnostic services.

7321.2 Mechanical Repairers, Motor Vehicle Manufacturing

Mechanical Repairers perform major repairs and replacement of mechanical units on newly assembled motor vehicles. Apprentices are included in this group.

Profile Summary

APTITUDES

G	V	N	S	P	Q	K	F	M
3	3	4	3	3	4	3	3	3

INTERESTS
OMi

DATA PEOPLE THINGS (DPT)
361

PHYSICAL ACTIVITIES (PA)

V	C	H	B	L	S
2	1	3	4	1	3

ENVIRONMENTAL CONDITIONS (EC)
L1, H3, D1

EDUCATION/TRAINING
4

Examples of Job Titles

Mechanical Upgrader, Automobile Manufacturing

Motor Repairer, Automobile Manufacturing

Descriptor Profile

Main Characteristics

Occupations in this group are characterized by the following aptitudes, interests and worker functions as they relate to main duties:

- **General learning ability** to understand and apply mechanical repair principles and procedures to ensure that motor vehicles run properly

- **Verbal ability** to complete reports to record problems and work performed

- **Spatial perception** to visualize the sequence of parts assembly and relative positions of machinery components

- **Form perception** to inspect motors in operation, and to test systems and components using testing devices to diagnose and isolate faults

- **Motor co-ordination** and **finger** and **manual dexterity** to repair and replace mechanical units and components using hand and power tools

- **Objective interest** in **precision working** to test and adjust units to specifications for proper performance, and to inspect and test mechanical units, such as engines, transmissions, axles and brake systems, to locate faults and malfunctions

- **Methodical interest** in **speaking** with supervisors to confirm findings on faults and malfunctions to determine whether to repair or replace units

- **Innovative interest** in **compiling** information to diagnose faults and malfunctions and to inspect and test mechanical units

7321.2
Subgroup 2 of 2

Physical Activities

Vision
   2 Near vision

Colour Discrimination
   1 Relevant

Hearing
   3 Other sound discrimination

Body Position
   4 Other body positions

Limb Co-ordination
   1 Upper limb co-ordination

Strength
   3 Medium

Environmental Conditions

Location
   L1 Regulated inside climate

Hazards
   H3 Equipment, machinery, tools

Discomforts
   D1 Noise

Employment Requirements

Education/Training
   4

- Completion of secondary school is usually required.

- On-the-job training of two-to-three years is provided by employers.

Workplaces/Employers

Motor vehicle manufacturing companies

Occupational Options

Mechanical repairers employed in motor vehicle manufacturing may progress to motor vehicle mechanic positions through an apprenticeship program, or with experience, they may progress to supervisory positions in motor vehicle manufacturing.

Similar Occupations Classified Elsewhere

Motor Vehicle Assemblers, Inspectors and Testers (9482)

Motor Vehicle Body Repairers (7322)

Supervisors of automobile assembly metal repairers (in 9221 *Supervisors, Motor Vehicle Assembling*)

Supervisors of motor vehicle mechanics (in 7216 *Contractors and Supervisors, Mechanic Trades*)

7322 Motor Vehicle Body Repairers

Motor Vehicle Body Repairers fix and restore damaged motor vehicle body parts and interior finishing. This group also includes metal repairers who repair defective automobile body parts and damage to the bodies of newly assembled cars. Apprentices are included in this group.

Profile Summary

APTITUDES

G	V	N	S	P	Q	K	F	M
3	4	4	3	3	4	3	3	3

INTERESTS
OMi

DATA PEOPLE THINGS (DPT)
481

PHYSICAL ACTIVITIES (PA)

V	C	H	B	L	S
2	1	1	4	2	3

ENVIRONMENTAL CONDITIONS (EC)
L1, H1, H3, H6, H7, D1, D3, D4

EDUCATION/TRAINING
2, 4, 5, 6, R

Examples of Job Titles

Autobody Repairer
Automotive Body Mechanic
Automotive Body Technician
Body Repairer, Motor Vehicle
Metal Finisher, Motor Vehicle Manufacturing
Metal Repairer, Motor Vehicle Manufacturing
Motor Vehicle Body Technician
Painter, Motor Vehicle Repair

Descriptor Profile

Main Characteristics

Occupations in this group are characterized by the following aptitudes, interests and worker functions as they relate to main duties:

- **General learning ability** to repair and replace front-end components, body components, doors and frames, and underbody components and to repair and replace interior components such as seat-frame assemblies, carpets and floorboard insulation

- **Spatial perception** to inspect repaired vehicles and test-drive vehicles for proper handling

- **Form perception** to hammer out dents, buckles and other defects using blocks and hammers

- **Motor co-ordination** and **finger and manual dexterity** to file, grind and sand repaired body surfaces using hand and power tools, to remove damaged fenders, panels and grills using wrenches and cutting torches and to bolt and weld replacement parts into place

- **Objective interest** in **precision working** to fill holes, dents and seams using soldering equipment and plastic filler, and to apply primers and repaint surfaces using brushes and spray guns

- **Methodical interest** in **computing** to review damage reports and estimates of repair costs and in planning work to be performed

- **Innovative interest** in repairing damaged components and straightening bent frames using frame and underbody pulling and anchoring equipment

7322

Physical Activities

Vision
  2 Near vision

Colour Discrimination
  1 Relevant

Hearing
  1 Limited

Body Position
  4 Other body positions

Limb Co-ordination
  2 Multiple limb co-ordination

Strength
  3 Medium

Environmental Conditions

Location
  L1 Regulated inside climate

Hazards
  H1 Dangerous chemical substances
  H3 Equipment, machinery, tools
  H6 Flying particles, falling objects
  H7 Fire, steam, hot surfaces

Discomforts
  D1 Noise
  D3 Odours
  D4 Non-toxic dusts

Employment Requirements

Education/Training
  2, 4, 5, 6, R

Motor vehicle body repairers:

- Completion of secondary school is usually required.

- Completion of a three-to-four year apprenticeship program *or* a combination of over three years of work experience in the trade and completion of a high school or college automotive body repair program is usually required to be eligible for trade certification.

- Trade certification is compulsory in Newfoundland, Ontario and Alberta and available, but voluntary, in Nova Scotia, Prince Edward Island, New Brunswick, Manitoba, Saskatchewan, British Columbia, the Northwest Territories and the Yukon.

- Interprovincial trade certification (Red Seal) is also available to qualified motor vehicle body repairers.

Metal repairers, motor vehicle manufacturing:

- Completion of secondary school may be required.

- One-to-two years of on-the-job training in body repair is provided by employers.

Workplaces/Employers

Automobile appraisal centers

Automobile dealerships

Automobile repair companies

Motor vehicle manufacturers

Occupational Options

Red Seal trade certification allows for interprovincial mobility of motor vehicle body repair tradespersons.

With experience, motor vehicle body repair tradespersons may progress to supervisory positions.

Metal repairers employed in motor vehicle manufacturing may progress to motor vehicle repairer positions through an apprenticeship program, or, with experience, they may progress to supervisory positions in motor vehicle manufacturing.

Similar Occupations Classified Elsewhere

Motor vehicle mechanics (in 7321 *Motor Vehicle Mechanics, Technicians and Mechanical Repairers*)

Supervisors of motor vehicle body repairers (in 7216 *Contractors and Supervisors, Mechanic Trades*)

Supervisors of automobile manufacturing metal repairers (in 9221 *Supervisors, Motor Vehicle Assembling*)

7331 Oil and Solid Fuel Heating Mechanics

Oil and Solid Fuel Heating Mechanics install and maintain oil, coal and wood heating systems in residential and commercial buildings. Apprentices are included in this group.

Profile Summary

APTITUDES

G	V	N	S	P	Q	K	F	M
3	4	4	3	3	4	3	3	3

INTERESTS
OIM

DATA PEOPLE THINGS (DPT)
261

PHYSICAL ACTIVITIES (PA)

V	C	H	B	L	S
2	1	1	4	1	4

ENVIRONMENTAL CONDITIONS (EC)
L1, H3

EDUCATION/TRAINING
4+, 5, R

Examples of Job Titles

Heating System Mechanic

Heating Technician

Oil Burner Apprentice

Oil Burner Installer

Oil Burner Mechanic

Wood Burner Installer

Descriptor Profile

Main Characteristics

Occupations in this group are characterized by the following aptitudes, interests and worker functions as they relate to main duties:

- **General learning ability** to understand and apply knowledge of heating-unit installation and maintenance principles and procedures, and to install, maintain and repair oil, coal and wood heating systems

- **Spatial perception** to read and interpret drawings and specifications to determine work to be done

- **Form perception** to lay out and assemble heating system components for oil burners

- **Motor co-ordination** to position, install and connect oil burner components such as control devices and thermostats to motors and electric power outlets using hand and power tools

- **Objective interest** in **precision working** to test installed units and adjust controls for proper functioning

- **Innovative interest** in **analyzing** information to troubleshoot and repair malfunctioning oil burners

- **Methodical interest** in **speaking** when scheduling and performing maintenance service on oil and solid-fuel heating systems

7331

Physical Activities

Vision
   2   Near vision

Colour Discrimination
   1   Relevant

Hearing
   1   Limited

Body Position
   4   Other body positions

Limb Co-ordination
   1   Upper limb co-ordination

Strength
   4   Heavy

Environmental Conditions

Location
   L1   Regulated inside climate

Hazards
   H3   Equipment, machinery, tools

Employment Requirements

Education/Training
4+, 5, R

- Some secondary school education is usually required.

- Completion of a three-to-four year apprenticeship program *or* a combination of over four years of work experience in the trade and some college or industry courses in heating-system installation and repair is usually required for trade certification.

- Trade certification is available, but not compulsory, in Newfoundland, Nova Scotia, Prince Edward Island, New Brunswick, British Columbia, the Northwest Territories and the Yukon.

- Interprovincial trade certification (Red Seal) is also available to qualified oil and solid-fuel heating mechanics.

Workplaces/Employers

Heating-systems installation and service companies

Occupational Options

Red Seal trade certification allows for interprovincial mobility.

Progression to supervisory positions is possible with experience.

Similar Occupations Classified Elsewhere

Refrigeration and Air Conditioning Mechanics (7313)

Supervisors of oil and solid-fuel heating mechanics (in 7216 *Contractors and Supervisors, Mechanic Trades*)

7332.1 Small Appliance Servicers and Repairers

Electric Appliance Servicers and Repairers service and repair small, domestic electric appliances. Apprentices are included in this group.

Profile Summary

APTITUDES

G	V	N	S	P	Q	K	F	M
3	3	3	3	3	4	3	3	3

INTERESTS
OMi

DATA PEOPLE THINGS (DPT)
364

PHYSICAL ACTIVITIES (PA)

V	C	H	B	L	S
2	1	3	3	1	2

ENVIRONMENTAL CONDITIONS (EC)
L1, H3, H4, D1

EDUCATION/TRAINING
4, R

Examples of Job Titles

Appliance Repair Apprentice
Appliance Service Technician
Appliance Servicer
Service Technician
Vacuum Cleaner Repairer

Descriptor Profile

Main Characteristics

Occupations in this group are characterized by the following aptitudes, interests and worker functions as they relate to main duties:

- **General learning ability** to repair small appliances such as power tools, kitchen toasters and electric lawn and garden equipment

- **Verbal ability** to consult customers and refer to work orders to determine why appliances do not work properly

- **Numerical ability** to prepare cost estimates of work performed

- **Spatial perception** to refer to schematic drawings and product manuals

- **Form perception** to recognize structural and mechanical defects

- **Motor co-ordination** and **finger** and **manual dexterity** to handle parts and tools and to pick up and position small parts

- **Objective interest** in operating soldering equipment and hand tools to replace and repair parts

- **Methodical interest** in compiling information to prepare reports of work done

- **Innovative interest** in speaking with customers to discuss why appliances are not working and to provide cost estimates for repairs

7332.1

Physical Activities

Vision
  2   Near vision

Colour Discrimination
  1   Relevant

Hearing
  3   Other sound discrimination

Body Position
  3   Sitting, standing, walking

Limb Co-ordination
  1   Upper limb co-ordination

Strength
  2   Light

Environmental Conditions

Location
  L1 Regulated inside climate

Hazards
  H3 Equipment, machinery, tools
  H4 Electricity

Discomforts
  D1 Noise

Employment Requirements

Education/Training
  4, R

- Small appliance repairers usually require some specialized college or high school courses or several months of on-the-job training.

- Appliance repair trade certification is compulsory in Alberta and available, but voluntary, in New Brunswick and the Northwest Territories.

Workplaces/Employers

Appliance service companies

Repair departments of retail and wholesale establishments

Repair shops

Occupational Options

Progression to supervisory positions is possible with experience.

Similar Occupations Classified Elsewhere

Electronic Service Technicians (Household and Business Equipment) (2242)

Supervisors of electric appliance servicers and repairers (in 7216 *Contractors and Supervisors, Mechanic Trades*)

7332.2 Major Appliance Repairers/Technicians

Electric Appliance Repairers service and repair major domestic electric appliances. Apprentices are included in this group.

Profile Summary

APTITUDES

G	V	N	S	P	Q	K	F	M
3	3	3	3	3	4	3	3	3

INTERESTS
OMI

DATA PEOPLE THINGS (DPT)
364

PHYSICAL ACTIVITIES (PA)

V	C	H	B	L	S
2	1	3	4	1	3

ENVIRONMENTAL CONDITIONS (EC)
L1, H3, H4

EDUCATION/TRAINING
5, 6, R

Examples of Job Titles

Appliance Repair Apprentice
Appliance Service Technician
Appliance Servicer
Dishwasher Repairer
Refrigerator Repairer
Service Technician
Stove Repairer
Washing Machine Servicer

Descriptor Profile

Main Characteristics

Occupations in this group are characterized by the following aptitudes, interests and worker functions as they relate to main duties:

- **General learning ability** to repair major appliances such as refrigerators and window air conditioners either in repair shops or in customers' residences

- **Verbal ability** to consult customers and refer to work orders to determine why appliances do not work properly

- **Numerical ability** to prepare cost estimates of work performed

- **Spatial** and **form perception** to refer to schematic diagrams and product manuals, and to disassemble appliances using hand tools

- **Motor co-ordination** and **finger** and **manual dexterity** to replace components and subcomponents and to reassemble appliances using hand tools and soldering and brazing equipment

- **Objective interest** in **operating** test equipment, such as meters and gauges to measure resistance, current, voltage and pressure, and to operate hand tools and soldering and brazing equipment

- **Methodical interest** in **speaking** to customers during service calls to repair appliances; and in planning service routes and preparing written accounts of work performed

- **Innovative interest** in **compiling** information to diagnose faults by checking controls, condensers, timer sequences, fans and other components

7332.2

Physical Activities

Vision
  2 Near vision

Colour Discrimination
  1 Relevant

Hearing
  3 Other sound discrimination

Body Position
  4 Other body positions

Limb Co-ordination
  1 Upper limb co-ordination

Strength
  3 Medium

Environmental Conditions

Location
  L1 Regulated inside climate

Hazards
  H3 Equipment, machinery, tools
  H4 Electricity

Employment Requirements

Education/Training
5, 6, R

- Major-appliance service/repair technicians require some secondary school education and completion of a college program in appliance repair
  or
  completion of a three-year apprenticeship program in appliance repair.

- Appliance-repair trade certification is compulsory in Alberta and available, but voluntary, in New Brunswick and the Northwest Territories.

Workplaces/Employers

Appliance service companies

Repair departments of retail and wholesale establishments

Repair shops

Occupational Options

Progression to supervisory positions is possible with experience.

Similar Occupations Classified Elsewhere

Electronic Service Technicians (Household and Business Equipment) (2242)

Supervisors of electric appliance servicers and repairers (in 7216 Contractors and Supervisors, Mechanic Trades)

7333 Electrical Mechanics

Electrical Mechanics maintain, test and repair electric motors, transformers, switchgears and other electrical apparatus. Apprentices are included in this group.

Profile Summary

APTITUDES

G	V	N	S	P	Q	K	F	M
3	4	4	3	3	4	3	3	3

INTERESTS
OMI

DATA PEOPLE THINGS (DPT)
281

PHYSICAL ACTIVITIES (PA)

V	C	H	B	L	S
2	1	3	4	1	2

ENVIRONMENTAL CONDITIONS (EC)
L1, H3, H4, H7, D1

EDUCATION/TRAINING
4+, 5, R

Examples of Job Titles

- Armature Winder Repairer
- Coil Winder and Repairer
- Electric Motor Repairer
- Electrical Mechanic
- Electrical Transformer Repairer
- Industrial Motor Winder Repairer
- Power Transformer Repairer
- Transformer Repairer

Descriptor Profile

Main Characteristics

Occupations in this group are characterized by the following aptitudes, interests and worker functions as they relate to main duties:

- **General learning ability** to test, observe and repair electric motors, transformers, switchgears and other electrical equipment

- **Spatial perception** to visualize relationship of parts and components when servicing and repairing

- **Form perception** to recognize mechanical defects when testing, repairing and replacing faulty wiring and components in switchgears, and when replacing and reconditioning shafts, bearings, commutators and other components

- **Motor co-ordination** to perform some machining to recondition and modify shafts, commutators and other parts

- **Finger** and **manual dexterity** to wind, assemble and install coils for motors and transformers

- **Objective interest** in **precision working** to perform static and dynamic balancing of armatures and rotors by welding, brazing and soldering electrical connections, and by aligning and adjusting parts

- **Methodical interest** in testing repaired motors, transformers, switchgears and other electrical apparatus to make sure they work properly

- **Innovative interest** in **analyzing** information to troubleshoot and repair motors, transformers, switchgears, generators and other electrical equipment

7333

Physical Activities

Vision
 2 Near vision

Colour Discrimination
 1 Relevant

Hearing
 3 Other sound discrimination

Body Position
 4 Other body positions

Limb Co-ordination
 1 Upper limb co-ordination

Strength
 2 Light

Environmental Conditions

Location
 L1 Regulated inside climate

Hazards
 H3 Equipment, machinery, tools
 H4 Electricity
 H7 Fire, steam, hot surfaces

Discomforts
 D1 Noise

Employment Requirements

Education/Training
4+, 5, R

- Completion of secondary school may be required.

- Completion of a three-to-four year apprenticeship program *or* a combination of over four years of work experience in the trade and some college or industry courses in electrical mechanics is usually required for trade certification.

- Trade certification as an electrical mechanic or electric motor winder is available, but not compulsory, in New Brunswick, Manitoba, Alberta, British Columbia and the Yukon.

Workplaces/Employers

Electrical repair shops

Maintenance departments of manufacturing companies

Service shops of electrical equipment manufacturers

Occupational Options

Although specialization may occur, workers in this group are expected to be proficient in repairing all types of electrical apparatus.

Progression to supervisory positions is possible with experience.

Similar Occupations Classified Elsewhere

Assemblers, Fabricators and Inspectors, Industrial Electrical Motors and Transformers (9485)

Industrial Electricians (7242)

Aircraft electrical mechanics (in 7315 *Aircraft Mechanics and Aircraft Inspectors*)

Supervisors of electrical mechanics (in 7216 *Contractors and Supervisors, Mechanic Trades*)

Remarks

Electrical mechanics may specialize in working with certain types of apparatus such as electric motors or transformers, or in performing certain functions such as winding coils.

7334 Motorcycle and Other Related Mechanics

Mechanics in this group test, repair and service motorcycles, motor scooters, snowmobiles, fork lifts and all-terrain vehicles. Apprentices are included in this group.

Profile Summary

APTITUDES

G	V	N	S	P	Q	K	F	M
3	3	3	3	3	4	3	3	3

INTERESTS
OMi

DATA PEOPLE THINGS (DPT)
261

PHYSICAL ACTIVITIES (PA)

V	C	H	B	L	S
2	1	3	4	1	3

ENVIRONMENTAL CONDITIONS (EC)
L1, H3, D1

EDUCATION/TRAINING
4+, 5, R

Examples of Job Titles

All-Terrain Vehicle Repairer
Motor Scooter Repairer
Motorcycle Mechanic
Snowmobile Repairer

Descriptor Profile

Main Characteristics

Occupations in this group are characterized by the following aptitudes, interests and worker functions as they relate to main duties:

- **General learning ability** to understand and apply principles of motor vehicle construction and operation to repair and service motorcycles, motor scooters, snowmobiles, fork lifts and all-terrain vehicles

- **Verbal ability** to advise customers on work done and condition of equipment

- **Numerical ability** to determine cost estimates of repairs

- **Spatial** and **form perception** to inspect and test engine and other mechanical components using test devices to diagnose and isolate faults

- **Motor co-ordination** and **finger** and **manual dexterity** to adjust, repair and replace mechanical and electrical parts and components using hand tools and equipment

- **Objective interest** in **precision working** to test and adjust repaired systems to make sure they work properly

- **Methodical interest** in **analyzing** information to perform scheduled maintenance service on equipment

- **Innovative interest** in **speaking** with supervisor to discuss work to be done and to review work orders

7334

Physical Activities

Vision
2 Near vision

Colour Discrimination
1 Relevant

Hearing
3 Other sound discrimination

Body Position
4 Other body positions

Limb Co-ordination
1 Upper limb co-ordination

Strength
3 Medium

Environmental Conditions

Location
L1 Regulated inside climate

Hazards
H3 Equipment, machinery, tools

Discomforts
D1 Noise

Employment Requirements

Education/Training
4+, 5, R

- Some secondary school education is usually required.

- For motorcycle mechanics, completion of a three-to-four year apprenticeship program
  or
  a combination of over three years of work experience in the trade and some high school or college courses in motorcycle repair is usually required to be eligible for trade certification.

- Other mechanics in this group may require several years of on-the-job training.

- Motorcycle-mechanic trade certification is compulsory in Ontario and Alberta and available, but voluntary, in British Columbia.

Workplaces/Employers

Service establishments

Service shops of motorcycle dealers and retailers

Occupational Options

Progression to supervisory positions is possible with experience.

Similar Occupations Classified Elsewhere

Other Small Engine and Equipment Mechanics (7335)

Supervisors of motorcycle and related equipment mechanics (in 7216 *Contractors and Supervisors, Mechanic Trades*)

7335 Other Small Engine and Equipment Mechanics

Mechanics in this group test, repair and service small gasoline- and diesel-powered equipment such as garden tractors, outboard motors, lawn mowers and other related equipment. Apprentices are included in this group.

Profile Summary

APTITUDES

G	V	N	S	P	Q	K	F	M
3	3	3	3	3	4	4	3	3

INTERESTS
OMi

DATA PEOPLE THINGS (DPT)
261

PHYSICAL ACTIVITIES (PA)

V	C	H	B	L	S
2	1	3	4	1	3

ENVIRONMENTAL CONDITIONS (EC)
L1, H3, D1

EDUCATION/TRAINING
4+, 5, R

Examples of Job Titles

Air-Cooled Engine Mechanic
Lawn Mower Repairer, Gasoline Powered
Motor Boat Mechanic
Outboard Motor Mechanic
Small Engine Repairer
Small Equipment Mechanic Apprentice
Small Equipment Repairer

Descriptor Profile

Main Characteristics

Occupations in this group are characterized by the following aptitudes, interests and worker functions as they relate to main duties:

- **General learning ability** to inspect, test, repair and service engines, motors and other mechanical components

- **Verbal ability** to advise customers on work done and condition of equipment

- **Numerical ability** to determine cost estimates of repairs

- **Spatial perception** to understand and visualize relationships and arrangement of parts in engines, motors and other components

- **Form perception** to detect faults in parts when inspecting and testing components

- **Finger** and **manual dexterity** to adjust, repair and replace mechanical and electrical parts and components using hand tools and equipment

- **Objective interest** in **precision working** to use test devices to diagnose and isolate faults, and to test and adjust repaired equipment to make sure it is working properly

- **Methodical interest** in **analyzing** information to perform scheduled maintenance service on equipment

- **Innovative interest** in **speaking** with supervisor to discuss work to be done and to review work orders

7335

Physical Activities

Vision
  2 Near vision

Colour Discrimination
  1 Relevant

Hearing
  3 Other sound discrimination

Body Position
  4 Other body positions

Limb Co-ordination
  1 Upper limb co-ordination

Strength
  3 Medium

Environmental Conditions

Location
  L1 Regulated inside climate

Hazards
  H3 Equipment, machinery, tools

Discomforts
  D1 Noise

Employment Requirements

Education/Training
  4+, 5, R

- Some secondary school education is usually required.

- Completion of a three-to-four year apprenticeship program in small engine or equipment repair or a combination of several years of work experience in the trade and some high school or college courses in small-engine or equipment repair is usually required for trade certification.

- Small-engine or equipment-mechanic trade certification is available, but not compulsory, in Newfoundland, Prince Edward Island, New Brunswick, Ontario, British Columbia and the Northwest Territories.

Workplaces/Employers

Dealer service shops

Service establishments

Occupational Options

Progression to supervisory positions is possible with experience.

Similar Occupations Classified Elsewhere

Motorcycle and Other Related Mechanics (7334)

Supervisors of small-engine and equipment mechanics (in 7216 *Contractors and Supervisors, Mechanic Trades*)

7341 Upholsterers

Upholsterers cover furniture, fixtures and similar items with fabric, leather and other upholstery materials.

Profile Summary

APTITUDES

G	V	N	S	P	Q	K	F	M
3	3	3	2	3	4	3	3	3

INTERESTS
OMI

DATA PEOPLE THINGS (DPT)
361

PHYSICAL ACTIVITIES (PA)

V	C	H	B	L	S
2	1	1	4	2	3

ENVIRONMENTAL CONDITIONS (EC)
L1, H3, D4

EDUCATION/TRAINING
4, 5, 6

Examples of Job Titles

Aircraft Upholsterer
Automobile Upholsterer
Custom Upholsterer
Furniture Upholsterer
Upholsterer
Upholstery Repairer

Descriptor Profile

Main Characteristics

Occupations in this group are characterized by the following aptitudes, interests and worker functions as they relate to main duties:

- **General learning ability** to understand and apply upholstering techniques and procedures and to select appropriate tools and materials in order to cover furniture, fixtures and similar items

- **Numerical ability** to provide cost estimates for upholstering furniture and other items

- **Spatial perception** to lay out, measure and cut materials according to sketches and design specifications; may make patterns from sketches, customer descriptions and blueprints

- **Motor co-ordination** and **manual dexterity** to operate sewing machines and sew materials by hand in order to seam cushions and join sections of covering materials and to replace worn-out webbing, springs and other furniture parts using hand and power tools

- **Finger dexterity** to tack, glue and sew ornamental trim, braids and buttons on upholstered items

- **Objective interest** in **precision working** to lay out and cut materials and to lay out, cut, fabricate and install upholstery in aircraft, motor vehicles, railway cars, boats and ships

- **Methodical interest** in **compiling** information to install padding and underlays and to fasten covering materials to furniture frames

- **Innovative interest** in **speaking** with customers to discuss upholstery fabric, colour and style; may repair furniture frames and refinish wood surfaces

7341

Physical Activities

Vision
  2   Near vision

Colour Discrimination
  1   Relevant

Hearing
  1   Limited

Body Position
  4   Other body positions

Limb Co-ordination
  2   Multiple limb co-ordination

Strength
  3   Medium

Environmental Conditions

Location
  L1 Regulated inside climate

Hazards
  H3 Equipment, machinery, tools

Discomforts
  D4 Non-toxic dusts

Employment Requirements

Education/Training
  4, 5, 6

- Some secondary school education is usually required.

- Completion of college or other specialized courses or program in furniture upholstering and repair *or* several years of on-the-job training, including working as an upholsterer helper, is usually required.

Workplaces/Employers

Furniture, aircraft, motor vehicle and other manufacturing companies

Furniture repair shops

Self-employment

Occupational Options

Progression to supervisory positions is possible with experience.

Similar Occupations Classified Elsewhere

Furniture and Fixture Assemblers and Inspectors (9492)

Furniture Finishers and Refinishers (9494)

Upholsterer helpers (in 9619 *Other Labourers in Processing, Manufacturing and Utilities*)

Supervisors of upholsterers in furniture manufacturing (in 9224 *Supervisors, Furniture and Fixtures Manufacturing*)

7342.1 Tailors and Dressmakers

Tailors and Dressmakers make, alter and repair tailored clothing, dresses, coats and other made-to-measure garments.

Profile Summary

APTITUDES

G	V	N	S	P	Q	K	F	M
3	3	4	3	3	4	3	2	3

INTERESTS
OIM

DATA PEOPLE THINGS (DPT)
261

PHYSICAL ACTIVITIES (PA)

V	C	H	B	L	S
2	1	2	4	1	2

ENVIRONMENTAL CONDITIONS (EC)
L1, H3

EDUCATION/TRAINING
2+, 4+

Examples of Job Titles

Alterations Dressmaker
Custom Tailor
Dressmaker
Tailor

Descriptor Profile

Main Characteristics

Occupations in this group are characterized by the following aptitudes, interests and worker functions as they relate to main duties:

- **General learning ability** to apply techniques of tailoring and dressmaking to make made-to-measure garments such as suits, dresses and coats according to customers' and clothing manufacturers' specifications

- **Spatial perception** to visualize the fit and drape of assembled garments from measurements, sketches and patterns and to design garments and draft patterns

- **Form perception** to perceive detail in style designs, patterns and material

- **Finger dexterity** to assemble, baste and sew garment parts using needle and thread and sewing machines

- **Objective interest** in **precision working** to finish and repair garments using needle and thread and to measure customers for size

- **Innovative interest** in **analyzing** information to perform specialized hand and machine sewing operations, and to alter original patterns to fit customers' measurements

- **Methodical interest** in **speaking** with customers to determine materials, styles and designs of garments, as well as to discuss garment repairs

7342.1
Subgroup 1 of 4

Physical Activities

Vision
  2 Near vision

Colour Discrimination
  1 Relevant

Hearing
  2 Verbal interaction

Body Position
  4 Other body positions

Limb Co-ordination
  1 Upper limb co-ordination

Strength
  2 Light

Environmental Conditions

Location
  L1 Regulated inside climate

Hazards
  H3 Equipment, machinery, tools

Employment Requirements

Education/Training
  2+, 4+

- Completion of secondary school may be required.

- Tailors and dressmakers require demonstrated ability to sew, style and fit men's or women's garments and may require completion of college or other courses in tailoring or dressmaking.

Workplaces/Employers

Clothing alteration shops

Clothing retailers

Garment manufacturing companies

Self-employment

Similar Occupations Classified Elsewhere

Machine Operators and Related Workers in Fabric, Fur and Leather Products Manufacturing (945)

7342.2 Furriers

Furriers make, alter and repair fur coats and other fur garments and accessories.

Profile Summary

APTITUDES

G	V	N	S	P	Q	K	F	M
3	3	4	2	2	4	3	2	3

INTERESTS
OIM

DATA PEOPLE THINGS (DPT)
281

PHYSICAL ACTIVITIES (PA)

V	C	H	B	L	S
2	1	2	4	1	2

ENVIRONMENTAL CONDITIONS (EC)
L1, H3, D4

EDUCATION/TRAINING
2+, 4+

Examples of Job Titles

Custom Furrier
Furrier

Descriptor Profile

Main Characteristics

Occupations in this group are characterized by the following aptitudes, interests and worker functions as they relate to main duties:

- **General learning ability** to apply the techniques of furriery to make, alter, restyle and repair natural fur garments and accessories

- **Verbal ability** to determine customers' sizes and style preferences

- **Spatial perception** to arrange pelts on patterns for cutting in order to achieve best appearance and symmetry

- **Form perception** to inspect pelts for texture and quality and to notice minor items relevant to styles, designs and patterns

- **Finger dexterity** to cut pelts according to patterns, and to sew fur parts and linings together to produce finished articles

- **Objective interest** in **precision working** to join furs together using sewing machines, and to lay out, stretch and trim sewn parts to conform to patterns

- **Innovative interest** in **analyzing** pelts to grade, sort and match furs

- **Methodical interest** in preparing skins by cutting off unusable parts

7342.2
Subgroup 2 of 4

Physical Activities

Vision
   2 Near vision

Colour Discrimination
   1 Relevant

Hearing
   2 Verbal interaction

Body Position
   4 Other body positions

Limb Co-ordination
   1 Upper limb co-ordination

Strength
   2 Light

Environmental Conditions

Location
   L1 Regulated inside climate

Hazards
   H3 Equipment, machinery, tools

Discomforts
   D4 Non-toxic dusts

Employment Requirements

Education/Training
   2+, 4+

- Completion of secondary school may be required.

- Furriers require several years of experience in selecting pelts and making, fitting, styling and altering fur garments and accessories.

Workplaces/Employers

Clothing alteration shops

Clothing retailers

Garment manufacturing companies

Self-employment

Similar Occupations Classified Elsewhere

Machine Operators and Related Workers in Fabric, Fur and Leather Products Manufacturing (945)

7342.3 Milliners

Milliners make, alter and repair hats.

Profile Summary

APTITUDES

G	V	N	S	P	Q	K	F	M
3	3	4	3	3	4	3	2	3

INTERESTS
OIM

DATA PEOPLE THINGS (DPT)
281

PHYSICAL ACTIVITIES (PA)

V	C	H	B	L	S
2	1	2	4	1	2

ENVIRONMENTAL CONDITIONS (EC)
L1, H3

EDUCATION/TRAINING
2+

Examples of Job Titles

Milliner

Descriptor Profile

Main Characteristics

Occupations in this group are characterized by the following aptitudes, interests and worker functions as they relate to main duties:

- **General learning ability** to apply knowledge of millinery techniques and to plan and create original and fashionable designs

- **Spatial perception** to visualize shape, arrangement and relationship of materials, trimmings and ornaments

- **Form perception** to make accurate visual comparisons of completed hats against existing, or original, designs and specifications

- **Finger dexterity** to hand-sew linings, ribbons, veils and other trimmings to hats

- **Objective interest** in **precision working** to shape, wire, sew, glue and block materials using hat forms, needle and thread, sewing machines, steamers and hand irons

- **Innovative interest** in **analyzing** information to alter hats to customers' specifications by changing shapes, ornaments and trimmings

- **Methodical interest** in cutting materials following patterns and using scissors

7342.3
Subgroup 3 of 4

Physical Activities

Vision
   2 Near vision

Colour Discrimination
   1 Relevant

Hearing
   2 Verbal interaction

Body Position
   4 Other body positions

Limb Co-ordination
   1 Upper limb co-ordination

Strength
   2 Light

Environmental Conditions

Location
   L1 Regulated inside climate

Hazards
   H3 Equipment, machinery, tools

Employment Requirements

Education/Training
   2+

- Completion of secondary school may be required.

- Milliners require demonstrated ability to sew, style and fit hats and caps.

Workplaces/Employers

Clothing alteration shops

Clothing retailers

Garment manufacturing companies

Self-employment

Similar Occupations Classified Elsewhere

Machine Operators and Related Workers in Fabric, Fur and Leather Products Manufacturing (945)

7342.4 Seamstresses

Seamstresses fit, alter and repair garments.

Profile Summary

APTITUDES

G	V	N	S	P	Q	K	F	M
3	3	4	3	3	4	3	2	3

INTERESTS
OMI

DATA PEOPLE THINGS (DPT)
361

PHYSICAL ACTIVITIES (PA)

V	C	H	B	L	S
2	1	2	4	1	2

ENVIRONMENTAL CONDITIONS (EC)
L1, H3

EDUCATION/TRAINING
2+

Examples of Job Titles

Seamstress

Descriptor Profile

Main Characteristics

Occupations in this group are characterized by the following aptitudes, interests and worker functions as they relate to main duties:

- **General learning ability** to fit, alter and repair garments according to customers' requests by hand and using sewing machines

- **Spatial perception** to position and pin sections on fabric, cut fabric according to patterns and visualize fit of garments when making alterations

- **Form perception** to perceive detail in designs, patterns and materials

- **Finger dexterity** to sew garments using needle and thread and to baste and pin fabric parts in preparation for final sewing

- **Objective interest** in **precision working** to make alterations while maintaining the drape and proportion of garments

- **Methodical interest** in **speaking** with customers to determine alterations and repairs required

- **Innovative interest** in **compiling** information from marks on garments and from garment repair tags to make alterations and repairs

7342.4

Physical Activities

Vision
   2 Near vision

Colour Discrimination
   1 Relevant

Hearing
   2 Verbal interaction

Body Position
   4 Other body positions

Limb Co-ordination
   1 Upper limb co-ordination

Strength
   2 Light

Environmental Conditions

Location
   L1 Regulated inside climate

Hazards
   H3 Equipment, machinery, tools

Employment Requirements

Education/Training
   2+

- Completion of secondary school may be required.

- Seamstresses require demonstrated ability to sew, alter and repair garments.

Workplaces/Employers

Clothing alteration shops

Clothing retailers

Garment manufacturing companies

Self-employment

Similar Occupations Classified Elsewhere

Machine Operators and Related Workers in Fabric, Fur and Leather Products Manufacturing (945)

7343.1 Shoemakers

Shoemakers make specialized and custom shoes and boots.

Profile Summary

APTITUDES

G	V	N	S	P	Q	K	F	M
3	3	4	3	3	4	3	2	3

INTERESTS
OIM

DATA PEOPLE THINGS (DPT)
361

PHYSICAL ACTIVITIES (PA)

V	C	H	B	L	S
2	1	2	1	1	2

ENVIRONMENTAL CONDITIONS (EC)
L1, H3, D3

EDUCATION/TRAINING
2+

Examples of Job Titles

Bootmaker
Custom Shoemaker
Orthopaedic Shoemaker
Shoemaker

Descriptor Profile

Main Characteristics

Occupations in this group are characterized by the following aptitudes, interests and worker functions as they relate to main duties:

- **General learning ability** to understand and apply custom-shoemaking techniques to make specialized footwear

- **Verbal ability** to discuss type of footwear to be made with customers; may supervise other shoemakers and shoe repairers

- **Spatial** and **form perception** to select patterns, leather and other materials and to outline and cut patterns

- **Finger dexterity** to select and assemble lasts, fasten insoles to lasts, and sew and glue other parts into place

- **Objective interest** in **precision working** to trim, dress and otherwise finish boots and shoes

- **Innovative interest** in **compiling** information from customers to estimate custom-footwear costs

- **Methodical interest** in **speaking** with customers to obtain their measurements and receive payment

7343.1
Subgroup 1 of 2

Physical Activities

Vision
   2   Near vision

Colour Discrimination
   1   Relevant

Hearing
   2   Verbal interaction

Body Position
   1   Sitting

Limb Co-ordination
   1   Upper limb co-ordination

Strength
   2   Light

Environmental Conditions

Location
   L1   Regulated inside climate

Hazards
   H3   Equipment, machinery, tools

Discomforts
   D3   Odours

Employment Requirements

Education/Training
   2+

- Some secondary school may be required.

- Extensive on-the-job training is provided for shoemakers.

- Shoemakers may require experience as shoe repairers.

Workplaces/Employers

Custom shoemaking establishments

Self-employment

Similar Occupations Classified Elsewhere

Labourers in shoe manufacturing (in 9619 *Other Labourers in Processing, Manufacturing and Utilities*)

Workers who cut fabric or leather to form shoe parts on a production basis (in 9452 *Fabric, Fur and Leather Cutters*)

Workers who operate sewing machines to make shoes on a production basis (in 9451 *Sewing Machine Operators*)

7343.2 Shoe Repairers

Shoe Repairers mend footwear.

Profile Summary

APTITUDES

G	V	N	S	P	Q	K	F	M
3	3	4	3	3	5	3	3	3

INTERESTS
OMI

DATA PEOPLE THINGS (DPT)
561

PHYSICAL ACTIVITIES (PA)

V	C	H	B	L	S
2	1	2	1	1	2

ENVIRONMENTAL CONDITIONS (EC)
L1, H3, D3

EDUCATION/TRAINING
2

Examples of Job Titles

Shoe Repairer

Descriptor Profiles

Main Characteristics

Occupations in this group are characterized by the following aptitudes, interests and worker functions as they relate to main duties:

- **General learning** and **verbal ability** to repair and refinish shoes according to customer specifications

- **Form perception** to perceive detail to determine the nature of damages and type of shoes

- **Motor co-ordination** and **finger** and **manual dexterity** to restitch ripped portions and sew patches over shoe uppers by hand and machine

- **Objective interest** in **precision working** to repair soles, heels and other parts of footwear using sewing, buffing and other shoe repair machines, materials and equipment

- **Methodical interest** in **speaking** to customers to estimate footwear-repair costs and receive payment

- **Innovative interest** in **copying** information to remove damaged parts in order to repair shoes, belts, luggage, purses and similar products

7343.2

Physical Activities

Vision
  2   Near vision

Colour Discrimination
  1   Relevant

Hearing
  2   Verbal interaction

Body Position
  1   Sitting

Limb Co-ordination
  1   Upper limb co-ordination

Strength
  2   Light

Environmental Conditions

Location
  L1   Regulated inside climate

Hazards
  H3   Equipment, machinery, tools

Discomforts
  D3   Odours

Employment Requirements

Education/Training
2

- Some secondary school may be required.

- Several months of on-the-job training is provided for shoe repairers.

Workplaces/Employers

Self-employment

Shoe repair shops

Occupational Options

Shoe repairers may progress to shoemakers with experience.

Similar Occupations Classified Elsewhere

Labourers in shoe manufacturing (in 9619 *Other Labourers in Processing, Manufacturing and Utilities*)

Workers who cut fabric or leather to form shoe parts on a production basis (in 9452 *Fabric, Fur and Leather Cutters*)

Workers who operate sewing machines to make shoes on a production basis (in 9451 *Sewing Machine Operators*)

7344.1 Jewellers and Related Workers

Jewellers and Related Workers fabricate, assemble, repair and appraise fine jewellery.

Profile Summary

APTITUDES

G	V	N	S	P	Q	K	F	M
3	3	3	2	2	4	3	2	3

INTERESTS
OIM

DATA PEOPLE THINGS (DPT)
281

PHYSICAL ACTIVITIES (PA)

V	C	H	B	L	S
1	1	2	1	1	1

ENVIRONMENTAL CONDITIONS (EC)
L1, H3

EDUCATION/TRAINING
5, 6

Examples of Job Titles

Diamond Cutter
Gem Cutter
Gemologist
Pearl Cutter
Precious Stone Setter

Descriptor Profile

Main Characteristics

Occupations in this group are characterized by the following aptitudes, interests and worker functions as they relate to main duties:

- **General learning ability** to understand the composition and structure of precious stones and metals to fabricate and repair precious and semi-precious metal jewellery such as rings, brooches, pendants, bracelets and lockets; may supervise other jewellers

- **Spatial perception** to visualize designs to set precious and semi-precious stones in jewellery mountings according to specifications

- **Form perception** to detect peculiarities affecting stone values

- **Finger dexterity** to mark cutting lines, cut and polish precious stones and solder intricate and fine pieces of jewellery to form rings, bracelets and brooches

- **Objective interest** in **precision working** to examine, cut, shape and polish diamonds and precious and synthetic gems using optical instruments, lathes, laps and cutting disks

- **Innovative interest** in **analyzing** information to appraise gemstones and diamonds and to identify rare specimens

- **Methodical interest** in cutting, sawing and filing articles in preparation for further processing

7344.1

Physical Activities

Vision
 1 Close visual acuity

Colour Discrimination
 1 Relevant

Hearing
 2 Verbal interaction

Body Position
 1 Sitting

Limb Co-ordination
 1 Upper limb co-ordination

Strength
 1 Limited

Environmental Conditions

Location
 L1 Regulated inside climate

Hazards
 H3 Equipment, machinery, tools

Employment Requirements

Education/Training
5, 6

- Completion of secondary school is usually required.

- Completion of a college or other program, or apprenticeship training in jewellery repair, is usually required.

- Experience as a jewellery assembler may be required.

Workplaces/Employers

Jewellery and watch repair shops

Jewellery, clock and watch manufacturers

Jewellery retail stores

Self-employment

Occupational Options

Mobility is possible among the various jewellery occupations in this group.

There is little mobility between the jewellery occupations and the watch repairers in the 7344 group.

Similar Occupations Classified Elsewhere

Jewellery and clock and watch production assemblers (in 9498 *Other Assemblers and Inspectors*)

Silversmiths and jewellery artisans (in 5244 *Artisans and Craftspersons*)

7344.2 Watch Repairers

Watch Repairers clean, adjust, repair and fabricate parts for clocks and watches.

Profile Summary

APTITUDES

G	V	N	S	P	Q	K	F	M
3	3	3	3	2	4	3	2	3

INTERESTS
OIM

DATA PEOPLE THINGS (DPT)
281

PHYSICAL ACTIVITIES (PA)

V	C	H	B	L	S
1	0	2	1	1	1

ENVIRONMENTAL CONDITIONS (EC)
L1, H3

EDUCATION/TRAINING
5, 6, R

Examples of Job Titles

Clock Repairer
Watch Repairer
Watchmaker

Descriptor Profile

Main Characteristics

Occupations in this group are characterized by the following aptitudes, interests and worker functions as they relate to main duties:

- **General learning ability** to understand the principles of clockwork mechanisms, to apply the techniques to fabricate and fit parts to make watches and clocks, and to make repairs and adjust timepieces and clock-operated devices; may supervise other watch repairers

- **Form perception** to examine clocks and watches and perform repairs and adjustments

- **Finger dexterity** to work with minute parts to repair and replace damaged parts, and to lubricate and adjust mechanisms

- **Objective interest** in **precision working** when using watchmaking instruments to fabricate, repair and replace timepieces and to test, adjust and regulate timepiece movements

- **Innovative interest** in **analyzing** information to identify the causes of malfunctions and to fabricate and fit parts

- **Methodical interest** in cleaning, polishing and lubricating timepieces and other parts

7344.2

Physical Activities

Vision
1 Close visual acuity

Colour Discrimination
0 Not relevant

Hearing
2 Verbal interaction

Body Position
1 Sitting

Limb Co-ordination
1 Upper limb co-ordination

Strength
1 Limited

Environmental Conditions

Location
L1 Regulated inside climate

Hazards
H3 Equipment, machinery, tools

Employment Requirements

Education/Training
5, 6, R

- Completion of secondary school is usually required.

- Completion of a college or other program, or apprenticeship training in watch repair, is usually required.

- Experience as a jewellery, clock or watch assembler may be required.

- A watch repairer certificate is compulsory in Quebec and Ontario.

Workplaces/Employers

Clock and watch manufacturers

Jewellery retail stores

Self-employment

Watch repair shops

Occupational Options

There is little mobility between the jewellery occupations and the watch repairers in the 7344 group.

Similar Occupations Classified Elsewhere

Jewellery and clock- and watch-production assemblers (in 9498 *Other Assemblers and Inspectors*)

Silversmiths and jewellery artisans (in 5244 *Artisans and Craftspersons*)

7351 Stationary Engineers and Auxiliary Equipment Operators

Stationary Engineers and Auxiliary Equipment Operators run and maintain various types of stationary engines and auxiliary equipment such as boilers, turbines, generators, compressors and other equipment to provide heat, ventilation, refrigeration, light and power for buildings, industrial plants and other work sites.

Profile Summary

APTITUDES

G	V	N	S	P	Q	K	F	M
3	3	3	3	4	4	3	4	3

INTERESTS
Oim

DATA PEOPLE THINGS (DPT)
282

PHYSICAL ACTIVITIES (PA)

V	C	H	B	L	S
2	0	1	4	1	2

ENVIRONMENTAL CONDITIONS (EC)
L1, H3, D1

EDUCATION/TRAINING
4, 5, 6, R

Examples of Job Titles

Auxiliary Plant Operator
Boiler Operator
Power Engineer
Power Engineer Apprentice
Stationary Engineer
Stationary Engineer Apprentice
Steam Plant Operator

Descriptor Profile

Main Characteristics

Occupations in this group are characterized by the following aptitudes, interests and worker functions as they relate to main duties:

- **General learning ability** to operate and maintain stationary engines such as boilers, turbines, generators, compressors and other equipment that provide heat, ventilation, refrigeration, light and power for buildings, industrial plants and other work sites

- **Spatial perception** to visualize the relationship of components in stationary engines to make adjustments and minor repairs

- **Motor co-ordination** and **manual dexterity** to clean and lubricate generators, turbines, pumps and compressors, and to perform other routine equipment maintenance using lubricants and hand tools

- **Objective interest** in **controlling** and operating automated and computerized control systems, stationary engines and auxiliary equipment

- **Innovative interest** in **analyzing** information from instrument readings to detect leaks and other equipment malfunctions

- **Methodical interest** in recording instrument readings, in monitoring and inspecting plant equipment, switches, valves, gauges, alarms, meters and other instruments to measure temperature, pressure and fuel flow, and in ensuring plant equipment is operating normally

7351

Physical Activities

Vision
  2 Near vision

Colour Discrimination
  0 Not relevant

Hearing
  1 Limited

Body Position
  4 Other body positions

Limb Co-ordination
  1 Upper limb co-ordination

Strength
  2 Light

Environmental Conditions

Location
  L1 Regulated inside climate

Hazards
  H3 Equipment, machinery, tools

Discomforts
  D1 Noise

Employment Requirements

Education/Training
  4, 5, 6, R

- Completion of secondary school is usually required.

- Completion of a regulated apprenticeship program in stationary or power engineering or on-the-job training and correspondence courses, high school courses or a college training program in stationary or power engineering are required.

- Provincial or territorial certification according to class (4th, 3rd, 2nd and 1st class and an additional 5th class in Manitoba, Saskatchewan and the Northwest Territories) is required.

Workplaces/Employers

Commercial establishments

Governments

Hospitals

Industrial and manufacturing plants

Universities

Occupational Options

Progression from lower to higher classes for stationary or power engineers is dependent on further training and experience.

Similar Occupations Classified Elsewhere

Power Systems and Power Station Operators (7352)

Professional engineers (in 213 *Civil, Mechanical, Electrical and Chemical Engineers* and 214 *Other Engineers*)

Supervisors of stationary engineers and auxiliary equipment operators (in 9212 *Supervisors, Petroleum, Gas and Chemical Processing and Utilities*)

7352.1 Power Systems Operators

Power Systems Operators monitor and operate switchboards and related equipment in electrical control centers to control the distribution of electrical power in transmission networks. Apprentices are included in this group.

Profile Summary

APTITUDES

G	V	N	S	P	Q	K	F	M
3	3	3	4	3	3	4	4	4

INTERESTS
Omi

DATA PEOPLE THINGS (DPT)
262

PHYSICAL ACTIVITIES (PA)

V	C	H	B	L	S
2	0	2	3	0	1

ENVIRONMENTAL CONDITIONS (EC)
L1, H5*

EDUCATION/TRAINING
4, 5, R

Examples of Job Titles

Apprentice Power Dispatcher
Chief Operator, Area Dispatch
Distribution Control Operator
Nuclear Reactor Operator
Power Plant Operator
Power System Operator

Descriptor Profile

Main Characteristics

Occupations in this group are characterized by the following aptitudes, interests and worker functions as they relate to main duties:

- **General learning ability** to monitor and operate computerized and pneumatically controlled switchboards and auxiliary equipment in electrical control centers

- **Verbal** and **numerical ability** to co-ordinate and schedule generating station and substation power loads and line voltages to meet distribution demands during daily operations, system outages, repairs, and importing and exporting of power

- **Form perception** to monitor and inspect station instruments, meters and alarms to ensure that transmission voltages and line loadings are within prescribed limits, and to detect equipment failure, line disturbances and outages

- **Clerical perception** to complete and maintain station records, logs and reports

- **Objective interest** in **controlling** the distribution and regulating the flow of electrical power in transmission networks by operating switchboards and auxiliary equipment

- **Methodical interest** in **speaking** to issue work and test permits to electrical and mechanical maintenance personnel; and in assisting during routine system testing

- **Innovative interest** in **analyzing** information to direct generating station and substation power loads and line voltages to meet distribution demands, and to assist maintenance and technical personnel to locate and isolate system problems

7352.1
Subgroup 1 of 2

Physical Activities

Vision
   2 Near vision

Colour Discrimination
   0 Not relevant

Hearing
   2 Verbal interaction

Body Position
   3 Sitting, standing, walking

Limb Co-ordination
   0 Not relevant

Strength
   1 Limited

Environmental Conditions

Location
   L1 Regulated inside climate

Hazards
   H5*Radiation

Employment Requirements

Education/Training
   4, 5, R

- Completion of secondary school is usually required for power system operators.

- Power-system operators require completion of a three-to-five year power-system-operator apprenticeship program
or
over three years of work experience in the trade and some college or industry courses in electrical and electronic technology.

- Trade certification is available but not mandatory for power system operators in Newfoundland.

Workplaces/Employers

Electric power utilities

Large manufacturing facilities

Occupational Options

Progression to supervisory positions is possible with experience.

Similar Occupations Classified Elsewhere

Stationary Engineers and Auxiliary Equipment Operators (7351)

Supervisors of power system and power station operators (in 9212 *Supervisors, Petroleum, Gas and Chemical Processing and Utilities*)

Remarks

*Environmental Conditions

- For some occupations in this group, **H**azards H5 (Radiation) may apply.

7352.2 Power Station Operators

Power Station Operators run reactors, turbines, boilers, generators and other related equipment in electrical generating stations and substations. Apprentices are included in this group.

Profile Summary

APTITUDES

G	V	N	S	P	Q	K	F	M
3	3	3	4	3	3	4	4	4

INTERESTS
Omi

DATA PEOPLE THINGS (DPT)
262

PHYSICAL ACTIVITIES (PA)

V	C	H	B	L	S
2	0	2	3	1	2

ENVIRONMENTAL CONDITIONS (EC)
L1, H3, H4*, D1

EDUCATION/TRAINING
4, 5, R

Examples of Job Titles

Apprentice Power Dispatcher
Diesel Station Operator
Generating Station Operator
Nuclear Reactor Operator
Power Dispatcher

Descriptor Profile

Main Characteristics

Occupations in this group are characterized by the following aptitudes, interests and worker functions as they relate to main duties:

- **General learning ability** to operate reactors, turbines, boilers, generators, condensers and auxiliary equipment in hydro, thermal and nuclear power plants

- **Verbal and numerical ability** to communicate with systems operators to regulate water levels, transmission loads, frequency and line voltages

- **Form perception** to monitor and inspect power plant equipment and equipment indicators to detect operating problems

- **Clerical perception** to complete and maintain station records, logs and reports

- **Objective interest** in **controlling** switching operations, starting up and shutting down power plant equipment

- **Methodical interest** in **speaking** with systems operators to regulate and co-ordinate transmission loads, frequency and line voltages

- **Innovative interest** in **analyzing** information to make adjustments and minor repairs

Physical Activities

Vision
  2 Near vision

Colour Discrimination
  0 Not relevant

Hearing
  2 Verbal interaction

Body Position
  3 Sitting, standing, walking

Limb Co-ordination
  1 Upper limb co-ordination

Strength
  2 Light

Environmental Conditions

Location
  L1 Regulated inside climate

Hazards
  H3 Equipment, machinery, tools
  H4*Electricity

Discomforts
  D1 Noise

Employment Requirements

Education/Training
  4, 5, R

- Completion of secondary school is usually required for power station operators.

- Power station operators require an apprenticeship program in stationary or power engineering
or
several years of work experience in the trade and some high school, correspondence or college courses in stationary or power engineering.

- Power station operators require a provincial or territorial power engineering or stationary engineering certificate according to class.

Workplaces/Employers

Electric power utilities

Large manufacturing facilities

Occupational Options

Progression to supervisory positions is possible with experience.

Similar Occupations Classified Elsewhere

Stationary Engineers and Auxiliary Equipment Operators (7351)

Supervisors of power system and power station operators (in 9212 Supervisors, Petroleum, Gas and Chemical Processing and Utilities)

Remarks

*Environmental Conditions

- For some occupations in this group, Hazards H4 (Electricity) may also apply.

7361.1 Railway Locomotive Engineers

Railway Locomotive Engineers operate railway locomotives to transport passengers and freight.

Profile Summary

APTITUDES

G	V	N	S	P	Q	K	F	M
3	3	3	3	3	4	4	4	3

INTERESTS
OMi

DATA PEOPLE THINGS (DPT)
363

PHYSICAL ACTIVITIES (PA)

V	C	H	B	L	S
4	1	3	1	2	2

ENVIRONMENTAL CONDITIONS (EC)
L4, D1, D2

EDUCATION/TRAINING
4, R

Examples of Job Titles

Freight Railway Engineer
Locomotive Engineer, Railway
Railway Engineer
Switch Engineer

Descriptor Profile

Main Characteristics

Occupations in this group are characterized by the following aptitudes, interests and worker functions as they relate to main duties:

- **General learning ability** to understand and apply railway procedures, rules and regulations

- **Verbal ability** to communicate with train crews and traffic control personnel to give and receive information and instructions concerning stops, delays and oncoming trains

- **Spatial perception** to visualize the relationship of moving trains to other objects, to judge distances and to visualize the proper function of train and track systems

- **Form perception** to inspect equipment for wear and defects, and to observe tracks to see that they are clear of obstacles

- **Manual dexterity** to move controls in response to visual signals

- **Objective interest** in **operating** locomotives to transport passengers and freight on railways; and in operating communication systems

- **Methodical interest** in **speaking - signalling** with train crews and traffic controllers to ensure safe operation and scheduling of trains

- **Innovative interest** in **compiling** information to inspect assigned locomotives and test operating controls and equipment

7361.1

Physical Activities

Vision
    4 Total visual field

Colour Discrimination
    1 Relevant

Hearing
    3 Other sound discrimination

Body Position
    1 Sitting

Limb Co-ordination
    2 Multiple limb co-ordination

Strength
    2 Light

Environmental Conditions

Location
    L4 In a vehicle or cab

Discomforts
    D1 Noise
    D2 Vibration

Employment Requirements

Education/Training
    4, R

- Completion of secondary school is usually required.

- Experience as a conductor is required for railway locomotive engineers.

- Level A Certificate of the Canadian Rail Operating Rules is required for railway locomotive engineers.

Workplaces/Employers

Railway transport companies

Occupational Options

Mobility among railway transport companies or among establishments employing locomotive engineers may be limited due to seniority provisions of collective agreements.

Similar Occupations Classified Elsewhere

Supervisors, Railway Transport Operations (7221)

7361.2 Yard Locomotive Engineers

Yard Locomotive Engineers operate locomotives within yards of railway, industrial and other establishments.

Profile Summary

APTITUDES

G	V	N	S	P	Q	K	F	M
3	4	4	3	4	4	4	4	3

INTERESTS
OMi

DATA PEOPLE THINGS (DPT)
363

PHYSICAL ACTIVITIES (PA)

V	C	H	B	L	S
4	1	3	1	2	2

ENVIRONMENTAL CONDITIONS (EC)
L3, L4, D1, D2

EDUCATION/TRAINING
4

Examples of Job Titles

Railway Hostler
Yard Engineer, Railway

Descriptor Profile

Main Characteristics

Occupations in this group are characterized by the following aptitudes, interests and worker functions as they relate to main duties:

- **General learning ability** to understand and apply railway procedures, rules and regulations

- **Spatial perception** to visualize the relationship of moving trains to other objects, to judge distances and to visualize the proper functioning of train and track systems

- **Manual dexterity** to move controls in response to visual signals when switching cars

- **Objective interest** in **operating** locomotives to switch, couple and uncouple cars for loading and unloading

- **Methodical interest** in **speaking - signalling** to perform switching operations according to written switching orders and dispatched instructions

- **Innovative interest** in **compiling** information to inspect locomotives, replenish fuel and perform routine maintenance on locomotives

7361.2
Subgroup 2 of 2

Physical Activities

Vision
 4 Total visual field

Colour Discrimination
 1 Relevant

Hearing
 3 Other sound discrimination

Body Position
 1 Sitting

Limb Co-ordination
 2 Multiple limb co-ordination

Strength
 2 Light

Environmental Conditions

Location
 L3 Outside
 L4 In a vehicle or cab

Discomforts
 D1 Noise
 D2 Vibration

Employment Requirements

Education/Training
 4

- Completion of secondary school is usually required.

- Experience as a conductor may be required for yard locomotive engineers.

- Experience as a railway yard worker may be required for yard locomotive engineers.

Workplaces/Employers

Industrial and commercial users of rail transport

Railway transport companies

Occupational Options

Mobility among railway transport companies or among establishments employing locomotive engineers may be limited due to seniority provisions of collective agreements.

Similar Occupations Classified Elsewhere

Supervisors, Railway Transport Operations (7221)

7362.1 Railway Conductors

Railway Conductors co-ordinate and supervise the activities of passenger and freight train crews.

Profile Summary

APTITUDES

G	V	N	S	P	Q	K	F	M
3	3	4	4	4	3	4	4	4

INTERESTS
DMs

DATA PEOPLE THINGS (DPT)
137

PHYSICAL ACTIVITIES (PA)

V	C	H	B	L	S
3	0	2	3	0	1

ENVIRONMENTAL CONDITIONS (EC)
L1, L4

EDUCATION/TRAINING
4, R

Examples of Job Titles

Freight Train Conductor
Passenger Train Conductor
Railway Conductor
Train Conductor

Descriptor Profile

Main Characteristics

Occupations in this group are characterized by the following aptitudes, interests and worker functions as they relate to main duties:

- **General learning ability** to understand orders, operating procedures and regulations, and to communicate with train crews by radio, signals and other means to give and receive train operation information

- **Verbal ability** to receive orders and explain them to brakemen/women, locomotive engineers and other crew members, and to announce approaching train stops

- **Clerical perception** to prepare train run reports

- **Directive interest** in **supervising** the activities of passenger and freight train crew members (except locomotive engineers) to ensure that trains run according to schedules, orders and operating rules

- **Methodical interest** in **co-ordinating** the activities of passenger and freight train crews

- **Social interest** in **handling** money to collect fares on passenger trains and in answering passenger inquiries

7362.1

Physical Activities

Vision
　　3　Near and far vision

Colour Discrimination
　　0　Not relevant

Hearing
　　2　Verbal interaction

Body Position
　　3　Sitting, standing, walking

Limb Co-ordination
　　0　Not relevant

Strength
　　1　Limited

Environmental Conditions

Location
　　L1　Regulated inside climate
　　L4　In a vehicle or cab

Employment Requirements

Education/Training
　　4, R

- Completion of secondary school is usually required.

- Experience as a brakeman/woman is required for conductors.

- Level A Certificate of the Canadian Rail Operating Rules is required for railway conductors.

Workplaces/Employers

Railway transport companies

Occupational Options

With experience, railway conductors may progress to locomotive engineers.

Similar Occupations Classified Elsewhere

Railway and Yard Locomotive Engineers (7361)

Supervisors, Railway Transport Operations (7221)

7362.2 Brakemen/women

Brakemen/women check train brakes and other systems and equipment before train departures, and assist railway conductors in activities en route.

Profile Summary

APTITUDES

G	V	N	S	P	Q	K	F	M
3	4	4	4	4	4	4	4	3

INTERESTS
OMi

DATA PEOPLE THINGS (DPT)
564

PHYSICAL ACTIVITIES (PA)

V	C	H	B	L	S
4	1	3	4	2	3

ENVIRONMENTAL CONDITIONS (EC)
L1, L3, L4, H3, D1

EDUCATION/TRAINING
4, R

Examples of Job Titles

Brakeman/woman
Front-End Brakeman/woman
Road Freight Brakeman/woman
Trail-End Brakeman/woman

Descriptor Profile

Main Characteristics

Occupations in this group are characterized by the following aptitudes, interests and worker functions as they relate to main duties:

- **General learning ability** to understand orders received from traffic controllers, to observe signals and track conditions and to open and close track switches

- **Manual dexterity** to check systems and equipment, such as air-conditioning and heating systems, and brakes and brake hoses, before departure

- **Objective interest** in **operating** to set and release hand brakes, to connect air brake hoses, and to couple and switch passenger and freight cars; and in making minor repairs to couplings, air hoses and wheel-bearing boxes

- **Methodical interest** in **copying** information to check systems and equipment such as air conditioning and heating systems, and brakes and brake hoses before departure

- **Innovative interest** in **speaking - signalling** to communicate with train crews by radio, signals and other means to aid operations, and to assist in collecting fares and helping passengers on and off trains

7362.2
Subgroup 2 of 2

Physical Activities

Vision
    4   Total visual field

Colour Discrimination
    1   Relevant

Hearing
    3   Other sound discrimination

Body Position
    4   Other body positions

Limb Co-ordination
    2   Multiple limb co-ordination

Strength
    3   Medium

Environmental Conditions

Location
    L1 Regulated inside climate
    L3 Outside
    L4 In a vehicle or cab

Hazards
    H3 Equipment, machinery, tools

Discomforts
    D1 Noise

Employment Requirements

Education/Training
    4, R

- Completion of secondary school is usually required.

- Experience as a railway worker is usually required for brakemen/women.

- Level B Certificate of the Canadian Rail Operating Rules is required for brakemen/women.

Workplaces/Employers

Railway transport companies

Occupational Options

With experience, brakemen/women may progress to railway conductors.

Similar Occupations Classified Elsewhere

Railway and Yard Locomotive Engineers (7361)

Supervisors, Railway Transport Operations (7221)

7371 Crane Operators

Crane Operators use cranes and draglines to lift, move, position and place machinery, equipment and other large objects at construction and industrial sites, ports, railway yards and other locations. Apprentices are included in this group.

Profile Summary

APTITUDES

G	V	N	S	P	Q	K	F	M
3	4	5	3	4	4	3	4	3

INTERESTS
OMi

DATA PEOPLE THINGS (DPT)
683

PHYSICAL ACTIVITIES (PA)

V	C	H	B	L	S
4	0	1	1	2	2

ENVIRONMENTAL CONDITIONS (EC)
L4, H8, D1

EDUCATION/TRAINING
4, 5, R

Examples of Job Titles

Boom Truck Crane Operator
Bridge Crane Operator
Climbing Crane Operator
Construction Crane Operator
Crane Operator
Dragline Crane Operator
Gantry Crane Operator
Mobile Crane Operator
Tower Crane Operator
Tractor Crane Operator

Descriptor Profile

Main Characteristics

Occupations in this group are characterized by the following aptitudes, interests and worker functions as they relate to main duties:

- **General learning ability** to operate mobile and tower cranes to lift, move, position and place equipment and materials at construction sites, shipyards, industrial yards and other locations

- **Spatial perception** to visualize the relative positions of objects and materials being moved

- **Motor co-ordination** and **manual dexterity** to operate cranes equipped with dredging attachments to dredge waterways and other areas, and to operate pile-driving cranes to drive pilings into earth to provide support for buildings and other structures

- **Objective interest** in operating gantry cranes to load and unload ship cargo at port side; locomotive cranes to move objects and materials at railway yards; bridge and overhead cranes to lift, move and place plant machinery and materials; and offshore oil-rig cranes to unload and reload supply vessels

- **Methodical interest** in performing routine maintenance work such as cleaning and lubricating cranes

- **Innovative interest** in **comparing** information to lift, move and place equipment and materials using cranes mounted on boats and barges

7371

Physical Activities

Vision
　4　Total visual field

Colour Discrimination
　0　Not relevant

Hearing
　1　Limited

Body Position
　1　Sitting

Limb Co-ordination
　2　Multiple limb co-ordination

Strength
　2　Light

Environmental Conditions

Location
　L4　In a vehicle or cab

Hazards
　H8　Dangerous locations

Discomforts
　D1　Noise

Employment Requirements

Education/Training
　4, 5, R

- Some secondary school education is required.

- Completion of a one-to-three year apprenticeship program
  or
  high school, college or industry courses in crane operating are usually required.

- Trade certification as a general crane operator is compulsory in Quebec and available, but voluntary, in Newfoundland, Saskatchewan and British Columbia.

- Internal company certification as a crane operator may be required by some employers.

- Boom truck crane operator trade certification is compulsory in Alberta.

- Mobile crane operator trade certification is compulsory in Ontario and Alberta.

- Tower-crane-operator trade certification is compulsory in Ontario, Alberta and British Columbia.

- Mobile crane operators may require a provincial licence to drive mobile cranes on public roads.

- Interprovincial trade certification (Red Seal) is also available to mobile crane operators.

Workplaces/Employers

Cargo handlers

Construction companies

Industrial companies

Railway companies

Occupational Options

Progression to supervisory positions is possible with experience.

Red Seal trade certification for mobile crane operators allows for interprovincial mobility.

Similar Occupations Classified Elsewhere

Heavy Equipment Operators (Except Crane) (7421)

Supervisors of crane operators (in 7217 *Contractors and Supervisors, Heavy Construction Equipment Crews*)

7372.1 Drillers - Surface Mining, Quarrying and Construction

Drillers in this group operate mobile drilling machines to bore blast holes in open-pit mines and quarries, and to bore holes for blasting and for building foundations at construction sites.

Profile Summary

APTITUDES

G	V	N	S	P	Q	K	F	M
3	4	4	3	4	4	3	4	3

INTERESTS
OMi

DATA PEOPLE THINGS (DPT)
582

PHYSICAL ACTIVITIES (PA)

V	C	H	B	L	S
4	1	1	4	2	3

ENVIRONMENTAL CONDITIONS (EC)
L3, L4, H3, H6, H8, D1, D2, D4

EDUCATION/TRAINING
2

Examples of Job Titles

Construction Driller
Driller, Construction
Foundation Drill Operator
Open-Pit Driller
Rotary Drilling Machine Operator

Descriptor Profile

Main Characteristics

Occupations in this group are characterized by the following aptitudes, interests and worker functions as they relate to main duties:

- **General learning ability** to operate machines to drill blast holes in rock at road and other construction sites

- **Spatial perception** to visualize positioning of drilling equipment, the locations of drill bits in drill holes, and the nature of rock formations penetrated

- **Motor co-ordination** and **manual dexterity** to drive and operate tracked and truck-mounted drills equipped with augers and other attachments to drill holes for building foundations and pilings

- **Objective interest** in **controlling** the operation of tracked and truck-mounted rotary drills, air-track drills and other drilling machines to bore large blast holes to specified depths at staked positions in open-pit mines and quarries

- **Methodical interest** in **copying** information to scale loose rock from walls, remove dust, install roof bolts and timbers, and clear broken rock from drilling areas as safety precautions; may measure locations and stake out patterns of holes to be drilled, load blast holes with explosives and detonate explosives to dislodge coal, ore and rock

- **Innovative interest** in servicing drilling equipment and making minor repairs

7372.1
Subgroup 1 of 2

Physical Activities

Vision
  4   Total visual field

Colour Discrimination
  1   Relevant

Hearing
  1   Limited

Body Position
  4   Other body positions

Limb Co-ordination
  2   Multiple limb co-ordination

Strength
  3   Medium

Environmental Conditions

Location
  L3   Outside
  L4   In a vehicle or cab

Hazards
  H3   Equipment, machinery, tools
  H6   Flying particles, falling objects
  H8   Dangerous locations

Discomforts
  D1   Noise
  D2   Vibration
  D4   Non-toxic dusts

Employment Requirements

Education/Training
2

- Some secondary school education is required.

- On-the-job training is provided.

- Experience as a heavy equipment operator may be required for drillers.

Workplaces/Employers

Drilling and blasting contractors

Mining, quarrying and construction companies

Occupational Options

Progression to supervisory positions is possible with experience.

Drillers often perform both drilling and blasting activities.

Similar Occupations Classified Elsewhere

Water Well Drillers (7373)

Oil and gas well drillers (in 8232 Oil and Gas Well Drillers, Servicers, Testers and Related Workers)

Supervisors of construction drillers and blasters (in 7217 Contractors and Supervisors, Heavy Construction Equipment Crews)

Supervisors of surface mining drillers and blasters (in 8221 Supervisors, Mining and Quarrying)

Underground mine drillers and blasters (in 8231 Underground Production and Development Miners)

7372.2 Blasters - Surface Mining, Quarrying and Construction

Blasters in this group fill blast holes with explosives and detonate explosives to dislodge coal, ore and rock and to demolish structures.

Profile Summary

APTITUDES

G	V	N	S	P	Q	K	F	M
3	4	4	3	3	4	3	3	3

INTERESTS
OID

DATA PEOPLE THINGS (DPT)
261

PHYSICAL ACTIVITIES (PA)

V	C	H	B	L	S
3	1	1	4	1	3

ENVIRONMENTAL CONDITIONS (EC)
L3, H1, H6, H8, D1, D4

EDUCATION/TRAINING
2, R

Examples of Job Titles

Blaster, Construction
Blaster, Surface Mining
Construction Blaster
Open-Pit Blaster

Descriptor Profile

Main Characteristics

Occupations in this group are characterized by the following aptitudes, interests and worker functions as they relate to main duties:

- **General learning ability** to understand and apply the principles, techniques and safety regulations that apply to the use, handling and firing of explosives

- **Spatial** and **form perception** to read instructions and diagrams, to lay out drill patterns and to determine depth and diameter of blast holes

- **Motor co-ordination** and **finger and manual dexterity** to load explosives in blast holes by hand, to press handles or buttons to detonate charges, to handle, store and transport explosives and accessories according to regulations, and to ensure that safety procedures are followed

- **Objective interest** in **precision working** to connect electrical wires, detonating cords and fuses into series, and to connect the series to blasting machines; may operate air-track, rotary, down-the-hole and other drilling machines

- **Innovative interest** in **analyzing** information to conduct field tests to determine the type and quantity of explosives required

- **Directive interest** in **speaking** with other workers to direct them in assembling primer charges using selected detonators, fuses, detonating cords and other materials, and to direct bulk-explosive trucks to load holes; may direct drilling of blast holes

7372.2
Subgroup 2 of 2

Physical Activities

Vision
   3 Near and far vision

Colour Discrimination
   1 Relevant

Hearing
   1 Limited

Body Position
   4 Other body positions

Limb Co-ordination
   1 Upper limb co-ordination

Strength
   3 Medium

Environmental Conditions

Location
   L3 Outside

Hazards
   H1 Dangerous chemical substances
   H6 Flying particles, falling objects
   H8 Dangerous locations

Discomforts
   D1 Noise
   D4 Non-toxic dusts

Employment Requirements

Education/Training
   2, R

- Some secondary school education is required.

- On-the-job training is provided.

- Experience as a blaster helper in surface mining and quarrying or construction may be required for blasters.

- Provincial blasting licence is usually required for blasters.

Workplaces/Employers

Drilling and blasting contractors

Mining, quarrying and construction companies

Occupational Options

Progression to supervisory positions is possible with experience.

Blasters often perform both drilling and blasting activities.

Similar Occupations Classified Elsewhere

Water Well Drillers (7373)

Oil and gas well drillers (in 8232 *Oil and Gas Well Drillers, Servicers, Testers and Related Workers*)

Supervisors of construction drillers and blasters (in 7217 *Contractors and Supervisors, Heavy Construction Equipment Crews*)

Supervisors of surface mining drillers and blasters (in 8221 *Supervisors, Mining and Quarrying*)

Underground mine drillers and blasters (in 8231 *Underground Production and Development Miners*)

7373 Water Well Drillers

Water Well Drillers operate a variety of mobile water-well drilling rigs and equipment to drill residential, commercial and industrial water wells. Apprentices are included in this group.

Profile Summary

APTITUDES

G	V	N	S	P	Q	K	F	M
3	4	4	3	4	4	3	4	3

INTERESTS
OMi

DATA PEOPLE THINGS (DPT)
662

PHYSICAL ACTIVITIES (PA)

V	C	H	B	L	S
3	0	1	4	2	3

ENVIRONMENTAL CONDITIONS (EC)
L3, H3, D1, D2, D5

EDUCATION/TRAINING
4+, 5, R

Examples of Job Titles

Cable Tool Driller - Water Well
Churn Drill Operator - Water Well
Water Well Driller
Water Well Driller Apprentice

Descriptor Profile

Main Characteristics

Occupations in this group are characterized by the following aptitudes, interests and worker functions as they relate to main duties:

- **General learning ability** to install, test, maintain and repair water-well pumps, piping systems and equipment, and to perform pumping tests for assessing well performance; may provide other drilling services such as repair and dismantling of existing water-well structures, and drilling elevator shafts and hydro pole holes

- **Spatial perception** to visualize the positioning of drilling equipment

- **Motor co-ordination** and **manual dexterity** to operate controls of water-well drilling equipment

- **Objective interest** in **controlling** water-well drilling rigs and other equipment to drill, bore and dig for residential, commercial and industrial water wells and to install well screens, casings and other well fixtures

- **Methodical interest** in **comparing** information to perform routine maintenance work on water-well drilling rigs and equipment

- **Innovative interest** in **speaking** to review client needs and proposed locations for water wells

7373

Physical Activities

Vision
   3   Near and far vision

Colour Discrimination
   0   Not relevant

Hearing
   1   Limited

Body Position
   4   Other body positions

Limb Co-ordination
   2   Multiple limb co-ordination

Strength
   3   Medium

Environmental Conditions

Location
   L3 Outside

Hazards
   H3 Equipment, machinery, tools

Discomforts
   D1 Noise
   D2 Vibration
   D5 Wetness

Employment Requirements

Education/Training
   4+, 5, R

- Some secondary school education is usually required.

- Completion of a two-to-three year water-well drilling apprenticeship program
or
two-to-three years of work experience in the trade combined with college or industry courses in water-well drilling are usually required to be eligible for trade certification.

- Trade certification is compulsory in New Brunswick and available, but voluntary, in Alberta and British Columbia.

Workplaces/Employers

Governments

Self-employment

Water-well drilling contractors

Occupational Options

Mobility is possible among the various well drilling operators in this group.

Progression to supervisory positions is possible with experience.

Similar Occupations Classified Elsewhere

Surface mining, quarrying and construction drillers (in 7372 *Drillers and Blasters - Surface Mining, Quarrying and Construction*)

Water-well drilling contractors and supervisors of water-well drillers (in 7217 *Contractors and Supervisors, Heavy Construction Equipment Crews*)

Remarks

Water well drillers may specialize in a specific method of drilling such as cable, rotary, auger, hammer or reverse circulation drilling.

7381 Printing Press Operators

Printing Press Operators set up and operate sheet- and web-fed presses to print illustrations, designs and text on paper, plastic, sheet metal and other material.

Profile Summary

APTITUDES

G	V	N	S	P	Q	K	F	M
3	3	4	3	3	3	3	3	3

INTERESTS
MOi

DATA PEOPLE THINGS (DPT)
660

PHYSICAL ACTIVITIES (PA)

V	C	H	B	L	S
2	1	1	4	1	3

ENVIRONMENTAL CONDITIONS (EC)
L1, D1, D3

EDUCATION/TRAINING
4, 5, 6, R

Examples of Job Titles

Apprentice Pressman/woman
Assistant Pressman/woman
First Pressman/woman
Flexographic Press Operator
Offset Press Operator
Printing Press Operator
Rotogravure Pressman/woman - Printing

Descriptor Profile

Main Characteristics

Occupations in this group are characterized by the following aptitudes, interests and worker functions as they relate to main duties:

- **General learning ability** to understand and operate sheet- and web-fed presses to print illustrations and text; may direct press crews to set up, operate and shut down large presses

- **Motor co-ordination** and **manual dexterity** to mount plates and cylinders, to make necessary adjustments and to operate presses at slow speeds to check samples for ink coverage, alignment and registration

- **Finger dexterity** to fill ink fountains and make measurements, adjustments and settings to control colour and viscosity

- **Methodical interest** in **comparing** information to monitor regular press runs for quality consistency and make adjustments; and in removing and cleaning plates at the end of press runs

- **Objective interest** in **setting up** and adjusting in-line binding and finishing equipment

- **Innovative interest** in **speaking** with supervisor to review job orders to determine job specifications, such as production time, colour sequence and quantities required, and to advise press crew of these specifications

7381

Physical Activities

Vision
   2 Near vision

Colour Discrimination
   1 Relevant

Hearing
   1 Limited

Body Position
   4 Other body positions

Limb Co-ordination
   1 Upper limb co-ordination

Strength
   3 Medium

Environmental Conditions

Location
   L1 Regulated inside climate

Discomforts
   D1 Noise
   D3 Odours

Employment Requirements

Education/Training
   4, 5, 6, R

- Completion of secondary school is usually required.

- Completion of a college program in printing technology
  or
  a four-year apprenticeship program in printing
  or
  a combination of on-the-job training and specialized high school, college or industry courses is usually required.

- Trade certification is available, but not compulsory, in Ontario, Alberta and the Northwest Territories.

Workplaces/Employers

Commercial printing companies

In-house printing departments of public- and private-sector publishing companies

Magazines

Newspapers

Occupational Options

Progression to supervisory positions, such as pressroom supervisor, is possible with experience.

Similar Occupations Classified Elsewhere

Supervisors, Printing and Related Occupations (7218)

Operators of laser printers, computerized high-speed colour copiers and printing machines (in 9471 *Printing Machine Operators*)

Screen printing artisans (in 5244 *Artisans and Craftspersons*)

Textile printers (in 9443 *Textile Dyeing and Finishing Machine Operators*)

7382　Commercial Divers

Commercial Divers perform underwater activities related to construction, inspection, search, salvage, repair and photography.

Profile Summary

APTITUDES

G	V	N	S	P	Q	K	F	M
3	3	4	3	3	5	3	3	3

INTERESTS
OIM

DATA PEOPLE THINGS (DPT)
364

PHYSICAL ACTIVITIES (PA)

V	C	H	B	L	S
4	0	3	4	2	4

ENVIRONMENTAL CONDITIONS (EC)
L3, H1, H3, H6, H8, D5

EDUCATION/TRAINING
5, R

Examples of Job Titles

Commercial Diver
Diver
Offshore Diver
Skin Diver, Commercial
Underwater Contractor
Underwater Welder
Underwater Worker

Descriptor Profile

Main Characteristics

Occupations in this group are characterized by the following aptitudes, interests and worker functions as they relate to main duties:

- **General learning ability** to perform offshore oil and gas exploration and extraction duties such as underwater surveys, non-destructive testing, blasting and construction; may supervise and train other divers

- **Spatial** and **form perception** to inspect vessels, buoyage systems, pipelines, sluice gates, plant intakes and outfalls and other materials, both visually and by non-destructive testing

- **Motor co-ordination** and **manual dexterity** to perform construction duties such as welding and installing pilings for cofferdams and footings for piers, and to maintain these and other structures using hand tools, power tools and pneumatic equipment

- **Objective interest** in **operating** underwater video, sonar, recording and related equipment for scientific and exploratory purposes; and in operating winches, derricks and cranes to manipulate cables and chains to raise sunken objects

- **Innovative interest** in **speaking - signalling** to participate in search-and-rescue, salvage, recovery and clean-up operations

- **Methodical interest** in **compiling** information to check and maintain diving equipment such as helmets, masks, air tanks, harnesses and gauges; and in setting up and detonating explosives to remove obstructions and break up or refloat submerged objects

7382

Physical Activities

Vision
 4 Total visual field

Colour Discrimination
 0 Not relevant

Hearing
 3 Other sound discrimination

Body Position
 4 Other body positions

Limb Co-ordination
 2 Multiple limb co-ordination

Strength
 4 Heavy

Environmental Conditions

Location
 L3 Outside

Hazards
 H1 Dangerous chemical substances
 H3 Equipment, machinery, tools
 H6 Flying particles, falling objects
 H8 Dangerous locations

Discomforts
 D5 Wetness

Employment Requirements

Education/Training
 5, R

- Completion of secondary school education is usually required.

- Completion of a recognized commercial-diving-school program is required.

- Military or police diving experience may be required.

- A Category I commercial diver's licence issued by the National Energy Board (NEB) or its equivalent is required.

- A provincial blaster's licence is usually required for the setting and detonation of explosives.

Workplaces/Employers

Commercial diving contractors

Oil and gas companies with offshore operations

Shipping and marine construction companies

7383.1 Gunsmiths

Gunsmiths repair, service, modify, calibrate and fabricate firearms.

Profile Summary

APTITUDES

G	V	N	S	P	Q	K	F	M
3	4	4	3	3	4	3	3	3

INTERESTS
OIM

DATA PEOPLE THINGS (DPT)
261

PHYSICAL ACTIVITIES (PA)

V	C	H	B	L	S
1	0	2	1	1	2

ENVIRONMENTAL CONDITIONS (EC)
L1, H3

EDUCATION/TRAINING
4, 5, R

Examples of Job Titles

Gunsmith
Small Arms Repairer

Descriptor Profile

Main Characteristics

Occupations in this group are characterized by the following aptitudes, interests and worker functions as they relate to main duties:

- **General learning ability** to fabricate, repair and modify firearms

- **Spatial** and **form perception** to read blueprints and interpret customers' specifications when fabricating and repairing firearms

- **Motor co-ordination** and **finger** and **manual dexterity** to use hand and power tools such as chisels, files, scrapers and broaching and grinding machines to fabricate, repair and finish firearms

- **Objective interest** in **precision working** to assemble parts, attach and adjust sights, and test completed firearms to determine strength characteristics, correct alignment and assembly

- **Innovative interest** in **analyzing** to examine and repair parts of guns such as barrels, firing mechanisms, sights and stocks

- **Methodical interest** in **speaking** with customers to determine specifications when fabricating and repairing firearms

7383.1
Subgroup 1 of 5

Physical Activities

Vision
 1 Close visual acuity

Colour Discrimination
 0 Not relevant

Hearing
 2 Verbal interaction

Body Position
 1 Sitting

Limb Co-ordination
 1 Upper limb co-ordination

Strength
 2 Light

Environmental Conditions

Location
 L1 Regulated inside climate

Hazards
 H3 Equipment, machinery, tools

Employment Requirements

Education/Training
 4, 5, R

- Some secondary school education is required.

- Completion of two-to-three year apprenticeship program in a relevant trade
 or
 college, high school or industry courses combined with several years of related work experience
 or
 several years of on-the-job training are required.

- Provincial trade certification or licence may be required for some occupations in this group.

Workplaces/Employers

Firearms fabrication and repair establishments

Self-employment

Occupational Options

There is little or no mobility among occupations in this group.

Progression to supervisory positions is possible with experience.

7383.2 Locksmiths

Locksmiths repair, service, install, calibrate and fabricate locks and keys.

Profile Summary

APTITUDES

G	V	N	S	P	Q	K	F	M
3	3	4	3	3	4	3	3	3

INTERESTS
OMi

DATA PEOPLE THINGS (DPT)
281

PHYSICAL ACTIVITIES (PA)

V	C	H	B	L	S
2	0	1	4	1	2

ENVIRONMENTAL CONDITIONS (EC)
L1, L3

EDUCATION/TRAINING
4, 5, R

Examples of Job Titles

Locksmith

Descriptor Profile

Main Characteristics

Occupations in this group are characterized by the following aptitudes, interests and worker functions as they relate to main duties:

- **General learning ability** to repair, install and adjust locks, make keys and change lock combinations

- **Spatial perception** to visualize the placement of parts when installing and adjusting locks

- **Form perception** to perceive detail when detecting physical defects in worn and damaged tumblers, springs and other parts

- **Motor co-ordination** to insert new and repaired tumblers into locks to change combinations

- **Finger** and **manual dexterity** to cut new and duplicate keys using key-cutting machines

- **Objective interest** in **precision working** to manipulate lockpicks in cylinders to open jammed locks and locks without keys, and to fabricate parts

- **Methodical interest** in replacing worn and damaged parts by chiselling, filing, scraping and other tooling to correct dimensions

- **Innovative interest** in **analyzing** to disassemble locks such as padlocks and door locks to locate defects

7383.2
Subgroup 2 of 5

Physical Activities

Vision
  2 Near vision

Colour Discrimination
  0 Not relevant

Hearing
  1 Limited

Body Position
  4 Other body positions

Limb Co-ordination
  1 Upper limb co-ordination

Strength
  2 Light

Environmental Conditions

Location
  L1 Regulated inside climate
  L3 Outside

Employment Requirements

Education/Training
  4, 5, R

- Some secondary school education is required.

- Completion of two-to-three year locksmith-apprenticeship program
  or
  college, high school or industry courses combined with several years of related work experience
  or
  several years of on-the-job training are required.

- Provincial trade certification or licence may be required for some occupations in this group.

Workplaces/Employers

Lock service companies

Self-employment

Occupational Options

There is little or no mobility among occupations in this group.

Progression to supervisory positions is possible with experience.

7383.3 Recreational Vehicle Repairers

Recreational Vehicle Repairers service and repair recreational vehicles.

Profile Summary

APTITUDES

G	V	N	S	P	Q	K	F	M
3	4	4	3	3	4	3	3	3

INTERESTS
OIM

DATA PEOPLE THINGS (DPT)
261

PHYSICAL ACTIVITIES (PA)

V	C	H	B	L	S
2	0	2	4	1	2

ENVIRONMENTAL CONDITIONS (EC)
L1, L3, H3

EDUCATION/TRAINING
4, 5, R

Examples of Job Titles

Recreation Vehicle Repairer

Descriptor Profile

Main Characteristics

Occupations in this group are characterized by the following aptitudes, interests and worker functions as they relate to main duties:

- **General learning ability** to repair and replace electrical wiring, plumbing, propane gas lines, windows, doors, cabinets and structural frames

- **Spatial perception** to visualize relationships and arrangements of parts in vehicle mechanisms and assemblies when repairing and replacing electrical wiring, plumbing and propane gas lines

- **Form perception** to detect defects when repairing and replacing damaged exterior panels and sealing leaks, and to install accessories such as air conditioners, T.V. antennas and awnings

- **Motor co-ordination** to check for leaks in water, refrigeration and propane gas systems using pressure gauges, manometers and gas leak detectors

- **Finger** and **manual dexterity** to use materials such as insulating tape, electrical connectors, caulking compounds, copper and plastic piping and fittings, and to use hand and plumbing tools when repairing wiring, propane gas lines and plumbing

- **Objective interest** in **precision working** to inspect and test functional units, wiring, piping and components such as switches, electric motors and valves to determine specific repairs and replacements

- **Innovative interest** in **analyzing** to disassemble and repair or replace stoves, heaters, pumps and other malfunctioning units, and to repair wiring and test electrical systems

- **Methodical interest** in **speaking** with owners to discuss nature of malfunctions and damages to assess extent of repairs required; and in inspecting new vehicles before delivery according to manufacturers' instructions and motor vehicle regulations

7383.3

Physical Activities

Vision
  2 Near vision

Colour Discrimination
  0 Not relevant

Hearing
  2 Verbal interaction

Body Position
  4 Other body positions

Limb Co-ordination
  1 Upper limb co-ordination

Strength
  2 Light

Environmental Conditions

Location
  L1 Regulated inside climate
  L3 Outside

Hazards
  H3 Equipment, machinery, tools

Employment Requirements

Education/Training
  4, 5, R

- Some secondary school education is required.

- Completion of two-to-three year apprenticeship program in recreational vehicle mechanics
  or
  college, high school or industry courses combined with several years of related work experience
  or
  several years of on-the-job training are required.

- Provincial trade certification or licence may be required for some occupations in this group.

Workplaces/Employers

Recreational vehicle repair shops

Self-employment

Occupational Options

There is little or no mobility among occupations in this group.

Progression to supervisory positions is possible with experience.

7383.4 Safe and Vault Servicers

Safe and Vault Servicers repair, service and install safes and vaults and calibrate and service locks and locking devices.

Profile Summary

APTITUDES

G	V	N	S	P	Q	K	F	M
3	4	4	3	4	4	3	4	3

INTERESTS
OMi

DATA PEOPLE THINGS (DPT)
581

PHYSICAL ACTIVITIES (PA)

V	C	H	B	L	S
2	0	1	4	1	4

ENVIRONMENTAL CONDITIONS (EC)
L1, H3

EDUCATION/TRAINING
4, 5, R

Examples of Job Titles

Safe and Vault Servicer

Descriptor Profile

Main Characteristics

Occupations in this group are characterized by the following aptitudes, interests and worker functions as they relate to main duties:

- **General learning ability** to install, repair and maintain safes and vaults in banks and other establishments

- **Spatial perception** to install vaults, vault doors, safes and deposit boxes in prepared vault shells according to blueprints

- **Motor co-ordination** and **manual dexterity** to remove and repair vaults, safes and locking devices using hand tools, machines and equipment such as drill presses and welding and cutting apparatus

- **Objective interest** in **precision working** to adjust safe and vault combinations to obtain new number sequences

- **Methodical interest** in **copying** information to remove interior and exterior paint finishes and spray on new finishes

- **Innovative interest** in testing and repairing locks and locking devices

7383.4

Physical Activities

Vision
　2　Near vision

Colour Discrimination
　0　Not relevant

Hearing
　1　Limited

Body Position
　4　Other body positions

Limb Co-ordination
　1　Upper limb co-ordination

Strength
　4　Heavy

Environmental Conditions

Location
　L1　Regulated inside climate

Hazards
　H3　Equipment, machinery, tools

Employment Requirements

Education/Training
4, 5, R

- Some secondary school education is required.

- Completion of a two-to-three year apprenticeship program in a relevant trade
  or
  college, high school or industry courses combined with several years of related work experience
  or
  several years of on-the-job training are required.

- Provincial trade certification or licence may be required for some occupations in this group.

Workplaces/Employers

Safe and vault service establishments

Self-employment

Occupational Options

There is little or no mobility among occupations in this group.

Progression to supervisory positions is possible with experience.

7383.5 Saw Fitters

Saw Fitters repair and service saw blades.

Profile Summary

APTITUDES

G	V	N	S	P	Q	K	F	M
3	4	4	3	3	4	3	4	3

INTERESTS
OMi

DATA PEOPLE THINGS (DPT)
582

PHYSICAL ACTIVITIES (PA)

V	C	H	B	L	S
2	0	1	3	1	2

ENVIRONMENTAL CONDITIONS (EC)
L1, H3, D1, D2

EDUCATION/TRAINING
4, 5, R

Examples of Job Titles

Saw Fitter

Descriptor Profile

Main Characteristics

Occupations in this group are characterized by the following aptitudes, interests and worker functions as they relate to main duties:

- **General learning ability** to repair, set and sharpen bandsaws, chainsaws, circular saws and other types of saw blades

- **Spatial perception** to fit and repair saw blades according to specifications

- **Motor co-ordination** and **manual dexterity** to straighten twists and kinks in blades using presses and hammers, and to adjust cutting widths of blades by setting teeth using special tools

- **Objective interest** in **controlling** presses and milling machines to cut teeth in blades; and in using power grinders and setting machines to sharpen and set blade teeth

- **Methodical interest** in **copying** to ensure that saw blades conform to specifications using micrometers and other measuring instruments, and to adjust saw-filing machines to match blades with angles of saws being repaired and sharpened

- **Innovative interest** in repairing defective blades and welding new teeth to blades

7383.5

Physical Activities

Vision
   2 Near vision

Colour Discrimination
   0 Not relevant

Hearing
   1 Limited

Body Position
   3 Sitting, standing, walking

Limb Co-ordination
   1 Upper limb co-ordination

Strength
   2 Light

Environmental Conditions

Location
   L1 Regulated inside climate

Hazards
   H3 Equipment, machinery, tools

Discomforts
   D1 Noise
   D2 Vibration

Employment Requirements

Education/Training
   4, 5, R

- Some secondary school education is required.

- Completion of a two-to-three year apprenticeship program in saw repair
  or
  college, high school or industry courses combined with several years of related work experience
  or
  several years of on-the-job training are required.

- Provincial trade certification or licence may be required for some occupations in this group.

Workplaces/Employers

Saw repair shops

Self-employment

Occupational Options

There is little or no mobility among occupations in this group.

Progression to supervisory positions is possible with experience.

7411 Truck Drivers

Truck Drivers operate heavy trucks to transport goods and materials over urban, interurban, provincial and international routes.

Profile Summary

APTITUDES

G	V	N	S	P	Q	K	F	M
3	4	4	3	4	4	3	4	3

INTERESTS
MOd

DATA PEOPLE THINGS (DPT)
563

PHYSICAL ACTIVITIES (PA)

V	C	H	B	L	S
4	1	1	1	2	2

ENVIRONMENTAL CONDITIONS (EC)
L4, D1, D2

EDUCATION/TRAINING
2, R

Examples of Job Titles

Bulk-Goods Truck Driver
Dump Truck Driver
Flatbed Truck Driver
Logging Truck Driver
Long-Haul Truck Driver
Moving Van Driver
Tow Truck Driver
Truck Driver
Truck Driver, Heavy Truck
Truck Driver, Tractor-trailer

Descriptor Profile

Main Characteristics

Occupations in this group are characterized by the following aptitudes, interests and worker functions as they relate to main duties:

- **General learning ability** to operate and drive straight and articulated trucks to transport goods and materials

- **Spatial perception** to visualize relationship among own vehicle, other moving vehicles and stationary objects, and to judge speed and distance when manoeuvring vehicle in confined and congested areas

- **Motor co-ordination** and **manual dexterity** to manipulate controls and to respond rapidly in response to visual stimuli when operating levers, pedals, steering wheels and other controls

- **Methodical interest** in **copying** to record cargo information, distance travelled, fuel consumption and other information in log books or on on-board computers, and to obtain special permits and other documents required to transport cargo on international routes

- **Objective interest** in **driving** straight and articulated trucks to transport goods and materials; may drive as part of a team or convoy, may transport hazardous products and dangerous goods, and may drive lighter, special purpose trucks

- **Directive interest** in **speaking** with others to oversee all aspects and functions of vehicles such as condition of equipment, loading and unloading, and safety and security of cargo, as well as to receive and relay information to a central dispatcher

7411

Physical Activities

Vision
　4　Total visual field

Colour Discrimination
　1　Relevant

Hearing
　1　Limited

Body Position
　1　Sitting

Limb Co-ordination
　2　Multiple limb co-ordination

Strength
　2　Light

Environmental Conditions

Location
　L4　In a vehicle or cab

Discomforts
　D1　Noise
　D2　Vibration

Employment Requirements

Education/Training
　2, R

- Some secondary school education is usually required.

- On-the-job training is provided.

- A driver's licence appropriate to the class of vehicle being driven is required.

- Air brake endorsement is required for drivers who operate vehicles equipped with air brakes.

- Drivers who transport hazardous products or dangerous goods must be certified by employers.

Workplaces/Employers

Manufacturing and distribution companies

Moving companies

Self-employment

Transportation companies

Occupational Options

Progression to supervisory positions or to non-driving occupations, such as truck driving instructors, safety officers or truck dispatchers, is possible with additional training or experience.

Similar Occupations Classified Elsewhere

Supervisors, Motor Transport and Other Ground Transit Operators (7222)

Drivers of light trucks (in 7414 *Delivery Drivers*)

Truck dispatchers (in 1475 *Dispatchers and Radio Operators*)

Truck driving instructors (in 4131 *College and Other Vocational Instructors*)

Snowplough, road oiler and garbage truck drivers (in 7422 *Public Works Maintenance Equipment Operators*)

7412.1 Bus and Streetcar Drivers

Bus and Streetcar Drivers transport passengers on established routes.

Profile Summary

APTITUDES

G	V	N	S	P	Q	K	F	M
3	4	4	3	4	4	3	4	3

INTERESTS
OMS

DATA PEOPLE THINGS (DPT)
563

PHYSICAL ACTIVITIES (PA)

V	C	H	B	L	S
4	1	1	1	2	2

ENVIRONMENTAL CONDITIONS (EC)
L4

EDUCATION/TRAINING
4, R

Examples of Job Titles

Bus Driver
Ground Transportation Driver
Sightseeing Tour Driver
Streetcar Operator
Transit Operator

Descriptor Profile

Main Characteristics

Occupations in this group are characterized by the following aptitudes, interests and worker functions as they relate to main duties:

- **General learning ability** to drive buses and streetcars to transport passengers along established routes to local destinations

- **Spatial perception** to visualize relationship among own vehicle and other moving vehicles and stationary objects and to judge speeds and distances accurately

- **Motor co-ordination** and **manual dexterity** to make rapid and accurate movements when manipulating bus and vehicle controls

- **Objective interest** in **driving** buses, streetcars and sightseeing tour buses to transport passengers along established routes, locally and over long distances; and in driving buses to transport goods to intercity and long-distance destinations

- **Methodical interest** in **copying** information to report delays, mechanical problems and accidents; and in collecting fares and recording transactions

- **Social interest** in **speaking** with passengers to provide information on fares, schedules and stops; may provide passengers with information on points of interest during trips

7412.1
Subgroup 1 of 3

Physical Activities

Vision
    4   Total visual field

Colour Discrimination
    1   Relevant

Hearing
    1   Limited

Body Position
    1   Sitting

Limb Co-ordination
    2   Multiple limb co-ordination

Strength
    2   Light

Environmental Conditions

Location
    L4   In a vehicle or cab

Employment Requirements

Education/Training
    4, R

- Completion of secondary school may be required.

- Up to three months of on-the-job training, including classroom instruction, is usually provided.

- A minimum of one year of safe driving experience is required.

- Bus drivers require a Class B, C, E or F driver's licence in Ontario and a Class 2 driver's licence elsewhere.

Workplaces/Employers

Municipal governments

Private transportation companies

Occupational Options

Progression to transit supervisory or inspector positions is possible with experience.

Similar Occupations Classified Elsewhere

Supervisors and inspectors of bus drivers, subway operators and other transit operators (in 7222 *Supervisors, Motor Transport and Other Ground Transit Operators*)

7412.2 School Bus Drivers

School Bus Drivers transport students by bus on established routes to and from schools.

Profile Summary

APTITUDES

G	V	N	S	P	Q	K	F	M
3	4	4	3	4	4	3	4	3

INTERESTS
OMS

DATA PEOPLE THINGS (DPT)
563

PHYSICAL ACTIVITIES (PA)

V	C	H	B	L	S
4	1	1	1	2	2

ENVIRONMENTAL CONDITIONS (EC)
L4, D1

EDUCATION/TRAINING
4, R

Examples of Job Titles

Bus Driver
School Bus Driver

Descriptor Profile

Main Characteristics

Occupations in this group are characterized by the following aptitudes, interests and worker functions as they relate to main duties:

- **General learning ability** to operate buses and understand and apply motor vehicle safety regulations

- **Spatial perception** to visualize relationship among own vehicle and other moving vehicles and stationary objects and to judge speeds and distances accurately

- **Motor co-ordination** and **manual dexterity** to make rapid and accurate movements when manipulating bus controls

- **Objective interest** in **driving** school buses to transport children to and from schools and on excursions

- **Methodical interest** in **copying** information to record delays; and in inspecting buses for cleanliness before departures

- **Social interest** in **speaking** to ensure children's safety when boarding buses, leaving buses and crossing streets while buses are stopped

Physical Activities

Vision
  4   Total visual field

Colour Discrimination
  1   Relevant

Hearing
  1   Limited

Body Position
  1   Sitting

Limb Co-ordination
  2   Multiple limb co-ordination

Strength
  2   Light

Environmental Conditions

Location
  L4   In a vehicle or cab

Discomforts
  D1   Noise

Employment Requirements

Education/Training
  4, R

- Completion of secondary school may be required.

- Up to three months of on-the-job training, including classroom instruction, is usually provided for all occupations in this group.

- A minimum of one year of safe driving experience is required.

- Bus drivers require a Class B, C, E or F driver's licence in Ontario and a Class 2 driver's licence elsewhere.

Workplaces/Employers

Municipal governments

Occupational Options

Progression to transit supervisory or inspector positions is possible with experience.

Similar Occupations Classified Elsewhere

Supervisors and inspectors of bus drivers, subway operators and other transit operators (in 7222 *Supervisors, Motor Transport and Other Ground Transit Operators*)

7412.3 Subway Train and Light Rail Transit Operators

Subway Train and Light Rail Transit Operators transport passengers on established routes.

Profile Summary

APTITUDES

G	V	N	S	P	Q	K	F	M
3	4	4	4	4	4	3	4	3

INTERESTS
OMs

DATA PEOPLE THINGS (DPT)
563

PHYSICAL ACTIVITIES (PA)

V	C	H	B	L	S
4	1	1	1	1	1

ENVIRONMENTAL CONDITIONS (EC)
L4

EDUCATION/TRAINING
4, R

Examples of Job Titles

Light Rail Transit Operator
Subway Train Operator

Descriptor Profile

Main Characteristics

Occupations in this group are characterized by the following aptitudes, interests and worker functions as they relate to main duties:

- **General learning ability** to understand and apply knowledge and skills needed to operate subway trains and light rail transit vehicles

- **Motor co-ordination** and **manual dexterity** to operate controls that open and close vehicle doors

- **Objective interest** in **driving - operating** subway and rail transit vehicles as part of two-person crews

- **Methodical interest** in **copying** information to report delays, malfunctions and accidents; and in observing signals at crossings and arrival and departure points

- **Social interest** in **speaking** with control units when reporting delays, malfunctions and accidents; and in directing passengers during emergency evacuation procedures

Physical Activities

Vision
 4 Total visual field

Colour Discrimination
 1 Relevant

Hearing
 1 Limited

Body Position
 1 Sitting

Limb Co-ordination
 1 Upper limb co-ordination

Strength
 1 Limited

Environmental Conditions

Location
 L4 In a vehicle or cab

Employment Requirements

Education/Training
 4, R

- Completion of secondary school may be required.

- Up to three months of on-the-job training, including classroom instruction, is usually provided.

- A minimum of one year of safe driving experience is required.

- Experience as a public transit bus driver is usually required for subway and light rail transit operators.

Workplaces/Employers

Municipal governments

Occupational Options

Progression to transit supervisory or inspector positions is possible with experience.

Similar Occupations Classified Elsewhere

Supervisors and inspectors of bus drivers, subway operators and other transit operators (in 7222 *Supervisors, Motor Transport and Other Ground Transit Operators*)

7413.1 Taxi and Limousine Drivers

Taxi and Limousine Drivers operate automobiles and limousines to transport passengers.

Profile Summary

APTITUDES

G	V	N	S	P	Q	K	F	M
4	4	4	3	4	4	3	4	3

INTERESTS
OMS

DATA PEOPLE THINGS (DPT)
563

PHYSICAL ACTIVITIES (PA)

V	C	H	B	L	S
4	1	2	1	2	3

ENVIRONMENTAL CONDITIONS (EC)
L4

EDUCATION/TRAINING
2, R

Examples of Job Titles

Airport Limousine Driver
Limousine Driver
Taxi Driver

Descriptor Profile

Main Characteristics

Occupations in this group are characterized by the following aptitudes, interests and worker functions as they relate to main duties:

- **General learning ability** to operate motor vehicles, to understand and follow motor vehicle and safety regulations, to know the location of streets and important buildings, and to select the best routes according to traffic conditions

- **Spatial perception** to visualize the relationship between own vehicle, other moving vehicles and stationary objects and to judge distances accurately

- **Motor co-ordination** and **manual dexterity** to make precise movements when manipulating gear shifts, levers, brakes and other controls and to help passengers with luggage and in boarding vehicles

- **Objective interest** in picking up and **driving** passengers to their destinations

- **Methodical interest** in **copying** information to record transactions and collect flat-rate and taximeter fares

- **Social interest** in **speaking** to maintain contact with dispatchers

7413.1

Physical Activities

Vision
   4   Total visual field

Colour Discrimination
   1   Relevant

Hearing
   2   Verbal interaction

Body Position
   1   Sitting

Limb Co-ordination
   2   Multiple limb co-ordination

Strength
   3   Medium

Environmental Conditions

Location
   L4   In a vehicle or cab

Employment Requirements

Education/Training
   2, R

- Some secondary school education is usually required.

- A minimum of one year of safe driving experience is usually required.

- A Class G driver's licence is required in Ontario, and a Class 4 driver's licence elsewhere.

- Taxi and limousine drivers require good knowledge of the geographical area to be covered.

- Taxi drivers usually require a municipal permit.

Workplaces/Employers

Self-employment

Taxi and transportation service companies

Occupational Options

Mobility from taxi or limousine driver to chauffeur is possible with experience.

Similar Occupations Classified Elsewhere

Supervisors, Motor Transport and Other Ground Transit Operators (7222)

Taxi dispatchers (in 1475 *Dispatchers and Radio Operators*)

7413.2 Chauffeurs

Chauffeurs drive automobiles and limousines to transport personnel and visitors of businesses, government and other organizations, and members of private households.

Profile Summary

APTITUDES

G	V	N	S	P	Q	K	F	M
4	4	4	3	4	4	3	4	3

INTERESTS
OMS

DATA PEOPLE THINGS (DPT)
563

PHYSICAL ACTIVITIES (PA)

V	C	H	B	L	S
4	1	2	1	2	3

ENVIRONMENTAL CONDITIONS (EC)
L4

EDUCATION/TRAINING
2, R

Examples of Job Titles

Chauffeur

Descriptor Profile

Main Characteristics

Occupations in this group are characterized by the following aptitudes, interests and worker functions as they relate to main duties:

- **General learning ability** to operate motor vehicles, to understand and follow motor vehicle and safety regulations, to know the location of streets and important buildings, and to select the best routes according to traffic conditions

- **Spatial perception** to visualize the relationship among own vehicle, other moving vehicles and stationary objects and to judge distances accurately

- **Motor co-ordination** and **manual dexterity** to make precise movements when manipulating gear shifts, levers, brakes and other controls

- **Objective interest** in **driving** employers to destinations in automobiles and limousines, and to meet and pick up employers according to requests, appointments and schedules

- **Methodical interest** in **copying** to clean and make minor repairs to vehicles, and to take vehicles for servicing

- **Social interest** in **speaking** to perform business and personal errands for employers such as delivering and picking up mail, business documents and parcels

Physical Activities

Vision
    4   Total visual field

Colour Discrimination
    1   Relevant

Hearing
    2   Verbal interaction

Body Position
    1   Sitting

Limb Co-ordination
    2   Multiple limb co-ordination

Strength
    3   Medium

Environmental Conditions

Location
    L4 In a vehicle or cab

Employment Requirements

Education/Training
    2, R

- Some secondary school education is usually required.

- A minimum of one year of safe driving experience is usually required.

- A Class G driver's licence is required in Ontario, and a Class 4 driver's licence elsewhere.

Workplaces/Employers

Businesses

Government

Organizations

Private individuals

Similar Occupations Classified Elsewhere

Supervisors, Motor Transport and Other Ground Transit Operators (7222)

Taxi dispatchers (in 1475 *Dispatchers and Radio Operators*)

7414 Delivery Drivers

Delivery Drivers operate automobiles, vans and light trucks to pick up and deliver various products.

Profile Summary

APTITUDES

G	V	N	S	P	Q	K	F	M
4	4	4	3	4	4	3	4	3

INTERESTS
MOs

DATA PEOPLE THINGS (DPT)
563

PHYSICAL ACTIVITIES (PA)

V	C	H	B	L	S
4	1	1	3	2	3

ENVIRONMENTAL CONDITIONS (EC)
L4

EDUCATION/TRAINING
2, R

Examples of Job Titles

Bread Deliverer
Canteen Driver
Delivery Driver
Driver Salesperson
Dry Cleaning Driver
Milk Deliverer
Newspaper Delivery Driver
Pizza Delivery Driver
Route Driver
Vending Machine Driver-Supplier

Descriptor Profile

Main Characteristics

Occupations in this group are characterized by the following aptitudes, interests and worker functions as they relate to main duties:

- **General learning ability** to operate and drive automobiles, vans and light trucks, and to pick up and deliver various products such as fast food, newspapers, magazines, bakery and dairy products and dry cleaning

- **Spatial perception** to visualize relationship among own vehicle, other moving vehicles and stationary objects; to visualize the movement and placement of objects and materials in vehicles; and to judge speed and distance when manoeuvring vehicles in confined and congested areas

- **Motor co-ordination** and **manual dexterity** to manipulate controls in response to visual stimuli when operating levers, pedals, steering wheels and other controls

- **Methodical interest** in **copying** to record information on pick-ups and deliveries, vehicle mileage, fuel costs and any problems

- **Objective interest** in **driving** automobiles, vans and light trucks

- **Social interest** in **speaking** to customers to sell products over established routes and accept and make payments for goods

7414

Physical Activities

Vision
  4 Total visual field

Colour Discrimination
  1 Relevant

Hearing
  1 Limited

Body Position
  3 Sitting, standing, walking

Limb Co-ordination
  2 Multiple limb co-ordination

Strength
  3 Medium

Environmental Conditions

Location
  L4 In a vehicle or cab

Employment Requirements

Education/Training
2, R

- Some secondary school education is required.

- A driver's licence appropriate to the class of vehicle being driven is required.

- One year of safe driving experience is usually required.

Workplaces/Employers

Dairies

Drug stores

Dry cleaners

Mobile caterers

Newspapers

Retail establishments

Take-out food stores

Occupational Options

Progression to supervisory positions is possible with experience.

Similar Occupations Classified Elsewhere

Couriers and Messengers (1463)

Drivers of heavy trucks (in 7411 *Truck Drivers*)

Garbage truck drivers (in 7422 *Public Works Maintenance Equipment Operators*)

Supervisors of delivery drivers (in 7222 *Supervisors, Motor Transport and Other Ground Transit Operators*)

7421 Heavy Equipment Operators (Except Crane)

Heavy Equipment Operators operate heavy equipment used in the construction and maintenance of roads, bridges, airports, gas and oil pipelines, tunnels, buildings and other structures; in surface mining and quarrying activities; and in material handling work. Apprentices are included in this group.

Profile Summary

APTITUDES

G	V	N	S	P	Q	K	F	M
3	4	4	3	4	5	3	4	3

INTERESTS
OMi

DATA PEOPLE THINGS (DPT)
683

PHYSICAL ACTIVITIES (PA)

V	C	H	B	L	S
4	0	1	1	2	2

ENVIRONMENTAL CONDITIONS (EC)
L4, H3, H8, D1, D2, D4

EDUCATION/TRAINING
2, 4, 5, R

Examples of Job Titles

Backhoe Operator
Bulldozer Operator
Excavator Operator
Gradall Operator
Grader Operator
Heavy Equipment Operator
Loader Operator
Side-Boom Tractor Operator

Descriptor Profile

Main Characteristics

Occupations in this group are characterized by the following aptitudes, interests and worker functions as they relate to main duties:

- **General learning ability** to operate heavy equipment such as backhoes, bulldozers, loaders and graders to excavate, move, load and grade earth, rock, gravel and other materials during construction and related activities

- **Spatial perception** to manoeuvre construction equipment to avoid other moving and stationary objects, and to operate heavy equipment with pile-driver heads to drive pilings into the earth to support buildings and other structures

- **Motor co-ordination** and **manual dexterity** to manipulate hand levers, foot pedals and steering devices

- **Objective interest** in **operating** bulldozers and heavy dredging, paving and surfacing equipment to deepen waterways, reclaim earth fill, lay, spread and compact concrete, asphalt and other surface materials during highway and road construction; and in operating power shovels to excavate rock, ore and other materials from open-pit mines, strip mines, quarries and construction pits

- **Methodical interest** in **comparing** information to move, load and unload cargo and to clear brush and stumps before logging activities using bulldozers and other heavy equipment

- **Innovative interest** in conducting pre-operational checks on equipment and in cleaning, lubricating and refilling equipment, and in building roads at logging and surface mining sites using bulldozers and other heavy equipment

7421

Physical Activities

Vision
  4 Total visual field

Colour Discrimination
  0 Not relevant

Hearing
  1 Limited

Body Position
  1 Sitting

Limb Co-ordination
  2 Multiple limb co-ordination

Strength
  2 Light

Environmental Conditions

Location
  L4 In a vehicle or cab

Hazards
  H3 Equipment, machinery, tools
  H8 Dangerous locations

Discomforts
  D1 Noise
  D2 Vibration
  D4 Non-toxic dusts

Employment Requirements

Education/Training
2, 4, 5, R

- Some secondary school education is required.

- Completion of a one-to-two year apprenticeship program
  or
  some high school, college or industry courses in heavy equipment operating combined with on-the-job training are required.

- Internal company certification may be required by some employers.

- Trade certification is compulsory in Quebec and available, but voluntary, in Newfoundland.

Workplaces/Employers

Construction companies

Heavy equipment contractors

Pipeline, logging and cargo handling companies

Public works departments

Occupational Options

Progression to supervisory positions is possible with experience.

Similar Occupations Classified Elsewhere

Contractors and Supervisors, Heavy Construction Equipment Crews (7217)

Crane Operators (7371)

Logging Machinery Operators (8241)

Underground Production and Development Miners (8231)

Fork-lift and industrial truck operators (in 7452 *Material Handlers*)

7422 Public Works Maintenance Equipment Operators

Public Works Maintenance Equipment Operators use vehicles and equipment to maintain streets, highways and sewer systems, and operate garbage trucks to remove garbage and refuse.

Profile Summary

APTITUDES

G	V	N	S	P	Q	K	F	M
4	4	4	3	4	4	3	4	3

INTERESTS
OMs

DATA PEOPLE THINGS (DPT)
683

PHYSICAL ACTIVITIES (PA)

V	C	H	B	L	S
4	1	1	1	2	2*

ENVIRONMENTAL CONDITIONS (EC)
L4, H3, D1, D2, D3*, D5

EDUCATION/TRAINING
2, R

Examples of Job Titles

Garbage Truck Driver
Municipal Maintenance-Equipment Operator
Oil Spreader Operator
Public Works Maintenance-Equipment Operator
Road-Oiling Truck Driver
Salt Truck Operator
Sand Spreader Operator
Sanitation Truck Driver
Sewer-Flushing Truck Operator
Snow Removal Equipment Operator
Street Flusher Operator
Street Sweeper Operator

Descriptor Profile

Main Characteristics

Occupations in this group are characterized by the following aptitudes, interests and worker functions as they relate to main duties:

- **General learning ability** to understand and operate vehicles and equipment to maintain streets and sewers, and to remove garbage and refuse

- **Spatial perception** to visualize relationship among own vehicle, other moving vehicles and stationary objects, and to visualize the movement and placement of objects and materials when removing sand, litter and trash

- **Motor co-ordination** and **manual dexterity** to manipulate levers, pedals, steering wheels and other controls when removing garbage, refuse and snow from streets, highways, parking lots and similar areas

- **Objective interest** in **driving** garbage trucks, street cleaning equipment such as street sweepers and other vehicles equipped with rotating brushes, snowploughs and plough blades; sewer maintenance equipment such as rodders and sewer jet cleaners; and trucks equipped with road-sanding, road-oiling and other similar apparatus

- **Methodical interest** in **comparing** information to check, lubricate, refuel and clean equipment, to maintain and repair sewer systems, and to remove garbage and dump loads at designated areas

- **Social interest** in reporting any malfunctions to supervisors

7422

Physical Activities

Vision
 4 Total visual field

Colour Discrimination
 1 Relevant

Hearing
 1 Limited

Body Position
 1 Sitting

Limb Co-ordination
 2 Multiple limb co-ordination

Strength
 2* Light

Environmental Conditions

Location
 L4 In a vehicle or cab

Hazards
 H3 Equipment, machinery, tools

Discomforts
 D1 Noise
 D2 Vibration
 D3* Odours
 D5 Wetness

Employment Requirements

Education/Training
 2, R

- Some secondary school may be required.

- Experience as a public works labourer is usually required.

- On-the-job training is provided.

- A driver's licence appropriate to a specific type of equipment may be required.

Workplaces/Employers

Municipal, provincial and federal public works departments

Private contractors under contract with government public works departments

Occupational Options

Progression to supervisory positions is possible with experience.

Similar Occupations Classified Elsewhere

Heavy Equipment Operators (Except Crane) (7421)

Public Works and Maintenance Labourers (7621)

Truck Drivers (7411)

Supervisors of public works maintenance-equipment operators (in 7217 *Contractors and Supervisors, Heavy Construction Equipment Crews*)

Remarks

*Physical Activities

- For some occupations in this group, **S**trength 3 (Medium) may apply.

*Environmental Conditions

- For some occupations in this group, **D**iscomforts D3 (Odours) may also apply.

7431 Railway Yard Workers

Railway Yard Workers regulate yard traffic, couple and uncouple trains and perform related yard activities.

Profile Summary

APTITUDES

G	V	N	S	P	Q	K	F	M
3	4	5	4	4	4	4	4	4

INTERESTS
OMi

DATA PEOPLE THINGS (DPT)
684

PHYSICAL ACTIVITIES (PA)

V	C	H	B	L	S
4	1	1	4	2	3

ENVIRONMENTAL CONDITIONS (EC)
L1, L3, H8, D1, D4

EDUCATION/TRAINING
2, R

Examples of Job Titles

Car Controller, Railway
Control Tower Operator, Railway
Signal Tower Operator, Railway
Switch Tender, Railway
Towerman/woman, Railway
Yard Coupler, Railway
Yard Worker, Railway

Descriptor Profile

Main Characteristics

Occupations in this group are characterized by the following aptitudes, interests and worker functions as they relate to main duties:

- **General learning ability** to understand procedures and regulations to operate centralized traffic control (CTC) systems, regulate yard traffic, and couple and uncouple trains

- **Spatial perception** to visualize relative positions and movements of trains on sections of railway to activate train switches that regulate railway traffic

- **Form perception** to align locomotives and cars for coupling, uncoupling and servicing using car retarders, turntables and track switches

- **Motor co-ordination** and **finger** and **manual dexterity** to operate switches, keys, buttons and other control devices

- **Objective interest** in operating control panel switches from railway yard towers to set traffic signals

- **Methodical interest** in comparing information to lubricate moving parts of railway cars and locomotives

- **Innovative interest** in switching cars according to instructions that indicate locations, dispositions and number of cars

7431

Physical Activities

Vision
- 4 Total visual field

Colour Discrimination
- 1 Relevant

Hearing
- 1 Limited

Body Position
- 4 Other body positions

Limb Co-ordination
- 2 Multiple limb co-ordination

Strength
- 3 Medium

Environmental Conditions

Location
- L1 Regulated inside climate
- L3 Outside

Hazards
- H8 Dangerous locations

Discomforts
- D1 Noise
- D4 Non-toxic dusts

Employment Requirements

Education/Training
2, R

- Some secondary school education is usually required.

- Experience as a railway labourer is required.

- On-the-job training is provided.

- Level B Certificate of the Canadian Rail Operating Rules is required.

Workplaces/Employers

Railway transport companies

Occupational Options

Progression to a position such as brakeman is possible with experience.

Similar Occupations Classified Elsewhere

Railway and Motor Transport Labourers (7622)

Railway Conductors and Brakemen/women (7362)

Railway Track Maintenance Workers (7432)

Supervisors of railway yard workers (in 7221 *Supervisors, Railway Transport Operations*)

7432 Railway Track Maintenance Workers

Railway Track Maintenance Workers operate machines and equipment to lay, maintain and repair railway tracks.

Profile Summary

APTITUDES

G	V	N	S	P	Q	K	F	M
3	4	5	3	4	5	3	4	3

INTERESTS
OMi

DATA PEOPLE THINGS (DPT)
684

PHYSICAL ACTIVITIES (PA)

V	C	H	B	L	S
3	0	1	4	1	3

ENVIRONMENTAL CONDITIONS (EC)
L3, H3, D1, D2

EDUCATION/TRAINING
2

Examples of Job Titles

Ballast Regulator Operator, Railway
Equipment Operator, Railway
Machine Operator, Railway
Rail Saw Operator
Section Worker, Railway
Spike Machine Operator, Railway
Tie Tamper Operator, Railway
Track Patroller, Railway
Trackman/woman, Railway

Descriptor Profile

Main Characteristics

Occupations in this group are characterized by the following aptitudes, interests and worker functions as they relate to main duties:

- **General learning ability** to operate machines and equipment, such as tie cutters, tie injectors, tie anchors, rail lifters, spike drivers, spike pullers, rail saws and tie cranes, to lay, maintain and repair railway tracks

- **Spatial perception** to judge distances and positions when patrolling assigned track sections to identify and report damaged and broken track

- **Motor co-ordination** and **manual dexterity** to shovel ice and snow from track switch boxes and to operate hand and foot controls of equipment

- **Objective interest** in operating machines and equipment to align tracks and to transfer, spread, level and tamp ballast around ties

- **Methodical interest** in **comparing** information to clean machines and equipment, clear snow from tracks and perform other track maintenance duties

- **Innovative interest** in making minor repairs to machines and equipment

7432

Physical Activities

Vision
   3 Near and far vision

Colour Discrimination
   0 Not relevant

Hearing
   1 Limited

Body Position
   4 Other body positions

Limb Co-ordination
   1 Upper limb co-ordination

Strength
   3 Medium

Environmental Conditions

Location
   L3 Outside

Hazards
   H3 Equipment, machinery, tools

Discomforts
   D1 Noise
   D2 Vibration

Employment Requirements

Education/Training
  2

- Some secondary school education is usually required.

- On-the-job training is provided.

Workplaces/Employers

Railway transport companies

Similar Occupations Classified Elsewhere

Railway and Motor Transport Labourers (7622)

Railway Yard Workers (7431)

Supervisors, Railway Transport Operations (7221)

7433 Deck Crew, Water Transport

Deck Crew in this group stand watch, operate and maintain deck equipment and perform other deck and bridge duties aboard ships and self-propelled vessels under the direction of deck officers.

Profile Summary

APTITUDES

G	V	N	S	P	Q	K	F	M
4	4	4	4	4	4	3	4	3

INTERESTS
OMi

DATA PEOPLE THINGS (DPT)
683

PHYSICAL ACTIVITIES (PA)

V	C	H	B	L	S
4	1	3	4	1	4

ENVIRONMENTAL CONDITIONS (EC)
L3, L4, H4, D1

EDUCATION/TRAINING
2

Examples of Job Titles

Able Seaman/woman
Boatswain - Military
Deckhand
Ordinary Seaman/woman
Tunnel Operator, Ship
Wheelsman/woman

Descriptor Profile

Main Characteristics

Occupations in this group are characterized by the following aptitudes, interests and worker functions as they relate to main duties:

- **General learning ability** to serve as members of deck crews aboard ships performing duties such as standing watch, steering, operating, maintaining and repairing deck equipment

- **Motor co-ordination** and **manual dexterity** to handle mooring lines, and splice and repair ropes, wire cables and cordage

- **Objective interest** in **operating** deck equipment such as winches, cranes, derricks and hawsers; and in steering ships and self-propelled vessels under the direction of officers on watch

- **Methodical interest** in **comparing** to clean, chip and paint deck surfaces

- **Innovative interest** in repairing deck equipment, ropes, wire cables and cordage

7433

Physical Activities

Vision
    4   Total visual field

Colour Discrimination
    1   Relevant

Hearing
    3   Other sound discrimination

Body Position
    4   Other body positions

Limb Co-ordination
    1   Upper limb co-ordination

Strength
    4   Heavy

Environmental Conditions

Location
    L3 Outside
    L4 In a vehicle or cab

Hazards
    H4 Electricity

Discomforts
    D1 Noise

Employment Requirements

Education/Training
  2

- Some secondary school education is required.

- On-the-job training is provided.

- Senior positions in this group, such as able seaman/woman, require experience.

Workplaces/Employers

Federal government departments including the Canadian Forces

Marine transportation companies

Occupational Options

Training and testing for various endorsements and certification, including the Marine Emergency Duty (MED) certificate, occur following employment as a deck crew member.

Progression to deck officer positions is possible with experience, additional training and deck-officer certification by Transport Canada.

Similar Occupations Classified Elsewhere

Boat Operators (7436)

Deck Officers, Water Transport (2273)

Engineer Officers, Water Transport (2274)

Engine Room Crew, Water Transport (7434)

Fishing Vessel Deckhands (8441)

7434 Engine Room Crew, Water Transport

Water Transport Engine Room Crew assists ship engineer officers to operate, maintain and repair engines, machinery and auxiliary equipment aboard ships and self-propelled vessels.

Profile Summary

APTITUDES

G	V	N	S	P	Q	K	F	M
3	3	3	4	4	4	3	4	3

INTERESTS
MOi

DATA PEOPLE THINGS (DPT)
684

PHYSICAL ACTIVITIES (PA)

V	C	H	B	L	S
2	0	3	4	1	2

ENVIRONMENTAL CONDITIONS (EC)
L1, L4, H3, H8, D1

EDUCATION/TRAINING
2

Examples of Job Titles

Engine Room Crew, Ship
Greaser, Engine Room
Marine Engine Oiler
Marine Engineering Mechanic - Military
Ship Boiler Tender
Ship Stoker

Descriptor Profile

Main Characteristics

Occupations in this group are characterized by the following aptitudes, interests and worker functions as they relate to main duties:

- **General learning ability** to assist ship engineers in performing routine maintenance work and repair engines, machinery and auxiliary equipment

- **Motor co-ordination** and **manual dexterity** to clean engine parts and keep engine rooms clean

- **Methodical interest** in **comparing** to monitor engine machinery and equipment indicators, record variables and report abnormalities to the ship engineer on watch

- **Objective interest** in operating and maintaining off-loading liquid pumps and valves

- **Innovative interest** in lubricating moving parts of engines, machinery and auxiliary equipment

7434

Physical Activities

Vision
   2 Near vision

Colour Discrimination
   0 Not relevant

Hearing
   3 Other sound discrimination

Body Position
   4 Other body positions

Limb Co-ordination
   1 Upper limb co-ordination

Strength
   2 Light

Environmental Conditions

Location
   L1 Regulated inside climate
   L4 In a vehicle or cab

Hazards
   H3 Equipment, machinery, tools
   H8 Dangerous locations

Discomforts
   D1 Noise

Employment Requirements

Education/Training
   2

- Some secondary school education is required.

- On-the-job training is provided.

Workplaces/Employers

Federal government departments including the Canadian Forces

Marine transportation companies

Occupational Options

Training and testing for various endorsements and certification, including the Marine Emergency Duty (MED) certificate, occur following employment as an engine room crew member.

Progression to ship engineer officer positions is possible with experience, additional training and certification by Transport Canada.

Similar Occupations Classified Elsewhere

Deck Crew, Water Transport (7433)

Deck Officers, Water Transport (2273)

Engineer Officers, Water Transport (2274)

7435.1 Lock Equipment Operators

Lock Equipment Operators operate lock gates, bridges and similar equipment along canal systems.

Profile Summary

APTITUDES
G	V	N	S	P	Q	K	F	M
3	3	4	3	3	4	4	4	3

INTERESTS
OMd

DATA PEOPLE THINGS (DPT)
664

PHYSICAL ACTIVITIES (PA)
V	C	H	B	L	S
4	0	2	1	0	1

ENVIRONMENTAL CONDITIONS (EC)
L1

EDUCATION/TRAINING
2

Examples of Job Titles

Cable Ferry Operator
Canal Operator
Loading Bridge Operator
Lockmaster

Descriptor Profile

Main Characteristics

Occupations in this group are characterized by the following aptitudes, interests and worker functions as they relate to main duties:

- **General learning ability** to operate controls to open and close lock gates

- **Verbal ability** to maintain good public relations with persons using lock facilities such as ships' crews, pleasure-boat operators and sightseers

- **Spatial** and **form perception** observe progress of vessels passing through locks

- **Manual dexterity** to operate controls, telecommunication equipment and portable loudspeakers to direct movements of vessels in lock areas

- **Objective interest** in **operating** controls to raise, lower and turn bridges

- **Methodical interest** in **comparing** information to record data concerning weather conditions and registration of vessels passing through locks

- **Directive interest** in **speaking** with captains and crews to direct movements of vessels in lock areas and to institute emergency procedures to assist vessels in difficulty

7435.1
Subgroup 1 of 3

Physical Activities

Vision
 4 Total visual field

Colour Discrimination
 0 Not relevant

Hearing
 2 Verbal interaction

Body Position
 1 Sitting

Limb Co-ordination
 0 Not relevant

Strength
 1 Limited

Environmental Conditions

Location
 L1 Regulated inside climate

Employment Requirements

Education/Training
 2

- Some secondary school education is usually required.
- On-the-job training is provided.

Workplaces/Employers

Cable ferry companies

Federal government

Ferry terminals

Occupational Options

There is little or no mobility among workers in the 7435 group.

7435.2 Cable Ferry Operators

Cable Ferry Operators operate cable ferries.

Profile Summary

APTITUDES
G	V	N	S	P	Q	K	F	M
3	3	4	3	3	5	4	4	3

INTERESTS
OMd

DATA PEOPLE THINGS (DPT)
663

PHYSICAL ACTIVITIES (PA)
V	C	H	B	L	S
4	0	1	3	1	2

ENVIRONMENTAL CONDITIONS (EC)
L4, D1, D2

EDUCATION/TRAINING
2

Examples of Job Titles

Cable Ferry Operator
Lockmaster

Descriptor Profile

Main Characteristics

Occupations in this group are characterized by the following aptitudes, interests and worker functions as they relate to main duties:

- **General learning ability** to operate and maintain cable ferries to transport passengers, vehicles and freight across narrow waterways

- **Spatial** and **form perception** to operate gates and loading ramps

- **Manual dexterity** to refuel, inspect, lubricate and perform emergency repairs to engines, cables, winches, pontoons and other equipment using hand tools and lubricants

- **Objective interest** in **operating** cable ferries across narrow waterways to opposite terminals

- **Methodical interest** in **comparing** to perform routine maintenance and repairs to engines, cables and winches

- **Directive interest** in **signalling** passengers and motor vehicles to embark and disembark

7435.2
Subgroup 2 of 3

Physical Activities

Vision
  4   Total visual field

Colour Discrimination
  0   Not relevant

Hearing
  1   Limited

Body Position
  3   Sitting, standing, walking

Limb Co-ordination
  1   Upper limb co-ordination

Strength
  2   Light

Environmental Conditions

Location
  L4 In a vehicle or cab

Discomforts
  D1 Noise
  D2 Vibration

Employment Requirements

Education/Training
  2

- Some secondary school education is usually required.

- On-the-job training is provided.

Workplaces/Employers

Cable ferry companies

Federal government

Provincial governments

Occupational Options

There is little or no mobility among workers in the 7435 group.

7435.3 Ferry Terminal Workers

Ferry Terminal Workers perform work at ferry terminals.

Profile Summary

APTITUDES

G	V	N	S	P	Q	K	F	M
4	4	4	4	4	4	4	4	4

INTERESTS
OMd

DATA PEOPLE THINGS (DPT)
664

PHYSICAL ACTIVITIES (PA)

V	C	H	B	L	S
4	0	1	4	1	3

ENVIRONMENTAL CONDITIONS (EC)
L1, L3, H3, D1

EDUCATION/TRAINING
2

Examples of Job Titles

Bridgeman/woman

Ferry Terminal Worker

Linesman/woman, Canal Lock System

Descriptor Profile

Main Characteristics

Occupations in this group are characterized by the following aptitudes, interests and worker functions as they relate to main duties:

- **General learning ability** to perform duties at ferry terminals

- **Spatial** and **form perception** to adjust levels of landing bridges

- **Objective interest** in **operating** controls to adjust landing bridges, to position and remove gangplanks, to open and close doors and gates, and to secure and remove docking devices

- **Methodical interest** in **comparing** to inspect security of gangplanks, maintain equipment and clean work area

- **Directive interest** in **signalling** passengers and motor vehicles to embark and disembark; may collect tickets and fares from passengers

7435.3
Subgroup 3 of 3

Physical Activities

Vision
    4   Total visual field

Colour Discrimination
    0   Not relevant

Hearing
    1   Limited

Body Position
    4   Other body positions

Limb Co-ordination
    1   Upper limb co-ordination

Strength
    3   Medium

Environmental Conditions

Location
    L1 Regulated inside climate
    L3 Outside

Hazards
    H3 Equipment, machinery, tools

Discomforts
    D1 Noise

Employment Requirements

Education/Training
2

- Some secondary school education is usually required.
- On-the-job training is provided.

Workplaces/Employers

Federal government

Ferry terminals

Provincial governments

Occupational Options

There is little or no mobility among workers in the 7435 group.

7436　Boat Operators

Boat Operators use small boats and crafts to transport passengers and freight, to sort and transport logs and to perform other duties.

Profile Summary

APTITUDES

G	V	N	S	P	Q	K	F	M
4	4	5	3	4	5	3	4	3

INTERESTS
MOs

DATA PEOPLE THINGS (DPT)
663

PHYSICAL ACTIVITIES (PA)

V	C	H	B	L	S
4	1	3	1	1	2

ENVIRONMENTAL CONDITIONS (EC)
L3, L4, H3, H8, D1

EDUCATION/TRAINING
2, R

Examples of Job Titles

Boomboat Operator
Charter Boat Operator
Launch Master
Motor Boat Operator
Scow Captain
Sightseeing Boat Operator
Small Craft Operator
Water Taxi Operator

Descriptor Profile

Main Characteristics

Occupations in this group are characterized by the following aptitudes, interests and worker functions as they relate to main duties:

- **General learning ability** to operate motorboats, launches, small ferry boats and other similar vessels to transport passengers and freight

- **Spatial perception** to visualize relative position of own boat with other boats, buoys and lights; may perform other duties such as patrolling beaches and measuring depth of water

- **Motor co-ordination** and **manual dexterity** to manoeuvre crafts by moving levers and helm to change speed and direction, and to service boats and equipment using hand and power tools, paint, brushes and cleaning equipment

- **Methodical interest** in **comparing** to maintain boats and equipment on board such as engines, winches, derricks, fire extinguishers and life preservers; may perform other duties such as checking for oil spills and other pollutants around ports and harbours, and sorting logs, forming log booms and salvaging lost logs

- **Objective interest** in **driving** boats, launches, ferries and other small vessels

- **Social interest** in **speaking - signalling** to perform special operations such as making soundings, conducting sightseeing tours and operating charter services and water taxis

7436

Physical Activities

Vision
    4   Total visual field

Colour Discrimination
    1   Relevant

Hearing
    3   Other sound discrimination

Body Position
    1   Sitting

Limb Co-ordination
    1   Upper limb co-ordination

Strength
    2   Light

Environmental Conditions

Location
    L3 Outside
    L4 In a vehicle or cab

Hazards
    H3 Equipment, machinery, tools
    H8 Dangerous locations

Discomforts
    D1 Noise

Employment Requirements

Education/Training
    2, R

- Some secondary school education is required.

- On-the-job training is provided.

- Master of a Small Craft or Master of a Small Passenger Craft certificate, issued by Transport Canada, is required.

Workplaces/Employers

Canal, port and harbour authorities

Logging companies

Marine companies that provide sightseeing tours or water taxi services

Occupational Options

Mobility among boat operators in this group is possible.

Progression to deck officer positions is possible with additional training, experience and certification.

Similar Occupations Classified Elsewhere

Deck Crew, Water Transport (7433)

Cable ferry operators (in 7435 *Lock and Cable Ferry Operators and Related Occupations*)

Ferry boat deck officers and ship pilots (in 2273 *Deck Officers, Water Transport*)

7437 Air Transport Ramp Attendants

Air Transport Ramp Attendants operate ramp-servicing vehicles and equipment, handle cargo and passenger baggage and perform other ground support duties at airports.

Profile Summary

APTITUDES

G	V	N	S	P	Q	K	F	M
4	4	4	3	4	4	4	4	3

INTERESTS
MOi

DATA PEOPLE THINGS (DPT)
683

PHYSICAL ACTIVITIES (PA)

V	C	H	B	L	S
4	0	1	4	2	4

ENVIRONMENTAL CONDITIONS (EC)
L3, L4, D1

EDUCATION/TRAINING
3, 4, R

Examples of Job Titles

Aircraft Groomer
Airport Ramp Attendant
Baggage Handler, Air Transport
Cargo Attendant, Air Transport
Ramp Agent, Air Transport
Ramp Attendant, Air Transport
Station Attendant, Air Transport

Descriptor Profile

Main Characteristics

Occupations in this group are characterized by the following aptitudes, interests and worker functions as they relate to main duties:

- **General learning ability** to operate ramp-servicing vehicles and equipment such as towing tractors, food-service trucks, de-icer sprayers and lavatory-servicing trucks

- **Spatial perception** to judge speed and relative distance when operating ramp-service vehicles and positioning passenger-loading stairs

- **Manual dexterity** to load and unload cargo and baggage, and to transport freight among aircraft and airport warehouses

- **Methodical interest** in **comparing** to sort and route cargo and passenger baggage, to clean and prepare aircraft interiors and to wash aircraft exteriors

- **Objective interest** in **driving** ramp-servicing vehicles; and in operating aircraft cargo doors, in marshalling and towing aircraft to gate positions for passenger boarding and deplaning, and in loading and unloading cargo

- **Innovative interest** in sorting and loading cargo and baggage to achieve proper balance according to instructions forwarded by load planners

7437

Physical Activities

Vision
   4   Total visual field

Colour Discrimination
   0   Not relevant

Hearing
   1   Limited

Body Position
   4   Other body positions

Limb Co-ordination
   2   Multiple limb co-ordination

Strength
   4   Heavy

Environmental Conditions

Location
   L3 Outside
   L4 In a vehicle or cab

Discomforts
   D1 Noise

Employment Requirements

Education/Training
   3, 4, R

- Completion of secondary school is usually required.

- Experience operating baggage transporting equipment or warehouse experience may be required.

- A driver's licence and a good driving record is usually required.

Workplaces/Employers

Airline and air services companies

Federal government

Occupational Options

There is mobility among jobs in this group.

Similar Occupations Classified Elsewhere

Material Handlers (7452)

Baggage handlers in accommodation and in rail, water and motor transportation [in 6672 *Other Attendants in Accommodation and Travel (Except Airline Travel)*]

Aircraft load planners (in 6433 *Airlines Sales and Service Agents*)

7441 Residential and Commercial Installers and Servicers

Residential and Commercial Installers and Servicers install and service interior and exterior prefabricated products, such as windows, doors, electrical appliances, water heaters, fences, play structures and septic systems, at residential and commercial properties.

Profile Summary

APTITUDES

G	V	N	S	P	Q	K	F	M
3	4	4	3	3	4	3	4	3

INTERESTS
OMi

DATA PEOPLE THINGS (DPT)
684

PHYSICAL ACTIVITIES (PA)

V	C	H	B	L	S
3	1	1	4	1	4

ENVIRONMENTAL CONDITIONS (EC)
L1, L2, L3, H3, D1

EDUCATION/TRAINING
2, R

Examples of Job Titles

Aluminium Window Installer
Eavestrough Installer
Electric Appliance Installer
Exterior Cladder
Fence Erector
Kitchen Cupboard and Vanity Installer
Recreation Structure Erector
Siding Installer
Sign Installer
Swimming Pool Installer
Water Conditioner Servicer
Water Heater Servicer
Window Installer

Descriptor Profile

Main Characteristics

Occupations in this group are characterized by the following aptitudes, interests and worker functions as they relate to main duties:

- **General learning ability** to install and service interior and exterior prefabricated products

- **Spatial** and **form perception** to read blueprints and work order specifications to determine layout and installation procedures

- **Motor co-ordination** and **manual dexterity** to use hand and power tools to install interior prefabricated products such as doors, windows, kitchen cupboards, bathroom vanities, water heaters and household appliances, and exterior prefabricated products such as siding, shutters, awnings, fences, decks, septic systems, signs and play structures

- **Objective interest** in **operating** equipment and tools to install and service interior and exterior prefabricated products

- **Methodical interest** in **comparing** information to measure and mark guidelines for installations

- **Innovative interest** in repairing and servicing interior and exterior prefabricated products

7441

Physical Activities

Vision
   3 Near and far vision

Colour Discrimination
   1 Relevant

Hearing
   1 Limited

Body Position
   4 Other body positions

Limb Co-ordination
   1 Upper limb co-ordination

Strength
   4 Heavy

Environmental Conditions

Location
   L1 Regulated inside climate
   L2 Unregulated inside climate
   L3 Outside

Hazards
   H3 Equipment, machinery, tools

Discomforts
   D1 Noise

Employment Requirements

Education/Training
   2, R

- Some secondary school education is usually required.

- On-the-job training and several months of related installing, repairing or servicing experience are usually required.

- A driver's licence may be required.

Workplaces/Employers

Companies specializing in specific product installation and service

Occupational Options

There is some mobility among the various types of installers and servicers in this group.

Similar Occupations Classified Elsewhere

Central air-conditioner and refrigerator installers (in 7313 *Refrigeration and Air Conditioning Mechanics*)

Supervisors of workers in this group (in 7219 *Contractors and Supervisors, Other Construction Trades, Installers, Repairers and Servicers*)

7442.1 Waterworks Maintenance Workers

Waterworks Maintenance Workers maintain and repair waterworks equipment and facilities.

Profile Summary

APTITUDES

G	V	N	S	P	Q	K	F	M
3	4	4	4	4	4	3	4	3

INTERESTS
MOi

DATA PEOPLE THINGS (DPT)
571

PHYSICAL ACTIVITIES (PA)

V	C	H	B	L	S
3	0	1	4	1	3

ENVIRONMENTAL CONDITIONS (EC)
L1, L3, H3, D5

EDUCATION/TRAINING
2

Examples of Job Titles

Pipeline Maintenance Worker
Pipeline Patrolman/woman
Utility Plant Maintenance Worker
Waterworks Maintenance Worker

Descriptor Profile

Main Characteristics

Occupations in this group are characterized by the following aptitudes, interests and worker functions as they relate to main duties:

- **General learning ability** to maintain and repair waterworks equipment and facilities

- **Motor co-ordination** and **manual dexterity** to install water meters using hand and power tools

- **Methodical interest** in **copying** to check, clean and lubricate waterworks equipment such as pumping equipment, chlorination equipment and compressors

- **Objective interest** in **precision working** to search and locate reported water leaks and repair water mains, valves and outlets

- **Innovative interest** in **assisting** to adjust and repair waterworks equipment under the direction of qualified tradespersons

7442.1
Subgroup 1 of 2

Physical Activities

Vision
  3   Near and far vision

Colour Discrimination
  0   Not relevant

Hearing
  1   Limited

Body Position
  4   Other body positions

Limb Co-ordination
  1   Upper limb co-ordination

Strength
  3   Medium

Environmental Conditions

Location
  L1 Regulated inside climate
  L3 Outside

Hazards
  H3 Equipment, machinery, tools

Discomforts
  D5 Wetness

Employment Requirements

Education/Training
  2

- Some secondary school education is usually required.

- Several years of experience as a labourer in the same company may be required.

- On-the-job training is provided.

Workplaces/Employers

Waste treatment plants

Water filtration and distribution plants

Occupational Options

Mobility among jobs in the 7442 group normally occurs within the same area of work, such as within waste-water treatment plants, within water filtration and distribution plants or within gas distribution plants.

Progression to supervisory positions is possible with experience.

Similar Occupations Classified Elsewhere

Gas Fitters (7253)

Water and Waste Plant Operators (9424)

Supervisors of water and gas maintenance workers (in 7216 *Contractors and Supervisors, Mechanic Trades*)

7442.2 Gas Maintenance Workers

Gas Maintenance Workers check and perform routine maintenance and minor repairs to exterior and underground gas mains and distribution lines.

Profile Summary

APTITUDES
G	V	N	S	P	Q	K	F	M
3	4	4	4	4	3	3	4	3

INTERESTS
MOi

DATA PEOPLE THINGS (DPT)
561

PHYSICAL ACTIVITIES (PA)
V	C	H	B	L	S
3	0	1	4	2	3

ENVIRONMENTAL CONDITIONS (EC)
L3, H1, H3, D3

EDUCATION/TRAINING
2

Examples of Job Titles

Gas Leak Locator
Gas Maintenance Worker
Utility Plant Maintenance Worker

Descriptor Profile

Main Characteristics

Occupations in this group are characterized by the following aptitudes, interests and worker functions as they relate to main duties:

- **General learning ability** to maintain and repair gas mains and distribution lines, and to conduct routine surveys of gas mains and distribution lines to detect and locate escaping gas

- **Clerical perception** to keep records of work performed and location and condition of pipelines

- **Motor co-ordination** and **manual dexterity** to dig ground to expose gas lines and repair damaged pipes, and to locate escaping gas using gas-detecting devices

- **Methodical interest** in **copying** to check and lubricate gas pipeline valves

- **Objective interest** in **precision working** to investigate reports of gas leaks to determine the exact location and extent of leaks

- **Innovative interest** in **speaking** with supervisor to provide information on underground gas distribution lines; and in observing excavation work to ensure that underground gas facilities are protected

7442.2

Physical Activities

Vision
 3 Near and far vision

Colour Discrimination
 0 Not relevant

Hearing
 1 Limited

Body Position
 4 Other body positions

Limb Co-ordination
 2 Multiple limb co-ordination

Strength
 3 Medium

Environmental Conditions

Location
 L3 Outside

Hazards
 H1 Dangerous chemical substances
 H3 Equipment, machinery, tools

Discomforts
 D3 Odours

Employment Requirements

Education/Training
 2

- Some secondary school education is usually required.

- Several years of experience as a labourer in the same company may be required.

- On-the-job training is provided.

Workplaces/Employers

Gas distribution companies

Occupational Options

Mobility among jobs in the 7442 group normally occurs within the same area of work, such as within waste-water treatment plants, within water filtration and distribution plants or within gas distribution plants.

Progression to supervisory positions is possible with experience.

Similar Occupations Classified Elsewhere

Gas Fitters (7253)

Water and Waste Plant Operators (9424)

Supervisors of water and gas maintenance workers (in 7216 *Contractors and Supervisors, Mechanic Trades*)

7443 Automotive Mechanical Installers and Servicers

Automotive Mechanical Installers and Servicers install replacement automotive mechanical parts such as mufflers, exhaust pipes, shock absorbers, springs and radiators, and perform routine maintenance service such as oil changes, lubrication and tire repairs on automobiles, trucks and heavy equipment.

Profile Summary

APTITUDES

G	V	N	S	P	Q	K	F	M
4	4	4	4	4	5	4	4	3

INTERESTS
MOi

DATA PEOPLE THINGS (DPT)
674

PHYSICAL ACTIVITIES (PA)

V	C	H	B	L	S
4	1	1	4	2	3

ENVIRONMENTAL CONDITIONS (EC)
L1, L2, L3, H3, H8*

EDUCATION/TRAINING
2

Examples of Job Titles

Crane Greaser
Heavy Equipment Servicer
Muffler Installer
Radiator Installer
Shock Absorber Installer
Spring Installer
Tire Repairer

Descriptor Profile

Main Characteristics

Occupations in this group are characterized by the following aptitudes, interests and worker functions as they relate to main duties:

- **General learning ability** to install and service automotive mechanical parts and perform routine maintenance services on automobiles, trucks and heavy equipment

- **Motor co-ordination** to grease booms, pulleys, buckets and other components of heavy equipment

- **Manual dexterity** to add and replace hydraulic and transmission fluids in motor vehicles, trucks and heavy equipment, and to drive automobiles and service trucks to construction, logging and other industrial sites

- **Methodical interest** in **comparing** to change engine oil and lubricate running gears and moving parts of automobiles, trucks and heavy equipment

- **Objective interest** in **operating** equipment to install replacement mufflers, exhaust pipes, shock absorbers and radiators, and to replace oil, air and fuel filters on motor vehicles, trucks and heavy equipment

- **Innovative interest** in **assisting** mechanics to repair and balance tires and perform other duties

7443

Physical Activities

Vision
    4   Total visual field

Colour Discrimination
    1   Relevant

Hearing
    1   Limited

Body Position
    4   Other body positions

Limb Co-ordination
    2   Multiple limb co-ordination

Strength
    3   Medium

Environmental Conditions

Location
    L1 Regulated inside climate
    L2 Unregulated inside climate
    L3 Outside

Hazards
    H3 Equipment, machinery, tools
    H8* Dangerous locations

Employment Requirements

Education/Training
2

- Some secondary school may be required.

- Several months of on-the-job training are usually required.

Workplaces/Employers

Automobile and truck service and repair shops

Construction, mining and logging companies

Service departments of industrial establishments

Occupational Options

There is some mobility among installers and servicers in this group.

Progression to supervisory positions is possible with experience.

Similar Occupations Classified Elsewhere

Heavy-Duty Equipment Mechanics (7312)

Motor Vehicle Mechanics, Technicians and Mechanical Repairers (7321)

Supervisors of workers in this group (in 7216 *Contractors and Supervisors, Mechanic Trades*)

Remarks

*Environmental Conditions

- For some occupations in this group, Hazards H8 (Dangerous locations) may also apply.

7444 Pest Controllers and Fumigators

Pest Controllers and Fumigators inspect buildings and outside areas for pest infestation and spray chemical treatments to kill noxious and destructive insects, rodents and other pests, and set cage traps to capture and remove animals.

Profile Summary

APTITUDES

G	V	N	S	P	Q	K	F	M
3	4	4	4	3	5	4	4	3

INTERESTS
OMi

DATA PEOPLE THINGS (DPT)
664

PHYSICAL ACTIVITIES (PA)

V	C	H	B	L	S
3	0	1	4	1	2

ENVIRONMENTAL CONDITIONS (EC)
L1, L3, H1

EDUCATION/TRAINING
4, R

Examples of Job Titles

Animal Control Trapper
Exterminator, Pests
Fumigator, Pests
Nuisance Control Trapper
Pest Control Operator
Pest Control Technician
Pest Controller

Descriptor Profile

Main Characteristics

Occupations in this group are characterized by the following aptitudes, interests and worker functions as they relate to main duties:

- **General learning ability** to fumigate households, spray chemicals, discharge toxic gases and set mechanical traps to kill insects, rodents and other pests that infest buildings and surrounding areas

- **Form perception** to inspect buildings and outside areas at regular intervals and at the specific request of property owners to detect signs of infestation

- **Manual dexterity** to install barriers such as needle strips, netting and other devices to keep animals off properties

- **Objective interest** in operating mechanical and electric sprayers; and in preparing and spraying chemical mixtures on infested areas

- **Methodical interest** in comparing to determine type of treatment required; and in cleaning out areas using rakes, shovels, brooms and mops

- **Innovative interest** in speaking with customers to provide cost estimates and to advise on how to prevent pest infestation

7444

Physical Activities

Vision
   3 Near and far vision

Colour Discrimination
   0 Not relevant

Hearing
   1 Limited

Body Position
   4 Other body positions

Limb Co-ordination
   1 Upper limb co-ordination

Strength
   2 Light

Environmental Conditions

Location
   L1 Regulated inside climate
   L3 Outside

Hazards
   H1 Dangerous chemical substances

Employment Requirements

Education/Training
   4, R

- Completion of secondary school is usually required.

- Completion of courses in pest control or extermination or several months of on-the-job training are usually required.

- A provincial pesticide applicator's licence is required in all provinces.

Workplaces/Employers

Pest control companies

Self-employment

Occupational Options

Progression to supervisory positions is possible with experience.

Similar Occupations Classified Elsewhere

Supervisors of pest controllers and fumigators (in 7219 *Contractors and Supervisors, Other Construction Trades, Installers, Repairers and Servicers*)

7445 Other Repairers and Servicers

Other Repairers and Servicers include workers not elsewhere classified who repair and service products such as cameras, scales, musical instruments, coin machines, vending machines, sporting goods and other miscellaneous products and equipment.

Profile Summary

APTITUDES

G	V	N	S	P	Q	K	F	M
3	4	4	3	3	4	3	3	3

INTERESTS
OMi

DATA PEOPLE THINGS (DPT)
384

PHYSICAL ACTIVITIES (PA)

V	C	H	B	L	S
2	0	1	4	1	2

ENVIRONMENTAL CONDITIONS (EC)
L1, H3

EDUCATION/TRAINING
2, 4

Examples of Job Titles

Bicycle Repairer
Camera Repairer
Meter Repairer
Piano Repairer
Scale Repairer
Sewing Machine Servicer
Sporting Goods Repairer
Vending Machine Repairer

Descriptor Profile

Main Characteristics

Occupations in this group are characterized by the following aptitudes, interests and worker functions as they relate to main duties:

- **General learning ability** to understand and apply the principles of installation, repair and adjustment of products and equipment

- **Spatial** and **form perception** to visualize the relationship and arrangement of parts in products to be repaired, and to examine products for wear

- **Motor co-ordination** and **finger** and **manual dexterity** to repair and replace defective and worn-out parts and components

- **Objective interest** in operating hand, power and specially designed tools

- **Methodical interest** in compiling information to test and adjust repaired products to ensure that they work properly

- **Innovative interest** in inspecting products to determine the need for repairs

7445

Physical Activities

Vision
   2 Near vision

Colour Discrimination
   0 Not relevant

Hearing
   1 Limited

Body Position
   4 Other body positions

Limb Co-ordination
   1 Upper limb co-ordination

Strength
   2 Light

Environmental Conditions

Location
   L1 Regulated inside climate

Hazards
   H3 Equipment, machinery, tools

Employment Requirements

Education/Training
   2, 4

- Some secondary school education is usually required.

- Completion of college or other courses relevant to a particular equipment or product repair
or
several months of on-the-job training are usually required.

Workplaces/Employers

Product specialty repair shops

Service establishments

Occupational Options

Some mobility may occur among workers in this group.

Progression to supervisory positions is possible with experience.

Similar Occupations Classified Elsewhere

Locksmiths (in 7383 *Other Trades and Related Occupations*)

Supervisors of workers in this group (in 7219 *Contractors and Supervisors, Other Construction Trades, Installers, Repairers and Servicers*)

7451 Longshore Workers

Longshore Workers transfer cargo throughout dock areas and to and from ships and other vessels.

Profile Summary

APTITUDES

G	V	N	S	P	Q	K	F	M
3	4	4	3	4	4	3	4	3

INTERESTS
OMi

DATA PEOPLE THINGS (DPT)
683

PHYSICAL ACTIVITIES (PA)

V	C	H	B	L	S
4	0	1	4	2	4

ENVIRONMENTAL CONDITIONS (EC)
L3, L4, H3, D1, D2

EDUCATION/TRAINING
2

Examples of Job Titles

Dockworker
Longshore Worker
Longshoreman/woman
Ship Loader Operator
Stevedore
Tanker Loader

Descriptor Profile

Main Characteristics

Occupations in this group are characterized by the following aptitudes, interests and worker functions as they relate to main duties:

- **General learning ability** to transfer cargo, such as containers, crated items and pallet-mounted machinery, around docks and to move cargo within range of cranes and hoists

- **Spatial perception** to visualize relationships, movements and placement of objects when operating mechanical towers to load vessels with materials such as coal and ore

- **Motor co-ordination** and **manual dexterity** to connect hoses and operate equipment to transfer liquid materials into storage tanks on vessels

- **Objective interest** in **driving** industrial trucks, tractors and other mobile equipment to transfer cargo; and in operating equipment, winches and other hoisting devices to transfer bulk materials such as grain to the holds of vessels, and in loading and unloading cargo on and off ships and other vessels

- **Methodical interest** in **comparing** to open and close hatches and in cleaning holds of ships

- **Innovative interest** in performing other activities, such as lashing, shoring and rigging cargo, aboard ships

7451

Physical Activities

Vision
   4   Total visual field

Colour Discrimination
   0   Not relevant

Hearing
   1   Limited

Body Position
   4   Other body positions

Limb Co-ordination
   2   Multiple limb co-ordination

Strength
   4   Heavy

Environmental Conditions

Location
   L3 Outside
   L4 In a vehicle or cab

Hazards
   H3 Equipment, machinery, tools

Discomforts
   D1 Noise
   D2 Vibration

Employment Requirements

Education/Training
2

- Some secondary school education may be required.
- On-the-job training is provided.

Workplaces/Employers

Marine cargo handling companies

Shipping agencies

Shipping lines

Occupational Options

Progression to foreman/woman or supervisor of longshore workers is possible with experience.

Similar Occupations Classified Elsewhere

Material Handlers (7452)

Longshore crane operators (in 7371 *Crane Operators*)

Supervisors of longshore workers (in 7217 *Contractors and Supervisors, Heavy Construction Equipment Crews*)

7452.1 Material Handlers (Manual)

Material Handlers (Manual) handle, move, load and unload materials by hand.

Profile Summary

APTITUDES

G	V	N	S	P	Q	K	F	M
4	4	4	4	4	4	3	4	3

INTERESTS
MOi

DATA PEOPLE THINGS (DPT)
686

PHYSICAL ACTIVITIES (PA)

V	C	H	B	L	S
3	0	1	4	2	4

ENVIRONMENTAL CONDITIONS (EC)
L1, L2, L3

EDUCATION/TRAINING
2

Examples of Job Titles

Bin Filler
Coal Handler
Freight Handler (Except Airline)
Furniture Mover
Lumber Piler, Building Supplies
Material Handler
Railway Car Loader
Stockpiler
Storage Worker
Truck Loader
Warehouseman/woman

Descriptor Profile

Main Characteristics

Occupations in this group are characterized by the following aptitudes, interests and worker functions as they relate to main duties:

- **General learning ability** to understand loading schedules and instructions

- **Motor co-ordination** and **manual dexterity** to load, unload and move products and materials by hand and by using basic material-handling equipment

- **Methodical interest** in **comparing** information to perform other material-handling activities such as counting, weighing, sorting, packing and unpacking

- **Objective interest** in **feeding - offbearing** to move household appliances and furniture on and off moving trucks and vans

- **Innovative interest** in arranging articles in vans to form compact loads and secure articles to prevent damage and breakage

7452.1
Subgroup 1 of 2

Physical Activities

Vision
 3 Near and far vision

Colour Discrimination
 0 Not relevant

Hearing
 1 Limited

Body Position
 4 Other body positions

Limb Co-ordination
 2 Multiple limb co-ordination

Strength
 4 Heavy

Environmental Conditions

Location
 L1 Regulated inside climate
 L2 Unregulated inside climate
 L3 Outside

Employment Requirements

Education/Training
 2

- Some secondary school education may be required.

- Physical strength is required for manual material handlers who work with heavy materials.

Workplaces/Employers

Manufacturing and processing companies

Retail and wholesale warehouses

Transportation, storage and moving companies

Similar Occupations Classified Elsewhere

Heavy Equipment Operators (Except Crane) (7421)

Longshore Workers (7451)

Airline freight attendants (in 7437 *Air Transport Ramp Attendants*)

Supervisors of material handlers (in 7217 *Contractors and Supervisors, Heavy Construction Equipment Crews*)

Warehouse supervisors (in 1215 *Supervisors, Recording, Distributing and Scheduling Occupations*)

7452.2 Material Handlers (Equipment Operators)

Material Handlers (Equipment Operators) handle, move, load and unload materials by using different types of material handling equipment.

Profile Summary

APTITUDES

G	V	N	S	P	Q	K	F	M
4	4	4	4	4	4	3	4	3

INTERESTS
OMi

DATA PEOPLE THINGS (DPT)
684

PHYSICAL ACTIVITIES (PA)

V	C	H	B	L	S
3	0	1	4	2	3

ENVIRONMENTAL CONDITIONS (EC)
L1, L2, L3, L4, H1*, H3, D1, D2

EDUCATION/TRAINING
2

Examples of Job Titles

Conveyor Console Operator
Fork-Lift Truck Operator
Freight Handler (Except Airline)
Material Handler

Descriptor Profile

Main Characteristics

Occupations in this group are characterized by the following aptitudes, interests and worker functions as they relate to main duties:

- **General learning ability** to operate winches and other loading devices to load and unload materials on and off trucks, railway cars and loading docks of warehouses and industrial establishments

- **Motor co-ordination** and **manual dexterity** to connect hoses and pipes; to operate equipment to load and unload liquid petroleum, chemical and other products into and from tank cars, tank trucks and storage tanks; and to operate equipment to load and unload materials such as coal, ore and grain into and from railway cars, trucks and other vehicles

- **Objective interest** in **operating** winches and other loading devices, industrial trucks, tractors, conveyors, loaders and other equipment to transport materials, grain and other materials from transportation vehicles to storage tanks, elevators, bins and other storage areas

- **Methodical interest** in **comparing** information to transport materials to and from transportation vehicles and loading docks, and to store and retrieve materials in warehouses; may assist in taking inventory and weighing and checking materials, opening containers and crates and filling warehouse orders

- **Innovative interest** in performing minor repairs to conveyors and other loading and unloading equipment

7452.2

Physical Activities

Vision
   3 Near and far vision

Colour Discrimination
   0 Not relevant

Hearing
   1 Limited

Body Position
   4 Other body positions

Limb Co-ordination
   2 Multiple limb co-ordination

Strength
   3 Medium

Environmental Conditions

Location
   L1 Regulated inside climate
   L2 Unregulated inside climate
   L3 Outside
   L4 In a vehicle or cab

Hazards
   H1*Dangerous chemical substances
   H3 Equipment, machinery, tools

Discomforts
   D1 Noise
   D2 Vibration

Employment Requirements

Education/Training
2

- Some secondary school education may be required.

- Physical strength is required for manual material handlers who work with heavy materials.

Workplaces/Employers

Manufacturing and processing companies

Retail and wholesale warehouses

Transportation, storage and moving companies

Similar Occupations Classified Elsewhere

Heavy Equipment Operators (Except Crane) (7421)

Longshore Workers (7451)

Airline freight attendants (in 7437 *Air Transport Ramp Attendants*)

Supervisors of material handlers (in 7217 *Contractors and Supervisors, Heavy Construction Equipment Crews*)

Warehouse supervisors (in 1215 *Supervisors, Recording, Distributing and Scheduling Occupations*)

Remarks

*Environmental Conditions

- For some occupations in this group, Hazards H1 (Dangerous chemical substances) may also apply.

7611 Construction Trades Helpers and Labourers

Construction Trades Helpers and Labourers assist skilled tradespersons and perform labouring activities at construction sites.

Profile Summary

APTITUDES

G	V	N	S	P	Q	K	F	M
4	4	4	4	4	5	4	4	4

INTERESTS
MOi

DATA PEOPLE THINGS (DPT)
674

PHYSICAL ACTIVITIES (PA)

V	C	H	B	L	S
3	0	1	4	1	4

ENVIRONMENTAL CONDITIONS (EC)
L2, L3, H1, H3, H6, H8, D1, D2, D3, D4

EDUCATION/TRAINING
1, 2

Examples of Job Titles

Asphalt Spreader
Bricklayer Helper
Carpenter Helper
Concrete Mixer Helper
Construction Helper
Construction Labourer
Demolition Worker
Drywall Sander
Flagman/woman
Glazier Helper
Labourer, Concrete Paving
Labourer, Excavation
Pipeline Mandrel Operator
Plumber Assistant
Roofer Helper
Stabber, Pipeline Construction

Descriptor Profile

Main Characteristics

Occupations in this group are characterized by the following aptitudes, interests and worker functions as they relate to main duties:

- **General learning ability** to assist tradespersons, such as carpenters, bricklayers, cement finishers, roofers and glaziers, in construction activities, to help heavy equipment operators secure special attachments to equipment, to guide operators in moving equipment, and to provide assistance in other activities

- **Spatial perception** to erect and dismantle concrete forms, scaffolding, ramps, catwalks, shoring and barricades

- **Form perception** to level earth to fine grade specifications using rakes and shovels

- **Motor co-ordination** and **manual dexterity** to load and unload construction materials, to move materials to work areas, to mix, pour and spread materials, such as concrete and asphalt, and to oil and grease hoists and similar equipment

- **Methodical interest** in **comparing** to sort, clean and pile salvaged materials; in removing rubble and other debris using rakes, shovels, wheelbarrows and other equipment; and in directing traffic at, or near, construction sites

- **Objective interest** in **operating** pneumatic hammers, vibrators and tampers; and in tending and feeding machines and equipment such as mixers, compressors and pumps

- **Innovative interest** in **assisting** to drill and blast rock, to align pipes and perform related activities during oil and gas pipeline construction and to demolish buildings using prying bars and other tools

7611

Physical Activities

Vision
   3 Near and far vision

Colour Discrimination
   0 Not relevant

Hearing
   1 Limited

Body Position
   4 Other body positions

Limb Co-ordination
   1 Upper limb co-ordination

Strength
   4 Heavy

Environmental Conditions

Location
   L2 Unregulated inside climate
   L3 Outside

Hazards
   H1 Dangerous chemical substances
   H3 Equipment, machinery, tools
   H6 Flying particles, falling objects
   H8 Dangerous locations

Discomforts
   D1 Noise
   D2 Vibration
   D3 Odours
   D4 Non-toxic dusts

Employment Requirements

Education/Training
1, 2

- Some experience as a general construction labourer may be required for construction trade helpers.

- Some pipeline workers, such as stabbers, mandrel operators and pre-heater tenders, usually require one season of experience in oil and gas pipeline construction.

Workplaces/Employers

Construction companies

Trade and labour contractors

Occupational Options

Mobility is possible among workers in this group.

Similar Occupations Classified Elsewhere

Other Trades Helpers and Labourers (7612)

Public Works and Maintenance Labourers (7621)

7612 Other Trades Helpers and Labourers

Other Trades Helpers and Labourers include workers not elsewhere classified who assist skilled tradespersons and perform labouring activities in the installation, maintenance and repair of industrial machinery, refrigeration, heating and air-conditioning equipment; in the maintenance and repair of transportation and heavy equipment; in the installation and repair of telecommunication and power cables; and in other repair and service work settings.

Profile Summary

APTITUDES

G	V	N	S	P	Q	K	F	M
4	4	4	4	4	4	3	4	3

INTERESTS
OMs

DATA PEOPLE THINGS (DPT)
674

PHYSICAL ACTIVITIES (PA)

V	C	H	B	L	S
3	1*	1	4	1	3*

ENVIRONMENTAL CONDITIONS (EC)
L1*, L2*, L3*, H1*, H3, H4*, H8*, D1*, D3*, D4

EDUCATION/TRAINING
2

Examples of Job Titles

Aerial Spraying Assistant
Aircraft Mechanic Helper
Cable Installer Helper
Diesel Mechanic Helper
Ground Worker - Telecommunications
Mechanic's Helper - Automotive
Millwright Helper
Refrigeration Mechanic Helper
Splicer Helper - Telecommunications
Surveyor Helper

Descriptor Profile

Main Characteristics

Occupations in this group are characterized by the following aptitudes, interests and worker functions as they relate to main duties:

- **General learning ability** to assist skilled tradespersons in the installation, maintenance and repair of industrial machinery and other equipment, and to perform other labouring and elementary tasks

- **Motor co-ordination** and **manual dexterity** to move tools, equipment and other materials to and from work areas, and to assist in land-surveying activities such as holding and moving stakes and rods, clearing brush and debris and transporting surveying tools to work areas

- **Objective interest** in **operating** tools and equipment for the mechanical, electrical and body repairs of aircraft, railway cars, automobiles, heavy equipment and motorcycles when assisting skilled tradespersons

- **Methodical interest** in **comparing** information to mix fertilizers, herbicides and pesticides and to load mixtures into airplanes for aerial spraying

- **Social interest** in **assisting** skilled tradespersons to repair electrical appliances, small engines and other similar equipment; to repair, maintain and install industrial machinery and equipment, refrigeration, heating and air-conditioning equipment, elevators, stationary electric-power generating and distribution equipment; and to splice overhead and underground communications and electric-power transmission cables

7612

Physical Activities

Vision
   3 Near and far vision

Colour Discrimination
   1* Relevant

Hearing
   1 Limited

Body Position
   4 Other body positions

Limb Co-ordination
   1 Upper limb co-ordination

Strength
   3* Medium

Environmental Conditions

Location
   L1* Regulated inside climate
   L2* Unregulated inside climate
   L3* Outside

Hazards
   H1* Dangerous chemical substances
   H3 Equipment, machinery, tools
   H4* Electricity
   H8* Dangerous locations

Discomforts
   D1* Noise
   D3* Odours
   D4 Non-toxic dusts

Employment Requirements

Education/Training
2

- Some secondary school education may be required.

- On-the-job training is provided.

Workplaces/Employers

Manufacturing, utility and service companies

Occupational Options

There is little or no mobility among occupations in this group.

Similar Occupations Classified Elsewhere

Construction Trades Helpers and Labourers (7611)

Remarks

*Physical Activties

- For some occupations in this group, **Colour Discrimination** 0 (Not relevant) and **Strength** 4 (Heavy) may also apply.

*Environmental Conditions

- For some occupations in this group, the following **Location** L2 (Unregulated inside climate) and L3 (Outside), **Hazards** H1 (Dangerous chemical substances), H4 (Electricity) and H8 (Dangerous locations) and **Discomforts** D1 (Noise) and D3 (Odours) may also apply.

7621 Public Works and Maintenance Labourers

Public Works and Maintenance Labourers perform a variety of labouring activities to maintain sidewalks, streets, roads and similar areas.

Profile Summary

APTITUDES
G	V	N	S	P	Q	K	F	M
4	4	5	4	4	5	4	4	4

INTERESTS
Moi

DATA PEOPLE THINGS (DPT)
674

PHYSICAL ACTIVITIES (PA)
V	C	H	B	L	S
3	0	1	4	2	4

ENVIRONMENTAL CONDITIONS (EC)
L3, H1*, H3, D1*, D2*, D3*, D4*

EDUCATION/TRAINING
1, 2

Examples of Job Titles

Garbage Collector
Municipal Labourer
Parking Meter Collector
Public Works Labourer
Road Maintenance Worker
Sewer Maintenance Worker
Sidewalk Cleaner

Descriptor Profile

Main Characteristics

Occupations in this group are characterized by the following aptitudes, interests and worker functions as they relate to main duties:

- **General learning ability** to clean and maintain sidewalks, streets, roads and public grounds of municipalities and other areas as members of crews

- **Form perception** to load and unload trucks with supplies and equipment and to collect and load refuse on garbage trucks

- **Motor co-ordination** to shovel cement and other materials into cement mixers, to spread concrete and asphalt on road surfaces using shovels, rakes and hand tampers, and to perform other activities to assist in the maintenance and repair of roads

- **Finger dexterity** to collect money from coin boxes of parking meters along established routes

- **Manual dexterity** to spread sand and salt on sidewalks for snow and ice control; to dig ditches and trenches using shovels and other hand tools; to cut trees, trim branches, rake leaves, apply fertilizers and insecticides by hand; and to water public lawns, trees and shrubs

- **Methodical interest** in **comparing** to sweep debris and shovel snow from streets, building grounds and other areas; and in loading snow and debris into carts or trucks

- **Objective interest** in **operating** jackhammers and drills to break up pavement and power mowers and cutters to cut lawns and grass along roadsides; may operate mobile sidewalk-cleaning equipment

- **Innovative interest** in **assisting** in routine maintenance and repair of equipment; and in assisting equipment operators to secure attachments to equipment and trucks, and in assisting skilled tradespersons such as carpenters, plumbers and mechanics

7621

Physical Activities

Vision
- 3 Near and far vision

Colour Discrimination
- 0 Not relevant

Hearing
- 1 Limited

Body Position
- 4 Other body positions

Limb Co-ordination
- 2 Multiple limb co-ordination

Strength
- 4 Heavy

Environmental Conditions

Location
- L3 Outside

Hazards
- H1*Dangerous chemical substances
- H3 Equipment, machinery, tools

Discomforts
- D1*Noise
- D2*Vibration
- D3*Odours
- D4*Non-toxic dusts

Employment Requirements

Education/Training
1, 2

- Several weeks of on-the-job training are provided.

Workplaces/Employers

Municipal, provincial and federal government public works departments

Private contractors under contract to governments

Occupational Options

Progression to supervisory positions or to public works maintenance-equipment operator positions is possible with experience.

Similar Occupations Classified Elsewhere

Public Works Maintenance Equipment Operators (7422)

Railway and Motor Transport Labourers (7622)

Construction labourers (in 7611 *Construction Trades Helpers and Labourers*)

Park labourers (in 8612 *Landscaping and Grounds Maintenance Labourers*)

Remarks

* Environmental Conditions

- For some occupations in this group, the following Hazards H1 (Dangerous chemical substances) and Discomforts D1 (Noise), D2 (Vibration), D3 (Odours) and D4 (Non-toxic dusts) may also apply.

7622.1 Railway Labourers

Railway Labourers perform a variety of tasks to assist track maintenance workers and railway yard workers.

Profile Summary

APTITUDES

G	V	N	S	P	Q	K	F	M
4	4	5	4	4	5	4	4	4

INTERESTS
OMs

DATA PEOPLE THINGS (DPT)
677

PHYSICAL ACTIVITIES (PA)

V	C	H	B	L	S
3	0	1	4	1	4

ENVIRONMENTAL CONDITIONS (EC)
L3, H3, D1

EDUCATION/TRAINING
2

Examples of Job Titles

Car Checker, Railway
Railway Labourer
Signal Gang Helper

Descriptor Profile

Main Characteristics

Occupations in this group are characterized by the following aptitudes, interests and worker functions as they relate to main duties:

- **General learning ability** to understand and follow instructions concerning track maintenance

- **Motor co-ordination** and **manual dexterity** to cut vegetation growth from tracks using scythes and mowers

- **Objective interest** in **handling** to transport tools and equipment on push and hand cars

- **Methodical interest** in **comparing** to check freight cars for physical damage and cleanliness

- **Social interest** in **assisting** railway track maintenance workers to lay, maintain and repair railway tracks

7622.1

Physical Activities

Vision
  3 Near and far vision

Colour Discrimination
  0 Not relevant

Hearing
  1 Limited

Body Position
  4 Other body positions

Limb Co-ordination
  1 Upper limb co-ordination

Strength
  4 Heavy

Environmental Conditions

Location
  L3 Outside

Hazards
  H3 Equipment, machinery, tools

Discomforts
  D1 Noise

Employment Requirements

Education/Training
2

- Some secondary school education is usually required.

Workplaces/Employers

Railway transport companies

Occupational Options

With experience, railway labourers may progress to railway track maintenance workers or railway yard workers.

Similar Occupations Classified Elsewhere

Material Handlers (7452)

Rail car oilers and greasers (in 7431 *Railway Yard Workers*)

7622.2 Motor Transport Labourers

Motor Transport Labourers perform a variety of tasks to assist motor transport operators.

Profile Summary

APTITUDES

G	V	N	S	P	Q	K	F	M
4	4	5	4	4	5	4	4	4

INTERESTS
MOs

DATA PEOPLE THINGS (DPT)
677

PA

V	C	H	B	L	S
3	0	1	4	1	4

ENVIRONMENTAL CONDITIONS (EC)
L1, L2, L3

EDUCATION/TRAINING
2

Examples of Job Titles

Delivery Truck Helper
Furniture Mover Helper
Moving Van Helper
Truck Driver Helper

Descriptor Profile

Main Characteristics

Occupations in this group are characterized by the following aptitudes, interests and worker functions as they relate to main duties:

- **General learning ability** to understand and follow instructions concerning material handling and packaging

- **Motor co-ordination** and **finger** and **manual dexterity** to load and stack material, tie bundles and affix labels to packaging

- **Methodical interest** in **comparing** information to sort articles by condition, size, shape and colour

- **Objective interest** in **handling** to perform labouring duties in warehouses

- **Social interest** in **assisting** truck and delivery drivers to load and unload vehicles

7622.2
Subgroup 2 of 2

Physical Activities

Vision
   3 Near and far vision

Colour Discrimination
   0 Not relevant

Hearing
   1 Limited

Body Position
   4 Other body positions

Limb Co-ordination
   1 Upper limb co-ordination

Strength
   4 Heavy

Environmental Conditions

Location
     L1 Regulated inside climate
     L2 Unregulated inside climate
     L3 Outside

Employment Requirements

Education/Training
2

- Some secondary school education is usually required.

Workplaces/Employers

Motor transport companies

Similar Occupations Classified Elsewhere

Material Handlers (7452)

Rail car oilers and greasers (in 7431 *Railway Yard Workers*)

Occupations Unique to Primary Industry

Occupations Unique to Primary Industry

MAJOR GROUP 82
SKILLED OCCUPATIONS IN PRIMARY INDUSTRY

821	**Supervisors, Logging and Forestry**
8211	Supervisors, Logging and Forestry

822	**Supervisors, Mining, Oil and Gas**
8221	Supervisors, Mining and Quarrying
8222	Supervisors, Oil and Gas Drilling and Service

823	**Underground Miners, Oil and Gas Drillers and Related Workers**
8231	Underground Production and Development Miners
8232	Oil and Gas Well Drillers, Servicers, Testers and Related Workers
	8232.1 Oil and Gas Well Drillers and Well Servicers
	8232.2 Oil and Gas Well Loggers, Testers and Related Workers

824	**Logging Machinery Operators**
8241	Logging Machinery Operators
	8241.1 Cable Yarding System Operators
	8241.2 Mechanical Harvester and Forwarder Operators
	8241.3 Mechanical Tree Processor and Loader Operators

825	**Contractors, Operators and Supervisors in Agriculture, Horticulture and Aquaculture**
8251	Farmers and Farm Managers
8252	Agricultural and Related Service Contractors and Managers
8253	Farm Supervisors and Specialized Livestock Workers
	8253.1 Farm Supervisors
	8253.2 Specialized Livestock Workers
8254	Nursery and Greenhouse Operators and Managers
8255	Landscaping and Grounds Maintenance Contractors and Managers
8256	Supervisors, Landscape and Horticulture
8257	Aquaculture Operators and Managers

826	**Fishing Vessel Masters and Skippers and Fishermen/women**
8261	Fishing Masters and Officers
8262	Fishing Vessel Skippers and Fishermen/women

MAJOR GROUP 84
INTERMEDIATE OCCUPATIONS IN PRIMARY INDUSTRY

841   Mine Service Workers and Operators in Oil and Gas Drilling
8411   Underground Mine Service and Support Workers
8412   Oil and Gas Well Drilling Workers and Services Operators
      8412.1   Oil and Gas Well Drilling Workers
      8412.2   Oil and Gas Well Services Operators

842   Logging and Forestry Workers
8421   Chainsaw and Skidder Operators
8422   Silviculture and Forestry Workers

843   Agriculture and Horticulture Workers
8431   General Farm Workers
8432   Nursery and Greenhouse Workers

844   Other Fishing and Trapping Occupations
8441   Fishing Vessel Deckhands
8442   Trappers and Hunters
      8442.1   Trappers
      8442.2   Hunters

MAJOR GROUP 86
LABOURERS IN PRIMARY INDUSTRY

861   Primary Production Labourers
8611   Harvesting Labourers
8612   Landscaping and Grounds Maintenance Labourers
8613   Aquaculture and Marine Harvest Labourers
      8613.1   Aquaculture Support Workers
      8613.2   Marine Plant Gatherers
      8613.3   Shellfish Harvesters
8614   Mine Labourers
8615   Oil and Gas Drilling, Servicing and Related Labourers
8616   Logging and Forestry Labourers

8211 Supervisors, Logging and Forestry

Supervisors in this group supervise and co-ordinate the activities of workers engaged in logging and silvicultural operations.

Profile Summary

APTITUDES

G	V	N	S	P	Q	K	F	M
3	3	3	3	4	3	4	4	4

INTERESTS
DSi

DATA PEOPLE THINGS (DPT)
138

PHYSICAL ACTIVITIES (PA)

V	C	H	B	L	S
3	0	2	3	0	1

ENVIRONMENTAL CONDITIONS (EC)
L1, L3, H1*, H8, D1, D4

EDUCATION/TRAINING
5+, 6+, R

Examples of Job Titles

Forest Operations Supervisor
Forestry Crew Supervisor
Hook Tender
Logging Contractor
Logging Foreman/woman
Production Supervisor, Logging
Silviculture Supervisor
Woods Foreman/woman

Descriptor Profile

Main Characteristics

Occupations in this group are characterized by the following aptitudes, interests and worker functions as they relate to main duties:

- **General learning ability** to supervise and co-ordinate the activities of logging and forestry workers, often in several work locations over several square kilometres

- **Verbal ability** to communicate with technical, professional and management forestry personnel regarding harvesting and management plans, procedures and schedules

- **Clerical perception** to prepare production and other reports

- **Directive interest** in **supervising** silvicultural activities such as scarification, planting and vegetation control, ensuring that government regulations are met; and in hiring new workers

- **Social interest** in training new workers and instructing workers in safety, recognition of unsafe work conditions and modification of work procedures

- **Innovative interest** in **co-ordinating** information to resolve work problems and recommend measures to improve work methods, and to schedule work crews, equipment and transportation for several work locations

8211

Physical Activities

Vision
   3   Near and far vision

Colour Discrimination
   0   Not relevant

Hearing
   2   Verbal interaction

Body Position
   3   Sitting, standing, walking

Limb Co-ordination
   0   Not relevant

Strength
   1   Limited

Environmental Conditions

Location
   L1   Regulated inside

Climate
   L3   Outside

Hazards
   H1*Dangerous chemical substances
   H8 Dangerous locations

Discomforts
   D1 Noise
   D4 Non-toxic dusts

Employment Requirements

Education/Training
5+, 6+, R

- Completion of secondary school is usually required.

- Completion of a one-to-three year college program for forestry technologists or technicians may be required.

- Formal company training and several months of on-the-job training are provided.

- Several years of experience as a logger, silvicultural worker or logging machinery operator are usually required.

- A chemical application licence may be required.

- An industrial first-aid certificate may be required.

Workplaces/Employers

Government agencies

Logging companies

Logging contractors

Similar Occupations Classified Elsewhere

Chainsaw and Skidder Operators (8421)

Forestry Technologists and Technicians (2223)

Logging Machinery Operators (8241)

Silviculture and Forestry Workers (8422)

Logging and forestry managers [in 0811 *Primary Production Managers (Except Agriculture)*]

Remarks

* Environmental Conditions

- For some occupations in this group, Hazards H1 (Dangerous chemical substances) may also apply.

8221 Supervisors, Mining and Quarrying

Supervisors in this group supervise and co-ordinate the activities of workers engaged in underground and surface mining operations and quarries.

Profile Summary

APTITUDES

G	V	N	S	P	Q	K	F	M
3	3	4	3	3	4	4	4	4

INTERESTS
DSi

DATA PEOPLE THINGS (DPT)
138

PHYSICAL ACTIVITIES (PA)

V	C	H	B	L	S
3	0	2	3	0	1

ENVIRONMENTAL CONDITIONS (EC)
L1, L2, L3, H8, D1, D4

EDUCATION/TRAINING
6+, 7+, R

Examples of Job Titles

Fill Foreman/woman
Foreman/woman, Underground Mine
Level Boss
Mine Captain
Mine Foreman/woman
Mine Supervisor
Shift Boss
Shift Foreman/woman
Supervisor, Mine
Supervisor, Quarry
Supervisor, Surface Mine
Track Boss
Yard Boss

Descriptor Profile

Main Characteristics

Occupations in this group are characterized by the following aptitudes, interests and worker functions as they relate to main duties:

- **General learning ability** to establish methods to meet work schedules and recommend measures to improve productivity

- **Verbal ability** to train workers in job duties, safety procedures and company policies, to recommend personnel actions such as hirings and promotions, and to prepare production and other reports

- **Spatial** and **form perception** to oversee the safety of mining and quarrying operations

- **Directive interest** in **supervising** the activities of heavy equipment operators, drillers, blasters and other workers in surface mining and quarrying, and of workers who extract coal, minerals and ore, operate underground conveyances and perform other services in support of underground mining; and in requisitioning materials and supplies

- **Social interest** in conferring with managerial and technical personnel, other departments and contractors to resolve problems and co-ordinate activities

- **Innovative interest** in **co-ordinating** and scheduling the activities of workers; and in resolving work problems

8221

Physical Activities

Vision
   3 Near and far vision

Colour Discrimination
   0 Not relevant

Hearing
   2 Verbal interaction

Body Position
   3 Sitting, standing, walking

Limb Co-ordination
   0 Not relevant

Strength
   1 Limited

Environmental Conditions

Location
   L1 Regulated inside climate
   L2 Unregulated inside climate
   L3 Outside

Hazards
   H8 Dangerous locations

Discomforts
   D1 Noise
   D4 Non-toxic dusts

Employment Requirements

Education/Training
6+, 7+, R

- Completion of secondary school is required.

- Completion of a college or university program in mining technology or engineering may be required for some positions in this group.

- Several years of experience in the occupations supervised is usually required.

- Provincial certification as an underground mine supervisor, shift boss or coal mining supervisor may be required.

Workplaces/Employers

Coal, metal and non-metallic mineral mines

Quarries

Occupational Options

There is mobility among employers especially for supervisors with post-secondary diplomas or degrees.

Mobility among surface mining, underground mining, coal or metal mining sectors may be somewhat limited by differences in production technologies and licensing requirements.

Similar Occupations Classified Elsewhere

Drillers and Blasters - Surface Mining, Quarrying and Construction (7372)

Heavy Equipment Operators (Except Crane) (7421)

Mine Labourers (8614)

Underground Production and Development Miners (8231)

Underground Mine Service and Support Workers (8411)

Mine managers [in 0811 *Primary Production Managers (Except Agriculture)*]

8222 Supervisors, Oil and Gas Drilling and Service

Supervisors in this group supervise and co-ordinate the activities of workers engaged in drilling for oil or gas, operating service rigs and providing oil- and gas-well services.

Profile Summary

APTITUDES

G	V	N	S	P	Q	K	F	M
3	3	3	3	4	4	3	4	3

INTERESTS
Dio

DATA PEOPLE THINGS (DPT)
138

PHYSICAL ACTIVITIES (PA)

V	C	H	B	L	S
3	0	2	3	0	1

ENVIRONMENTAL CONDITIONS (EC)
L1, L3, H1*, H8, D1, D3

EDUCATION/TRAINING
4+, 6+, R

Examples of Job Titles

Fracturing Supervisor
Multi-Service Operator
Rig Manager
Tool Pusher
Well-Services Crew Supervisor

Descriptor Profile

Main Characteristics

Occupations in this group are characterized by the following aptitudes, interests and worker functions as they relate to main duties:

- **General learning ability** to establish methods to meet work schedules, to co-ordinate activities with other departments and to recommend measures to improve productivity

- **Verbal ability** to train workers in job duties, safety procedures and company policies, to recommend personnel actions, such as hirings and promotions, and to prepare production and other reports

- **Directive interest** in supervising the activities of workers who drill for oil and gas, operate service rigs and provide oil- and gas-well services; and in requisitioning materials and supplies

- **Innovative interest** in co-ordinating and scheduling the activities of workers; and in resolving work problems

- **Objective interest** in understanding the functioning of equipment and machinery used in oil and gas drilling and services; may set up machines and equipment

8222

Physical Activities

Vision
3   Near and far vision

Colour Discrimination
0   Not relevant

Hearing
2   Verbal interaction

Body Position
3   Sitting, standing, walking

Limb Co-ordination
0   Not relevant

Strength
1   Limited

Environmental Conditions

Location
L1   Regulated inside climate
L3   Outside

Hazards
H1*Dangerous chemical substances
H8   Dangerous locations

Discomforts
D1   Noise
D3   Odours

Employment Requirements

Education/Training
4+, 6+, R

- Completion of secondary school is required.

- Drilling supervisors, including rig managers and tool pushers, require completion of college or Petroleum Industry Training Service (PITS) courses for drillers and supervisors.

- For drilling supervisors, extensive experience of eight years or more in the occupations supervised is required.

- Well-services supervisors require completion of college or industry courses in the services provided.

- A college diploma in petroleum engineering technology may be required.

- For well-services supervisors, several years experience in the occupations supervised is required.

- Certificates in first aid, hydrogen-sulphide awareness, blowout prevention, Workplace Hazardous Materials Information System (WHMIS), Transportation of Dangerous Goods (TDG) or other safety subjects are required and are obtained by completing short courses.

Workplaces/Employers

Drilling and well service contractors

Petroleum producing companies

Occupational Options

There is little mobility for supervisors from well services to well drilling.

Similar Occupations Classified Elsewhere

Oil and Gas Well Drillers, Servicers, Testers and Related Workers (8232)

Oil and Gas Well Drilling Workers and Services Operators (8412)

Primary Production Managers (Except Agriculture) (0811)

Remarks

*Environmental Conditions

- For some occupations in this group, **Hazards** H1 (Dangerous chemical substances) may also apply.

8231 Underground Production and Development Miners

Underground Production and Development Miners drill, blast, operate mining machinery and perform related duties to extract coal and ore in underground mines, and to construct tunnels, passageways and shafts to facilitate mining operations.

Profile Summary

APTITUDES

G	V	N	S	P	Q	K	F	M
3	4	4	3	3	4	3	3	3

INTERESTS
OIM

DATA PEOPLE THINGS (DPT)
682

PHYSICAL ACTIVITIES (PA)

V	C	H	B	L	S
3	0	1	4	1	3

ENVIRONMENTAL CONDITIONS (EC)
L2, H1*, H3, H6, H8, D1, D2, D4

EDUCATION/TRAINING
4, 5, R

Examples of Job Titles

Blaster - Underground Mining
Chute Blaster
Diamond Driller - Underground Mining
Drift Miner
Driller
Faceman/woman, Coal Mine
Jumbo Drill Operator
Miner
Mining Machine Operator
Mucking Machine Operator
Raise Miner
Roadheader Operator
Scooptram Operator
Shot Firer

Descriptor Profile

Main Characteristics

Occupations in this group are characterized by the following aptitudes, interests and worker functions as they relate to main duties:

- **General learning ability** to set up and operate mining machinery to shear coal, rock and ore from working faces, and to perform duties required to ensure safety and to support the mining advance

- **Spatial** and **form perception** to set up and operate drills and drilling machines to produce designated patterns of blasting holes

- **Motor co-ordination** and **finger and manual dexterity** to scale loose rock from walls and roofs, to drill and install rock bolts, to extend and install air and water pipes, to operate ore loading machinery and to construct timber supports and cribbing

- **Objective interest** in **controlling** the operations of diamond drills and other specialized drills, such as raise-boring machinery, to test geological formations and produce underground passageways

- **Innovative interest** in **comparing** information to load explosives, set fuses and detonate explosives to produce desired blasting patterns and rock fragmentation in underground mines

- **Methodical interest** in performing routine maintenance of mining machinery and in loading and hauling ore from stopes, drifts and drawpoints to ore passes using scooptrams, load-haul dump (LHD) machines and mucking machines

8231

Physical Activities

Vision
   3 Near and far vision

Colour Discrimination
   0 Not relevant

Hearing
   1 Limited

Body Position
   4 Other body positions

Limb Co-ordination
   1 Upper limb co-ordination

Strength
   3 Medium

Environmental Conditions

Location
   L2 Unregulated inside climate

Hazards
   H1* Dangerous chemical substances
   H3 Equipment, machinery, tools
   H6 Flying particles, falling objects
   H8 Dangerous locations

Discomforts
   D1 Noise
   D2 Vibration
   D4 Non-toxic dusts

Employment Requirements

Education/Training
   4, 5, R

- Completion of secondary school is usually required.

- Formal training of up to six weeks, followed by extended periods of specialized training as a helper or in support occupations, is usually provided.

- Previous experience as a mine labourer or in other mine occupations is usually required.

- Provincial blasting licence may be required.

- May be certified in the basic common core program or as an underground hard-rock miner in Ontario.

- Company licensing or certification is often required for occupations in this group.

Workplaces/Employers

Coal, metal and non-metallic mineral underground mines

Specialized contractors in mine construction, shaft sinking and tunnelling

Occupational Options

Mobility is possible to other occupational groups in underground mining such as underground service and support occupations.

There is mobility among employers within each of the three following sectors: underground coal mining, underground hard-rock mining and underground potash, salt or soft-rock mining.

Mobility among these sectors is somewhat limited by differences in production technologies.

Progression to mining supervisor is possible with experience.

Similar Occupations Classified Elsewhere

Drillers and Blasters - Surface Mining, Quarrying and Construction (7372)

Mine Labourers (8614)

Supervisors, Mining and Quarrying (8221)

Underground Mine Service and Support Workers (8411)

Remarks

*Environmental Conditions

- For some occupations in this group, **Hazards** H1 (Dangerous chemical substances) may also apply.

8232.1 Oil and Gas Well Drillers and Well Servicers

Oil and Gas Well Drillers and Well Servicers control the operation of drilling and hoisting equipment on drilling and service rigs, and direct the activities of rig crews under the supervision of rig managers.

Profile Summary

APTITUDES

G	V	N	S	P	Q	K	F	M
3	3	4	4	4	4	3	4	3

INTERESTS
ODm

DATA PEOPLE THINGS (DPT)
362

PHYSICAL ACTIVITIES (PA)

V	C	H	B	L	S
3	0	2	4	1	3

ENVIRONMENTAL CONDITIONS (EC)
L3, H1, H3, H6, H8, D1, D2, D3, D5

EDUCATION/TRAINING
4+, 6+, R

Examples of Job Titles

Assistant Driller
Directional Drilling Operator
Downhole Tool Operator
Driller
Service Rig Operator

Descriptor Profile

Main Characteristics

Occupations in this group are characterized by the following aptitudes, interests and worker functions as they relate to main duties:

- **General learning ability** to understand the functioning of equipment and machinery to oversee drilling and service rig operations, and to direct the activities of rig crews under the supervision of rig managers

- **Verbal ability** to train and arrange for training of crews

- **Objective interest** in **controlling** the operations of drilling and service-rig drilling and hoisting machinery

- **Directive interest** in **speaking** with members of rig crews to direct them in setting up rigs, drilling and completing and servicing oil and gas exploration and producing wells

- **Methodical interest** in **compiling** information to maintain records of drilling and servicing operations

Physical Activities

Vision
   3 Near and far vision

Colour Discrimination
   0 Not relevant

Hearing
   2 Verbal interaction

Body Position
   4 Other body positions

Limb Co-ordination
   1 Upper limb co-ordination

Strength
   3 Medium

Environmental Conditions

Location
   L3 Outside

Hazards
   H1 Dangerous chemical substances
   H3 Equipment, machinery, tools
   H6 Flying particles, falling objects
   H8 Dangerous locations

Discomforts
   D1 Noise
   D2 Vibration
   D3 Odours
   D5 Wetness

Employment Requirements

Education/Training
4+, 6+, R

- Completion of secondary school is usually required.

- Oil and gas well drillers and servicers require three-to-six months of formal on-the-job training, college or Petroleum Industry Training Service (PITS) courses and four or more years of work experience in subordinate rig crew positions.

- A college diploma in drilling may be required.

- Offshore work requires several years of experience in an equivalent position on land.

- Certificates in first aid, hydrogen-sulphide awareness, blowout prevention, Workplace Hazardous Materials Information System (WHMIS) and Transportation of Dangerous Goods (TDG) are required.

- Provincial blaster's licence may be required for well perforation services.

Workplaces/Employers

Drilling and well service contractors

Petroleum producing companies

Occupational Options

Mobility between jobs on drilling and service rigs is limited by the differences in the machinery, tools and operations performed, but mobility is possible especially from drilling to service rigs.

Progression to crew supervisors or managers is possible with experience.

Similar Occupations Classified Elsewhere

Oil and Gas Well Drilling Workers and Services Operators (8412)

Supervisors, Oil and Gas Drilling and Service (8222)

Water Well Drillers (7373)

8232.2 Oil and Gas Well Loggers, Testers and Related Workers

Oil and Gas Well Loggers, Testers and Related Workers operate specialized mechanical and electronic equipment, tools and instruments to provide services in conjunction with well drilling, completion and servicing.

Profile Summary

APTITUDES

G	V	N	S	P	Q	K	F	M
3	3	4	3	4	4	3	4	3

INTERESTS
OMi

DATA PEOPLE THINGS (DPT)
382

PHYSICAL ACTIVITIES (PA)

V	C	H	B	L	S
4	1	1	4	2	3

ENVIRONMENTAL CONDITIONS (EC)
L3, L4, H1, H3, H8, D1, D3

EDUCATION/TRAINING
4+, 6+, R

Examples of Job Titles

Drill Stem Tester
Electric Line Operator
Logging and Perforating Operator
Slickline Operator
Well Testing Operator
Wireline Operator

Descriptor Profile

Main Characteristics

Occupations in this group are characterized by the following aptitudes, interests and worker functions as they relate to main duties:

- **General learning ability** to understand the function of equipment and machinery, and to operate recorders and computers in mobile testing and logging units to collect data in order to provide services in conjunction with well drilling, completion and servicing

- **Spatial perception** to lower, position and retrieve equipment and instruments

- **Motor co-ordination** and **manual dexterity** to assemble and attach equipment, tools and recorders to drill stems and wirelines

- **Objective interest** in **controlling** the operation of wirelines, unit controls, and equipment and instruments in mobile testing and logging units

- **Methodical interest** in driving well-service and wireline trucks to well sites

- **Innovative interest** in **compiling** information to direct the operations of wireline and unit controls to conduct required procedures and tests; may perform limited data interpretation

8232.2

Physical Activities

Vision
   4   Total visual field

Colour Discrimination
   1   Relevant

Hearing
   1   Limited

Body Position
   4   Other body positions

Limb Co-ordination
   2   Multiple limb co-ordination

Strength
   3   Medium

Environmental Conditions

Location
   L3 Outside
   L4 In a vehicle or cab

Hazards
   H1 Dangerous chemical substance
   H3 Equipment, machinery, tools
   H8 Dangerous locations

Discomforts
   D1 Noise
   D3 Odours

Employment Requirements

Education/Training
   4+, 6+, R

- Completion of secondary school is usually required.

- Oil- and gas-well loggers, testers and related workers require three-to-six months of formal on-the-job training, and several year's experience in subordinate logging and testing positions or on drilling and servicing rigs.

- Completion of a college program in electronics or engineering technology may be required for open-hole well logging.

- Certificates in first aid, hydrogen-sulphide awareness, blowout prevention, Workplace Hazardous Materials Information System (WHMIS) and Transportation of Dangerous Goods (TDG) are required.

- Provincial blaster's licence may be required for well perforation services.

Workplaces/Employers

Well logging or testing companies

Occupational Options

Mobility between jobs on drilling and service rigs is limited by the differences in the machinery, tools and operations performed, but mobility is possible especially from drilling to service rigs.

Progression to crew supervisors or managers is possible with experience.

Similar Occupations Classified Elsewhere

Oil and Gas Well Drilling Workers and Services Operators (8412)

Supervisors, Oil and Gas Drilling and Service (8222)

Water Well Drillers (7373)

8241.1 Cable Yarding System Operators

Cable Yarding System Operators run cable yarding systems to yard trees at logging sites.

Profile Summary

APTITUDES

G	V	N	S	P	Q	K	F	M
3	4	5	3	4	5	3	4	3

INTERESTS
Omi

DATA PEOPLE THINGS (DPT)
683

PHYSICAL ACTIVITIES (PA)

V	C	H	B	L	S
4	0	1	4	2	3

ENVIRONMENTAL CONDITIONS (EC)
L3, L4, H3, H6, H8, D1, D2, D3, D4

EDUCATION/TRAINING
2+, 4+, R

Examples of Job Titles

Grapple Operator
Linehorse Operator
Rigging Slinger
Steelspar Operator
Yarder Operator

Descriptor Profile

Main Characteristics

Occupations in this group are characterized by the following aptitudes, interests and worker functions as they relate to main duties:

- **General learning ability** to understand and apply the techniques of sorting, hoisting and moving logs, and to understand the operations of mobile equipment and boats

- **Spatial perception** to observe relative paths and positions of moving logs, and to operate and drive mobile logging equipment

- **Motor co-ordination** to drive and operate mobile logging equipment and to balance while working on log booms and climbing log piles

- **Manual dexterity** to move hand controls of logging equipment and to use hand and power tools

- **Objective interest** in **driving - operating** machines to transport trees from logging areas to landing and log-loading sites in mountainous terrain; and in assisting mechanics with major breakdowns and dismantling equipment

- **Methodical interest** in **comparing** information to clean and maintain yarder machinery; and in ensuring proper equipment conditions and normal operations

- **Innovative interest** in making minor repairs

8241.1
Subgroup 1 of 3

Physical Activities

Vision
    4   Total visual field

Colour Discrimination
    0   Not relevant

Hearing
    1   Limited

Body Position
    4   Other body positions

Limb Co-ordination
    2   Multiple limb co-ordination

Strength
    3   Medium

Environmental Conditions

Location
    L3 Outside
    L4 In a vehicle or cab

Hazards
    H3 Equipment, machinery, tools
    H6 Flying particles, falling objects
    H8 Dangerous locations

Discomforts
    D1 Noise
    D2 Vibration
    D3 Odours
    D4 Non-toxic dusts

Employment Requirements

Education/Training
2+, 4+, R

- Completion of secondary school may be required.

- From three-to-16 months of on-the-job training is provided, depending on the complexity of machinery operated and the type of woodlands operation.

- Experience requirements vary depending on the complexity of machinery operated. Cable yarder operators usually require three- to-five years of logging experience.

- Certification as a heavy equipment operator may be required.

- Provincial air-brake certification may be required in British Columbia, depending on the type of equipment operated.

- Workplace Hazardous Materials Information System (WHMIS) certification may be required.

- Company certification to operate mobile logging machinery may be required.

Workplaces/Employers

Logging companies

Logging contractors

Occupational Options

There is some mobility among jobs in this group from less complex to more complex machinery operation.

There is some mobility among employers, particularly in similar types of woodland operations.

Progression to logging and forestry supervisory positions is possible with experience.

Self-employment as a logging contractor is possible with investment in equipment.

Similar Occupations Classified Elsewhere

Chainsaw and Skidder Operators (8421)

Heavy Equipment Operators (Except Crane) (7421)

Silviculture and Forestry Workers (8422)

Supervisors, Logging and Forestry (8211)

Truck Drivers (7411)

8241.2 Mechanical Harvester and Forwarder Operators

Mechanical Harvester and Forwarder Operators use equipment to fell and process trees at logging sites.

Profile Summary

APTITUDES

G	V	N	S	P	Q	K	F	M
3	4	5	3	4	5	3	4	3

INTERESTS
Omi

DATA PEOPLE THINGS (DPT)
683

PHYSICAL ACTIVITIES (PA)

V	C	H	B	L	S
4	0	1	3	2	3

ENVIRONMENTAL CONDITIONS (EC)
L3, L4, H3, H6, H8, D1, D2, D3, D4

EDUCATION/TRAINING
2+, 4+, R

Examples of Job Titles

Feller Buncher Operator
Feller Forwarder Operator
Shortwood Harvester Operator
Treelength Forwarder Operator

Descriptor Profile

Main Characteristics

Occupations in this group are characterized by the following aptitudes, interests and worker functions as they relate to main duties:

- **General learning ability** to assess site and terrain to apply correct and safe procedures while driving heavy equipment in logging areas

- **Spatial perception** to visualize area and direction of falling trees to avoid injury to other trees and personnel

- **Objective interest** in **driving - operating** heavy equipment to perform a combination of felling, slashing, bucking, bunching and forwarding operations in logging areas

- **Methodical interest** in **comparing** information to regulate rate of machine operation and to ensure logs are cut to specified lengths

- **Innovative interest** in servicing machinery and making minor repairs

8241.2
Subgroup 2 of 3

Physical Activities

Vision
    4   Total visual field

Colour Discrimination
    0   Not relevant

Hearing
    1   Limited

Body Position
    3   Sitting, standing, walking

Limb Co-ordination
    2   Multiple limb co-ordination

Strength
    3   Medium

Environmental Conditions

Location
    L3 Outside
    L4 In a vehicle or cab

Hazards
    H3 Equipment, machinery, tools
    H6 Flying particles, falling objects
    H8 Dangerous locations

Discomforts
    D1 Noise
    D2 Vibration
    D3 Odours
    D4 Non-toxic dusts

Employment Requirements

Education/Training
    2+, 4+, R

- Completion of secondary school may be required.

- From three-to-16 months of on-the-job training is provided, depending on the complexity of machinery operated and the type of woodlands operation.

- Experience requirements vary depending on the complexity of machinery operated. Mechanical harvester and forwarder operators may require logging experience as a chainsaw and skidder operator. Feller buncher operators usually require three-to-five years of logging experience.

- Certification as a heavy equipment operator may be required.

- Provincial air-brake certification may be required in British Columbia, depending on the type of equipment operated.

- Workplace Hazardous Materials Information System (WHMIS) certification may be required

- Company certification to operate mobile logging machinery may be required.

Workplaces/Employers

Logging companies

Logging contractors

Occupational Options

There is some mobility among jobs in this group from less complex to more complex machinery operation.

There is some mobility among employers, particularly in similar types of woodland operations.

Progression to logging and forestry supervisory positions is possible with experience.

Self-employment as a logging contractor is possible with investment in equipment.

Similar Occupations Classified Elsewhere

Chainsaw and Skidder Operators (8421)

Heavy Equipment Operators (Except Crane) (7421)

Silviculture and Forestry Workers (8422)

Supervisors, Logging and Forestry (8211)

Truck Drivers (7411)

8241.3 Mechanical Tree Processor and Loader Operators

Mechanical Tree Processor and Loader Operators run machinery to process and load trees at logging sites.

Profile Summary

APTITUDES

G	V	N	S	P	Q	K	F	M
3	4	5	3	4	5	3	4	3

INTERESTS
Omi

DATA PEOPLE THINGS (DPT)
684

PHYSICAL ACTIVITIES (PA)

V	C	H	B	L	S
4	0	1	3	2	3

ENVIRONMENTAL CONDITIONS (EC)
L3, L4, H3, H6, H8, D1, D2, D3, D4

EDUCATION/TRAINING
2, 4, R

Examples of Job Titles

Chipping Machine Operator
Delimber Operator
Loader Operator
Log Processor Operator
Slasher Operator - Logging

Descriptor Profile

Main Characteristics

Occupations in this group are characterized by the following aptitudes, interests and worker functions as they relate to main duties:

- **General learning ability** to understand and apply correct and safe procedures for operating tree-processing and loading machinery

- **Spatial perception** to visualize amount of area required to manoeuvre and operate tree-processing equipment

- **Objective interest** in **operating** a variety of machines that perform a combination of slashing, bucking, chipping, sorting and loading logs and trees at landing sites

- **Methodical interest** in **comparing** information to position felled whole and delimbed trees for processing

- **Innovative interest** in servicing machinery and making minor repairs

8241.3
Subgroup 3 of 3

Physical Activities

Vision
  4 Total visual field

Colour Discrimination
  0 Not relevant

Hearing
  1 Limited

Body Position
  3 Sitting, standing, walking

Limb Co-ordination
  2 Multiple limb co-ordination

Strength
  3 Medium

Environmental Conditions

Location
  L3 Outside
  L4 In a vehicle or cab

Hazards
  H3 Equipment, machinery, tools
  H6 Flying particles, falling objects
  H8 Dangerous locations

Discomforts
  D1 Noise
  D2 Vibration
  D3 Odours
  D4 Non-toxic dusts

Employment Requirements

Education/Training
  2, 4, R

- Completion of secondary school may be required.

- From three-to-16 months of on-the-job training is provided, depending on the complexity of machinery operated and the type of woodlands operation.

- Experience requirements vary depending on the complexity of machinery operated. Mechanical tree-processor and loader operators usually require one-to-three years of logging experience.

- Certification as a heavy equipment operator may be required.

- Provincial air-brake certification may be required in British Columbia, depending on the type of equipment operated.

- Workplace Hazardous Materials Information System (WHMIS) certification may be required.

- Company certification to operate mobile logging machinery may be required.

Workplaces/Employers

Logging companies

Logging contractors

Occupational Options

There is some mobility among jobs in this group from less complex to more complex machinery operation.

There is some mobility among employers, particularly in similar types of woodland operations.

Progression to logging and forestry supervisory positions is possible with experience.

Self-employment as a logging contractor is possible with investment in equipment.

Similar Occupations Classified Elsewhere

Chainsaw and Skidder Operators (8421)

Heavy Equipment Operators (Except Crane) (7421)

Silviculture and Forestry Workers (8422)

Supervisors, Logging and Forestry (8211)

Truck Drivers (7411)

8251 Farmers and Farm Managers

Farmers and Farm Managers control the operation and function of farms, such as growing crops, raising and breeding livestock, poultry and other animals, and marketing farm products.

Profile Summary

APTITUDES

G	V	N	S	P	Q	K	F	M
3	3	3	4	3	4	3	4	3

INTERESTS
DMO

DATA PEOPLE THINGS (DPT)
133

PHYSICAL ACTIVITIES (PA)

V	C	H	B	L	S
3	0	2	4	2	3

ENVIRONMENTAL CONDITIONS (EC)
L1, L3, L4*, H1, H2*, H3, D3, D4

EDUCATION/TRAINING
1+, 6+

Examples of Job Titles

Apiarist
Apple Grower
Breeder, Domestic Animals
Chicken Farmer
Dairy Farmer
Feedlot Manager
Fruit Farmer
Fur Farmer
Grape Grower
Hog Breeder
Horse Breeder
Market Gardener
Potato Farmer
Rancher
Seed Grower
Sod Farmer
Vegetable Grower
Vineyard Manager
Wheat Farmer

Descriptor Profile

Main Characteristics

Occupations in this group are characterized by the following aptitudes, interests and worker functions as they relate to main duties:

- **General learning ability** to manage the operation of farms, ranches and orchards

- **Verbal ability** to establish marketing programs

- **Numerical ability** to develop and keep financial and production records

- **Directive interest** in **supervising** and hiring farm workers; and in determining amounts and kinds of crops and livestock, and in purchasing farm machinery, livestock, seed, feed and other supplies

- **Methodical interest** in **co-ordinating** information to plant, cultivate and harvest crops; and in raising and breeding livestock and poultry

- **Objective interest** in **driving - operating** and maintaining farm machinery, equipment and buildings

8251

Physical Activities

Vision
   3 Near and far vision

Colour Discrimination
   0 Not relevant

Hearing
   2 Verbal interaction

Body Position
   4 Other body positions

Limb Co-ordination
   2 Multiple limb co-ordination

Strength
   3 Medium

Environmental Conditions

Location
   L1 Regulated inside climate
   L3 Outside
   L4* In a vehicle or cab

Hazards
   H1 Dangerous chemical substances
   H2* Biological agents
   H3 Equipment, machinery, tools

Discomforts
   D3 Odours
   D4 Non-toxic dusts

Employment Requirements

Education/Training
1+, 6+

- Extensive farming experience (obtained as a farmer, farm supervisor or specialized livestock worker or by working on a family farm) is usually required.

- A college diploma in agriculture may be required.

Workplaces/Employers

Farms

Self-employment

Similar Occupations Classified Elsewhere

Agricultural and Related Service Contractors and Managers (8252)

Farm Supervisors and Specialized Livestock Workers (8253)

Nursery and Greenhouse Operators and Managers (8254)

Supervisors, Landscape and Horticulture (8256)

Remarks

Farmers and farm managers may manage farms specializing in particular crops such as wheat, apples or potatoes, or raise particular livestock such as beef cattle, hogs or chickens.

*Environmental Conditions

- For some occupations in this group, **Location** L4 (In a vehicle or cab) and **Hazards** H2 (Biological agents) may also apply.

8252 Agricultural and Related Service Contractors and Managers

Agricultural Contractors and Managers operate establishments that provide agricultural services such as livestock and poultry breeding, soil preparation, crop planting, crop spraying, cultivating and harvesting.

Profile Summary

APTITUDES

G	V	N	S	P	Q	K	F	M
3	4	4	3	4	4	3	4	3

INTERESTS
OMi

DATA PEOPLE THINGS (DPT)
117

PHYSICAL ACTIVITIES (PA)

V	C	H	B	L	S
3	0	2	3	0	1

ENVIRONMENTAL CONDITIONS (EC)
L1, H1*, H2*

EDUCATION/TRAINING
1+, 4+, R

Examples of Job Titles

Artificial Inseminator
Crop Dusting Contractor
Livestock Breeding Service Manager
Manager, Artificial Insemination Service
Manager, Crop Harvesting Service

Descriptor Profile

Main Characteristics

Occupations in this group are characterized by the following aptitudes, interests and worker functions as they relate to main duties:

- **General learning ability** to manage businesses that provide livestock services, such as artificial insemination, spraying and shearing of livestock, and disinfecting of pens, barns and poultry houses, and that provide crop services such as plowing, irrigating, cultivating, spraying and harvesting

- **Objective interest** in **handling** machinery and equipment; and in participating in the provision of services

- **Methodical interest** in **co-ordinating** and maintaining financial and operational records; and in hiring and training workers

- **Innovative interest** in **negotiating** with farmers and farm managers regarding services

8252

Physical Activities

Vision
   3 Near and far vision

Colour Discrimination
   0 Not relevant

Hearing
   2 Verbal interaction

Body Position
   3 Sitting, standing, walking

Limb Co-ordination
   0 Not relevant

Strength
   1 Limited

Environmental Conditions

Location
   L1 Regulated inside climate

Hazards
   H1*Dangerous chemical substances
   H2*Biological agents

Employment Requirements

Education/Training
1+, 4+, R

- Several years of experience related to the agricultural service offered are usually required.

- Contractors and managers providing certain services, such as artificial insemination and pesticide application, may require training certificates and provincial licensing.

Workplaces/Employers

Establishments that provide agricultural services

Self-employment

Similar Occupations Classified Elsewhere

Farmers and Farm Managers (8251)

Farm Supervisors and Specialized Livestock Workers (8253)

Nursery and Greenhouse Operators and Managers (8254)

Pest Controllers and Fumigators (7444)

Pet Groomers and Animal Care Workers (6483)

Supervisors, Landscape and Horticulture (8256)

Remarks

* Environmental Conditions

- For some occupations in this group, **Hazards** H1 (Dangerous chemical substances) and H2 (Biological agents) may apply.

8253.1 Farm Supervisors

Farm Supervisors oversee the work of general farm workers and harvesting labourers and perform general farm duties.

Profile Summary

APTITUDES

G	V	N	S	P	Q	K	F	M
3	4	4	4	3	4	3	3	3

INTERESTS
DMi

DATA PEOPLE THINGS (DPT)
137

PHYSICAL ACTIVITIES (PA)

V	C	H	B	L	S
3	0	2	3	1	3

ENVIRONMENTAL CONDITIONS (EC)
L1, L2, L3, H2*, H3, D3

EDUCATION/TRAINING
1, 5, 6

Examples of Job Titles

Farm Foreman/woman
Farm Supervisor
Feedlot Foreman/woman
Hog Operation Supervisor
Poultry Farm Foreman/woman
Ranch Foreman/woman
Vegetable Farm Foreman/woman

Descriptor Profile

Main Characteristics

Occupations in this group are characterized by the following aptitudes, interests and worker functions as they relate to main duties:

- **General learning ability** to supervise the work of general farm workers and harvesting labourers and to perform general farm duties

- **Directive interest** in **supervising** and co-ordinating the work of general farm workers and harvesting labourers; and in supervising breeding programs and harvest operations

- **Methodical interest** in **handling** equipment to perform general farm duties; and in maintaining quality control and production records

- **Innovative interest** in **co-ordinating** information to develop work schedules and establish procedures

Physical Activities

Vision
   3 Near and far vision

Colour Discrimination
   0 Not relevant

Hearing
   2 Verbal interaction

Body Position
   3 Sitting, standing, walking

Limb Co-ordination
   1 Upper limb co-ordination

Strength
   3 Medium

Environmental Conditions

Location
   L1 Regulated inside climate
   L2 Unregulated, inside climate
   L3 Outside

Hazards
   H2*Biological agents
   H3 Equipment, machinery, tools

Discomforts
   D3 Odours

Employment Requirements

Education/Training
   1, 5, 6

- Farm supervisors may require a college certificate or other specialized training in agriculture or livestock husbandry.

Workplaces/Employers

General farms

Specialized farms

Similar Occupations Classified Elsewhere

Agricultural and Related Service Contractors and Managers (8252)

Farmers and Farm Managers (8251)

General Farm Workers (8431)

Harvesting Labourers (8611)

Remarks

Farm supervisors may specialize in dairy, poultry, swine, beef, sheep, fruit, vegetable, mixed, speciality and equine farms.

*Environmental Conditions

- For some occupations in this group, **Hazards** H2 (Biological agents) may also apply.

8253.2 Specialized Livestock Workers

Specialized Livestock Workers carry out feeding, health and breeding programs on dairy, beef, sheep, poultry and hog farms, and may also supervise general farm workers and harvesting labourers.

Profile Summary

APTITUDES

G	V	N	S	P	Q	K	F	M
3	4	4	4	3	4	3	3	3

INTERESTS
MId

DATA PEOPLE THINGS (DPT)
137

PHYSICAL ACTIVITIES (PA)

V	C	H	B	L	S
3	0	1	4	2	3

ENVIRONMENTAL CONDITIONS (EC)
L1, L2, L3, H2, H3, D3

EDUCATION/TRAINING
1, 5, 6

Examples of Job Titles

Cattle Herdsperson
Dairy Herdsperson
Horse Trainer
Shepherd
Swine Herdsperson

Descriptor Profile

Main Characteristics

Occupations in this group are characterized by the following aptitudes, interests and worker functions as they relate to main duties:

- **General learning ability** to carry out pasture and pen breeding programs, and to recognize and treat certain livestock health problems

- **Methodical interest** in **handling equipment** to perform general farm duties; and in maintaining livestock performance records and in training horses

- **Innovative interest** in **co-ordinating** information to formulate feeding programs

- **Directive interest** in **supervising** feeding, health and breeding programs; may supervise general farm workers and harvesting labourers

8253.2
Subgroup 2 of 2

Physical Activities

Vision
- 3 Near and far vision

Colour Discrimination
- 0 Not relevant

Hearing
- 1 Limited

Body Position
- 4 Other body positions

Limb Co-ordination
- 2 Multiple limb co-ordination

Strength
- 3 Medium

Environmental Conditions

Location
- L1 Regulated inside climate
- L2 Unregulated inside climate
- L3 Outside

Hazards
- H2 Biological agents
- H3 Equipment, machinery, tools

Discomforts
- D3 Odours

Employment Requirements

Education/Training
1, 5, 6

- Specialized livestock workers may require a college certificate or other specialized training in agriculture or livestock husbandry.

Workplaces/Employers

General farms

Specialized farms

Similar Occupations Classified Elsewhere

Agricultural and Related Service Contractors and Managers (8252)

Farmers and Farm Managers (8251)

General Farm Workers (8431)

Harvesting Labourers (8611)

Remarks

Specialized livestock workers usually specialize in one type of farm animal such as beef cattle, dairy cattle or swine.

8254 Nursery and Greenhouse Operators and Managers

Nursery and Greenhouse Operators and Managers plan, organize, direct and control the activities of nursery and greenhouse staff who grow and market trees, shrubs, flowers and plants.

Profile Summary

APTITUDES

G	V	N	S	P	Q	K	F	M
3	3	3	4	4	4	3	4	3

INTERESTS
DMs

DATA PEOPLE THINGS (DPT)
138

PHYSICAL ACTIVITIES (PA)

V	C	H	B	L	S
3	1	2	3	0	1

ENVIRONMENTAL CONDITIONS (EC)
L1

EDUCATION/TRAINING
6+

Examples of Job Titles

Christmas Tree Farm Operator
Flower Grower
Greenhouse Farmer
Greenhouse Manager
Greenhouse Operator
Nursery Farmer
Nursery Manager
Nursery Operator
Plant Grower

Descriptor Profile

Main Characteristics

Occupations in this group are characterized by the following aptitudes, interests and worker functions as they relate to main duties:

- **General learning ability** to manage the operations of nurseries and greenhouses and to establish the environmental conditions required to grow trees, shrubs, flowers and plants

- **Verbal** and **numerical ability** to maintain records on stock, finances and personnel and to develop marketing plans

- **Directive interest** in **supervising** staff in planting, transplanting, feeding and spraying stock; and in hiring staff and overseeing training, in setting work schedules and in determining types and quantities of stock

- **Methodical interest** in **co-ordinating** information to organize nursery and greenhouse operations; and in ordering materials such as fertilizer, garden and lawn-care equipment, and other nursery and greenhouse accessories

- **Social interest** in providing information to customers on gardening and the care of trees, shrubs, flowers, plants and lawns

8254

Physical Activities

Vision
   3 Near and far vision

Colour Discrimination
   1 Relevant

Hearing
   2 Verbal interaction

Body Position
   3 Sitting, standing, walking

Limb Co-ordination
   0 Not relevant

Strength
   1 Limited

Environmental Conditions

Location
   L1 Regulated inside climate

Employment Requirements

Education/Training
   6+

- Completion of a college program in horticulture is usually required.

- Experience as a nursery or greenhouse supervisor is required.

Workplaces/Employers

Greenhouses

Nurseries

Similar Occupations Classified Elsewhere

Nursery and Greenhouse Workers (8432)

Supervisors, Landscape and Horticulture (8256)

Turf growers (in 8251 *Farmers and Farm Managers*)

8255 Landscaping and Grounds Maintenance Contractors and Managers

Landscaping and Grounds Maintenance Contractors and Managers plan, organize, direct and control the operations of landscaping, interior plantscaping, lawn-care and tree-service departments and establishments.

Profile Summary

APTITUDES

G	V	N	S	P	Q	K	F	M
2	3	3	2	3	4	4	4	4

INTERESTS
DOM

DATA PEOPLE THINGS (DPT)
138

PHYSICAL ACTIVITIES (PA)

V	C	H	B	L	S
3	1	2	3	0	1

ENVIRONMENTAL CONDITIONS (EC)
L1, L3

EDUCATION/TRAINING
4+, 6+

Examples of Job Titles

Grounds Maintenance Contractor
Grounds Maintenance Manager
Interior Plantscaping Contractor
Landscape Service Contractor
Landscaping Contractor
Landscaping Manager
Lawn Care Manager
Lawn Maintenance Contractor
Tree Service Contractor

Descriptor Profile

Main Characteristics

Occupations in this group are characterized by the following aptitudes, interests and worker functions as they relate to main duties:

- **General learning ability** to plan, organize, direct and control the operations of landscaping, interior plantscaping, lawn-care and tree-service establishments

- **Verbal** and **numerical ability** to maintain financial and personnel records and to tender bids on contracts for landscaping and grounds maintenance work

- **Spatial perception** to prepare proposals containing sketches and layouts

- **Directive interest** in **supervising** and hiring staff; and in controlling the operations of maintenance services

- **Objective interest** in organizing and directing the planting and maintenance of trees, gardens, lawns, shrubs and hedges, and the construction and installation of fences, decks, patios, walkways and retaining walls

- **Methodical interest** in **co-ordinating** information to plan and estimate the materials and labour requirements for contracts

8255

Physical Activities

Vision
   3 Near and far vision

Colour Discrimination
   1 Relevant

Hearing
   2 Verbal interaction

Body Position
   3 Sitting, standing, walking

Limb Co-ordination
   0 Not relevant

Strength
   1 Limited

Environmental Conditions

Location
   L1 Regulated inside climate
   L3 Outside

Employment Requirements

Education/Training
4+, 6+

- A college diploma or specialized courses in landscaping and horticulture are usually required.

- Experience as a landscape or horticulture supervisor or as a landscape or horticulture technician is required.

Workplaces/Employers

Lawn-care establishments

Self-employment

Tree-service establishments

Similar Occupations Classified Elsewhere

Contractors and Supervisors, Other Construction Trades, Installers, Repairers and Servicers (7219)

Landscape Architects (2152)

Landscape and Horticulture Technicians and Specialists (2225)

Nursery and Greenhouse Operators and Managers (8254)

Supervisors, Landscape and Horticulture (8256)

8256 Supervisors, Landscape and Horticulture

Supervisors, Landscape and Horticulture oversee and co-ordinate the activities of workers in the following groups: *Landscaping and Grounds Maintenance Labourers* (8612) and *Nursery and Greenhouse Workers* (8432).

Profile Summary

APTITUDES

G	V	N	S	P	Q	K	F	M
3	3	4	4	4	4	4	4	4

INTERESTS
DSM

DATA PEOPLE THINGS (DPT)
134

PHYSICAL ACTIVITIES (PA)

V	C	H	B	L	S
3	1	2	3	0	1

ENVIRONMENTAL CONDITIONS (EC)
L1, L3, H1*

EDUCATION/TRAINING
4, R

Examples of Job Titles

Cemetery Foreman/woman
Greenhouse Supervisor
Grounds Keeper Supervisor
Landscaping Foreman/woman
Horticulture Worker Supervisor
Nursery Foreman/woman
Park Caretaker
Park Supervisor, Grounds Maintenance
Supervisor, Nursery Workers
Supervisor, Park Labourers

Descriptor Profile

Main Characteristics

Occupations in this group are characterized by the following aptitudes, interests and worker functions as they relate to main duties:

- **General learning ability** to supervise and co-ordinate the activities of workers to provide landscaping and horticultural services and to establish work procedures; may perform the same duties as workers

- **Verbal ability** to train workers in job duties and company policies, and to prepare progress and other reports

- **Directive interest** in **supervising** workers who maintain lawns, gardens, athletic fields, golf courses, cemeteries, parks, interior plantscapes and other landscaped areas, who spread topsoil and lay sod, who spray, prune, cut and remove trees and shrubs, who construct landscape and landscape structures and who plant, cultivate and harvest trees, shrubs, flowers and plants

- **Social interest** in **co-ordinating** information to resolve work-related problems, to establish work schedules and to co-ordinate activities with other units

- **Methodical interest** in **operating** equipment for landscaping and grounds maintenance; and in requisitioning supplies and materials and in submitting progress and other reports

8256

Physical Activities

Vision
   3 Near and far vision

Colour Discrimination
   1 Relevant

Hearing
   2 Verbal interaction

Body Position
   3 Sitting, standing, walking

Limb Co-ordination
   0 Not relevant

Strength
   1 Limited

Environmental Conditions

Location
   L1 Regulated inside climate
   L3 Outside

Hazards
   H1*Dangerous chemical substances

Employment Requirements

Education/Training
   4, R

- Completion of secondary school is usually required.

- Experience in the occupation supervised is required.

- A provincial licence to apply chemical fertilizers, fungicides, herbicides and pesticides may be required.

Workplaces/Employers

Cemeteries

Greenhouses

Landscaping companies

Landscaping departments of public- and private-sector establishments

Lawn-care companies

Nurseries

Tree-service companies

Similar Occupations Classified Elsewhere

Landscape Architects (2152)

Landscaping and Grounds Maintenance Contractors and Managers (8255)

Nursery and Greenhouse Operators and Managers (8254)

Remarks

*Environmental Conditions

- For some occupations in this group, Hazards H1 (Dangerous chemical substances) may apply.

8257 Aquaculture Operators and Managers

Aquaculture Operators and Managers control the operations of facilities that cultivate and harvest fish, shellfish and marine plants for replenishment of wildlife stocks and commercial sale.

Profile Summary

APTITUDES

G	V	N	S	P	Q	K	F	M
3	3	4	4	3	4	4	4	3

INTERESTS
DMO

DATA PEOPLE THINGS (DPT)
134

PHYSICAL ACTIVITIES (PA)

V	C	H	B	L	S
3	0	2	4	2	2

ENVIRONMENTAL CONDITIONS (EC)
L1, L3, D3, D5

EDUCATION/TRAINING
4+, 6, R

Examples of Job Titles

Aquaculture Manager
Aquaculture Operator
Fish Farm Manager
Fish Farm Operator
Fish Farmer
Fish Hatchery Manager
Fish Hatchery Operator
Mussel Grower
Oyster Grower
Salmon Grower
Trout Farmer

Descriptor Profile

Main Characteristics

Occupations in this group are characterized by the following aptitudes, interests and worker functions as they relate to main duties:

- **General learning ability** to manage the operations of fish hatcheries, fish farms and other aquatic farms, to co-ordinate selection and maintenance of brood stock and to scuba dive to inspect sea farm operations

- **Verbal ability** to collect and record growth and production data, to maintain financial records and to establish marketing strategies and inventory and quality control methods

- **Form perception** to conduct and supervise stock examinations to identify diseases and parasites, and to identify species' requirements

- **Directive interest** in **supervising** and training workers, technicians and technologists; and in selecting and overseeing preparation of sites for species cultivation, and supervising the processing of products

- **Methodical interest** in **co-ordinating** information to monitor environments and maintain optimum conditions, to apply prescribed medicinal substances to control and prevent infection, to determine food requirements and to structure feeding regimes

- **Objective interest** in **operating** and maintaining cultivating and harvesting equipment; and in designing and constructing pens, floating stations, collector strings and fences for sea farms

8257

Physical Activities

Vision
  3 Near and far vision

Colour Discrimination
  0 Not relevant

Hearing
  2 Verbal interaction

Body Position
  4 Other body positions

Limb Co-ordination
  2 Multiple limb co-ordination

Strength
  2 Light

Environmental Conditions

Location
  L1 Regulated inside climate
  L3 Outside

Discomforts
  D3 Odours
  D5 Wetness

Employment Requirements

Education/Training
  4+, 6, R

- Completion of secondary school is usually required.

- A college diploma in aquaculture or a related field
  or
  several years of experience in fishing or aquaculture operations are usually required.

- A commercial aquaculture or fish hatchery licence, permit or lease is required for self-employed aquaculture operators and managers.

Workplaces/Employers

Commercial aquatic farms

Public or private fish hatcheries

Self-employment

Similar Occupations Classified Elsewhere

Aquaculture technicians (in 2221 *Biological Technologists and Technicians*)

Aquaculture support workers (in 8613 *Aquaculture and Marine Harvest Labourers*)

8261 Fishing Masters and Officers

Fishing Masters and Officers manage and operate saltwater and freshwater fishing vessels greater than 100 gross tonnes to pursue and catch fish and other marine life.

Profile Summary

APTITUDES

G	V	N	S	P	Q	K	F	M
3	3	3	2	3	4	3	4	3

INTERESTS
DOi

DATA PEOPLE THINGS (DPT)
133

PHYSICAL ACTIVITIES (PA)

V	C	H	B	L	S
4	1	3	3	1	2

ENVIRONMENTAL CONDITIONS (EC)
L4, H8

EDUCATION/TRAINING
2+, 4, R

Examples of Job Titles

Captain, Fishing Vessel
Captain, Offshore Fishing Vessel
Deck Officer, Fishing Vessel
First Mate, Fishing Vessel
Fishing Master
Master, Fishing Vessel
Mate, Fishing Vessel
Trawler Captain

Descriptor Profile

Main Characteristics

Occupations in this group are characterized by the following aptitudes, interests and worker functions as they relate to main duties:

- **General learning ability** to command fishing vessels to catch fish and other marine life

- **Verbal ability** to record fishing progress, crew activities, weather and sea conditions in ships' logs

- **Numerical ability** to plot courses and compute navigational positions using compasses, charts, tables and other aids

- **Spatial perception** to interpret charts and tables

- **Directive interest** in **supervising** crew activities; and in directing fishing operations and in selecting and training vessel crews

- **Objective interest** in **operating** navigational instruments and electronic fishing aids such as colour and paper sounders; and in steering vessels

- **Innovative interest** in **co-ordinating** information to determine optimum fishing areas

8261

Physical Activities

Vision
    4   Total visual field

Colour Discrimination
    1   Relevant

Hearing
    3   Other sound discrimination

Body Position
    3   Sitting, standing, walking

Limb Co-ordination
    1   Upper limb co-ordination

Strength
    2   Light

Environmental Conditions

Location
    L4   In a vehicle or cab

Hazards
    H8   Dangerous locations

Employment Requirements

Education/Training
2+, 4, R

- Some secondary school education is usually required.

- One-to-two years of experience as a fishing vessel deckhand is required.

- Captains require one year of service as officer of the watch.

- A Fishing Master's Certificate is required for all occupations in this group.

- A commercial fishing licence is required.

Workplaces/Employers

Establishments operating commercial fishing vessels

Occupational Options

Completion of Department of Transport examinations is required to advance from Fishing Master Class IV through Class I. Training programs are provided in provincial training centres.

Progression to merchant or government vessel officer positions (which require a Marine Officer Certificate) is possible with additional training and experience.

Similar Occupations Classified Elsewhere

Deck Officers, Water Transport (2273)

Fishing Vessel Skippers and Fishermen/women (8262)

Fishing vessel engineers requiring a Department of Transport licence (in 2274 *Engineer Officers, Water Transport*)

8262 Fishing Vessel Skippers and Fishermen/women

Fishing Vessel Skippers and Fishermen/women operate fishing vessels to pursue and catch fish and other marine life.

Profile Summary

APTITUDES

G	V	N	S	P	Q	K	F	M
4	4	4	4	4	4	3	4	3

INTERESTS
ODi

DATA PEOPLE THINGS (DPT)
133

PHYSICAL ACTIVITIES (PA)

V	C	H	B	L	S
4	1	3	4	2	3

ENVIRONMENTAL CONDITIONS (EC)
L1, L3, L4, H3, H8, D1, D3, D5

EDUCATION/TRAINING
2+, R

Examples of Job Titles

Fisherman/woman
Fishing Vessel Skipper
Inshore Fisherman/woman
Lobster Fisherman/woman
Longliner, Fisherman/woman
Seiner, Fisherman/woman

Descriptor Profile

Main Characteristics

Occupations in this group are characterized by the following aptitudes, interests and worker functions as they relate to main duties:

- **General learning ability** to operate fishing vessels to pursue and catch fish and other marine life

- **Motor co-ordination** and **manual dexterity** to maintain engines, fishing gear and other equipment

- **Objective interest** in **operating** navigational instruments and fishing gear; and in steering vessels; may transport fish to processing plants and fish buyers

- **Directive interest** in **supervising** crews and directing fishing operations; and in selecting areas for fishing, in recording financial transactions, fishing activities, weather and sea conditions, and in estimating costs and planning budgets for each fishing season

- **Innovative interest** in **co-ordinating** information to plot courses and compute navigational positions using compasses, charts and other aids; and in establishing fish marketing plans

8262

Physical Activities

Vision
    4   Total visual field

Colour Discrimination
    1   Relevant

Hearing
    3   Other sound discrimination

Body Position
    4   Other body positions

Limb Co-ordination
    2   Multiple limb co-ordination

Strength
    3   Medium

Environmental Conditions

Location
    L1 Regulated inside climate
    L3 Outside
    L4 In a vehicle or cab

Hazards
    H3 Equipment, machinery, tools
    H8 Dangerous locations

Discomforts
    D1 Noise
    D3 Odours
    D5 Wetness

Employment Requirements

Education/Training
    2+, R

- Several years of experience as fishing vessel crew member or helper are usually required.

- A commercial fishing licence is required.

- Licences are required for each species of fish pursued.

Workplaces/Employers

Self-employed owner-operators of fishing vessels

Occupational Options

Progression to master or mate on fishing vessels over 100 gross tonnes is possible with additional training, licensing and experience.

Similar Occupations Classified Elsewhere

Fishing Masters and Officers (8261)

Fishing Vessel Deckhands (8441)

8411 Underground Mine Service and Support Workers

Underground Mine Service and Support Workers perform a range of duties related to the operation of ore passes, chutes and conveyor systems, the construction and support of underground structures, passages and roadways, and the supply of materials and supplies to support underground mining.

Profile Summary

APTITUDES

G	V	N	S	P	Q	K	F	M
3	4	4	3	4	5	3	4	3

INTERESTS
OMd

DATA PEOPLE THINGS (DPT)
674

PHYSICAL ACTIVITIES (PA)

V	C	H	B	L	S
4	0	1	4	2	4

ENVIRONMENTAL CONDITIONS (EC)
L2, H3, H6, H8, D1, D2, D4

EDUCATION/TRAINING
4, R

Examples of Job Titles

Backfiller
Blaster Helper
Cage Tender
Conveyor Operator
Crusher Operator
Driller Helper
Haulageman/woman
Lamp Keeper
Materialman/woman
Mine Construction Worker
Nipper
Orepass Tender
Pipe Worker
Raise Miner Helper
Skip Tender
Timberman/woman
Trainman/woman

Descriptor Profile

Main Characteristics

Occupations in this group are characterized by the following aptitudes, interests and worker functions as they relate to main duties:

- **General learning ability** to operate and maintain ore chutes and conveyor systems to control the flow of ore and coal in underground mines

- **Motor co-ordination** and **manual dexterity** to attach and extend ventilation and water pipes and perform related mine services, and to supply and maintain backfill distribution of sand, rock and other materials

- **Objective interest** in **operating** construction equipment such as bulldozers, graders and backhoes to build and maintain underground passages and haulageways, in using construction and mining tools to construct wood and metal supports and structures, and in operating diesel and electric track-haulage equipment, such as ore trains, to distribute personnel and supplies and to convey ore from ore passes to primary crushers and skips

- **Methodical interest** in **comparing** information to maintain supply storage areas and equipment and supplies such as explosives, drill bits, fire extinguishers, lamps and batteries; and in performing routine maintenance

- **Directive interest** in **assisting** miners in setting up and operating drilling and other mining machinery

8411

Physical Activities

Vision
    4   Total visual field

Colour Discrimination
    0   Not relevant

Hearing
    1   Limited

Body Position
    4   Other body positions

Limb Co-ordination
    2   Multiple limb co-ordination

Strength
    4   Heavy

Environmental Conditions

Location
    L2   Unregulated inside climate

Hazards
    H3   Equipment, machinery, tools
    H6   Flying particles, falling objects
    H8   Dangerous locations

Discomforts
    D1   Noise
    D2   Vibration
    D4   Non-toxic dusts

Employment Requirements

Education/Training
    4, R

- Completion of secondary school is usually required.

- Previous formal training of up to six weeks followed by periods of on-the-job training as a helper or in support occupations is usually required.

- Previous experience as a mine labourer is usually required.

- May be certified in the basic common core program in Ontario.

- Company licensing or certification is often required for occupations in this group.

Workplaces/Employers

Coal, metal and non-metallic mineral mines

Occupational Options

Mobility to other occupational groups in underground mining is possible.

There is mobility among employers within each of the three following sectors: underground coal mining, underground hard-rock mining, and underground potash, salt or soft-rock mining.

Mobility among these sectors is somewhat limited by differences in production technologies.

Similar Occupations Classified Elsewhere

Drillers and Blasters - Surface Mining, Quarrying and Construction (7372)

Mine Labourers (8614)

Underground Production and Development Miners (8231)

8412.1 Oil and Gas Well Drilling Workers

Oil and Gas Well Drilling Workers operate drilling and service rig machinery as members of rig crews.

Profile Summary

APTITUDES

G	V	N	S	P	Q	K	F	M
3	4	4	4	4	4	3	4	3

INTERESTS
OMd

DATA PEOPLE THINGS (DPT)
362

PHYSICAL ACTIVITIES (PA)

V	C	H	B	L	S
3	0	1	4	1	3

ENVIRONMENTAL CONDITIONS (EC)
L3, H1, H3, H6, H8, D1, D3, D5

EDUCATION/TRAINING
2, R

Examples of Job Titles

Blender Operator
Derrickman/woman
Motorman/woman
Pumpman/woman

Descriptor Profile

Main Characteristics

Occupations in this group are characterized by the following aptitudes, interests and worker functions as they relate to main duties:

- **General learning ability** to operate drilling and service rig machinery as members of rig crews

- **Motor co-ordination** and **manual dexterity** to align and manipulate sections of pipe and drill stems from platforms on rig derricks during removals and replacements of strings of pipe and drill stems and bits

- **Objective interest** in **controlling** and maintaining drilling mud systems and pumps during drilling and mixing of mud chemicals and additives; and in operating and maintaining diesel motors, transmissions and other mechanical equipment

- **Methodical interest** in **compiling** information to record mud flows and volumes and to take samples; and in assisting in setting up, taking down and transporting rigs

- **Directive interest** in **speaking** with floor hands and labourers to supervise their activities

8412.1
Subgroup 1 of 2

Physical Activities

Vision
    3   Near and far vision

Colour Discrimination
    0   Not relevant

Hearing
    1   Limited

Body Position
    4   Other body positions

Limb Co-ordination
    1   Upper limb co-ordination

Strength
    3   Medium

Environmental Conditions

Location
    L3 Outside

Hazards
    H1 Dangerous chemical substances
    H3 Equipment, machinery, tools
    H6 Flying particles, falling objects
    H8 Dangerous locations

Discomforts
    D1 Noise
    D3 Odours
    D5 Wetness

Employment Requirements

Education/Training
   2, R

- Completion of secondary school may be required.

- One year of experience as a floor hand, assistant or labourer is usually required.

- Certificates in first aid, hydrogen-sulphide awareness, blowout prevention, Workplace Hazardous Materials Information System (WHMIS), Transportation of Dangerous Goods (TDG) or in other safety concerns may be required.

Workplaces/Employers

Drilling and well service contractors

Petroleum producing companies

Occupational Options

Progression to oil and gas well driller or service rig operator is possible with experience.

Similar Occupations Classified Elsewhere

Oil and Gas Drilling, Servicing and Related Labourers (8615)

Oil and Gas Well Drillers, Servicers, Testers and Related Workers (8232)

Supervisors, Oil and Gas Drilling and Service (8222)

8412.2 Oil and Gas Well Services Operators

Oil and Gas Well Services Operators drive trucks and operate specialized hydraulic pumping systems to place cement in wells and to treat wells with chemicals, sand mixtures and gases to stimulate production.

Profile Summary

APTITUDES

G	V	N	S	P	Q	K	F	M
3	4	4	4	4	4	3	4	3

INTERESTS
OMi

DATA PEOPLE THINGS (DPT)
564

PHYSICAL ACTIVITIES (PA)

V	C	H	B	L	S
4	1	1	4	2	3

ENVIRONMENTAL CONDITIONS (EC)
L3, L4, H1, H3, H6, H8, D1, D3, D5

EDUCATION/TRAINING
2, R

Examples of Job Titles

Acid Truck Driver
Cementer
Chemical Services Operator
Coiled Tubing Operator
Formation Fracturing Operator
Nitrogen Operator
Pumper Operator

Descriptor Profile

Main Characteristics

Occupations in this group are characterized by the following aptitudes, interests and worker functions as they relate to main duties:

- **General learning ability** to drive trucks and operate specialized hydraulic pumping systems to place cement in wells and to treat wells with chemicals, sand mixtures and gases to stimulate production

- **Motor co-ordination** and **manual dexterity** to attach pumps and hoses to wellheads, and to adjust pumping procedures

- **Objective interest** in **operating** systems to pump chemicals, gases, sand, cement and other materials into wells

- **Methodical interest** in **speaking** to train assistants and helpers; and in driving trucks to well sites

- **Innovative interest** in **copying** information to read gauges to interpret conditions and adjust procedures; may mix chemicals and cement

Physical Activities

Vision
    4 Total visual field

Colour Discrimination
    1 Relevant

Hearing
    1 Limited

Body Position
    4 Other body positions

Limb Co-ordination
    2 Multiple limb co-ordination

Strength
    3 Medium

Environmental Conditions

Location
    L3 Outside
    L4 In a vehicle or cab

Hazards
    H1 Dangerous chemical substances
    H3 Equipment, machinery, tools
    H6 Flying particles, falling objects
    H8 Dangerous locations

Discomforts
    D1 Noise
    D3 Odours
    D5 Wetness

Employment Requirements

Education/Training
2, R

- Completion of secondary school may be required.

- Training of up to three months with an experienced operator is required for oil- and gas-well services operators.

- One year of experience as a floor hand, assistant or labourer is usually required.

- Certificates in first aid, hydrogen-sulphide awareness, blowout prevention, Workplace Hazardous Materials Information System (WHMIS), Transportation of Dangerous Goods (TDG) or in other safety concerns may be required.

Workplaces/Employers

Drilling and well service contractors

Petroleum producing companies

Occupational Options

Progression to oil and gas well driller or service rig operator is possible with experience.

Progression to supervisor of well services is possible for gas and oil well services operators.

Similar Occupations Classified Elsewhere

Oil and Gas Drilling, Servicing and Related Labourers (8615)

Oil and Gas Well Drillers, Servicers, Testers and Related Workers (8232)

Supervisors, Oil and Gas Drilling and Service (8222)

8421 Chainsaw and Skidder Operators

Chainsaw and Skidder Operators operate chainsaws to fell, delimb and buck trees, and operate skidders to move and yard the felled trees from logging sites to landing areas for processing and transportation.

Profile Summary

APTITUDES

G	V	N	S	P	Q	K	F	M
4	4	5	3	4	5	3	4	3

INTERESTS
OMi

DATA PEOPLE THINGS (DPT)
683

PHYSICAL ACTIVITIES (PA)

V	C	H	B	L	S
4	0	1	4	2	4

ENVIRONMENTAL CONDITIONS (EC)
L3, L4*, H3, H6, H8, D1, D2, D3, D4

EDUCATION/TRAINING
2, 4, 6, R

Examples of Job Titles

Bucker
Chainsaw Operator
Faller
Feller
Forest Worker - Logging
Grapple Skidder Operator
Landingman/woman
Pieceworker - Logging
Skidder Operator

Descriptor Profile

Main Characteristics

Occupations in this group are characterized by the following aptitudes, interests and worker functions as they relate to main duties:

- **General learning ability** to operate chainsaws to fell, delimb and buck trees, and operate skidders to move and yard the felled trees from logging sites to landing areas for processing and transportation

- **Spatial perception** to assess sites, terrain and weather before felling and yarding trees

- **Objective interest** in **driving** skidders to push trees and logs into bunches and drag logs to roadside loading areas; and in operating chainsaws

- **Methodical interest** in moving and yarding felled trees using cable and grapple skidders

- **Innovative interest** in **comparing** information to service, and make minor repairs to skidders and chainsaws; may work as members of teams rotating between chainsaw and skidder operations

8421

Physical Activities

Vision
   4 Total visual field

Colour Discrimination
   0 Not relevant

Hearing
   1 Limited

Body Position
   4 Other body positions

Limb Co-ordination
   2 Multiple limb co-ordination

Strength
   4 Heavy

Environmental Conditions

Location
   L3 Outside
   L4* In a vehicle or cab

Hazards
   H3 Equipment, machinery, tools
   H6 Flying particles, falling objects
   H8 Dangerous locations

Discomforts
   D1 Noise
   D2 Vibration
   D3 Odours
   D4 Non-toxic dusts

Employment Requirements

Education/Training
   2, 4, 6, R

- Completion of secondary school may be required.

- Completion of a college program for forest workers may be required.

- Formal training in chainsaw operation and maintenance and several months of on-the-job training are usually provided.

- Previous experience as a logging and forestry labourer or logging machine operator may be required. Experience requirements vary depending on the type and location of woodlands operations.

- Provincial accreditation or a forest worker program certificate is required in some provinces.

- Workplace Hazardous Materials Information System (WHIMS) certification may be required.

Workplaces/Employers

Logging companies

Logging contractors

Occupational Options

There is a trend toward company certification of chainsaw operators in larger companies.

There is some mobility among jobs within this group, because chainsaw and skidder operators often work in teams and rotate jobs.

Mobility may be limited from eastern and central forest zones to western forest zones where tree size or steep terrain may require different cutting and yarding methods.

Mobility is possible to logging machinery operators.

Progression to supervisory positions or self-employment as a logging contractor is possible with experience.

Similar Occupations Classified Elsewhere

Logging and Forestry Labourers (8616)

Logging Machinery Operators (8241)

Silviculture and Forestry Workers (8422)

Logging contractors and supervisors (in 8211 *Supervisors, Logging and Forestry*)

Remarks

Chainsaw operators often must own and maintain their own chainsaw.

*Environmental Conditions

- For some occupations in this group, **Location** L4 (In a vehicle or cab) may also apply.

8422 Silviculture and Forestry Workers

Silviculture and Forestry Workers perform duties related to reforestation and the management, improvement and conservation of forest lands.

Profile Summary

APTITUDES

G	V	N	S	P	Q	K	F	M
3	4	5	4	4	4	3	4	3

INTERESTS
OMi

DATA PEOPLE THINGS (DPT)
583

PHYSICAL ACTIVITIES (PA)

V	C	H	B	L	S
4	0	1	4	2	4

ENVIRONMENTAL CONDITIONS (EC)
L3, L4*, H1, H3, H6, H7, H8, D1, D2, D3, D4

EDUCATION/TRAINING
2, 4, 5, 6, R

Examples of Job Titles

Clearing Saw Operator
Forestry Crew Person
Forest Firefighter
Forestry Worker
Pieceworker, Silviculture
Scarification Equipment Operator
Silviculture Worker
Spacing Saw Operator
Thinning Saw Operator

Descriptor Profile

Main Characteristics

Occupations in this group are characterized by the following aptitudes, interests and worker functions as they relate to main duties:

- **General learning ability** to assess sites and select seedlings, and to perform duties related to reforestation, management, improvement and conservation of forest lands

- **Motor co-ordination** and **manual dexterity** to plant trees using manual planting tools

- **Objective interest** in **driving - operating** skidders, bulldozers and other prime movers to pull scarification and site-preparation equipment over areas to be regenerated; and in operating power thinning saws to thin and space trees in reforestation areas and chainsaws to thin young forest stands

- **Methodical interest** in **copying** information to control weeds and undergrowth using manual tools and chemicals; and in performing silvicultural duties such as collecting seed cones, pruning trees and marking trees for subsequent operations

- **Innovative interest** in fighting forest fires under the direction of fire suppression officers and forestry technicians

8422

Physical Activities

Vision
   4   Total visual field

Colour Discrimination
   0   Not relevant

Hearing
   1   Limited

Body Position
   4   Other body positions

Limb Co-ordination
   2   Multiple limb co-ordination

Strength
   4   Heavy

Environmental Conditions

Location
   L3 Outside
   L4* In a vehicle or cab

Hazards
   H1 Dangerous chemical substances
   H3 Equipment, machinery, tools
   H6 Flying particles, falling objects
   H7 Fire, steam, hot surfaces
   H8 Dangerous locations

Discomforts
   D1 Noise
   D2 Vibration
   D3 Odours
   D4 Non-toxic dusts

Employment Requirements

Education/Training
2, 4, 5, 6, R

- Completion of secondary school may be required.

- Completion of a college or other specialized program for silviculture workers or forestry crew workers may be required.

- Formal training in power saw operation and maintenance and several months of on-the-job training are usually provided.

- Experience as a logging and forestry labourer may be required.

- A chemicals application licence is required.

- Workplace Hazardous Materials Information System (WHMIS) and Transportation of Dangerous Goods (TDG) certificates may be required.

- A silvicultural worker's licence may be required.

Workplaces/Employers

Government services

Logging companies

Logging contractors

Occupational Options

There is some mobility among jobs in this group.

Progression to supervisory positions is possible with experience.

Progression to forestry technician or technologist is possible with additional education and training.

Similar Occupations Classified Elsewhere

Chainsaw and Skidder Operators (8421)

Forestry Technologists and Technicians (2223)

Logging and Forestry Labourers (8616)

Supervisors, Logging and Forestry (8211)

Remarks

*Environmental Conditions

- For some occupations in this group, Location L4 (In a vehicle or cab) may also apply.

8431 General Farm Workers

General Farm Workers plant, cultivate and harvest crops, raise livestock and poultry, and maintain and repair farm equipment and buildings. This group includes operators of farm machinery.

Profile Summary

APTITUDES

G	V	N	S	P	Q	K	F	M
4	4	4	4	4	4	3	4	3

INTERESTS
MOi

DATA PEOPLE THINGS (DPT)
683

PHYSICAL ACTIVITIES (PA)

V	C	H	B	L	S
3	1	1	4	2	3

ENVIRONMENTAL CONDITIONS (EC)
L1, L2, L3, L4, H1, H2, H3, D1, D2, D3, D4

EDUCATION/TRAINING
1, 4, 6

Examples of Job Titles

Beef Cattle Farm Worker
Cattle Ranch Labourer
Cowhand
Dairy Farm Worker
Farm Machinery Operator
Fruit Tree Pruner
General Farm Worker
Grain Farm Worker
Harvester Machine Operator
Hatchery Worker
Poultry Farm Worker
Vegetable Farm Worker

Descriptor Profile

Main Characteristics

Occupations in this group are characterized by the following aptitudes, interests and worker functions as they relate to main duties:

- **General learning ability** to plant, cultivate and harvest crops, raise livestock and poultry, and maintain and repair farm equipment and buildings

- **Motor co-ordination** and **manual dexterity** to plant, fertilize, cultivate, spray, irrigate and harvest crops

- **Methodical interest** in **comparing** information to prepare produce for market, to feed and tend livestock and poultry, and to clean stables, barns, barnyards and pens

- **Objective interest** in **driving - operating** and maintaining farm machinery and equipment

- **Innovative interest** in detecting disease and health problems in crops, livestock and poultry

8431

Physical Activities

Vision
   3 Near and far vision

Colour Discrimination
   1 Relevant

Hearing
   1 Limited

Body Position
   4 Other body positions

Limb Co-ordination
   2 Multiple limb co-ordination

Strength
   3 Medium

Environmental Conditions

Location
   L1 Regulated inside climate
   L2 Unregulated inside climate
   L3 Outside
   L4 In a vehicle or cab

Hazards
   H1 Dangerous chemical substances
   H2 Biological agents
   H3 Equipment, machinery, tools

Discomforts
   D1 Noise
   D2 Vibration
   D3 Odours
   D4 Non-toxic dusts

Employment Requirements

Education/Training
1, 4, 6

- There are no specific educational or training requirements. However, college certificate or other specialized courses related to farming, such as farm equipment mechanics, agricultural welding, tree pruning and pesticide application, are available.

- Basic farm knowledge, usually obtained from working on a family farm, may be required for employment.

Workplaces/Employers

Crop farms

Fruit and vegetable farms

Livestock farms

Specialty farms

Occupational Options

Progression to supervisory positions is possible with experience.

Similar Occupations Classified Elsewhere

Agricultural and Related Service Contractors and Managers (8252)

Harvesting Labourers (8611)

Farmers and Farm Managers (8251)

Farm Supervisors and Specialized Livestock Workers (8253)

Remarks

General farm workers can become specialized in a particular type of crop or livestock production through experience.

8432　Nursery and Greenhouse Workers

Nursery and Greenhouse Workers plant, cultivate and harvest trees, shrubs, flowers and plants, and serve nursery and greenhouse customers.

Profile Summary

APTITUDES

G	V	N	S	P	Q	K	F	M
4	4	4	4	4	5	3	4	3

INTERESTS
MOi

DATA PEOPLE THINGS (DPT)
684

PHYSICAL ACTIVITIES (PA)

V	C	H	B	L	S
3	1	1	4	2	3

ENVIRONMENTAL CONDITIONS (EC)
L1, L3, H1, H3

EDUCATION/TRAINING
2, 4, R

Examples of Job Titles

Forest Nursery Worker
Greenhouse Worker
Hothouse Worker
Hydroponics Worker
Nursery Worker

Descriptor Profile

Main Characteristics

Occupations in this group are characterized by the following aptitudes, interests and worker functions as they relate to main duties:

- **General learning ability** to plant, cultivate and harvest trees, shrubs, flowers and plants and to serve nursery and greenhouse customers

- **Methodical interest** in digging, cutting and transplanting trees, shrubs, flowers and plants and preparing them for sale and in providing information to customers about gardening

- **Objective interest** in operating equipment to spray against disease and pests; and in positioning and regulating greenhouse and outdoor irrigation systems; may operate tractors and other machinery and equipment to fertilize, cultivate, harvest and spray

- **Innovative interest** in comparing information to prepare soil and plant bulbs, seeds and cuttings; and in grafting and budding plants and in transplanting seedlings and root cuttings

8432

Physical Activities

Vision
   3   Near and far vision

Colour Discrimination
   1   Relevant

Hearing
   1   Limited

Body Position
   4   Other body positions

Limb Co-ordination
   2   Multiple limb co-ordination

Strength
   3   Medium

Environmental Conditions

Location
   L1 Regulated inside climate
   L3 Outside

Hazards
   H1 Dangerous chemical substances
   H3 Equipment, machinery, tools

Employment Requirements

Education/Training
   2, 4, R

- Completion of secondary school may be required.

- Completion of college courses in horticulture or a related field may be required.

- On-the-job training is provided.

- A provincial licence to apply chemical fertilizers, fungicides, herbicides and pesticides may be required.

Workplaces/Employers

Greenhouses

Indoor and outdoor nurseries

Occupational Options

Progression to supervisory positions such as greenhouse supervisor is possible with experience.

Similar Occupations Classified Elsewhere

General Farm Workers (8431)

Harvesting Labourers (8611)

Landscaping and Grounds Maintenance Labourers (8612)

Nursery and Greenhouse Operators and Managers (8254)

Silviculture and Forestry Workers (8422)

Supervisors, Landscape and Horticulture (8256)

8441 Fishing Vessel Deckhands

Fishing Vessel Deckhands perform manual tasks on commercial fishing voyages and maintain fishing vessels.

Profile Summary

APTITUDES

G	V	N	S	P	Q	K	F	M
4	4	4	4	3	5	3	4	3

INTERESTS
MOi

DATA PEOPLE THINGS (DPT)
684

PHYSICAL ACTIVITIES (PA)

V	C	H	B	L	S
3	0	1	4	2	3

ENVIRONMENTAL CONDITIONS (EC)
L3, L4, H8, D3, D5

EDUCATION/TRAINING
2, R

Examples of Job Titles

Crewman/woman, Fishing Vessel
Fishing Vessel Deckhand
Deckhand, Seiner
Icer, Fishing Vessel
Netmender, Fishing Vessel
Trawlerman/woman

Descriptor Profile

Main Characteristics

Occupations in this group are characterized by the following aptitudes, interests and worker functions as they relate to main duties:

- **General learning ability** to prepare nets, lines and other fishing tackle

- **Form perception** to observe defects in nets and other fishing equipment

- **Motor co-ordination** to handle mooring lines during docking; may steer vessels to and from fishing areas

- **Manual dexterity** to clean deck surfaces and fish holds

- **Methodical interest** in **comparing** information to clean, sort and pack fish in ice and stow catch in hold; may prepare and cook meals for crew members

- **Objective interest** in **operating - manipulating** fishing gear to catch fish and other marine life

- **Innovative interest** in repairing nets, splicing ropes and maintaining fishing gear and other deck equipment

8441

Physical Activities

Vision
   3   Near and far vision

Colour Discrimination
   0   Not relevant

Hearing
   1   Limited

Body Position
   4   Other body positions

Limb Co-ordination
   2   Multiple limb co-ordination

Strength
   3   Medium

Environmental Conditions

Location
   L3 Outside
   L4 In a vehicle or cab

Hazards
   H8 Dangerous locations

Discomforts
   D3 Odours
   D5 Wetness

Employment Requirements

Education/Training
   2, R

- There are no specific educational requirements.

- On-the-job training is provided.

- Trawlermen/women require at least one year of experience.

- Fishing vessel deckhands require a commercial fishing licence.

Workplaces/Employers

Establishments that operate commercial fishing vessels

Self-employed fishermen/women

Occupational Options

Fishing vessel deckhands may progress to watchkeeper or mate positions with additional training.

Fishing vessel deckhands may become skippers upon acquiring an entry licence and a boat.

Similar Occupations Classified Elsewhere

Fishing Masters and Officers (8261)

Fishing Vessel Skippers and Fishermen/women (8262)

Deck Officers, Water Transport (2273)

8442.1 Trappers

Trappers snare wild animals for pelts and live sale.

Profile Summary

APTITUDES

G	V	N	S	P	Q	K	F	M
4	4	5	4	4	5	3	4	3

INTERESTS
OMi

DATA PEOPLE THINGS (DPT)
684

PHYSICAL ACTIVITIES (PA)

V	C	H	B	L	S
4	0	1	4	2	4

ENVIRONMENTAL CONDITIONS (EC)
L3, H2, H3, H8

EDUCATION/TRAINING
1, 4, R

Examples of Job Titles

Fur Trapper
Game Trapper
Trapper

Descriptor Profile

Main Characteristics

Occupations in this group are characterized by the following aptitudes, interests and worker functions as they relate to main duties:

- **General learning ability** to trap live animals for sale to buyers and for relocation purposes, and to trap designated animals for bounty and other control programs; may specialize in trapping a particular kind of animal

- **Objective interest** in operating snowmobiles and travelling on foot, snowshoes and skis to patrol traplines; and in maintaining and repairing equipment

- **Methodical interest** in **comparing** information to remove catches and reset traps and snares; and in killing and skinning catches for pelts, and in treating and packing pelts for marketing

- **Innovative interest** in setting traps with bait and positioning traps along trails

8442.1

Physical Activities

Vision
    4 Total visual field

Colour Discrimination
    0 Not relevant

Hearing
    1 Limited

Body Position
    4 Other body positions

Limb Co-ordination
    2 Multiple limb co-ordination

Strength
    4 Heavy

Environmental Conditions

Location
    L3 Outside

Hazards
    H2 Biological agents
    H3 Equipment, machinery, tools
    H8 Dangerous locations

Employment Requirements

Education/Training
    1, 4, R

- Completion of trapping courses may be required in some provinces.

- A trapping licence may be required by some provincial governments.

Workplaces/Employers

Self-employment

Occupational Options

In some jurisdictions, trappers may be allocated trapping areas based on their experience.

Similar Occupations Classified Elsewhere

Animal control trappers or nuisance control trappers (in 7444 *Pest Controllers and Fumigators*)

Remarks

Trappers work on a seasonal basis.

8442.2 Hunters

Hunters catch wild animals for pelts and live sale.

Profile Summary

APTITUDES

G	V	N	S	P	Q	K	F	M
4	4	5	4	4	5	3	4	3

INTERESTS
OMi

DATA PEOPLE THINGS (DPT)
684

PHYSICAL ACTIVITIES (PA)

V	C	H	B	L	S
4	1	3	4	2	4

ENVIRONMENTAL CONDITIONS (EC)
L3, H2, H3, H8

EDUCATION/TRAINING
1, 4, R

Examples of Job Titles

Hunter
Sealer

Descriptor Profile

Main Characteristics

Occupations in this group are characterized by the following aptitudes, interests and worker functions as they relate to main duties:

- **General learning ability** to hunt wild animals for pelts and live sale

- **Objective interest** in **operating** boats and snowmobiles and travelling on foot to reach hunting areas; and in killing wild animals using firearms and other weapons and in maintaining hunting equipment

- **Methodical interest** in skinning animals for pelts using knives

- **Innovative interest** in **comparing** information to treat, pack and transport pelts to processing plants and public auctions

Physical Activities

Vision
    4   Total visual field

Colour Discrimination
    1   Relevant

Hearing
    3   Other sound discrimination

Body Position
    4   Other body positions

Limb Co-ordination
    2   Multiple limb co-ordination

Strength
    4   Heavy

Environmental Conditions

Location
    L3 Outside

Hazards
    H2 Biological agents
    H3 Equipment, machinery, tools
    H8 Dangerous locations

Employment Requirements

Education/Training
    1, 4, R

- Completion of hunting courses may be required in some provinces.

- A hunting licence may be required by provincial governments.

Workplaces/Employers

Self-employment

Similar Occupations Classified Elsewhere

Animal control trappers or nuisance control trappers (in 7444 *Pest Controllers and Fumigators*)

Remarks

Hunters work on a seasonal basis.

8611 Harvesting Labourers

Harvesting Labourers assist other farm workers to harvest, sort and pack crops.

Profile Summary

APTITUDES
G	V	N	S	P	Q	K	F	M
4	4	4	4	4	5	3	4	3

INTERESTS
Moi

DATA PEOPLE THINGS (DPT)
687

PHYSICAL ACTIVITIES (PA)
V	C	H	B	L	S
3	1	1	4	2	4

ENVIRONMENTAL CONDITIONS (EC)
L3

EDUCATION/TRAINING
1

Examples of Job Titles

Apple Picker
Berry Picker
Crop Farm Labourer
Fruit Picker
Harvest Hand
Tobacco Picker
Vegetable Packer

Descriptor Profile

Main Characteristics

Occupations in this group are characterized by the following aptitudes, interests and worker functions as they relate to main duties:

- **General learning ability** to assist other farm workers to harvest, sort and pack crops

- **Motor co-ordination** and **manual dexterity** to transplant seedlings, thin row crops, pick berries and prepare produce for market, and to bag grain, pull vegetables and connect irrigation piping

- **Methodical interest** in **comparing** information to sort and pack fruit and vegetables at farms, and to pick row and orchard crops

- **Objective interest** in **handling**, loading, unloading and transferring crates, supplies, farm produce, livestock and poultry

- **Innovative interest** in preparing vegetable produce for market

8611

Physical Activities

Vision
  3 Near and far vision

Colour Discrimination
  1 Relevant

Hearing
  1 Limited

Body Position
  4 Other body positions

Limb Co-ordination
  2 Multiple limb co-ordination

Strength
  4 Heavy

Environmental Conditions

Location
  L3 Outside

Employment Requirements

Education/Training
  1

- There are no specific educational or training requirements.

Workplaces/Employers

Crop farms

Fruit farms

Livestock farms

Specialty farms

Vegetable farms

Occupational Options

Progression to other farm worker positions is possible with experience.

Similar Occupations Classified Elsewhere

Farm Supervisors and Specialized Livestock Workers (8253)

Farmers and Farm Managers (8251)

General Farm Workers (8431)

8612 Landscaping and Grounds Maintenance Labourers

Landscaping and Grounds Maintenance Labourers perform manual work to assist in the construction of landscapes and related structures, and to maintain lawns, gardens, athletic fields, golf courses, cemeteries, parks and landscaped interiors and areas.

Profile Summary

APTITUDES

G	V	N	S	P	Q	K	F	M
4	4	5	4	4	5	3	4	3

INTERESTS
MOi

DATA PEOPLE THINGS (DPT)
684

PHYSICAL ACTIVITIES (PA)

V	C	H	B	L	S
3	1	1	4	2	3

ENVIRONMENTAL CONDITIONS (EC)
L3, H1, H3, D1, D2

EDUCATION/TRAINING
2, R

Examples of Job Titles

Bulb Planter
Cemetery Labourer
Gardening Helper
Golf Course Worker
Grass Cutter
Grounds Maintenance Worker
Landscape Labourer
Maintenance Worker, Parks
Sod Layer
Transplanter

Descriptor Profile

Main Characteristics

Occupations in this group are characterized by the following aptitudes, interests and worker functions as they relate to main duties:

- **General learning ability** to perform manual work to assist in the construction of landscapes and related structures and to maintain lawns, gardens, athletic fields, golf courses, cemeteries, parks and landscaped interiors and areas

- **Motor co-ordination** and **manual dexterity** to cut grass, rake, fertilize and water lawns, to weed gardens, to prune shrubs and trees and to perform other manual duties as directed by supervisors

- **Methodical interest** in spraying and dusting as directed to control insects and diseases and in performing other manual duties to clean and maintain landscaped environments

- **Objective interest** in operating power mowers, tractors, snowblowers, chainsaws, electric clippers, sod cutters, pruning saws and other equipment

- **Innovative interest** in comparing information to spread top soil, lay sod and plant flowers, grass, shrubs and trees; and in performing other duties to assist with the construction of landscapes and related structures

8612

Physical Activities

Vision
   3   Near and far vision

Colour Discrimination
   1   Relevant

Hearing
   1   Limited

Body Position
   4   Other body positions

Limb Co-ordination
   2   Multiple limb co-ordination

Strength
   3   Medium

Environmental Conditions

Location
   L3 Outside

Hazards
   H1 Dangerous chemical substances
   H3 Equipment, machinery, tools

Discomforts
   D1 Noise
   D2 Vibration

Employment Requirements

Education/Training
   2, R

- Some secondary school education may be required.

- A provincial licence to apply chemical fertilizers, fungicides, herbicides and pesticides may be required.

Workplaces/Employers

Cemeteries

Golf courses

Landscaping and lawn-care companies

Landscaping departments of governments and private establishments

Occupational Options

Progression to technical or supervisory occupations in landscaping and horticulture is possible with additional training or experience.

Similar Occupations Classified Elsewhere

Landscape and Horticulture Technicians and Specialists (2225)

Nursery and Greenhouse Workers (8432)

Residential and Commercial Installers and Servicers (7441)

Supervisors, Landscape and Horticulture (8256)

8613.1 Aquaculture Support Workers

Aquaculture Support Workers help workers and other labourers in aquaculture and fishing.

Profile Summary

APTITUDES

G	V	N	S	P	Q	K	F	M
4	4	4	4	4	4	4	3	4

INTERESTS
MOi

DATA PEOPLE THINGS (DPT)
684

PHYSICAL ACTIVITIES (PA)

V	C	H	B	L	S
3	0	1	4	1	3

ENVIRONMENTAL CONDITIONS (EC)
L1, L3, H2, D3, D5

EDUCATION/TRAINING
2

Examples of Job Titles

Aquaculture Support Worker
Fish Farm Helper
Fish Tagger
Fry Marker
Sea Farm Attendant
Wharf Worker - Fishing

Descriptor Profile

Main Characteristics

Occupations in this group are characterized by the following aptitudes, interests and worker functions as they relate to main duties:

- **General learning ability** to assist aquaculture technicians in the operations of fish hatcheries and other aquatic farms and to operate boats in marine aquaculture operations

- **Methodical interest** in **comparing** information to prepare stocks for market, to feed and vaccinate stocks and to perform culling and marking or banding techniques

- **Objective interest** in **operating**, maintaining and cleaning pumps, filters and other equipment; and in cleaning and maintaining enclosures

- **Innovative interest** in reporting any observed irregularities in stocks

8613.1
Subgroup 1 of 3

Physical Activities

Vision
   3 Near and far vision

Colour Discrimination
   0 Not relevant

Hearing
   1 Limited

Body Position
   4 Other body positions

Limb Co-ordination
   1 Upper limb co-ordination

Strength
   3 Medium

Environmental Conditions

Location
   L1 Regulated inside climate
   L3 Outside

Hazards
   H2 Biological agents

Discomforts
   D3 Odours
   D5 Wetness

Employment Requirements

Education/Training
2

- Some secondary school education is usually required.

Workplaces/Employers

Commercial aquatic farms

Public or private fish hatcheries

Similar Occupations Classified Elsewhere

Aquaculture Operators and Managers (8257)

Fishing Vessel Deckhands (8441)

Fishing Vessel Skippers and Fishermen/women (8262)

8613.2 Marine Plant Gatherers

Marine Plant Gatherers collect marine plants for further processing.

Profile Summary

APTITUDES

G	V	N	S	P	Q	K	F	M
4	4	4	4	4	4	4	3	4

INTERESTS
Moi

DATA PEOPLE THINGS (DPT)
687

PHYSICAL ACTIVITIES (PA)

V	C	H	B	L	S
3	0	1	4	1	3

ENVIRONMENTAL CONDITIONS (EC)
L3, D3, D5

EDUCATION/TRAINING
2

Examples of Job Titles

Dulse Gatherer

Marine Plant Gatherer

Seaweed Gatherer

Descriptor Profile

Main Characteristics

Occupations in this group are characterized by the following aptitudes, interests and worker functions as they relate to main duties:

- **General learning ability** to gather marine plants from beaches, rocks and shallow waters

- **Methodical interest** in **comparing** information to spread gatherings and transport them to processing plants

- **Objective interest** in **handling** equipment to rake seaweed, dulse and Irish moss; and in loading plants into carts, wagons and other receptacles

- **Innovative interest** in removing foreign objects from gatherings

8613.2
Subgroup 2 of 3

Physical Activities

Vision
   3 Near and far vision

Colour Discrimination
   0 Not relevant

Hearing
   1 Limited

Body Position
   4 Other body positions

Limb Co-ordination
   1 Upper limb co-ordination

Strength
   3 Medium

Environmental Conditions

Location
   L3 Outside

Discomforts
   D3 Odours
   D5 Wetness

Employment Requirements

Education/Training
2

- Some secondary school education is usually required.

Workplaces/Employers

Commercial aquatic farms

Self-employment

Similar Occupations Classified Elsewhere

Aquaculture Operators and Managers (8257)

Fishing Vessel Deckhands (8441)

Fishing Vessel Skippers and Fishermen/women (8262)

8613.3 Shellfish Harvesters

Shellfish Harvesters collect shellfish for sale in markets.

Profile Summary

APTITUDES

G	V	N	S	P	Q	K	F	M
4	4	4	4	4	4	4	3	4

INTERESTS
Moi

DATA PEOPLE THINGS (DPT)
687

PHYSICAL ACTIVITIES (PA)

V	C	H	B	L	S
3	0	1	4	1	3

ENVIRONMENTAL CONDITIONS (EC)
L3, D3, D5

EDUCATION/TRAINING
2, R

Examples of Job Titles

Clam Digger
Oyster Picker
Shellfish Harvester

Descriptor Profile

Main Characteristics

Occupations in this group are characterized by the following aptitudes, interests and worker functions as they relate to main duties:

- **General learning ability** to cultivate and harvest shellfish

- **Finger dexterity** to gather shellfish from wild and cultivated beds by hand and using shovels, forks and rakes

- **Methodical interest** in **comparing** information to clean, sort and transport shellfish to markets

- **Objective interest** in **handling** spades, forks and other instruments to dig clams from beds; and in picking oysters

- **Innovative interest** in selling catches to public at docks and in markets

Physical Activities

Vision
   3 Near and far vision

Colour Discrimination
   0 Not relevant

Hearing
   1 Limited

Body Position
   4 Other body positions

Limb Co-ordination
   1 Upper limb co-ordination

Strength
   3 Medium

Environmental Conditions

Location
   L3 Outside

Discomforts
   D3 Odours
   D5 Wetness

Employment Requirements

Education/Training
   2, R

- Some secondary school education is usually required.

- Shellfish harvesters require commercial fishing licences.

Workplaces/Employers

Self-employment

Similar Occupations Classified Elsewhere

Aquaculture Operators and Managers (8257)

Fishing Vessel Deckhands (8441)

Fishing Vessel Skippers and Fishermen/women (8262)

8614 Mine Labourers

Mine Labourers carry out general labouring duties to assist in the extraction of coal, minerals and ore, and perform other services in support of underground mining.

Profile Summary

APTITUDES

G	V	N	S	P	Q	K	F	M
4	4	5	4	4	5	4	4	3

INTERESTS
MOi

DATA PEOPLE THINGS (DPT)
684

PHYSICAL ACTIVITIES (PA)

V	C	H	B	L	S
3	0	1	4	1	4

ENVIRONMENTAL CONDITIONS (EC)
L2, H3, H6, H8, D1, D4

EDUCATION/TRAINING
3, 4, R

Examples of Job Titles

Mine Helper
Mine Labourer
Shoveller - Underground Mining

Descriptor Profile

Main Characteristics

Occupations in this group are characterized by the following aptitudes, interests and worker functions as they relate to main duties:

- **General learning ability** to carry out general labouring duties to assist in the extraction of coal, minerals and ore, and to perform other services in support of underground mining

- **Manual dexterity** to clear spills using hand and power tools

- **Methodical interest** in **comparing** information to load, move, sort and pile materials and supplies

- **Objective interest** in **operating** equipment and using hand tools to clean underground rooms, roadways, working areas and mining equipment and conveyances

- **Innovative interest** in assisting other mine workers in maintaining and constructing underground installations

8614

Physical Activities

Vision
   3 Near and far vision

Colour Discrimination
   0 Not relevant

Hearing
   1 Limited

Body Position
   4 Other body positions

Limb Co-ordination
   1 Upper limb co-ordination

Strength
   4 Heavy

Environmental Conditions

Location
   L2 Unregulated inside climate

Hazards
   H3 Equipment, machinery, tools
   H6 Flying particles, falling objects
   H8 Dangerous locations

Discomforts
   D1 Noise
   D4 Non-toxic dusts

Employment Requirements

Education/Training
   3, 4, R

- Completion of secondary school is usually required.

- A short period of introductory training is provided.

- Mine labourers are registered in the basic common core program in Ontario.

Workplaces/Employers

Coal, metal and non-metallic mineral mines

Occupational Options

There is mobility among jobs in this group.

Progression to underground production and development miner or underground mine service and support worker is possible with experience and training.

Similar Occupations Classified Elsewhere

Underground Mine Service and Support Workers (8411)

Underground Production and Development Miners (8231)

8615 Oil and Gas Drilling, Servicing and Related Labourers

Labourers in this group carry out general labouring duties and operate equipment to assist in the drilling and servicing of oil and gas wells. This group includes labourers who assist in geophysical prospecting for oil and gas.

Profile Summary

APTITUDES

G	V	N	S	P	Q	K	F	M
4	4	4	4	4	5	3	4	3

INTERESTS
MOi

DATA PEOPLE THINGS (DPT)
684

PHYSICAL ACTIVITIES (PA)

V	C	H	B	L	S
3	0	1	4	1	4

ENVIRONMENTAL CONDITIONS (EC)
L3, H1, H3, H6, H8, D1, D3, D5

EDUCATION/TRAINING
2, 4, R

Examples of Job Titles

Floorman/woman
Helper, Wireline
Labourer, Oil Field
Leasehand
Roughneck
Roustabout
Service Rig Helper
Shakerhand
Well Treatment Helper

Descriptor Profile

Main Characteristics

Occupations in this group are characterized by the following aptitudes, interests and worker functions as they relate to main duties:

- **General learning ability** to carry out general labouring duties and to assist in the drilling and servicing of oil and gas wells

- **Motor co-ordination** and **manual dexterity** to assist in setting up, taking down and transporting rigs and service equipment

- **Methodical interest** in **comparing** information to handle, sort and move drill tools, pipes, cement and other materials, and to clean up rig areas; may drive trucks to transport materials and well service equipment

- **Objective interest** in **operating** equipment to manipulate sections of pipes and drill stems at rig floors during drilling and for removal and replacement of strings of pipes, drill stems and bits

- **Innovative interest** in maintaining drilling equipment on drill floors

Physical Activities

Vision
   3 Near and far vision

Colour Discrimination
   0 Not relevant

Hearing
   1 Limited

Body Position
   4 Other body positions

Limb Co-ordination
   1 Upper limb co-ordination

Strength
   4 Heavy

Environmental Conditions

Location
   L3 Outside

Hazard
   H1 Dangerous chemical substances
   H3 Equipment, machinery, tools
   H6 Flying particles, falling objects
   H8 Dangerous locations

Discomforts
   D1 Noise
   D3 Odours
   D5 Wetness

Employment Requirements

Education/Training
2, 4, R

- Completion of secondary school may be required.

- Completion of introductory college or Petroleum Industry Training Service (PITS) courses may be required.

- Certificates in hydrogen-sulphide awareness, Workplace Hazardous Materials Information System (WHMIS) or Transportation of Dangerous Goods (TGD) may be required.

Workplaces/Employers

Drilling and well servicing contractors

Petroleum producing companies

Occupational Options

Progression to more senior operating positions is possible with experience.

Similar Occupations Classified Elsewhere

Oil and Gas Well Drilling Workers and Services Operators (8412)

Oil and Gas Well Drillers, Servicers, Testers and Related Workers (8232)

8616 Logging and Forestry Labourers

Logging and Forestry Labourers perform manual tasks such as attaching choker cables to logs, planting trees, clearing brush, spraying chemicals, cleaning up landing areas and assisting other workers in woodlands operations.

Profile Summary

APTITUDES

G	V	N	S	P	Q	K	F	M
4	4	5	4	4	5	4	4	3

INTERESTS
MOi

DATA PEOPLE THINGS (DPT)
684

PHYSICAL ACTIVITIES (PA)

V	C	H	B	L	S
3	0	1	4	2	4

ENVIRONMENTAL CONDITIONS (EC)
L3, H1, H3, H6, H8, D1, D2, D3, D4

EDUCATION/TRAINING
2, 4, R

Examples of Job Titles

Chokerman/woman
Forestry Labourer
Logging Labourer
Swamper, Seasonal
Tree Planter, Seasonal

Descriptor Profile

Main Characteristics

Occupations in this group are characterized by the following aptitudes, interests and worker functions as they relate to main duties:

- **General learning ability** to perform manual tasks such as attaching choker cables to logs, planting trees, clearing brush, spraying chemicals, cleaning up landing areas and assisting other workers in woodlands operations

- **Manual dexterity** to attach chokers and cables to felled trees for yarding

- **Methodical interest** in **comparing** information to clean up landing areas at logging sites

- **Objective interest** in **operating** chainsaws to clear trails through woodlands; and in using manual equipment and tools to spray herbicides from the ground and to plant trees

- **Innovative interest** in assisting other workers at logging sites

8616

Physical Activities

Vision
　3　Near and far vision

Colour Discrimination
　0　Not relevant

Hearing
　1　Limited

Body Position
　4　Other body positions

Limb Co-ordination
　2　Multiple limb co-ordination

Strength
　4　Heavy

Environmental Conditions

Location
　L3　Outside

Hazards
　H1　Dangerous chemical substances
　H3　Equipment, machinery, tools
　H6　Flying particles, falling objects
　H8　Dangerous locations

Discomforts
　D1　Noise
　D2　Vibration
　D3　Odours
　D4　Non-toxic dusts

Employment Requirements

Education/Training
　2, 4, R

- Completion of secondary school may be required.

- Completion of pre-employment safety courses may be required.

- Several weeks of formal and on-the-job training are provided.

- Workplace Hazardous Materials Information System (WHMIS) certification may be required.

- A chemicals application licence may be required.

Workplaces/Employers

Logging companies

Logging contractors

Occupational Options

There is mobility among jobs in this group.

Progression to other positions, such as silviculture and forestry worker, chainsaw and skidder operator or logging machinery operator is possible with experience.

Similar Occupations Classified Elsewhere

Chainsaw and Skidder Operators (8421)

Logging Machinery Operators (8241)

Silviculture and Forestry Workers (8422)

Occupations Unique to Processing, Manufacturing and Utilities

Occupations Unique to Processing, Manufacturing and Utilities

MAJOR GROUP 92
PROCESSING, MANUFACTURING AND UTILITIES SUPERVISORS AND SKILLED OPERATORS

921 Supervisors, Processing Occupations

9211 Supervisors, Mineral and Metal Processing
9212 Supervisors, Petroleum, Gas and Chemical Processing and Utilities
9213 Supervisors, Food, Beverage and Tobacco Processing
9214 Supervisors, Plastic and Rubber Products Manufacturing
9215 Supervisors, Forest Products Processing
9216 Supervisors, Textile Processing

922 Supervisors, Assembly and Fabrication

9221 Supervisors, Motor Vehicle Assembling
9222 Supervisors, Electronics Manufacturing
9223 Supervisors, Electrical Products Manufacturing
9224 Supervisors, Furniture and Fixtures Manufacturing
9225 Supervisors, Fabric, Fur and Leather Products Manufacturing
9226 Supervisors, Other Mechanical and Metal Products Manufacturing
9227 Supervisors, Other Products Manufacturing and Assembly

923 Central Control and Process Operators in Manufacturing and Processing

9231 Central Control and Process Operators, Mineral and Metal Processing
9232 Petroleum, Gas and Chemical Process Operators
9233 Pulping Control Operators
9234 Papermaking and Coating Control Operators

MAJOR GROUP 94-95
PROCESSING AND MANUFACTURING MACHINE OPERATORS AND ASSEMBLERS

941 Machine Operators and Related Workers in Metal and Mineral Products Processing

9411 Machine Operators, Mineral and Metal Processing
9412 Foundry Workers
    9412.1 Manual Mouldmakers
    9412.2 Manual Coremakers
    9412.3 Machine Mouldmakers and Coremakers
    9412.4 Metal Casters
    9412.5 Foundry Furnace Operators
9413 Glass Forming and Finishing Machine Operators and Glass Cutters
    9413.1 Glass Process Control Operators
    9413.2 Glass Forming Machine Operators
    9413.3 Glass Finishing Machine Operators
    9413.4 Glass Cutters

9414	Concrete, Clay and Stone Forming Operators	
	9414.1	Concrete Products Forming and Finishing Workers
	9414.2	Concrete Products Machine Operators
	9414.3	Clay Products Forming and Finishing Machine Operators
	9414.4	Stone Forming and Finishing Workers
9415	Inspectors and Testers, Mineral and Metal Processing	

942 Machine Operators and Related Workers in Chemical, Plastic and Rubber Processing

9421	Chemical Plant Machine Operators	
9422	Plastics Processing Machine Operators	
	9422.1	Mixing Machine Operators
	9422.2	Calendering Process Operators
	9422.3	Extruding Process Operators
	9422.4	Moulding Process Operators
9423	Rubber Processing Machine Operators and Related Workers	
	9423.1	Rubber Processing Machine Operators
	9423.2	Assemblers, Rubber Products
	9423.3	Rubber Products Inspectors
9424	Water and Waste Plant Operators	
	9424.1	Water Plant Operators
	9424.2	Waste Plant Operators

943 Machine Operators and Related Workers in Pulp and Paper Production and Wood Processing

9431	Sawmill Machine Operators	
9432	Pulp Mill Machine Operators	
9433	Papermaking and Finishing Machine Operators	
9434	Other Wood Processing Machine Operators	
9435	Paper Converting Machine Operators	
9436	Lumber Graders and Other Wood Processing Inspectors and Graders	
	9436.1	Lumber Graders
	9436.2	Other Wood Processing Inspectors and Graders

944 Machine Operators and Related Workers in Textile Processing

9441	Textile Fibre and Yarn Preparation Machine Operators
9442	Weavers, Knitters and Other Fabric-Making Occupations
9443	Textile Dyeing and Finishing Machine Operators
9444	Textile Inspectors, Graders and Samplers

945 Machine Operators and Related Workers in Fabric, Fur and Leather Products Manufacturing

9451	Sewing Machine Operators	
9452	Fabric, Fur and Leather Cutters	
	9452.1	Fabric Cutters
	9452.2	Fur Cutters
	9452.3	Leather Cutters
9453	Hide and Pelt Processing Workers	
9454	Inspectors and Testers, Fabric, Fur and Leather Products Manufacturing	

946   **Machine Operators and Related Workers in Food, Beverage and Tobacco Processing**

9461   Process Control and Machine Operators, Food and Beverage Processing
- 9461.1   Process Control Operators, Food and Beverage Processing
- 9461.2   Machine Operators, Food and Beverage Processing

9462   Industrial Butchers and Meat Cutters, Poultry Preparers and Related Workers
- 9462.1   Industrial Butchers
- 9462.2   Industrial Meat Cutters
- 9462.3   Poultry Preparers
- 9462.4   Trimmers

9463   Fish Plant Workers
- 9463.1   Fish Plant Machine Operators
- 9463.2   Fish Plant Cutters and Cleaners

9464   Tobacco Processing Machine Operators

9465   Testers and Graders, Food and Beverage Processing

947   **Printing Machine Operators and Related Occupations**

9471   Printing Machine Operators

9472   Camera, Platemaking and Other Pre-Press Occupations
- 9472.1   Graphic Arts Camera Operators
- 9472.2   Cylinder Preparers
- 9472.3   Film Strippers/Assemblers
- 9472.4   Platemakers
- 9472.5   Pre-Press Technicians
- 9472.6   Scanner Operators

9473   Binding and Finishing Machine Operators
- 9473.1   Binding Machine Operators
- 9473.2   Finishing Machine Operators

9474   Photographic and Film Processors

948   **Mechanical, Electrical and Electronics Assemblers**

9481   Aircraft Assemblers and Aircraft Assembly Inspectors
- 9481.1   Aircraft Assemblers
- 9481.2   Aircraft Assembly Inspectors

9482   Motor Vehicle Assemblers, Inspectors and Testers
- 9482.1   Motor Vehicle Assemblers
- 9482.2   Motor Vehicle Inspectors and Testers

9483   Electronics Assemblers, Fabricators, Inspectors and Testers
- 9483.1   Electronics Assemblers
- 9483.2   Electronics Fabricators
- 9483.3   Electronics Inspectors
- 9483.4   Electronics Testers

9484   Assemblers and Inspectors, Electrical Appliance, Apparatus and Equipment Manufacturing
- 9484.1   Assemblers, Electrical Appliance, Apparatus and Equipment Manufacturing
- 9484.2   Inspectors and Testers, Electrical Appliance, Apparatus and Equipment Manufacturing

9485 Assemblers, Fabricators and Inspectors, Industrial Electrical Motors and Transformers
    9485.1 Assemblers, Industrial Electrical Motors and Transformers
    9485.2 Electrical Fitters, Industrial Electrical Motors and Transformers
    9485.3 Inspectors, Industrial Electrical Motors and Transformers

9486 Mechanical Assemblers and Inspectors
    9486.1 Mechanical Assemblers
    9486.2 Mechanical Inspectors

9487 Machine Operators and Inspectors, Electrical Apparatus Manufacturing
    9487.1 Machine Operators, Electrical Apparatus Manufacturing
    9487.2 Inspectors and Testers, Electrical Apparatus Manufacturing

949 Other Assembly and Related Occupations

9491 Boat Assemblers and Inspectors
    9491.1 Boat Assemblers
    9491.2 Boat Inspectors

9492 Furniture and Fixture Assemblers and Inspectors
    9492.1 Furniture and Fixture Assemblers
    9492.2 Furniture and Fixture Inspectors

9493 Other Wood Products Assemblers and Inspectors
    9493.1 Other Wood Products Assemblers
    9493.2 Other Wood Products Inspectors

9494 Furniture Finishers and Refinishers
    9494.1 Furniture Finishers
    9494.2 Furniture Refinishers

9495 Plastics Products Assemblers, Finishers and Inspectors
    9495.1 Plastics Products Assemblers and Finishers
    9495.2 Plastics Products Inspectors

9496 Painters and Coaters, Manufacturing

9497 Plating, Metal Spraying and Related Operators

9498 Other Assemblers and Inspectors
    9498.1 Other Assemblers
    9498.2 Other Inspectors

951 Machining, Metalworking, Woodworking and Related Machine Operators

9511 Machining Tool Operators

9512 Forging Machine Operators

9513 Woodworking Machine Operators

9514 Metalworking Machine Operators

9515 Welding, Brazing and Soldering Machine Operators
    9515.1 Welding Machine Operators
    9515.2 Brazing and Soldering Machine Operators

9516 Other Metal Products Machine Operators

9517 Other Products Machine Operators

MAJOR GROUP 96
LABOURERS IN PROCESSING, MANUFACTURING AND UTILITIES

961 **Labourers in Processing, Manufacturing and Utilities**

9611 Labourers in Mineral and Metal Processing
9612 Labourers in Metal Fabrication
9613 Labourers in Chemical Products Processing and Utilities
9614 Labourers in Wood, Pulp and Paper Processing
9615 Labourers in Rubber and Plastic Products Manufacturing
9616 Labourers in Textile Processing
9617 Labourers in Food, Beverage and Tobacco Processing
9618 Labourers in Fish Processing
9619 Other Labourers in Processing, Manufacturing and Utilities

9211 Supervisors, Mineral and Metal Processing

Supervisors, Mineral and Metal Processing supervise and co-ordinate the activities of workers in the following groups: *Central Control and Process Operators, Mineral and Metal Processing* (9231), *Machine Operators and Related Workers in Metal and Mineral Products Processing* (941) and *Labourers in Mineral and Metal Processing* (9611).

Profile Summary

APTITUDES

G	V	N	S	P	Q	K	F	M
3	3	3	4	3	3	3	4	3

INTERESTS
Dio

DATA PEOPLE THINGS (DPT)
138

PHYSICAL ACTIVITIES (PA)

V	C	H	B	L	S
3	0	2	3	0	1

ENVIRONMENTAL CONDITIONS (EC)
L1, H5*, H7*, D1, D3

EDUCATION/TRAINING
3+

Examples of Job Titles

Blast Furnace Foreman/woman
Brick and Tile Foreman/woman
Cement Processing Supervisor
Coremaking Foreman/woman
Die Casting Supervisor
Foreman/woman, Lead Refining
Lime Preparation Foreman/woman
Melting and Roasting Department Supervisor
Metal Rolling Foreman/woman
Ore Milling Supervisor
Supervisor, Glass Cutters

Descriptor Profile

Main Characteristics

Occupations in this group are characterized by the following aptitudes, interests and worker functions as they relate to main duties:

- **General learning ability** to establish methods to meet work schedules, co-ordinate work activities with units and recommend work measures to improve productivity and product quality

- **Verbal ability** to train staff in job duties, safety procedures and company policies, and to recommend personnel actions such as hirings and promotions

- **Numerical ability** and **clerical perception** to requisition materials and supplies, and to prepare production and other reports

- **Directive interest** in **supervising** the activities of workers who operate single or multi-functional mineral and metal processing machinery and equipment; who operate mouldmaking and coremaking machines or manually make moulds and cores; who operate glass process control, forming and finishing machines; who operate concrete, clay and stone forming and finishing machines; and who operate cement process control machines and equipment

- **Innovative interest** in **co-ordinating** work activities and production schedules with units; and in resolving work problems

- **Objective interest** in understanding the functioning of equipment and machinery used in mineral and metal processing operations; may set up machines and equipment

9211

Physical Activities

Vision
   3 Near and far vision

Colour Discrimination
   0 Not relevant

Hearing
   2 Verbal interaction

Body Position
   3 Sitting, standing, walking

Limb Co-ordination
   0 Not relevant

Strength
   1 Limited

Environmental Conditions

Location
   L1 Regulated inside climate

Hazards
   H5*Radiation
   H7*Fire, steam, hot surfaces

Discomforts
   D1 Noise
   D3 Odours

Employment Requirements

Education/Training
   3+

- Completion of secondary school is usually required.

- Several years of experience as a worker in the unit or department being supervised are required.

Workplaces/Employers

Mineral, ore and metal processing plants such as:

Aluminium plants

Cement processing plants

Clay, glass and stone processing plants

Foundries

Metal refineries

Mineral ore mills

Steel mills

Uranium processing plants

Similar Occupations Classified Elsewhere

Supervisors, Mining and Quarrying (8221)

Supervisors, Other Mechanical and Metal Products Manufacturing (9226)

Remarks

*Environmental Conditions

- For some occupations in this group, **Hazards** H5 (Radiation) and H7 (Fire, steam, hot surfaces) may also apply.

9212 Supervisors, Petroleum, Gas and Chemical Processing and Utilities

Supervisors in this group supervise and co-ordinate the activities of workers in the following groups: *Petroleum, Gas and Chemical Process Operators (9232)*, *Chemical Plant Machine Operators (9421)*, *Labourers in Chemical Products Processing and Utilities (9613)*, *Water and Waste Plant Operators (9424)*, *Stationary Engineers and Auxiliary Equipment Operators (7351)* and *Power Systems and Power Station Operators (7352)*.

Profile Summary

APTITUDES

G	V	N	S	P	Q	K	F	M
3	3	3	4	3	3	3	4	3

INTERESTS
Dim

DATA PEOPLE THINGS (DPT)
138

PHYSICAL ACTIVITIES (PA)

V	C	H	B	L	S
3	0	2	3	0	1

ENVIRONMENTAL CONDITIONS (EC)
L1, H1*, D3

EDUCATION/TRAINING
3+, 4+, 5+, 6+, R

Examples of Job Titles

Chemical Processing Supervisor
Foreman/woman, Chemical
Foreman/woman, Cosmetics Processing
Foreman/woman, Natural Gas Plant
Foreman/woman, Water Purification Plant
Petroleum Processing Foreman/woman
Production Supervisor, Pharmaceuticals
Production Supervisor, Specialty Chemicals
Steam Engineer Leader
Supervisor, Petroleum Refining
Supervisor, Pipeline Operation
Supervisor, Power Station
Supervisor, Sewage Treatment Plant

Descriptor Profile

Main Characteristics

Occupations in this group are characterized by the following aptitudes, interests and worker functions as they relate to main duties:

- **General learning ability** to establish methods to meet work schedules, recommend measures to improve productivity and product quality, and provide information for maintenance plans to ensure that maintenance and production objectives are met

- **Verbal ability** to train staff in job duties, safety procedures and company policies, and to recommend personnel actions such as hirings and promotions

- **Numerical ability** and **clerical perception** to develop and manage operating budget for areas of responsibility, and to prepare production and other reports

- **Directive interest** in supervising activities of workers who operate petroleum refineries, chemical plants, water and waste disposal plants and equipment, pipelines, heating plants, and power stations and systems; may also supervise and schedule the activities of trade workers, labourers and other workers

- **Innovative interest** in co-ordinating work activities and production schedules with other units; and in resolving work problems and identifying, investigating and correcting potential environmental and safety problems

- **Methodical interest** in documenting potential safety problems and requisitioning materials and supplies

9212

Physical Activities

Vision
   3   Near and far vision

Colour Discrimination
   0   Not relevant

Hearing
   2   Verbal interaction

Body Position
   3   Sitting, standing, walking

Limb Co-ordination
   0   Not relevant

Strength
   1   Limited

Environmental Conditions

Location
   L1   Regulated inside climate

Hazards
   H1*Dangerous chemical substances

Discomforts
   D3   Odours

Employment Requirements

Education/Training
   3+, 4+, 5+, 6+, R

- Completion of secondary school is required.

- Post-secondary education in chemical processing or sciences may be required for some occupations in this group.

- Several years of experience as a senior operator in the same company or plant are usually required.

- Some occupations in this group may require a specific licence or certification, such as a stationary engineer's licence or refrigeration certification.

Workplaces/Employers

Chemical and pharmaceutical companies

Petroleum and natural gas processing companies

Pipeline and petrochemical companies

Water and waste treatment utilities

Occupational Options

There is some mobility among occupations with similar technological or licensing requirements within this group.

Similar Occupations Classified Elsewhere

Supervisors of telecommunications workers, power utility electricians and power line workers (in 7212 *Contractors and Supervisors, Electrical Trades and Telecommunications Occupations*)

Remarks

*Environmental Conditions

- For some occupations in this group, **Hazards** H1 (Dangerous chemical substances) may apply.

9213 Supervisors, Food, Beverage and Tobacco Processing

Supervisors in this group supervise and co-ordinate the activities of workers who operate processing machines, and package and grade food, beverage and tobacco products.

Profile Summary

APTITUDES

G	V	N	S	P	Q	K	F	M
3	3	3	4	4	3	4	4	4

INTERESTS
Dim

DATA PEOPLE THINGS (DPT)
138

PHYSICAL ACTIVITIES (PA)

V	C	H	B	L	S
3	0	2	3	0	1

ENVIRONMENTAL CONDITIONS (EC)
L1, D3

EDUCATION/TRAINING
3+

Examples of Job Titles

Foreman/woman, Poultry Graders
Packaging Supervisor
Production Supervisor
Supervisor, Bottling
Supervisor, Fish Processing
Supervisor, Food Product Testers
Supervisor, Meat Packing
Supervisor, Tobacco Processing
Supervisor, Vegetable Packing
Team Supervisor, Flour Milling

Descriptor Profile

Main Characteristics

Occupations in this group are characterized by the following aptitudes, interests and worker functions as they relate to main duties:

- **General learning ability** to establish methods to meet work schedules and recommend measures to improve productivity and product quality

- **Verbal ability** to train staff in job duties, safety procedures and company policies, and to recommend personnel actions such as hirings and promotions

- **Clerical perception** to prepare production and other reports

- **Directive interest** in supervising the activities of workers who process, package, test and grade food, beverage and tobacco products

- **Innovative interest** in co-ordinating work activities with other units in the food, beverage and tobacco processing industries; and in resolving work problems

- **Methodical interest** in scheduling activities of workers and requisitioning materials and supplies

9213

Physical Activities

Vision
   3 Near and far vision

Colour Discrimination
   0 Not relevant

Hearing
   2 Verbal interaction

Body Position
   3 Sitting, standing, walking

Limb Co-ordination
   0 Not relevant

Strength
   1 Limited

Environmental Conditions

Location
   L1 Regulated inside climate

Discomforts
   D3 Odours

Employment Requirements

Education/Training
   3+

- Completion of secondary school is usually required.

- Several years of experience in the food, beverage or tobacco processing industry are required.

Workplaces/Employers

Bakeries

Breweries

Dairies

Fish plants

Flour mills

Food, beverage and tobacco processing establishments

Meat plants

Sugar refineries

Similar Occupations Classified Elsewhere

Managers of food, beverage and tobacco processing (in 0911 *Manufacturing Managers*)

Supervisors of meat and fish inspectors (in 2222 *Agricultural and Fish Products Inspectors*)

9214 Supervisors, Plastic and Rubber Products Manufacturing

Supervisors in this group supervise and co-ordinate the activities of workers who operate processing machines and who fabricate, assemble and inspect rubber and plastic products.

Profile Summary

APTITUDES

G	V	N	S	P	Q	K	F	M
3	3	3	4	4	3	3	4	3

INTERESTS
Dio

DATA PEOPLE THINGS (DPT)
138

PHYSICAL ACTIVITIES (PA)

V	C	H	B	L	S
3	0	2	3	0	1

ENVIRONMENTAL CONDITIONS (EC)
L1, D1, D3

EDUCATION/TRAINING
2+, 4+

Examples of Job Titles

Foreman/woman, Blow Moulding

Foreman/woman, Calendering - Rubber and Plastic Manufacturing

Foreman/woman, Extruding - Rubber and Plastic Manufacturing

Supervisor, Injection Moulding

Supervisor, Plastic Products Manufacturing

Supervisor, Rubber Products Manufacturing

Supervisor, Tire Building

Descriptor Profile

Main Characteristics

Occupations in this group are characterized by the following aptitudes, interests and worker functions as they relate to main duties:

- **General learning ability** to establish methods to meet work schedules and recommend measures to improve productivity and product quality

- **Verbal ability** to train staff in job duties, safety procedures and company policies, and to recommend personnel actions such as hirings and promotions

- **Numerical ability** and **clerical perception** to requisition materials and supplies, and to prepare production and other reports

- **Directive interest** in **supervising** the activities of production workers who operate processing machines and who fabricate, assemble, finish and inspect plastic and rubber parts and products

- **Innovative interest** in **co-ordinating** work activities and production schedules with other departments; and in resolving work problems

- **Objective interest** in understanding the operation of processing machines and other equipment used in plastic and rubber products manufacturing; may set up machines and equipment

9214

Physical Activities

Vision
   3 Near and far vision

Colour Discrimination
   0 Not relevant

Hearing
   2 Verbal interaction

Body Position
   3 Sitting, standing, walking

Limb Co-ordination
   0 Not relevant

Strength
   1 Limited

Environmental Conditions

Location
   L1 Regulated inside climate

Discomforts
   D1 Noise
   D3 Odours

Employment Requirements

Education/Training
   2+, 4+

- Some secondary school education is usually required.

- Several years of experience as a machine operator or an assembler in rubber or plastic products manufacturing is usually required.

- Completion of a basic course in statistical process control (SPC) may be required for supervisors in plastic products manufacturing.

Workplaces/Employers

Plastic parts divisions of manufacturing companies

Rubber and plastic products manufacturing companies

Similar Occupations Classified Elsewhere

Labourers in Rubber and Plastic Products Manufacturing (9615)

Plastic Products Assemblers, Finishers and Inspectors (9495)

Plastics Processing Machine Operators (9422)

Rubber Processing Machine Operators and Related Workers (9423)

9215 Supervisors, Forest Products Processing

Supervisors in this group supervise and co-ordinate the activities of workers in the following groups: *Pulping Control Operators* (9233), *Papermaking and Coating Control Operators* (9234), *Labourers in Wood, Pulp and Paper Processing* (9614) and *Machine Operators and Related Workers in Pulp and Paper Production and Wood Processing* (943).

Profile Summary

APTITUDES

G	V	N	S	P	Q	K	F	M
3	3	3	3	4	3	3	4	3

INTERESTS
Dio

DATA PEOPLE THINGS (DPT)
138

PHYSICAL ACTIVITIES (PA)

V	C	H	B	L	S
3	0	2	3	0	1

ENVIRONMENTAL CONDITIONS (EC)
L1, D1, D3

EDUCATION/TRAINING
4+, 6+, R

Examples of Job Titles

Coating Room Foreman/woman - Pulp and Paper

Foreman/woman, Lumber Grading

Foreman/woman, Plywood Making

Foreman/woman, Shingle Mill

Foreman/woman, Waferboard

Foreman/woman, Wood Treating Plant

Paper Machine Foreman/woman

Paper Mill Foreman/woman

Pulp Mill Foreman/woman

Sawmill Foreman/woman

Shift Operating Supervisor - Pulp and Paper

Supervisor, Paper Converting

Tour Foreman/woman - Pulp and Paper

Descriptor Profile

Main Characteristics

Occupations in this group are characterized by the following aptitudes, interests and worker functions as they relate to main duties:

- **General learning ability** to establish methods to meet work schedules and recommend measures to improve productivity and product quality

- **Verbal ability** to train staff in job duties, safety procedures and company policies, to recommend personnel actions such as hirings and promotions, and to administer collective agreements

- **Numerical ability** and **clerical perception** to requisition materials and supplies, and to prepare production and other reports

- **Spatial perception** to monitor safety conditions and ensure that systems and equipment are operating efficiently

- **Directive interest** in supervising the activities of workers who operate pulp and paper mills, paper converting mills, sawmills, planing mills, plywood, waferboard and other wood and paper products mills; and in ensuring that proper maintenance and repairs are performed

- **Innovative interest** in co-ordinating work activities and production schedules with other departments; and in resolving work problems

- **Objective interest** in understanding the operation of equipment and machinery used in forest products processing; may set up machines and equipment

9215

Physical Activities

Vision
   3 Near and far vision

Colour Discrimination
   0 Not relevant

Hearing
   2 Verbal interaction

Body Position
   3 Sitting, standing, walking

Limb Co-ordination
   0 Not relevant

Strength
   1 Limited

Environmental Conditions

Location
   L1 Regulated inside climate

Discomforts
   D1 Noise
   D3 Odours

Employment Requirements

Education/Training
   4+, 6+, R

- Completion of secondary school is required.

- A college diploma in pulp and paper technology or a related discipline may be required for some pulp and paper supervisor positions.

- Several years of some combination of formal and on-the-job training are provided.

- Several years of experience in the most senior occupation being supervised are often required.

- Certificates, such as in lumber grading and industrial first aid, and a competency certificate in natural gas may be required.

Workplaces/Employers

Paper converting companies

Planing mills

Pulp and paper companies

Sawmills

Waferboard plants

Wood processing companies

Wood treatment plants

Occupational Options

Mobility is possible among positions employing similar technology or producing similar products.

Progression to managerial positions is possible with experience.

Similar Occupations Classified Elsewhere

Manufacturing Managers (0911)

9216 Supervisors, Textile Processing

Supervisors in this group supervise and co-ordinate the activities of workers who process fibre into yarn and thread; who weave, knit and fabricate textile products; who bleach, dye and finish textile products; and who inspect textile products.

Profile Summary

APTITUDES

G	V	N	S	P	Q	K	F	M
3	3	3	4	4	3	3	4	3

INTERESTS
Dio

DATA PEOPLE THINGS (DPT)
138

PHYSICAL ACTIVITIES (PA)

V	C	H	B	L	S
3	1	2	3	0	1

ENVIRONMENTAL CONDITIONS (EC)
L1, D1, D4

EDUCATION/TRAINING
3+, 6+

Examples of Job Titles

Dye Room Supervisor
Finishing Supervisor - Textiles
Foreman/woman, Textile Processing
Spinning Supervisor - Textiles
Supervisor, Knitting
Tufting Supervisor - Textiles
Weave Room Supervisor

Descriptor Profile

Main Characteristics

Occupations in this group are characterized by the following aptitudes, interests and worker functions as they relate to main duties:

- **General learning ability** to establish methods to meet work schedules and recommend measures to improve productivity and product quality

- **Verbal ability** to train staff in job duties, safety procedures and company policies, and to recommend personnel actions such as hirings and promotions

- **Numerical ability** and **clerical perception** to requisition materials and supplies, and to prepare production and other reports

- **Directive interest** in supervising the activities of production workers who operate machines to process fibre, yarn, thread and textiles, and who bleach, dye, finish and inspect textiles

- **Innovative interest** in co-ordinating work activities and production schedules with other departments; and in resolving work problems

- **Objective interest** in understanding the functioning of equipment and machinery used in textile processing; may set up machines and equipment

9216

Physical Activities

Vision
  3 Near and far vision

Colour Discrimination
  1 Relevant

Hearing
  2 Verbal interaction

Body Position
  3 Sitting, standing, walking

Limb Co-ordination
  0 Not relevant

Strength
  1 Limited

Environmental Conditions

Location
  L1 Regulated inside climate

Discomforts
  D1 Noise
  D4 Non-toxic dusts

Employment Requirements

Education/Training
  3+, 6+

- Completion of secondary school is usually required.

- A college diploma in textile technology or in a related field may be required for some supervisory positions.

- Several years experience as a textile mechanic or repairer, textile technician or operator in a process such as weaving, tufting or dyeing are usually required.

- Experience may be required in a specific process or with a specific type or model of equipment.

Workplaces/Employers

Textile companies

Occupational Options

There is mobility among jobs in this group.

Progression to managerial positions is possible with experience.

Similar Occupations Classified Elsewhere

Textile Machinery Mechanics and Repairers (7317)

Technologists and technicians in textile manufacturing (in 2233 *Industrial Engineering and Manufacturing Technologists and Technicians*)

Master dyers and textile colour technologists (in 2211 *Applied Chemical Technologists and Technicians*)

9221 Supervisors, Motor Vehicle Assembling

Supervisors in this group supervise and co-ordinate the activities of workers in motor vehicle production departments.

Profile Summary

APTITUDES

G	V	N	S	P	Q	K	F	M
3	3	3	4	3	3	4	4	4

INTERESTS
Dim

DATA PEOPLE THINGS (DPT)
138

PHYSICAL ACTIVITIES (PA)

V	C	H	B	L	S
3	1	2	3	0	1

ENVIRONMENTAL CONDITIONS (EC)
L1

EDUCATION/TRAINING
3+

Examples of Job Titles

Area Co-ordinator - Motor Vehicle Manufacturing

Assembly Foreman/woman - Motor Vehicle Manufacturing

Foreman/woman - Motor Vehicle Manufacturing

General Supervisor, Assembly - Motor Vehicle Manufacturing

Supervisor, Assembly - Motor Vehicle Manufacturing

Zone Supervisor, Assembly - Motor Vehicle Manufacturing

Descriptor Profile

Main Characteristics

Occupations in this group are characterized by the following aptitudes, interests and worker functions as they relate to main duties:

- **General learning ability** to establish methods to meet work schedules and recommend measures to improve productivity and product quality

- **Verbal ability** to train staff in job duties, safety procedures and company policies and to recommend personnel actions such as hirings and promotions

- **Clerical perception** to prepare production and other reports

- **Directive interest** in **supervising** the activities of workers in motor vehicle manufacturing production departments such as body shop, chassis, paint, trim and hardware and final assembly

- **Innovative interest** in **co-ordinating** work activities with other units; and in resolving work problems

- **Methodical interest** in requisitioning materials and supplies, and scheduling the activities of workers

Physical Activities

Vision
   3 Near and far vision

Colour Discrimination
   1 Relevant

Hearing
   2 Verbal interaction

Body Position
   3 Sitting, standing, walking

Limb Co-ordination
   0 Not relevant

Strength
   1 Limited

Environmental Conditions

Location
   L1 Regulated inside climate

Employment Requirements

Education/Training
   3+

- Completion of secondary school is usually required.

- Several years of experience as a production worker in motor vehicle manufacturing are required.

Workplaces/Employers

Automobile, van and light truck manufacturing plants

Similar Occupations Classified Elsewhere

Motor Vehicle Assemblers, Inspectors and Testers (9482)

Supervisors of engine assemblers (in 9226 *Supervisors, Other Mechanical and Metal Products Manufacturing*)

9222 Supervisors, Electronics Manufacturing

Supervisors in this group supervise and co-ordinate the activities of workers who assemble, fabricate, test, repair and inspect electronic parts, components and systems.

Profile Summary

APTITUDES

G	V	N	S	P	Q	K	F	M
3	3	3	3	4	3	3	4	3

INTERESTS

Dio

DATA PEOPLE THINGS (DPT)

138

PHYSICAL ACTIVITIES (PA)

V	C	H	B	L	S
3	1	2	3	0	1

ENVIRONMENTAL CONDITIONS (EC)

L1

EDUCATION/TRAINING

3+, 6+

Examples of Job Titles

Assembly Supervisor

Foreman/woman, Electronic Assembly

Foreman/woman, Final Assembly and Test

Foreman/woman, Printed Circuit Board Fabrication

Production Supervisor

Supervisor, Assembly and Test

Systems Test Foreman/woman

Test Supervisor

Descriptor Profile

Main Characteristics

Occupations in this group are characterized by the following aptitudes, interests and worker functions as they relate to main duties:

- **General learning ability** to establish methods to meet work schedules, co-ordinate work activities with other departments and recommend work measures to improve productivity

- **Verbal ability** to train workers in job duties, safety procedures and company policies, and to recommend personnel actions such as hirings and promotions

- **Numerical ability** and **clerical perception** to requisition materials and supplies, and to prepare production and other reports

- **Directive interest** in **supervising** the activities of workers who assemble, fabricate, inspect and test electronic and electromechanical assemblies, subassemblies, parts and components; and in ensuring that safety rules and regulations are followed

- **Innovative interest** in **co-ordinating** the activities and production schedules of workers, related helpers and labourers; and in resolving work problems

- **Objective interest** in understanding the functioning of equipment and machinery used in electronics manufacturing; may set up machines and equipment

9222

Physical Activities

Vision
   3 Near and far vision

Colour Discrimination
   1 Relevant

Hearing
   2 Verbal interaction

Body Position
   3 Sitting, standing, walking

Limb Co-ordination
   0 Not relevant

Strength
   1 Limited

Environmental Conditions

Location
   L1 Regulated inside climate

Employment Requirements

Education/Training
   3+, 6+

- Completion of secondary school is usually required.

- Several years of experience as an electronics assembler, fabricator, inspector or tester are usually required.

- Completion of a two-year college program in electronics may be required.

Workplaces/Employers

Electronics manufacturing plants

Similar Occupations Classified Elsewhere

Electrical and Electronics Engineering Technologists and Technicians (2241)

Electronic Service Technicians (Household and Business Equipment) (2242)

Electronics Assemblers, Fabricators, Inspectors and Testers (9483)

Supervisors, Electrical Products Manufacturing (9223)

9223 Supervisors, Electrical Products Manufacturing

Supervisors in this group supervise and co-ordinate the activities of workers who assemble, fabricate and inspect electrical components, appliances, motors and industrial equipment.

Profile Summary

APTITUDES

G	V	N	S	P	Q	K	F	M
3	3	3	3	4	3	3	4	3

INTERESTS
Dio

DATA PEOPLE THINGS (DPT)
138

PHYSICAL ACTIVITIES (PA)

V	C	H	B	L	S
3	1	2	3	0	1

ENVIRONMENTAL CONDITIONS (EC)
L1

EDUCATION/TRAINING
3+

Examples of Job Titles

Foreman/woman, Electrical Motor Assembly

Foreman/woman, Electrical Transformer Assembly

Foreman/woman, Switchgear Assembly

Supervisor, Electrical Appliance Assembly

Supervisor, Electrical Equipment Manufacturing

Descriptor Profile

Main Characteristics

Occupations in this group are characterized by the following aptitudes, interests and worker functions as they relate to main duties:

- **General learning ability** to establish methods to meet work schedules, co-ordinate work activities with other departments and recommend work measures to improve productivity

- **Verbal ability** to train staff in job duties, safety procedures and company policies, and to recommend personnel actions such as hirings and promotions

- **Numerical ability** and **clerical perception** to requisition materials and supplies, and to prepare production and other reports

- **Directive interest** in **supervising** the activities of workers who assemble, fabricate and inspect various types of electrical apparatus such as appliances, batteries, motors, transformers, generators, and switchgear and control equipment

- **Innovative interest** in **co-ordinating** the activities of workers and production schedules; and in resolving work problems

- **Objective interest** in understanding the functioning of equipment and machinery used to manufacture electrical components, appliances, motors and industrial equipment; may set up machines and equipment

9223

Physical Activities

Vision
   3   Near and far vision

Colour Discrimination
   1   Relevant

Hearing
   2   Verbal interaction

Body Position
   3   Sitting, standing, walking

Limb Co-ordination
   0   Not relevant

Strength
   1   Limited

Environmental Conditions

Location
   L1   Regulated inside climate

Employment Requirements

Education/Training
   3+

- Completion of secondary school is usually required.

- Several years of experience in the same company as an assembler, inspector or lead hand are required.

Workplaces/Employers

Electrical products manufacturing companies

Similar Occupations Classified Elsewhere

Supervisors, Electronics Manufacturing (9222)

Contractors and Supervisors, Electrical Trades and Telecommunications Occupations (7212)

9224 Supervisors, Furniture and Fixtures Manufacturing

Supervisors in this group supervise and co-ordinate the activities of workers who manufacture furniture and fixtures made of wood and other materials.

Profile Summary

APTITUDES

G	V	N	S	P	Q	K	F	M
3	3	3	4	3	3	4	4	4

INTERESTS
Dio

DATA PEOPLE THINGS (DPT)
138

PHYSICAL ACTIVITIES (PA)

V	C	H	B	L	S
3	1	2	3	0	1

ENVIRONMENTAL CONDITIONS (EC)
L1

EDUCATION/TRAINING
2+

Examples of Job Titles

Foreman/woman, Cabinetmakers

Foreman/woman, Desk Assembly

Foreman/woman, Furniture Assembly

Laminating Foreman/woman

Supervisor, Furniture and Fixture Manufacturing

Supervisor, Furniture Finishers

Supervisor, Woodworking Machine Operators

Woodworking Machine Operators Foreman/woman

Descriptor Profile

Main Characteristics

Occupations in this group are characterized by the following aptitudes, interests and worker functions as they relate to main duties:

- **General learning ability** to establish methods to meet work schedules, co-ordinate work activities with other departments and recommend work measures to improve productivity and product quality

- **Verbal ability** to train staff in job duties, safety procedures and company policies, and to recommend personnel actions such as hirings and promotions

- **Numerical ability** and **clerical perception** to requisition materials and supplies, and to prepare production and other reports

- **Directive interest** in **supervising** the activities of workers who assemble furniture and fixtures of various materials, operate woodworking machines and finish furniture to specified colour and finish

- **Innovative interest** in **co-ordinating** work activities and production schedules; and in resolving work problems

- **Objective interest** in understanding the operation of equipment and machinery used in the manufacture of furniture and fixtures made of wood and other materials

9224

Physical Activities

Vision
   3 Near and far vision

Colour Discrimination
   1 Relevant

Hearing
   2 Verbal interaction

Body Position
   3 Sitting, standing, walking

Limb Co-ordination
   0 Not relevant

Strength
   1 Limited

Environmental Conditions

Location
   L1 Regulated inside climate

Employment Requirements

Education/Training
   2+

- Some secondary school education is usually required.

- Experience in the same company, as a furniture and fixture assembler, woodworking machine operator or furniture finisher is usually required.

Workplaces/Employers

Furniture and fixtures manufacturing establishments

Similar Occupations Classified Elsewhere

Supervisors of millwork and wood product manufacturing other than furniture and fixture, and wood machining (in 9227 *Supervisors, Other Products Manufacturing and Assembly*)

9225 Supervisors, Fabric, Fur and Leather Products Manufacturing

Supervisors in this group supervise and co-ordinate the activities of workers in the following groups: *Sewing Machine Operators* (9451), *Fabric, Fur and Leather Cutters* (9452), *Hide and Pelt Processing Workers* (9453) and *Inspectors and Testers, Fabric, Fur and Leather Products Manufacturing* (9454).

Profile Summary

APTITUDES

G	V	N	S	P	Q	K	F	M
3	3	3	4	3	3	4	4	4

INTERESTS
Dio

DATA PEOPLE THINGS (DPT)
138

PHYSICAL ACTIVITIES (PA)

V	C	H	B	L	S
3	1	2	3	0	1

ENVIRONMENTAL CONDITIONS (EC)
L1

EDUCATION/TRAINING
2+

Examples of Job Titles

Boot and Shoe Foreman/woman

Canvas Products Manufacturing Foreman/woman

Cutting Department Foreman/woman, Fabric

Embroidery Supervisor, Fabric Products

Fur Dressing Foreman/woman

Hat and Cap Maker Foreman/woman

Sample Room Foreman/woman, Leather Products

Sewing Machine Operator Supervisor

Stitching Department Supervisor

Tannery Foreman/woman

Descriptor Profile

Main Characteristics

Occupations in this group are characterized by the following aptitudes, interests and worker functions as they relate to main duties:

- **General learning ability** to establish methods to meet work schedules, co-ordinate work activities with other units and recommend measures to improve productivity and product quality

- **Verbal ability** to train staff in job duties, safety procedures and company policies, and to recommend personnel actions such as hirings and promotions

- **Numerical ability** and **clerical perception** to requisition materials and supplies, and to prepare production and other reports

- **Directive interest** in **supervising** the activities of workers who cut and stitch fabric, fur or leather garments and other products in the manufacturing process

- **Innovative interest** in **co-ordinating** work activities and production schedules; and in resolving work problems

- **Objective interest** in understanding the operation of equipment and machinery used in fabric, fur and leather products manufacturing

9225

Physical Activities

Vision
   3 Near and far vision

Colour Discrimination
   1 Relevant

Hearing
   2 Verbal interaction

Body Position
   3 Sitting, standing, walking

Limb Co-ordination
   0 Not relevant

Strength
   1 Limited

Environmental Conditions

Location
   L1 Regulated inside climate

Employment Requirements

Education/Training
   2+

- Some secondary school education may be required.

- Several years of experience as a worker in the group being supervised are required.

Workplaces/Employers

Clothing and textile manufacturers

Fabric products manufacturers

Tanneries

Occupational Options

There is little mobility among the various types of supervisors in this group.

Similar Occupations Classified Elsewhere

Supervisors, Textile Processing (9216)

9226 Supervisors, Other Mechanical and Metal Products Manufacturing

Supervisors in this group supervise and co-ordinate the activities of workers who fabricate, assemble and inspect mechanical and metal products such as aircraft and aircraft parts, heavy trucks, buses, trailers, motor vehicle engines, transmissions, heating equipment, and commercial refrigeration and similar metal products.

Profile Summary

APTITUDES

G	V	N	S	P	Q	K	F	M
3	3	3	4	3	3	4	4	3

INTERESTS

Dio

DATA PEOPLE THINGS (DPT)

138

PHYSICAL ACTIVITIES (PA)

V	C	H	B	L	S
3	0	2	3	0	1

ENVIRONMENTAL CONDITIONS (EC)

L1, D1

EDUCATION/TRAINING

2+

Examples of Job Titles

Aircraft Assembly Foreman/woman

Engine Assembly Supervisor (Except Aircraft)

Foreman/woman, Metalworking Machine Operators

Foreman/woman, Mobile Home Assembly

Supervisor, Aircraft Assembly

Supervisor, Helicopter Assembly

Supervisor, Snowmobile Assembly

Truck Trailer Assembly Foreman/woman

Descriptor Profile

Main Characteristics

Occupations in this group are characterized by the following aptitudes, interests and worker functions as they relate to main duties:

- **General learning ability** to establish methods to meet work schedules, co-ordinate work activities with other departments and recommend measures to improve productivity and product quality

- **Verbal ability** to train staff in job duties, safety procedures and company policies, and to recommend personnel actions such as hirings and promotions

- **Numerical ability** and **clerical perception** to requisition materials and supplies, and to prepare production and other reports

- **Directive interest** in **supervising** the activities of workers who assemble and inspect products such as aircraft, buses, heavy trucks, transmissions, automobile engines, and refrigeration and heating equipment

- **Innovative interest** in **co-ordinating** work activities and production schedules; and in resolving work problems

- **Objective interest** in understanding the operation of equipment and machinery used in mechanical and metal products manufacturing; may set up machinery and equipment

9226

Physical Activities

Vision
   3 Near and far vision

Colour Discrimination
   0 Not relevant

Hearing
   2 Verbal interaction

Body Position
   3 Sitting, standing, walking

Limb Co-ordination
   0 Not relevant

Strength
   1 Limited

Environmental Conditions

Location
   L1 Regulated inside climate

Discomforts
   D1 Noise

Employment Requirements

Education/Training
   2+

- Completion of secondary school may be required.

- Several years of experience as an assembler or inspector in the same company are usually required.

Workplaces/Employers

Mechanical and metal products manufacturing companies

Similar Occupations Classified Elsewhere

Supervisors, Electrical Products Manufacturing (9223)

Supervisors, Motor Vehicle Assembling (9221)

Aircraft engine assembly supervisors (in 7216 *Contractors and Supervisors, Mechanic Trades*)

Supervisors of machine fitters (in 7214 *Contractors and Supervisors, Metal Forming, Shaping and Erecting Trades*)

9227 Supervisors, Other Products Manufacturing and Assembly

This group includes supervisors not elsewhere classified who oversee and co-ordinate the activities of workers assembling, fabricating and inspecting products such as jewellery, clocks and watches, millwork, sporting goods, toys and other miscellaneous products.

Profile Summary

APTITUDES

G	V	N	S	P	Q	K	F	M
3	3	3	4	4	3	3	3	3

INTERESTS
Dio

DATA PEOPLE THINGS (DPT)
138

PHYSICAL ACTIVITIES (PA)

V	C	H	B	L	S
3	0	2	3	0	1

ENVIRONMENTAL CONDITIONS (EC)
L1

EDUCATION/TRAINING
2+

Examples of Job Titles

Foreman/woman, Bicycle Assembly

Foreman/woman, Clock and Watch Assembly

Foreman/woman, Jewellery Manufacturing

Supervisor, Millwork Assembly

Supervisor, Silverware Manufacturing

Supervisor, Sports Equipment Assembly

Supervisor, Toy Manufacturing

Descriptor Profile

Main Characteristics

Occupations in this group are characterized by the following aptitudes, interests and worker functions as they relate to main duties:

- **General learning ability** to establish methods to meet work schedules, co-ordinate work activities with other departments and recommend measures to improve productivity and product quality

- **Verbal ability** to train workers in job duties, safety procedures and company policies, and to recommend personnel actions such as hirings and promotions

- **Numerical ability** and **clerical perception** to requisition materials and supplies, and to prepare production and other reports

- **Motor co-ordination** and **finger** and **manual dexterity** to demonstrate assembly and fabrication methods

- **Directive interest** in **supervising** the activities of workers who assemble, fabricate and inspect products such as jewellery, clocks, watches, bicycles, millwork, sporting goods and toys

- **Innovative interest** in **co-ordinating** work activities with other departments; and in resolving work problems

- **Objective interest** in understanding the functioning of equipment and machinery used to manufacture and assemble products such as jewellery, clocks, watches, bicycles, millwork, sporting goods and toys; may set up machinery and equipment

9227

Physical Activities

Vision
   3 Near and far vision

Colour Discrimination
   0 Not relevant

Hearing
   2 Verbal interaction

Body Position
   3 Sitting, standing, walking

Limb Co-ordination
   0 Not relevant

Strength
   1 Limited

Environmental Conditions

Location
   L1 Regulated inside climate

Employment Requirements

Education/Training
   2+

- Completion of secondary school may be required.

- Several years of experience as an assembler or inspector in the same company are usually required.

Workplaces/Employers

Manufacturing companies

Occupational Options

There is little mobility among different types of supervisors in this group.

Similar Occupations Classified Elsewhere

Supervisors of woodworking machine operators (in 9224 *Supervisors, Furniture and Fixtures Manufacturing*)

9231 Central Control and Process Operators, Mineral and Metal Processing

Central Control and Process Operators, Mineral and Metal Processing, operate and monitor multi-functional process control machinery and equipment to control the processing of mineral ores, metals and cement.

Profile Summary

APTITUDES
G	V	N	S	P	Q	K	F	M
3	3	3	3	3	3	4	4	4

INTERESTS
ODi

DATA PEOPLE THINGS (DPT)
262

PHYSICAL ACTIVITIES (PA)
V	C	H	B	L	S
3	0	2	3	1	1

ENVIRONMENTAL CONDITIONS (EC)
L1

EDUCATION/TRAINING
4

Examples of Job Titles

Blast Furnace Operator
Central Control Caster
Central Control Room Operator
Console Operator - Cement Manufacturing
Roaster Operator
Rolling Mill Control Operator

Descriptor Profile

Main Characteristics

Occupations in this group are characterized by the following aptitudes, interests and worker functions as they relate to main duties:

- **General learning ability** to co-ordinate and monitor the operation of a particular aspect of mineral ore, metal and cement processing production through control panels, computer terminals and other control systems, usually from central control rooms

- **Verbal ability** to provide and organize training for production crews

- **Numerical ability** to maintain shift logs of production and other data

- **Clerical perception** to prepare production and other reports

- **Objective interest** in **controlling** the operation of multi-functional processing machinery to grind, separate, filter, melt, roast, treat, refine and otherwise process mineral ores; and in starting up and shutting down production systems in cases of emergency or as required by schedules

- **Directive interest** in **speaking** to members of production crews including machine and process operators, tenders, assistants and helpers to co-ordinate and supervise their activities

- **Innovative interest** in **analyzing** computer printouts, video monitors and gauges to verify specified processing conditions and to make necessary adjustments

9231

Physical Activities

Vision
  3 Near and far vision

Colour Discrimination
  0 Not relevant

Hearing
  2 Verbal interaction

Body Position
  3 Sitting, standing, walking

Limb Co-ordination
  1 Upper limb co-ordination

Strength
  1 Limited

Environmental Conditions

Location
  L1 Regulated inside climate

Employment Requirements

Education/Training
4

- Completion of secondary school is usually required.

- On-the-job training is provided.

- Several years of experience as a machine or process operator, usually in the same company or production department, are required.

Workplaces/Employers

Mineral, ore and metal processing plants such as:

Aluminium plants

Cement processing plants

Metal refineries

Mineral ore mills

Steel mills

Uranium processing plants

Occupational Options

There is little mobility among the various types of central control and process operators within the mineral and metal processing industry.

With experience, central control and process operators may progress to supervisory positions in mineral and metal processing.

Similar Occupations Classified Elsewhere

Machine Operators, Mineral and Metal Processing (9411)

Supervisors, Mineral and Metal Processing (9211)

9232 Petroleum, Gas and Chemical Process Operators

Petroleum, Gas and Chemical Process Operators monitor and operate petroleum, petrochemical and chemical plants and monitor, adjust and maintain processing units and equipment in these plants.

Profile Summary

APTITUDES

G	V	N	S	P	Q	K	F	M
3	3	3	3	4	4	4	3	4

INTERESTS
Old

DATA PEOPLE THINGS (DPT)
262

PHYSICAL ACTIVITIES (PA)

V	C	H	B	L	S
2	0	1	3	1	2

ENVIRONMENTAL CONDITIONS (EC)
L1, H1, D1, D3

EDUCATION/TRAINING
4, 5, 6, R

Examples of Job Titles

Acid Plant Operator
Cell Room Operator, Chlor-alkali Plant
Chemical Process Operator
Chief Operator - Chemical Processing
Fractionator Operator
Gas Field Operator
Gas Plant Operator
Gas Recovery Operator
Lead Operator - Chemical Processing
Liquefaction Plant Operator
Master Operator - Chemical Processing
Petroleum Process Operator
Pharmaceutical Processing Operator
Pipeline Compressor Station Operator
Process Technician
Refinery Operator
Senior Operating Technician

Descriptor Profile

Main Characteristics

Occupations in this group are characterized by the following aptitudes, interests and worker functions as they relate to main duties:

- **General learning ability** to monitor and optimize physical and chemical processes for several processing units, and to monitor outside process equipment; may be cross-trained in a skilled trade and work in that trade during shift cycles; may rotate between different processing units during shift cycles

- **Numerical ability** to sample products, perform tests, record data, carry out statistical process control on process operations and write production logs

- **Finger dexterity** to adjust equipment, valves, pumps and controls, and process equipment

- **Objective interest** in **controlling** process start-up, shut-down and trouble shooting; and in operating electronic or computerized control panels from a central control room; and in shutting down, isolating and preparing process units or production equipment for maintenance

- **Innovative interest** in **analyzing** information to develop operator procedures for normal operations, start-up and shut-down of units; and in participating in safety audits and programs, and in providing emergency response when required

- **Directive interest** in **speaking** with team members and trainees to authorize or co-sign maintenance work orders; may work in a team with shared supervisory responsibilities and participate in training other workers

9232

Physical Activities

Vision
  2   Near vision

Colour Discrimination
  0   Not relevant

Hearing
  1   Limited

Body Position
  3   Sitting, standing, walking

Limb Co-ordination
  1   Upper limb co-ordination

Strength
  2   Light

Environmental Conditions

Location
  L1   Regulated inside climate

Hazards
  H1   Dangerous chemical substances

Discomforts
  D1   Noise
  D3   Odours

Employment Requirements

Education/Training
  4, 5, 6, R

- Completion of secondary school is required. Mathematics, chemistry and physics subjects are often specified.

- A college diploma in process operation, sciences or a related subject may be required for some positions.

- Petroleum and chemical process operators and process technicians require completion of several years of formal company training.

- Experience as a petroleum or chemical process operator in all the operating units controlled by the central control room is required for chief operators.

- Company certification as a petroleum process operator or technician may be required.

- A provincial stationary engineer licence, compressor operator or refrigeration certificate may be required when certain kinds of equipment are included in the process.

- Certification in the transportation of dangerous goods (TDG), first aid, firefighting or workplace hazardous materials information system (WHMIS) may be required.

Workplaces/Employers

Industrial, agricultural and specialty chemical companies

Petroleum and natural gas processing companies

Pharmaceutical companies

Pipeline and petrochemical companies

Occupational Options

There is considerable mobility among jobs within a company, often as part of a formal development or training program.

Mobility to other petroleum or chemical processing plants is possible, but may be limited by the usual practice of training and promoting workers from within the establishment.

Progression to supervisory or managerial positions is possible with experience.

Similar Occupations Classified Elsewhere

Chemical Plant Machine Operators (9421)

Supervisors, Petroleum, Gas and Chemical Processing and Utilities (9212)

Remarks

Occupations in this group may involve exposure to hazards of toxic, flammable or explosive chemicals and personal protective equipment may be required.

9233 Pulping Control Operators

Pulping Control Operators operate and monitor multi-functional process control machinery and equipment to control the processing of wood, scrap pulp and other cellulose materials in the production of pulp.

Profile Summary

APTITUDES

G	V	N	S	P	Q	K	F	M
3	3	3	4	3	3	4	4	4

INTERESTS
Old

DATA PEOPLE THINGS (DPT)
262

PHYSICAL ACTIVITIES (PA)

V	C	H	B	L	S
2	0	1	3	1	1

ENVIRONMENTAL CONDITIONS (EC)
L1, H7*, D3

EDUCATION/TRAINING
4, 5, 6, R

Examples of Job Titles

Beater Engineer
Bleach Plant Operator
Cook - Pulp and Paper
Digester Operator
Pulping Control Operator
Pulping Group Operator
Thermo-Mechanical Pulp Operator

Descriptor Profile

Main Characteristics

Occupations in this group are characterized by the following aptitudes, interests and worker functions as they relate to main duties:

- **General learning ability** to co-ordinate and monitor the operation of screening equipment, washing equipment, digesters, mixing tanks and other pulp-processing equipment from automated panel boards, in a central control room

- **Verbal** and **numerical ability** to complete and maintain production reports

- **Form** and **clerical perception** to observe panel indicators, gauges, video monitors and other instruments from a central control room in order to detect equipment malfunctions and ensure pulp processes are operating within prescribed production limits

- **Objective interest** in **controlling** the processing of wood, scrap pulp and other cellulose materials

- **Innovative interest** in **analyzing** instrument readings and production test samples to make adjustments to production process and equipment

- **Directive interest** in **signalling** to pulp machine operators to make required adjustments to pulp production process and equipment

9233

Physical Activities

Vision
  2 Near vision

Colour Discrimination
  0 Not relevant

Hearing
  1 Limited

Body Position
  3 Sitting, standing, walking

Limb Co-ordination
  1 Upper limb co-ordination

Strength
  1 Limited

Environmental Conditions

Location
  L1 Regulated inside climate

Hazards
  H7*Fire, steam, hot surfaces

Discomforts
  D3 Odours

Employment Requirements

Education/Training
4, 5, 6, R

- Completion of secondary school is required.

- A college or other program in forest products processing or a related subject may be required.

- Completion of several weeks of formal company training and several months of on-the-job training is required.

- Several years experience as a pulp mill machine operator within the same company is usually required.

- Certificate in industrial first aid may be required.

Workplaces/Employers

Pulp and paper companies

Occupational Options

There is limited mobility among jobs within this occupational group.

Progression to supervisory positions is possible with experience.

Similar Occupations Classified Elsewhere

Pulp Mill Machine Operators (9432)

Supervisors, Forest Products Processing (9215)

Remarks

*Environmental Conditions

- For some occupations in this group, **Hazards** H7 (Fire, steam, hot surfaces) may also apply.

9234 Papermaking and Coating Control Operators

Papermaking and Coating Control Operators operate and monitor multi-functional process control machinery and equipment to control the processing of paper, paper pulp and paperboard.

Profile Summary

APTITUDES

G	V	N	S	P	Q	K	F	M
3	3	4	3	4	4	4	4	4

INTERESTS
Old

DATA PEOPLE THINGS (DPT)
262

PHYSICAL ACTIVITIES (PA)

V	C	H	B	L	S
2	0	1	3	1	1

ENVIRONMENTAL CONDITIONS (EC)
L1, H1*, D3

EDUCATION/TRAINING
4, 5, R

Examples of Job Titles

Back Tender, Paper Machine
Control Operator, Paper Machine
Fourdrinier Machine Operator
Panelboard Operator - Pulp and Paper
Paper Coating Machine Operator
Paper Machine Operator

Descriptor Profile

Main Characteristics

Occupations in this group are characterized by the following aptitudes, interests and worker functions as they relate to main duties:

- **General learning ability** to operate, co-ordinate and monitor the operation of papermaking and papercoating process equipment from a central control room or from machine consoles and control panels in an equipment cabin to make paper from pulp stock, mix chemicals and dyes, and coat paper products

- **Verbal ability** to complete and maintain production reports

- **Spatial perception** to observe panel indicators, gauges, video monitors and other instruments to detect equipment malfunctions and ensure papermaking and coating processes are operating according to process specifications

- **Objective interest** in **controlling** process operations and machinery using distributed control systems and process computers

- **Innovative interest** in **analyzing** instrument readings and production test samples to make adjustments to production process and equipment

- **Directive interest** in **signalling** to other papermaking and finishing machine operators to make required adjustments to papermaking and coating process and equipment

9234

Physical Activities

Vision
2 Near vision

Colour Discrimination
0 Not relevant

Hearing
1 Limited

Body Position
3 Sitting, standing, walking

Limb Co-ordination
1 Upper limb co-ordination

Strength
1 Limited

Environmental Conditions

Location
L1 Regulated inside climate

Hazards
H1*Dangerous chemical substances

Discomforts
D3 Odours

Employment Requirements

Education/Training
4, 5, R

- Completion of secondary school is required.

- Completion of several weeks of formal company training and several months of on-the-job training is required.

- Several years experience as a papermaking and finishing machine operator within the same company is usually required.

- Certificate in industrial first aid may be required.

- Competency certificate in natural gas may be required.

Workplaces/Employers

Pulp and paper companies

Occupational Options

There is limited mobility among jobs within this occupational group.

Progression to supervisory positions is possible with experience.

Similar Occupations Classified Elsewhere

Papermaking and Finishing Machine Operators (9433)

Supervisors, Forest Products Processing (9215)

Remarks

*Environmental Conditions

- For some occupations in this group, Hazards H1 (Dangerous chemical substances) may also apply.

9411 Machine Operators, Mineral and Metal Processing

Machine Operators in this group run machinery to process mineral ore and metal products.

Profile Summary

APTITUDES

G	V	N	S	P	Q	K	F	M
3	4	4	4	4	4	3	4	3

INTERESTS
OMi

DATA PEOPLE THINGS (DPT)
584

PHYSICAL ACTIVITIES (PA)

V	C	H	B	L	S
2	0	1	2	1	2

ENVIRONMENTAL CONDITIONS (EC)
L1, L2*, H3, H5*, H7*, D1, D3, D4*

EDUCATION/TRAINING
2

Examples of Job Titles

Aluminium Classifier
Asbestos Drier
Billet Heater
Brick and Tile Crusher Operator
Cement Miller
Extrusion Press Operator
Foil Winding Machine Operator
Furnace Charger
Ladle Pourer
Lead Refiner
Lime Kiln Operator
Mica Sheet Laminator
Quenching Car Operator
Sintering Machine Operator
Slurry Equipment Operator
Steel Roller
Uranium Classifier Operator
Zinc Cell Operator

Descriptor Profile

Main Characteristics

Occupations in this group are characterized by the following aptitudes, interests and worker functions as they relate to main duties:

- **General learning ability** and **manual dexterity** to set up, prepare and adjust mineral ore, metal and cement processing machinery to carry out one step in the mineral ore and metal processing operation

- **Motor co-ordination** to make adjustments to machinery

- **Objective interest** in **operating** single-function machinery to grind, separate, filter, mix, melt, treat, cast, roll, refine and otherwise process mineral ores

- **Methodical interest** in **copying** to record production information and complete reports

- **Innovative interest** in observing gauges, meters, computer printouts, video monitors and products to make sure machines operate properly, and to verify specified processing conditions

9411

Physical Activities

Vision
  2   Near vision

Colour Discrimination
  0   Not relevant

Hearing
  1   Limited

Body Position
  2   Standing and/or walking

Limb Co-ordination
  1   Upper limb co-ordination

Strength
  2   Light

Environmental Conditions

Location
  L1 Regulated inside climate
  L2* Unregulated inside climate

Hazards
  H3 Equipment, machinery, tools
  H5* Radiation
  H7* Fire, steam, hot surfaces

Discomforts
  D1 Noise
  D3 Odours
  D4* Non-toxic dusts

Employment Requirements

Education/Training
  2

- Some secondary school education is required.

- On-the-job training is provided.

- Experience as a labourer in mineral and metal processing is usually required for machine operators.

Workplaces/Employers

Mineral, ore and metal processing plants such as:

Aluminum plants

Cement processing plants

Metal refineries

Mineral ore mills

Steel mills

Uranium processing plants

Occupational Options

There is little mobility among the various types of machine operators within the mineral and metal processing industry.

With experience, machine operators may progress to central control and process operators in mineral and metal processing.

Similar Occupations Classified Elsewhere

Central Control and Process Operators, Mineral and Metal Processing (9231)

Foundry Workers (9412)

Glass Forming and Finishing Machine Operators and Glass Cutters (9413)

Concrete, Clay and Stone Forming Operators (9414)

Inspectors and Testers, Mineral and Metal Processing (9415)

Labourers in Mineral and Metal Processing (9611)

Remarks

*Environmental Conditions

- For some occupations in this group, the following Location L2 (Unregulated inside climate), Hazards H5 (Radiation) and H7 (Fire, steam, hot surfaces), and Discomforts D4 (Non-toxic dusts) may also apply:

9412.1 Manual Mouldmakers

Manual Mouldmakers make foundry moulds by hand and operate furnaces in foundries.

Profile Summary

APTITUDES

G	V	N	S	P	Q	K	F	M
3	3	4	3	3	4	3	3	3

INTERESTS
OMI

DATA PEOPLE THINGS (DPT)
381

PHYSICAL ACTIVITIES (PA)

V	C	H	B	L	S
2	0	1	4	1	4

ENVIRONMENTAL CONDITIONS (EC)
L2, H3, H7, D1, D3

EDUCATION/TRAINING
2+

Examples of Job Titles

Bench Moulder
Manual Moulder
Pit Moulder
Sand Moulder

Descriptor Profile

Main Characteristics

Occupations in this group are characterized by the following aptitudes, interests and worker functions as they relate to main duties:

- **General learning ability** to understand characteristics of metal, and to make sand moulds using patterns, moulding boxes and sand and hand tools

- **Spatial perception** to visualize finished parts from drawings and patterns

- **Form perception** to examine moulds to ensure that they conform to specified standards

- **Motor co-ordination** and **finger** and **manual dexterity** to use hand tools and measuring instruments to prepare moulds; may pour molten metal into moulds to produce metal castings

- **Objective interest** in **precision working** when making sand moulds and repairing damaged impressions; and in operating ovens to dry moulds

- **Methodical interest** in **compiling** information to follow bench, floor and pit moulding methods

- **Innovative interest** in attaining set limits, tolerances and standards

9412.1

Physical Activities

Vision
  2 Near vision

Colour Discrimination
  0 Not relevant

Hearing
  1 Limited

Body Position
  4 Other body positions

Limb Co-ordination
  1 Upper limb co-ordination

Strength
  4 Heavy

Environmental Conditions

Location
  L2 Unregulated inside climate

Hazards
  H3 Equipment, machinery, tools
  H7 Fire, steam, hot surfaces

Discomforts
  D1 Noise
  D3 Odours

Employment Requirements

Education/Training
  2+

- Some secondary school education is usually required.

- Up to two years of on-the-job training are required.

Workplaces/Employers

Foundry departments of metal products manufacturing companies

Metal foundries

Occupational Options

There is some mobility among workers in the 9412 group.

Progression to supervisory positions is possible with experience.

Similar Occupations Classified Elsewhere

Foundry labourers (in 9611 *Labourers in Mineral and Metal Processing*)

Furnace operators who operate furnaces to convert and refine primary metals (in 9411 *Machine Operators, Mineral and Metal Processing*)

Operators of continuous casting of steel or other primary metals or casting of primary ingots (in 9231 *Central Control and Process Operators, Mineral and Metal Processing*)

Supervisors of foundry workers (in 9211 *Supervisors, Mineral and Metal Processing*)

9412.2 Manual Coremakers

Manual Coremakers make foundry cores by hand and operate furnaces in foundries.

Profile Summary

APTITUDES

G	V	N	S	P	Q	K	F	M
4	4	4	4	3	4	3	4	3

INTERESTS
OMI

DATA PEOPLE THINGS (DPT)
381

PHYSICAL ACTIVITIES (PA)

V	C	H	B	L	S
2	0	1	4	1	3

ENVIRONMENTAL CONDITIONS (EC)
L2, H3, H7, D1, D3

EDUCATION/TRAINING
2

Examples of Job Titles

Sand Coremaker

Descriptor Profile

Main Characteristics

Occupations in this group are characterized by the following aptitudes, interests and worker functions as they relate to main duties:

- **General learning ability** to make cores for use in moulds to form holes or void spaces in castings using core boxes, sand, hammer and wire, and other reinforcing materials

- **Form perception** to observe contours of patterns for hollows in metal castings

- **Motor co-ordination** and **manual dexterity** to use hand tools and measuring instruments, and to coat cores with protective materials

- **Objective interest** in **precision working** when assembling sections to form completed cores; and in operating ovens to bake cores

- **Methodical interest** in **compiling** information to patch cracked and chipped areas on cores; and in smoothing surfaces of cores

- **Innovative interest** in attaining set limits, tolerances and standards

9412.2
Subgroup 2 of 5

Physical Activities

Vision
  2 Near vision

Colour Discrimination
  0 Not relevant

Hearing
  1 Limited

Body Position
  4 Other body positions

Limb Co-ordination
  1 Upper limb co-ordination

Strength
  3 Medium

Environmental Conditions

Location
  L2 Unregulated inside climate

Hazards
  H3 Equipment, machinery, tools
  H7 Fire, steam, hot surfaces

Discomforts
  D1 Noise
  D3 Odours

Employment Requirements

Education/Training
  2

- Some secondary school education is usually required.

- Several months of on-the-job training are required.

Workplaces/Employers

Foundry departments of metal products manufacturing companies

Metal foundries

Occupational Options

There is some mobility among workers in the 9412 group.

Progression to supervisory positions is possible with experience.

Similar Occupations Classified Elsewhere

Foundry labourers (in 9611 *Labourers in Mineral and Metal Processing*)

Furnace operators who operate furnaces to convert and refine primary metals (in 9411 *Machine Operators, Mineral and Metal Processing*)

Operators of continuous casting of steel or other primary metals or casting of primary ingots (in 9231 *Central Control and Process Operators, Mineral and Metal Processing*)

Supervisors of foundry workers (in 9211 *Supervisors, Mineral and Metal Processing*)

9412.3 Machine Mouldmakers and Coremakers

Machine Mouldmakers and Coremakers operate machines to make foundry moulds and cores.

Profile Summary

APTITUDES

G	V	N	S	P	Q	K	F	M
4	4	4	4	4	4	3	4	3

INTERESTS
OMi

DATA PEOPLE THINGS (DPT)
682

PHYSICAL ACTIVITIES (PA)

V	C	H	B	L	S
2	0	1	4	1	3

ENVIRONMENTAL CONDITIONS (EC)
L2, H3, H7, D1, D3

EDUCATION/TRAINING
2

Examples of Job Titles

Ceramic Mouldmaker
Machine Coremaker

Descriptor Profile

Main Characteristics

Occupations in this group are characterized by the following aptitudes, interests and worker functions as they relate to main duties:

- **General learning ability** to set up, adjust and operate mouldmaking and coremaking machines to make sand and ceramic moulds and cores

- **Motor co-ordination** and **manual dexterity** to use hand tools and measuring instruments to prepare and measure moulds and cores

- **Objective interest** in **controlling** mouldmaking and coremaking machinery

- **Methodical interest** in **comparing** products with drawings and specifications to ensure that they conform to standards

- **Innovative interest** in attaining set limits, tolerances and standards

9412.3
Subgroup 3 of 5

Physical Activities

Vision
  2   Near vision

Colour Discrimination
  0   Not relevant

Hearing
  1   Limited

Body Position
  4   Other body positions

Limb Co-ordination
  1   Upper limb co-ordination

Strength
  3   Medium

Environmental Conditions

Location
  L2   Unregulated inside climate

Hazards
  H3   Equipment, machinery, tools
  H7   Fire, steam, hot surfaces

Discomforts
  D1   Noise
  D3   Odours

Employment Requirements

Education/Training
  2

- Some secondary school education is usually required.

- Several months of on-the-job training are required.

Workplaces/Employers

Foundry departments of metal products manufacturing companies

Metal foundries

Occupational Options

There is some mobility among workers in the 9412 group.

Progression to supervisory positions is possible with experience.

Similar Occupations Classified Elsewhere

Foundry labourers (in 9611 *Labourers in Mineral and Metal Processing*)

Furnace operators who operate furnaces to convert and refine primary metals (in 9411 *Machine Operators, Mineral and Metal Processing*)

Operators of continuous casting of steel or other primary metals or casting of primary ingots (in 9231 *Central Control and Process Operators, Mineral and Metal Processing*)

Supervisors of foundry workers (in 9211 *Supervisors, Mineral and Metal Processing*)

9412.4 Metal Casters

Metal Casters operate machines to cast molten metal for use in foundries.

Profile Summary

APTITUDES

G	V	N	S	P	Q	K	F	M
4	4	4	4	4	4	3	4	3

INTERESTS
OMi

DATA PEOPLE THINGS (DPT)
682

PHYSICAL ACTIVITIES (PA)

V	C	H	B	L	S
2	0	1	4	1	3

ENVIRONMENTAL CONDITIONS (EC)
L2, H3, H7, D1, D3

EDUCATION/TRAINING
2

Examples of Job Titles

Casting Machine Operator
Die Casting Machine Operator
Metal Caster

Descriptor Profile

Main Characteristics

Occupations in this group are characterized by the following aptitudes, interests and worker functions as they relate to main duties:

- **General learning ability** to set up and operate machines to cast ferrous and non-ferrous metal products

- **Motor co-ordination** and **manual dexterity** to hand ladle and pour molten metal into moulds to produce castings

- **Objective interest** in **controlling** the flow of molten metals to moulds and the flow of water and air to cooling systems; and in operating machines to cast ferrous and non-ferrous metal products

- **Methodical interest** in **comparing** products with drawings and specifications to ensure that they conform to standards

- **Innovative interest** in examining castings for defects and in attaining set limits, tolerances and standards

9412.4
Subgroup 4 of 5

Physical Activities

Vision
   2 Near vision

Colour Discrimination
   0 Not relevant

Hearing
   1 Limited

Body Position
   4 Other body positions

Limb Co-ordination
   1 Upper limb co-ordination

Strength
   3 Medium

Environmental Conditions

Location
   L2 Unregulated inside climate

Hazards
   H3 Equipment, machinery, tools
   H7 Fire, steam, hot surfaces

Discomforts
   D1 Noise
   D3 Odours

Employment Requirements

Education/Training
   2

- Some secondary school education is usually required.

- Several months of on-the-job training are required.

Workplaces/Employers

Foundry departments of metal products manufacturing companies

Metal foundries

Occupational Options

There is some mobility among workers in the 9412 group.

Progression to supervisory positions is possible with experience.

Similar Occupations Classified Elsewhere

Foundry labourers (in 9611 *Labourers in Mineral and Metal Processing*)

Furnace operators who operate furnaces to convert and refine primary metals (in 9411 *Machine Operators, Mineral and Metal Processing*)

Operators of continuous casting of steel or other primary metals or casting of primary ingots (in 9231 *Central Control and Process Operators, Mineral and Metal Processing*)

Supervisors of foundry workers (in 9211 *Supervisors, Mineral and Metal Processing*)

9412.5 Foundry Furnace Operators

Foundry Furnace Operators run furnaces to melt and cast metals in foundries.

Profile Summary

APTITUDES

G	V	N	S	P	Q	K	F	M
4	4	4	4	4	4	3	4	3

INTERESTS
OMi

DATA PEOPLE THINGS (DPT)
682

PHYSICAL ACTIVITIES (PA)

V	C	H	B	L	S
2	1	1	4	1	3

ENVIRONMENTAL CONDITIONS (EC)
L2, H3, H7, D1, D3

EDUCATION/TRAINING
2

Examples of Job Titles

Foundry Worker
Furnace Operator - Foundry
Melter - Foundry

Descriptor Profile

Main Characteristics

Occupations in this group are characterized by the following aptitudes, interests and worker functions as they relate to main duties:

- **General learning ability** to understand the characteristics of molten metals and to operate furnaces

- **Motor co-ordination** and **manual dexterity** to set furnace controls and use hand tools and measuring instruments

- **Objective interest** in **controlling** the injection of fuels and air into furnaces and the flow of electricity and coolants in order to operate furnaces

- **Methodical interest** in **comparing** test data from melts to ensure that products conform to standards

- **Innovative interest** in observing colour of molten metals and instrument readings in order to adjust controls, and in attaining set specifications

9412.5
Subgroup 5 of 5

Physical Activities

Vision
   2 Near vision

Colour Discrimination
   1 Relevant

Hearing
   1 Limited

Body Position
   4 Other body positions

Limb Co-ordination
   1 Upper limb co-ordination

Strength
   3 Medium

Environmental Conditions

Location
   L2 Unregulated inside climate

Hazards
   H3 Equipment, machinery, tools
   H7 Fire, steam, hot surfaces

Discomforts
   D1 Noise
   D3 Odours

Employment Requirements

Education/Training
  2

- Some secondary school education is usually required.

- Several months of on-the-job training are required.

Workplaces/Employers

Foundry departments of metal products manufacturing companies

Metal foundries

Occupational Options

There is some mobility among workers in the 9412 group.

Progression to supervisory positions is possible with experience.

Similar Occupations Classified Elsewhere

Foundry labourers (in 9611 *Labourers in Mineral and Metal Processing*)

Furnace operators who operate furnaces to convert and refine primary metals (in 9411 *Machine Operators, Mineral and Metal Processing*)

Operators of continuous casting of steel or other primary metals or casting of primary ingots (in 9231 *Central Control and Process Operators, Mineral and Metal Processing*)

Supervisors of foundry workers (in 9211 *Supervisors, Mineral and Metal Processing*)

9413.1 Glass Process Control Operators

Glass Process Control Operators run multi-functional process control machinery to melt, form and cut float glass and glass products.

Profile Summary

APTITUDES

G	V	N	S	P	Q	K	F	M
3	4	4	4	4	4	3	4	3

INTERESTS
OMi

DATA PEOPLE THINGS (DPT)
382

PHYSICAL ACTIVITIES (PA)

V	C	H	B	L	S
2	0	1	3	1	1

ENVIRONMENTAL CONDITIONS (EC)
L1

EDUCATION/TRAINING
2

Examples of Job Titles

Float Operator - Glass Forming
Mirror Maker

Descriptor Profile

Main Characteristics

Occupations in this group are characterized by the following aptitudes, interests and worker functions as they relate to main duties:

- **General learning ability** to operate multi-functional process control machinery through control panels, computer terminals and other control systems to mix and melt raw materials

- **Motor co-ordination** and **manual dexterity** to adjust controls in order to coat glass with silver and other metals and materials

- **Objective interest** in **controlling** machines that heat, anneal, temper and form float glass and glass products; may operate process control machinery to cut glass and assemble glass window units

- **Methodical interest** in **compiling** information to maintain shift logs of production and other data

- **Innovative interest** in observing gauges, computer printouts and video monitors to verify specified processing conditions, and to make adjustments as necessary

9413.1
Subgroup 1 of 4

Physical Activities

Vision
   2 Near vision

Colour Discrimination
   0 Not relevant

Hearing
   1 Limited

Body Position
   3 Sitting, standing, walking

Limb Co-ordination
   1 Upper limb co-ordination

Strength
   1 Limited

Environmental Conditions

Location
   L1 Regulated inside climate

Employment Requirements

Education/Training
   2

- Some secondary school education may be required.

- Experience as a machine operator helper in glass manufacturing is usually required.

Workplaces/Employers

Glass and glass-products manufacturing companies

Occupational Options

Mobility is possible among the various types of machine operators in the 9413 group.

Progression to supervisory positions is possible with experience.

Similar Occupations Classified Elsewhere

Glaziers (7292)

Glass blowers (in 5244 *Artisans and Craftspersons*)

Helpers and labourers in glass products manufacturing (in 9611 *Labourers in Mineral and Metal Processing*)

Neon sign makers (in 9484 *Assemblers and Inspectors, Electrical Appliance, Apparatus and Equipment Manufacturing*)

Production inspectors in glass products manufacturing (in 9415 *Inspectors and Testers, Mineral and Metal Processing*)

Supervisors of workers in this group (in 9211 *Supervisors, Mineral and Metal Processing*)

9413.2 Glass Forming Machine Operators

Glass Forming Machine Operators run single-function machines to melt and form glassware and glass products.

Profile Summary

APTITUDES

G	V	N	S	P	Q	K	F	M
3	4	4	4	4	4	3	4	3

INTERESTS
OMi

DATA PEOPLE THINGS (DPT)
382

PHYSICAL ACTIVITIES (PA)

V	C	H	B	L	S
2	0	1	2	1	2

ENVIRONMENTAL CONDITIONS (EC)
L2, H3, H7

EDUCATION/TRAINING
2

Examples of Job Titles

Bottle Machine Operator
Glass Blowing Machine Operator
Glass Moulder
Glass Pressing Machine Operator

Descriptor Profile

Main Characteristics

Occupations in this group are characterized by the following aptitudes, interests and worker functions as they relate to main duties:

- **General learning ability** to set up automatic glass feeding, flowing and forming machines

- **Motor co-ordination** and **manual dexterity** to spray and swab moulds with oil solutions to prevent adhesion of glass and to use measuring instruments

- **Objective interest** in **controlling** machines that press and blow molten glass into moulds to form containers such as bottles, jars and drinking glasses

- **Methodical interest** in **compiling** information to weigh, measure and check production samples using scales and gauges and by visual verification to ensure that samples conform to specifications

- **Innovative interest** in adjusting automatic glass feeding, flowing and forming machines to meet production specifications

9413.2
Subgroup 2 of 4

Physical Activities

Vision
   2 Near vision

Colour Discrimination
   0 Not relevant

Hearing
   1 Limited

Body Position
   2 Standing and/or walking

Limb Co-ordination
   1 Upper limb co-ordination

Strength
   2 Light

Environmental Conditions

Location
   L2 Unregulated inside climate

Hazards
   H3 Equipment, machinery, tools
   H7 Fire, steam, hot surfaces

Employment Requirements

Education/Training
2

- Some secondary school education may be required.

- Experience as a machine operator helper in glass manufacturing is usually required.

Workplaces/Employers

Glass and glass-products manufacturing companies

Occupational Options

Mobility is possible among the various types of machine operators in the 9413 group.

Progression to supervisory positions is possible with experience.

Similar Occupations Classified Elsewhere

Glaziers (7292)

Glass blowers (in 5244 *Artisans and Craftspersons*)

Helpers and labourers in glass products manufacturing (in 9611 *Labourers in Mineral and Metal Processing*)

Neon sign makers (in 9484 *Assemblers and Inspectors, Electrical Appliance, Apparatus and Equipment Manufacturing*)

Production inspectors in glass products manufacturing (in 9415 *Inspectors and Testers, Mineral and Metal Processing*)

Supervisors of workers in this group (in 9211 *Supervisors, Mineral and Metal Processing*)

9413.3 Glass Finishing Machine Operators

Glass Finishing Machine Operators run single-function machines to finish flat glass, glassware, bottles and other glass products.

Profile Summary

APTITUDES

G	V	N	S	P	Q	K	F	M
3	4	4	4	3	4	3	4	3

INTERESTS
OMi

DATA PEOPLE THINGS (DPT)
584

PHYSICAL ACTIVITIES (PA)

V	C	H	B	L	S
2	0	1	2	1	2

ENVIRONMENTAL CONDITIONS (EC)
L1, H3, H6, D1, D4

EDUCATION/TRAINING
2

Examples of Job Titles

Glass Beveller
Glass Finishing Machine Operator

Descriptor Profile

Main Characteristics

Occupations in this group are characterized by the following aptitudes, interests and worker functions as they relate to main duties:

- **General learning ability** to set up glass and glass-product finishing machines

- **Form perception** to inspect products visually for quality

- **Objective interest** in **operating** finishing machines to grind, drill, sand, bevel, decorate, wash and polish glass and glass products

- **Methodical interest** in **copying** to record manufacturing information such as quantities, sizes and types of goods produced

- **Innovative interest** in adjusting glass and glass-product finishing machines to meet production specifications

9413.3
Subgroup 3 of 4

Physical Activities

Vision
    2 Near vision

Colour Discrimination
    0 Not relevant

Hearing
    1 Limited

Body Position
    2 Standing and/or walking

Limb Co-ordination
    1 Upper limb co-ordination

Strength
    2 Light

Environmental Conditions

Location
    L1 Regulated inside climate

Hazards
    H3 Equipment, machinery, tools
    H6 Flying particles, falling objects

Discomforts
    D1 Noise
    D4 Non-toxic dusts

Employment Requirements

Education/Training
    2

- Some secondary school education may be required.

- Experience as a machine operator helper in glass manufacturing is usually required.

Workplaces/Employers

Glass and glass-products manufacturing companies

Occupational Options

Mobility is possible among the various types of machine operators in the 9413 group.

Progression to supervisory positions is possible with experience.

Similar Occupations Classified Elsewhere

Glaziers (7292)

Glass blowers (in 5244 *Artisans and Craftspersons*)

Helpers and labourers in glass products manufacturing (in 9611 *Labourers in Mineral and Metal Processing*)

Neon sign makers (in 9484 *Assemblers and Inspectors, Electrical Appliance, Apparatus and Equipment Manufacturing*)

Production inspectors in glass products manufacturing (in 9415 *Inspectors and Testers, Mineral and Metal Processing*)

Supervisors of workers in this group (in 9211 *Supervisors, Mineral and Metal Processing*)

9413.4 Glass Cutters

Glass Cutters cut flat glass of various thicknesses to specified sizes and shapes by hand.

Profile Summary

APTITUDES

G	V	N	S	P	Q	K	F	M
3	4	4	4	4	4	3	4	3

INTERESTS
OMi

DATA PEOPLE THINGS (DPT)
584

PHYSICAL ACTIVITIES (PA)

V	C	H	B	L	S
2	0	1	4	1	3

ENVIRONMENTAL CONDITIONS (EC)
L1, H3, D1, D4

EDUCATION/TRAINING
2

Examples of Job Titles

Glass Cutter, Hand
Glass Edger

Descriptor Profile

Main Characteristics

Occupations in this group are characterized by the following aptitudes, interests and worker functions as they relate to main duties:

- **General learning ability** to cut glass of various thicknesses to specified sizes and shapes by hand

- **Motor co-ordination** and **manual dexterity** to place sheets of glass on padded tables or in jigs, and to smooth rough edges using belt sanders and smoothing wheels

- **Objective interest** in **operating** equipment and using hand tools to cut glass along marked outlines and around patterns

- **Methodical interest** in **copying** to measure and mark glass, and to place patterns on or under glass for cutting

- **Innovative interest** in examining and marking defective glass to obtain best cuts

9413.4
Subgroup 4 of 4

Physical Activities

Vision
2 Near vision

Colour Discrimination
0 Not relevant

Hearing
1 Limited

Body Position
4 Other body positions

Limb Co-ordination
1 Upper limb co-ordination

Strength
3 Medium

Environmental Conditions

Location
L1 Regulated inside climate

Hazards
H3 Equipment, machinery, tools

Discomforts
D1 Noise
D4 Non-toxic dusts

Employment Requirements

Education/Training
2

- Some secondary school education may be required.

- Experience as a machine operator helper in glass manufacturing is usually required.

- Experience as a glass cutter helper is usually required for manual glass cutters.

Workplaces/Employers

Glass and glass-products manufacturing companies

Occupational Options

Mobility is possible among the various types of machine operators in the 9413 group.

Progression to supervisory positions is possible with experience.

Similar Occupations Classified Elsewhere

Glaziers (7292)

Glass blowers (in 5244 *Artisans and Craftspersons*)

Helpers and labourers in glass products manufacturing (in 9611 *Labourers in Mineral and Metal Processing*)

Neon sign makers (in 9484 *Assemblers and Inspectors, Electrical Appliance, Apparatus and Equipment Manufacturing*)

Production inspectors in glass products manufacturing (in 9415 *Inspectors and Testers, Mineral and Metal Processing*)

Supervisors of workers in this group (in 9211 *Supervisors, Mineral and Metal Processing*)

9414.1 Concrete Products Forming and Finishing Workers

Concrete Products Forming and Finishing Workers cast and finish concrete products.

Profile Summary

APTITUDES

G	V	N	S	P	Q	K	F	M
3	4	4	3	3	4	3	4	3

INTERESTS
OMi

DATA PEOPLE THINGS (DPT)
584

PHYSICAL ACTIVITIES (PA)

V	C	H	B	L	S
2	1	1	4	1	4

ENVIRONMENTAL CONDITIONS (EC)
L1, H1, H3, H6, H8, D1, D2, D4, D5

EDUCATION/TRAINING
2

Examples of Job Titles

Concrete Block Maker
Finisher - Concrete Products
Stonework Moulder

Descriptor Profile

Main Characteristics

Occupations in this group are characterized by the following aptitudes, interests and worker functions as they relate to main duties:

- **General learning ability** to build moulds for casting concrete products, and to operate equipment used to form, cut and finish concrete products

- **Spatial perception** to cement sections together to form odd-shaped fittings, and to position reinforcing rods and wire mesh in moulds and fill moulds with concrete from suspended pouring buckets

- **Form perception** to finish surfaces of castings using screeds and trowels

- **Motor co-ordination** and **manual dexterity** to construct clay models and moulds by hand and with hand tools, and to cut cured concrete pipe sections with saws and chisels

- **Objective interest** in operating equipment such as vibrating tables to settle concrete, electric vibrators to tamp concrete, and cranes and forklifts to remove castings from moulds

- **Methodical interest** in copying information to construct clay models and moulds, and to build wood forms

- **Innovative interest** in repairing wood forms, and in ensuring that products conform to specifications

9414.1
Subgroup 1 of 4

Physical Activities

Vision
   2 Near vision

Colour Discrimination
   1 Relevant

Hearing
   1 Limited

Body Position
   4 Other body positions

Limb Co-ordination
   1 Upper limb co-ordination

Strength
   4 Heavy

Environmental Conditions

Location
   L1 Regulated inside climate

Hazards
   H1 Dangerous chemical substances
   H3 Equipment, machinery, tools
   H6 Flying particles, falling objects
   H8 Dangerous locations

Discomforts
   D1 Noise
   D2 Vibration
   D4 Non-toxic dusts
   D5 Wetness

Employment Requirements

Education/Training
2

- Some secondary school education may be required.

- Experience as a helper or labourer in concrete manufacturing may be required.

- Mould makers in this group who construct and repair wooden forms may require some carpentry or woodworking experience.

Workplaces/Employers

Concrete products manufacturing companies

Occupational Options

Mobility is possible among workers within each of the concrete, clay and stone manufacturing sectors, but there is little or no mobility among these manufacturing sectors.

Progression to supervisory positions is possible with experience.

Similar Occupations Classified Elsewhere

Concrete workers in construction (in 7282 *Cement Finishers*)

Helpers and labourers in concrete, clay and stone products manufacturing (in 9611 *Labourers in Mineral and Metal Processing*)

Inspectors of concrete, clay and stone products (in 9415 *Inspectors and Testers, Mineral and Metal Processing*)

Sculptors (in 5136 *Painters, Sculptors and Other Visual Artists*)

Stone carvers, hand and craft potters (in 5244 *Artisans and Craftspersons*)

Stone masons (in 7281 *Bricklayers*)

Supervisors of workers in this group (in 9211 *Supervisors, Mineral and Metal Processing*)

9414.2 Concrete Products Machine Operators

Concrete Products Machine Operators run single-function machines to mix, drill, grind and cut concrete for manufacturing concrete products.

Profile Summary

APTITUDES

G	V	N	S	P	Q	K	F	M
3	4	4	3	3	4	3	4	3

INTERESTS
OMi

DATA PEOPLE THINGS (DPT)
584

PHYSICAL ACTIVITIES (PA)

V	C	H	B	L	S
2	1	1	4	1	3

ENVIRONMENTAL CONDITIONS (EC)
L1, H3, D1, D2

EDUCATION/TRAINING
2

Examples of Job Titles

Concrete Block Maker
Precast Concrete Moulder
Precast Concrete Slab Maker

Descriptor Profile

Main Characteristics

Occupations in this group are characterized by the following aptitudes, interests and worker functions as they relate to main duties:

- **General learning ability** to set up, adjust and operate single-function machines used in the manufacture of concrete products

- **Spatial perception** to visualize the interrelationship of parts when setting up machines

- **Form perception** to detect broken edges, cracks, wrinkles and other defects in products

- **Motor co-ordination** and **manual dexterity** to use measuring instruments and adjust machine controls

- **Objective interest** in **operating** single-function machines that mix, drill, grind and cut concrete to specifications

- **Methodical interest** in **copying** information to record manufacturing information such as quantities, sizes and types of goods produced

- **Innovative interest** in checking products for quality control and in performing ongoing machine adjustments

9414.2

Physical Activities

Vision
  2 Near vision

Colour Discrimination
  1 Relevant

Hearing
  1 Limited

Body Position
  4 Other body positions

Limb Co-ordination
  1 Upper limb co-ordination

Strength
  3 Medium

Environmental Conditions

Location
  L1 Regulated inside climate

Hazards
  H3 Equipment, machinery, tools

Discomforts
  D1 Noise
  D2 Vibration

Employment Requirements

Education/Training
  2

- Some secondary school education may be required.

- Experience as a helper or labourer in concrete manufacturing may be required.

Workplaces/Employers

Concrete products manufacturing companies

Occupational Options

Mobility is possible among workers within each of the concrete, clay and stone manufacturing sectors, but there is little or no mobility among these manufacturing sectors.

Progression to supervisory positions is possible with experience.

Similar Occupations Classified Elsewhere

Concrete workers in construction (in 7282 *Cement Finishers*)

Helpers and labourers in concrete, clay and stone products manufacturing (in 9611 *Labourers in Mineral and Metal Processing*)

Inspectors of concrete, clay and stone products (in 9415 *Inspectors and Testers, Mineral and Metal Processing*)

Sculptors (in 5136 *Painters, Sculptors and Other Visual Artists*)

Stone carvers, hand and craft potters (in 5244 *Artisans and Craftspersons*)

Stone masons (in 7281 *Bricklayers*)

Supervisors of workers in this group (in 9211 *Supervisors, Mineral and Metal Processing*)

9414.3 Clay Products Forming and Finishing Machine Operators

Clay Products Forming and Finishing Machine Operators run machines to mix, extrude, mould, press and bake clay in order to form clay products.

Profile Summary

APTITUDES
G	V	N	S	P	Q	K	F	M
3	4	4	3	3	4	3	4	3

INTERESTS
OMi

DATA PEOPLE THINGS (DPT)
584

PHYSICAL ACTIVITIES (PA)
V	C	H	B	L	S
2	1	1	4	1	3

ENVIRONMENTAL CONDITIONS (EC)
L2, H3, H7

EDUCATION/TRAINING
2

Examples of Job Titles

Asbestos Shingle Presser
Brick Presser Operator
Clay Press Operator
Finisher - Clay Products
Moulder, Clay Products

Descriptor Profile

Main Characteristics

Occupations in this group are characterized by the following aptitudes, interests and worker functions as they relate to main duties:

- **General learning ability** to set up and operate automatic machines that mix ingredients, extrude tempered clay mixtures and cut extruded clay into sections to make products such as bricks, drain tiles and porcelain insulators

- **Spatial perception** to visualize finished products from specifications

- **Form perception** to detect deviations from standards in materials and products

- **Motor co-ordination** and **manual dexterity** to fill moulds with slip to form pottery and porcelain ware such as jugs, cups, sinks and toilet bowls

- **Objective interest** in operating mechanical and hydraulic rams and hot presses

- **Methodical interest** in **copying** information to prepare and mix slip

- **Innovative interest** in operating kilns to bake products according to specifications

9414.3
Subgroup 3 of 4

Physical Activities

Vision
   2 Near vision

Colour Discrimination
   1 Relevant

Hearing
   1 Limited

Body Position
   4 Other body positions

Limb Co-ordination
   1 Upper limb co-ordination

Strength
   3 Medium

Environmental Conditions

Location
   L2 Unregulated inside climate

Hazards
   H3 Equipment, machinery, tools
   H7 Fire, steam, hot surfaces

Employment Requirements

Education/Training
   2

- Some secondary school education may be required.

- Experience as a helper or labourer in concrete, clay or stone products manufacturing may be required.

Workplaces/Employers

Clay products manufacturing companies

Occupational Options

Mobility is possible among workers within each of the concrete, clay and stone manufacturing sectors, but there is little or no mobility among these manufacturing sectors.

Progression to supervisory positions is possible with experience.

Similar Occupations Classified Elsewhere

Concrete workers in construction (in 7282 *Cement Finishers*)

Helpers and labourers in concrete, clay and stone products manufacturing (in 9611 *Labourers in Mineral and Metal Processing*)

Inspectors of concrete, clay and stone products (in 9415 *Inspectors and Testers, Mineral and Metal Processing*)

Sculptors (in 5136 *Painters, Sculptors and Other Visual Artists*)

Stone carvers, hand and craft potters (in 5244 *Artisans and Craftspersons*)

Stone masons (in 7281 *Bricklayers*)

Supervisors of workers in this group (in 9211 *Supervisors, Mineral and Metal Processing*)

9414.4 Stone Forming and Finishing Workers

Stone Forming and Finishing Workers operate machines to form, cut and finish stone products.

Profile Summary

APTITUDES
G	V	N	S	P	Q	K	F	M
3	4	4	3	3	4	3	4	3

INTERESTS
OMi

DATA PEOPLE THINGS (DPT)
584

PHYSICAL ACTIVITIES (PA)
V	C	H	B	L	S
2	0	1	4	1	4

ENVIRONMENTAL CONDITIONS (EC)
L1, H3, H6, H8, D1, D2, D4

EDUCATION/TRAINING
2

Examples of Job Titles

Finisher - Stone Products
Granite Cutter
Marble Cutter
Stone Driller
Stone Planner

Descriptor Profile

Main Characteristics

Occupations in this group are characterized by the following aptitudes, interests and worker functions as they relate to main duties:

- **General learning ability** to operate machines to form, cut and finish stone products, and to operate stone-dressing lathes to sharpen and dress grindstones used for grinding logs into pulp

- **Spatial perception** to visualize the size and shape of finished products from drawings and specifications

- **Form perception** to examine products for defects

- **Motor co-ordination** and **manual dexterity** to handle machine controls, hand tools, parts and materials

- **Objective interest** in **operating** machines to grind and polish surfaces of stone blocks, slabs and other stone products to specific shapes and designs, and to produce smooth finishes

- **Methodical interest** in **copying** information to operate blade and wire saws to cut blocks of stone to specified dimensions, and to operate machines to drill holes in blocks and slabs of stone according to specifications

- **Innovative interest** in operating sandblasting equipment to cut inscriptions and decorative designs on monument stones

9414.4
Subgroup 4 of 4

Physical Activities

Vision
2   Near vision

Colour Discrimination
0   Not relevant

Hearing
1   Limited

Body Position
4   Other body positions

Limb Co-ordination
1   Upper limb co-ordination

Strength
4   Heavy

Environmental Conditions

Location
L1   Regulated inside climate

Hazards
H3   Equipment, machinery, tools
H6   Flying particles, falling objects
H8   Dangerous locations

Discomforts
D1   Noise
D2   Vibration
D4   Non-toxic dusts

Employment Requirements

Education/Training
2

- Some secondary school education may be required.

- Experience as a helper or labourer in concrete, clay or stone products manufacturing may be required.

Workplaces/Employers

Stone products manufacturing companies

Occupational Options

Mobility is possible among workers within each of the concrete, clay and stone manufacturing sectors, but there is little or no mobility among these manufacturing sectors.

Progression to supervisory positions is possible with experience.

Similar Occupations Classified Elsewhere

Concrete workers in construction (in 7282 *Cement Finishers*)

Helpers and labourers in concrete, clay and stone products manufacturing (in 9611 *Labourers in Mineral and Metal Processing*)

Inspectors of concrete, clay and stone products (in 9415 *Inspectors and Testers, Mineral and Metal Processing*)

Sculptors (in 5136 *Painters, Sculptors and Other Visual Artists*)

Stone carvers, hand and craft potters (in 5244 *Artisans and Craftspersons*)

Stone masons (in 7281 *Bricklayers*)

Supervisors of workers in this group (in 9211 *Supervisors, Mineral and Metal Processing*)

9415 Inspectors and Testers, Mineral and Metal Processing

Inspectors and Testers, Mineral and Metal Processing, inspect, grade, sample and test raw materials and products from mineral ore and metal processing operations.

Profile Summary

APTITUDES

G	V	N	S	P	Q	K	F	M
3	4	4	4	3	4	4	4	3

INTERESTS
MOI

DATA PEOPLE THINGS (DPT)
587

PHYSICAL ACTIVITIES (PA)

V	C	H	B	L	S
2	0	1	2	1	2

ENVIRONMENTAL CONDITIONS (EC)
L1, L2*, H7*, D1*, D4*

EDUCATION/TRAINING
4

Examples of Job Titles

Asbestos Grader
Brick and Tile Inspector
Casting Inspector
Clay Products Grader
Fibreglass Tester
Glass Inspector
Heat Treating Inspector
Metal Processing Inspector
Mineral Sampler
Molten Metal Sampler
Sheet Steel Inspector
Steel Tester

Descriptor Profile

Main Characteristics

Occupations in this group are characterized by the following aptitudes, interests and worker functions as they relate to main duties:

- **General learning ability** and **form perception** to inspect mineral ore, metal, cement, glass, clay and concrete products at various stages of processing to ensure that they adhere to specifications

- **Manual dexterity** to test products for strength and durability

- **Methodical interest** in **copying** to grade and label raw materials and finished products according to size, thickness, composition and other classification criteria; and in completing inspection and test reports

- **Objective interest** in **handling** products to take samples during and after processing for routine analyses and subsequent laboratory analyses

- **Innovative interest** in testing products to ensure that they conform to specifications; and in advising supervisors and process and machine operators of problems and product deficiencies

9415

Physical Activities

Vision
  2 Near vision

Colour Discrimination
  0 Not relevant

Hearing
  1 Limited

Body Position
  2 Standing and/or walking

Limb Co-ordination
  1 Upper limb co-ordination

Strength
  2 Light

Environmental Conditions

Location
  L1 Regulated inside climate
  L2* Unregulated inside climate

Hazards
  H7*Fire, steam, hot surfaces

Discomforts
  D1*Noise
  D4*Non-Toxic Dusts

Employment Requirements

Education/Training
4

- Completion of secondary school is usually required.

- Experience as a machine or process operator in mineral and metal processing is usually required.

Workplaces/Employers

Mineral ore and metal processing plants such as:

Aluminium Plants

Cement processing plants

Clay, glass and stone processing plants

Foundries

Metal refineries

Mineral ore mills

Steel mills

Uranium processing plants

Similar Occupations Classified Elsewhere

Machine Operators, Mineral and Metal Processing (9411)

Quality control technologists and technicians (in 2211 *Applied Chemical Technologists and Technicians* and in 2212 *Geological and Mineral Technologists and Technicians*)

Remarks

*Environmental conditions

- For some occupations in this group, the following **L**ocation L2 (Unregulated inside climate), **H**azards H7 (Fire, steam, hot surfaces) and **D**iscomforts D1 (Noise) and D4 (Non-toxic dusts) may also apply.

9421 Chemical Plant Machine Operators

Chemical Plant Machine Operators monitor and operate units and machinery to blend, mix, process and package specialty chemicals, pharmaceuticals, cleaning and toiletry products.

Profile Summary

APTITUDES

G	V	N	S	P	Q	K	F	M
3	4	4	4	4	4	3	4	3

INTERESTS
OMi

DATA PEOPLE THINGS (DPT)
584

PHYSICAL ACTIVITIES (PA)

V	C	H	B	L	S
2	1	1	2	1	2

ENVIRONMENTAL CONDITIONS (EC)
L1, H1, H3, D1, D3

EDUCATION/TRAINING
4, 5, R

Examples of Job Titles

Batch Mixer - Chemical Processing
Blender - Chemical Processing
Capsule Machine Operator
Evaporator Operator - Chemical Processing
Formulations Blender Operator
Glue Blender
Granulator Machine Operator
Mixer - Chemical Processing
Screener - Chemical Processing
Soap Maker

Descriptor Profile

Main Characteristics

Occupations in this group are characterized by the following aptitudes, interests and worker functions as they relate to main duties:

- **General learning ability** to monitor meters, gauges and electronic instruments on one or more chemical or formulation units such as mixers, blenders, driers, tabletting, encapsulation, granulation and coating machines

- **Motor co-ordination** and **manual dexterity** to adjust processing machines and equipment

- **Objective interest** in **operating** to start up and shut down equipment; may operate equipment from control rooms or control consoles located near production units

- **Methodical interest** in **copying** to record production data, and to measure, weigh and load chemical ingredients following formulation cards

- **Innovative interest** in troubleshooting equipment, and in taking samples to perform routine chemical and physical tests of products

9421

Physical Activities

Vision
   2 Near vision

Colour Discrimination
   1 Relevant

Hearing
   1 Limited

Body Position
   2 Standing and/or walking

Limb Co-ordination
   1 Upper limb co-ordination

Strength
   2 Light

Environmental Conditions

Location
   L1 Regulated inside climate

Hazards
   H1 Dangerous chemical substances
   H3 Equipment, machinery, tools

Discomforts
   D1 Noise
   D3 Odours

Employment Requirements

Education/Training
   4, 5, R

- Completion of secondary school is usually required.

- Completion of several months to one year informal, on-the-job training within the company is required for most mixer and blender operators.

- Completion of more than one year of formal and informal company training may be required for some operators working in pharmaceutical, explosives and agricultural chemical or in specialty chemical plants.

- Previous experience in chemical products processing as an assistant, labourer or helper may be required for some occupations in this group.

- Certification in the transportation of dangerous goods (TDG), first aid, firefighting or workplace hazardous materials information system (WHMIS) may be required for some occupations in this group.

Workplaces/Employers

Chemical, cleaning compound, ink and adhesive industries

Chemical processing departments in other industries

Occupational Options

Mobility among employers producing similar products is possible for some of the more skilled operators in this group.

Progression to supervisory positions, or to process control occupations, is possible with experience.

Similar Occupations Classified Elsewhere

Petroleum, Gas and Chemical Process Operators (9232)

Supervisors, Petroleum, Gas and Chemical Processing and Utilities (9212)

Remarks

Personal protective equipment may be required when working with some types of chemicals or pharmaceuticals.

9422.1 Mixing Machine Operators

Mixing Machine Operators set up and operate plastic mixing machines used in the manufacture of plastic parts and products.

Profile Summary

APTITUDES
G	V	N	S	P	Q	K	F	M
3	4	4	3	3	4	4	4	3

INTERESTS
MOi

DATA PEOPLE THINGS (DPT)
584

PHYSICAL ACTIVITIES (PA)
V	C	H	B	L	S
3	1	1	2	1	3

ENVIRONMENTAL CONDITIONS (EC)
L1, H1, H3, D1, D3

EDUCATION/TRAINING
2, 4

Examples of Job Titles

Banbury Operator
Solution Mixer Operator

Descriptor Profile

Main Characteristics

Occupations in this group are characterized by the following aptitudes, interests and worker functions as they relate to main duties:

- **General learning ability** to set up and operate mixing machines used in the manufacture of plastic parts and products

- **Spatial** and **form perception** to visualize the interrelationship of parts to set up machines

- **Manual dexterity** to place weighed materials in machines and to unload mixtures into containers and conveyors for further processing

- **Methodical interest** in **copying** information to weigh resins, colorants and other chemicals according to formulas

- **Objective interest** in **operating** equipment to blend plastics and other chemicals

- **Innovative interest** in blending plastics and other chemicals to specified consistencies and thicknesses

9422.1
Subgroup 1 of 4

Physical Activities

Vision
   3   Near and far vision

Colour Discrimination
   1   Relevant

Hearing
   1   Limited

Body Position
   2   Standing and/or walking

Limb Co-ordination
   1   Upper limb co-ordination

Strength
   3   Medium

Environmental Conditions

Location
   L1   Regulated inside climate

Hazards
   H1   Dangerous chemical substances
   H3   Equipment, machinery, tools

Discomforts
   D1   Noise
   D3   Odours

Employment Requirements

Education/Training
   2, 4

- Completion of secondary school may be required.

- On-the-job training is provided.

- Several years of experience as a helper, tender or packer in the same company may be required.

- Completion of a statistical process control (SPC) course may be required.

Workplaces/Employers

Plastic products manufacturing companies

Occupational Options

Mobility among the various operators in the 9422 group is possible.

Progression to supervisory positions is possible with experience.

Similar Occupations Classified Elsewhere

Labourers in Rubber and Plastic Products Manufacturing (9615)

Plastic Products Assemblers, Finishers and Inspectors (9495)

Rubber Processing Machine Operators and Related Workers (9423)

Supervisors, Plastic and Rubber Products Manufacturing (9214)

9422.2 Calendering Process Operators

Calendering Process Operators set up and operate calendering machines used in the manufacture of plastic parts and products.

Profile Summary

APTITUDES

G	V	N	S	P	Q	K	F	M
3	4	4	3	3	4	4	4	3

INTERESTS
OMi

DATA PEOPLE THINGS (DPT)
582

PHYSICAL ACTIVITIES (PA)

V	C	H	B	L	S
3	0	1	2	1	2

ENVIRONMENTAL CONDITIONS (EC)
L1, H3, D1

EDUCATION/TRAINING
2, 4

Examples of Job Titles

Bag Machine Operator

Calender Operator - Rubber and Plastic Manufacturing

Descriptor Profile

Main Characteristics

Occupations in this group are characterized by the following aptitudes, interests and worker functions as they relate to main duties:

- **General learning ability** to operate calender machines that transform bales and slabs into continuous plastic sheets or films of specified thicknesses

- **Spatial** and **form perception** to set up machines and examine materials produced

- **Manual dexterity** to make adjustments to processing equipment

- **Objective interest** in **controlling** processing by adjusting calender rollers for production line changes

- **Methodical interest** in **copying** information to monitor quality of materials produced

- **Innovative interest** in troubleshooting and making minor adjustments to equipment

9422.2
Subgroup 2 of 4

Physical Activities

Vision
  3 Near and far vision

Colour Discrimination
  0 Not relevant

Hearing
  1 Limited

Body Position
  2 Standing and/or walking

Limb Co-ordination
  1 Upper limb co-ordination

Strength
  2 Light

Environmental Conditions

Location
  L1 Regulated inside climate

Hazards
  H3 Equipment, machinery, tools

Discomforts
  D1 Noise

Employment Requirements

Education/Training
  2, 4

- Completion of secondary school may be required.

- On-the-job training is provided.

- Several years of experience as a helper, tender or packer in the same company may be required.

- Completion of a statistical process control (SPC) course may be required.

Workplaces/Employers

Plastic products manufacturing companies

Occupational Options

Mobility among the various operators in the 9422 group is possible.

Progression to supervisory positions is possible with experience.

Similar Occupations Classified Elsewhere

Labourers in Rubber and Plastic Products Manufacturing (9615)

Plastic Products Assemblers, Finishers and Inspectors (9495)

Rubber Processing Machine Operators and Related Workers (9423)

Supervisors, Plastic and Rubber Products Manufacturing (9214)

9422.3 Extruding Process Operators

Extruding Process Operators set up and operate extruding machines used in the manufacture of plastic parts and products.

Profile Summary

APTITUDES

G	V	N	S	P	Q	K	F	M
3	4	4	3	3	4	4	4	3

INTERESTS
OMi

DATA PEOPLE THINGS (DPT)
582

PHYSICAL ACTIVITIES (PA)

V	C	H	B	L	S
3	0	1	2	1	2

ENVIRONMENTAL CONDITIONS (EC)
L1, H3, D1

EDUCATION/TRAINING
2, 4

Examples of Job Titles

Extruder Operator - Rubber and Plastic Manufacturing

Descriptor Profile

Main Characteristics

Occupations in this group are characterized by the following aptitudes, interests and worker functions as they relate to main duties:

- **General learning ability** to operate machines that extrude plastic compounds through nozzles and dies

- **Spatial** and **form perception** to set up extruding machines and examine materials produced

- **Manual dexterity** to make adjustments to processing equipment

- **Objective interest** in **controlling** processing by changing dies on extruding machines according to production line changes

- **Methodical interest** in **copying** information to monitor quality of materials produced

- **Innovative interest** in troubleshooting and making minor adjustments to equipment

9422.3
Subgroup 3 of 4

Physical Activities

Vision
　3　Near and far vision

Colour Discrimination
　0　Not relevant

Hearing
　1　Limited

Body Positio
　2　Standing and/or walking

Limb Co-ordination
　1　Upper limb co-ordination

Strength
　2　Light

Environmental Conditions

Location
　L1　Regulated inside climate

Hazards
　H3　Equipment, machinery, tools

Discomforts
　D1　Noise

Employment Requirements

Education/Training
2, 4

- Completion of secondary school may be required.

- On-the-job training is provided.

- Several years of experience as a helper, tender or packer in the same company may be required.

- Completion of a statistical process control (SPC) course may be required.

Workplaces/Employers

Plastic products manufacturing companies

Occupational Options

Mobility among the various operators in the 9422 group is possible.

Progression to supervisory positions is possible with experience.

Similar Occupations Classified Elsewhere

Labourers in Rubber and Plastic Products Manufacturing (9615)

Plastic Products Assemblers, Finishers and Inspectors (9495)

Rubber Processing Machine Operators and Related Workers (9423)

Supervisors, Plastic and Rubber Products Manufacturing (9214)

9422.4 Moulding Process Operators

Moulding Process Operators set up and operate moulding processing machines used in the manufacture of plastic parts and products.

Profile Summary

APTITUDES

G	V	N	S	P	Q	K	F	M
3	4	4	3	3	4	4	4	3

INTERESTS
OMi

DATA PEOPLE THINGS (DPT)
582

PHYSICAL ACTIVITIES (PA)

V	C	H	B	L	S
3	1	1	2	1	2

ENVIRONMENTAL CONDITIONS (EC)
L1, L2, H1, H3, H7

EDUCATION/TRAINING
2, 4

Examples of Job Titles

Blow Moulding Machine Operator
Injection Moulding Operator
Plastics Press Operator
Printing Roller Moulder

Descriptor Profile

Main Characteristics

Occupations in this group are characterized by the following aptitudes, interests and worker functions as they relate to main duties:

- **General learning ability** to operate moulding machines that mould plastic products according to specifications

- **Spatial** and **form perception** to set up moulding machines and examine materials produced

- **Manual dexterity** to change moulds

- **Objective interest** in **controlling** processing by adjusting equipment for production line changes

- **Methodical interest** in **copying** information to follow formulation cards in order to mix resin batches for injection moulding processes, and to monitor quality of materials produced

- **Innovative interest** in troubleshooting and making minor adjustments to equipment

9422.4

Physical Activities

Vision
   3   Near and far vision

Colour Discrimination
   1   Relevant

Hearing
   1   Limited

Body Position
   2   Standing and/or walking

Limb Co-ordination
   1   Upper limb co-ordination

Strength
   2   Light

Environmental Conditions

Location
   L1   Regulated inside climate
   L2   Unregulated inside climate

Hazards
   H1   Dangerous chemical substances
   H3   Equipment, machinery, tools
   H7   Fire, steam, hot surfaces

Employment Requirements

Education/Training
   2, 4

- Completion of secondary school may be required.

- On-the-job training is provided.

- Several years of experience as a helper, tender or packer in the same company may be required.

- Completion of a statistical process control (SPC) course may be required.

- Completion of courses in hydraulics, pneumatics and electronics systems may be required for moulding process operators.

Workplaces/Employers

Plastic products manufacturing companies

Occupational Options

Mobility among the various operators in the 9422 group is possible.

Progression to supervisory positions is possible with experience.

Similar Occupations Classified Elsewhere

Labourers in Rubber and Plastic Products Manufacturing (9615)

Plastic Products Assemblers, Finishers and Inspectors (9495)

Rubber Processing Machine Operators and Related Workers (9423)

Supervisors, Plastic and Rubber Products Manufacturing (9214)

9423.1 Rubber Processing Machine Operators

Rubber Processing Machine Operators operate processing machines used in the manufacture of rubber products.

Profile Summary

APTITUDES

G	V	N	S	P	Q	K	F	M
4	4	4	4	4	4	3	4	3

INTERESTS
OMi

DATA PEOPLE THINGS (DPT)
685

PHYSICAL ACTIVITIES (PA)

V	C	H	B	L	S
2	0	1	2	1	2

ENVIRONMENTAL CONDITIONS (EC)
L1, H3, H7*, D1, D3

EDUCATION/TRAINING
2

Examples of Job Titles

Banbury Operator
Calender Operator
Cracker Operator
Cure Operator
Extruder Operator
Rubber Processing Machine Operator

Descriptor Profile

Main Characteristics

Occupations in this group are characterized by the following aptitudes, interests and worker functions as they relate to main duties:

- **General learning ability** to set up and operate rubber processing machinery

- **Motor co-ordination** and **manual dexterity** to adjust machines to proper settings

- **Objective interest** in **tending** machinery used for mixing, calendering, extruding, moulding and curing rubber materials and rubber products

- **Methodical interest** in **comparing** to check and monitor product quality

- **Innovative interest** in making adjustments to machines and in training and helping train new workers

9423.1
Subgroup 1 of 3

Physical Activities

Vision
   2 Near vision

Colour Discrimination
   0 Not relevant

Hearing
   1 Limited

Body Position
   2 Standing and/or walking

Limb Co-ordination
   1 Upper limb co-ordination

Strength
   2 Light

Environmental Conditions

Location
   LI Regulated inside climate

Hazards
   H3 Equipment, machinery, tools
   H7*Fire, steam, hot surfaces

Discomforts
   D1 Noise
   D3 Odours

Employment Requirements

Education/Training
   2

- Some secondary school education is usually required.
- Experience as a labourer in the same company may be required.
- On-the-job training is provided.

Workplaces/Employers

Rubber products manufacturing companies

Tire manufacturers

Occupational Options

Mobility among the various labourers in the 9423 group is possible.

Progression to supervisory positions is possible with experience.

Similar Occupations Classified Elsewhere

Labourers in Rubber and Plastic Products Manufacturing (9615)

Plastic Products Assemblers, Finishers and Inspectors (9495)

Plastics Processing Machine Operators (9422)

Supervisors, Plastic and Rubber Products Manufacturing (9214)

Remarks

*Environmental Conditions

- For some occupations in this group, **Hazards** H7 (Fire, steam, hot surfaces) may also apply.

9423.2 Assemblers, Rubber Products

Assemblers in this group put together rubber products.

Profile Summary

APTITUDES

G	V	N	S	P	Q	K	F	M
4	4	4	4	4	4	3	4	3

INTERESTS
OMi

DATA PEOPLE THINGS (DPT)
684

PHYSICAL ACTIVITIES (PA)

V	C	H	B	L	S
2	0	1	4	1	4

ENVIRONMENTAL CONDITIONS (EC)
L1, H3, D1

EDUCATION/TRAINING
2

Examples of Job Titles

Assembler, Rubber Goods
Belt Builder, Rubber
Hose Builder, Rubber
Rubber Products Assembler
Tire Builder

Descriptor Profile

Main Characteristics

Occupations in this group are characterized by the following aptitudes, interests and worker functions as they relate to main duties:

- **General learning ability** to operate machines and equipment to assemble rubber products

- **Motor co-ordination** and **manual dexterity** to use hand tools to cut, shape, splice, fit and cement rubber materials to form rubber parts and products

- **Objective interest** in **operating** finishing machines and equipment to trim, grind and buff rubber parts and products into final form

- **Methodical interest** in **comparing** information to lay out and prepare rubber materials for assembly

- **Innovative interest** in training and helping train new workers

9423.2
Subgroup 2 of 3

Physical Activities

Vision
  2 Near vision

Colour Discrimination
  0 Not relevant

Hearing
  1 Limited

Body Position
  4 Other body positions

Limb Co-ordination
  1 Upper limb co-ordination

Strength
  4 Heavy

Environmental Conditions

Location
  L1 Regulated inside climate

Hazards
  H3 Equipment, machinery, tools

Discomforts
  D1 Noise

Employment Requirements

Education/Training
  2

- Some secondary school education is usually required.

- Experience as a labourer in the same company may be required.

- On-the-job training is provided.

Workplaces/Employers

Rubber products manufacturing companies

Tire manufacturers

Occupational Options

Mobility among the various labourers in the 9423 group is possible.

Progression to supervisory positions is possible with experience.

Similar Occupations Classified Elsewhere

Labourers in Rubber and Plastic Products Manufacturing (9615)

Plastic Products Assemblers, Finishers and Inspectors (9495)

Plastics Processing Machine Operators (9422)

Supervisors, Plastic and Rubber Products Manufacturing (9214)

9423.3 Rubber Products Inspectors

Rubber Products Inspectors examine products to ensure that they conform to specifications and quality standards.

Profile Summary

APTITUDES

G	V	N	S	P	Q	K	F	M
4	4	4	4	4	4	3	4	3

INTERESTS
OMD

DATA PEOPLE THINGS (DPT)
587

PHYSICAL ACTIVITIES (PA)

V	C	H	B	L	S
2	0	1	4	1	2

ENVIRONMENTAL CONDITIONS (EC)
L1

EDUCATION/TRAINING
2

Examples of Job Titles

Inspector - Rubber Manufacturing
Tire Inspector

Descriptor Profile

Main Characteristics

Occupations in this group are characterized by the following aptitudes, interests and worker functions as they relate to main duties:

- **General learning ability** to inspect rubber products for defects and to ensure that they conform to specifications and quality standards

- **Motor co-ordination** and **manual dexterity** to affix seals and tags to approved products

- **Objective interest** in **handling** to examine products visually; and in using instruments to check that products conform to specifications; may make minor adjustments and repairs to products

- **Methodical interest** in **copying** to fill out product inspection reports; and in marking defective products

- **Directive interest** in rerouting defective products for repair or recycle

9423.3
Subgroup 3 of 3

Physical Activities

Vision
  2 Near vision

Colour Discrimination
  0 Not relevant

Hearing
  1 Limited

Body Position
  4 Other body positions

Limb Co-ordination
  1 Upper limb co-ordination

Strength
  2 Light

Environmental Conditions

Location
  L1 Regulated inside climate

Employment Requirements

Education/Training
2

- Some secondary school education is usually required.

- Experience as a labourer in the same company may be required.

- On-the-job training is provided.

Workplaces/Employers

Rubber products manufacturing companies

Tire manufacturers

Occupational Options

Mobility among the various labourers in the 9423 group is possible.

Progression to supervisory positions is possible with experience.

Similar Occupations Classified Elsewhere

Labourers in Rubber and Plastic Products Manufacturing (9615)

Plastic Products Assemblers, Finishers and Inspectors (9495)

Plastics Processing Machine Operators (9422)

Supervisors, Plastic and Rubber Products Manufacturing (9214)

9424.1 Water Plant Operators

Water Plant Operators monitor and operate computerized control systems and equipment in water filtration and treatment plants to regulate the treatment and distribution of water.

Profile Summary

APTITUDES

G	V	N	S	P	Q	K	F	M
3	3	3	4	3	3	4	4	3

INTERESTS
OIM

DATA PEOPLE THINGS (DPT)
282

PHYSICAL ACTIVITIES (PA)

V	C	H	B	L	S
2	1	1	2	1	1

ENVIRONMENTAL CONDITIONS (EC)
L1, D1

EDUCATION/TRAINING
4

Examples of Job Titles

Operator, Water Purification Plant
Water Filtration Plant Operator
Water Treatment Plant Operator

Descriptor Profile

Main Characteristics

Occupations in this group are characterized by the following aptitudes, interests and worker functions as they relate to main duties:

- **General learning ability** to operate and monitor computerized control systems and equipment in water filtration and treatment plants

- **Verbal ability** to complete plant logs and reports

- **Numerical ability** and **clerical perception** to read flow meters, gauges and other recording instruments to measure water output, consumption levels, bacterial content, and chlorine and fluoride levels

- **Form perception** to inspect systems and equipment to detect malfunctions and to ensure that they are operating normally

- **Manual dexterity** to make adjustments to systems and equipment

- **Objective interest** in **controlling** systems and equipment to regulate the treatment and distribution of water

- **Innovative interest** in **analyzing** test results and instrument readings; and in making adjustments to systems and equipment as required

- **Methodical interest** in collecting and testing water samples for chemical and bacterial content, and in maintaining plant logs and reports

9424.1
Subgroup 1 of 2

Physical Activities

Vision
   2   Near vision

Colour Discrimination
   1   Relevant

Hearing
   1   Limited

Body Position
   2   Standing and/or walking

Limb Co-ordination
   1   Upper limb co-ordination

Strength
   1   Limited

Environmental Conditions

Location
   L1 Regulated inside climate

Discomforts
   D1 Noise

Employment Requirements

Education/Training
   4

- Completion of secondary school is usually required.

- College, high school or industry training courses in water treatment and pollution control are required.

- On-the-job training is provided.

- Previous experience as a labourer or utilities maintenance worker with the same employer may be required.

Workplaces/Employers

Industries

Institutions

Municipal governments

Occupational Options

There is limited mobility between water plant and waste plant operators.

Progression to supervisory positions is possible with experience.

Similar Occupations Classified Elsewhere

Supervisors, Petroleum, Gas and Chemical Processing and Utilities (9212)

Waterworks and Gas Maintenance Workers (7442)

Water and waste plant labourers (in 9613 *Labourers in Chemical Products Processing and Utilities*)

9424.2 Waste Plant Operators

Waste Plant Operators monitor and operate computerized control systems and equipment in waste water, sewage treatment and liquid waste plants to regulate the treatment and disposal of sewage and wastes.

Profile Summary

APTITUDES

G	V	N	S	P	Q	K	F	M
3	3	3	4	3	3	4	4	3

INTERESTS
OIM

DATA PEOPLE THINGS (DPT)
282

PHYSICAL ACTIVITIES (PA)

V	C	H	B	L	S
2	1	1	2	1	1

ENVIRONMENTAL CONDITIONS (EC)
L1, D1, D3

EDUCATION/TRAINING
4

Examples of Job Titles

Process Operator, Liquid Waste

Sewage Plant Operator

Waste-Water Treatment Plant Operator

Descriptor Profile

Main Characteristics

Occupations in this group are characterized by the following aptitudes, interests and worker functions as they relate to main duties:

- **General learning ability** to operate and monitor computerized control systems and equipment in waste-water treatment, sewage treatment and liquid waste plants

- **Verbal ability** to complete plant logs and reports

- **Numerical ability** and **clerical perception** to monitor and read gauges, meters and other recording instruments to detect equipment malfunctions

- **Form perception** to patrol plant to inspect pumps, motors, filters, chlorimeters and other equipment to ensure that systems are operating within prescribed limits

- **Manual dexterity** to adjust plant systems and equipment

- **Objective interest** in **controlling** systems and equipment to regulate flow of sewage through settling, aeration and digestion tanks, and to treat and dispose of sewage wastes

- **Innovative interest** in **analyzing** test results and instrument readings; and in making adjustments to systems and equipment as required

- **Methodical interest** in collecting and testing waste and sewage samples, and in maintaining plant logs and reports

9424.2
Subgroup 2 of 2

Physical Activities

Vision
  2 Near vision

Colour Discrimination
  1 Relevant

Hearing
  1 Limited

Body Position
  2 Standing and/or walking

Limb Co-ordination
  1 Upper limb co-ordination

Strengt
  1 Limited

Environmental Conditions

Location
  L1 Regulated inside climate

Discomforts
  D1 Noise
  D3 Odours

Employment Requirements

Education/Training
  4

- Completion of secondary school is usually required.

- College, high school or industry training courses in water treatment and pollution control are required.

- On-the-job training is provided.

- Previous experience as a labourer or utilities maintenance worker with the same employer may be required.

Workplaces/Employers

Industries

Institutions

Municipal governments

Occupational Options

There is limited mobility between water plant and waste plant operators.

Progression to supervisory positions is possible with experience.

Similar Occupations Classified Elsewhere

Supervisors, Petroleum, Gas and Chemical Processing and Utilities (9212)

Waterworks and Gas Maintenance Workers (7442)

Water and waste plant labourers (in 9613 *Labourers in Chemical Products Processing and Utilities*)

9431 Sawmill Machine Operators

Sawmill Machine Operators run, monitor and control automated lumbermill equipment to saw timber logs into rough lumber; to saw, trim and plane rough lumber into dressed lumber of various sizes; and to saw and split shingles and shakes.

Profile Summary

APTITUDES

G	V	N	S	P	Q	K	F	M
3	4	4	3	4	5	3	4	4

INTERESTS
OMi

DATA PEOPLE THINGS (DPT)
384

PHYSICAL ACTIVITIES (PA)

V	C	H	B	L	S
3	0	1	4	1	4

ENVIRONMENTAL CONDITIONS (EC)
L1, H3, H6, D1, D3, D4

EDUCATION/TRAINING
2, R

Examples of Job Titles

Circular Saw Operator
Edgerman/woman
Head Sawyer
Log Cut-Off Operator
Planer Operator
Resaw Operator
Shake Splitter
Trimmerman/woman

Descriptor Profile

Main Characteristics

Occupations in this group are characterized by the following aptitudes, interests and worker functions as they relate to main duties:

- **General learning ability** to operate automated lumbermill equipment from control rooms and equipment consoles to saw logs into rough lumber

- **Spatial perception** to monitor logs and lumber movement to ensure that cuts are made according to specifications

- **Manual dexterity** to start conveyor systems to move logs and lumber to and from saws, and to clean and lubricate equipment

- **Objective interest** in **operating** machines to saw, trim and plane rough lumber into dressed lumber of various sizes, and to saw and split shingles and shakes

- **Methodical interest** in **compiling** information while examining logs and rough lumber to determine size, condition, quality and other characteristics in order to decide what cuts are required

- **Innovative interest** in setting up and adjusting saw equipment, and replacing blades and bands using wrenches, gauges and other hand tools

9431

Physical Activities

Vision
   3   Near and far vision

Colour Discrimination
   0   Not relevant

Hearing
   1   Limited

Body Position
   4   Other body positions

Limb Co-ordination
   1   Upper limb co-ordination

Strength
   4   Heavy

Environmental Conditions

Location
   L1   Regulated inside climate

Hazards
   H3   Equipment, machinery, tools
   H6   Flying particles, falling objects

Discomforts
   D1   Noise
   D3   Odours
   D4   Non-toxic dusts

Employment Requirements

Education/Training
   2, R

- Completion of a secondary school may be required.

- Several weeks of on-the-job training are usually provided.

- Head sawyers and planer operators usually require several years of experience in other sawmill machine operating positions in the same company.

- A certificate in industrial first aid may be required.

Workplaces/Employers

Planing mills

Sawmills

Occupational Options

There is some mobility among jobs in this occupational group.

Progression to supervisory positions is possible with experience.

Similar Occupations Classified Elsewhere

Labourers in Wood, Pulp and Paper Processing (9614)

Lumber Graders and Other Wood Processing Inspectors and Graders (9436)

Other Wood Processing Machine Operators (9434)

Supervisors, Forest Products Processing (9215)

Woodworking Machine Operators (9513)

9432 Pulp Mill Machine Operators

Pulp Mill Machine Operators operate and monitor processing machinery and equipment to produce pulp.

Profile Summary

APTITUDES

G	V	N	S	P	Q	K	F	M
3	4	4	4	4	4	4	4	3

INTERESTS
OMi

DATA PEOPLE THINGS (DPT)
564

PHYSICAL ACTIVITIES (PA)

V	C	H	B	L	S
2	0	1	2	1	2

ENVIRONMENTAL CONDITIONS (EC)
L1, H3, H7*, D1, D3

EDUCATION/TRAINING
4, 5, 6, R

Examples of Job Titles

Assistant Bleacher Operator - Pulp and Paper
Assistant Digester Operator
Beater Operator
Cook's First Helper - Pulp and Paper
Field Operator - Pulp and Paper
Grinderman/woman - Pulp and Paper
Refiner Operator - Pulp and Paper
Screenman/woman - Pulp and Paper
Thermo-Mechanical Pulp Assistant Operator

Descriptor Profile

Main Characteristics

Occupations in this group are characterized by the following aptitudes, interests and worker functions as they relate to main duties:

- **General learning ability** to monitor machinery and equipment to carry out one or more cellulose processing steps, and to maintain and complete production reports

- **Manual dexterity** to collect processing samples and conduct titration tests, pH readings and other routine tests on pulp and solutions

- **Objective interest** in **operating** and monitoring screening equipment, digesters, mixing tanks, washers and other pulp processing machinery and equipment to carry out one or more cellulose processing step

- **Methodical interest** in **copying** to observe equipment and machinery panel indicators, gauges, level indicators and other instruments to detect malfunctions and to ensure that process steps are carried out according to specifications

- **Innovative interest** in **speaking** with pulping control operators to make process adjustments and start up or shut down machinery and equipment as required

9432

Physical Activities

Vision
   2 Near vision

Colour Discrimination
   0 Not relevant

Hearing
   1 Limited

Body Position
   2 Standing and/or walking

Limb Co-ordination
   1 Upper limb co-ordination

Strength
   2 Light

Environmental Conditions

Location
   L1 Regulated inside climate

Hazards
   H3 Equipment, machinery, tools
   H7*Fire, steam, hot surfaces

Discomforts
   D1 Noise
   D3 Odours

Employment Requirements

Education/Training
   4, 5, 6, R

- Completion of secondary school is required.

- A college diploma in forest products processing or a related subject may be required.

- Completion of several weeks of formal company training and several months of on-the-job training is required.

- Previous experience as a pulp mill labourer within the same company is usually required.

- A certificate in industrial first aid may be required.

Workplaces/Employers

Pulp and paper companies

Occupational Options

There is limited mobility among jobs within this occupational group.

Progression to pulping control operator is possible with experience.

Similar Occupations Classified Elsewhere

Labourers in Wood, Pulp and Paper Processing (9614)

Pulping Control Operators (9233)

Remarks

*Environmental Conditions

- For some occupations in this group, **Hazards** H7 (Fire, steam, hot surfaces) may also apply.

9433 Papermaking and Finishing Machine Operators

Papermaking and Finishing Machine Operators use process machinery and equipment and assist papermaking and coating control operators to produce, coat and finish paper.

Profile Summary

APTITUDES

G	V	N	S	P	Q	K	F	M
4	4	4	3	3	4	3	4	3

INTERESTS
OMi

DATA PEOPLE THINGS (DPT)
564

PHYSICAL ACTIVITIES (PA)

V	C	H	B	L	S
2	0	1	2	1	2

ENVIRONMENTAL CONDITIONS (EC)
L1, H3, D1, D3

EDUCATION/TRAINING
4, 5, R

Examples of Job Titles

Assistant Coating Operator - Pulp and Paper

Balerman/woman - Pulp and Paper

Calender Operator - Pulp and Paper

Embossing Calender Operator - Pulp and Paper

Fourth Hand - Pulp and Paper

Graderman/woman - Pulp and Paper

Sheeter Operator - Pulp and Paper

Winderman/woman - Pulp and Paper

Descriptor Profile

Main Characteristics

Occupations in this group are characterized by the following aptitudes, interests and worker functions as they relate to main duties:

- **General learning ability** to monitor papermaking and finishing process machinery and equipment, and to maintain and complete production reports

- **Spatial perception** to observe equipment and ensure that process steps are carried out according to specifications

- **Form perception** to inspect paper for wrinkles, holes, discolouration, streaks and other defects

- **Motor co-ordination** and **manual dexterity** to mount, position and thread paper rolls using hoists

- **Objective interest** in **operating** machinery and equipment to dry, laminate, coat, slit, trim, wind and carry out process steps; and in controlling process machinery using a distributed control system and process computers

- **Methodical interest** in **copying** to observe equipment and machinery, panel indicators, gauges, level indicators and other instruments to detect malfunctions

- **Innovative interest** in **speaking** with and assisting papermaking and coating control operators to make process adjustments and to start up or shut down process machines as required

9433

Physical Activities

Vision
2   Near vision

Colour Discrimination
0   Not relevant

Hearing
1   Limited

Body Position
2   Standing and/or walking

Limb Co-ordination
1   Upper limb co-ordination

Strength
2   Light

Environmental Conditions

Location
L1   Regulated inside climate

Hazards
H3   Equipment, machinery, tools

Discomforts
D1   Noise
D3   Odours

Employment Requirements

Education/Training
4, 5, R

- Completion of secondary school is required.

- Completion of several weeks of formal company training and several months of on-the-job training is required.

- Previous experience as a labourer within the same company is usually required.

- A certificate in industrial first aid may be required.

- A competency certificate in natural gas may be required.

Workplaces/Employers

Pulp and paper companies

Occupational Options

There is limited mobility among jobs within this occupational group.

Progression to papermaking and coating control operator occupations is possible with experience.

Similar Occupations Classified Elsewhere

Labourers in Wood, Pulp and Paper Processing (9614)

Papermaking and Coating Control Operators (9234)

Machine operators engaged in fabricating and assembling paper products (in 9435 *Paper Converting Machine Operators*)

9434 Other Wood Processing Machine Operators

Machine Operators in this group operate and tend process machinery and equipment to remove bark from logs, to produce wood chips, to preserve and treat wood, and to produce waferboard, particle board, hardboard, insulation board, plywood, veneer and similar wood products.

Profile Summary

APTITUDES

G	V	N	S	P	Q	K	F	M
3	4	4	4	4	4	3	4	3

INTERESTS
OMi

DATA PEOPLE THINGS (DPT)
584

PHYSICAL ACTIVITIES (PA)

V	C	H	B	L	S
3	0	1	4	1	3

ENVIRONMENTAL CONDITIONS (EC)
L1, L2, H1*, H3, H6, H7*, D1, D3, D4

EDUCATION/TRAINING
2, 4

Examples of Job Titles

Barker Operator
Chipper Operator
Lumber Kiln Operator
Particle Board Line Operator
Plywood Panel Assembler
Timber Treating Tank Operator
Veneer Drier Tender
Veneer Lathe Operator
Waferboard Press Operator
Wood Treater

Descriptor Profile

Main Characteristics

Occupations in this group are characterized by the following aptitudes, interests and worker functions as they relate to main duties:

- **General learning ability** to operate and tend process machinery and equipment to remove bark, knots and dirt from logs, to reduce logs and sawmill waste into wood chips and flakes, to stack and band lumber, to screen wood chips, and to produce waferboard, particle board, hardboard and insulation board, and to complete and maintain production reports

- **Motor co-ordination** and **manual dexterity** to assemble plywood panels and repair plywood and veneer mechanically and manually

- **Objective interest** in operating and tending conveyors, lathes, sanding machines and other equipment to peel and slice veneer from logs and log sections, and to glue, press, trim, sand and splice veneer sheets; and in operating kilns, treating tanks and other equipment to dry lumber and other wood products; and to treat chemically and impregnate wood products with preservatives

- **Methodical interest** in **copying** to observe equipment, panel indicators, video monitors and other instruments to detect malfunctions and ensure that machinery and equipment are operating according to specifications

- **Innovative interest** in setting up, adjusting, starting up and shutting down process equipment and machines as required

9434

Physical Activities

Vision
  3   Near and far vision

Colour Discrimination
  0   Not relevant

Hearing
  1   Limited

Body Position
  4   Other body positions

Limb Co-ordination
  1   Upper limb co-ordination

Strength
  3   Medium

Environmental Conditions

Location
  L1   Regulated inside climate
  L2   Unregulated inside climate

Hazards
  H1*Dangerous chemical substances
  H3   Equipment, machinery, tools
  H6   Flying particles, falling objects
  H7*Fire, steam, hot surfaces

Discomforts
  D1   Noise
  D3   Odours
  D4   Non-toxic dusts

Employment Requirements

Education/Training
  2, 4

- Completion of secondary school may be required.

- Several months of on-the-job training are provided.

- For lumber kiln operators, particle board operators and waferboard operators, some combination of college or company courses and up to a year of on-the-job training may be required.

- Previous experience as a labourer in wood processing may be required.

Workplaces/Employers

Planing mills

Sawmills

Waferboard plants

Wood processing plants

Wood rooms of pulp mills

Wood treatment plants

Occupational Options

There is some mobility among jobs in this group.

Progression to other positions in the wood, pulp and paper industries is possible with experience.

Similar Occupations Classified Elsewhere

Labourers in Wood, Pulp and Paper Processing (9614)

Supervisors, Forest Products Processing (9215)

Remarks

*Environmental Conditions

- For some occupations in this group, Hazards H1 (Dangerous chemical substances) and H7 (Fire, steam, hot surfaces) may also apply.

9435 Paper Converting Machine Operators

Paper Converting Machine Operators operate machines that fabricate and assemble paper products such as paper bags, containers, boxes, envelopes and similar articles.

Profile Summary

APTITUDES

G	V	N	S	P	Q	K	F	M
4	4	4	3	3	4	4	4	3

INTERESTS
MOi

DATA PEOPLE THINGS (DPT)
684

PHYSICAL ACTIVITIES (PA)

V	C	H	B	L	S
2	0	1	2	1	2

ENVIRONMENTAL CONDITIONS (EC)
L1, H3, D1

EDUCATION/TRAINING
3

Examples of Job Titles

Box Maker Operator
Carton Forming Machine Operator
Coremaker
Corrugator Operator
Envelope Maker Operator
Paper Bag Machine Operator

Descriptor Profile

Main Characteristics

Occupations in this group are characterized by the following aptitudes, interests and worker functions as they relate to main duties:

- **General learning ability** to operate machines that cut, fold, glue and clip paper and cardboard to make boxes, corrugated cartons and other articles

- **Spatial** and **form perception** to operate machines that press paper to form drinking cups and other containers

- **Manual dexterity** to clean and lubricate machines and perform other routine maintenance

- **Methodical interest** in **comparing** to operate machines that glue paper to cardboard and cut it to required lengths

- **Objective interest** in **operating** machines that cut, glue and fold paper to make envelopes and paper bags, and other paper converting machines to form products such as paper tubes, cards, paper towels and diapers

- **Innovative interest** in setting up machines

9435

Physical Activities

Vision
   2   Near vision

Colour Discrimination
   0   Not relevant

Hearing
   1   Limited

Body Position
   2   Standing and/or walking

Limb Co-ordination
   1   Upper limb co-ordination

Strength
   2   Light

Environmental Conditions

Location
   L1   Regulated inside climate

Hazards
   H3   Equipment, machinery, tools

Discomforts
   D1   Noise

Employment Requirements

Education/Training
   3

- Completion of secondary school is required by the pulp and paper industry and other large employers.

- Several weeks of on-the-job training are provided.

- Previous experience as a labourer within the same company may be required.

Workplaces/Employers

Paper products manufacturing companies

Occupational Options

There is some mobility among jobs in this occupational group.

Similar Occupations Classified Elsewhere

Papermaking and Finishing Machine Operators (9433)

Printing Machine Operators (9471)

Printing Press Operators (7381)

9436.1 Lumber Graders

Lumber Graders inspect and grade lumber to identify defects, to ensure that the lumber conforms to company specifications, and to classify lumber according to industry standards.

Profile Summary

APTITUDES

G	V	N	S	P	Q	K	F	M
4	4	4	4	3	4	4	3	4

INTERESTS
Moi

DATA PEOPLE THINGS (DPT)
587

PHYSICAL ACTIVITIES (PA)

V	C	H	B	L	S
3	0	1	4	1	3

ENVIRONMENTAL CONDITIONS (EC)
L1, L2, H3, D1, D3, D4

EDUCATION/TRAINING
4, R

Examples of Job Titles

Grader - Wood Processing

Grader Tallyman/woman - Wood Processing

Lumber Grader

Wood Measurer

Descriptor Profile

Main Characteristics

Occupations in this group are characterized by the following aptitudes, interests and worker functions as they relate to main duties:

- **General learning ability** to classify and sort lumber according to industry standards

- **Form perception** to examine lumber for knots, holes, splits and other defects

- **Finger dexterity** to use callipers, gauges and tape measures

- **Methodical interest** in **copying** information to complete and maintain reports, and tally and stamp lumber to indicate grade, wood types, moisture levels and other characteristics; and in measuring lumber to ensure that it meets specified thicknesses, lengths and widths

- **Objective interest** in **handling** to measure and stamp lumber

- **Innovative interest** in sorting lumber for further drying, trimming and remanufacturing

9436.1

Physical Activities

Vision
   3 Near and far vision

Colour Discrimination
   0 Not relevant

Hearing
   1 Limited

Body Position
   4 Other body positions

Limb Co-ordination
   1 Upper limb co-ordination

Strength
   3 Medium

Environmental Conditions

Location
   L1 Regulated inside climate
   L2 Unregulated inside climate

Hazards
   H3 Equipment, machinery, tools

Discomforts
   D1 Noise
   D3 Odours
   D4 Non-toxic dusts

Employment Requirements

Education/Training
   4, R

- Completion of secondary school is usually required.

- On-the-job training and up to two weeks of classroom training are provided for lumber graders.

- Previous experience as a sawmill machine operator, other wood processing operator or as a labourer in wood processing is usually required for graders in this group.

- Lumber graders require a lumber grader's licence issued by a provincial lumber association.

Workplaces/Employers

Planing mills

Sawmills

Waferboard plants

Wood processing companies

Wood treatment plants

Occupational Options

There is some mobility between employers processing similar wood products.

Similar Occupations Classified Elsewhere

Supervisors, Forest Products Processing (9215)

Forest product technologists (in 2211 *Applied Chemical Technologists and Technicians*)

Log scalers (in 2223 *Forestry Technologists and Technicians*)

Production technologists in sawmills (in 2233 *Industrial Engineering and Manufacturing Technologists and Technicians*)

9436.2 Other Wood Processing Inspectors and Graders

Inspectors and Graders in this group inspect and grade shingles, veneer, waferboard and similar wood products to identify defects, to ensure that they conform to company specifications and to classify them according to industry standards.

Profile Summary

APTITUDES

G	V	N	S	P	Q	K	F	M
4	4	4	4	3	4	4	3	4

INTERESTS
Moi

DATA PEOPLE THINGS (DPT)
587

PHYSICAL ACTIVITIES (PA)

V	C	H	B	L	S
3	0	1	4	1	3

ENVIRONMENTAL CONDITIONS (EC)
L1, D1, D3, D4

EDUCATION/TRAINING
4

Examples of Job Titles

Particle Board Grader
Plywood Grader
Plywood Inspector
Veneer Grader
Wood Measurer

Descriptor Profile

Main Characteristics

Occupations in this group are characterized by the following aptitudes, interests and worker functions as they relate to main duties:

- **General learning ability** to grade and label wood products according to quality standards

- **Form perception** to inspect plywood panels, veneer sheets, panelboard, shingles and similar wood products for straightness and for knots, holes, splits and other defects

- **Finger dexterity** to use standard measuring instruments

- **Methodical interest** in **copying** information to maintain and complete inspection and grading reports and mark defects; and in measuring wood products to ensure that they conform to specifications

- **Objective interest** in **handling** to measure, mark and sort wood products

- **Innovative interest** in sorting products for repair and re-processing

Physical Activities

Vision
    3   Near and far vision

Colour Discrimination
    0   Not relevant

Hearing
    1   Limited

Body Position
    4   Other body positions

Limb Co-ordination
    1   Upper limb co-ordination

Strength
    3   Medium

Environmental Conditions

Location
    L1   Regulated inside climate

Discomforts
    D1   Noise
    D3   Odours
    D4   Non-toxic dusts

Employment Requirements

Education/Training
4

- Completion of secondary school is usually required.

- Previous experience as a sawmill machine operator, other wood processing operator or as a labourer in wood processing is usually required for graders and inspectors in this group.

Workplaces/Employers

Planing mills

Sawmills

Waferboard plants

Wood processing companies

Wood treatment plants

Occupational Options

There is some mobility among employers processing similar wood products.

Similar Occupations Classified Elsewhere

Supervisors, Forest Products Processing (9215)

Forest product technologists (in 2211 *Applied Chemical Technologists and Technicians*)

Log scalers (in 2223 *Forestry Technologists and Technicians*)

Production technologists in sawmills (in 2233 *Industrial Engineering and Manufacturing Technologists and Technicians*)

9441 Textile Fibre and Yarn Preparation Machine Operators

Textile Fibre and Yarn Preparation Machine Operators prepare textile fibres and spin, wind and twist yarn and thread.

Profile Summary

APTITUDES

G	V	N	S	P	Q	K	F	M
4	4	5	4	4	5	3	4	3

INTERESTS
MOi

DATA PEOPLE THINGS (DPT)
664

PHYSICAL ACTIVITIES (PA)

V	C	H	B	L
2	1	1	2	1
				3

ENVIRONMENTAL CONDITIONS (EC)
L1, H3, D1, D4

EDUCATION/TRAINING
2

Examples of Job Titles

Card Tender
Opening and Blending Operator
Slasher Operator - Textiles
Spinning Operator - Textiles
Twisting Operator - Textiles
Warping Operator - Textiles
Wool Scourer

Descriptor Profile

Main Characteristics

Occupations in this group are characterized by the following aptitudes, interests and worker functions as they relate to main duties:

- **General learning ability** to operate and feed machines that wash, mix, blend, pick, card, lap, comb and draw fibres

- **Motor co-ordination** and **manual dexterity** to feed yarn texturizing machines and to tie broken threads

- **Methodical interest** in **comparing** to patrol work areas in order to check for defects and broken yarn

- **Objective interest** in **operating** yarn texturizing machines, spinning and twisting frames, and winding and reeling machines

- **Innovative interest** in **speaking** to notify supervisors and mechanics of equipment malfunctions; and in investigating machine stoppages

9441

Physical Activities

Vision
  2 Near vision

Colour Discrimination
  1 Relevant

Hearing
  1 Limited

Body Position
  2 Standing and/or walking

Limb Co-ordination
  1 Upper limb co-ordination

Strength
  3 Medium

Environmental Conditions

Location
  L1 Regulated inside climate

Hazards
  H3 Equipment, machinery, tools

Discomforts
  D1 Noise
  D4 Non-toxic dusts

Employment Requirements

Education/Training
2

- Some secondary school education may be required.

- Several months of on-the-job training may be provided.

Workplaces/Employers

Textile companies

Occupational Options

There is considerable mobility among occupations in this group.

Progression to supervisory positions is possible with experience.

Similar Occupations Classified Elsewhere

Supervisors, Textile Processing (9216)

9442 Weavers, Knitters and Other Fabric-Making Occupations

Workers in this group operate machines to process yarn and thread into woven, non-woven and knitted products as well as to quilt and embroider fabrics. This group also includes workers who perform activities such as reproducing patterns, drawing in and tying warps and setting up looms.

Profile Summary

APTITUDES

G	V	N	S	P	Q	K	F	M
3	4	4	4	3	4	3	3	3

INTERESTS
OMi

DATA PEOPLE THINGS (DPT)
662

PHYSICAL ACTIVITIES (PA)

V	C	H	B	L	S
2	1	1	2	1	2

ENVIRONMENTAL CONDITIONS (EC)
L1, H3, D1, D4

EDUCATION/TRAINING
2

Examples of Job Titles

Carpet Weaver
Drawer-in
Drawing-in Machine Operator
Embroidery Machine Operator
Hosiery Knitter
Knitter
Knitting Machine Operator
Loom Operator
Mattress Sewing Machine Operator
Pinning Machine Operator
Quilting Machine Operator
Tufting Operator
Warp-Knitting Machine Tender
Warp Tier-in
Weaver

Descriptor Profile

Main Characteristics

Occupations in this group are characterized by the following aptitudes, interests and worker functions as they relate to main duties:

- **General learning ability** to operate machines to process yarn and thread into woven, non-woven and knitted products such as cloth, lace, carpets, rope, industrial fabric, hosiery and knitted garments, and to quilt and embroider fabrics

- **Form perception** to patrol machines and check fabrics and products for defects, and to verify efficient operations

- **Motor co-ordination** and **finger dexterity** to repair minor mechanical problems such as broken and defective needles

- **Manual dexterity** to set up looms and other processing machines, and to operate looms in order to weave yarn and thread into textile fabrics and products

- **Objective interest** in **controlling** machines that produce twine, ropes and nets; knitting machines that produce knitted fabrics, hosiery, garments and other products; carpet tufting machines; felt making needle-punch machines; and other machines that produce textile products

- **Methodical interest** in **comparing** to read loom patterns and prepare loom pattern mechanisms for processing

- **Innovative interest** in **speaking** to notify supervisors and repairers of mechanical malfunctions; and in investigating machine stoppages, and in operating automatic multi-needle machines to embroider material and sew yard goods, quilts and mattress coverings

9442

Physical Activities

Vision
  2   Near vision

Colour Discrimination
  1   Relevant

Hearing
  1   Limited

Body Position
  2   Standing and/or walking

Limb Co-ordination
  1   Upper limb co-ordination

Strength
  2   Light

Environmental Conditions

Location
  L1 Regulated inside climate

Hazards
  H3 Equipment, machinery, tools

Discomforts
  D1 Noise
  D4 Non-toxic dusts

Employment Requirements

Education/Training
  2

- On-the-job training is provided for periods up to several months, depending on the complexity of the product, whether equipment set-up and maintenance is done by the operator, and on the number of machines operated.

- Previous experience as a labourer in the same company may be required for some operators in this group.

Workplaces/Employers

Garment manufacturing companies

Mattress manufacturing companies

Textile companies

Occupational Options

Movement among employers may be limited by differences in machines and products.

Progression to textile machinery mechanics and repairers or to supervisory positions is possible with experience.

Similar Occupations Classified Elsewhere

Sewing Machine Operators (9451)

Supervisors, Textile Processing (9216)

Textile Machinery Mechanics and Repairers (7317)

9443 Textile Dyeing and Finishing Machine Operators

Textile Dyeing and Finishing Machine Operators bleach, dye and finish yarn, thread, cloth and textile products.

Profile Summary

APTITUDES

G	V	N	S	P	Q	K	F	M
4	4	4	4	4	4	4	4	3

INTERESTS
OMi

DATA PEOPLE THINGS (DPT)
664

PHYSICAL ACTIVITIES (PA)

V	C	H	B	L	S
2	1	1	2	1	2

ENVIRONMENTAL CONDITIONS (EC)
L1, H1, H3, H7*, D1, D3

EDUCATION/TRAINING
2

Examples of Job Titles

Autoclave Tender - Textiles
Bleaching Range Operator
Carpet Drying Machine Tender
Coater Operator - Textiles
Dye Range Operator

Descriptor Profile

Main Characteristics

Occupations in this group are characterized by the following aptitudes, interests and worker functions as they relate to main duties:

- **General learning ability** and **manual dexterity** to set up machines for proper processing

- **Objective interest** in **operating** machines to bleach, dye, coat and finish fabric, thread, yarn and other textile products

- **Methodical interest** in **comparing** to examine products for defects and to ensure that products adhere to quality standards; and in mixing dyes and chemicals according to established formulas

- **Innovative interest** in **speaking** to notify supervisors and mechanics of equipment malfunctions

9443

Physical Activities

Vision
    2   Near vision

Colour Discrimination
    1   Relevant

Hearing
    1   Limited

Body Position
    2   Standing and/or walking

Limb Co-ordination
    1   Upper limb co-ordination

Strength
    2   Light

Environmental Conditions

Location
    L1   Regulated inside climate

Hazards
    H1   Dangerous chemical substances
    H3   Equipment, machinery, tools
    H7* Fire, steam, hot surfaces

Discomforts
    D1   Noise
    D3   Odours

Employment Requirements

Education/Training
2

- Completion of secondary school may be required.

- On-the-job training is provided for periods up to several months, depending on the complexity of the process and the number of machines operated.

Workplaces/Employers

Textile manufacturing companies

Occupational Options

Progression is possible within the group to operate more complex dye ranges and textile printing equipment.

Progression to supervisory positions usually requires completion of a college program in textiles, chemistry or a related subject.

Similar Occupations Classified Elsewhere

Supervisors, Textile Processing (9216)

Master dyers and textile colour technologists (in 2211 *Applied Chemical Technologists and Technicians*)

Remarks

* Environmental Conditions

- For some occupations in this group, **Hazards** H7 (Fire, steam, hot surfaces) may also apply.

9444 Textile Inspectors, Graders and Samplers

Textile Inspectors, Graders and Samplers prepare samples and inspect and grade textile products.

Profile Summary

APTITUDES

G	V	N	S	P	Q	K	F	M
3	4	4	4	3	4	4	4	3

INTERESTS
Moi

DATA PEOPLE THINGS (DPT)
587

PHYSICAL ACTIVITIES (PA)

V	C	H	B	L	S
2	1	1	2	1	2

ENVIRONMENTAL CONDITIONS (EC)
L1, D4

EDUCATION/TRAINING
2

Examples of Job Titles

Cloth Grader
Cloth Inspector
Inspector - Textiles
Perch Operator
Quality Control Inspector - Textiles
Sampler - Textiles
Textile Grader
Yarn Inspector

Descriptor Profile

Main Characteristics

Occupations in this group are characterized by the following aptitudes, interests and worker functions as they relate to main duties:

- **General learning ability** to examine fabric and textile products to make sure they conform to quality standards

- **Form perception** to note slight differences, defects and irregularities in textile products

- **Manual dexterity** to examine fabrics and use testing, inspection and measuring instruments

- **Methodical interest** in **copying** information to sort products by styles, colours, sizes, lengths and other criteria; and in marking defects and recording information on inspected products

- **Objective interest** in **handling** textiles to measure and weigh products; may package products

- **Innovative interest** in grading products and in repairing minor defects

9444

Physical Activities

Vision
   2 Near vision

Colour Discrimination
   1 Relevant

Hearing
   1 Limited

Body Position
   2 Standing and/or walking

Limb Co-ordination
   1 Upper limb co-ordination

Strength
   2 Light

Environmental Conditions

Location
   L1 Regulated inside climate

Discomforts
   D4 Non-toxic dusts

Employment Requirements

Education/Training
   2

- Some secondary school education may be required.
- On-the-job training is provided.
- Experience as a weaver, knitter or other fabric-making operator may be required for inspection of more valuable and complex products.

Workplaces/Employers

Textile companies

Similar Occupations Classified Elsewhere

Supervisors, Textile Processing (9216)

9451 Sewing Machine Operators

Sewing Machine Operators sew fabric, fur, leather and synthetic materials to produce and repair garments and other articles.

Profile Summary

APTITUDES

G	V	N	S	P	Q	K	F	M
4	4	4	3	3	5	3	3	3

INTERESTS
OMi

DATA PEOPLE THINGS (DPT)
684

PHYSICAL ACTIVITIES (PA)

V	C	H	B	L	S
1	1	1	1	2	2

ENVIRONMENTAL CONDITIONS (EC)
L1, H3, D1

EDUCATION/TRAINING
2

Examples of Job Titles

Fur Sewing Machine Operator
Leather Products Sewing Machine Operator
Lining Stitcher
Sample Maker
Sample Sewer
Serging Machine Operator
Sewing Machine Operator
Shoe Sewer

Descriptor Profile

Main Characteristics

Occupations in this group are characterized by the following aptitudes, interests and worker functions as they relate to main duties:

- **General learning ability** to operate sewing machines to join sections of garments and other articles into finished products on a piecework or production basis

- **Spatial perception** to position articles and materials in machines

- **Form perception** to examine finished products for defects

- **Motor co-ordination** and **finger** and **manual dexterity** to thread and operate a variety of sewing machines

- **Objective interest** in **operating** single-, double- and multi-needle sewing machines, serging machines to sew and overcast edges of materials simultaneously, and stitching machines to sew leather parts together for garments, handbags, shoes and other articles

- **Methodical interest** in **comparing** to select threads according to specifications and colours of fabrics, and to operate fur sewing machines to join pelt strips to required sizes and shapes and to join pelts into garment sections and shells

- **Innovative interest** in operating tackers, buttonhole makers and fusing, hemmer and other machines to finish garments and other articles, and in using sewing machines, sergers and other machines to repair garments and other articles during manufacturing

9451

Physical Activities

Vision
1 Close visual acuity

Colour Discrimination
1 Relevant

Hearing
1 Limited

Body Position
1 Sitting

Limb Co-ordination
2 Multiple limb co-ordination

Strength
2 Light

Environmental Conditions

Location
L1 Regulated inside climate

Hazards
H3 Equipment, machinery, tools

Discomforts
D1 Noise

Employment Requirements

Education/Training
2

- Some secondary school education is usually required.

- Experience operating a sewing machine is usually required.

- On-the-job training may be provided.

Workplaces/Employers

Clothing manufacturing companies

Footwear manufacturing companies

Fur products manufacturing companies

Furriers

Textile and leather products manufacturing companies

Occupational Options

Sewing machine operators may progress to supervisory positions with experience.

Similar Occupations Classified Elsewhere

Fabric, Fur and Leather Cutters (9452)

Tailors, Dressmakers, Furriers and Milliners (7342)

Supervisors of sewing machine operators (in 9225 *Supervisors, Fabric, Fur and Leather Products Manufacturing*)

9452.1 Fabric Cutters

Fabric Cutters make parts for garments, linens and other articles.

Profile Summary

APTITUDES

G	V	N	S	P	Q	K	F	M
3	4	4	4	4	4	3	4	3

INTERESTS
MOi

DATA PEOPLE THINGS (DPT)
581

PHYSICAL ACTIVITIES (PA)

V	C	H	B	L	S
2	0	1	2	1	2

ENVIRONMENTAL CONDITIONS (EC)
L1, H3, D4

EDUCATION/TRAINING
2

Examples of Job Titles

Clothing Cutter
Computer Cutter
Fabric Cutter
Sample Cutter

Descriptor Profile

Main Characteristics

Occupations in this group are characterized by the following aptitudes, interests and worker functions as they relate to main duties:

- **General learning ability** to cut fabrics to make parts for garments, linens and other articles

- **Motor co-ordination** and **manual dexterity** to place patterns on top of layers of fabric, and to cut fabrics using electric and manual knives and cutters

- **Methodical interest** in **copying** information to cut fabrics while following patterns

- **Objective interest** in **precision working** to activate computerized cutting devices to cut layers of fabric; may cut fabric samples

- **Innovative interest** in adjusting guides, cutting blades and other mechanisms for specific operations

9452.1
Subgroup 1 of 3

Physical Activities

Vision
   2   Near vision

Colour Discrimination
   0   Not relevant

Hearing
   1   Limited

Body Position
   2   Standing and/or walking

Limb Co-ordination
   1   Upper limb co-ordination

Strength
   2   Light

Environmental Conditions

Location
   L1   Regulated inside climate

Hazards
   H3   Equipment, machinery, tools

Discomforts
   D4   Non-toxic dusts

Employment Requirements

Education/Training
2

- Some secondary school education is usually required.

- Experience as a fabric cutter is required for fabric sample cutters.

- Some on-the-job training is provided for occupations in this group.

Workplaces/Employers

Clothing and textile manufacturers

Manufacturers of fabric products

Occupational Options

There is little mobility among the different kinds of cutters in the 9452 group.

Progression to supervisory positions is possible with experience.

Similar Occupations Classified Elsewhere

Supervisors, Fabric, Fur and Leather Products Manufacturing (9225)

Tailors, Dressmakers, Furriers and Milliners (7342)

9452.2 Fur Cutters

Fur Cutters make parts for garments and other fur articles.

Profile Summary

APTITUDES

G	V	N	S	P	Q	K	F	M
3	4	4	4	4	4	3	4	3

INTERESTS
MOi

DATA PEOPLE THINGS (DPT)
581

PHYSICAL ACTIVITIES (PA)

V	C	H	B	L	S
2	0	1	2	1	2

ENVIRONMENTAL CONDITIONS (EC)
L1, H3, D4

EDUCATION/TRAINING
2+

Examples of Job Titles

Fur Cutter
Sample Cutter

Descriptor Profile

Main Characteristics

Occupations in this group are characterized by the following aptitudes, interests and worker functions as they relate to main duties:

- **General learning ability** to cut fur pelts to make parts for garments and other fur articles

- **Motor co-ordination** and **manual dexterity** to use furriers' knives and cutters

- **Methodical interest** in **copying** to cut fur skins in diagonal strips to specified lengths and shapes of pelts; may sort and match skins

- **Objective interest** in **precision working** with cutting devices to cut fur skins; may prepare fur samples

- **Innovative interest** in numbering pelts to indicate their location on patterns

9452.2
Subgroup 2 of 3

Physical Activities

Vision
  2 Near vision

Colour Discrimination
  0 Not relevant

Hearing
  1 Limited

Body Position
  2 Standing and/or walking

Limb Co-ordination
  1 Upper limb co-ordination

Strength
  2 Light

Environmental Conditions

Location
  L1 Regulated inside climate

Hazards
  H3 Equipment, machinery, tools

Discomforts
  D4 Non-toxic dusts

Employment Requirements

Education/Training
  2+

- Some secondary school education is usually required.

- Experience as a fur cutter is required for fur sample cutters.

- Several years of on-the-job training are provided for fur cutters.

Workplaces/Employers

Fur products manufacturers

Furriers

Occupational Options

There is little mobility among the different kinds of cutters in the 9452 group.

Progression to supervisory positions is possible with experience.

Similar Occupations Classified Elsewhere

Supervisors, Fabric, Fur and Leather Products Manufacturing (9225)

Tailors, Dressmakers, Furriers and Milliners (7342)

9452.3 Leather Cutters

Leather Cutters make parts for shoes, garments and other leather articles.

Profile Summary

APTITUDES

G	V	N	S	P	Q	K	F	M
3	4	4	4	4	4	3	4	3

INTERESTS
OMi

DATA PEOPLE THINGS (DPT)
581

PHYSICAL ACTIVITIES (PA)

V	C	H	B	L	S
2	0	1	2	1	2

ENVIRONMENTAL CONDITIONS (EC)
L1, H3, D4

EDUCATION/TRAINING
2

Examples of Job Titles

Die Cutter
Glove Cutter
Leather Cutter
Sample Cutter
Shoe Cutter

Descriptor Profile

Main Characteristics

Occupations in this group are characterized by the following aptitudes, interests and worker functions as they relate to main duties:

- **General learning ability** to cut leather to make parts for shoes, garments and other articles

- **Motor co-ordination** and **manual dexterity** to use cutting machines and equipment

- **Objective interest** in **precision working** with machines and by hand to make leather products; may cut leather samples

- **Methodical interest** in **copying** to select leather and cutting dies for goods and shoe parts according to specifications

- **Innovative interest** in positioning leather on cutting beds of machines, and in maximizing usage according to skins' grains, flaws and stretch

9452.3
Subgroup 3 of 3

Physical Activities

Vision
  2 Near vision

Colour Discrimination
  0 Not relevant

Hearing
  1 Limited

Body Position
  2 Standing and/or walking

Limb Co-ordination
  1 Upper limb co-ordination

Strength
  2 Light

Environmental Conditions

Location
  L1 Regulated inside climate

Hazards
  H3 Equipment, machinery, tools

Discomforts
  D4 Non-toxic dusts

Employment Requirements

Education/Training
  2

- Some secondary school education is usually required.

- Experience as a leather cutter is required for leather sample cutters.

- Some on-the-job training is provided for occupations in this group.

Workplaces/Employers

Leather garment and other products manufacturers

Shoe manufacturers

Occupational Options

There is little mobility among the different kinds of cutters in the 9452 group.

Progression to supervisory positions is possible with experience.

Similar Occupations Classified Elsewhere

Supervisors, Fabric, Fur and Leather Products Manufacturing (9225)

Tailors, Dressmakers, Furriers and Milliners (7342)

9453 Hide and Pelt Processing Workers

Hide and Pelt Processing Workers prepare hides, pelts and skins to produce leather stock and finished furs.

Profile Summary

APTITUDES

G	V	N	S	P	Q	K	F	M
4	4	4	4	3	4	3	4	3

INTERESTS
OMI

DATA PEOPLE THINGS (DPT)
684

PHYSICAL ACTIVITIES (PA)

V	C	H	B	L	S
2	1	1	4	1	3

ENVIRONMENTAL CONDITIONS (EC)
L1, H1, H3, D3, D4, D5

EDUCATION/TRAINING
2

Examples of Job Titles

Beating Machine Tender
Leather Buffer
Leather Stretcher
Pelt Dresser
Pickler
Shaving Machine Tender
Splitter
Tanner

Descriptor Profile

Main Characteristics

Occupations in this group are characterized by the following aptitudes, interests and worker functions as they relate to main duties:

- **General learning ability** to trim, scrape, clean, tan, buff and dye animal hides, pelts and skins to produce leather stock and finished furs

- **Form perception** to examine hides, skins and pelts for defects

- **Motor co-ordination** and **manual dexterity** to cut particles of flesh and fat from hides and pelts using hand and powered cutting knives, and to remove loose hair from hides and pelts

- **Objective interest** in operating machines to remove flesh and hair from hides, skins and pelts, and to polish and roughen hides and skins to specified finishes

- **Methodical interest** in **comparing** information to shave hides to uniform thicknesses, and to shear fur and wool hides to produce pelts with hair of specified and uniform lengths

- **Innovative interest** in preparing solutions in vats and revolving drums, in immersing hides and skins in solutions to clean, de-hair, pickle, dye, oil and tan them, in immersing pelts in solutions to clean, soften and preserve them, and in tinting and dying furs to enhance their natural shades

Physical Activities

Vision
  2 Near vision

Colour Discrimination
  1 Relevant

Hearing
  1 Limited

Body Position
  4 Other body positions

Limb Co-ordination
  1 Upper limb co-ordination

Strength
  3 Medium

Environmental Conditions

Location
  L1 Regulated inside climate

Hazards
  H1 Dangerous chemical substances
  H3 Equipment, machinery, tools

Discomforts
  D3 Odours
  D4 Non-toxic dusts
  D5 Wetness

Employment Requirements

Education/Training
  2

- On-the-job training is usually provided.

Workplaces/Employers

Fur dressing businesses

Leather and fur dyeing establishments

Leather tanning companies

Occupational Options

There is some mobility among jobs in this group.

Progression to supervisory positions is possible with experience.

Similar Occupations Classified Elsewhere

Supervisors of hide and pelt processing workers (in 9225 *Supervisors, Fabric, Fur and Leather Products Manufacturing*)

9454 Inspectors and Testers, Fabric, Fur and Leather Products Manufacturing

Inspectors and Testers in this group inspect and grade hides, pelts and leather, garments and other manufactured fabric, fur and leather products.

Profile Summary

APTITUDES

G	V	N	S	P	Q	K	F	M
4	4	4	3	3	4	3	3	4

INTERESTS
Moi

DATA PEOPLE THINGS (DPT)
587

PHYSICAL ACTIVITIES (PA)

V	C	H	B	L	S
2	1	1	3	1	2

ENVIRONMENTAL CONDITIONS (EC)
L1

EDUCATION/TRAINING
2+

Examples of Job Titles

Clothing Inspector
Cushion and Cover Inspector
Fur Grader
Garment Inspector
Hide Grader
Leather Goods Inspector
Pelt Grader
Seconds Inspector-Grader
Shirt Inspector

Descriptor Profile

Main Characteristics

Occupations in this group are characterized by the following aptitudes, interests and worker functions as they relate to main duties:

- **General learning ability** to inspect and grade animal hides, pelts and leather according to size, condition and weight

- **Spatial** and **form perception** to inspect garments and similar products for defects such as seam splits, puckers, missing buttons, and colour and shape variations

- **Motor co-ordination** and **finger dexterity** to trim excess material and loose threads using scissors, to remove lint using brushes and lint removers, to repair minor defects and to remove spots using cleaning solutions

- **Methodical interest** in **copying** to record information on the number and nature of defects, and to tag products according to sizes, styles and quality

- **Objective interest** in **handling** to measure products and verify fit by placing garments over forms

- **Innovative interest** in grading and sorting finished products

9454

Physical Activities

Vision
   2 Near vision

Colour Discrimination
   1 Relevant

Hearing
   1 Limited

Body Position
   3 Sitting, standing, walking

Limb Co-ordination
   1 Upper limb co-ordination

Strength
   2 Light

Environmental Conditions

Location
   L1 Regulated inside climate

Employment Requirements

Education/Training
   2+

- Some secondary school education may be required.

- Work experience in the manufacture of the products under examination is usually required.

Workplaces/Employers

Garment, fur and leather products manufacturers

Leather tanning and fur dressing establishments

Occupational Options

There is little mobility among the different inspectors and testers in this group.

Similar Occupations Classified Elsewhere

Textile Inspectors, Graders and Samplers (9444)

9461.1 Process Control Operators, Food and Beverage Processing

Process Control Operators run multi-functional process control machinery to process and package food and beverage products.

Profile Summary

APTITUDES

G	V	N	S	P	Q	K	F	M
3	4	4	4	3	4	3	4	3

INTERESTS
OMI

DATA PEOPLE THINGS (DPT)
682

PHYSICAL ACTIVITIES (PA)

V	C	H	B	L	S
2	0	1	3	1	1

ENVIRONMENTAL CONDITIONS (EC)
L1, D1, D3

EDUCATION/TRAINING
2+

Examples of Job Titles

Control-Room Operator, Food and Beverage Processing

Descriptor Profile

Main Characteristic

Occupations in this group are characterized by the following aptitudes, interests and worker functions as they relate to main duties:

- **General learning ability** to operate multi-functional process control systems and equipment to process and package food and beverage products

- **Form perception** to observe gauges, computer printouts and video monitors

- **Motor co-ordination** and **manual dexterity** to adjust temperature and pressure controls, and to turn valves to start machines and processing equipment

- **Objective interest** in **controlling** multi-functional processing equipment through control panels, computer terminals and other control systems to process and package food and beverage products

- **Methodical interest** in **comparing** information to monitor equipment in order to verify specified processing conditions, and to maintain shift logs of production and other data

- **Innovative interest** in adjusting process variables such as cooking times, ingredient inputs, flow rates and temperature settings

9461.1
Subgroup 1 of 2

Physical Activities

Vision
    2   Near vision

Colour Discrimination
    0   Not relevant

Hearing
    1   Limited

Body Position
    3   Sitting, standing, walking

Limb Co-ordination
    1   Upper limb co-ordination

Strength
    1   Limited

Environmental Conditions

Location
    L1   Regulated inside climate

Discomforts
    D1 Noise
    D3 Odours

Employment Requirements

Education/Training
2+

- Completion of secondary school may be required.

- Experience as a machine operator, food and beverage processing, is usually required for process control operators.

Workplaces/Employers

Bakeries

Breweries

Dairies

Flour mills

Food and beverage processing establishments

Fruit and vegetable processing plants

Meat plants

Sugar refineries

Occupational Options

There is little mobility among the various types of process control operators within the food and beverage processing industry.

Process control operators may progress to supervisory positions in food and beverage processing with experience.

Similar Occupations Classified Elsewhere

Bakers (6252)

Butchers and Meat Cutters, Retail and Wholesale (6251)

Fish Plant Workers (9463)

Industrial Butchers and Meat Cutters, Poultry Preparers and Related Workers (9462)

Labourers in Fish Processing (9618)

Labourers in Food, Beverage and Tobacco Processing (9617)

Supervisors, Food, Beverage and Tobacco Processing (9213)

9461.2 Machine Operators, Food and Beverage Processing

Machine Operators run single-function machines to process and package food and beverage products.

Profile Summary

APTITUDES

G	V	N	S	P	Q	K	F	M
3	4	4	4	3	4	3	4	3

INTERESTS
OMi

DATA PEOPLE THINGS (DPT)
684

PHYSICAL ACTIVITIES (PA)

V	C	H	B	L	S
2	0	1	2	1	2

ENVIRONMENTAL CONDITIONS (EC)
L1, H3, H7*, D1, D3

EDUCATION/TRAINING
2

Examples of Job Titles

Bakery Machine Operator
Bottling Machine Operator
Brewer
Canning Machine Operator
Chocolate Refiner
Fermenter Operator
Freezer Operator
Fryer Operator
Meat Grinder
Mixer Operator, Dry Foods
Pasteurizer Operator
Sugar Boiler

Descriptor Profile

Main Characteristics

Occupations in this group are characterized by the following aptitudes, interests and worker functions as they relate to main duties:

- **General learning ability** to operate single-function machines to process and package food and beverage products

- **Form perception** to check products for defects

- **Motor co-ordination** and **manual dexterity** to adjust machines so they operate correctly

- **Objective interest** in operating processing and packaging machines and equipment

- **Methodical interest** in **comparing** information to make sure products conform to company standards; and in recording production data such as quantities, weights, sizes, dates and types of packaged products

- **Innovative interest** in setting up and adjusting processing and packaging machines

9461.2
Subgroup 2 of 2

Physical Activities

Vision
2 Near vision

Colour Discrimination
0 Not relevant

Hearing
1 Limited

Body Position
2 Standing and/or walking

Limb Co-ordination
1 Upper limb co-ordination

Strength
2 Light

Environmental Conditions

Location
L1 Regulated inside climate

Hazards
H3 Equipment, machinery, tools
H7*Fire, steam, hot surfaces

Discomforts
D1 Noise
D3 Odours

Employment Requirements

Education/Training
2

- Completion of secondary school may be required

- Experience as a labourer in food and beverage processing may be required for machine operators.

Workplaces/Employers

Bakeries

Breweries

Dairies

Flour mills

Food and beverage processing establishments

Fruit and vegetable processing plants

Meat plants

Sugar refineries

Occupational Options

There is mobility among machine operators within the food and beverage processing industry.

Machine operators may progress to process control operators or supervisors in food and beverage processing with experience.

Similar Occupations Classified Elsewhere

Bakers (6252)

Butchers and Meat Cutters, Retail and Wholesale (6251)

Fish Plant Workers (9463)

Industrial Butchers and Meat Cutters, Poultry Preparers and Related Workers (9462)

Labourers in Fish Processing (9618)

Labourers in Food, Beverage and Tobacco Processing (9617)

Supervisors, Food, Beverage and Tobacco Processing (9213)

Remarks

*Environmental Conditions

- For some occupations in this group, **Hazards**, H7 (Fire, steam, hot surfaces) may also apply.

9462.1 Industrial Butchers

Industrial Butchers prepare meat for further processing, packaging and marketing.

Profile Summary

APTITUDES

G	V	N	S	P	Q	K	F	M
3	4	4	4	4	5	4	4	3

INTERESTS
OMd

DATA PEOPLE THINGS (DPT)
684

PHYSICAL ACTIVITIES (PA)

V	C	H	B	L	S
2	0	1	4	1	4

ENVIRONMENTAL CONDITIONS (EC)
L1, H2, H3, D1, D3, D5

EDUCATION/TRAINING
2

Examples of Job Titles

Industrial Butcher
Slaughterer

Descriptor Profile

Main Characteristics

Occupations in this group are characterized by the following aptitudes, interests and worker functions as they relate to main duties:

- **General learning ability** to apply the techniques of slaughtering and skinning livestock; may slaughter cattle, calves and sheep as prescribed by religious laws

- **Manual dexterity** to use stunning devices and knives to stun, slaughter and skin animals

- **Objective interest** in **operating** equipment to split carcasses into smaller portions to facilitate handling

- **Methodical interest** in **comparing** information to remove viscera and other inedible parts from carcasses

- **Directive interest** in preparing meat for further processing, packaging and marketing

9462.1
Subgroup 1 of 4

Physical Activities

Vision
    2   Near vision

Colour Discrimination
    0   Not relevant

Hearing
    1   Limited

Body Position
    4   Other body positions

Limb Co-ordination
    1   Upper limb co-ordination

Strength
    4   Heavy

Environmental Conditions

Location
    L1 Regulated inside climate

Hazards
    H2 Biological agents
    H3 Equipment, machinery, tools

Discomforts
    D1 Noise
    D3 Odours
    D5 Wetness

Employment Requirements

Education/Training
2

- Completion of secondary school may be required.

- On-the-job training is usually provided for industrial butchers.

Workplaces/Employers

Meat and poultry slaughtering establishments

Processing and packing plants

Occupational Options

Progression to supervisory positions is possible with experience.

Similar Occupations Classified Elsewhere

Butchers and Meat Cutters, Retail and Wholesale (6251)

Meat graders (in 9465 Testers and Graders, Food and Beverage Processing)

Meat inspectors (in 2222 Agricultural and Fish Products Inspectors)

Supervisors, meat packing (in 9213 Supervisors, Food, Beverage and Tobacco Processing)

9462.2 Industrial Meat Cutters

Industrial Meat Cutters prepare meat and poultry for further processing, packaging and marketing.

Profile Summary

APTITUDES

G	V	N	S	P	Q	K	F	M
3	4	4	4	4	5	4	4	3

INTERESTS
OMd

DATA PEOPLE THINGS (DPT)
681

PHYSICAL ACTIVITIES (PA)

V	C	H	B	L	S
2	0	1	2	1	4

ENVIRONMENTAL CONDITIONS (EC)
L1, H2, H3, D1, D3, D5*

EDUCATION/TRAINING
4, 5

Examples of Job Titles

Beef Boner
Ham Cutter
Industrial Meat Cutter

Descriptor Profile

Main Characteristics

Occupations in this group are characterized by the following aptitudes, interests and worker functions as they relate to main duties:

- **General learning ability** to cut beef, lamb, pork and veal carcasses or sides and quarters of carcasses into basic cuts

- **Manual dexterity** to use knives, cleavers, saws and other butcher's tools

- **Objective interest** in **precision working** to remove bones from meat

- **Methodical interest** in **comparing** information to cut meat and poultry into specific cuts for institutional, commercial and other wholesale use

- **Directive interest** in preparing meats for further cutting, processing and packaging

9462.2

Physical Activities

Vision
  2 Near vision

Colour Discrimination
  0 Not relevant

Hearing
  1 Limited

Body Position
  2 Standing and/or walking

Limb Co-ordination
  1 Upper limb co-ordination

Strength
  4 Heavy

Environmental Conditions

Location
  L1 Regulated inside climate

Hazards
  H2 Biological agents
  H3 Equipment, machinery, tools

Discomforts
  D1 Noise
  D3 Odours
  D5*Wetness

Employment Requirements

Education/Training
  4, 5

- Completion of secondary school may be required.

- For industrial meat cutters, completion of a program in industrial meat cutting
  or
  experience as an industrial butcher or trimmer is required.

Workplaces/Employers

Meat and poultry slaughtering establishments

Processing and packing plants

Occupational Options

Industrial meat cutters may progress to inspecting, testing and grading jobs.

Progression to supervisory positions is possible with experience.

Similar Occupations Classified Elsewhere

Butchers and Meat Cutters, Retail and Wholesale (6251)

Meat graders (in 9465 *Testers and Graders, Food and Beverage Processing*)

Meat inspectors (in 2222 *Agricultural and Fish Products Inspectors*)

Supervisors, meat packing (in 9213 *Supervisors, Food, Beverage and Tobacco Processing*)

Remarks

*Environmental Conditions

- For some occupations in this group, **Discomforts** D5 (Wetness) may also apply.

9462.3 Poultry Preparers

Poultry preparers prepare poultry for further processing, packaging and marketing.

Profile Summary

APTITUDES

G	V	N	S	P	Q	K	F	M
3	4	4	4	4	5	4	4	3

INTERESTS
OMd

DATA PEOPLE THINGS (DPT)
684

PHYSICAL ACTIVITIES (PA)

V	C	H	B	L	S
2	0	1	2	1	2

ENVIRONMENTAL CONDITIONS (EC)
L1, H2, H3, D1, D3, D4, D5

EDUCATION/TRAINING
2

Examples of Job Titles

Poultry Preparer

Descriptor Profile

Main Characteristics

Occupations in this group are characterized by the following aptitudes, interests and worker functions as they relate to main duties:

- **General learning ability** to slaughter poultry

- **Manual dexterity** to use mechanical devices, knives and other butcher's tools

- **Objective interest** in **operating** equipment to remove feathers and singe and wash poultry

- **Methodical interest** in **comparing** information to remove inedible parts

- **Directive interest** in preparing poultry for further processing and packaging

9462.3
Subgroup 3 of 4

Physical Activities

Vision
   2 Near vision

Colour Discrimination
   0 Not relevant

Hearing
   1 Limited

Body Position
   2 Standing and/or walking

Limb Co-ordination
   1 Upper limb co-ordination

Strength
   2 Light

Environmental Conditions

Location
   L1 Regulated inside climate

Hazards
   H2 Biological agents
   H3 Equipment, machinery, tools

Discomforts
   D1 Noise
   D3 Odours
   D4 Non-toxic dusts
   D5 Wetness

Employment Requirements

Education/Training
2

- Completion of secondary school may be required.

- On-the-job training is usually provided for poultry preparers.

Workplaces/Employers

Meat and poultry slaughtering establishments

Processing and packing plants

Occupational Options

Progression to supervisory positions is possible with experience.

Similar Occupations Classified Elsewhere

Butchers and Meat Cutters, Retail and Wholesale (6251)

Meat graders (in 9465 *Testers and Graders, Food and Beverage Processing*)

Meat inspectors (in 2222 *Agricultural and Fish Products Inspectors*)

Supervisors, meat packing (in 9213 *Supervisors, Food, Beverage and Tobacco Processing*)

9462.4 Trimmers

Trimmers prepare meat and poultry for further processing, packaging and marketing.

Profile Summary

APTITUDES

G	V	N	S	P	Q	K	F	M
3	4	4	4	4	5	4	4	3

INTERESTS
OMd

DATA PEOPLE THINGS (DPT)
684

PHYSICAL ACTIVITIES (PA)

V	C	H	B	L	S
2	0	1	2	1	2

ENVIRONMENTAL CONDITIONS (EC)
L1, H2, H3, D1, D3, D5*

EDUCATION/TRAINING
2

Examples of Job Titles

Meat Trimmer

Descriptor Profile

Main Characteristics

Occupations in this group are characterized by the following aptitudes, interests and worker functions as they relate to main duties:

- **General learning ability** to remove skin, excess fat, bruises and other blemishes from carcasses and meat portions

- **Manual dexterity** to use butcher and electric knives

- **Objective interest** in **operating** equipment to trim meats and fat from bones

- **Methodical interest** in **comparing** information to trim meat into specified shapes

- **Directive interest** in preparing meat for further processing, packaging and marketing

9462.4

Physical Activities

Vision
   2 Near vision

Colour Discrimination
   0 Not relevant

Hearing
   1 Limited

Body Position
   2 Standing and/or walking

Limb Co-ordination
   1 Upper limb co-ordination

Strength
   2 Light

Environmental Conditions

Location
   L1 Regulated inside climate

Hazards
   H2 Biological agents
   H3 Equipment, machinery, tools

Discomforts
   D1 Noise
   D3 Odours
   D5*Wetness

Employment Requirements

Education/Training
2

- Completion of secondary school may be required.

- On-the-job training is usually provided for trimmers.

Workplaces/Employers

Meat and poultry slaughtering establishments

Processing and packing plants

Occupational Options

Progression to supervisory positions is possible with experience.

Similar Occupations Classified Elsewhere

Butchers and Meat Cutters, Retail and Wholesale (6251)

Meat graders (in 9465 *Testers and Graders, Food and Beverage Processing*)

Meat inspectors (in 2222 *Agricultural and Fish Products Inspectors*)

Supervisors, meat packing (in 9213 *Supervisors, Food, Beverage and Tobacco Processing*)

Remarks

*Environmental Conditions

- For some occupations in this group, **D**iscomforts D5 (Wetness) may also apply.

9463.1 Fish Plant Machine Operators

Fish Plant Machine Operators set up and operate machinery to process and package fish products.

Profile Summary

APTITUDES

G	V	N	S	P	Q	K	F	M
4	4	5	4	4	5	4	4	3

INTERESTS
OMi

DATA PEOPLE THINGS (DPT)
684

PHYSICAL ACTIVITIES (PA)

V	C	H	B	L	S
2	0	1	2	1	2

ENVIRONMENTAL CONDITIONS (EC)
L1, H3, D1, D3

EDUCATION/TRAINING
2

Examples of Job Titles

Fish Cake Maker
Fish Canning Machine Operator
Fish Cutting Machine Operator
Fish Plant Worker
Shellfish Processor
Shellfish Separator Tender

Descriptor Profile

Main Characteristics

Occupations in this group are characterized by the following aptitudes, interests and worker functions as they relate to main duties:

- **General learning ability** to set up and operate machinery to process and package fish products

- **Form perception** to check products and packaging for defects

- **Manual dexterity** to repair and maintain equipment

- **Objective interest** in **operating** machines that process and package fish products

- **Methodical interest** in **comparing** information to make sure products and packaging conform to company standards; and in recording production information such as quantities, weights, dates and types of products

- **Innovative interest** in adjusting machinery to operate properly

9463.1
Subgroup 1 of 2

Physical Activities

Vision
2   Near vision

Colour Discrimination
0   Not relevant

Hearing
1   Limited

Body Position
2   Standing and/or walking

Limb Co-ordination
1   Upper limb co-ordination

Strength
2   Light

Environmental Conditions

Location
L1   Regulated inside climate

Hazards
H3   Equipment, machinery, tools

Discomforts
D1   Noise
D3   Odours

Employment Requirements

Education/Training
2

- Some secondary school education may be required.
- On-the-job training is required.

Workplaces/Employers

Fish processing plants

Occupational Options

Progression to supervisory positions is possible with experience.

Similar Occupations Classified Elsewhere

Labourers in Fish Processing (9618)

Supervisors, Food, Beverage and Tobacco Processing (9213)

9463.2 Fish Plant Cutters and Cleaners

Fish Plant Cutters and Cleaners cut, trim and clean fish by hand.

Profile Summary

APTITUDES

G	V	N	S	P	Q	K	F	M
4	4	5	4	4	5	4	4	3

INTERESTS
Moi

DATA PEOPLE THINGS (DPT)
687

PHYSICAL ACTIVITIES (PA)

V	C	H	B	L	S
2	0	1	2	1	3

ENVIRONMENTAL CONDITIONS (EC)
L1, H2, H3, D3, D5

EDUCATION/TRAINING
2

Examples of Job Titles

Fish Cleaner and Cutter
Fish Plant Worker
Shellfish Shucker
Trimmer

Descriptor Profile

Main Characteristics

Occupations in this group are characterized by the following aptitudes, interests and worker functions as they relate to main duties:

- **General learning ability** to cut, clean and trim fish before marketing and further processing

- **Manual dexterity** to use knives to scrape away scales, cut fish, separate fillets and remove scrap parts

- **Methodical interest** in **comparing** information to cut fish sections according to specifications; and in placing fish in containers for weighing

- **Objective interest** in **handling** lobsters and other crustaceans using knives to disjoint and remove meat in preparation for canning and further processing

- **Innovative interest** in checking fish fillets to determine optimal number and size of fillet sections

9463.2
Subgroup 2 of 2

Physical Activities

Vision
  2 Near vision
Colour Discrimination
  0 Not relevant
Hearing
  1 Limited
Body Position
  2 Standing and/or walking
Limb Co-ordination
  1 Upper limb co-ordination
Strength
  3 Medium

Environmental Conditions

Location
  L1 Regulated inside climate
Hazards
  H2 Biological agents
  H3 Equipment, machinery, tools
Discomforts
  D3 Odours
  D5 Wetness

Employment Requirements

Education/Training
  2

- Some secondary school education may be required.
- On-the-job training is required.

Workplaces/Employers

Fish processing plants

Occupational Options

Progression to supervisory positions is possible with experience.

Similar Occupations Classified Elsewhere

Labourers in Fish Processing (9618)

Supervisors, Food, Beverage and Tobacco Processing (9213)

9464 Tobacco Processing Machine Operators

Tobacco Processing Machine Operators prepare and treat raw tobacco leaves, and produce and package tobacco products such as cigarettes and cigars.

Profile Summary

APTITUDES

G	V	N	S	P	Q	K	F	M
4	4	4	4	4	5	4	4	3

INTERESTS
MOi

DATA PEOPLE THINGS (DPT)
684

PHYSICAL ACTIVITIES (PA)

V	C	H	B	L	S
2	0	1	2	1	2

ENVIRONMENTAL CONDITIONS (EC)
L1, H3, D1, D3, D4

EDUCATION/TRAINING
2

Examples of Job Titles

Cigar Maker

Cigarette Machine Tender

Cleaning and Classifying Operator - Tobacco Processing

Conveyor Tender - Tobacco Processing

Dryer Tender - Tobacco Processing

Module Tender - Tobacco Processing

Tobacco Blender

Tobacco Packaging Machine Tender

Descriptor Profile

Main Characteristics

Occupations in this group are characterized by the following aptitudes, interests and worker functions as they relate to main duties:

- **General learning ability** to operate machines that blend, flavour, condition, dry, flatten, strip and cut raw tobacco leaves

- **Manual dexterity** to clear blockages on machines

- **Methodical interest** in **comparing** to clean machines and immediate work areas; and in advising supervisors of mechanical malfunctions and product irregularities

- **Objective interest** in operating equipment to process tobacco; and in tending processing machines

- **Innovative interest** in setting and adjusting temperature, speed, tension and pressure of processing equipment

9464

Physical Activities

Vision
  2 Near vision

Colour Discrimination
  0 Not relevant

Hearing
  1 Limited

Body Position
  2 Standing and/or walking

Limb Co-ordination
  1 Upper limb co-ordination

Strength
  2 Light

Environmental Conditions

Location
  L1 Regulated inside climate

Hazards
  H3 Equipment, machinery, tools

Discomforts
  D1 Noise
  D3 Odours
  D4 Non-toxic dusts

Employment Requirements

Education/Training
  2

- Some secondary school education may be required.

- Experience as a labourer in the tobacco processing industry may be required.

Workplaces/Employers

Leaf tobacco processing plants

Tobacco products plants

Occupational Options

Progression to supervisory positions in the tobacco processing industry is possible with experience.

Similar Occupations Classified Elsewhere

Supervisors, Food, Beverage and Tobacco Processing (9213)

Tobacco testers and graders (in 9465 Testers and Graders, Food and Beverage Processing)

9465 Testers and Graders, Food and Beverage Processing

Testers and Graders in this group test and grade ingredients and finished food, beverage and tobacco products to ensure that they conform to company standards.

Profile Summary

APTITUDES
G	V	N	S	P	Q	K	F	M
3	4	4	4	3	4	4	4	4

INTERESTS
Mlo

DATA PEOPLE THINGS (DPT)
587

PHYSICAL ACTIVITIES (PA)
V	C	H	B	L	S
2	1	1	2	1	2

ENVIRONMENTAL CONDITIONS (EC)
L1, D3

EDUCATION/TRAINING
2

Examples of Job Titles

Beef Grader
Beer Tester
Cheese Grader
Fish Grader
Milk Grader
Poultry Grader
Product Tester, Food and Beverage Processing
Tobacco Grader

Descriptor Profile

Main Characteristics

Occupations in this group are characterized by the following aptitudes, interests and worker functions as they relate to main duties:

- **General learning ability** and **form perception** to examine ingredients and finished products by sight, touch, taste and smell to ensure that they conform to company standards

- **Methodical interest** in **copying** information to conduct routine tests for product specifications such as colour, alcohol content, carbonation, fat content and packaging

- **Innovative interest** in grading and sorting raw materials and finished products, and in advising supervisors of ingredient and product deficiencies

- **Objective interest** in **handling** to weigh materials and take samples of products at various stages of processing

9465

Physical Activities

Vision
  2   Near vision

Colour Discrimination
  1   Relevant

Hearing
  1   Limited

Body Position
  2   Standing and/or walking

Limb Co-ordination
  1   Upper limb co-ordination

Strength
  2   Light

Environmental Conditions

Location
  L1   Regulated inside climate

Discomforts
  D3   Odours

Employment Requirements

Education/Training
  2

- Completion of secondary school may be required.

- Experience as a machine operator or labourer in the food and beverage processing industry may be required.

- On-the-job training is usually provided.

Workplaces/Employers

Bakeries

Breweries

Dairies

Fish plants

Flour mills

Food, beverage and tobacco processing plants

Fruit and vegetable processing plants

Meat plants

Sugar refineries

Occupational Options

There is little mobility among the various types of testers and graders in this group.

Progression to supervisory positions is possible with experience.

Similar Occupations Classified Elsewhere

Agricultural and Fish Products Inspectors (2222)

Supervisors, Food, Beverage and Tobacco Processing (9213)

Quality control technologists and technicians (in 2211 *Applied Chemical Technologists and Technicians*)

9471 Printing Machine Operators

Printing Machine Operators operate laser printers, computerized high-speed colour copiers and other printing machines to print text, illustrations and designs on a wide variety of materials such as paper, plastic, glass, leather and metal.

Profile Summary

APTITUDES
G	V	N	S	P	Q	K	F	M
3	4	4	4	3	4	4	4	3

INTERESTS
MOI

DATA PEOPLE THINGS (DPT)
584

PHYSICAL ACTIVITIES (PA)
V	C	H	B	L	S
2	1	1	4	1	3

ENVIRONMENTAL CONDITIONS (EC)
L1

EDUCATION/TRAINING
2, 4

Examples of Job Titles

Colour Copier Operator
Electronic Sign Maker Operator
Laser Printer Operator
Printing and Finishing Machine Operator
Printing Machine Operator
Screen Print Operator
Silk-Screening Machine Operator
Wallpaper Printer

Descriptor Profile

Main Characteristics

Occupations in this group are characterized by the following aptitudes, interests and worker functions as they relate to main duties:

- **General learning ability** to review work orders to determine job specifications such as ink colours and quantities

- **Form perception** to monitor printing machines during print run

- **Manual dexterity** to clean machines and replace worn parts

- **Methodical interest** in **copying** information to input codes and to key programming data on console keyboards of computerized printer

- **Objective interest** in **operating** printing machines

- **Innovative interest** in setting up and making adjustments to printing machines, such as filling ink and paint reservoirs and loading stock

9471

Physical Activities

Vision
   2 Near vision

Colour Discrimination
   1 Relevant

Hearing
   1 Limited

Body Position
   4 Other body positions

Limb Co-ordination
   1 Upper limb co-ordination

Strength
   3 Medium

Environmental Conditions

Location
   L1 Regulated inside climate

Employment Requirements

Education/Training
   2, 4

- Completion of secondary school may be required.
- Completion of college or other courses in printing may be required.
- On-the-job training is provided.

Workplaces/Employers

Commercial printing companies

In-house printing facilities of large establishments

Rapid printing services

Similar Occupations Classified Elsewhere

Printing Press Operators (7381)

Supervisors, Printing and Related Occupations (7218)

Textile printing machine operators (in 9443 *Textile Dyeing and Finishing Machine Operators*)

9472.1 Graphic Arts Camera Operators

Graphic Arts Camera Operators convert photographs to film for printing.

Profile Summary

APTITUDES

G	V	N	S	P	Q	K	F	M
3	3	3	3	2	4	3	4	4

INTERESTS
OMI

DATA PEOPLE THINGS (DPT)
582

PHYSICAL ACTIVITIES (PA)

V	C	H	B	L	S
2	1	1	3	1	2

ENVIRONMENTAL CONDITIONS (EC)
L1, H3

EDUCATION/TRAINING
4, 5, 6, R

Examples of Job Titles

Camera Operator, Graphic Arts

Descriptor Profile

Main Characteristics

Occupations in this group are characterized by the following aptitudes, interests and worker functions as they relate to main duties:

- **General learning** and **verbal ability** to study work orders to determine photographic techniques required to transfer desired effects to film

- **Numerical ability** to compute lens and copy-board settings for same size, enlarged and reduced negatives

- **Spatial perception** to mount photographs and art work copies on vacuum copy boards

- **Form perception** to focus camera lenses and obtain optimum contrast ranges

- **Motor co-ordination** to adjust cameras

- **Objective interest** in **controlling** to set up and adjust black and white or colour separation cameras to convert graphic art and photographs into film for assembly and exposure onto printing plates and cylinders

- **Methodical interest** in **copying** information to produce films according to specifications, and to compare developed films with copies

- **Innovative interest** in determining equipment adjustments required to transfer desired effects to film

9472.1

Physical Activities

Vision
   2 Near vision

Colour Discrimination
   1 Relevant

Hearing
   1 Limited

Body Position
   3 Sitting, standing, walking

Limb Co-ordination
   1 Upper limb co-ordination

Strength
   2 Light

Environmental Conditions

Location
   L1 Regulated inside climate

Hazards
   H3 Equipment, machinery, tools

Employment Requirements

Education/Training
4, 5, 6, R

- Completion of secondary school is required.

- Completion of a college program in graphic arts technology
  or
  a four-to-five year apprenticeship program in printing and graphic arts
  or
  a combination of on-the-job training and specialized college, industry or other courses is required.

- Trade certification for some occupations in the 9472 group is available, but not compulsory, in Ontario, Alberta and the Northwest Territories.

Workplaces/Employers

Colour graphics, platemaking and cylinder preparation companies

Commercial printing companies

In-house printing departments of public- and private-sector establishments

Magazines

Newspapers

Similar Occupations Classified Elsewhere

Graphic Arts Technicians (5223)

Graphic Designers and Illustrating Artists (5241)

Supervisors, Printing and Related Occupations (7218)

Typesetters and desktop publishing operators (in 1423 *Typesetters and Related Occupations*)

9472.2 Cylinder Preparers

Cylinder Preparers get ready, engrave and etch cylinders for printing presses.

Profile Summary

APTITUDES

G	V	N	S	P	Q	K	F	M
3	3	3	3	2	4	3	3	3

INTERESTS
OMI

DATA PEOPLE THINGS (DPT)
581

PHYSICAL ACTIVITIES (PA)

V	C	H	B	L	S
2	1	1	3	1	2

ENVIRONMENTAL CONDITIONS (EC)
L1, H1, H3, H6, D4

EDUCATION/TRAINING
4, 5, 6, R

Examples of Job Titles

Cylinder Preparer - Printing
Printing Plate Engraver

Descriptor Profile

Main Characteristics

Occupations in this group are characterized by the following aptitudes, interests and worker functions as they relate to main duties:

- **General learning** and **verbal ability** to read work sheets to determine sizes and diameters of cylinders required

- **Numerical ability** to measure diameters of cylinders using micrometers to calculate depths of cuts required

- **Spatial perception** to visualize positions of engraved and etched patterns on plates and cylinders

- **Form perception** to examine surfaces of cylinders for flaws using magnifying scopes to ensure surfaces can be etched

- **Motor co-ordination** and **finger** and **manual dexterity** to use hand tools and to paint cylinders with acid-resistant coatings to control etchings in acid baths

- **Objective interest** in **precision working** to etch and engrave cylinders using hand tools, etching machines, photogravure and laser processes to produce cylinders for gravure presses

- **Methodical interest** in **copying** information to grind and polish press cylinders to desired sizes

- **Innovative interest** in exposing and laying down carbon tissue, and in examining and correcting flaws and faults

9472.2
Subgroup 2 of 6

Physical Activities

Vision
    2   Near vision

Colour Discrimination
    1   Relevant

Hearing
    1   Limited

Body Position
    3   Sitting, standing, walking

Limb Co-ordination
    1   Upper limb co-ordination

Strength
    2   Light

Environmental Conditions

Location
    L1 Regulated inside climate

Hazards
    H1 Dangerous chemical substances
    H3 Equipment, machinery, tools
    H6 Flying particles, falling objects

Discomforts
    D4 Non-toxic dusts

Employment Requirements

Education/Training
4, 5, 6, R

- Completion of secondary school is required.

- Completion of a college program in graphic arts technology
  or
  a four-to-five year apprenticeship program in printing and graphic arts
  or
  a combination of on-the-job training and specialized college, industry or other courses is required.

- Trade certification for some occupations in the 9472 group is available, but not compulsory, in Ontario, Alberta and the Northwest Territories.

Workplaces/Employers

Colour graphics, platemaking and cylinder preparation companies

Commercial printing companies

In-house printing departments of public- and private-sector establishments

Magazines

Newspapers

Similar Occupations Classified Elsewhere

Graphic Arts Technicians (5223)

Graphic Designers and Illustrating Artists (5241)

Supervisors, Printing and Related Occupations (7218)

Typesetters and desktop publishing operators (in 1423 *Typesetters and Related Occupations*)

9472.3 Film Strippers/Assemblers

Film Strippers/Assemblers put film and negatives together to prepare printing plates and cylinders.

Profile Summary

APTITUDES

G	V	N	S	P	Q	K	F	M
3	3	3	3	2	4	3	4	4

INTERESTS
OMI

DATA PEOPLE THINGS (DPT)
581

PHYSICAL ACTIVITIES (PA)

V	C	H	B	L	S
2	1	1	3	1	1

ENVIRONMENTAL CONDITIONS (EC)
L1, H3

EDUCATION/TRAINING
4, 5, 6, R

Examples of Job Titles

Film Stripper/Assembler

Descriptor Profile

Main Characteristics

Occupations in this group are characterized by the following aptitudes, interests and worker functions as they relate to main duties:

- **General learning** and **verbal ability** to read work orders to determine treatment of negatives

- **Numerical ability** to calculate and plot registration points and reference lines to ensure accurate registrations

- **Spatial perception** to visualize layouts and position negative components into place

- **Form perception** to examine negatives and composite negatives for flaws

- **Motor co-ordination** to retouch imperfections as required

- **Objective interest** in **precision working** to assemble and position pieces of film by hand and using automated equipment

- **Methodical interest** in **copying** to produce flats and composite negatives for printing plates and cylinders according to work orders

- **Innovative interest** in determining desired layouts

9472.3
Subgroup 3 of 6

Physical Activities

Vision
  2 Near vision

Colour Discrimination
  1 Relevant

Hearing
  1 Limited

Body Position
  3 Sitting, standing, walking

Limb Co-ordination
  1 Upper limb co-ordination

Strength
  1 Limited

Environmental Conditions

Location
  L1 Regulated inside climate

Hazards
  H3 Equipment, machinery, tools

Employment Requirements

Education/Training
4, 5, 6, R

- Completion of secondary school is required.

- Completion of a college program in graphic arts technology
  or
  a four-to-five year apprenticeship program in printing and graphic arts
  or
  a combination of on-the-job training and specialized college, industry or other courses is required.

- Trade certification for some occupations in the 9472 group is available, but not compulsory, in Ontario, Alberta and the Northwest Territories.

Workplaces/Employers

Colour graphics, platemaking and cylinder preparation companies

Commercial printing companies

In-house printing departments of public and private sector establishments

Magazines

Newspapers

Similar Occupations Classified Elsewhere

Graphic Arts Technicians (5223)

Graphic Designers and Illustrating Artists (5241)

Supervisors, Printing and Related Occupations (7218)

Typesetters and desktop publishing operators (in 1423 *Typesetters and Related Occupations*)

9472.4 Platemakers

Platemakers prepare printing plates for printing presses.

Profile Summary

APTITUDES

G	V	N	S	P	Q	K	F	M
3	3	3	3	2	4	3	4	4

INTERESTS
OMI

DATA PEOPLE THINGS (DPT)
581

PHYSICAL ACTIVITIES (PA)

V	C	H	B	L	S
2	0	1	3	1	2

ENVIRONMENTAL CONDITIONS (EC)
L1, H1, H3

EDUCATION/TRAINING
4, 5, 6, R

Examples of Job Titles

Platemaker

Descriptor Profile

Main Characteristics

Occupations in this group are characterized by the following aptitudes, interests and worker functions as they relate to main duties:

- **General learning, verbal** and **numerical ability** to read work orders and calculate machine settings

- **Spatial perception** to align negatives over sensitized plates and position them in vacuum frames of exposing tables

- **Form perception** to inspect negatives and processed material for imperfections

- **Motor co-ordination** to adjust equipment controls

- **Objective interest** in **precision working** to operate vacuum frames, plate processors and step-and-repeat machines to produce printing plates

- **Methodical interest** in **copying** information to mix chemicals in order to prepare platemaking solutions according to specifications

- **Innovative interest** in making adjustments to vacuum frames, plate processors and step-and-repeat machines

9472.4

Physical Activities

Vision
 2 Near vision

Colour Discrimination
 0 Not relevant

Hearing
 1 Limited

Body Position
 3 Sitting, standing, walking

Limb Co-ordination
 1 Upper limb co-ordination

Strength
 2 Light

Environmental Conditions

Location
 L1 Regulated inside climate

Hazards
 H1 Dangerous chemical substances
 H3 Equipment, machinery, tools

Employment Requirements

Education/Training
4, 5, 6, R

- Completion of secondary school is required.

- Completion of a college program in graphic arts technology
or
a four-to-five year apprenticeship program in printing and graphic arts
or
a combination of on-the-job training and specialized college, industry or other courses is required.

- Trade certification for some occupations in the 9472 group is available, but not compulsory, in Ontario, Alberta and the Northwest Territories.

Workplaces/Employers

Colour graphics, platemaking and cylinder preparation companies

Commercial printing companies

In-house printing departments of public- and private-sector establishments

Magazines

Newspapers

Similar Occupations Classified Elsewhere

Graphic Arts Technicians (5223)

Graphic Designers and Illustrating Artists (5241)

Supervisors, Printing and Related Occupations (7218)

Typesetters and desktop publishing operators (in 1423 *Typesetters and Related Occupations*)

9472.5 Pre-Press Technicians

Pre-Press Technicians operate computerized studio systems that allow changes to be made to negatives and page layouts in preparation for printing.

Profile Summary

APTITUDES

G	V	N	S	P	Q	K	F	M
3	3	3	3	2	4	3	4	4

INTERESTS
OMI

DATA PEOPLE THINGS (DPT)
382

PHYSICAL ACTIVITIES (PA)

V	C	H	B	L	S
2	1	1	1	1	1

ENVIRONMENTAL CONDITIONS (EC)
L1

EDUCATION/TRAINING
4, 5, 6, R

Examples of Job Titles

Dot Etcher

Pre-Press Technician

Studio Image Processing System Operator

Descriptor Profile

Main Characteristics

Occupations in this group are characterized by the following aptitudes, interests and worker functions as they relate to main duties:

- **General learning** and **numerical ability** to operate various computer-controlled systems to perform colour separations, retouching and editing that allow changes to be made to negatives for printing purposes

- **Spatial perception** to visualize page layouts

- **Form perception** to identify areas of colour negatives requiring changes

- **Motor co-ordination** to adjust equipment controls

- **Objective interest** in **controlling** systems to alter shapes, sizes and positions of illustrations and text electronically

- **Methodical interest** in **compiling** information to perform colour separations, retouching and editing

- **Innovative interest** in planning page layouts

9472.5

Physical Activities

Vision
    2   Near vision

Colour Discrimination
    1   Relevant

Hearing
    1   Limited

Body Position
    1   Sitting

Limb Co-ordination
    1   Upper limb co-ordination

Strength
    1   Limited

Environmental Conditions

Location
    L1   Regulated inside climate

Employment Requirements

Education/Training
    4, 5, 6, R

- Completion of secondary school is required.

- Completion of a college program in graphic arts technology
  or
  a four-to-five year apprenticeship program in printing and graphic arts
  or
  a combination of on-the-job training and specialized college, industry or other courses is required.

- Trade certification for some occupations in the 9472 group is available, but not compulsory, in Ontario, Alberta and the Northwest Territories.

Workplaces/Employers

Colour graphics, platemaking and cylinder preparation companies

Commercial printing companies

In-house printing departments of public- and private-sector establishments

Magazines

Newspapers

Similar Occupations Classified Elsewhere

Graphic Arts Technicians (5223)

Graphic Designers and Illustrating Artists (5241)

Supervisors, Printing and Related Occupations (7218)

Typesetters and desktop publishing operators (in 1423 *Typesetters and Related Occupations*)

9472.6 Scanner Operators

Scanner Operators run computerized scanning equipment to prepare printing plates and cylinders for printing presses.

Profile Summary

APTITUDES

G	V	N	S	P	Q	K	F	M
3	3	3	3	2	4	3	4	4

INTERESTS
OMI

DATA PEOPLE THINGS (DPT)
582

PHYSICAL ACTIVITIES (PA)

V	C	H	B	L	S
2	1	1	1	1	1

ENVIRONMENTAL CONDITIONS (EC)
L1

EDUCATION/TRAINING
4, 5, 6, R

Examples of Job Titles

Scanner Operator

8

Descriptor Profile

Main Characteristics

Occupations in this group are characterized by the following aptitudes, interests and worker functions as they relate to main duties:

- **General learning ability** to operate computerized scanning machines to make colour separations and corrections from colour copies and transparencies for use in preparing printing plates and cylinders

- **Numerical ability** to read co-ordinates of scanning devices in order to identify locations of marked areas and to set machines on co-ordinates

- **Spatial perception** to position scanners over areas requiring colour separation and correction

- **Form perception** to observe oscilloscopes to determine density of local areas of separations

- **Motor co-ordination** to adjust equipment controls

- **Objective interest** in **controlling** computerized scanning machines to make required colour separations and corrections

- **Methodical interest** in **copying** information to follow preparation procedures

- **Innovative interest** in identifying areas requiring correction and in determining preparation procedures

9472.6

Physical Activities

Vision
   2 Near Vision

Colour Discrimination
   1 Relevant

Hearing
   1 Limited

Body Position
   1 Sitting

Limb Co-ordination
   1 Upper limb co-ordination

Strength
   1 Limited

Environmental Conditions

Location
   L1 Regulated inside climate

Employment Requirements

Education/Training
   4, 5, 6, R

- Completion of secondary school is required.

- Completion of a college program in graphic arts technology
or
a four-to-five year apprenticeship program in printing and graphic arts
or
a combination of on-the-job training and specialized college, industry or other courses is required.

- Trade certification for some occupations in the 9472 group is available, but not compulsory, in Ontario, Alberta and the Northwest Territories.

Workplaces Employers

Colour graphics, platemaking and cylinder preparation companies

Commercial printing companies

In-house printing departments of public- and private-sector establishments

Magazines

Newspapers

Similar Occupations Classified Elsewhere

Graphic Arts Technicians (5223)

Graphic Designers and Illustrating Artists (5241)

Supervisors, Printing and Related Occupations (7218)

Typesetters and desktop publishing operators (in 1423 *Typesetters and Related Occupations*)

9473.1 Binding Machine Operators

Binding Machine Operators set up, run and oversee the operation of specific machines, equipment and computerized units that bind printed material.

Profile Summary

APTITUDES

G	V	N	S	P	Q	K	F	M
3	3	4	3	3	4	3	4	3

INTERESTS
OMi

DATA PEOPLE THINGS (DPT)
582

PHYSICAL ACTIVITIES (PA)

V	C	H	B	L	S
2	0	1	2	1	2

ENVIRONMENTAL CONDITIONS (EC)
L1, H3, D1

EDUCATION/TRAINING
4, 5, 6

Examples of Job Titles

- Binder - Printing
- Binder and Finisher
- Bindery Assistant
- Bindery Operator
- Bookbinder, Machine
- Bookbinding Machine Operator
- Cerlox Binder Operator
- Cutter Operator - Printing
- Gathering Machine Operator - Printing
- Perforator Operator
- Stitcher Operator

Descriptor Profile

Main Characteristics

Occupations in this group are characterized by the following aptitudes, interests and worker functions as they relate to main duties:

- **General learning ability** to set up and operate various specialized equipment and machines that cut, fold, gather, stitch and trim brochures, magazines, books, business forms and other printed material

- **Verbal ability** to read production specifications

- **Spatial perception** to understand the function of machines and visualize the relationship of moving parts to detect malfunctions

- **Form perception** to detect imperfect bindings, incomplete cuts, incorrect stitch lengths, and torn, loose and uneven pages

- **Motor co-ordination** to use measuring devices and adjust controls to regulate size of cut and machine speed

- **Manual dexterity** to use hand tools to set up and maintain equipment

- **Objective interest** in **controlling** computerized units to start, stop and regulate machines and equipment

- **Methodical interest** in **copying** to perform work according to production specifications

- **Innovative interest** in making adjustments to machines and equipment

9473.1
Subgroup 1 of 2

Physical Activities

Vision
  2 Near vision

Colour Discrimination
  0 Not relevant

Hearing
  1 Limited

Body Position
  2 Standing and/or walking

Limb Co-ordination
  1 Upper limb co-ordination

Strength
  2 Light

Environmental Conditions

Location
  L1 Regulated inside climate

Hazards
  H3 Equipment, machinery, tools

Discomforts
  D1 Noise

Employment Requirements

Education/Training
  4, 5, 6

- Completion of secondary school is required.

- Completion of a college program in graphic arts technology
  or
  a four-year apprenticeship program in printing
  or
  a combination of on-the-job training and specialized college, industry or other courses may be required.

Workplaces/Employers

Binderies

Commercial printing companies

In-house printing, binding and finishing departments of public- and private-sector establishments

Magazines

Newspapers

Publishing companies

Occupational Options

There is mobility among various types of binding machine operators in this group.

Progression to supervisory positions is possible with experience.

Similar Occupations Classified Elsewhere

Supervisors, Printing and Related Occupations (7218)

Feeders, loaders, offbearers and similar occupations (in 9619 *Other Labourers in Processing, Manufacturing and Utilities*)

Hand bookbinders (in 5244 *Artisans and Craftspersons*)

9473.2 Finishing Machine Operators

Finishing Machine Operators set up, run and oversee the operation of specific machines, equipment and computerized units that finish printed material. This group includes workers who perform finishing operations in the paper, carton and packaging industries, and those who encode and stamp plastic cards.

Profile Summary

APTITUDES
G	V	N	S	P	Q	K	F	M
3	3	4	3	3	4	3	4	3

INTERESTS
OMi

DATA PEOPLE THINGS (DPT)
582

PHYSICAL ACTIVITIES (PA)
V	C	H	B	L	S
2	1	1	2	1	2

ENVIRONMENTAL CONDITIONS (EC)
L1, H3, D1

EDUCATION/TRAINING
4, 5, 6

Examples of Job Titles

Finishing Machine Operator
Gold Leaf Stamper
Laminating Machine Operator

Descriptor Profile

Main Characteristics

Occupations in this group are characterized by the following aptitudes, interests and worker functions as they relate to main duties:

- **General learning ability** to set up and operate various specialized equipment and machines that die cut, emboss, imprint, laminate, gold stamp and perform other finishing operations on printed material

- **Verbal ability** to review work order specifications

- **Spatial perception** to understand the functioning of machines and visualize the relationship of moving parts in order to detect malfunctions

- **Form perception** to check samples for quality

- **Motor co-ordination** to use measuring devices and adjust controls to regulate machines

- **Manual dexterity** to use hand tools to set up and maintain equipment

- **Objective interest** in **controlling** computerized units to start, stop and regulate machines and equipment

- **Methodical interest** in **copying** to perform work according to specifications

- **Innovative interest** in applying decorations and lettering to bound books, and in making adjustments to machines and equipment

9473.2
Subgroup 2 of 2

Physical Activities

Vision
   2 Near vision

Colour Discrimination
   1 Relevant

Hearing
   1 Limited

Body Position
   2 Standing and/or walking

Limb Co-ordination
   1 Upper limb co-ordination

Strength
   2 Light

Environmental Conditions

Location
   L1 Regulated inside climate

Hazards
   H3 Equipment, machinery, tools

Discomforts
   D1 Noise

Employment Requirements

Education/Training
   4, 5, 6

- Completion of secondary school is required.

- Completion of a college program in graphic arts technology
or
a four-year apprenticeship program in printing
or
a combination of on-the-job training and specialized college, industry or other courses may be required.

Workplaces/Employers

Binderies

Commercial printing companies

In-house printing, binding and finishing departments of public- and private-sector establishments

Newspapers

Magazines

Publishing companies

Occupational Options

Progression to supervisory positions is possible with experience.

Similar Occupations Classified Elsewhere

Supervisors, Printing and Related Occupations (7218)

Feeders, loaders, offbearers and similar occupations (in 9619 *Other Labourers in Processing, Manufacturing and Utilities*)

Hand bookbinders (in 5244 *Artisans and Craftspersons*)

9474 Photographic and Film Processors

Photographic and Film Processors process and finish still photographic film and motion picture film.

Profile Summary

APTITUDES

G	V	N	S	P	Q	K	F	M
3	4	4	3	3	4	3	3	3

INTERESTS
OMI

DATA PEOPLE THINGS (DPT)
584

PHYSICAL ACTIVITIES (PA)

V	C	H	B	L	S
2	1	1	2	1	1

ENVIRONMENTAL CONDITIONS (EC)
L1, H1

EDUCATION/TRAINING
3+, 4, 5, 6

Examples of Job Titles

Dark Room Technician
Film Developer
Film Printing Machine Operator
Film Processor
Photofinisher
Photograph Developer
Photograph Inspector
Photographic Processor

Descriptor Profile

Main Characteristics

Occupations in this group are characterized by the following aptitudes, interests and worker functions as they relate to main duties:

- **General learning ability** to process and finish still photographic film and motion picture film

- **Spatial** and **form perception** to inspect rolls of photographic prints to make sure they conform to specifications, and to inspect motion picture film for defects in developing and printing

- **Motor co-ordination** and **finger and manual dexterity** to splice film and mount film on reels

- **Objective interest** in operating equipment to develop negatives and slides, print photographs, develop motion picture film and transfer film to video tape; and in operating photographic enlarging equipment to produce prints and enlargements from negatives

- **Methodical interest** in copying information to measure and mix chemicals required for processing; and in tending automatic equipment in retail establishments to develop colour negatives, prints and slides

- **Innovative interest** in retouching photographic negatives and original prints to correct defects

9474

Physical Activities

Vision
   2   Near vision

Colour Discrimination
   1   Relevant

Hearing
   1   Limited

Body Position
   2   Standing and/or walking

Limb Co-ordination
   1   Upper limb co-ordination

Strength
   1   Limited

Environmental Conditions

Location
   L1   Regulated inside climate

Hazards
   H1   Dangerous chemical substances

Employment Requirements

Education/Training
3+, 4, 5, 6

- Completion of secondary school is usually required.

- For employment in film processing laboratories, completion of a college or other specialized program *or* extensive related experience is required.

- For employment as a film printing machine operator in retail outlets, on-the-job training is provided.

Workplaces/Employers

Film processing laboratories

Retail photofinishing establishments

Occupational Options

There is mobility among occupations within laboratory processing operations.

Progression is possible from automatic machine tenders in retail establishments to laboratory processing occupations.

Similar Occupations Classified Elsewhere

Film strippers and assemblers and negative retouchers in the printing or graphic arts industry (in 9472 *Camera, Platemaking and Other Pre-Press Occupations*)

Supervisors of photographic and film processors (in 7218 *Supervisors, Printing and Related Occupations*)

9481.1 Aircraft Assemblers

Aircraft Assemblers put together, fit and install prefabricated parts to manufacture fixed-wing and rotary-wing aircraft and aircraft subassemblies.

Profile Summary

APTITUDES

G	V	N	S	P	Q	K	F	M
3	3	3	3	3	4	3	3	3

INTERESTS

OMI

DATA PEOPLE THINGS (DPT)

381

PHYSICAL ACTIVITIES (PA)

V	C	H	B	L	S
3	0	1	4	1	4

ENVIRONMENTAL CONDITIONS (EC)

L1, H3, D1

EDUCATION/TRAINING

5, 6

Examples of Job Titles

Aircraft Assembler
Airframe Assembler
Bench and Structural Assembler
Bench Fitter Mechanic
Rigger, Aircraft Assembly
Wing Tank Mechanic

Descriptor Profile

Main Characteristics

Occupations in this group are characterized by the following aptitudes, interests and worker functions as they relate to main duties:

- **General learning ability** to assemble, fit and install prefabricated parts to manufacture fixed-wing and rotary-wing aircraft and aircraft subassemblies

- **Verbal ability** and **spatial** and **form perception** to read and interpret aircraft assembly diagrams

- **Numerical ability** to compute dimensions and locate reference points from specifications when laying out work

- **Motor co-ordination** and **finger** and **manual dexterity** to use hand and power tools when drilling and riveting aircraft units and assemblies, and to assemble aircraft components

- **Objective interest** in **precision working** to assemble and fit prefabricated parts to form subassemblies while working at benches or directly on aircraft structures; and to assemble, fit and install prefabricated parts and subassemblies such as aircraft skins, flight controls, rigging, hydraulics and other mechanical systems

- **Methodical interest** in **compiling** information from assembly diagrams and specifications

- **Innovative interest** in making adjustments to assemblies and components

9481.1
Subgroup 1 of 2

Physical Activities

Vision
   3   Near and far vision

Colour Discrimination
   0   Not relevant

Hearing
   1   Limited

Body Position
   4   Other body positions

Limb Co-ordination
   1   Upper limb co-ordination

Strength
   4   Heavy

Environmental Conditions

Location
   L1   Regulated inside climate

Hazards
   H3   Equipment, machinery, tools

Discomforts
   D1   Noise

Employment Requirements

Education/Training
5, 6

- Completion of secondary school is required.

- Completion of a college or other program in aviation or aeronautical technology, with emphasis in aircraft manufacturing, may be required.

- Aircraft assemblers receive several months of on-the-job and classroom training.

Workplaces/Employers

Aircraft and aircraft subassembly manufacturers

Occupational Options

Aircraft assemblers may progress to supervisory positions with experience.

Similar Occupations Classified Elsewhere

Aircraft Mechanics and Aircraft Inspectors (7315)

Aircraft engine assemblers (in 7316 *Machine Fitters*)

Aircraft painters (in 9496 *Painters and Coaters, Manufacturing*)

Supervisors of aircraft assemblers or inspectors (in 9226 *Supervisors, Other Mechanical and Metal Product Manufacturing*)

9481.2 Aircraft Assembly Inspectors

Aircraft Assembly Inspectors examine aircraft assemblies for adherence to engineering specifications.

Profile Summary

APTITUDES

G	V	N	S	P	Q	K	F	M
3	3	3	3	3	3	3	3	3

INTERESTS
OMI

DATA PEOPLE THINGS (DPT)
381

PHYSICAL ACTIVITIES (PA)

V	C	H	B	L	S
3	1	1	3	1	2

ENVIRONMENTAL CONDITIONS (EC)
L1

EDUCATION/TRAINING
5+, 6+

Examples of Job Titles

Aircraft Inspector, Assembly

Descriptor Profile

Main Characteristics

Occupations in this group are characterized by the following aptitudes, interests and worker functions as they relate to main duties:

- **General learning ability** to inspect aircraft assemblies to make sure they adhere to engineering specifications

- **Verbal ability** to complete detailed inspection reports

- **Numerical ability** and **clerical perception** to take accurate measurements

- **Spatial perception** to visualize complete assemblies as represented in assembly diagrams

- **Form perception** to observe assembly defects

- **Motor co-ordination** and **finger** and **manual dexterity** to use measuring and testing equipment

- **Objective interest** in **precision working** to set and adjust controls on measuring and testing equipment

- **Methodical interest** in **compiling data** from drawings and specifications; and in checking assembled units with standards specified on drawings and production orders

- **Innovative interest** in inspecting assemblies for alignment, symmetry, dimensions, fit and quality of workmanship

9481.2

Physical Activities

Vision
 3 Near and far vision

Colour Discrimination
 1 Relevant

Hearing
 1 Limited

Body Position
 3 Sitting, standing, walking

Limb Co-ordination
 1 Upper limb co-ordination

Strength
 2 Light

Environmental Conditions

Location
 L1 Regulated inside climate

Employment Requirements

Education/Training
 5+, 6+

- Completion of secondary school is required.

- Completion of a college or other program in aviation or aeronautical technology, with emphasis in aircraft manufacturing, may be required.

- Aircraft assembly inspectors require experience as aircraft assemblers.

Workplaces/Employers

Aircraft and aircraft subassembly manufacturers

Occupational Options

Aircraft assembly inspectors may progress to supervisory positions with experience.

Similar Occupations Classified Elsewhere

Aircraft Mechanics and Aircraft Inspectors (7315)

Aircraft engine assemblers (in 7316 *Machine Fitters*)

Aircraft painters (in 9496 *Painters and Coaters, Manufacturing*)

Supervisors of aircraft assemblers or inspectors (in 9226 *Supervisors, Other Mechanical and Metal Products Manufacturing*)

9482.1 Motor Vehicle Assemblers

Motor Vehicle Assemblers put together and install prefabricated motor vehicle parts and components to form subassemblies and finished motor vehicles.

Profile Summary

APTITUDES

G	V	N	S	P	Q	K	F	M
4	4	5	4	4	5	4	4	3

INTERESTS
OMi

DATA PEOPLE THINGS (DPT)
584

PHYSICAL ACTIVITIES (PA)

V	C	H	B	L	S
3	0	1	4	1	4

ENVIRONMENTAL CONDITIONS (EC)
L1, H3, D1

EDUCATION/TRAINING
4

Examples of Job Titles

Auto Assembly Worker
Body Assembler
Car Assembler
Door Fitter
Light Truck Assembler
Motor Vehicle Assembler
Transmission Installer
Van Assembler

Descriptor Profile

Main Characteristics

Occupations in this group are characterized by the following aptitudes, interests and worker functions as they relate to main duties:

- **General learning ability** to assemble and install prefabricated motor vehicle parts and components to form subassemblies and finished motor vehicles

- **Manual dexterity** to bolt, screw, clip, weld, solder and otherwise fasten motor vehicle parts and components together using hand and power tools and equipment

- **Objective interest** in **operating** automated assembly equipment, and in using hand and power tools and such other aids as overhead joists, to position and install parts and subassemblies such as engines, transmissions, door panels and instrument panels

- **Methodical interest** in **copying** information to connect cables, tubes and wires to complete assemblies and installations; and in tending automated assembling equipment such as robotic and fixed automation equipment

- **Innovative interest** in fitting and adjusting parts such as doors, hoods and trunk lids

9482.1
Subgroup 1 of 2

Physical Activities

Vision
  3 Near and far vision

Colour Discrimination
  0 Not relevant

Hearing
  1 Limited

Body Position
  4 Other body positions

Limb Co-ordination
  1 Upper limb co-ordination

Strength
  4 Heavy

Environmental Conditions

Location
  L1 Regulated inside climate

Hazards
  H3 Equipment, machinery, tools

Discomforts
  D1 Noise

Employment Requirements

Education/Training
  4

- Completion of secondary school is usually required.

- Skills required for this occupation are normally acquired through on-the-job training.

Workplaces/Employers

Automobile, van and light truck manufacturers

Occupational Options

Mobility is possible among jobs in the same production department.

Progression to supervisory positions is possible with experience.

Similar Occupations Classified Elsewhere

Supervisors, Motor Vehicle Assembling (9221)

Assemblers of heavy trucks, trailers and buses (in 9486 *Mechanical Assemblers and Inspectors*)

Automobile assembly painters and coaters (in 9496 *Painters and Coaters, Manufacturing*)

Automotive engine, clutch and transmission assemblers (in 9486 *Mechanical Assemblers and Inspectors*)

9482.2 Motor Vehicle Inspectors and Testers

Motor Vehicle Inspectors and Testers inspect and test parts, subassemblies and finished products to ensure that they operate properly and conform to quality standards.

Profile Summary

APTITUDES
G	V	N	S	P	Q	K	F	M
3	3	4	3	3	4	4	4	4

INTERESTS
OMI

DATA PEOPLE THINGS (DPT)
583

PHYSICAL ACTIVITIES (PA)
V	C	H	B	L	S
3	1	1	3	2	2

ENVIRONMENTAL CONDITIONS (EC)
L1, D1

EDUCATION/TRAINING
4

Examples of Job Titles

Assembly Inspector
Chassis Inspector
Test Driver

Descriptor Profile

Main Characteristics

Occupations in this group are characterized by the following aptitudes, interests and worker functions as they relate to main duties:

- **General learning ability** to test motor vehicle electrical assemblies, equipment and wiring using testing devices such as meters, analyzers and timing lights

- **Verbal ability** to report motor vehicle defects

- **Spatial perception** to visualize the relationship and arrangement of vehicle parts and components

- **Form perception** to check motor vehicle exterior priming and colour coats, sealers and glazes for defects

- **Objective interest** in **driving** to test motor vehicles on roll testing devices to ensure that transmissions, axles, engines and brakes function properly

- **Methodical interest** in **copying** to record motor vehicle defects; and in marking defects to be repaired

- **Innovative interest** in inspecting fully assembled motor vehicles for defects and ensuring that previously noted defects have been corrected

9482.2
Subgroup 2 of 2

Physical Activities

Vision
   3 Near and far vision

Colour Discrimination
   1 Relevant

Hearing
   1 Limited

Body Position
   3 Sitting, standing, walking

Limb Co-ordination
   2 Multiple limb co-ordination

Strength
   2 Light

Environmental Conditions

Location
   L1 Regulated inside climate

Discomforts
   D1 Noise

Employment Requirements

Education/Training
   4

- Completion of secondary school is usually required.

- Skills required for this occupation are normally acquired through on-the-job training.

Workplaces/Employers

Automobile, van and light truck manufacturers

Occupational Options

Mobility is possible among jobs in the same production department.

Progression to supervisory positions is possible with experience.

Similar Occupations Classified Elsewhere

Supervisors, Motor Vehicle Assembling (9221)

Assemblers of heavy trucks, trailers and buses (in 9486 *Mechanical Assemblers and Inspectors*)

Automobile assembly painters and coaters (in 9496 *Painters and Coaters, Manufacturing*)

Automotive engine, clutch and transmission assemblers (in 9486 *Mechanical Assemblers and Inspectors*)

9483.1 Electronics Assemblers

Electronics Assemblers put together electronic equipment, parts and components.

Profile Summary

APTITUDES

G	V	N	S	P	Q	K	F	M
3	4	4	3	3	4	3	3	3

INTERESTS
OMi

DATA PEOPLE THINGS (DPT)
581

PHYSICAL ACTIVITIES (PA)

V	C	H	B	L	S
1	1	1	1	1	1

ENVIRONMENTAL CONDITIONS (EC)
L1, H3

EDUCATION/TRAINING
2

Examples of Job Titles

Capacitor Assembler
Circuit Board Assembler
Component Inserting Machine Operator
Electronics Assembler
Wave Soldering Machine Operator
Wiring and Assembly Operator

Descriptor Profile

Main Characteristics

Occupations in this group are characterized by the following aptitudes, interests and worker functions as they relate to main duties:

- **General learning ability** to assemble electronic equipment, parts and components

- **Spatial perception** to visualize assemblies and final products from drawings

- **Form perception** to detect irregularities on printed circuit boards and examine products for defects

- **Motor co-ordination** and **finger** and **manual dexterity** to use hand and small power tools to install, mount, fasten, align and adjust parts, components, wiring and harnesses to subassemblies and assemblies

- **Objective interest** in **precision working** to assemble microcircuits requiring fine hand assembly, and to use microscopes and adhere to clean-room procedures; and in operating automatic and semi-automatic machines to position, solder and clean components on printed circuit boards

- **Methodical interest** in **copying** information to solder and assemble manually, various electronic components such as resistors, diodes, transistors, capacitors, integrated circuits, wires and other electronic parts onto printed circuit boards

- **Innovative interest** in verifying dimensions and alignment of parts

9483.1

Physical Activities

Vision
  1 Close visual acuity

Colour Discrimination
  1 Relevant

Hearing
  1 Limited

Body Position
  1 Sitting

Limb Co-ordination
  1 Upper limb co-ordination

Strength
  1 Limited

Environmental Conditions

Location
  L1 Regulated inside climate

Hazards
  H3 Equipment, machinery, tools

Employment Requirements

Education/Training
  2

- Some secondary school education is required.

Workplaces/Employers

Electronics manufacturing plants

Occupational Options

Progression from electronics assembler to electronics inspector or tester is possible with additional training and experience.

Similar Occupations Classified Elsewhere

Assemblers and Inspectors, Electrical Appliance, Apparatus and Equipment Manufacturing (9484)

Electronic Service Technicians (Household and Business Equipment) (2242)

9483.2 Electronics Fabricators

Electronics Fabricators make electronic equipment, parts and components.

Profile Summary

APTITUDES

G	V	N	S	P	Q	K	F	M
3	4	4	3	3	4	3	3	3

INTERESTS
OMi

DATA PEOPLE THINGS (DPT)
584

PHYSICAL ACTIVITIES (PA)

V	C	H	B	L	S
2	1	1	2	1	2

ENVIRONMENTAL CONDITIONS (EC)
L1, H3

EDUCATION/TRAINING
2

Examples of Job Titles

Wafer Fabrication Operator
Wave Soldering Machine Operator

Descriptor Profile

Main Characteristics

Occupations in this group are characterized by the following aptitudes, interests and worker functions as they relate to main duties:

- **General learning ability** to operate equipment and machines to fabricate electronic equipment, parts and components

- **Spatial perception** to set up process equipment

- **Form perception** to examine equipment, parts and components for defects

- **Motor co-ordination** and **finger** and **manual dexterity** to adjust controls to start, stop and regulate equipment

- **Objective interest** in **operating** process equipment including automatic and semi-automatic machines to fabricate, solder, clean, seal and stamp components; and in performing other process operations as specified

- **Methodical interest** in **copying** information to monitor process equipment and adhere to clean-room procedures

- **Innovative interest** in adjusting equipment used to fabricate products

9483.2

Physical Activities

Vision
　2　Near vision

Colour Discrimination
　1　Relevant

Hearing
　1　Limited

Body Position
　2　Standing and/or walking

Limb Co-ordination
　1　Upper limb co-ordination

Strength
　2　Light

Environmental Conditions

Location
　L1　Regulated inside climate

Hazards
　H3　Equipment, machinery, tools

Employment Requirements

Education/Training
2

- Some secondary school education is required.

Workplaces/Employers

Electronics manufacturing plants

Occupational Options

Progression from electronics component fabricator to electronics inspector or tester is possible with additional training and experience.

Similar Occupations Classified Elsewhere

Assemblers and Inspectors, Electrical Appliance, Apparatus and Equipment Manufacturing (9484)

Electronic Service Technicians (Household and Business Equipment) (2242)

9483.3 Electronics Inspectors

Electronics Inspectors inspect electronic and electromechanical assemblies, subassemblies, parts and components to ensure that they conform to prescribed standards.

Profile Summary

APTITUDES

G	V	N	S	P	Q	K	F	M
3	3	3	3	3	4	3	3	3

INTERESTS
Mid

DATA PEOPLE THINGS (DPT)
587

PHYSICAL ACTIVITIES (PA)

V	C	H	B	L	S
1	1	1	2	1	1

ENVIRONMENTAL CONDITIONS (EC)
L1

EDUCATION/TRAINING
2, 4

Examples of Job Titles

Electronics Inspector

Inspector, Printed Circuit Board Assembly

Descriptor Profile

Main Characteristics

Occupations in this group are characterized by the following aptitudes, interests and worker functions as they relate to main duties:

- **General learning ability** to inspect electronic components and assemblies, while products are being assembled and fabricated, in order to ensure that they conform to specifications

- **Verbal ability** to summarize inspection results

- **Numerical ability** to check mechanical dimensions

- **Form perception** to check final assemblies for finish, labelling and packaging

- **Motor co-ordination** and **finger** and **manual dexterity** to perform "go-no-go" electrical tests

- **Methodical interest** in **copying** information to collect and record inspection results, and to mark acceptable and defective assemblies

- **Innovative interest** in identifying defective components and assemblies

- **Directive interest** in **handling** assemblies during inspection; and in returning faulty assemblies to production for repair

9483.3
Subgroup 3 of 4

Physical Activities

Vision
1   Close visual acuity

Colour Discrimination
1   Relevant

Hearing
1   Limited

Body Position
2   Standing and/or walking

Limb Co-ordination
1   Upper limb co-ordination

Strength
1   Limited

Environmental Conditions

Location
L1   Regulated inside climate

Employment Requirements

Education/Training
2, 4

- Some secondary school education is required.

- Electronics inspectors may require experience as an electronics assembler or component fabricator.

Workplaces/Employers

Electronics manufacturing plants

Similar Occupations Classified Elsewhere

Assemblers and Inspectors, Electrical Appliance, Apparatus and Equipment Manufacturing (9484)

Electronic Service Technicians (Household and Business Equipment) (2242)

9483.4 Electronics Testers

Electronics Testers test electronic and electromechanical assemblies, subassemblies, parts and components to ensure that they conform to prescribed standards.

Profile Summary

APTITUDES

G	V	N	S	P	Q	K	F	M
3	3	3	4	4	4	3	3	3

INTERESTS
OMI

DATA PEOPLE THINGS (DPT)
684

PHYSICAL ACTIVITIES (PA)

V	C	H	B	L	S
2	1	1	2	1	2

ENVIRONMENTAL CONDITIONS (EC)
L1, H4

EDUCATION/TRAINING
2, 4

Examples of Job Titles

Crystal Final Tester
Tester, Electronic Components

Descriptor Profile

Main Characteristics

Occupations in this group are characterized by the following aptitudes, interests and worker functions as they relate to main duties:

- **General learning ability** to operate various test equipment and tools to perform simple electrical and continuity testing of electronic components, parts and systems

- **Verbal** and **numerical ability** to maintain test reports

- **Objective interest** in **operating** automatic testing equipment to locate circuit and wiring faults, shorts and component defects; may conduct life tests (burn-ins) on components, subassemblies and assemblies

- **Methodical interest** in **comparing** information from test results to ensure that specifications are met; and in setting parts and products aside for repairs

- **Innovative interest** in setting up automatic testing equipment, and in replacing components and parts as tests indicate

9483.4

Physical Activities

Vision
  2 Near vision

Colour Discrimination
  1 Relevant

Hearing
  1 Limited

Body Position
  2 Standing and/or walking

Limb Co-ordination
  1 Upper limb co-ordination

Strength
  2 Light

Environmental Conditions

Location
  L1 Regulated inside climate

Hazards
  H4 Electricity

Employment Requirements

Education/Training
  2, 4

- Some secondary school education is required.

- Electronics testers may require post-secondary courses in basic electronic theory, testing techniques and testing equipment.

- Electronics testers may require experience as an electronics assembler or component fabricator.

Workplaces/Employers

Electronics manufacturing plants

Similar Occupations Classified Elsewhere

Assemblers and Inspectors, Electrical Appliance, Apparatus and Equipment Manufacturing (9484)

Electronic Service Technicians (Household and Business Equipment) (2242)

9484.1 Assemblers, Electrical Appliance, Apparatus and Equipment Manufacturing

Assemblers in this group put together prefabricated parts to produce household, commercial and industrial appliances and equipment. This group includes workers who set up and prepare assembly lines for operation.

Profile Summary

APTITUDES
G	V	N	S	P	Q	K	F	M
3	4	4	4	4	4	3	3	3

INTERESTS
MOi

DATA PEOPLE THINGS (DPT)
584

PHYSICAL ACTIVITIES (PA)
V	C	H	B	L	S
2	1	1	4	1	3

ENVIRONMENTAL CONDITIONS (EC)
L1, H3, D1

EDUCATION/TRAINING
2

Examples of Job Titles

Assembler, Electrical Appliances
Circuit Breaker Assembler
Clothes Dryer Assembler, Electric
Coffeemaker Assembler
Dishwasher Assembler
Hair Dryer Assembler
Lawnmower Assembler, Electric
Production Assembler, Electrical Equipment
Refrigerator Assembler, Electric

Descriptor Profile

Main Characteristics

Occupations in this group are characterized by the following aptitudes, interests and worker functions as they relate to main duties:

- **General learning ability** to assemble prefabricated parts on assembly lines and at work benches, using screw guns and other hand and power tools

- **Motor co-ordination** and **finger dexterity** to wind coils and armatures for small motors and transformers

- **Manual dexterity** to position and fasten components, such as springs, toggles and other parts, into assembly casings

- **Methodical interest** in **copying** information to assemble small and large household appliances, and small transformers, motors and transmissions used in appliances and other electrical products

- **Objective interest** in **operating** equipment to assemble circuit breakers, switches and other electrical control equipment; and in setting up assembly lines with materials and supplies

- **Innovative interest** in setting up and adjusting production tools, and in performing minor repairs to products rejected from production assembly lines

9484.1

Physical Activities

Vision
    2   Near vision

Colour Discrimination
    1   Relevant

Hearing
    1   Limited

Body Position
    4   Other body positions

Limb Co-ordination
    1   Upper limb co-ordination

Strength
    3   Medium

Environmental Conditions

Location
    L1 Regulated inside climate

Hazards
    H3 Equipment, machinery, tools

Discomforts
    D1 Noise

Employment Requirements

Education/Training
2

- Some secondary school education is usually required.
- On-the-job training is provided.

Workplaces/Employers

Electric appliance manufacturing companies

Electrical equipment manufacturing companies

Occupational Options

With experience, assemblers may progress to inspecting and testing positions.

Progression to supervisory positions is possible with experience.

Similar Occupations Classified Elsewhere

Electric Appliance Servicers and Repairers (7332)

Electrical Mechanics (7333)

Machine Operators and Inspectors, Electrical Apparatus Manufacturing (9487)

Supervisors, Electrical Products Manufacturing (9223)

Assemblers of electronic products, such as televisions, radios and computers (in 9483 *Electronics Assemblers, Fabricators, Inspectors and Testers*)

Assemblers of heavy-duty electric motors, transformers and related equipment (in 9485 *Assemblers, Fabricators and Inspectors, Industrial Electrical Motors and Transformers*)

9484.2 Inspectors and Testers, Electrical Appliance, Apparatus and Equipment Manufacturing

Inspectors and Testers in this group inspect and test assembled products.

Profile Summary

APTITUDES

G	V	N	S	P	Q	K	F	M
3	3	3	4	4	3	3	3	3

INTERESTS
MOi

DATA PEOPLE THINGS (DPT)
584

PHYSICAL ACTIVITIES (PA)

V	C	H	B	L	S
2	1	1	2	1	2

ENVIRONMENTAL CONDITIONS (EC)
L1, D1

EDUCATION/TRAINING
2, 4, 6

Examples of Job Titles

Inspector, Electrical Appliance Assembly

Inspector, Electrical Controls Assembly

Descriptor Profile

Main Characteristics

Occupations in this group are characterized by the following aptitudes, interests and worker functions as they relate to main duties:

- **General learning ability** to inspect and test assembled products

- **Verbal ability** to summarize inspection results

- **Numerical ability** and **clerical perception** to record inspection results

- **Form perception** to check products at different stages of production for visual defects

- **Motor co-ordination** and **finger** and **manual dexterity** to check products at different stages of production for faulty electrical and mechanical connections

- **Methodical interest** in **copying** information to collect and record inspection results; and in marking acceptable and defective assemblies

- **Objective interest** in operating automatic and other testing equipment to ensure product quality

- **Innovative interest** in identifying and returning faulty assemblies to production for repairs

Physical Activities

Vision
  2   Near vision

Colour Discrimination
  1   Relevant

Hearing
  1   Limited

Body Positio
  2   Standing and/or walking

Limb Co-ordination
  1   Upper limb co-ordination

Strength
  2   Light

Environmental Conditions

Location
  L1   Regulated inside climate

Discomforts
  D1   Noise

Employment Requirements

Education/Training
2, 4, 6

- Some secondary school education is usually required.

- On-the-job training is provided.

- Inspectors may require experience as an assembler in the same company.

- Some types of inspectors may require completion of an electronics college program

Workplaces/Employers

Electric appliance manufacturing companies

Electrical equipment manufacturing companies

Occupational Options

Progression to supervisory positions is possible with experience.

Similar Occupations Classified Elsewhere

Electric Appliance Servicers and Repairers (7332)

Electrical Mechanics (7333)

Machine Operators and Inspectors, Electrical Apparatus Manufacturing (9487)

Supervisors, Electrical Products Manufacturing (9223)

Assemblers of electronic products, such as televisions, radios and computers (in 9483 *Electronics Assemblers, Fabricators, Inspectors and Testers*)

Assemblers of heavy-duty electric motors, transformers and related equipment (in 9485 *Assemblers, Fabricators and Inspectors, Industrial Electrical Motors and Transformers*)

9485.1 Assemblers, Industrial Electrical Motors and Transformers

Assemblers, Industrial Electrical Motors and Transformers, assemble and fit heavy-duty industrial electrical equipment.

Profile Summary

APTITUDES

G	V	N	S	P	Q	K	F	M
3	4	3	3	3	4	3	3	3

INTERESTS
OMI

DATA PEOPLE THINGS (DPT)
384

PHYSICAL ACTIVITIES (PA)

V	C	H	B	L	S
2	1	1	4	1	3

ENVIRONMENTAL CONDITIONS (EC)
L1, H3, D1

EDUCATION/TRAINING
4

Examples of Job Titles

Assembler and Wirer, Motors and Generators

Coil Winder, Transformer

Power Transformer Assembler

Transformer Winder

Winder, AC and DC Armatures

Descriptor Profile

Main Characteristics

Occupations in this group are characterized by the following aptitudes, interests and worker functions as they relate to main duties:

- **General learning** and **numerical ability** to assemble and fit metal and other prefabricated parts, according to blueprints, in order to build heavy-duty electric motors and transformers

- **Spatial** and **form perception** to set up production machinery and equipment, and to assemble and fit motor and transformer auxiliary equipment such as bushings, tap changes, conduit boxes, heating devices, protective equipment and cooling equipment

- **Motor co-ordination** and **finger** and **manual dexterity** to make electrical connections using crimping, brazing and soldering equipment

- **Objective interest** in operating overhead cranes to assemble windings into transformer cores; and in assembling stators and armatures for heavy-duty electric motors, and in compressing steel laminations to build transformer cores

- **Methodical interest** in compiling data from drawings, work orders and specifications to determine fabrication and assembly procedures; may perform basic tests on electric motors

- **Innovative interest** in adjusting production machinery and equipment such as coil winding machines for the manufacture of heavy-duty electrical equipment

9485.1
Subgroup 1 of 3

Physical Activities

Vision
    2   Near vision

Colour Discrimination
    1   Relevant

Hearing
    1   Limited

Body Position
    4   Other body positions

Limb Co-ordination
    1   Upper limb co-ordination

Strength
    3   Medium

Environmental Conditions

Location
    L1 Regulated inside climate

Hazards
    H3 Equipment, machinery, tools

Discomforts
    D1 Noise

Employment Requirements

Education/training
    4

- Completion of secondary school is usually required.

- College courses in electricity or electro-technology may be required.

- Several years of on-the-job training are usually provided.

- Set-up persons and lead-hands in this group may require experience as an assembler, fitter or wirer in the same company.

Workplaces/Employers

Manufacturers of heavy-duty electrical equipment such as:

Control equipment

Industrial electric motors

Railway locomotives

Transformers

Transit vehicles

Occupational Options

Progression to supervisory positions is possible with experience.

Similar Occupations Classified Elsewhere

Assemblers and Inspectors, Electrical Appliance, Apparatus and Equipment Manufacturing (9484)

Electrical Mechanics (7333)

Supervisors, Electrical Products Manufacturing (9223)

Assemblers of small electric motors, transformers, circuit breakers or similar products (in 9484 *Assemblers and Inspectors, Electrical Appliance, Apparatus and Equipment Manufacturing*)

Electrical technicians who test heavy-duty electric motors, transformers or other industrial electrical equipment (in 2241 *Electrical and Electronics Engineering Technologists and Technicians*)

9485.2 Electrical Fitters, Industrial Electrical Motors and Transformers

Electrical Fitters, Industrial Electrical Motors and Transformers, assemble, fabricate, fit and wire heavy-duty industrial electrical equipment.

Profile Summary

APTITUDES

G	V	N	S	P	Q	K	F	M
3	4	3	3	3	4	3	3	3

INTERESTS
OMI

DATA PEOPLE THINGS (DPT)
384

PHYSICAL ACTIVITIES (PA)

V	C	H	B	L	S
2	1	1	4	1	2

ENVIRONMENTAL CONDITIONS (EC)
L1, H4

EDUCATION/TRAINING
4

Examples of Job Titles

Assembler, Switchgear and Control Panel
Control Panel Assembler
Electrical Fitter
Fitter and Assembler, AC and DC Motors
Panelboard Assembler - Industrial Electric Equipment
Switchgear Fitter Wirer
Wirer, Electric Switchgear Panels

Descriptor Profile

Main Characteristics

Occupations in this group are characterized by the following aptitudes, interests and worker functions as they relate to main duties:

- **General learning** and **numerical ability** to assemble, fabricate, fit and wire heavy-duty industrial electrical equipment

- **Spatial** and **form perception** to interpret engineering drawings, electrical schematics and blueprints

- **Motor co-ordination** and **manual dexterity** to assemble panelboard and switchboard cabinets, and to install bus bars used to carry heavy electric current

- **Finger dexterity** to wire electrical connections for switchboards and panelboards

- **Objective interest** in **operating** equipment to fit motor starters, contactors, capacitors, circuit breakers, voltage regulators, printed circuit boards and other electrical control devices into switchboards and panelboards in order to produce automated processing control equipment, electrical distribution panels and other industrial electrical control equipment; may operate metal fabricating equipment to fabricate or modify bus bars

- **Methodical interest** in **compiling** data from engineering drawings, electrical schematics and blueprints to determine specifications

- **Innovative interest** in adjusting parts as required

9485.2
Subgroup 2 of 3

Physical Activities

Vision
2   Near vision

Colour Discrimination
1   Relevant

Hearing
1   Limited

Body Position
4   Other body positions

Limb Co-ordination
1   Upper limb co-ordination

Strength
2   Light

Environmental Conditions

Location
L1   Regulated inside climate

Hazards
H4   Electricity

Employment Requirements

Education/Training
4

- Completion of secondary school is usually required.

- College courses in electricity or electro-technology may be required.

- Several years of on-the-job training are usually provided.

- Lead-hands in this group may require experience as an assembler, fitter or wirer in the same company.

Workplaces/Employers

Manufacturers of heavy-duty electrical equipment such as:

Control equipment

Industrial electric motors

Railway locomotives

Transformers

Transit vehicles

Occupational Options

Progression to supervisory positions is possible with experience.

Similar Occupations Classified Elsewhere

Assemblers and Inspectors, Electrical Appliance, Apparatus and Equipment Manufacturing (9484)

Electrical Mechanics (7333)

Supervisors, Electrical Products Manufacturing (9223)

Assemblers of small electric motors, transformers, circuit breakers or similar products (in 9484 *Assemblers and Inspectors, Electrical Appliance, Apparatus and Equipment Manufacturing*)

Electrical technicians who test heavy-duty electric motors, transformers or other industrial electrical equipment (in 2241 *Electrical and Electronics Engineering Technologists and Technicians*)

9485.3 Inspectors, Industrial Electrical Motors and Transformers

Inspectors, Industrial Electrical Motors and Transformers inspect heavy-duty industrial electrical equipment.

Profile Summary

APTITUDES

G	V	N	S	P	Q	K	F	M
3	3	3	3	3	4	4	4	4

INTERESTS
MId

DATA PEOPLE THINGS (DPT)
387

PHYSICAL ACTIVITIES (PA)

V	C	H	B	L	S
2	1	1	2	0	1

ENVIRONMENTAL CONDITIONS (EC)
L1

EDUCATION/TRAINING
4

Examples of Job Titles

Inspector and Tester, AC and DC Motors

Inspector, Electrical Control Panel

Transformer Inspector

Descriptor Profile

Main Characteristics

Occupations in this group are characterized by the following aptitudes, interests and worker functions as they relate to main duties:

- **General learning** and **numerical ability** to check final assembly of electric motors, transformers and control equipment to ensure that they adhere to quality control standards

- **Verbal ability** to summarize inspection results

- **Spatial perception** to visualize the arrangements of parts and configuration of finished products from blueprints

- **Form perception** to detect product defects

- **Methodical interest** in **compiling** information to collect and record inspection results

- **Innovative interest** in troubleshooting to resolve production problems

- **Directive interest** in **handling** equipment for inspection purposes; and in monitoring production

9485.3
Subgroup 3 of 3

Physical Activities

Vision
  2 Near vision

Colour Discrimination
  1 Relevant

Hearing
  1 Limited

Body Position
  2 Standing and/or walking

Limb Co-ordination
  0 Not relevant

Strength
  1 Limited

Environmental Conditions

Location
  L1 Regulated inside climate

Employment Requirements

Education/Training
4

- Completion of secondary school is usually required.

- College courses in electricity or electro-technology may be required.

- Several years of on-the-job training are usually provided.

- Inspectors in this group may require experience as an assembler, fitter or wirer in the same company.

Workplaces/Employers

Manufacturers of heavy electrical equipment such as:

Control equipment

Industrial electric motors

Railway locomotives

Transformers

Transit vehicles

Occupational Options

Progression to supervisory positions is possible with experience.

Similar Occupations Classified Elsewhere

Assemblers and Inspectors, Electrical Appliance, Apparatus and Equipment Manufacturing (9484)

Electrical Mechanics (7333)

Supervisors, Electrical Products Manufacturing (9223)

Assemblers of small electric motors, transformers, circuit breakers or similar products (in 9484 *Assemblers and Inspectors, Electrical Appliance, Apparatus and Equipment Manufacturing*)

Electrical technicians who test heavy-duty electric motors, transformers or other industrial electrical equipment (in 2241 *Electrical and Electronics Engineering Technologists and Technicians*)

9486.1 Mechanical Assemblers

Mechanical Assemblers put together products such as trucks, buses, snowmobiles, garden tractors, automotive engines, transmissions, outboard motors, gear boxes, hydraulic pumps and sewing machines.

Profile Summary

APTITUDES
G	V	N	S	P	Q	K	F	M
4	4	4	4	3	4	3	4	3

INTERESTS
OMi

DATA PEOPLE THINGS (DPT)
584

PHYSICAL ACTIVITIES (PA)
V	C	H	B	L	S
2	1	1	4	1	3

ENVIRONMENTAL CONDITIONS (EC)
L1, H3, D1

EDUCATION/TRAINING
2

Examples of Job Titles

Automotive Engine Assembler
Garden Machinery Assembler
Gear-Box Assembler
Gear-Case Assembler
Hydraulic Hoist Assembler
Mechanical Assembler
Sewing Machine Assembler
Snowmobile Assembler
Tractor Assembler
Transmission Assembler
Truck Assembler
Truck Trailer Assembler
Vending Machine Assembler

Descriptor Profile

Main Characteristics

Occupations in this group are characterized by the following aptitudes, interests and worker functions as they relate to main duties:

- **General learning ability** to assemble, fit and install prefabricated parts to form subassemblies, and to finish products using hand and power tools

- **Form perception**, **motor co-ordination** and **manual dexterity** to connect cables, tubes and wires, and to fasten parts together using bolting and riveting equipment and other fastening and joining techniques

- **Objective interest** in **operating** automated assembling equipment and small cranes to transport and position larger parts; and in tending automated assembling equipment such as robotics and fixed automation equipment

- **Methodical interest** in **copying** information to assemble mechanical products

- **Innovative interest** in **positioning**, aligning and adjusting parts for proper fit and assembly

9486.1

Subgroup 1 of 2

Physical Activities

Vision
  2 Near vision

Colour Discrimination
  1 Relevant

Hearing
  1 Limited

Body Position
  4 Other body positions

Limb Co-ordination
  1 Upper limb co-ordination

Strength
  3 Medium

Environmental Conditions

Location
  L1 Regulated inside climate

Hazards
  H3 Equipment, machinery, tools

Discomforts
  D1 Noise

Employment Requirements

Education/Training
2

- Some secondary school education is required.

- Up to two years of on-the-job training are provided.

Workplaces/Employers

Machinery manufacturers

Mechanical products manufacturing companies

Transportation equipment manufacturers

Occupational Options

There is little or no mobility among the various assemblers and inspectors in the 9486 group.

Progression to supervisory positions is possible with experience.

Similar Occupations Classified Elsewhere

Aircraft Assemblers and Aircraft Assembly Inspectors (9481)

Motor Vehicle Assemblers, Inspectors and Testers (9482)

Industrial machinery, heavy equipment and aircraft engine assemblers (in 7316 *Machine Fitters*)

Supervisors of mechanical assemblers and inspectors (in 9226 *Supervisors, Other Mechanical and Metal Products Manufacturing*)

9486.2 Mechanical Inspectors

Mechanical Inspectors check and inspect subassemblies and finished products to ensure proper quality and that they conform to product specifications.

Profile Summary

APTITUDES

G	V	N	S	P	Q	K	F	M
3	4	4	4	3	4	3	4	3

INTERESTS
OMd

DATA PEOPLE THINGS (DPT)
587

PHYSICAL ACTIVITIES (PA)

V	C	H	B	L	S
2	1	1	4	1	2

ENVIRONMENTAL CONDITIONS (EC)
L1, D1

EDUCATION/TRAINING
2

Examples of Job Titles

Truck Assembly Inspector

Descriptor Profile

Main Characteristics

Occupations in this group are characterized by the following aptitudes, interests and worker functions as they relate to main duties:

- **General learning ability** to check subassemblies and inspect finished products for proper quality

- Form perception, motor co-ordination and **manual dexterity** to check mechanical assemblies and subassemblies for alignment and proper functioning

- **Objective interest** in **handling** equipment to test and check electrical assemblies and wiring for proper connections

- **Methodical interest** in **copying** information to ensure subassemblies and finished products conform to product specifications

- **Directive interest** in performing minor adjustments and repairs

9486.2
Subgroup 2 of 2

Physical Activities

Vision
    2   Near vision

Colour Discrimination
    1   Relevant

Hearing
    1   Limited

Body Position
    4   Other body positions

Limb Co-ordination
    1   Upper limb co-ordination

Strength
    2   Light

Environmental Conditions

Location
    L1   Regulated inside climate

Discomforts
    D1   Noise

Employment Requirements

Education/Training
    2

- Some secondary school education is required.

- Up to two years of on-the-job training are provided.

- Experience as a mechanical assembler may be required for inspectors.

Workplaces/Employers

Machinery manufacturers

Mechanical products manufacturing companies

Transportation equipment manufacturers

Occupational Options

There is little or no mobility among the various assemblers and inspectors in the 9486 group.

Progression to supervisory positions is possible with experience.

Similar Occupations Classified Elsewhere

Aircraft Assemblers and Aircraft Assembly Inspectors (9481)

Motor Vehicle Assemblers, Inspectors and Testers (9482)

Industrial machinery, heavy equipment and aircraft engine assemblers (in 7316 *Machine Fitters*)

Supervisors of mechanical assemblers and inspectors (in 9226 *Supervisors, Other Mechanical and Metal Products Manufacturing*)

9487.1 Machine Operators, Electrical Apparatus Manufacturing

Machine Operators, Electrical Apparatus Manufacturing, operate machinery and equipment to fabricate complete products and parts for use in the assembly of electric appliances, equipment and apparatus such as batteries, fuses and plugs.

Profile Summary

APTITUDES

G	V	N	S	P	Q	K	F	M
4	4	4	4	4	5	3	4	3

INTERESTS
MOi

DATA PEOPLE THINGS (DPT)
584

PHYSICAL ACTIVITIES (PA)

V	C	H	B	L	S
2	1	1	4	1	2

ENVIRONMENTAL CONDITIONS (EC)
L1, H1, H3, D1

EDUCATION/TRAINING
2

Examples of Job Titles

Assembly Machine Setter - Electrical Equipment Manufacturing

Battery Repairer, Production Line

Dry Charge Machine Operator

Epoxy Coating Machine Operator

Machine Operator, Electrical Appliance Manufacturing

Machine Set-Up Operator, Electrical Equipment Manufacturing

Descriptor Profile

Main Characteristics

Occupations in this group are characterized by the following aptitudes, interests and worker functions as they relate to main duties:

- **General learning ability** to operate machinery and equipment to fabricate complete products and parts for use in the assembly of electric appliances and equipment

- **Motor co-ordination** and **manual dexterity** to position lead-acid storage batteries on assembly lines and insert battery contents into casings, to load machinery with glass tubes, bulbs and other parts to produce incandescent, fluorescent and other types of light bulbs and tubes, and to remove and pack finished products

- **Methodical interest** in **copying** information to operate and feed machinery and equipment to produce wiring devices such as fuses, plugs, caps, sockets, connectors and switches

- **Objective interest** in **operating** machinery to assemble, test and package dry-cell batteries, to fabricate plates for lead-acid storage batteries, and to apply protective coatings to items such as freezer cabinets, small electric motors and transformer assemblies

- **Innovative interest** in setting up and adjusting production machinery and equipment for operation, and in performing minor repairs to items rejected from production lines

9487.1
Subgroup 1 of 2

Physical Activities

Vision
  2 Near vision

Colour Discrimination
  1 Relevant

Hearing
  1 Limited

Body Position
  4 Other body positions

Limb Co-ordination
  1 Upper limb co-ordination

Strength
  2 Light

Environmental Conditions

Location
  L1 Regulated inside climate

Hazards
  H1 Dangerous chemical substance
  H3 Equipment, machinery, tools

Discomforts
  D1 Noise

Employment Requirements

Education/Training
  2

- Some secondary school education is usually required.

- On-the-job training is provided.

Workplaces/Employers

Electric appliance manufacturing companies

Electrical equipment manufacturing companies

Occupational Options

With experience, machine operators may progress to inspecting and testing positions.

Progression to supervisory positions is possible with experience.

Similar Occupations Classified Elsewhere

Assemblers and Inspectors, Electrical Appliance, Apparatus and Equipment Manufacturing (9484)

Supervisors, Electrical Products Manufacturing (9223)

9487.2 Inspectors and Testers, Electrical Apparatus Manufacturing

Inspectors and Tester, Electrical Apparatus Manufacturing, inspect and test completed parts and production items.

Profile Summary

APTITUDES

G	V	N	S	P	Q	K	F	M
3	4	4	4	4	5	3	4	3

INTERESTS
MOd

DATA PEOPLE THINGS (DPT)
587

PHYSICAL ACTIVITIES (PA)

V	C	H	B	L	S
2	1	1	2	1	2

ENVIRONMENTAL CONDITIONS (EC)
L1, D1

EDUCATION/TRAINING
2

Examples of Job Titles

Inspector, Electrical Dry Battery
Inspector, Electrical Light Bulbs

Descriptor Profile

Main Characteristics

Occupations in this group are characterized by the following aptitudes, interests and worker functions as they relate to main duties:

- **General learning ability** to inspect and test completed electrical parts and production items

- **Verbal ability** to summarize inspection results

- **Motor co-ordination** and **manual dexterity** to check in-process and completed production items for mechanical defects

- **Methodical interest** in **copying** information to collect and record inspection results; and in marking acceptable and defective assemblies

- **Objective interest** in operating testing equipment to maintain quality of products

- **Directive interest** in **handling** products during inspections to identify and return faulty assemblies to production for repairs

9487.2
Subgroup 2 of 2

Physical Activities

Vision
  2 Near vision

Colour Discrimination
  1 Relevant

Hearing
  1 Limited

Body Position
  2 Standing and/or walking

Limb Co-ordination
  1 Upper limb co-ordination

Strength
  2 Light

Environmental Conditions

Location
  L1 Regulated inside climate

Discomforts
  D1 Noise

Employment Requirements

Education/Training
  2

- Some secondary school education is usually required.
- On-the-job training is provided.
- Inspectors may require experience as an assembler in the same company.

Workplaces/Employers

Electric appliance manufacturing companies

Electrical equipment manufacturing companies

Occupational Options

Progression to supervisory positions is possible with experience.

Similar Occupations Classified Elsewhere

Assemblers and Inspectors, Electrical Appliance, Apparatus and Equipment Manufacturing (9484)

Supervisors, Electrical Products Manufacturing (9223)

9491.1 Boat Assemblers

Boat Assemblers put together wood, fibreglass and metal boats such as sailboats, motorboats, canoes and cabin cruisers.

Profile Summary

APTITUDES

G	V	N	S	P	Q	K	F	M
3	4	4	3	3	5	3	4	3

INTERESTS
OMi

DATA PEOPLE THINGS (DPT)
584

PHYSICAL ACTIVITIES (PA)

V	C	H	B	L	S
3	0	1	4	1	4

ENVIRONMENTAL CONDITIONS (EC)
L1, H3, D1

EDUCATION/TRAINING
2

Examples of Job Titles

Aluminium Boat Assembler
Boat Assembler
Canoe Assembler
Fibreglass Boat Assembler
Motorboat Assembler
Sailboat Assembler

Descriptor Profile

Main Characteristics

Occupations in this group are characterized by the following aptitudes, interests and worker functions as they relate to main duties:

- **General learning ability** to assemble wood, fibreglass and metal boats

- **Spatial** and **form perception** to visualize how various boat components fit together to form complete products

- **Motor co-ordination** and **manual dexterity** to cut, shape and join timber pieces to make wood boats using hand and power tools and to caulk decks and hulls using caulking guns

- **Objective interest** in operating equipment and using hand tools to install trims, rudders, seats, engine mounts and other accessories

- **Methodical interest** in copying information to assemble pre-cut timber pieces to make wood boats, and to assemble prefabricated parts and sections of fibreglass, metal and other material to form complete boats

- **Innovative interest** in fitting parts and sections to form complete assemblies; may repair boats

9491.1
Subgroup 1 of 2

Physical Activities

Vision
   3   Near and far vision

Colour Discrimination
   0   Not relevant

Hearing
   1   Limited

Body Position
   4   Other body positions

Limb Co-ordination
   1   Upper limb co-ordination

Strength
   4   Heavy

Environmental Conditions

Location
   L1   Regulated inside climate

Hazards
   H3   Equipment, machinery, tools

Discomforts
   D1   Noise

Employment Requirements

Education/Training
2

- Some secondary school education may be required.

- On-the-job training is provided.

- Experience as a helper or labourer in the same company may be required for boat assemblers.

Workplaces/Employers

Boat and marine craft manufacturing companies

Occupational Options

Progression to supervisory positions is possible with experience.

Similar Occupations Classified Elsewhere

Builders of customized wooden boats (in 7271 *Carpenters*)

Canoe craftspersons (in 5244 *Artisans and Craftspersons*)

Helpers and labourers in boat manufacturing (in 9619 *Other Labourers in Processing, Manufacturing and Utilities*)

Supervisors of boat assemblers and inspectors (in 9227 *Supervisors, Other Products Manufacturing and Assembly*)

Workers who fabricate, assemble and fit steel and other metal components to build ships (in 7263 *Structural Metal and Platework Fabricators and Fitters*)

9491.2 Boat Inspectors

Boat Inspectors check assembled boats to ensure product quality.

Profile Summary

APTITUDES

G	V	N	S	P	Q	K	F	M
3	3	4	3	3	5	3	4	3

INTERESTS
MOi

DATA PEOPLE THINGS (DPT)
587

PHYSICAL ACTIVITIES (PA)

V	C	H	B	L	S
3	0	1	4	1	2

ENVIRONMENTAL CONDITIONS (EC)
L1, D1

EDUCATION/TRAINING
2

Examples of Job Titles

Boat Inspector

Descriptor Profile

Main Characteristics

Occupations in this group are characterized by the following aptitudes, interests and worker functions as they relate to main duties:

- **General learning ability** to inspect assembled boats for defects and to ensure that they conform to quality standards

- **Spatial perception** to verify conformity with plans and specifications

- **Form perception** to examine assembled boats for defects

- **Methodical interest** in **copying** to record information on inspected products and mark defects

- **Objective interest** in **handling** measuring devices to verify alignments

- **Innovative interest** in making minor adjustments and repairs

9491.2

Physical Activities

Vision
  3 Near and far vision

Colour Discrimination
  0 Not relevant

Hearing
  1 Limited

Body Position
  4 Other body positions

Limb Co-ordination
  1 Upper limb co-ordination

Strength
  2 Light

Environmental Conditions

Location
  L1 Regulated inside climate

Discomforts
  D1 Noise

Employment Requirements

Education/Training
2

- Some secondary school education may be required.

- On-the-job training is provided.

- Experience as a boat assembler may be required for boat inspectors.

Workplaces/Employers

Boat and marine craft manufacturing companies

Occupational Options

Progression to supervisory positions is possible with experience.

Similar Occupations Classified Elsewhere

Builders of customized wooden boats (in 7271 *Carpenters*)

Canoe craftspersons (in 5244 *Artisans and Craftspersons*)

Helpers and labourers in boat manufacturing (in 9619 *Other Labourers in Processing, Manufacturing and Utilities*)

Supervisors of boat assemblers and inspectors (in 9227 *Supervisors, Other Products Manufacturing and Assembly*)

Workers who fabricate, assemble and fit steel and other metal components to build ships (in 7263 *Structural Metal and Platework Fabricators and Fitters*)

9492.1 Furniture and Fixture Assemblers

Furniture and Fixture Assemblers put together parts to form subassemblies and complete articles of furniture and fixtures.

Profile Summary

APTITUDES

G	V	N	S	P	Q	K	F	M
4	4	4	3	4	4	3	4	4

INTERESTS
OMi

DATA PEOPLE THINGS (DPT)
584

PHYSICAL ACTIVITIES (PA)

V	C	H	B	L	S
2	0	1	4	1	3

ENVIRONMENTAL CONDITIONS (EC)
L1, H3, D1, D4

EDUCATION/TRAINING
2

Examples of Job Titles

Chair Assembler
Desk Assembler
Fixture Assembler
Furniture Assembler
Metal Furniture Assembler
Table Assembler
Wood Furniture Assembler

Descriptor Profile

Main Characteristics

Occupations in this group are characterized by the following aptitudes, interests and worker functions as they relate to main duties:

- **General learning ability** to form subassemblies and complete articles of furniture and fixtures

- **Spatial perception** to visualize how furniture components fit together to form complete products

- **Motor co-ordination** to prepare, sand and trim wood furniture and fixture parts using hand and power tools

- **Objective interest** in **operating** equipment, and using hand and power tools to install hardware, such as hinges and clasps, on furniture and fixtures

- **Methodical interest** in **copying** information to assemble wood and metal furniture and fixtures to form subassemblies and complete articles, and to assemble combinations of parts made of wood, metal, plastic, cane and other materials to form subassemblies

- **Innovative interest** in reinforcing assembled furniture and fixtures with dowels and other supports

9492.1
Subgroup 1 of 2

Physical Activities

Vision
   2 Near vision

Colour Discrimination
   0 Not relevant

Hearing
   1 Limited

Body Position
   4 Other body positions

Limb Co-ordination
   1 Upper limb co-ordination

Strength
   3 Medium

Environmental Conditions

Location
   L1 Regulated inside climate

Hazards
   H3 Equipment, machinery, tools

Discomforts
   D1 Noise
   D4 Non-toxic dusts

Employment Requirements

Education/Training
2

- Some secondary school education may be required.

- On-the-job training is provided.

- Experience as a labourer in the same company may be required.

Workplaces/Employers

Furniture manufacturing companies

Occupational Options

Mobility is possible among jobs in the 9492 group.

Progression to supervisory positions is possible with experience.

Similar Occupations Classified Elsewhere

Furniture Finishers and Refinishers (9494)

Other Wood Products Assemblers and Inspectors (9493)

Woodworking Machine Operators (9513)

Supervisors of workers in this group (in 9224 *Supervisors, Furniture and Fixtures Manufacturing*)

9492.2 Furniture and Fixture Inspectors

Furniture and Fixture Inspectors examine furniture and fixture subassemblies and finished products to ensure product quality.

Profile Summary

APTITUDES

G	V	N	S	P	Q	K	F	M
4	4	4	3	4	4	3	4	4

INTERESTS
MOi

DATA PEOPLE THINGS (DPT)
587

PHYSICAL ACTIVITIES (PA)

V	C	H	B	L	S
2	1	1	4	1	2

ENVIRONMENTAL CONDITIONS (EC)
L1, D1

EDUCATION/TRAINING
2

Examples of Job Titles

Assembly Inspector - Furniture Manufacturing

Furniture Inspector

Descriptor Profile

Main Characteristics

Occupations in this group are characterized by the following aptitudes, interests and worker functions as they relate to main duties:

- **General learning ability** to inspect furniture and fixture subassemblies and finished products to ensure that they conform to quality standards

- **Spatial perception** to verify conformity with plans and specifications

- **Motor co-ordination** to use measuring and marking devices

- **Methodical interest** in **copying** to record information on inspected products and mark defective parts and products

- **Objective interest** in **handling** furniture and fixture subassemblies and finished products for inspection purposes

- **Innovative interest** in making minor adjustments and repairs

9492.2
Subgroup 2 of 2

Physical Activities

Vision
  2 Near vision

Colour Discrimination
  1 Relevant

Hearing
  1 Limited

Body Position
  4 Other body positions

Limb Co-ordination
  1 Upper limb co-ordination

Strength
  2 Light

Environmental Conditions

Location
  L1 Regulated inside climate

Discomforts
  D1 Noise

Employment Requirements

Education/Training
  2

- Some secondary school education may be required.

- On-the-job training is provided.

- Experience as a labourer in the same company may be required.

Workplaces/Employers

Furniture manufacturing companies

Occupational Options

Mobility is possible among jobs in the 9492 group.

Progression to supervisory positions is possible with experience.

Similar Occupations Classified Elsewhere

Furniture Finishers and Refinishers (9494)

Other Wood Products Assemblers and Inspectors (9493)

Woodworking Machine Operators (9513)

Supervisors of workers in this group (in 9224 *Supervisors, Furniture and Fixtures Manufacturing*)

9493.1 Other Wood Products Assemblers

Workers in this group assemble a variety of wood products and millwork, such as window sashes and doors.

Profile Summary

APTITUDES

G	V	N	S	P	Q	K	F	M
4	4	5	4	4	4	3	4	3

INTERESTS
OMi

DATA PEOPLE THINGS (DPT)
584

PHYSICAL ACTIVITIES (PA)

V	C	H	B	L	S
2	0	1	4	1	3

ENVIRONMENTAL CONDITIONS (EC)
L1, H3, D1, D4

EDUCATION/TRAINING
2

Examples of Job Titles

Bench Assembler, Wood Products
Crate Builder, Wood
Manufactured Housing Production Worker
Millwork Assembler
Pallet Maker, Wood
Prefabricated Housing Assembler
Wood Products Assembler
Wooden Box Assembler
Wooden Door Maker

Descriptor Profile

Main Characteristics

Occupations in this group are characterized by the following aptitudes, interests and worker functions as they relate to main duties:

- **General learning ability** to assemble a variety of wood products and millwork such as window sashes and doors

- **Motor co-ordination** and **manual dexterity** to trim and sand joints, moulding and other wood parts to be assembled using hand and power tools, and to install hardware such as knobs and hinges

- **Objective interest** in **operating** assembly line equipment such as jigs, overhead cranes and hand and power tools to assemble door panels, trusses, modular components and other parts to make prefabricated housing

- **Methodical interest** in **copying** information to assemble wood products such as window sashes, doors, boxes, pallets, ladders and barrels using glue, staples, screws, bolts and other fasteners

- **Innovative interest** in reinforcing assembled products with dowelling and other supports

9493.1

Physical Activities

Vision
   2 Near vision

Colour Discrimination
   0 Not relevant

Hearing
   1 Limited

Body Position
   4 Other body positions

Limb Co-ordination
   1 Upper limb co-ordination

Strength
   3 Medium

Environmental Conditions

Location
   L1 Regulated inside climate

Hazards
   H3 Equipment, machinery, tools

Discomforts
   D1 Noise
   D4 Non-toxic dusts

Employment Requirements

Education/Training
2

- Experience as a labourer in the same company may be required.
- On-the-job training is provided.

Workplaces/Employers

Wood and millwork products manufacturing companies

Similar Occupations Classified Elsewhere

Cabinetmakers (7272)

Carpenters (7271)

Furniture and Fixture Assemblers and Inspectors (9492)

Supervisors, Other Products Manufacturing and Assembly (9227)

Woodworking Machine Operators (9513)

Labourers in wood products manufacturing (in 9619 *Other Labourers in Processing, Manufacturing and Utilities*)

9493.2 Other Wood Products Inspectors

Inspectors in this group examine wood products to ensure product quality.

Profile Summary

APTITUDES

G	V	N	S	P	Q	K	F	M
4	4	5	4	4	4	3	4	3

INTERESTS
MOi

DATA PEOPLE THINGS (DPT)
587

PHYSICAL ACTIVITIES (PA)

V	C	H	B	L	S
2	0	1	4	1	2

ENVIRONMENTAL CONDITIONS (EC)
L1, D1

EDUCATION/TRAINING
2

Examples of Job Titles

Sash and Door Inspector
Wood Products Assembling Inspector

Descriptor Profile

Main Characteristics

Occupations in this group are characterized by the following aptitudes, interests and worker functions as they relate to main duties:

- **General learning ability** to inspect wood products to ensure that they conform to quality standards

- **Motor co-ordination** and **manual dexterity** to use measuring and marking devices

- **Methodical interest** in **copying** to record information on inspected products and mark defective parts and products

- **Objective interest** in **handling** wood products for inspection purposes

- **Innovative interest** in making minor adjustments and repairs

9493.2

Physical Activities

Vision
  2 Near vision

Colour Discrimination
  0 Not relevant

Hearing
  1 Limited

Body Position
  4 Other body positions

Limb Co-ordination
  1 Upper limb co-ordination

Strength
  2 Light

Environmental Conditions

Location
  L1 Regulated inside climate

Discomforts
  D1 Noise

Employment Requirements

Education/Training
2

- Experience as a labourer in the same company may be required.

- Inspectors may require related assembly experience.

- On-the-job training is provided.

Workplaces/Employers

Wood and millwork products manufacturing companies

Similar Occupations Classified Elsewhere

Cabinetmakers (7272)

Carpenters (7271)

Furniture and Fixture Assemblers and Inspectors (9492)

Supervisors, Other Products Manufacturing and Assembly (9227)

Woodworking Machine Operators (9513)

Labourers in wood products manufacturing (in 9619 *Other Labourers in Processing, Manufacturing and Utilities*)

9494.1 Furniture Finishers

Furniture Finishers finish new wood and metal furniture to specified colours and finishes.

Profile Summary

APTITUDES

G	V	N	S	P	Q	K	F	M
4	4	4	4	4	4	3	4	3

INTERESTS
OMI

DATA PEOPLE THINGS (DPT)
684

PHYSICAL ACTIVITIES (PA)

V	C	H	B	L	S
2	1	1	4	1	3

ENVIRONMENTAL CONDITIONS (EC)
L1, H1, H3, D3, D4

EDUCATION/TRAINING
2, 4

Examples of Job Titles

Finishing Machine Operator
Furniture Finisher
Furniture Polisher
Furniture Stainer
Touch-Up Person - Furniture Finishing
Trimmer - Furniture Finishing
Wash-Off Operator - Furniture Finishing
Wood Finisher

Descriptor Profile

Main Characteristics

Occupations in this group are characterized by the following aptitudes, interests and worker functions as they relate to main duties:

- **General learning ability** to set up and operate finishing machines or finish furniture by hand

- **Motor co-ordination** and **manual dexterity** to apply lacquers and other sealers, to spray metal furniture with paint and other materials, and to clean and polish furniture

- **Objective interest** in operating equipment to sand metal furniture to prepare for finish; and in using brushes and spray guns

- **Methodical interest** in **comparing** information to stain and finish wood to specified colours with stains, paints and other materials and to apply toners, highlights, glazes and shaders to obtain desired finish

- **Innovative interest** in decorating wood surfaces and marking them to create antique and other effects using hand and power tools

Physical Activities

Vision
    2 Near vision

Colour Discrimination
    1 Relevant

Hearing
    1 Limited

Body Position
    4 Other body positions

Limb Co-ordination
    1 Upper limb co-ordination

Strength
    3 Medium

Environmental Conditions

Location
    L1 Regulated inside climate

Hazards
    H1 Dangerous chemical substances
    H3 Equipment, machinery, tools

Discomforts
    D3 Odours
    D4 Non-toxic dusts

Employment Requirements

Education/Training
  2, 4

- Some secondary school education is required.

- College, high school or industry courses in furniture finishing may be required.

- On-the-job training is provided.

Workplaces/Employers

Furniture manufacturing plants

Furniture refinishing and repair shops

Retail furniture stores

Similar Occupations Classified Elsewhere

Painters and Decorators (7294)

Upholsterers (7341)

9494.2 Furniture Refinishers

Furniture Refinishers refinish repaired, used and old furniture.

Profile Summary

APTITUDES

G	V	N	S	P	Q	K	F	M
4	4	4	4	4	4	3	4	3

INTERESTS
OMI

DATA PEOPLE THINGS (DPT)
684

PHYSICAL ACTIVITIES (PA)

V	C	H	B	L	S
2	1	1	4	1	3

ENVIRONMENTAL CONDITIONS (EC)
L1, H1, H3, D3, D4

EDUCATION/TRAINING
2, 4

Examples of Job Titles

Furniture Refinisher
Furniture Stripper

Descriptor Profile

Main Characteristics

Occupations in this group are characterized by the following aptitudes, interests and worker functions as they relate to main duties:

- **General learning ability** to refinish repaired, used and old furniture

- **Motor co-ordination** and **manual dexterity** to strip old finishes from wood surfaces using steel wool, sandpaper and solvents, to smooth gouges with wood fillers, to sand wood, and to polish and wax refinished surfaces

- **Objective interest** in **operating** equipment to sand and grind metal surfaces to prepare for coatings, and to paint metal surfaces using electrostatic methods, spray guns and other painting equipment; may perform duties of furniture finisher

- **Methodical interest** in **comparing** to match colours to obtain original finishes

- **Innovative interest** in applying appropriate finishes to stripped wood; and in making minor repairs

9494.2

Physical Activities

Vision
2 Near vision

Colour discrimination
1 Relevant

Hearing
1 Limited

Body Position
4 Other body positions

Limb Co-ordination
1 Upper limb co-ordination

Strength
3 Medium

Environmental Conditions

Location
L1 Regulated inside climate

Hazards
H1 Dangerous chemical substances
H3 Equipment, machinery, tools

Discomforts
D3 Odours
D4 Non-toxic dusts

Employment Requirements

Education/Training
2, 4

- Some secondary school education is required.

- College, high school or industry courses in furniture refinishing may be required.

- On-the-job training is provided.

Workplaces/Employers

Furniture refinishing shops

Self-employment

Similar Occupations Classified Elsewhere

Painters and Decorators (7294)

Upholsterers (7341)

9495.1 Plastic Products Assemblers and Finishers

Plastic Products Assemblers and Finishers put together and finish plastic parts and products.

Profile Summary

APTITUDES

G	V	N	S	P	Q	K	F	M
4	4	4	4	4	4	3	4	3

INTERESTS
OMi

DATA PEOPLE THINGS (DPT)
584

PHYSICAL ACTIVITIES (PA)

V	C	H	B	L	S
2	0	1	4	1	3

ENVIRONMENTAL CONDITIONS (EC)
L1, H1*, H3, H7*, D1, D3

EDUCATION/TRAINING
2

Examples of Job Titles

Fibreglass Laminator
Plastic Bottle Trimmer
Plastic Parts Assembler
Plastic Tank Assembler
Plastics Assembler
Plastics Fabricator
Plastics Grinder
Plastics Trimmer
Skylight Assembler

Descriptor Profile

Main Characteristics

Occupations in this group are characterized by the following aptitudes, interests and worker functions as they relate to main duties:

- **General learning ability** to assemble and finish plastic parts and products

- **Motor co-ordination** and **manual dexterity** to operate spray guns in order to apply resin mixtures to metal and wood moulds to form plastic products

- **Objective interest** in operating machines, equipment and hand tools to cut, shape, splice and fit plastic materials to form parts and assemblies, and in operating finishing equipment to trim, grind and buff products into final form

- **Methodical interest** in copying information to assemble composite materials on patterns to form parts and assemblies using bonding agents

- **Innovative interest** in loading and operating autoclave ovens to cure and bond parts and subassemblies

9495.1
Subgroup 1 of 2

Physical Activities

Vision
  2 Near vision

Colour Discrimination
  0 Not relevant

Hearing
  1 Limited

Body Position
  4 Other body positions

Limb Co-ordination
  1 Upper limb co-ordination

Strength
  3 Medium

Environmental Conditions

Location
  L1 Regulated inside climate

Hazards
  H1*Dangerous chemical substances
  H3 Equipment, machinery, tools
  H7*Fire, steam, hot surfaces

Discomforts
  D1 Noise
  D3 Odours

Employment Requirements

Education/Training
  2

- Some secondary school education is usually required.

- Experience as a labourer in the same company may be required.

- On-the-job training is provided.

Workplaces/Employers

Plastic parts divisions of aircraft and other manufacturing companies

Plastic products manufacturing companies

Occupational Options

Mobility among the various workers in the 9495 group is possible.

Progression to supervisory positions is possible with experience.

Similar Occupations Classified Elsewhere

Labourers in Rubber and Plastic Products Manufacturing (9615)

Plastics Processing Machine Operators (9422)

Rubber Processing Machine Operators and Related Workers (9423)

Supervisors, Plastic and Rubber Products Manufacturing (9214)

Remarks

*Environmental Conditions

- For some occupations in this group, **Hazards** H1 (Dangerous chemical substances) and H7 (Fire, steam, hot surfaces) may also apply.

9495.2 Plastic Products Inspectors

Plastic Products Inspectors examine plastic parts and products.

Profile Summary

APTITUDES

G	V	N	S	P	Q	K	F	M
4	4	4	4	4	4	3	4	3

INTERESTS
MOi

DATA PEOPLE THINGS (DPT)
587

PHYSICAL ACTIVITIES (PA)

V	C	H	B	L	S
2	0	1	2	1	2

ENVIRONMENTAL CONDITIONS (EC)
L1, D1

EDUCATION/TRAINING
2

Examples of Job Titles

Plastic Products Inspector and Tester
Plastics Inspector

Descriptor Profile

Main Characteristics

Occupations in this group are characterized by the following aptitudes, interests and worker functions as they relate to main duties:

- **General learning ability** to inspect plastic products for defects and to ensure that they conform to specifications and quality standards

- **Motor co-ordination** and **manual dexterity** to affix seals and tags to approved products

- **Methodical interest** in **copying** information to mark defective products and prepare reports on inspected products

- **Objective interest** in **handling** products for inspection; and in using instruments to inspect plastic products

- **Innovative interest** in making minor adjustments and repairs to products, and in rerouting defective products for repair or recycle

9495.2
Subgroup 2 of 2

Physical Activities

Vision
  2 Near vision

Colour Discrimination
  0 Not relevant

Hearing
  1 Limited

Body Position
  2 Standing and/or walking

Limb Co-ordination
  1 Upper limb co-ordination

Strength
  2 Light

Environmental Conditions

Location
  L1 Regulated inside climate

Discomforts
  D1 Noise

Employment Requirements

Education/Training
  2

- Some secondary school education is usually required.

- Experience as a labourer in the same company may be required.

- On-the-job training is provided.

Workplaces/Employers

Plastic parts divisions of aircraft and other manufacturing companies

Plastic products manufacturing companies

Occupational Options

Mobility among the various workers in the 9495 group is possible.

Progression to supervisory positions is possible with experience.

Similar Occupations Classified Elsewhere

Labourers in Rubber and Plastic Products Manufacturing (9615)

Plastics Processing Machine Operators (9422)

Rubber Processing Machine Operators and Related Workers (9423)

Supervisors, Plastic and Rubber Products Manufacturing (9214)

9496 Painters and Coaters, Manufacturing

Painters and Coaters, Manufacturing, use equipment to apply paint, enamel, lacquer and other non-metallic protective and decorative coatings to surfaces of products.

Profile Summary

APTITUDES

G	V	N	S	P	Q	K	F	M
4	4	4	4	3	4	3	3	3

INTERESTS
OMi

DATA PEOPLE THINGS (DPT)
584

PHYSICAL ACTIVITIES (PA)

V	C	H	B	L	S
2	1	1	4	1	2

ENVIRONMENTAL CONDITIONS (EC)
L1, H1, D3

EDUCATION/TRAINING
2, 4, 5

Examples of Job Titles

Aircraft Painter
Assembly Painter
Automobile Painter
Coating Machine Operator
Dip Tank Attendant
Industrial Product Painter
Manufacturing Painter
Paint Machine Operator
Paint Systems Operator
Production Painter
Spray Paint Operator
Spray Painter

Descriptor Profile

Main Characteristics

Occupations in this group are characterized by the following aptitudes, interests and worker functions as they relate to main duties:

- **General learning ability** to tend and operate machines, and use brushes and spray equipment to apply paint, enamel, lacquer and other non-metallic protective and decorative coatings to surfaces of products

- **Form perception** to observe surface coatings for proper thickness, smoothness and quality

- **Motor co-ordination** and **finger dexterity** to paint small items and apply touch-ups using brushes

- **Manual dexterity** to operate hand-held spray guns to spray-paint and coat stationary items or items moving on conveyors

- **Objective interest** in operating equipment to clean, wash and prepare items for paint, lacquer and other protective and decorative coatings; and in operating automated spray paint, dip and flow coating equipment and other mechanized painting and product coating application equipment

- **Methodical interest** in copying information to mix paints using automated paint-mixing equipment according to predetermined formulas, and to clean and maintain painting and coating equipment

- **Innovative interest** in selecting appropriate paints; may prepare and apply stencils, decals and other decorative items on finished products

Physical Activities

Vision
    2 Near vision

Colour Discrimination
    1 Relevant

Hearing
    1 Limited

Body Position
    4 Other body positions

Limb Co-ordination
    1 Upper limb co-ordination

Strength
    2 Light

Environmental Conditions

Location
    L1 Regulated inside climate

Hazards
    H1 Dangerous chemical substances

Discomforts
    D3 Odours

Employment Requirements

Education/Training
    2, 4, 5

- Some secondary school education is usually required.

- Several months of on-the-job training are usually provided.

- Some industrial painters, such as aircraft painters, require specialized training or college courses.

Workplaces/Employers

Manufacturing companies

Occupational Options

Progression to supervisory positions is possible with experience.

Similar Occupations Classified Elsewhere

Furniture Finishers and Refinishers (9494)

Plating, Metal Spraying and Related Operators (9497)

Autobody repair painters or repainters (in 7322 *Motor Vehicle Body Repairers*)

Construction painters (in 7294 *Painters and Decorators*)

Supervisors of manufacturing painters and coaters (in 9214 *Supervisors, Plastic and Rubber Products Manufacturing* and in 922 *Supervisors, Assembly and Fabrication*)

9497 Plating, Metal Spraying and Related Operators

Workers in this group operate machines and equipment to deposit metallized substances on metal and other articles for decorative, protective and restorative coatings.

Profile Summary

APTITUDES

G	V	N	S	P	Q	K	F	M
3	4	4	4	3	4	3	4	3

INTERESTS
OMi

DATA PEOPLE THINGS (DPT)
584

PHYSICAL ACTIVITIES (PA)

V	C	H	B	L	S
2	1	1	2	1	2

ENVIRONMENTAL CONDITIONS (EC)
L1, H1, H3, H7

EDUCATION/TRAINING
2

Examples of Job Titles

Anodizer
Electroplater Operator
Galvanizer
Metal Coater Operator
Metal Dipper
Metal Electroplater
Metal Spray Operator
Sherardizer

Descriptor Profile

Main Characteristics

Occupations in this group are characterized by the following aptitudes, interests and worker functions as they relate to main duties:

- **General learning ability** to operate machines and equipment to deposit metallized substances on metal and other articles for decorative, protective and restorative coatings

- **Form perception** to find defects in plating when checking for proper thicknesses

- **Motor co-ordination** and **manual dexterity** to operate spray equipment to build up worn and damaged parts, and to bond protective and decorative coatings on metal objects

- **Objective interest** in **operating** electroplating and hot-dip metal plating equipment to coat metal and other objects

- **Methodical interest** in **copying** information to prepare and mix metallizing solutions according to formulas and specifications; and in tending automatic metal coating machines that convey objects through a series of cleaning, rinsing and plating solutions

- **Innovative interest** in checking the proper thicknesses of plating using micrometers, callipers and other devices

9497

Physical Activities

Vision
   2   Near vision

Colour Discrimination
   1   Relevant

Hearing
   1   Limited

Body Position
   2   Standing and/or walking

Limb Co-ordination
   1   Upper limb co-ordination

Strength
   2   Light

Environmental Conditions

Location
   L1   Regulated inside climate

Hazards
   H1   Dangerous chemical substances
   H3   Equipment, machinery, tools
   H7   Fire, steam, hot surfaces

Employment Requirements

Education/Training
   2

- Some secondary school education is usually required.

- Experience in operating production machinery or equipment may be required.

- Three-to-six months of on-the-job training are usually required.

Workplaces/Employers

Customized metal plating and coating shops

Metal products manufacturing companies

Occupational Options

Progression to supervisory positions is possible with experience.

Similar Occupations Classified Elsewhere

Production painters (in 9496 *Painters and Coaters, Manufacturing*)

Supervisors of operators in this group (in 9226 *Supervisors, Other Mechanical and Metal Products Manufacturing*)

9498.1 Other Assemblers

Workers in this group assemble products such as jewellery, silverware, clocks and watches, musical instruments, sporting goods and toys.

Profile Summary

APTITUDES

G	V	N	S	P	Q	K	F	M
4	4	4	4	4	4	3	3	3

INTERESTS
OMi

DATA PEOPLE THINGS (DPT)
584

PHYSICAL ACTIVITIES (PA)

V	C	H	B	L	S
2	1	1	4	1	3

ENVIRONMENTAL CONDITIONS (EC)
L1, H3

EDUCATION/TRAINING
2

Examples of Job Titles

Antenna Assembler
Bicycle Assembler
Eyeglass Frame Assembler
Golf Club Assembler
Lamp Shade Assembler
Skate Maker
Venetian Blind Assembler
Watch Assembler

Descriptor Profile

Main Characteristics

Occupations in this group are characterized by the following aptitudes, interests and worker functions as they relate to main duties:

- **General learning ability** to assemble products such as jewellery, silverware, clocks and watches, musical instruments, sporting goods and toys

- **Motor co-ordination** and **manual dexterity** to cut, shape and fit materials to form parts and components

- **Finger dexterity** to screw, clip, glue, bond, weld and otherwise assemble parts and components

- **Objective interest** in **operating** equipment and using hand tools to bring products to final form by sanding, trimming, grinding and cleaning

- **Methodical interest** in **copying** information to assemble parts and components to form products

- **Innovative interest** in making minor adjustments and repairs

9498.1
Subgroup 1 of 2

Physical Activities

Vision
2   Near vision

Colour Discrimination
1   Relevant

Hearing
1   Limited

Body Position
4   Other body position

Limb Co-ordination
1   Upper limb co-ordination

Strength
3   Medium

Environmental Conditions

Location
L1   Regulated inside climate

Hazards
H3   Equipment, machinery, tools

Employment Requirements

Education/Training
2

- Some secondary school education is usually required.

- Experience as a manufacturing labourer in the same company may be required.

- On-the-job training is provided.

Workplaces/Employers

Manufacturing companies

Occupational Options

There is little or no mobility among the various assemblers in the 9498 group.

Progression to supervisory positions is possible with experience.

Similar Occupations Classified Elsewhere

Other Products Machine Operators (9517)

Supervisors, Other Products Manufacturing and Assembly (9227)

9498.2 Other Inspectors

Workers in this group inspect products such as jewellery, silverware, clocks and watches, musical instruments, sporting goods and toys.

Profile Summary

APTITUDES

G	V	N	S	P	Q	K	F	M
4	4	4	4	4	4	3	3	3

INTERESTS
MOi

DATA PEOPLE THINGS (DPT)
587

PHYSICAL ACTIVITIES (PA)

V	C	H	B	L	S
2	1	1	2	0	1

ENVIRONMENTAL CONDITIONS (EC)
L1

EDUCATION/TRAINING
2

Examples of Job Titles

Camera Assembly Inspector
Jewellery Inspector
Piano Assembly Inspector
Toy Inspector

Descriptor Profile

Main Characteristics

Occupations in this group are characterized by the following aptitudes, interests and worker functions as they relate to main duties:

- **General learning ability** to check manufactured items for defects to ensure that they conform to specifications

- Motor co-ordination and finger and **manual dexterity** to affix seals and tags to approved items

- **Methodical interest** in **copying** information to complete reports on inspected products

- **Objective interest** in **handling** to inspect manufactured items visually; and in using sample models and instruments for inspection purposes

- **Innovative interest** in returning defective products for repair or recycle

9498.2
Subgroup 2 of 2

Physical Activities

Vision
    2   Near vision

Colour Discrimination
    1   Relevant

Hearing
    1   Limited

Body Position
    2   Standing and/or walking

Limb Co-ordination
    0   Not relevant

Strength
    1   Limited

Environmental Conditions

Location
    L1   Regulated inside climate

Employment Requirements

Education/Training
    2

- Some secondary school education is usually required.

- Experience as a manufacturing labourer in the same company may be required.

- On-the-job training is provided.

Workplaces/Employers

Manufacturing companies

Occupational Options

There is little or no mobility among the various inspectors in the 9498 group.

Progression to supervisory positions is possible with experience.

Similar Occupations Classified Elsewhere

Other Products Machine Operators (9517)

Supervisors, Other Products Manufacturing and Assembly (9227)

9511 Machining Tool Operators

Machining Tool Operators set up and operate or tend metal-cutting machines designed for repetitive machining work. This group includes workers who etch and chemically mill metal pieces.

Profile Summary

APTITUDES

G	V	N	S	P	Q	K	F	M
3	3	3	3	3	4	3	3	3

INTERESTS
OMi

DATA PEOPLE THINGS (DPT)
580

PHYSICAL ACTIVITIES (PA)

V	C	H	B	L	S
2	0	1	2	1	3

ENVIRONMENTAL CONDITIONS (EC)
L1, H1*, H3, H6, D1, D2*

EDUCATION/TRAINING
2, 4

Examples of Job Titles

- Aircraft Parts Etcher
- Boring Mill Operator
- Lathe Machining Operator
- Machining Tool Operator
- Metal Grinder Operator, Production
- Milling Machine Set-Up Operator
- Numerical Control (NC) Machine Tool Operator
- Production Gear Cutter
- Radial Drill Operator

Descriptor Profile

Main Characteristics

Occupations in this group are characterized by the following aptitudes, interests and worker functions as they relate to main duties:

- **General learning ability** to set up and operate or tend metal-cutting machines designed for repetitive machining work
- **Verbal ability** to study job orders
- **Numerical ability** and **form perception** to measure and verify dimensions of machined parts using precision instruments
- **Spatial perception** to interpret blueprints in order to determine future machining operations
- **Motor co-ordination** and **finger** and **manual dexterity** to immerse metal parts and work pieces in etching solutions to remove unwanted portions
- **Objective interest** in operating and tending machines to perform repetitive machining operations such as turning, milling, drilling, boring, planing, honing, broaching and grinding
- **Methodical interest** in **copying** information to prepare etching solutions
- **Innovative interest** in **setting up** metal-cutting machines

9511

Physical Activities

Vision
   2 Near vision

Colour Discrimination
   0 Not relevant

Hearing
   1 Limited

Body Position
   2 Standing and/or walking

Limb Co-ordination
   1 Upper limb co-ordination

Strength
   3 Medium

Environmental Conditions

Location
   L1 Regulated inside climate

Hazards
   H1*Dangerous chemical substances
   H3 Equipment, machinery, tools
   H6 Flying particles, falling objects

Discomforts
   D1 Noise
   D2*Vibration

Employment Requirements

Education/Training
   2, 4

- Some secondary school education is required.

- College or other courses in machining may be required.

- Several months of on-the-job training are provided.

- Senior positions in this group, such as set-up operator, require experience as a machine operator.

Workplaces/Employers

Machine shops

Metal products and other manufacturing companies

Occupational Options

Experienced machining tool operators may become machinists through apprenticeship training.

Similar Occupations Classified Elsewhere

Machinists and Machining and Tooling Inspectors (7231)

Tool and Die Makers (7232)

Supervisors of machining tool operators (in 9226 *Supervisors, Other Mechanical and Metal Products Manufacturing*)

Remarks

*Environmental Conditions

- For some occupations in this group, **Hazards** H1 (Dangerous chemical substances) and **Discomforts** D2 (Vibration) may also apply.

9512   Forging Machine Operators

Forging Machine Operators operate forging machines to form and shape metal into various shapes and sizes, and to produce desired strength, hardness and other characteristics.

Profile Summary

APTITUDES

G	V	N	S	P	Q	K	F	M
4	4	4	4	3	4	4	4	3

INTERESTS
OMd

DATA PEOPLE THINGS (DPT)
584

PHYSICAL ACTIVITIES (PA)

V	C	H	B	L	S
3	1	1	4	1	4

ENVIRONMENTAL CONDITIONS (EC)
L2, H3, H7, D1

EDUCATION/TRAINING
2

Examples of Job Titles

Bending Machine Operator
Cold Drawn Operator
Cold Press Operator
Forging Press Operator
Hot Press Operator
Manipulator Operator
Trip Hammer Operator
Upsetter Operator

Descriptor Profile

Main Characteristics

Occupations in this group are characterized by the following aptitudes, interests and worker functions as they relate to main duties:

- **General learning ability** to operate forging machines to form and shape metal into various shapes and sizes, and to produce desired strength, hardness and other characteristics

- **Form perception** to examine finished forgings for defects

- **Manual dexterity** to place metal pieces in furnaces using hand tongs and remove from furnaces when colour of metals indicate proper forging temperatures, and to position heated and cold metal pieces on dies of presses and other forging machinery

- **Objective interest** in operating gas- and oil-fired furnaces to heat metals to proper temperatures before forging; and in positioning and adjusting dies on anvils of forging machine using hand tools, overhead cranes or other hoisting devices

- **Methodical interest** in copying information to operate presses and other machines to perform hot and cold forging by flattening, straightening, twisting, forming, drawing, upsetting, splitting, cutting, punching, piercing, bending, coining and other operations

- **Directive interest** in loading and unloading furnaces with automatic conveyors

Physical Activities

Vision
 3 Near and far vision

Colour Discrimination
 1 Relevant

Hearing
 1 Limited

Body Position
 4 Other body positions

Limb Co-ordination
 1 Upper limb co-ordination

Strength
 4 Heavy

Environmental Conditions

Location
 L2 Unregulated inside climate

Hazards
 H3 Equipment, machinery, tools
 H7 Fire, steam, hot surfaces

Discomforts
 D1 Noise

Employment Requirements

Education/Training
 2

- Some secondary school education is usually required.
- On-the-job training is provided.

Workplaces/Employers

Fabricated metal products industries

Machinery industries

Transportation equipment industries

Occupational Options

Progression to blacksmith, die setting or supervisory positions is possible with experience.

Similar Occupations Classified Elsewhere

Blacksmiths and Die Setters (7266)

Supervisors of forging machine operators (in 9226 *Supervisors, Other Mechanical and Metal Products Manufacturing*)

9513 Woodworking Machine Operators

Woodworking Machine Operators set up, program and operate one or more woodworking machines to fabricate and repair parts for furniture, fixtures and other wood products.

Profile Summary

APTITUDES

G	V	N	S	P	Q	K	F	M
4	4	4	4	3	4	3	4	3

INTERESTS
OMi

DATA PEOPLE THINGS (DPT)
560

PHYSICAL ACTIVITIES (PA)

V	C	H	B	L	S
2	0	1	4	1	3

ENVIRONMENTAL CONDITIONS (EC)
L1, H1, H3, H6, D1, D3, D4

EDUCATION/TRAINING
2

Examples of Job Titles

Band Saw Operator - Woodworking

Boring Machine Operator - Woodworking

Drill Operator - Woodworking

Drum Sander - Woodworking

Edge Bander Operator - Woodworking

Glue Machine Operator - Woodworking

Lathe Operator - Woodworking

Planer Operator - Woodworking

Rough Mill Operator - Woodworking

Shaper - Woodworking

Woodworking Machine Operator

Descriptor Profile

Main Characteristics

Occupations in this group are characterized by the following aptitudes, interests and worker functions as they relate to main duties:

- **General learning ability** to read and interpret specifications to set up, program and operate woodworking machines

- **Form perception** to notice slight differences in size and finish of products when examining them for defects

- **Motor co-ordination** and **manual dexterity** to use manual woodworking machines such as saws, routers, planers, drills and sanders, and to operate gluing machines to glue pieces of wood together and press and affix wood veneer to wood surfaces

- **Objective interest** in **setting up**, programming and operating one or more computerized or manual woodworking machine to fabricate and repair parts for furniture, fixtures and other wood products; and in operating preset, special-purpose woodworking machines to fabricate products such as coat hangers, mop handles, clothes pins and other products

- **Methodical interest** in **speaking** with supervisors to follow verbal instructions

- **Innovative interest** in **copying** to tend preset, special-purpose machines; may clean and lubricate equipment, and replace parts as necessary

9513

Physical Activities

Vision
  2 Near vision

Colour Discrimination
  0 Not relevant

Hearing
  1 Limited

Body Position
  4 Other body positions

Limb Co-ordination
  1 Upper limb co-ordination

Strength
  3 Medium

Environmental Conditions

Location
  L1 Regulated inside climate

Hazards
  H1 Dangerous chemical substances
  H3 Equipment, machinery, tools
  H6 Flying particles, falling objects

Discomforts
  D1 Noise
  D3 Odours
  D4 Non-toxic dusts

Employment Requirements

Education/Training
2

- Some secondary school education is usually required.

- On-the-job training is usually provided.

- Experience as a labourer in the same company may be required.

Workplaces/Employers

Fixture manufacturing companies

Furniture manufacturing companies

Wood-products manufacturing establishments

Occupational Options

Mobility is common among jobs in this group.

Progression to supervisory positions is possible with experience.

Similar Occupations Classified Elsewhere

Cabinetmakers (7272)

Carpenters (7271)

Supervisors of woodworking machine operators (in 9224 *Supervisors, Furniture and Fixtures Manufacturing*)

9514 Metalworking Machine Operators

Light Metalworking Machine Operators shape sheet and other light metal into parts and products. Heavy Metalworking Machine Operators shape and form steel and other heavy metal into parts and products.

Profile Summary

APTITUDES

G	V	N	S	P	Q	K	F	M
3	4	4	4	3	4	3	4	3

INTERESTS
OMi

DATA PEOPLE THINGS (DPT)
560

PHYSICAL ACTIVITIES (PA)

V	C	H	B	L	S
2	0	1	4	1	3

ENVIRONMENTAL CONDITIONS (EC)
L1, H3, H6, D1

EDUCATION/TRAINING
2

Examples of Job Titles

Brake Press Operator
Disk Flange Operator
Metalworking Machine Operator
Power Press Operator
Punch Press Operator
Rolls Operator
Saw Operator
Shear Operator
Vertical Press Operator

Descriptor Profile

Main Characteristics

Occupations in this group are characterized by the following aptitudes, interests and worker functions as they relate to main duties:

- **General learning ability** to read specifications to set up and operate metalworking machines

- **Form perception** to check products for correct shapes, dimensions and other specifications

- **Motor co-ordination** and **manual dexterity** to operate machines and equipment that weld, solder, bolt, screw and rivet metal parts together; may select and transport material to work areas manually or using cranes or hoists

- **Objective interest** in setting up and operating light or heavy metalworking machines such as shears, power presses, saws, plate rolls, drills, brakes, slitters, punch presses and CNC (computer numerical control) equipment to cut bend, roll, ream, punch, drill and otherwise shape metal stock into parts and products

- **Methodical interest** in **speaking** with supervisors to follow verbal instructions

- **Innovative interest** in **copying** information to tend computerized equipment; may clean and lubricate equipment, and replace parts as required

9514

Physical Activities

Vision
  2 Near vision

Colour Discrimination
  0 Not relevant

Hearing
  1 Limited

Body Position
  4 Other body positions

Limb Co-ordination
  1 Upper limb co-ordination

Strength
  3 Medium

Environmental Conditions

Location
  L1 Regulated inside climate

Hazards
  H3 Equipment, machinery, tools
  H6 Flying particles, falling objects

Discomforts
  D1 Noise

Employment Requirements

Education/Training
  2

- Some secondary school education is required.

- On-the-job training is usually provided.

- Previous experience as a labourer or helper in the same company may be required.

Workplaces/Employers

Boiler and platework manufacturing companies

Heavy machinery manufacturing companies

Light metal products manufacturing companies

Sheet-metal products manufacturing companies

Sheet-metal shops

Shipbuilding industry

Structural steel fabrication companies

Occupational Options

There is little or no mobility between operators of light and heavy metalworking machines.

Progression to structural metal fabricator or supervisory positions is possible with experience.

Similar Occupations Classified Elsewhere

Sheet Metal Workers (7261)

Structural Metal and Platework Fabricators and Fitters (7263)

Supervisors of metalworking machine operators (in 9226 *Supervisors, Other Mechanical and Metal Products Manufacturing*)

9515.1 Welding Machine Operators

Welding Machine Operators run previously set-up welding machines.

Profile Summary

APTITUDES

G	V	N	S	P	Q	K	F	M
3	4	4	3	3	5	4	4	3

INTERESTS
OMi

DATA PEOPLE THINGS (DPT)
684

PHYSICAL ACTIVITIES (PA)

V	C	H	B	L	S
2	0	1	2	1	2

ENVIRONMENTAL CONDITIONS (EC)
L1, H3, D1

EDUCATION/TRAINING
2

Examples of Job Titles

Production Welder

Spot Welder

Descriptor Profiles

Main Characteristics

Occupations in this group are characterized by the following aptitudes, interests and worker functions as they relate to main duties:

- **General learning ability** to understand specifications and operate previously set-up welding machines

- **Spatial** and **form perception** and **manual dexterity** to mount and center parts in jaws of holding clamps, to set welding machine controls according to specifications and to operate machines using console controls

- **Objective interest** in **operating** previously set-up welding machines such as spot, butt and seam resistance, and gas- and arc-welding machines

- **Methodical interest** in **comparing** machine settings to job specifications

- **Innovative interest** in repairing and fabricating metal parts

9515.1
Subgroup 1 of 2

Physical Activities

Vision
2 Near vision

Colour Discrimination
0 Not relevant

Hearing
1 Limited

Body Position
2 Standing and/or walking

Limb Co-ordination
1 Upper limb co-ordination

Strength
2 Light

Environmental Conditions

Location
L1 Regulated inside climate

Hazards
H3 Equipment, machinery, tools

Discomforts
D1 Noise

Employment Requirements

Education/Training
2

- Some secondary school education may be required.

- Several months of on-the-job training are usually provided.

- Experience as a machine operator helper may be required.

Workplaces/Employers

Aircraft manufacturing companies

Heavy machinery manufacturing companies

Metal products manufacturing companies

Transportation equipment manufacturing companies

Similar Occupations Classified Elsewhere

Welders (7265)

Remarks

In data provided by Statistics Canada, groups 7265 and 9515 are combined to form 9510 *Welders and Soldering Machine Operators.*

9515.2 Brazing and Soldering Machine Operators

Brazing and Soldering Machine Operators run previously set-up brazing and soldering machines.

Profile Summary

APTITUDES

G	V	N	S	P	Q	K	F	M
3	4	4	3	3	5	4	4	3

INTERESTS
OMi

DATA PEOPLE THINGS (DPT)
684

PHYSICAL ACTIVITIES (PA)

V	C	H	B	L	S
2	0	1	2	1	2

ENVIRONMENTAL CONDITIONS (EC)
L1, H3, D1

EDUCATION/TRAINING
2

Examples of Job Titles

Brazer Operator
Brazing Machine Operator
Soldering Machine Operator

Descriptor Profile

Main Characteristics

Occupations in this group are characterized by the following aptitudes, interests and worker functions as they relate to main duties:

- **General learning ability** to understand work orders, diagrams and layouts, and to operate previously set-up brazing and soldering machines

- **Spatial** and **form perception** and **manual dexterity** to align and clamp parts together, and to position them in fixtures, jigs and vises

- **Objective interest** in **operating** previously set-up brazing and soldering machines to bond metal parts and to fill holes, indentations and seams of metal articles with solder

- **Methodical interest** in **comparing** to select torch tips, braze alloy and flux according to type and thickness of metal as specified by work orders

- **Innovative interest** in fabricating and repairing metal parts

9515.2

Physical Activities

Vision
  2 Near vision

Colour Discrimination
  0 Not relevant

Hearing
  1 Limited

Body Position
  2 Standing and/or walking

Limb Co-ordination
  1 Upper limb co-ordination

Strength
  2 Light

Environmental Conditions

Location
  L1 Regulated inside climate

Hazards
  H3 Equipment, machinery, tools

Discomforts
  D1 Noise

Employment Requirements

Education/Training
2

- Some secondary school education may be required.

- Several months of on-the-job training are usually provided.

- Experience as a machine operator helper may be required.

Workplaces/Employers

Aircraft manufacturing companies

Heavy machinery manufacturing companies

Metal products manufacturing companies

Transportation equipment manufacturing companies

Similar Occupations Classified Elsewhere

Welders (7265)

Remarks

In data provided by Statistics Canada, groups 7265 and 9515 are combined to form 9510 *Welders and Soldering Machine Operators*.

9516 Other Metal Products Machine Operators

Metal Products Machine Operators not elsewhere classified operate one or more automatic and multi-purpose machines to produce metal parts and products such as wires, nails, bolts and chains.

Profile Summary

APTITUDES

G	V	N	S	P	Q	K	F	M
4	4	4	4	4	4	4	4	3

INTERESTS
MOd

DATA PEOPLE THINGS (DPT)
684

PHYSICAL ACTIVITIES (PA)

V	C	H	B	L	S
2	0	1	2	1	2

ENVIRONMENTAL CONDITIONS (EC)
L1, H3, D1

EDUCATION/TRAINING
2

Examples of Job Titles

Bolt Machine Operator
Bullet Maker
Can Forming Machine Operator
Chain Making Machine Operator
Metal Cable Maker Operator
Nail Making Machine Tender
Spring Machine Operator
Wire Screen Maker
Wire Weaver

Descriptor Profile

Main Characteristics

Occupations in this group are characterized by the following aptitudes, interests and worker functions as they relate to main duties:

- **General learning ability** to operate and tend automatic and multi-purpose machines to produce metal parts and products

- **Manual dexterity** to clean, polish, file and otherwise finish products

- **Methodical interest** in **comparing** information to check products for quality and other specifications

- **Objective interest** in **operating** automatic and multi-purpose machines, including wire looms, to produce wire screening, fencing, tinware, metal baskets, racks, hooks, metal tubing and other metal articles

- **Directive interest** in fitting and assembling components using hand and power tools; may clean and lubricate machinery

9516

Physical Activities

Vision
   2 Near vision

Colour Discrimination
   0 Not relevant

Hearing
   1 Limited

Body Position
   2 Standing and/or walking

Limb Co-ordination
   1 Upper limb co-ordination

Strength
   2 Light

Environmental Conditions

Location
   L1 Regulated inside climate

Hazards
   H3 Equipment, machinery, tools

Discomforts
   D1 Noise

Employment Requirements

Education/Training
2

- Some secondary school education may be required.

- On-the-job training is provided.

- Experience as a labourer in the same company may be required.

Workplaces/Employers

Metal products manufacturing companies

Occupational Options

There is some mobility among machine operators in this group.

Progression to supervisory positions is possible with experience.

Similar Occupations Classified Elsewhere

Forging Machine Operators (9512)

Metalworking Machine Operators (9514)

Machining Tool Operators (9511)

Supervisors of machine operators in this group (in 9226 *Supervisors, Other Mechanical and Metal Products Manufacturing*)

9517 Other Products Machine Operators

Machine Operators not elsewhere classified operate machines to cut, press, stamp, mould, treat, finish and otherwise fabricate jewellery, buttons, pencils, crayons, non-prescription lenses, brushes, notions and other products.

Profile Summary

APTITUDES

G	V	N	S	P	Q	K	F	M
4	4	4	4	4	5	4	4	3

INTERESTS
MOd

DATA PEOPLE THINGS (DPT)
684

PHYSICAL ACTIVITIES (PA)

V	C	H	B	L	S
2	0	1	4	1	3

ENVIRONMENTAL CONDITIONS (EC)
L1, H3, D1

EDUCATION/TRAINING
2

Examples of Job Titles

Brush Making Machine Operator
Button Machine Operator
Crayon Making Machine Tender
Jewellery Annealer
Prism Maker Operator
Skate Press Operator
Sports Ball Moulder
Stuffing Machine Tender
Tennis Ball Maker Operator

Descriptor Profile

Main Characteristics

Occupations in this group are characterized by the following aptitudes, interests and worker functions as they relate to main duties:

- **General learning ability** to operate and monitor machines that fabricate components and products; may make routine changes of dies, nozzles and other machinery attachments

- **Manual dexterity** to load supplies into hoppers of dispensing units and manually align, feed and otherwise place materials into machines

- **Methodical interest** in **comparing** to clean work stations by removing scraps, dust, shavings and other by-products

- **Objective interest** in operating machines to cut, press, stamp, mould, treat, finish and otherwise fabricate components and products

- **Directive interest** in monitoring machines for proper operation by watching for jammed materials, defective units and other irregularities

9517

Physical Activities

Vision
   2 Near vision

Colour Discrimination
   0 Not relevant

Hearing
   1 Limited

Body Position
   4 Other body positions

Limb Co-ordination
   1 Upper limb co-ordination

Strength
   3 Medium

Environmental Conditions

Location
   L1 Regulated inside climate

Hazards
   H3 Equipment, machinery, tools

Discomforts
   D1 Noise

Employment Requirements

Education/Training
   2

- Some secondary school may be required.
- On-the-job training is provided.
- Experience as a labourer in the same company may be required.

Workplaces/Employers

Manufacturing companies

Occupational Options

Progression to supervisory positions is possible with experience.

Similar Occupations Classified Elsewhere

Other Assemblers and Inspectors (9498)

Supervisors of machine operators in this group (in 9227 *Supervisors, Other Products Manufacturing and Assembly*)

9611 Labourers in Mineral and Metal Processing

Labourers in this group perform material handling, clean-up, packaging and other routine activities in mineral ore and metal processing.

Profile Summary

APTITUDES

G	V	N	S	P	Q	K	F	M
4	4	4	4	4	5	4	4	3

INTERESTS
MOi

DATA PEOPLE THINGS (DPT)
684

PHYSICAL ACTIVITIES (PA)

V	C	H	B	L	S
3	1	1	4	2	4

ENVIRONMENTAL CONDITIONS (EC)
L1, H3, H6, H7, D1, D4

EDUCATION/TRAINING
2

Examples of Job Titles

Asbestos Worker
Billet Pusher
Brick and Tile Kiln Cleaner
Casting Helper
Foundry Labourer
Furnace Helper
Glass Packer
Kiln Labourer
Metal Pourer Helper
Rolling Mill Worker
Salt Screening Labourer
Tailings Labourer

Descriptor Profile

Main Characteristics

Occupations in this group are characterized by the following aptitudes, interests and worker functions as they relate to main duties:

- **General learning ability** to perform material handling, clean-up, packaging and other activities to assist process and machine operators in mineral ore and metal processing

- **Manual dexterity** to feed conveyors, crushers and other equipment, to open valves and start pumps, to skim dross from furnaces and to stack, bundle and transport materials manually

- **Methodical interest** in **comparing** information to clean work areas and equipment

- **Objective interest** in **operating** forklifts and other powered equipment to transport raw materials, finished products and scrap materials throughout plant

- **Innovative interest** in sorting and stamping materials

9611

Physical Activities

Vision
   3 Near and far vision

Colour Discrimination
   1 Relevant

Hearing
   1 Limited

Body Position
   4 Other body positions

Limb Co-ordination
   2 Multiple limb co-ordination

Strength
   4 Heavy

Environmental Conditions

Location
   L1 Regulated inside climate

Hazards
   H3 Equipment, machinery, tools
   H6 Flying particles, falling objects
   H7 Fire, steam, hot surfaces

Discomforts
   D1 Noise
   D4 Non-toxic dusts

Employment Requirements

Education/Training
2

- Some secondary school education is usually required.

Workplaces/Employers

Mineral, ore and metal processing plants such as:

Aluminium plants

Cement processing plants

Clay, glass and stone processing plants

Foundries

Metal refineries

Mineral ore mills

Steel mills

Uranium processing plants

Occupational Options

Progression to machine and process operator positions is possible with experience.

Similar Occupations Classified Elsewhere

Labourers in Metal Fabrication (9612)

Machine Operators, Mineral and Metal Processing (9411)

9612 Labourers in Metal Fabrication

Labourers in this group remove excess metal and unwanted materials from metal products and perform other labouring activities.

Profile Summary

APTITUDES

G	V	N	S	P	Q	K	F	M
4	4	4	4	4	5	4	4	3

INTERESTS
MOi

DATA PEOPLE THINGS (DPT)
684

PHYSICAL ACTIVITIES (PA)

V	C	H	B	L	S
3	0	1	4	1	4

ENVIRONMENTAL CONDITIONS (EC)
L1, H3, H6, D1

EDUCATION/TRAINING
2

Examples of Job Titles

Chipper-Grinder
Forge Helper
Grinder-Deburrer
Labourer, Metal Fabrication
Metal Cleaner
Metalworking Machine Helper
Plater Helper
Shipfitter Helper
Shotblast Operator
Wheelabrator Operator
Wire Drawer Helper

Descriptor Profile

Main Characteristics

Occupations in this group are characterized by the following aptitudes, interests and worker functions as they relate to main duties:

- **General learning ability** to remove excess metal and unwanted materials from metal parts, castings and other metal products, and to assist structural steel and platework fitters, sheet-metal workers, metal machine operators and other metal workers

- **Manual dexterity** to immerse metal products in cleaning solutions, and to transport raw materials and finished metal products manually or by using hoists and other devices; may grind and chip excess metal from metal products using hand tools

- **Methodical interest** in **comparing** information to clean work areas and equipment; and in loading and unloading vehicles using hand carts and dollies

- **Objective interest** in **operating** metal-cleaning equipment such as wheelabrators, deburrers and shotblasters to remove excess welds, rust, scale and other material from surfaces of metal parts, castings and other metal products

- **Innovative interest** in sorting metal sheets and parts, scrap metal and other materials

9612

Physical Activities

Vision
  3 Near and far vision

Colour Discrimination
  0 Not relevant

Hearing
  1 Limited

Body Position
  4 Other body positions

Limb Co-ordination
  1 Upper limb co-ordination

Strength
  4 Heavy

Environmental Conditions

Location
  L1 Regulated inside climate

Hazards
  H3 Equipment, machinery, tools
  H6 Flying particles, falling objects

Discomforts
  D1 Noise

Employment Requirements

Education/Training
2

- Some secondary school education may be required.

Workplaces/Employers

Heavy machinery manufacturing plants

Metal products manufacturing companies

Sheet-metal fabrication shops

Shipbuilding companies

Structural steel, boiler and platework fabrication plants

Occupational Options

There is some mobility between occupations in this group.

Progression to metalworking machine operator positions is possible with experience.

Similar Occupations Classified Elsewhere

Labourers in Mineral and Metal Processing (9611)

Metal machine operators (in several groups in 951 *Machining, Metalworking, Woodworking and Related Machine Operators*)

9613 Labourers in Chemical Products Processing and Utilities

Labourers in this group carry out a variety of material handling, cleaning and routine labouring activities.

Profile Summary

APTITUDES

G	V	N	S	P	Q	K	F	M
4	4	4	4	4	5	3	4	3

INTERESTS
MOi

DATA PEOPLE THINGS (DPT)
684

PHYSICAL ACTIVITIES (PA)

V	C	H	B	L	S
3	0	1	4	1	4

ENVIRONMENTAL CONDITIONS (EC)
L1, H1, H3, D1, D3

EDUCATION/TRAINING
2

Examples of Job Titles

Cleaner, Filter - Chemical Processing
Cleaner, Still - Chemical Processing
Coating Machine Feeder
Helper - Chemical Processing
Labourer - Gas Utility
Loader - Chemical Processing
Retort Unloader
Water Intake Tender
Waterworks Labourer

Descriptor Profile

Main Characteristics

Occupations in this group are characterized by the following aptitudes, interests and worker functions as they relate to main duties:

- **General learning ability** to carry out a variety of material handling, cleaning and labouring activities

- **Motor co-ordination** and **manual dexterity** to feed and unload production machinery and equipment, to move and pile materials and products manually and to perform general duties such as basic construction, painting and other manual tasks

- **Methodical interest** in **comparing** information to clean production areas and chemical processing machines and equipment

- **Objective interest** in **operating** equipment to move and pile materials and products; and in assisting workers to operate processing plant equipment

- **Innovative interest** in sorting materials and products, and in assisting other workers to repair and maintain processing, gas distribution, water filtration and waste-water plant equipment

9613

Physical Activities

Vision
   3 Near and far vision

Colour Discrimination
   0 Not relevant

Hearing
   1 Limited

Body Position
   4 Other body positions

Limb Co-ordination
   1 Upper limb co-ordination

Strength
   4 Heavy

Environmental Conditions

Location
   L1 Regulated inside climate

Hazards
   H1 Dangerous chemical substances
   H3 Equipment, machinery, tools

Discomforts
   D1 Noise
   D3 Odours

Employment Requirements

Education/Training
   2

- Completion of secondary school may be required.

Workplaces/Employers

Chemical companies

Electrical, water and waste treatment utilities

Petroleum and natural gas processing companies

Pharmaceutical companies

Pipeline and petrochemical companies

Occupational Options

Considerable mobility is possible among jobs in this occupational group.

Progression to operator positions in the chemical or utility industry is possible with experience and appropriate entry qualifications.

Similar Occupations Classified Elsewhere

Chemical Plant Machine Operators (9421)

Petroleum Gas and Chemical Process Operators (9232)

Power Systems and Power Station Operators (7352)

Water and Waste Plant Operators (9424)

9614 Labourers in Wood, Pulp and Paper Processing

Labourers in this group carry out general labouring and routine wood-processing activities, and assist pulp mill and papermaking machine operators.

Profile Summary

APTITUDES

G	V	N	S	P	Q	K	F	M
4	4	5	4	4	5	4	4	3

INTERESTS
MOi

DATA PEOPLE THINGS (DPT)
684

PHYSICAL ACTIVITIES (PA)

V	C	H	B	L	S
3	0	1	4	2	4

ENVIRONMENTAL CONDITIONS (EC)
L1, L2, L4, H3, H6, D1, D2, D3, D4

EDUCATION/TRAINING
3

Examples of Job Titles

- Beater Operator Helper - Pulp and Paper
- Chip Bin Attendant - Wood Processing
- Conveyor Cleaner - Pulp and Paper
- Green Chainman/woman - Wood Processing
- Grinder Feeder - Pulp and Paper
- Labourer - Pulp and Paper
- Labourer - Wood Processing
- Lumber Straightener - Wood Processing
- Plywood Drier Feeder
- Sheeter Helper, Pulp and Paper
- Utility Man/Woman - Pulp and Paper

Descriptor Profile

Main Characteristics

Occupations in this group are characterized by the following aptitudes, interests and worker functions as they relate to main duties:

- **General learning ability** to carry out general labouring and routine wood-processing activities, and to assist other wood processing workers in operating various machines and equipment

- **Manual dexterity** to feed logs onto conveyors and into hoppers of grinding machines and align logs manually; to use tools and equipment, feed conveyors, saws, drying machines and other equipment to process lumber, shingles, veneer, plywood and similar wood products; and to pile and transport wood products manually during various stages of wood processing

- **Methodical interest** in **comparing** information to clean work areas and wood processing machines and equipment using shovels, hoses and other tools

- **Objective interest** in **operating** forklifts and other equipment to load processing materials onto conveyors and into processing tanks, to remove and transport wastes, to pile and transport wood products, and to remove scrap lumber and wood chips for reprocessing

- **Innovative interest** in sorting lumber, veneer sheets, panelboards and similar wood products

9614

Physical Activities

Vision
    3 Near and far vision

Colour Discrimination
    0 Not relevant

Hearing
    1 Limited

Body Position
    4 Other body positions

Limb Co-ordination
    2 Multiple limb co-ordination

Strength
    4 Heavy

Environmental Conditions

Location
    L1 Regulated inside climate
    L2 Unregulated inside climate
    L4 In a vehicle or cab

Hazards
    H3 Equipment, machinery, tools
    H6 Flying particles, falling objects

Discomforts
    D1 Noise
    D2 Vibration
    D3 Odours
    D4 Non-toxic dusts

Employment Requirements

Education/Training
    3

- Completion of secondary school is required by the pulp and paper industry and by other large employers.

Workplaces/Employers

Paper converting companies

Planing mills

Pulp and paper companies

Sawmills

Waferboard plants

Wood processing companies

Wood treatment plants

Occupational Options

There is considerable mobility among jobs within individual establishments.

Progression to machine or plant operating positions is possible with experience.

Similar Occupations Classified Elsewhere

Machine Operators and Related Workers in Pulp and Paper Production and Wood Processing (943)

9615 Labourers in Rubber and Plastic Products Manufacturing

Labourers in this group assist machine operators, move materials and perform routine tasks.

Profile Summary

APTITUDES

G	V	N	S	P	Q	K	F	M
4	5	5	4	4	5	4	4	4

INTERESTS
MOi

DATA PEOPLE THINGS (DPT)
687

PHYSICAL ACTIVITIES (PA)

V	C	H	B	L	S
3	0	1	4	1	4

ENVIRONMENTAL CONDITIONS (EC)
L1, H3, D1, D3

EDUCATION/TRAINING
2

Examples of Job Titles

Belt Builder Helper
Labourer, Plastics Manufacturing
Labourer, Rubber Manufacturing
Machine-Offbearer, Rubber Manufacturing
Machine Operator Helper
Mould Cleaner, Rubber Manufacturing
Moulded Products Stripper, Rubber and Plastics Manufacturing
Roll Changer, Rubber Manufacturing
Spreader Operator Helper, Plastics Manufacturing

Descriptor Profile

Main Characteristics

Occupations in this group are characterized by the following aptitudes, interests and worker functions as they relate to main duties:

- **General learning ability** to assist machine operators and assemblers in performing their duties, and in setting up and dismantling machinery and equipment

- **Methodical interest** in **comparing** information to clean and lubricate machinery and equipment, and to prepare raw materials for mixing processes

- **Objective interest** in **handling** to transport materials and tools to and from work areas using handcarts and other conveyances

- **Innovative interest** in monitoring machines to watch for jammed materials and defective products

9615

Physical Activities

Vision
   3   Near and far vision

Colour Discrimination
   0   Not relevant

Hearing
   1   Limited

Body Position
   4   Other body positions

Limb Co-ordination
   1   Upper limb co-ordination

Strength
   4   Heavy

Environmental Conditions

Location
   L1 Regulated inside climate

Hazards
   H3 Equipment, machinery, tools

Discomforts
   D1 Noise
   D3 Odours

Employment Requirements

Education/Training
2

- Some secondary school education may be required.

Workplaces/Employers

Rubber and plastic products manufacturing companies

Occupational Options

Progression to machine operator or assembler positions in rubber and plastic products manufacturing is possible with experience.

Similar Occupations Classified Elsewhere

Plastic Products Assemblers, Finishers and Inspectors (9495)

Plastics Processing Machine Operators (9422)

Rubber Processing Machine Operators and Related Workers (9423)

Supervisors, Plastic and Rubber Products Manufacturing (9214)

9616 Labourers in Textile Processing

Labourers in this group perform a variety of manual duties to assist in the processing of fibres and the production of textile fabrics and other textile products.

Profile Summary

APTITUDES

G	V	N	S	P	Q	K	F	M
4	4	5	4	4	4	4	4	3

INTERESTS
Moi

DATA PEOPLE THINGS (DPT)
686

PHYSICAL ACTIVITIES (PA)

V	C	H	B	L	S
3	0	1	4	1	4

ENVIRONMENTAL CONDITIONS (EC)
L1, D1, D4

EDUCATION/TRAINING
2

Examples of Job Titles

Doffer

Dyeing and Finishing Machine Loader

Helper - Textiles

Textile Machine Cleaner

Waste Machine Feeder

Yarn Handler

Descriptor Profile

Main Characteristics

Occupations in this group are characterized by the following aptitudes, interests and worker functions as they relate to main duties:

- **General learning ability** to perform a variety of manual duties to assist in processing fibres into yarns and threads

- **Manual dexterity** to push carts, trucks and cans of fibres from one work area to another

- **Methodical interest** in **comparing** information to clean textile machines and work areas

- **Objective interest** in **feeding - offbearing** to load and off-load machines

- **Innovative interest** in assisting with weaving, knitting, bleaching, dyeing and finishing of textile fabrics and other textile products

9616

Physical Activities

Vision
   3 Near and far vision

Colour Discrimination
   0 Not relevant

Hearing
   1 Limited

Body Position
   4 Other body positions

Limb Co-ordination
   1 Upper limb co-ordination

Strength
   4 Heavy

Environmental Conditions

Location
   L1 Regulated inside climate

Discomforts
   D1 Noise
   D4 Non-toxic dusts

Employment Requirements

Education/Training
2

- Some secondary school education may be required.

Workplaces/Employers

Textile companies

Occupational Options

Progression to machine operator positions is possible with experience.

Similar Occupations Classified Elsewhere

Machine Operators and Related Workers in Textile Processing (944)

9617 Labourers in Food, Beverage and Tobacco Processing

Labourers in this group perform material handling, clean-up, packaging and other routine activities related to food, beverage and tobacco processing.

Profile Summary

APTITUDES

G	V	N	S	P	Q	K	F	M
4	5	5	4	4	5	4	4	4

INTERESTS
MOi

DATA PEOPLE THINGS (DPT)
686

PHYSICAL ACTIVITIES (PA)

V	C	H	B	L	S
3	0	1	4	1	4

ENVIRONMENTAL CONDITIONS (EC)
L1, H3, D1, D3

EDUCATION/TRAINING
2

Examples of Job Titles

Bottle Washer
Brewery Worker
Cigarette Packer
Dairy Helper
Food Processing Labourer
Meat Packager
Potato Chip Sorter
Production Helper

Descriptor Profile

Main Characteristics

Occupations in this group are characterized by the following aptitudes, interests and worker functions as they relate to main duties:

- **General learning ability** to perform material handling, clean-up, packaging and other routine activities related to food, beverage and tobacco processing, and to assist process control and machine operators in performing their duties

- **Manual dexterity** to transport raw materials, finished products and packaging materials throughout the plant and warehouse manually, and to pack goods into bags, boxes and other containers

- **Methodical interest** in **comparing** information to clean work areas and equipment; and in measuring ingredients

- **Objective interest** in **feeding - offbearing** to dump ingredients into hoppers of mobile tank trucks and mixing and grinding machines, to feed flattened boxes into forming machines to construct containers, to remove filled containers from conveyors, and to feed and unload tobacco processing machines

- **Innovative interest** in checking products and packaging for basic quality defects

9617

Physical Activities

Vision
   3 Near and far vision

Colour Discrimination
   0 Not relevant

Hearing
   1 Limited

Body Position
   4 Other body positions

Limb Co-ordination
   1 Upper limb co-ordination

Strength
   4 Heavy

Environmental Conditions

Location
   L1 Regulated inside climate

Hazards
   H3 Equipment, machinery, tools

Discomforts
   D1 Noise
   D3 Odours

Employment Requirements

Education/Training
2

- Some secondary school education may be required.

Workplaces/Employers

Bakeries

Breweries

Dairies

Flour mills

Food, beverage and tobacco processing plants

Fruit and vegetable processing plants

Meat plants

Sugar refineries

Occupational Options

There is some mobility among occupations in this group.

Labourers in food, beverage and tobacco processing may progress to machine or process operating positions with experience.

Similar Occupations Classified Elsewhere

Labourers in Fish Processing (9618)

Process Control and Machine Operators, Food and Beverage Processing (9461)

Tobacco Processing Machine Operators (9464)

9618 Labourers in Fish Processing

Labourers in this group perform clean-up, packaging, material handling and other routine activities related to fish processing.

Profile Summary

APTITUDES

G	V	N	S	P	Q	K	F	M
4	4	5	4	4	5	3	4	3

INTERESTS
MOi

DATA PEOPLE THINGS (DPT)
686

PHYSICAL ACTIVITIES (PA)

V	C	H	B	L	S
3	0	1	4	2	4

ENVIRONMENTAL CONDITIONS (EC)
L2, L3, D3, D5

EDUCATION/TRAINING
2

Examples of Job Titles

Cannery Labourer
Fish Briner
Fish Plant Labourer
Fish Salter
Fish Weigher
Shellfish Labourer
Shellfish Packer

Descriptor Profile

Main Characteristics

Occupations in this group are characterized by the following aptitudes, interests and worker functions as they relate to main duties:

- **General learning ability** to perform clean-up, packaging, material handling and other routine activities related to fish processing

- **Motor co-ordination** and **manual dexterity** to unload fish and shellfish from fishing vessels and transport them by hand or forklift truck to work areas in fish processing plants, to immerse fresh fish fillets in brine solutions in order to condition them for wrapping or freezing, and to pack fish in ice

- **Methodical interest** in **comparing** information to clean work areas and equipment, and to record weights

- **Objective interest** in **feeding - offbearing** to dump ingredients into hoppers of mixing and grinding machines; and in transporting supplies and packaging materials throughout plants and storage areas manually and with powered equipment

- **Innovative interest** in sorting and weighing fish and shellfish, and in measuring ingredients

9618

Physical Activities

Vision
   3 Near and far vision

Colour Discrimination
   0 Not relevant

Hearing
   1 Limited

Body Position
   4 Other body positions

Limb Co-ordination
   2 Multiple limb co-ordination

Strength
   4 Heavy

Environmental Conditions

Location
   L2 Unregulated inside climate
   L3 Outside

Discomforts
   D3 Odours
   D5 Wetness

Employment Requirements

Education/Training
   2

- Some secondary school education may be required.

Workplaces/Employers

Fish processing and packaging plants

Occupational Options

Progression to other occupations in the fish processing industry is possible with experience.

Similar Occupations Classified Elsewhere

Fish Plant Workers (9463)

Supervisors of labourers in fish processing (in 9213 *Supervisors, Food, Beverage and Tobacco Processing*)

9619 Other Labourers in Processing, Manufacturing and Utilities

This group includes labourers not elsewhere classified who perform material handling, clean-up, packaging and other elemental activities in processing, manufacturing and utilities.

Profile Summary

APTITUDES

G	V	N	S	P	Q	K	F	M
4	4	4	4	4	5	4	4	4

INTERESTS
MOi

DATA PEOPLE THINGS (DPT)
687

PHYSICAL ACTIVITIES (PA)

V	C	H	B	L	S
3	0	1	4	1	4

ENVIRONMENTAL CONDITIONS (EC)
L1, H3

EDUCATION/TRAINING
2

Examples of Job Titles

Bindery Helper
Box Packer
Carton Marker
Chair Sander
Clothing Plant Labourer
Electrical Products Labourer
Film Cutter - Film Processing
Furniture Packer
Garment Folder
Labourer, Shoe Manufacturing
Lens Blocker
Packager, Machine
Seed Packager
Upholsterer Helper

Descriptor Profile

Main Characteristics

Occupations in this group are characterized by the following aptitudes, interests and worker functions as they relate to main duties:

- **General learning ability** to perform material handling, clean-up, packaging and other elemental activities in processing, manufacturing and utilities, and to assist machine operators, assemblers and other workers

- **Manual dexterity** to pack, crate and package materials and products

- **Methodical interest** in **comparing** information to clean work areas and equipment

- **Objective interest** in **handling** to transport raw materials, finished products and equipment throughout plant manually and using powered equipment

- **Innovative interest** in checking and weighing materials and products

9619

Physical Activities

Vision
　3　Near and far vision

Colour Discrimination
　0　Not relevant

Hearing
　1　Limited

Body Position
　4　Other body positions

Limb Co-ordination
　1　Upper limb co-ordination

Strength
　4　Heavy

Environmental Conditions

Location
　L1　Regulated inside climate

Hazards
　H3　Equipment, machinery, tools

Employment Requirements

Education/Training
2

- Some secondary school education may be required.

Workplaces/Employers

Clothing manufacturing companies

Electrical and electronic products manufacturing companies

Footwear manufacturing companies

Furniture manufacturing companies

Printing and packaging companies

Occupational Options

There is some mobility among occupations in this group.

Progression to machine operating positions is possible with experience.

Similar Occupations Classified Elsewhere

Supervisors of labourers in this group (in 9227 *Supervisors, Other Products Manufacturing and Assembly*)